The Dictionary of

Second Edition

The Dictionary of

Second Edition

Joseph A. Angelo, Jr.

FITZROY DEARBORN PUBLISHERS

CHICAGO • LONDON

The Dictionary of Space Technology, Second Edition

Fitzroy Dearborn Publishers
919 Michigan Avenue
Chicago, Illinois
U.S.A.

or

Fitzroy Dearborn Publishers
310 Regent Street
London WIR 5AJ
England

Library of Congress Cataloging-in-Publication Data is available.

ISBN 1-57958-149-8

Text design by Robert Yaffe
Illustrations redrawn by Jeremy Eagle from original material courtesy of sources cited

Printed in the United States of America

This book is printed on acid-free paper.

This book is dedicated to my beloved daughter, Jennifer April Angelo (1975–1993). Her life, though tragically brief, was filled with such love and compassion for others that she will always serve as my inspiration. Young people, like Jennifer, can make this world a better place, and they most certainly deserve to inherit the stars!

INTRODUCTION

The first edition of this book appeared shortly after the space shuttle *Columbia* flew its inaugural mission (called STS-1) in April 1981. The book's overall purpose was to open the language of space, especially that of the space shuttle era, to all who wished to join humanity's march to the stars. Much has transpired since the first edition was published.

The far-traveling *Voyager 2* spacecraft successfully encountered distant Uranus (1986) and Neptune (1989). It then departed the solar system to join its spacecraft-twin (*Voyager 1*) on separate trajectories through interstellar space, each carrying a recorded message from the planet Earth. The Hubble Space Telescope was launched by space shuttle (1990), experienced operational problems, and then was repaired by other space shuttle missions (1993 and 1997). "Rescued" on orbit, Hubble now provides an incredibly beautiful view of the universe and some of its most interesting wonders.

The cold war between the former Soviet Union and the United States ended. Cooperation in space has replaced decades of confrontation and politically stimulated competition. In fact, as the revised manuscript was being completed, American astronauts and their Russian cosmonaut companions orbited Earth onboard the Mir space station during a series of joint missions. These Shuttle-Mir cooperative activities were promoted as the initial part of the International Space Station program—the most extensive international technology effort ever undertaken.

A robot mini-rover (called Sojourner) landed on Mars in July 1997 and was guided successfully over interplanetary distances by enthusiastic human controllers at the Jet Propulsion Laboratory of the National Aeronautics and Space Administration (NASA). The machine explorer cautiously traversed the Martian surface at Ares Vallis—an ancient riverbed that contains many interesting geologic features and rock specimens.

Launched from Cape Canaveral, Florida in December 1996, this NASA mission, called the Mars Pathfinder, is just the first of an exciting series of missions to the Red Planet that will highlight the first decade of the 21st century and our entry into the next millennium.

However, this period also has had its moments of great pain and sorrow. Like many others, I braved the uncommon cold that morning in January 1986 to watch the *Challenger* lift off on what was to be its final mission. From the beach, I personally witnessed the telltale, erratic plumes as they spread across the blue Florida sky—and I knew immediately that something was wrong, terribly wrong. The *Challenger* had exploded and its brave crew of seven perished on the pathway to the stars.

But somehow good emerges, even out of the most profound tragedy. For example, the night following the *Challenger* accident, I had to lecture my space technology class, which contained about 50 graduate students from the Kennedy Space Center and Cape Canaveral Air Force Station. Although I thoroughly enjoyed teaching the class and its exceptionally qualified complement of students, this was going to be an extremely difficult night—especially since many of my students were directly involved in the *Challenger*'s launch. I tossed away the planned lecture and gave a very special address on the emergence of humanity's extraterrestrial civilization, emphasizing the fact that despite this tragedy, we could not turn our back on the stars. As the lecture ended and the students departed the teaching auditorium, I noticed that three of my former students were sitting in the back of the large room. Somewhat puzzled, I approached them and inquired in a friendly, slightly humorous tone: "Didn't we graduate you fellows last year?" Without hesitating, they spontaneously and unanimously responded, "Yes, but we needed to be inspired again!"

That is what this revised book is all about. Space is inspirational! Space technology continues to exert a significant influence on all areas of human activity and is stimulating a terrestrial renaissance that will lead to the creation of our extraterrestrial civilization. This revised book opens up, once again, the rapidly evolving language of space technology to all who wish to participate in, or at least understand, this grandest of human adventures. The revised book serves as a well-illustrated guide to an exciting assortment of U.S. and foreign space activities (defense-related, scientific, and commercial) that have occurred since the beginning of the space age (1957), are now being conducted, or will happen as we make the transition into the next millennium. Encyclopedic entries have been provided for those terms that are considered especially important.

A quote from a special friend and space visionary, the late Dr. Krafft A. Ehricke, precisely captures the spirit and continued purpose of this revised edition: "The space engineer is intrinsically the environmentalist's most powerful ally. Contributions in space are essential to preventing the pollution of mankind's future by resignation and despair . . . Space is not an option. It is an imperative—an economic, an environmental, and, above all, a human imperative."

Finally, I wish once again to express my most sincere appreciation to NASA and the United States Air Force, which generously provided much of the material that made this revision possible. Special thanks also are given to the public relations staff at the National Reconnaissance Office, the Washington, D.C. office of the European Space Agency, and the library staff at the Florida Institute of Technology. A very special public acknowledgment is also made to my editors at Facts On File for their unwavering support and patience during the production of this revised edition. Finally, this revision would never have been possible without the loving support and constant encouragement of my wife, Joan. Whatever success this new edition enjoys is very much her success; whatever limitations that might appear are solely my own.

—Joseph A. Angelo, Jr.
Cape Canaveral, 1998

A Symbol for (atomic) MASS NUMBER.

aberration 1. In optics, a specific deviation from a perfect image, such as spherical aberration, astigmatism, coma, curvature of field, and distortion. For example, spherical aberration results in a point of light (i.e., a point image) appearing as a circular disk at the focal point of a spherical lens or curved mirror. This occurs because the focal points of light rays far from the optical axis are different from the focal points of light rays passing through or near the center of the lens or mirror. Light rays passing near the center of a spherical lens or curved mirror have longer focal lengths than those passing near the edges of the optical system. 2. In astronomy, the apparent angular displacement of the position of a celestial body in the direction of motion of the observer. This effect is caused by the combination of the velocity of the observer and the velocity of light (c), which is approximately 300,000 kilometers per second (km/s) (approximately 186,410 miles per second). An observer on Earth would have Earth's orbital velocity around the sun (V_E), which is approximately 30 km/s. As a result of this effect in the course of a year, the light from a "fixed" star appears to move in a small ellipse around its mean position on the celestial sphere.

abiotic Not involving living things; not produced by living organisms.

ablation A form of MASS TRANSFER COOLING that involves the removal of a special surface material (called an ABLATIVE MATERIAL) from a body, such as a REENTRY VEHICLE, a planetary probe or a reusable aerospace vehicle (such as the space shuttle orbiter), by melting, vaporization, sublimation,

chipping, or other erosive process, due to the aerodynamic heating effects of moving through a planetary atmosphere at very high speed. The rate at which ablation occurs is a function of the reentering body's passage through the aerothermal environment, a high-temperature environment caused by atmospheric friction. Ablation is also a function of other factors including: (1) the amount of thermal energy (i.e., heat) needed to raise the temperature of the ablative material to the ablative temperature (including phase change); (2) the heat blocking action created by BOUNDARY LAYER thickening due to the injection of mass; and (3) the thermal energy dissipated into the interior of the body by conduction at the ablative temperature. To promote maximum thermal protection, the ablative material should not easily conduct heat into the reentry body. To minimize MASS loss during the ablative cooling process, the ablative material also should have a high value for its effective heat of ablation—a thermophysical property that describes the efficiency with which thermal energy (joules [J]) is removed per unit mass (kilograms [kg]) lost or "ablated." Contemporary fiberglass-resin ablative materials can achieve over 10^7 J/kg thermal energy removal efficiencies through sublimation processes during reentry. Ablative cooling generally is considered to be the least massive-intensive approach to reentry vehicle thermal protection. However, these mass savings are achieved at the expense of heat shield (and possibly reentry vehicle) reusability.

ablative cooling Temperature reduction achieved by VAPORIZATION or MELTING of special surface materials.
See also: ABLATION.

1

ablative material A special material designed to provide thermal protection to a reentry body traveling at HYPERSONIC speed in a planetary atmosphere. Ablative materials are used on the surfaces of REENTRY VEHICLES and planetary probes to absorb thermal energy (i.e., heat) by removing MASS. This mass loss process prevents HEAT TRANSFER to the rest of the vehicle and maintains the temperatures of the vehicle's structure and interior (including crew compartment for missions involving humans or other living creatures) within acceptable levels. Ablative materials absorb thermal energy by increasing in temperature and then by undergoing changes in their physical state through MELTING, VAPORIZATION, or SUBLIMATION. This absorbed thermal energy is then dissipated from the vehicle's surface by a loss of mass (generally in either the liquid or VAPOR phase) during high-speed flow interactions with the atmosphere.

The departing ablative material also can block part of the aerodynamic heat transfer to the remaining surface material in a manner similar to TRANSPIRATION COOLING. Modern fiberglass-resin compound ablative materials can achieve over 10 million joules (J) of effective thermal energy transfer per kilogram (kg) of ablative material mass removed (10^7 J/kg).

ablative shield 1. In general, a shield that evaporates when heated, thereby absorbing thermal energy and protecting the underlying structure from heat damage. 2. In SPACE DEFENSE, a protective shield that evaporates when heated by a LASER beam attack. This shield contains special material that absorbs the incoming laser beam energy and vaporizes—thereby protecting the SPACE SYSTEM that is located behind it from heat damage or destruction.

Figure 1. An aborted Juno II rocket, seconds before explosion at Cape Canaveral AFS (July 16, 1959) *(Courtesy of U.S. Air Force)*

ablative shock The process by which a mechanical SHOCK WAVE is generated at the surface of an object that has been exposed to an intense pulse (or pulses) of ELECTROMAGNETIC RADIATION (for example, an intense LASER beam). A thin layer of the object's surface material rapidly and explosively evaporates. The departing plume of vaporized material exerts pressure against the surface, generating a mechanical shock at the surface. This shock wave then propagates deeper into the object and can cause MELTING, VAPORIZATION, and spallation of other near-surface material as well as structural failure within the object.

See also: SPALLING.

ablator A special material designed to provide thermal protection through the process of ABLATION (i.e., ABLATIVE COOLING).

abort 1. To cancel, cut short, or break off an action, operation, or procedure with an aircraft, space vehicle, or the like, especially because of equipment failure. For example, the lunar landing mission was *aborted* during the *Apollo 13* flight. 2. In defense, failure to accomplish a military mission for any reason other than enemy action. The abort may occur at any point from the initiation of an operation to arrival at the target or destination. 3. An aircraft, space vehicle, or planetary probe that aborts. 4. An act or instance of aborting. 5. To cancel or cut short a flight, after it has been launched. (See Figure 1.)

abort modes (Space Transportation System) An abort mode is the sequence of events that occurs during an interrupted or prematurely terminated flight.

Selection of an abort mode during ascent may become necessary if a failure affects SPACE SHUTTLE vehicle performance, such as the failure of a main engine or an ORBITAL MANEUVERING SYSTEM. Other failures requiring early termination of a space shuttle flight, such as a cabin leak, also might require the selection of an abort mode.

There are two basic types of ascent abort modes for space shuttle missions: *intact aborts* and *contingency aborts*. Intact aborts are designed to provide a safe return of the ORBITER vehicle and its crew to a planned landing site. Contingency aborts are designed to permit flight crew survival following more severe failures when an intact abort is not possible. A contingency abort generally would result in a ditch operation.

Figure 2. Transatlantic-landing abort mode for the space shuttle *(NASA)*

There are four types of intact aborts: Abort-to-Orbit (ATO), Abort-Once-Around (AOA), Transatlantic-Landing (TAL), and Return-to-Launch-Site (RTLS).

The *Abort-to-Orbit* (ATO) mode is designed to allow the *orbiter* vehicle to achieve a temporary orbit that is lower than the nominal orbit. This abort mode requires less performance and provides time to evaluate problems and then choose either an early deorbit maneuver or an orbital maneuvering system thrusting maneuver to raise the orbit and continue the mission.

The *Abort-Once-Around* (AOA) mode is designed to allow the orbiter vehicle to fly once around Earth and make a normal entry and landing. This abort mode generally involves two orbital maneuvering system thrusting sequences, with the second sequence being a deorbit maneuver. The atmospheric entry sequence would be similar to a normal mission entry.

The *Transatlantic-Landing* (TAL) mode is designed to permit an intact landing on the other side of the Atlantic Ocean at emergency landing sites in Morocco, the Gambia, or Spain. This abort mode results in a BALLISTIC TRAJECTORY that does not require an orbital maneuvering system burn. (See Figure 2.)

Finally, the *Return-to-Launch-Site* (RTLS) mode involves flying downrange to dissipate propellant and then turning around under power to return the orbiter vehicle, its crew, and payload directly to a landing at or near the Kennedy Space Center launch site.

The type of failure (e.g., loss of one main engine) and the time of the failure determine which type of abort mode would be selected. For example, if the problem is a space shuttle main engine failure, the flight crew and MISSION CONTROL CENTER (at the NASA Johnson Space Center in Houston) select the best option available at the time when the main engine fails.

See also: SPACE TRANSPORTATION SYSTEM.

abrasion The loss of surface material due to frictional forces.

absentee ratio With respect to a hypothetical constellation of orbiting space weapon platforms, the ratio of the number of platforms not in position to participate in a battle to the number that are. In recent space defense studies, typical absentee ratios for KINETIC ENERGY WEAPON systems were approximately 10 to 30, depending on the details of the space platform orbits and the postulated space battle scenarios.

absolute 1. Pertaining to measurements or units of measurement relative to a universal constant, natural datum, or fundamental physical relationship of space, time, and mass; for example, ABSOLUTE TEMPERATURE. In any given system of measurement, an absolute unit is one for which the constant of proportionality is unity (i.e., "1"). For example, all base units with the Système International (SI) system are absolute. 2. Complete, as in *absolute vacuum*.

See also: SI UNITS.

absolute altimeter An instrument designed to indicate the true vertical height of an aircraft, aerospace vehicle, or spacecraft above the planet's surface.

absolute pressure In engineering, the total pressure exerted on the boundary (i.e., walls) of a system. This term is used to indicate the PRESSURE (normal component of force per unit area exerted by a fluid on a system boundary) above the hypothetical absolute zero value of pressure that is theoretically obtainable in empty space. The ATMOSPHERIC PRESSURE is defined as the pressure exerted on a system boundary by a planetary atmosphere (location dependent). The term "(positive) gage pressure" is used to identify the difference for a particular system between the absolute pressure and the atmospheric pressure, which is generally used as the reference. However, in vacuum system technology work on Earth, the atmospheric pressure exceeds the absolute pressure of the system. So the terms "vacuum" and negative gage pressure (NGP) often are used to describe the amount by which the

atmospheric pressure exceeds the absolute pressure of the vacuum system.

In traditional engineering units, absolute pressure usually is expressed in pounds-force per square inch-absolute (psia), while gage pressure is designated pounds-force per square inch-gage (psig).

See also: PRESSURE.

absolute temperature Temperature value relative to absolute zero. In thermodynamics, absolute temperature values are expressed in degrees Kelvin (K) (SI unit system) or degrees Rankine (R) (traditional engineering unit system).

See also: ABSOLUTE TEMPERATURE SCALE.

absolute temperature scale The absolute temperature scale in the international system (SI) of units is the Kelvin scale (symbol: K). By international agreement, a reference value of 273.16° K has been assigned to the TRIPLE POINT of water. The Celsius (formerly Centigrade) scale (symbol: C) is a relative temperature scale that is related to the absolute Kelvin scale by the formula:

$$T_C = T_K - 273.16$$

The Celsius scale was originally developed such that 1° C = 1° K, but using the ice point of water (273.15° K) to establish 0° C. However, from decisions at the International Practical Temperature Scale Agreements of 1968, the triple point of water was established as 273.16° K or 0.01° C, consequently shifting the zero point of the Celsius scale slightly so that now 0° K actually corresponds to -273.15° C.

A second absolute temperature scale in use is the Rankine scale (symbol: R). In this case, the triple point for water is fixed by international agreement at 491.69° R. The Fahrenheit scale (symbol: F) is a relative temperature scale related to the absolute Rankine scale by the formula:

$$T_F = T_R - 459.67$$

Similarly, the Fahrenheit relative temperature scale was developed such that 1° F = 1° R, but because by international agreement the triple point of water (491.69° R) represents 32.02° F on the Fahrenheit relative temperature scale, 0° F now corresponds to 459.67° R.

These tiny differences between absolute zero and the corresponding Celsius and Fahrenheit temperatures are artifacts from early measurements in thermodynamics in which 0° C and 32.00° F were based on the ice point of water (namely, 273.15° K and 491.67° R, respectively).

The two absolute temperature scales are related to each other by the formula:

$$1 \text{ K} = \frac{9}{5} \text{ R}$$

In physics and engineering, absolute temperatures are very useful for expressing levels of temperature, that is, for describing how far an object is above an absolute datum, as well as for expressing temperature intervals or differentials. The relative temperature scales (Celsius and Fahrenheit) are also convenient and commonly used to express temperature differences and intervals. However, in thermodynamics and aerospace applications, it is often good practice to interpret the temperature (symbol: T) as meaning absolute temperature (i.e., K or R), unless otherwise identified as given in terms of relative temperature values (namely, C or F).

The absolute temperature scales emerged in the 19th century, as the science of thermodynamics became more rigorously established. The Scottish engineer William Rankine (1820–72) developed the Rankine scale, while the Scottish physicist Lord William Thomson Kelvin (1824–1907) proposed what is now called the Kelvin temperature scale. An absolute temperature scale, such as the Rankine or Kelvin scale, proved essential in performing accurate thermodynamic calculations. On the other hand, the earlier relative temperature scales, namely the Fahrenheit or Celsius scales, remained convenient in day-to-day applications, such as cooking, weather forecasting, medicine, and general commerce. The Fahrenheit relative temperature scale was created by the Dutch-German physicist Gabriel Fahrenheit (1686–1736) in the early part of the 18th century. In 1742 the Swiss scientist Anders Celsius (1701–44) developed a "centigrade" (i.e., 100-step) relative temperature scale that he based on the freezing and boiling points of water.

absorbed dose (symbol: D) When ionizing radiation passes through matter, some of its energy is imparted to the matter. The amount of energy absorbed per unit mass of irradiated material is called the absorbed dose. The traditional unit of absorbed dose is the RAD (an acronym for *r*adiation *a*bsorbed *d*ose); while the SI derived unit for absorbed dose is called the GRAY (symbol: Gy). One

gray is defined as 1 joule (J) of energy deposited per kilogram (kg) of irradiated matter, while 1 rad is defined as 100 ergs of energy deposited per gram of irradiated matter.

$$1 \text{ Gy} = 1 \text{ J/kg}$$
$$1 \text{ rad} = 100 \text{ ergs/gm}$$

The traditional and SI units of absorbed dose are related as follows:

$$100 \text{ rad} = 1 \text{ Gy}$$

The absorbed dose often is loosely referred to in radiation protection activities as "dose" (although this use is neither precise nor correct) and also is frequently confused with the term DOSE EQUIVALENT (symbol: H).

See also: DOSE EQUIVALENT.

absorptance (absorptivity) In radiation heat transfer, the absorptance (commonly used symbol, α) of a body is defined as the ratio of the incident radiant energy absorbed by the body to the total radiant energy falling upon the body. For the special case of an ideal BLACKBODY, all the radiant energy incident upon this blackbody is absorbed, regardless of the wavelength or direction. Since in this special case all the incident radiant energy is absorbed, the absorptance for a blackbody has a value of unity, that is, $\alpha_{blackbody} = 1$. All other real-world solid objects have an absorptance of less than one. Compare this term with REFLECTANCE and TRANSMITTANCE.

absorption 1. In general, the taking up or assimilation of one substance by another; for example, a process in which one or more soluble components of a gas mixture are dissolved in a liquid. 2. In heat transfer, the process by which incident radiant energy is absorbed and converted into other forms of energy. 3. In vacuum technology, the process of a gas entering the interior of a solid. 4. In physics and nuclear technology, a nuclear interaction in which an incident neutron disappears as a free particle upon interacting with an atomic nucleus.

absorption line A gap, dip, or dark line occurring in a spectrum caused by the absorption of electromagnetic radiation (radiant energy) at a specific wavelength by an absorbing substance, such as a planetary atmosphere or a monoatomic gas.

See also: ABSORPTION SPECTRUM.

absorption spectrum (pl: spectra) The array of absorption lines and bands that results from the passage of electromagnetic radiation (i.e., radiant energy) from a continuously emitting high-temperature source through a selectively absorbing medium that is cooler than the source. The absorption spectrum is characteristic of the absorbing medium, just as an emission spectrum is characteristic of the radiating source.

An absorption spectrum formed by a monoatomic gas (e.g., helium, He) exhibits discrete dark lines, while one formed by a polyatomic gas (e.g., carbon dioxide, CO_2) exhibits ordered arrays (bands) of dark lines, which appear regularly spaced and very close together. This type of absorption often is referred to as line absorption. Line spectra occur because the atoms of the absorbing gas are making transitions between specific energy levels. In contrast, the absorption spectrum formed by a selectively absorbing liquid or solid is generally continuous in nature, that is, there is a continuous wavelength region over which the radiation is absorbed.

See also: ELECTROMAGNETIC SPECTRUM.

abundance (of elements in universe) Contemporary analyses of solar and stellar spectra have shown that hydrogen (H) and helium (He) are by far the most abundant elements in the universe. All other elements taken together make up only some 2% of the mass of the observable universe. The *cosmic abundance* of an element can be defined as its percentage of the total mass found in the universe. Using elemental abundances found in our own solar system as a guide and incorporating other astrophysical data (i.e., observed stellar spectra), the estimated cosmic abundance of the most common materials in the universe is:

Element	Abundance (percentage of total mass)
Hydrogen (H)	73.0
Helium (He)	25
Oxygen (O)	0.8
Carbon (C)	0.3
Nitrogen (N)	0.1
Neon (Ne)	<0.1
Silicon (Si)	<0.1
Magnesium (Mg)	<0.1

accelerated life test(s) A series of procedures and methods developed to help approximate, in a rela-

tively short time, the deteriorating effects and potential failure modes that would be encountered under normal, long-term service conditions. Consider, for example, a spacecraft component (e.g., a vent valve) that is required to perform an open-and-close cycle (an operation taking about 1 minute) once every 30 days, during a mission planned to last 10 years. This mechanical device might first be tested on Earth (under simulated aerospace environment conditions) by opening and closing it 100 or more times using an accelerated life test program. During this test program, the time required to open or close the device would be kept identical to that anticipated during the actual mission (here about 1 minute). However, the frequency at which the open-close cycles are performed would be greatly accelerated. In fact, the total sequence of 100 or more open-close cycles might be performed in a month. Aerospace engineers would monitor the performance of the device to see if it was in danger of failing. Such accelerated life tests are intended to help detect critical design flaws and material incompatibilities (e.g., excessive wear or friction) that eventually might impact the performance of a spacecraft component or subsystem over its anticipated operational lifetime.

acceleration (usual symbol: a) The rate of change of VELOCITY. Acceleration typically has the units of meters per second per second (m/s^2).

acceleration of gravity (symbol: g) The acceleration due to gravity at Earth's surface; by international agreement, g has the standard value of 9.80665 meters per second per second (32.1740 feet per second per second).

accelerator A device used in nuclear physics for increasing the velocity and energy of charged elementary particles, such as electrons or protons, through the application of electromagnetic forces.

accelerometer A TRANSDUCER that measures acceleration or gravitational forces capable of imparting acceleration.

acceptance test(s) In aerospace, the required formal tests conducted to demonstrate the acceptability of a unit, component, or system for delivery. These tests demonstrate performance to purchase specification requirements and serve as quality-control screens to detect deficiencies of workmanship and materials.

access control The set of procedures for providing systematic, reliable, and generally automatic use of communication lines, channels, and networks for information transfer or for information processing by computer systems. In computer system security, the process of limiting access to an electronic data processing system to authorized persons only—usually through the use of a password, key, or special card that enables the holder to access the controlled system.

accident In aerospace operations, an unplanned event that results in the injury or death of personnel, damage to an aerospace vehicle or spacecraft, or damage to property or the environment; also, an unplanned event that could lead to an unsafe situation or operational mode.
See also: CHALLENGER ACCIDENT.

acclimation (acclimitization) In general, the physiological and behavioral adjustments of an organism in response to changes in its environment. Specifically, the adjustments of a human being to a new environment; the bodily changes that tend to increase efficiency and reduce energy loss. Also called *acclimatization*.

accretion The gradual accumulation of small particles of dust and gas into larger material bodies, generally due to the influence of gravity. For example, in the early stages of star formation, matter begins to collect, or *accrete*, in a giant interstellar cloud of gas and dust (called a nebula) and eventually forms into a star with small quantities of residual matter collecting into one or more planets orbiting this new star.
See also: ACCRETION DISK.

accretion disk A rotating disk of matter, such as small particles, dust, and gases, surrounding an astronomical object, such as a neutron star, which is accumulated gravitationally by the object.
See also: ACCRETION.

accumulator In general, a device or mechanism that stores up or accumulates something. For example, in hydraulics, an accumulator stores fluid under pressure; in computer science, an accumula-

tor stores a number and subsequently replaces that number with the new number that results when the originally stored number is operated upon (e.g., added, subtracted, multiplied, squared, etc.) by the computer system.

accustomization The process of learning the skills and techniques for living and functioning with a minimum amount of discomfort in a new or harsh environment.

acoustic Arising from or associated with sound. For example, an *acoustic wave.*

acoustic absorber An array of acoustic resonators distributed along the wall of a combustion chamber, designed to prevent OSCILLATORY COMBUSTION by increasing damping in the engine system.

acoustics The scientific study of sound, including its production, propagation, and interaction with materials.

acoustic velocity The speed at which sound waves travel in a particular medium. Also called *the speed of sound.* For example, sound travels at approximately 331 meters per second through air that is at 0° Celsius and 1 atmosphere pressure.

acquisition 1. The process of locating the orbit of a satellite or the trajectory of a space probe so that tracking or telemetry data can be gathered. 2. The process of pointing an antenna or telescope so that it is properly oriented to gather tracking or telemetry data from a satellite or space probe. 3. The process of searching for and detecting a potentially threatening object in space. An *acquisition sensor* is designed to search a large area of space and to distinguish potential targets from other objects against the background of space.

acquisition and tracking radar A radar system that locks onto a strong signal and tracks the object reflecting the signal.

acronym A word formed from the first letters of a name, such as *LDEF,* which means *Long Duration Exposure Facility,* or a word formed by combining the initial parts of a series of words, such as *radar,* which means *radio detection and ranging.* Acronyms are used very often in the aerospace industry.

activation analysis A method for identifying and measuring chemical elements in a sample of material. The sample is first made radioactive by bombarding (i.e., by irradiating) it with neutrons, protons, or other nuclear particles. The newly formed radioactive atoms in the sample then experience radioactive decay, giving off characteristic nuclear radiations, such as gamma rays of specific energy levels, which tell what kinds of atoms are present and how many.

activation energy (symbol: E_{act}) In general, the energy required to initiate a reaction. In chemistry, the minimum energy needed for a chemical reaction to occur. Often expressed as joules per mole of reactants (J/ml).

active 1. In general, transmitting a signal—as, for example, an *active* satellite. 2. In surveillance and remote sensing, an adjective applied to actions or equipment that emit signals or energy capable of being detected. 3. In physics and nuclear technology, radioactive—as for example, an *active* isotope of the element cesium.

active control The automatic activation of various control functions and equipment onboard an aerospace vehicle or satellite. For example, to achieve active attitude control of a satellite, the satellite's current attitude is measured automatically and compared with a reference or desired value. Any significant difference between the satellite's current attitude and the reference or desired attitude produces an error signal, which is then used to initiate appropriate corrective maneuvers by onboard actuators. Since both the measurements and the automatically imposed corrective maneuvers will not be perfect, the active control cycle usually continues through a number of iterations until the difference between the satellite's actual and desired attitude is within preselected, tolerable limits.

active defense The employment of limited offensive action and counterattacks to deny a contested area or position to the enemy. Compare with PASSIVE DEFENSE.

active discrimination In ballistic missile defense (BMD), the illumination of a potential target with electromagnetic radiation, in order to determine from the characteristics of the reflected radiation whether this object is a genuine threat object (e.g., an enemy reentry vehicle or post-boost vehicle) or just a decoy. Radar and laser radar systems are examples of active discrimination devices.
See also: BALLISTIC MISSILE DEFENSE.

active galaxies At the center of some galaxies is a small highly luminous region, or "active nucleus." In such a galaxy, this small active central region (about the size of our solar system) emits more energy than is emitted from all the stars in that galaxy taken collectively. The emitted energy can extend over a wide portion of the electromagnetic spectrum, from radio waves to X rays. Objects that have been referred to as active galaxies include quasars, BL Lac objects, and Seyfert galaxies. Also called *active galactic nuclei (AGN) objects.*

active homing guidance A system of homing guidance wherein the missile carries within itself both the source for illuminating the target and the receiver for detecting the signal reflected by the target. Active homing guidance systems also can be used to assist space systems in rendezvous and docking operations.

active microwave instrument A microwave instrument, such as a radar altimeter, which provides its own source of illumination. For example, by measuring the radar returns from the ocean or sea, a radar altimeter on a spacecraft can be used to deduce wave height, which is an indirect measure of surface windspeed.
See also: REMOTE SENSING.

active remote sensing A remote sensing technique that supplies its own source of electromagnetic radiation to illuminate a target.
See also: REMOTE SENSING.

active satellite A satellite that transmits a signal, in contrast to a PASSIVE SATELLITE.

active sensor A sensor that illuminates a target, producing return secondary radiation that is then detected in order to track and possibly identify the target. A LIDAR is an example of an active sensor.

active tracking system A system that requires the addition of a transponder or transmitter on board the space vehicle or missile to repeat, transmit, or retransmit information to the tracking equipment.

activity The rate of disintegration or decay of radioactive nuclei.
See also: RADIOACTIVITY.

actuation time The elapsed time from receipt of a signal to the first motion of the device being activated.

actuator A servomechanism that supplies and transmits energy for the operation of other mechanisms, systems, or process control equipment.

acute radiation dose Total ionizing radiation dose received at one time or over a period so short that biological recovery cannot occur prior to the onset of acute radiation syndrome (i.e., radiation sickness).

adapter Any device used or designed primarily to fit or adjust one component to another; for example, a fitting to join two pipes that have different threads or different diameters.

adapter skirt A flange or extension on a launch vehicle stage or section that provides a means of fitting on another stage or section.

adaptive control system A control system that continuously monitors the dynamic response of the system being controlled and then automatically adjusts critical system parameters to satisfy preassigned response criteria—thereby producing the same response over a wide range of environmental conditions.

adaptive optics Optical systems that can be modified (e.g., by controlling the shape of a mirror) to compensate for distortions. An example is the use of information from a beam of light passing through the atmosphere to compensate for the distortion experienced by another beam of light on its passage through the atmosphere. Adaptive optics systems are used in observational astronomy to eliminate the "twinkling" of stars and in ballistic missile defense to reduce the dispersive effect of the atmosphere on laser beam weapons. At visible and near-infrared wavelengths, the angular resolution of Earth-based telescopes with apertures greater than 10 to 20 centimeters is limited by turbulence in Earth's atmosphere rather than by the inherent, diffraction-limited image size of the system. Large telescopes can be equipped with adap-

tive optics systems to compensate for atmospheric turbulence effects and can achieve imaging on scales that approach the diffraction limit. These adaptive optics systems continuously measure the wavefront errors resulting from atmospheric turbulence. Then, using a pointlike reference source situated above the distorting layers of Earth's atmosphere, compensation is achieved by rapidly adjusting a deformable optical element located in or near a pupil plane of the optical system.

adaptive preferential defense A ballistic missile defense (BMD) tactic designed to increase the value of the defense system. The defense determines, in the early midcourse phase of ballistic missile trajectories, the intended target of each reentry vehicle (RV) that has survived the first layers of the defensive system. Then those targets that the defense wishes to protect are defended by preferentially attacking those reentry vehicles (i.e., warheads) aimed at these targets. To further optimize the number of surviving targets, those that have the fewest warheads aimed at them are defended first.
See also: BALLISTIC MISSILE DEFENSE.

additive A material or substance added to something else for a specific purpose. For example, a substance can be added to a rocket propellant to achieve a more even rate of combustion.

adhesion Molecular attraction that holds the surfaces of two substances together.

adiabatic In general, without gain or loss of heat; in thermodynamics, a process in which heat (thermal energy) is neither added to nor removed from the system involved. When an adiabatic process is also reversible, it is called isentropic (meaning constant entropy (s) or simply $\Delta s = 0$).

adiabatic demagnetization cooling A thermodynamic process based on the *magnetocaloric effect* which is used to achieve very low temperatures, that is, less than 1° Kelvin (<1° K). Experiments with paramagnetic materials have indicated that for a reversible adiabatic process, a decrease in the magnetic field also causes a decrease in temperature. This phenomenon is called the magnetocaloric effect. Therefore, to achieve very low temperatures, a paramagnetic salt is first cooled with liquid helium down to a few degrees Kelvin and a

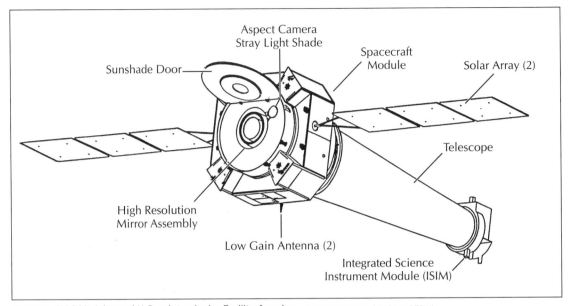

Figure 3. NASA's Advanced X-Ray Astrophysics Facility–Imaging   *(Drawing courtesy of NASA and TRW)*

strong magnetic field is applied. The paramagnetic salt then is thermally isolated and the magnetic field reduced to zero. As a result of the magnetocaloric effect, the temperature of the paramagnetic salt also decreases to a very low value, typically down to 0.001° K and below.

adiabatic process A change of state (condition) of a thermodynamic system in which there is no heat transfer across the boundaries of the system. For example, an adiabatic compression process results in "warming" (i.e., raising the internal energy level of) the working fluid, while an adiabatic expansion process results in "cooling" (i.e., decreasing the internal energy level of) the working fluid.

adiabatic wall In a thermodynamic system, a boundary that is a perfect heat insulator (i.e., neither transports nor absorbs thermal energy); in boundary layer theory, the wall condition in which the temperature gradient at the wall is zero.

adsorbent A material that takes up gases or liquids by adsorption. For example, activated carbon is a highly adsorbent form of carbon used to remove odors and toxic substances from liquid or gaseous streams.

adsorption The adhesion of a thin film of liquid or gas to the surface of a solid substance. The solid does not combine chemically with the adsorbed substance.

Advanced X-Ray Astrophysics Facility–Imaging (AXAF-I) NASA's Advanced X-Ray Astrophysics Facility–Imaging (AXAF-I) will complement visual and radiofrequency observations made from other space-based observatories, such as the Hubble Space Telescope. The basic objectives of the AXAF-I are to determine the positions of X-ray sources; their physical properties, such as composition and structure; and the cosmic processes involved in X-ray production. The AXAF-I will study stellar structure and evolution, large-scale galactic phenomena, active galaxies, clusters of galaxies, quasars, and cosmology. This approximately 4,500-kilogram (10,000-pound) facility will be launched by the space shuttle in the late 1990s into LOW EARTH ORBIT (LEO) and then be carried into a highly elliptical, high-altitude orbit by an upper stage. The final AXAF-I orbit will have an apogee of approximately 100,000 kilometers (km) (62,000 miles [mi]) and a perigee of about 10,000 km (6,200 mi). This high-altitude orbit provides a greater X-ray source observing efficiency, since at lower orbital altitudes Earth's trapped radiation belts can effectively obscure low-intensity X-ray signals coming from deep space. The major instrument in the AXAF-I telescope is called the high-resolution mirror assembly (HRMA). This device uses four pairs of accurately shaped mirrors to focus X rays from deep-space sources onto the imaging instruments located at the other end of the 10-meter (38.8-foot)-long telescope. The HRMA's mirrors are slightly angled so that X rays will graze off their surfaces, much like a stone skipping on a pond. Because of their high energy levels and short wavelengths, these cosmic source X rays ordinarily are absorbed by conventional mirrors when they strike the mirror's surface at angles larger than a few degrees. When placed in orbit, the AXAF-I will represent a major new astrophysics facility supporting high-resolution X-ray astronomy. (See Figure 3.)

See also: X-RAY ASTRONOMY.

advection In meteorology and environmental science, the transport of an atmospheric property or material (e.g., a pollutant) primarily by horizontal motion in the atmosphere, as, for example, the movement of cold air from the polar regions to the temperate regions of the biosphere. There is a general distinction between the terms "advection" and "CONVECTION." Advection is used to describe predominantly horizontal, large-scale motions of the atmosphere, while convection is used to describe predominantly vertical, locally induced motions within the atmosphere.

Aegis A totally integrated shipboard weapon system that combines computers, radars, and missiles to provide a defense umbrella for surface shipping. The system is capable of automatically detecting, tracking, and destroying airborne, seaborne, and land-launched weapons.

Figure 4. An Aeroassist Orbital Transfer Vehicle (AOTV)   *(Artist's Concept courtesy of NASA)*

aeolian Pertaining to, carried by, or caused by the wind. For example, aeolian sand dunes on the surface of Mars. Also called *eolian*.

aerial 1. (adjective) of or pertaining to the air, atmosphere, or aviation. 2. (noun) an antenna.

aero- Of or pertaining to the air, the atmosphere, aircraft, or flight through the atmosphere.

aeroassist The use of atmospheric lift and drag to maneuver a spacecraft. Aeroassist allows spacecraft to change direction or slow down while flying through a planet's atmosphere. As shown in Figure 4, for example, an Aeroassist Orbit Transfer Vehicle (AOTV) slows itself with a balloonlike drag device while passing through the upper regions of Earth's atmosphere before it swings out into a low-altitude parking orbit. The key advantage of an aeroassist maneuver versus an all-propellant "braking" equivalent is that it results in a large saving of propellant mass compared to what would be required to perform the necessary braking and/or orbital capture engine firings.

aerobrake A structure to deflect airflow around a spacecraft and provide aeroassist. In August 1993 NASA's Magellan spacecraft became the first planetary exploration mission to use aerobraking as a way of changing its orbit around the target planet. Although this spacecraft was not designed for flight through the Venusian atmosphere, it was flown over 700 times through the upper atmosphere of Venus to half its orbital period, thereby eliminating the need for large propulsive burns. This successful aerobraking maneuver enabled the Magellan to achieve another mission objective, the creation of a map of the planet's polar gravity field from a near-circular orbit.

See also: AEROASSIST; MAGELLAN MISSION.

aerodynamic forces The forces exerted by a moving gas upon a body completely immersed in it. The lift (symbol: L) is the component of the aerodynamic force acting in a direction normal (i.e., perpendicular) to the flight path; the drag (symbol: D) is the component of the aerodynamic force in a direction parallel and opposite to the flight path. (See Figure 5.) In general, the lift and the drag can be expressed as functions of the body's (vehicle's) velocity (symbol: V), the mass density (symbol: ρ) of the air (or other gaseous fluid through which the

vehicle is moving), and a charateristic surface area (A) representative of the body or flight vehicle. In a very simplified form, the lift and drag are expressed as:

$$(\text{LIFT}) \; \mathbf{L} = 0.5 \, C_L \, \rho \, A \, \mathbf{V}^2$$

and

$$(\text{DRAG}) \; \mathbf{D} = 0.5 \, C_D \, \rho \, A \, \mathbf{V}^2$$

where C_L is called the lift coefficient and C_D the drag coefficient. These coefficients generally are strong functions of a body's speed (often expressed in Mach number) and the angle of attack (symbol: α). The angle of attack is defined as the angle between a reference line fixed with respect to an airframe and a line in the direction of movement of the body. For low-flight speeds, the values of the lift and drag coefficients are determined primarily by the angle of attack. At high (i.e., supersonic) velocities, these coefficients are a function of both angle of attack and Mach number. For a typical ballistic missile, the angle of attack is usually very low (i.e., $\alpha < 1^0$).

In summary, the aerodynamic forces acting upon a body flying through the atmosphere are dependent on the velocity of the object, its geometric characteristics (i.e., size and shape), and the thermophysical properties of the atmosphere (e.g., temperature and density) at flight altitude.

aerodynamic heating The surface heating of a solid body produced by the passage of air or other gases over the body. It is caused by friction and by compression processes and is significant mainly at very high velocities, that is, at high Mach numbers (M), such as M greater than 3 or 4. For an aerospace vehicle, such as the space shuttle, or for a ballistic missile reentry vehicle traveling from outer space through Earth's atmosphere, peak aerodynamic

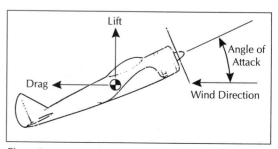

Figure 5   *(NASA)*

heating generally occurs in stagnation point regions on the object, such as on a wing's leading edge or on the blunt surfaces of a nose cone.

aerodynamic missile A missile that uses aerodynamic forces to maintain its flight path, generally employing propulsion guidance.

aerodynamics The branch of science that deals with the motion of gases (especially air) and with the forces acting on solid bodies when they move through gases or when gases move against or around solid bodies.

aerodynamic skip An atmospheric entry abort caused by entering a planet's atmosphere at an excessively shallow angle. This results in a trajectory back out into space rather than downward toward the planet. The process is analogous to a stone skipping across the surface of a pond.

aerodynamic throat area The effective flow area of a nozzle's throat; generally, the effective flow area is less than the geometric flow area because the flow is not uniform.
See also: NOZZLE.

aerodynamic vehicle A vehicle that has lifting and control surfaces to provide stability, control, and maneuverability while flying through a planet's atmosphere. For aerodynamic missiles, the flight profile both during and after thrust depends primarily on AERODYNAMIC FORCES. A glider or an airplane is capable of flight only within a sensible (measurable) atmosphere, and such vehicles rely on aerodynamic forces to keep them aloft.

aeroelasticity The mechanical response of structurally elastic bodies to AERODYNAMIC FORCES.

aeronautics The science of flight within the atmosphere; the engineering principles associated with the design and construction of craft for flight within the atmosphere; the theory and practice of operating craft within the atmosphere.

aeropause The region of Earth's atmosphere above which aircraft cannot function.

aerosol(s) In general, very small solid particles or droplets of liquid suspended in a gas; with respect to Earth's environment, the very small dust particles and droplets of liquid (other than water or ice) in the atmosphere that range in size from 0.001 to larger than 100 micrometers in radius. Aerosols include smoke, dust, haze, and fumes. They are important in the atmosphere as nuclei for the condensation of water droplets and ice crystals, as participants in various chemical cycles, and as absorbers and scatterers of solar radiation, thereby influencing the radiation budget (i.e., the overall balance of incoming versus outgoing radiant energy) of the Earth-atmosphere system, which in turn influences the climate on the surface of Earth.
See also: GLOBAL CHANGE.

aerospace A term, derived from *aeronautics* and *space*, meaning of or pertaining to Earth's atmospheric envelope and outer space beyond it; these two separate physical entities are taken as a single realm for activities involving the launch, guidance, control, and recovery of vehicles and systems that can travel in both physical regions. For example, the space shuttle orbiter is called an "aerospace" vehicle because it operates both in the atmosphere and in outer space.

aerospace control The national defense role that encompasses all actions taken to secure and control the aerospace environment and to deny the use of that environment to the enemy.

aerospace control operations The employment of aerospace forces, supported by ground and naval forces, as appropriate, to achieve military objectives in vital aerospace areas. Such operations include destruction of enemy aerospace and surface-to-air forces, interdiction of enemy aerospace operations, protection of vital air lines of communication, and the establishment of local military superiority in areas of air and space operations. (See Figure 6.)

aerospace defense 1. An inclusive term encompassing air defense and space defense. 2. All defensive measures designed to destroy attacking enemy aircraft, missiles, and/or space vehicles after they leave Earth's surface, or to nullify or reduce the effectiveness of attacks by such systems.

aerospace ground equipment (AGE) All equipment needed on the ground to make an aerospace system operational in its intended environment.

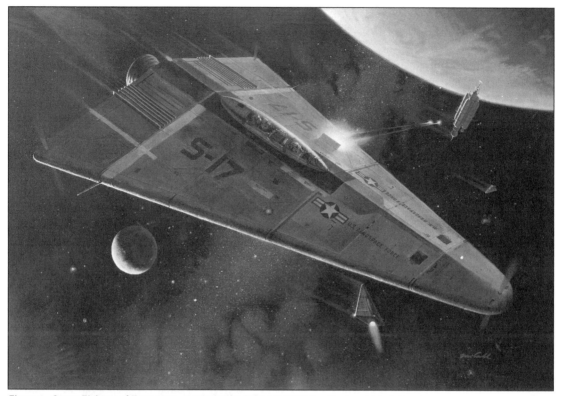

Figure 6. *Space Fighters of Tomorrow*—a painting by Robert T. McCall   *(Courtesy of U.S. Air Force)*

aerospace medicine That branch of medical science dealing with the effects of flight through the atmosphere or in space on the human body and with the prevention or cure of physiological or psychological illnesses arising from these effects.

aerospace technology transfer The generation of innovation in virtually all branches of science and technology as a result of the pursuit of aerospace technology goals and applications. Specifically, the secondary or "spin-off" applications of aerospace technologies in such diverse fields as health and longevity, sports, wildlife research, pollution, control, search and rescue operations, archaeology, and many other areas that help improve the quality of life on Earth.

aerospace vehicle A vehicle, such as the space shuttle orbiter, that is capable of operating both within Earth's atmosphere and in outer space.

aerospike nozzle An annular nozzle that allows a gas to expand from one surface—a centerbody

spike or plug—to ambient pressure. Also called a *plug nozzle* or a *spike nozzle*.

aerozine A liquid rocket fuel consisting of a mixture of hydrazine (N_2H_4) and unsymmetrical dimethylhydrazine (UDMH), chemical formula: $(CH_3)_2NNH_2$. For example, aerozine 50 is a 50–50 blend of hydrazine and UDMH.

afterbody 1. A companion body that trails a satellite or spacecraft. 2. A portion or section of a launch vehicle, rocket, or missile that enters the atmosphere unprotected behind the nose cone or other component that is protected for atmospheric entry. 3. The aft section of a vehicle.

afterburner A device used for increasing the thrust of a jet engine by burning additional fuel in the uncombined oxygen present in the turbine exhaust gases.

afterburning 1. In rocketry, the characteristic of some rocket motors to burn irregularly for some time after the main burning and thrust generation have ceased. 2. In aeronautics, the process of fuel injection and combustion in the exhaust gases of a turbojet engine (aft or to the rear of the turbine). The function of an AFTERBURNER—a device for augmenting the thrust of a jet engine by burning additional fuel in the uncombined oxygen in the exhaust gases from the turbine.

aft flight deck That part of the space shuttle orbiter cabin on the upper deck where payload controls can be located.
See also: SPACE TRANSPORTATION SYSTEM.

aft skirt The component of the space shuttle Solid Rocket Booster (SRB) used for mounting the thrust vector control system and for supporting the aft cluster of the four booster separation motors.
See also: SPACE TRANSPORTATION SYSTEM.

Agena An upper-stage LAUNCH VEHICLE used in combination with Thor or Atlas first stages, Agena was developed originally for the U.S. Air Force. Agena A, the first version of this upper stage, was followed by Agena B, which had a larger fuel capacity and engines that could restart in space. The later Agena D was standardized to provide a launch vehicle for a variety of military and NASA payloads. For example, NASA used the Atlas-Agena vehicles to launch large Earth-orbiting satellites as well as lunar and interplanetary space probes; Thor-Agena vehicles launched scientific satellites, such as the ORBITING GEOPHYSICAL OBSERVATORY (OGO), and applications satellites, such as Nimbus meteorological satellites. In Project Gemini, the Agena D vehicle, modified to suit specialized requirements of space rendezvous and docking maneuvers, became the Gemini Agena Target Vehicle (GATV).
See also: LAUNCH VEHICLE.

age of Moon The elapsed time, usually expressed in days, since the last new Moon.

agglutinate(s) Common particle type in lunar sediment; agglutinates consist of small rock, mineral, and glass fragments bonded together with glass.
See also: MOON.

agglutination In general, the process of uniting solid particles coated with a thin layer of adhesive material or of arresting solid particles by impact on a surface coated with an adhesive.

agility In ballistic missile defense (BMD), the ability of a pointing system for a sensor or a weapon to shift rapidly and accurately from one target to another.

agravic Of or pertaining to a condition in which there is no gravitation. In reality, absolute agravic conditions do not exist in the universe, since all objects within the universe attract each other gravitationally (no matter how weakly).

air The mixture of gases comprising Earth's atmosphere.
See also: ATMOSPHERE.

airborne optical adjunct In ballistic missile defense (BMD), a set of sensors designed to detect, track, and discriminate an incoming warhead. These sensors, typically optical or infrared devices, would be flown onboard a long-endurance aerial platform (either human-crewed or remotely piloted) stationed high above the clouds.

airborne particulates Total suspended matter found in Earth's atmosphere as solid pieces or liquid droplets. Airborne particulates include wind-blown dust, emissions from industrial processes, smoke from the combustion of wood and coal, and the exhaust of motor vehicles.

air-breather An aerodynamic vehicle propelled by the combustion of fuel that is oxidized by air taken in from the atmosphere; an *air-breathing vehicle.* Cruise missiles and jet aircraft are examples of air-breathers, while rockets carry their own supply of oxidizer and operate independently of the surrounding atmospheric environment.

air-breathing missile A missile with an engine requiring the intake of air for combustion of its fuel, as in a ramjet or turbojet. It can be contrasted with the rocket-engine missile, which carries its own oxidizer and can operate beyond the atmosphere.

air breakup The breakup of a reentry body or rocket (e.g., scientific sounding rocket) after reentry into the atmosphere. Air breakup sometimes is accomplished by detonating a small explosive charge inside the reentry body or rocket. The air breakup process can retard the fall of certain pieces, thereby increasing the chances of recovery of selected components (i.e., a scientific instrument capsule) by reducing the severity of ground impact.

airburst An explosion of a bomb or projectile above the surface as distinguished from an explosion on contact with the surface or after surface penetration.

aircraft A vehicle designed to be supported by air, either by the dynamic action of the air on the surfaces of the vehicle or else by its own buoyancy. Aircraft include fixed-wing airplanes, gliders, helicopters, free and captive balloons, and airships.

air defense All defensive measures designed to destroy attacking enemy aircraft or missiles in Earth's atmosphere or to nullify or reduce the effectiveness of such attacks.

airflow A flow or stream of air. Airflow can occur in a wind tunnel and in the intake portion of a jet engine; relative airflow occurs past the wing or other component of a moving aircraft. Airflow usually is measured in terms of mass or volume per unit time.

airfoil A device (e.g., wing or canard) designed to provide an aerodynamic force (e.g., lift) when it moves through the air. (See Figure 7.)
  See also: WING.

Air Force Space Command (AFSPC) Air Force Space Command, with headquarters at Peterson Air Force Base, Colorado, is an air force major command and the air force component of both the U.S. Space Command for space forces and the U.S. Strategic Command for intercontinental ballistic missile (ICBM) forces. AFSPC was established on September 1, 1982. The primary purpose of air force space operations is to enhance United States military operations by ensuring access to and use of space. Space operations include tactical warning and attack assessment, space surveillance, spacelift, satellite control, counterspace, and direct support of combat forces.

Air Force Space Command operates military space systems, including weather, communications, navigational, and missile warning satellites, providing support anywhere conflict might occur. The command also operates ground-based radars and missile warning satellites to provide ballistic missile attack warning for the North American continent. In addition, AFSPC operates the national launch centers (i.e., Cape Canaveral Air Force Station, Florida, and Vandenberg Air Force Base, California) to provide military, civil, and commercial access to space (*spacelift*). AFSPC operates a worldwide network of surveillance radars and telescopes that provide continuous information on the location of Earth-orbiting satellites and hazardous space debris. Finally, AFSPC maintains the U.S. land-based intercontinental ballistic missile force.

  See also: CAPE CANAVERAL AIR FORCE STATION; CHEYENNE MOUNTAIN AIR STATION; UNITED STATES SPACE COMMAND; VANDENBERG AIR FORCE BASE.

airframe The assembled structural and aerodynamic components of an aircraft or rocket vehicle that support the different systems and subsystems integral to the vehicle. The term "airframe," a carryover from aviation technology, is still appropriate for rocket vehicles, since a major function of the airframe is performed during the rocket's flight within the atmosphere.

airglow A faint general luminosity in Earth's sky, most apparent at night. As a relatively steady (visible) radiant emission from the upper atmosphere, it is distinguished from the sporadic emission of aurorae. Airglow is a chemiluminescence that occurs during recombination of ionized atmospheric atoms and molecules that have collided with high-energy particles and radiation, primarily from the Sun. Airglow includes emissions from the oxygen molecule (O_2), the nitrogen molecule (N_2), the hydroxyl radical (OH), atomic oxygen (O), and sodium (Na).

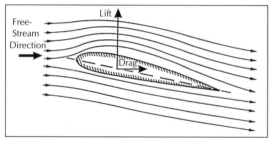

Figure 7. Basic forces generated by an airfoil in an airstream   *(Drawing courtesy of NASA)*

air launch The process of launching a guided missile from an aircraft while it is in flight. For example, while in aerial combat a pilot may choose to launch an air-to-air guided missile at an enemy aircraft.

airlock In general, a small chamber with "airtight" doors that is capable of being pressurized and depressurized. This device serves as a passageway for crew members and equipment between two places of different pressure levels—for example, between a spacecraft cabin and outer space.

airplane A heavier-than-air, fixed-wing vehicle capable of flight through the atmosphere. Aerodynamic forces are used in conjunction with a powerplant (e.g., jet engine or propeller) to achieve motion through the air.

air pollution The presence of contaminant or pollutant substances in the air that do not disperse properly and interfere with human health or welfare, or produce other harmful environmental effects.

airscoop A hood or open end of an air duct that projects into the airstream around an aircraft or missile in such a way as to use the motion of the vehicle to capture air for use in an engine, a ventilator, and so on.

air sounding The act of measuring atmospheric phenomena or determining atmospheric conditions at altitude, especially by means of sensors carried by balloons or SOUNDING ROCKETS.

air surveillance The systematic observation of airspace by electronic, visual, or other means, primarily for the purpose of identifying and determining the movements of aircraft and missiles, friendly and enemy, in the airspace under observation.

air-to-air missile (AAM) A missile launched from an airborne vehicle at a target above the surface of Earth (i.e., at a target in the air).

air-to-surface missile (ASM) A missile launched from an airborne vehicle at a surface target. Sometimes referred to as an *AGM* or *air-to-ground missile.*

air-to-underwater missile (AUM) A missile launched from an airborne vehicle toward an underwater target, such as a submarine.

albedo In general, the ratio of the electromagnetic energy reflected by a surface to the total amount of electromagnetic energy incident upon the surface. Specifically, the fraction of total solar radiation incident upon Earth that is reflected by the planet —for example, the albedo of Earth is 30%. With respect to the Moon, a high albedo indicates a light-colored region, while a low albedo indicates a dark region. Lunar maria ("seas") have a low albedo; lunar highlands have a high albedo.

algorithm A special mathematical procedure or rule for solving a particular type of problem.

alien In the context of advanced space technology and science fiction, an extraterrestrial; an inhabitant (presumably intelligent) of another world.

alien life-form (ALF) A contemporary phrase used to describe extraterrestrial beings.

all-inertial guidance The guidance of a rocket vehicle or missile entirely by use of inertial devices; the equipment used for this.

allowable load (or stress) Load that, if exceeded, produces failure of the structural element under consideration. Failure may be defined as buckling, yielding, ultimate, or fatigue, whichever condition prevents the component from performing its intended function. Allowable load sometimes is referred to as criterion load or stress; allowable stress is equivalent to material strength.

alloy A substance that has metallic properties and is composed of two or more chemical elements, at least one of which is an elemental metal. For example, brass is an alloy of zinc (Zn) and copper (Cu); while steel is an alloy of iron (Fe) and carbon (C) and often small amounts of other elements.

Alpha Centauri The star system nearest to our own Sun, approximately 4.3 light-years away. It is actually a triple star system, with two stars orbiting around each other and the third star, called Proxima Centauri, revolving around the pair at some distance. In various celestial configurations,

Proxima Centauri becomes the closest known star to our solar system—approximately 4.2 light-years away.

alphanumeric (*alpha*bet plus *numeric*) Including letters and numerical digits; for example, ALPH67DJ10.

alpha particle (symbol: α) A positively charged particle emitted by certain radioactive nuclides. It is made up of two neutrons and two protons bound together and thus is identical to the nucleus of a helium (He) atom that has been stripped of its orbital electrons. Alpha particles are the least penetrating of the three common types of radiation (alpha, beta, and gamma); they are stopped easily by materials such as a thin sheet of paper or even a few centimeters of air.

altimeter An instrument for measuring height (i.e., altitude) above a reference point, such as sea level. A *barometric altimeter* is an instrument that displays the height of an aircraft or aerospace vehicle above a specified pressure datum; a *radio/radar altimeter* is an instrument that displays the distance between an aircraft datum and the surface vertically below as determined by a reflected radio/radar transmission.

altitude The vertical distance (i.e., height) of a level, a point, or an object (considered as a point), measured from mean sea level. In astronomy, the angle between the horizon and a celestial object. In space navigation, the height above the mean surface of the reference celestial object—this is in contrast to the *distance* from the reference celestial body, which is designated as the distance from the center of the celestial object.

altitude acclimatization A slow physiological adaptation resulting from prolonged exposure to significantly reduced atmospheric pressure.

altitude chamber A chamber within which the air pressure and temperature can be adjusted to simulate different conditions that occur at different altitudes; used for crew training, experimentation, and aerospace system testing. Also called *hypobaric chamber*.

altitude engine Rocket engine that is designed to operate at high-altitude conditions.

altitude sickness The syndrome of depression, anorexia, nausea, vomiting, and collapse, due to decreased atmospheric pressure, occurring in an individual exposed to an altitude beyond that to which acclimatization has occurred.

ambient The surroundings, especially of or pertaining to the environment around an aircraft, aerospace vehicle, or other aerospace object (e.g., nose cone or planetary probe) in flight but is unaffected by the body. The natural conditions in a given environment, such as *ambient pressure* or *ambient temperature*.

amorphous In planetary geology, a rock that lacks crystal structure; without form.

ampere (symbol: A) The SI UNIT of electric current, defined as the constant current that—if maintained in two straight parallel conductors of infinite length, of negligible circular cross sections and placed 1 meter apart in a vacuum—would produce a force between these conductors equal to 2×10^{-7} newtons per meter of length. The unit is named after the French physicist André M. Ampère (1775–1836).

amplifier A device capable of reproducing an input electrical or electromagnetic radiation signal with increased intensity, or *gain*. The energy required to increase the intensity of the input signal is drawn from an external source. If the output signal is a linear function of the input signal, the device is called a *linear amplifier*; otherwise, it is called a *nonlinear amplifier*.

amplitude The maximum value of the displacement of a wave or other periodic phenomenon from a reference position.

amplitude modulation (AM) In telemetry and communications, a form of modulation in which the amplitude of the carrier wave is varied, or "modulated," about its unmodulated value. The amount of modulation is proportional to the amplitude of the signal wave. The frequency of the carrier wave is kept constant. Compare with FREQUENCY MODULATION.

analog (device) A device that depicts values by a continuously variable physical property, such as voltage, pressure, or position. An analog representation of a signal can vary continuously over a range, while a digital representation of the same signal is restricted to a discrete set of numbers. A mercury-filled thermometer is an example of a simple analog device. As the temperature varies, the mercury moves within the device continuously to indicate all new temperature values (within the range of temperatures for the particular thermometer).

analog computer A computing device that processes continuously variable physical (analog) data, such as voltage or pressure variations. Specialized analog computers are used in selected scientific and industrial applications. However, the vast majority of modern computers are digital devices that process discrete data, such as binary numbers. A slide rule is an example of a simple analog computer.
See also: DIGITAL COMPUTER.

analog processing Problem solving in an analog computer by means of direct manipulation of the magnitudes of a physical quantity. For example, the magnitudes of different voltage pulses may be compared, added, subtracted, and so on, in the course of solving a problem.

analog-to-digital converter (ADC) A device that transforms continuously variable analog data or signals into discrete, digitized signals. In the ADC device, the incoming analog signal is sampled, digitized, and encoded.

ancient astronaut theory A contemporary hypothesis that Earth was visited in the past by extraterrestrial explorers. Although *unproven* in the context of traditional scientific investigation, this hypothesis has given rise to many popular stories, books, and motion pictures—all speculations that seek to link such phenomena as ancient civilizations, unresolved mysteries from the past, and unidentified flying objects (UFOs) with extraterrestrial sources.
See also: UNIDENTIFIED FLYING OBJECT.

androgynous interface A nonpolar interface; one that physically can join with another of the same design; literally, having both male and female characteristics.

android A term from science fiction describing a robot with near-human form or features.

Andromeda Galaxy The Great Spiral Galaxy in Andromeda is our neighboring galaxy and the most distant object visible to the naked eye of an observer on Earth. It is comparable in size to our own Milky Way Galaxy and is some 2.2 million light-years (670 kiloparsecs) away. The Andromeda Galaxy is also called *M31*.

anechoic chamber A test enclosure especially designed for experiments in acoustics. The interior walls of the chamber are covered with special materials (typically sound-absorbing, pyramid-shaped surfaces) that absorb sufficiently well the sound incident upon the walls, thereby creating an essentially "sound-free" condition in the frequency range(s) of interest.

aneroid A thin, disk-shaped metallic box or capsule, partially evacuated of air and sealed. This device expands or contracts in response to changes in atmospheric (or ambient gaseous) pressure and therefore serves as the sensing element in various types of pressure gages, such as barometers and altimeters.

angle The inclination of two intersecting lines to each other, measured by the arc of a circle intercepted between the two lines forming the angle. The center of this circle is the point of intersection. There are many types of angles: an *acute angle* is less than 90°; a *right angle* is precisely 90°; an *obtuse angle* is greater than 90° but less than 180°; and a *straight angle* is 180°.

angle of attack The angle (commonly used symbol: α) between a reference line fixed with respect to an airframe and a line in the direction of movement of the body.
See also: aerodynamic forces.

angle of incidence The angle at which a ray of energy or electromagnetic radiation impinges on a surface. It usually is measured between the direction of propagation and a perpendicular to the surface at the point of incidence and, therefore, has a value lying between 0° and 90°.

angle of reflection The angle at which a reflected ray of energy or eletromagnetic radiation leaves a reflecting surface. It usually is measured between the direction of the outgoing ray and a perpendicular to the surface at the point of reflection. Compare with ANGLE OF INCIDENCE.

angstrom (symbol: Å) A unit of length commonly used to measure wavelengths of electromagnetic radiation in the visible, near-infrared, and near-ultraviolet portions of the spectrum.

$$1 \text{ angstrom (Å)} = 10^{-10} \text{ meter} = 0.1 \text{ nanometer}$$

This unit is named after Anders Jonas Ångstrom 1814–1874), a Swedish physicist, who quantitatively described the solar spectrum in 1868.

angular acceleration (symbol: α) The rate of change of angular velocity.

angular frequency (symbol: ω) The frequency of a periodic quantity expressed in radians per second. It is equal to the frequency (in hertz or cycles per second) times 2π radians per cycle.

angular measure Units of angle expressed in terms of degrees (°), arc minutes (ζ'), and arc seconds (''), where $1° = 60'$ and $1' = 60''$, while $360° = 2\pi$ (a full circle). In the case of the Keplerian (orbital) element called the right ascension of the ascending node (Ω), angular measure is expressed in terms of hours, minutes, and seconds. This particular orbital element describes the rotation of the orbit plane from the reference axis and helps uniquely specify the position and path of a satellite (natural or human-made) in its orbit as a function of time.
See also: KEPLERIAN ELEMENTS.

angular momentum (symbol: L) A measure of a body's tendency to continue rotating at a particular rate around a particular axis; it is the product of the angular velocity (ω) of an object and its moment of inertia (I) about the axis of rotation; that is, $L = I \, \omega$.

angular resolution The angle between two points that can just be distinguished by a detector and a collimator. The normal human eye has an angular resolution of about 1 arc minute (1'). A collimator is a device (often cylindrical in form) that produces a certain size beam of particles or light.

angular velocity (symbol: ω) The change of angle per unit time; the rate of change of angular dis-

placement. It is normally expressed in radians per second.

anisotropic Exhibiting different properties along axes in different directions; an anisotropic radiator would, for example, emit different amounts of radiation in different directions as compared to an isotropic radiator, which emits radiation uniformly in all directions.

annealing The application of thermal energy (heat) to a material to relieve stresses, change certain properties, improve machinability, or to realign atoms in a distorted crystal lattice as might have been caused, for example, by radiation damage. The heated material then is cooled at a suitable rate to achieve the desired effect.

annihilation The conversion of a particle and its corresponding antiparticle into electromagnetic radiation (annihilation radiation) upon collision. This annihilation radiation has a minimum energy equivalent to the rest masses (m_0) of the colliding particles. For example, when a positron and an electron collide, the minimum annihilation radiation consists of a pair of gamma rays, each of approximately 0.511-million electron volts (MeV) energy. The energy of annihilation is derived from the mass of the disappearing particles according to the famous Einstein mass-energy equivalence formula, $E = m_0 c^2$.
See also: ANTIMATTER.

annular Pertaining to an annulus or ring; ring-shaped.

annular nozzle A nozzle with an annular (or ring-shaped) throat formed by an outer wall and a centerbody wall.
See also: NOZZLE.

anode The positive electrode in a system (e.g., an electrolytic cell or a discharge tube) whereby electrons leave the system.

anodize To produce a protective oxide film on a metal (generally aluminum) by electrochemical means.

anomaly 1. In general, a deviation from the norm. 2. In geodesy, a deviation of an observed value from a theoretical value, due to an abnormality in the observed quantity. 3. In remote sensing, an area on an image that is considerably different from the surrounding general area. For example, an oasis or concentration of vegetation in an image of the desert; a single hill or small mountain in the middle of a flat plain; a dry, high patch of land in the middle of a swamp; or a warm, thermally active spot in a frigid polar landscape. 4. In celestial mechanics and astronomy, the angle used to define the position (at a particular time) of a celestial object such as a planet or artificial satellite in an elliptical orbit about its primary. The *true anomaly* of a planet, for example, is the angle between the focus (the Sun), the planet, and the point of closest approach (i.e., the perihelion) in the direction of the planet's motion.

Antarctic Space Analog Program (ASAP) A NASA-sponsored program involving the use of Antarctica as a test bed for space technologies, equipment, and procedures that may be used to explore the Moon and Mars. Antarctica, like the Moon and Mars, has remote and hostile locations that are difficult for humans to explore but can be reached by sophisticated robotic systems. The harsh, isolated environment of Antarctica is suitable for testing and demonstrating the advanced "telepresence technologies" necessary for eventual human-interactive robot exploration of Mars in the next century.

antenna A conductor by which electromagnetic waves (e.g., radio, radar or microwave) are transmitted or received. Sometimes called an *aerial.*

antenna array A system of antennas coupled together to obtain directional effects or to increase sensitivity.

anthropogenic Human made; in the context of environmental science, emissions that are produced as a result of human activities.

anthropometry The branch of science dealing with the measurement of the human body. Among other applications in aerospace, this field supports improved spacesuit design. It also assists in the development of more efficient and comfortable "human operator" workstations.
See also: SPACESUIT; TELEOPERATION.

antiballistic missile (ABM) system A missile system designed to intercept and destroy a strategic offensive ballistic missile or its deployed reentry vehicles.
See also: BALLISTIC MISSILE DEFENSE.

anti-extrusion ring Ring installed on the low-pressure side of a seal or packing to prevent extrusion of the sealing material; sometimes called a *backup ring.*

anti-G suit A device worn by air crew to counteract the effects on the human body of positive acceleration.

antimatter Matter in which the ordinary nuclear particles (e.g., electrons, protons, and neutrons) are conceived of as being replaced by the corresponding antiparticles (i.e., positrons, antiprotons, antineutrons, etc.). For example, an antiparticle hydrogen atom would consist of a negatively charged antiproton with an orbital positron (positively charged electron). Normal matter and antimatter mutually annihilate each other upon contact and are converted into pure energy, called *annihilation radiation.* Although individual antiparticles have been discovered and their behavior observed in laboratories, bulk quantities of naturally occurring antimatter have yet to be found in the universe. Sometimes called *mirror matter.*
See also: ANNIHILATION.

antimissile missile (AMM) A missile launched against a hostile missile in flight. For example, a Patriot missile being fired against an incoming Scud missile during Desert Storm operations in the Gulf War.
See also: BALLISTIC MISSILE DEFENSE.

antiparticle Every elementary particle has a corresponding real (or hypothetical) antiparticle, which has equal mass but opposite electric charge (or other property, as in the case of the neutron and antineutron). The antiparticle of the electron is the positron; of the proton, the antiproton; and so on. However, the photon is its own antiparticle. When a particle and its corresponding antiparticle collide, they are converted into energy in a process called ANNIHILATION.
See also: ANTIMATTER.

antipodal Located at the opposite point on a celestial body. For example, Earth's North Pole is antipodal to its South Pole.

antiradiation missile (ARM) A missile that homes passively on a radiation source, such as an enemy radar signal.

antirotation device Mechanical device (e.g., a key) used in rotating machinery to prevent rotation of one component relative to an adjacent component.

antisatellite (ASAT) operations Defensive and offensive operations designed to neutralize, disrupt, or threaten hostile satellites or important satellite control elements, such as a ground station or a relay satellite system.

antisatellite (ASAT) weapon A weapon system designed to destroy satellites in space. The ASAT weapon may be launched from the ground or an aircraft or may be based in space. The target satellite may be destroyed by nuclear or conventional explosion, collision at high velocity (i.e., a kinetic energy weapon), or directed energy beam.

antislosh baffle A device provided in a tank to dampen liquid motion. This device can take many forms, including flat ring, truncated cone, and vane.

antisubmarine rocket (ASROC) A surface–ship-launched, rocket-propelled, nuclear depth charge or homing torpedo.

antivortex baffles Assemblies installed in the propellant tanks of liquid-fueled rockets to prevent gas from entering the engine(s). The baffles minimize the rotating action as the propellants flow out the bottom of the tanks. Without these baffles, the rotating propellants would create a vortex similar to a whirlpool in a bathtub drain.

apareon That point on a Mars-centered orbit at which a satellite or spacecraft is at its greatest distance from the planet. The term "apareon" is analogous to the term "apogee."

apastron 1. That point in a body's orbit around a star at which it is at a maximum distance from the star. 2. Also, that point in the orbit of one member of a binary star system at which the stars are farthest apart. (That point at which they are closest together is called *periastron*.)

aperture 1. The diameter of the objective of a telescope or other optical instrument. 2. An opening, especially that opening in the front of a camera or optical instrument through which light passes. 3. Concerning a unidirectional antenna, that portion of a plane surface near the antenna, perpendicular to the direction of maximum radiation, through which the major portion of the electromagnetic radiation passes.

aperture synthesis The use of a variable-aperture radio interferometer to mimic the "full dish" of a huge radio telescope.
See also: RADIOASTRONOMY.

aphelion The point in an object's orbit around the Sun that is most distant from the Sun. (The orbital point nearest the Sun is called the *perihelion*.)

apoapsis That point in an orbit farthest from the orbited central body or center of attraction.
See also: ORBITS OF OBJECTS IN SPACE.

apocynthion That point in the lunar orbit of a spacecraft or satellite launched from Earth that is farthest from the Moon. Compare with APOLUNE.

apogee 1. In general, the point at which a missile trajectory or a satellite orbit is farthest from the center of the gravitational field of the controlling body or bodies. 2. Specifically, the point that is farthest from Earth in a geocentric orbit. The term is applied to both the orbit of the Moon around Earth as well as to the orbits of artificial satellites around Earth. At apogee, the velocity of the orbiting object is at a minimum. To enlarge or "circularize" the orbit, a spacecraft's thruster (i.e., the apogee kick motor) is fired at apogee, giving the space vehicle and its payload the necessary increase in velocity. Opposite of *perigee*. 3. The highest altitude reached by a sounding rocket launched from Earth's surface.
See also: ORBITS OF OBJECTS IN SPACE.

apogee motor A rocket motor attached to a satellite or spacecraft that is used for boosting the payload from an initial parking orbit to an orbit of high apogee (e.g., a geosynchronous orbit). The apogee motor is designed to fire when the space vehicle is at apogee—the orbital point farthest from Earth. This burn of the apogee motor establishes a new orbit farther from Earth or permits the spacecraft to achieve escape velocity. Also called *apogee kick motor* or *apogee rocket*.

apojove The farthest point in an orbit around the planet Jupiter.

Apollo Lunar Surface Experiments Package (ALSEP) Scientific devices and equipment placed on the Moon by the Apollo astronauts and left there to transmit data back to Earth. Experiments included the study of meteorite impacts, lunar surface characteristics, seismic activity on the Moon, solar wind interaction, and analysis of the very tenuous lunar atmosphere.

Apollo Project On May 25, 1961 President John F. Kennedy proposed that the United States establish as a national goal a human lunar landing and return by the end of the decade. In response to this presidential initiative, NASA instituted the Apollo Project (which was preceded by the Mercury and Gemini projects). A giant new rocket, the Saturn V, would be needed to send astronauts and their equipment safely to the lunar surface. The Saturn V first stage used a cluster of five F-1 engines that generated some 33,360,000 newtons (7.5 million pounds-force [lb_{force}]) of thrust. The second stage used a cluster of five J-2 engines that developed a combined thrust of 4.4 million newtons (1 million lb_{force}). The third stage of this "moon rocket" was powered by a single J-2 engine with 889,600 newtons (200,000 lb_{force}) thrust capability.

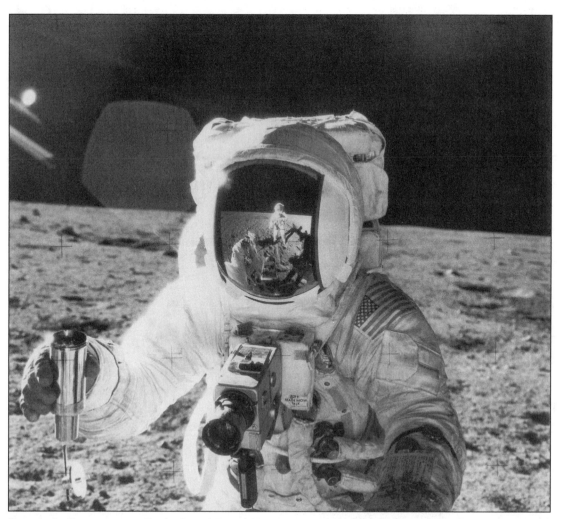

Figure 8. *Apollo 12* astronauts Charles Conrad, Jr., and Alan L. Bean on the lunar surface (November 1969) *(NASA)*

APOLLO PROJECT SUMMARY

Spacecraft Name	Crew	Date	Flight Time (Hrs., Min., Sec.)	Revolutions	Remarks
Apollo 7	Walter H. Schirra Donn Eisele Walter Cunningham	10/11–22/68	260:8:45	163	First manned Apollo flight demonstrated the spacecraft, crew, and support elements. All performed as required.
Apollo 8	Frank Borman James A. Lovell, Jr. William Anders	12/21–27/68	147:00:41	10 rev. of Moon	History's first manned flight to the vicinity of another celestial body.
Apollo 9	James A. McDivitt David R. Scott Russell L. Schweikart	3/3–13/69	241:00:53	151	First all-up manned Apollo flight (with *Saturn V* and command, service and lunar modules). First Apollo extravehicular activity. First docking of command service module with lunar module.
Apollo 10	Thomas P. Stafford John W. Young Eugene A. Cernan	5/18–26/69	192:03:23	31 rev. of Moon	Apollo LM descended to within 14.5 km of Moon and later rejoined command service module. First rehearsal in lunar environment.
Apollo 11	Neil A. Armstrong Michael Collins Edwin E. Aldrin, Jr.	7/16–24/69	195:18:35	30 rev. of Moon	First landing of men on the Moon. Total stay time: 21 hrs. 36 min.
Apollo 12	Charles Conrad, Jr. Richard F. Gordon, Jr. Alan L. Bean	11/14–24/69	244:36:25	45 rev. of Moon	Second manned exploration of the Moon. Total stay time: 31 hrs. 31 min.
Apollo 13	James A. Lovell, Jr. John L. Swigert, Jr. Fred W. Haise, Jr.	4/11–17/70	142:54:41	–	Mission aborted because of service module oxygen tank failure.
Apollo 14	Alan B. Shepard, Jr. Stuart A. Roosa Edgar D. Mitchell	1/31–2/9/71	216:01:59	34 rev. of Moon	First manned landing in and exploration of lunar highlands. Total stay time: 33 hrs. 31 min.
Apollo 15	David R. Scott Alfred M. Worden James B. Irwin	7/26–8/7/71	295:11:53	74 rev. of Moon	First use of lunar roving vehicle. Total stay time: 66 hrs. 55 min.
Apollo 16	John W. Young Thomas K. Mattingly II Charles M. Duke, Jr.	4/16–27/72	265:51:05	64 rev. of Moon	First use of remote-controlled television camera to record liftoff of the lunar module ascent stage from the lunar surface. Total stay time: 71 hrs. 2 min.
Apollo 17	Eugene A. Cernan Ronald E. Evans Harrison H. Schmitt	12/7–19/72	301:51:59	75 rev. of Moon	Last manned lunar landing and exploration of the Moon in the Apollo program returned 110 kg of lunar samples to Earth Total stay time: 75 hrs

Source: NASA.

From October 1961 through April 1968, a variety of unmanned flight tests of the Saturn 1B and V launch vehicles and the Apollo spacecraft/lunar module were conducted successfully. These unmanned tests included the *Apollo 4, 5,* and *6* missions (November 1967 to April 1968) which involved Earth orbital trajectories.

On January 27, 1967 tragedy struck the U.S. space program when a fire erupted inside an Apollo spacecraft during ground testing at Complex 34, Cape Canaveral Air Force Station (AFS), Florida. This flash fire caused the deaths of Astronauts Virgil (Gus) Grissom, Edward White II, and Roger Chafee. As a result of this accident, major modifications had to be made to the Apollo spacecraft prior to its first crewed mission in space.

Liftoff of the first crewed Apollo launch, *Apollo 7,* occurred on October 11, 1968. A Saturn 1B vehicle left Complex 34 at Cape Canaveral AFS carrying Astronauts Walter Schirra, Donn Eisele, and Walter Cunningham on an 11-day mission that tested the Apollo spacecraft's performance in Earth orbit. All subsequent Apollo missions were flown from Complex 39 at the NASA Kennedy Space Center, which is adjacent to Cape Canaveral AFS.

Apollo 8, with Astronauts Frank Borman, William Anders, and James Lovell, lifted off on December 21, 1968. This flight involved the first voyage by human beings from Earth to the vicinity of another planetary body. In 147 hours *Apollo 8* took its crew on a faultless, 800,000-kilometer (km) (500,000-mile [mi]) space flight, which included 10 lunar orbits.

Apollo 9 took place in March 1969 and was the first all-up flight of the Apollo/Saturn V space vehicle configuration (i.e., all lunar mission equipment was flown together for the first time, including a flight article lunar module instead of the lunar module test article used in the *Apollo 8* mission). An article is one version of a piece of aerospace equipment in the class of such equipment. While in Earth orbit, the *Apollo 9* astronauts demonstrated key docking and rendezvous maneuvers between the Apollo spacecraft and the lunar module.

The *Apollo 10* mission in May 1969 successfully completed the second human flight that orbited the Moon. In a dress rehearsal for the actual lunar landing mission (which occurred in *Apollo 11*), the *Apollo 10* astronauts came within 14.5 km (9 mi) of the lunar surface and spent nearly 62 hours (31 revolutions) in lunar orbit.

The *Apollo 11* mission achieved the national goal set by President Kennedy in 1961—namely landing human beings on the surface of the Moon and returning them safely to Earth within the decade of the 1960s. On July 20, 1969 Astronauts Neil Armstrong and Edwin (Buzz) Aldrin flew the lunar module to the surface of the Moon, touching down safely in the Sea of Tranquility. While Armstrong and then Aldrin became the first two persons to walk on another world, Astronaut Michael Collins, the command module pilot orbited above.

Four months later, in November 1969, the crew of the *Apollo 12* repeated the journey to the lunar surface, this time landing at and exploring a site in the Ocean of Storms. Their lunar surface activities included a visit to the *Surveyor III* spacecraft landing site. (See Figure 8).

Apollo 13 was launched on April 11, 1970. Its crew was scheduled to land on the Fra Mauro upland area of the Moon. However, a rupture of the service module oxygen tank on April 13 caused a life-threatening power failure of the command and service module electrical system. Using their lunar module (*Aquarius*) as a "lifeboat," Astronauts Lovell, John Swigert, and Fred Haise skillfully maneuvered their disabled spacecraft around the Moon and came back to Earth on a "free-return" trajectory. They abandoned the severely damaged service module and the "lifesaving" lunar module just prior to reentry into Earth's atmosphere and rode the Apollo command module to a safe splashdown and recovery in the Pacific Ocean on April 17.

Apollo 14 was retargeted to accomplish the mission planned for *Apollo 13*. The *Apollo 14* spacecraft was launched on January 31, 1971, and the lunar module touched down on February 5 on the Fra Mauro formation, just 18.3 meters (m) (60 feet [ft]) from the targeted point. The astronauts carried out numerous experiments and conducted successful exploration and specimen collections in the lunar highlands. The return flight to Earth was normal, and the Apollo capsule touched down in the South Pacific on February 9.

The fourth successful lunar landing mission, *Apollo 15,* was launched on July 26, 1971. The astronauts landed at the Hadley Apennine site. During their extended (approximately 67-hour) stay on the lunar surface, they used the electric-powered Lunar Rover vehicle for the first time. About 77 kilograms (170 pounds) of surface samples were collected and extensive science experiments performed during this mission. Slashdown in the Pacific Ocean occurred on August 7.

Apollo 16 (the fifth successful lunar landing mission) was launched on April 16, 1972. The astronauts explored the Decartes highlands and returned approximately 93.5 kg (210 lb) of Moon rocks and soil samples. A Lunar Rover vehicle was used again to assist in surface exploration activities. The liftoff of the lunar module from the Moon's surface was recorded for the first time with the help of a remote-controlled television camera.

The final Apollo mission to the Moon, *Apollo 17,* was launched on December 7, 1972. During this 12-day mission, the astronauts explored the Taurus-Littrow landing site, emplaced geophysical instruments, and collected 108 kg (240 lb) of lunar soil and rock samples. Astronauts Eugene Cernan and Harrison Schmitt were the last human beings to walk on the surface of the Moon in the 20th century.

The Apollo Project and its exciting missions to the Moon represent one of the greatest triumphs of both human technology and the human spirit.

See also: GEMINI PROJECT; MERCURY PROJECT; MOON.

Apollo-Soyuz Test Project (ASTP) Joint U.S.-Soviet space mission (July 1975) centering on the rendezvous and docking of the *Apollo 18* spacecraft and the *Soyuz 19* spacecraft. Both the Soyuz and Apollo spacecraft were launched on July 15, 1975; the U.S. *Apollo 18* spacecraft lifted off approximately 7 1/2 hours after the Soviets launched the *Soyuz 19* spacecraft. The Russian cosmonauts (Aleskey Leonov and Valeriy Kubasov) maneuvered their *Soyuz 19* spacecraft to the planned orbit for docking at an altitude of 222 kilometers (138 miles) over Europe. The *Apollo 18* astronauts (Thomas Stafford, Vance Brand, and Donald [Deke] Slayton) then completed the rendezvous sequence, eventually docking with the Soyuz spacecraft on July 17. During the next two days the crews accomplished four transfer operations between the two spacecraft and completed five scheduled experiments. Following the first undocking, a joint solar eclipse experiment was performed. Then the Apollo spacecraft accomplished a second successful docking, this time with the Soyuz apparatus locking the two spacecraft together. The final undocking occurred on July 19. The two spacecraft moved to a station-keeping distance and a joint ultraviolet absorption experiment was performed, involving a complicated series of orbital maneuvers. Afterward, the *Apollo 18* spacecraft entered a separate orbit, and

unilateral activities were conducted by both the Soyuz and Apollo crews. The Soyuz landed safely on July 21, after six mission days, and the Apollo flight was concluded successfully on July 24, nine days after launch. The primary objectives of this international mission were met, including rendezvous, docking, crew transfer, and control center–crew interaction.

apolune That point in the lunar orbit of a spacecraft or satellite launched from the Moon that is farthest from the Moon. Compare with APOCYNTHION.

aposelene The farthest point in an orbit around the Moon.

apparent In astronomy, observed. True values are reduced from apparent (observed) values by eliminating those factors, such as refraction, and flight time, that can affect the observation.

applied research Research concerned with the practical application of knowledge, material, and/or techniques directed toward a solution to an existing or anticipated (space technology) problem.
See also: BASIC RESEARCH.

approach The maneuvers of a spacecraft or aerospace vehicle from its normal orbital position (sometimes called its *stationkeeping* position) toward another orbiting object (e.g., a satellite, space station, or spacecraft) for the purpose of conducting rendezvous and docking or capture operations.

appulse 1. The apparent near approach of one celestial body to another. For example, the apparent close approach (on the celestial sphere) of a planet or asteroid to a star, without the occurrence of an occultation. 2. A penumbral eclipse of the Moon.

apsis (plural: apsides) In orbital mechanics, either of the two orbital points nearest (*periapsis*) or farthest (*apoapsis*) from the center of gravitational attraction. The apsides are called the *perigee* and *apogee* for an orbit around Earth and the *perihelion* and *aphelion* for an orbit around the Sun. The straight line connecting these two points is called the *line of apsides* and represents the major axis of an elliptical orbit.
See also: ORBITS OF OBJECTS IN SPACE.

arc 1. In mathematics, a part of a curved line, such as a portion of a circle. 2. In physics, a luminous glow that appears when an electric current passes through ionized air or gas. 3. In planetary science, an auroral arc.

arc discharge A luminous, gaseous electrical discharge in which charge transfer occurs continuously along a narrow channel of high ion density. An arc discharge requires a continuous source of electric potential difference across the terminals of the arc. The intense ionization needed to maintain the high current is provided by the evaporation of the electrodes.

architecture 1. In aerospace engineering, the overall design of a system: its elements, their functions, and their interrelationships. 2. In computer science, the overall logic structure of a computer or computer-based system. 3. In ballistic missile defense (BMD), a description of all functional activities to be performed to achieve the desired level of defense, the system elements needed to perform the functions, and the allocation of performance levels among those systems.

arc-jet engine A type of electric rocket engine in which the propellant gas is heated by passing through an electric arc. (See Figure 9.) In general, the cathode is located axially in the arc-jet engine, and the anode is formed into a combined plenum chamber/constrictor/nozzle configuration. The main problems associated with arc-jet engines are electrode erosion and low overall efficiency. Electrode erosion occurs as a result of the intense heating experienced by the electrodes and can seriously limit the thruster lifetime. The electrode erosion problem can be reduced by careful design of the electrodes. Overall arc-jet engine efficiency is dominated by "frozen-flow" losses, which are the result of dissociation and ionization of the propellant. These "frozen-flow" losses are much more difficult to reduce since they are dependent on the thermodynamics of the flow and heating processes. A high-power arc-jet engine with exhaust velocities between 8×10^3 and 2×10^4 meters per second is an attractive option for propelling an orbital transfer vehicle. Recent research has demonstrated a 30 kilowatt (kW)–class arc-jet engine operating for approximately 600 hours with ammonia as propellant.

See also: ELECTRIC PROPULSION.

arc-minute One/sixtieth (1/60th) of a degree of angle. This unit of angle is associated with precise measurements of motions and positions of celestial objects as occurs in the science of astrometry.

$$1° = 60 \text{ arc-min} = 60'$$

See also: ARC-SECOND; ASTROMETRY.

Figure 9. Diagram showing major components and dimensions of a contemporary 30-kW class arc-jet engine *(NASA)*

arc-second One/three thousand six hundreth (1/3,600th) of a degree of angle. This unit of angle is associated with very precise measurements of stellar motions and positions in the science of astrometry.

$$1' \text{ (arc-min)} = 60 \text{ arc-sec} = 60''$$

See also: ARC-MINUTE; ASTROMETRY.

area defense A ballistic missile defense (BMD) that covers a large area. The term usually implies the capability of protecting "soft" targets (e.g., not hardened missile silos or bunkers).
See also: BALLISTIC MISSILE DEFENSE.

area ratio Ratio of the geometric flow area of the nozzle exit to the geometric flow area of the nozzle throat; also called *expansion area ratio* or simply *expansion ratio*.
See also: NOZZLE.

Arecibo Observatory The world's largest radio/radar telescope with a 305-meter- (1,000-foot-) diameter dish. It is located in the tropical jungles of Puerto Rico, filling a spherical bowl that was formed naturally by the collapse of huge limestone caves. When it operates as a radiowave receiver, the Arecibo telescope listens for signals from celestial objects at the farthest reaches of the universe. As a radar transmitter/receiver, it assists astronomers and planetary scientists by bouncing signals off the Moon, off nearby planets and their satellites, and even off layers of Earth's ionosphere.
See also: RADAR ASTRONOMY; RADIOASTRONOMY.

areocentric With Mars as the center.

areodesy The branch of science that determines by careful observation and precise measurement the size and shape of the planet Mars and the exact position of points and features on the surface of the planet. Compare with GEODESY.

areographic Referring to positions on Mars measured in latitude from the Martian equator and in longitude from the reference meridian.

areography The study of the surface features of Mars; the "geography" of Mars.

Ares The planet Mars. This name for the fourth planet in our solar system is derived from the ancient Greek word Ares (Αρες)—their name for the mythological god of war (who was called Mars by the Romans). Today the term "Ares" is seldom used for Mars, except in combined forms, such as areocentric and areodesy.

argument of periapsis The argument (angular distance) of periapsis from the ascending node.
See also: ORBITS OF OBJECTS IN SPACE.

Ariane The Ariane family of launch vehicles evolved from a European desire, first expressed in the early 1960s, to achieve and maintain an independent access to space. Early manifestation of the efforts that ultimately resulted in the creation of Arianespace (the international company that now markets the Ariane launch vehicles) included France's Diamant launch vehicle program (with operations at Hammaguir, Algeria, in the Sahara Desert) and the Europa launch vehicle program, which operated out of the Woomera range in Australia, before moving to Kourou, French Guiana, in 1970. These early efforts eventually yielded the first Ariane flight on December 24, 1979. That mission, called L01, was followed by 10 more *Ariane-1* flights over the next six years. The initial Ariane vehicle family (*Ariane-1* through *Ariane-4*) centered on a three-stage launch vehicle configuration with evolving capabilities. The *Ariane-1* vehicle gave way in 1984 to the more powerful *Ariane-2* and *Ariane-3* vehicle configurations. These configurations, in turn, were replaced in June 1988 with the successful launch of the *Ariane-4* vehicle—a launcher that has been called Europe's "space workhorse." *Ariane-4* vehicles are designed to orbit satellites with a total mass values of up to 4,700 kilograms (kg) (10,350 pounds-mass [lbm]). The various launch vehicle versions differ according to the number and type of strap-on boosters and the size of the fairings.

On October 30, 1997, a new more powerful launcher, called *Ariane-5*, joined the Ariane family, when its second qualification flight (called V502 or Ariane 502) successfully took place at the Guiana Space Center in Kourou. Twenty-seven minutes into this flight, the Maqsat-H and Maqsat-B platforms, carrying instruments to analyze the new launch vehicle's performance, and the TeamSat technology satellite were injected into orbit. Following an additional *Ariane-5* qualification

Ariane Launch Vehicle Evolution

arianespace

1981	1984	1988	1995–98
Ariane 1	*Ariane 2* *Ariane 3*	*Ariane 4*	*Ariane 5*

Ariane 1

Fairing
Diam= 3.0 M

Vehicle Equipment Bay

Cyrogenic 3rd Stage
8T
H_2/O_2

2nd Stage
34T
UH25 + N_2O_4

1st Stage
144T
UH25 + N_2O_4

Ariane 3

Larger Fairing
Diam= 3.2 M

SYLDA

Stretched
3rd Stage
Capacity: 10.7T

2 Solid
Strap-On
Boosters

Ariane 4

New Fairing
Diam= 4 M

Spelda
New Vehicle
Equipment Bay
Structure

Stretched
1st Stage

Ariane 5

Fairing
Diam= 5.4 M

Speltra

Vehicle
Equipment
Bay

2 Solid
Strap-On
Boosters

	Ariane 1	Ariane 2	Ariane 3	Ariane 4	Ariane 5
Height: M(Ft)	48 (156)	49 (160)	49 (160)	58 (191)	54 (177)
Approximate Liftoff Mass: T (Klbs)	210 (462)	217 (477)	240 (528)	470 (1,034)	725 (1,595)
GTO Payload Mass: KG (lb)	1,800 (3,960)	2,200 (4,840)	2,700 (5,940)	4,520 (9,965)	6,800 (15,000)

Figure 10. Ariane Launch Vehicle Evolution   *(Arianespace)*

flight in 1998 under European Space Agency (ESA) and French Space Agency (CNES) responsibility, Arianespace will manage commercial flights of this new launch vehicle.

The *Ariane-5* launch vehicle is an advanced "two-stage" system, consisting of a powerful liquid hydrogen/liquid oxygen-fueled main engine (called the Vulcain) and two strap-on-solid propellant rockets. It will be capable of placing a satellite payload of 5,900 kilograms (kg) (13,000 pounds-mass [lbm]) (dual satellite launch) or 6,800 kilograms (kg) (14,950 pounds-mass [lbm]) (single satellite launch) into geostationary transfer orbit, and approximately 20,000 kilograms (kg) (44,000 pounds-mass [lbm]) into low Earth orbit. (See Figure 10.)

Ariane vehicles are launched from Kourou, French Guiana, in South America. Kourou was chosen in part because it is close to Earth's equator, which makes the site ideal for launching most satellites. Following the first firing of a Diamant rocket by CNES (the French Space Agency) in 1970, Europe decided to use Kourou for its Europa launch vehicles. In 1975 ESA took over the existing European facilities at the Guiana Space Center to build the ELA-1 complex (the Ensemble de Lancement Ariane, or Ariane Launch Complex) for its *Ariane-1, 2,* and *3* launch vehicles. ESA next created the ELA-2 complex for the *Ariane-4* vehicle. The *Ariane-5* vehicle is launched from a new complex, called ELA-3, whose facilities spread over 21 square kilometers (km²) (8.1 square miles [mi²]). In all, the "European spaceport" at Kourou covers 960 square kilometers (km²) (370.6 square miles [m²]) and has a workforce of over 1,000 persons.

See also: EUROPEAN SPACE AGENCY.

articulated Segmented or jointed and thereby able to accommodate motion.

artificial gravity A simulated gravity established within a spacecraft, space station, or space settlement, as by rotating the crew cabin or habitable modules about an axis of the space vehicle or station, the centrifugal force generated being similar to the force of gravity.

artificial intelligence (AI) A term commonly taken to mean the study of thinking and perceiving as general information-processing functions—or the science of *machine intelligence (MI)*. Computer systems now have been programmed to diagnose diseases; prove theorems; analyze electronic circuits; play complex games such as chess, poker, and backgammon; solve differential equations; assemble mechanical equipment using robotic manipulator arms and end effectors (i.e., the robot "hands" at the end of the manipulator arms); pilot uncrewed vehicles across complex terrestrial terrain as well as through the vast reaches of interplanetary space; analyze the structure of complex organic molecules; understand human speech patterns; and even write other computer programs. All of these computer-accomplished functions require a degree of "intelligence" similar to mental activities performed by the human brain. In time, a general theory of intelligence may emerge from the current efforts of scientists and engineers now engaged in the field of artificial intelligence. This general theory would help guide the design and development of even "smarter" robot spacecraft and exploratory probes, permitting a more thorough exploration of the distant regions of the solar system and beyond.

Artificial intelligence includes a number of elements or subdisciplines, including planning and problem solving; perception; natural language; expert systems; automation; teleoperation and robotics; distributed data management; and cognition and learning, among others.

All artificial intelligence involves elements of planning and problem solving. The problem-solving function implies a wide range of tasks, including decision making, optimization, dynamic resource allocation, and many other calculations or logical operations.

Perception is the process of obtaining data from one or more sensors and processing or analyzing the data to assist in making some subsequent decision or taking some subsequent action. The basic problem in perception is to extract from a large amount of (remotely) sensed data some feature or characteristic that then permits object identification.

One of the most challenging problems in the evolution of the digital computer has been the communication that must occur between the human operator and the machine. The human operator would like to use an everyday, or "natural," language to gain access to the computer system. The process of communication between machines and people is very complex and frequently requires sophisticated computer hardware and software.

An expert system permits the scientific or technical expertise of a particular human being to be stored in a computer system for subsequent use by other human beings who have not had the equivalent professional or technical experience. Expert systems have been developed for use in such diverse fields as medical diagnosis, mineral exploration, and mathematical problem solving. To create an expert system, a team of software specialists will collaborate with a scientific expert to construct a computer-based interactive dialogue system that is capable, at least to some extent, of making the expert's professional knowledge and experience available to other individuals. In this case, the computer system, or "thinking machine," not only stores the scientific or professional expertise of one human being but also permits ready access to this valuable knowledge base because of its artificial intelligence, which guides other human users.

Automatic devices are those that operate without direct human control. NASA has used many such automated "smart" machines to explore other objects within our solar system. For example, the two Viking landers placed on the Martian surface in 1976 represent one of the great triumphs of robotic space exploration. After separation from the Viking orbiter spacecraft, the lander (protected by an aeroshell) descended into the thin Martian atmosphere at speeds of approximately 16,000 kilometers (10,000 miles) per hour. It was slowed down by aerodynamic drag until its aeroshell was discarded. The lander slowed down further by releasing parachutes and finally achieved a gentle landing by automatically firing retrorockets. This entire sequence was accomplished automatically by both Viking landers. The plunge of the Galileo Probe into the Jovian atmosphere in December 1995 is another example of advanced automation in support of space exploration.

Teleoperation implies that a human operator is in remote control of a mechanical system. Control signals can be sent by means of "hardwire" (if the device under control is nearby) or via electromagnetic signals (e.g., laser or radio frequency) if the robot system is some distance away. Of course, in dealing with great distances in interplanetary exploration, eventually even electromagnetic-wave transmission cannot accommodate real-time control. When the device to be controlled on another world is light-minutes or even light-hours away, teleoperation must yield to increasing levels of autonomous, machine-intelligence-dependent robotic operation.

Robotic devices are computer-controlled mechanical systems that are capable of manipulating or controlling other machine devices. Robots may be mobile or fixed in place and either fully automatic or teleoperated.

Frequently large quantities of data are involved in the operation of automatic robotic devices. The field of distributed data management is concerned with ways of organizing cooperation among independent but mutually interacting databases.

Finally, in the field of artificial intelligence, the concept of cognition and learning refers to the development of a machine intelligence that can deal with new facts, unexpected events, and even contradictory information. Today's "smart" machines handle new data by means of preprogrammed methods or logic steps. Tomorrow's "smarter" machines will have the ability to learn, possibly even to understand, as they encounter new situations and are forced to change their mode of operation.

See also: ROBOTICS.

artificial satellite An early aerospace term used to describe an object, such as a spacecraft, built by human beings and placed in orbit around Earth or other planetary body. *Sputnik 1,* launched by the Soviets on October 4, 1957, was the first artificial satellite to be placed in orbit around Earth.

ascending node That point at which a planet, planetoid, or comet crosses to the north side of the ecliptic; that point at which a satellite or spacecraft crosses to the north side of the equatorial plane of its primary. Sometimes called *northbound node.* The opposite is the DESCENDING NODE.

See also: ORBITS OF OBJECTS IN SPACE.

asperities Minute irregularities or roughnesses on the surface of a component, usually the result of the surface-refinishing process.

assembly A number of parts and/or subassemblies joined together to perform a specific function and capable of disassembly. The distinction between an assembly and a subassembly is determined by the particular application. A grouping used in one application as a complete assembly also may be used in another application as a subassembly to form part of a larger assembly.

asteroid A small, solid object orbiting the Sun independently of a planet. The majority of the asteroids—which are also called *minor planets* or *planetoids*—have orbits that lie in the "main asteroid belt" between Mars and Jupiter. Most asteroids travel around the Sun at distances of 2.2 to 3.3 astronomical units and possess orbital periods between three and six years. There are more than 500 main-belt asteroids over 50 kilometers (km) in diameter and thousands that are smaller. Approximately 2,000 of these have fairly well-known orbits and have been assigned names. For example, Ceres (which has a diameter of about 1,000 km) was discovered in 1801 by the Italian astronomer Giuseppe Piazzi (1746–1826). He named this asteroid (the first discovered) after the Roman goddess of agriculture.

In the 20th century, asteroids with orbits that cross Earth's orbit also have been discovered. These "Earth-crossers," or inner solar system asteroids, are divided into three groups: Aten, Apollo, and Amor (where each group takes on the name of its principal asteroid). Some scientists have postulated that the impact of an Earth-crossing asteroid may have been responsible for the disappearance of the dinosaurs and many other animal species on Earth some 65 million years ago.

Asteroids have been classified on the basis of their spectral characteristics—that is, by how much light of different colors they reflect. The three major classifications are: C-type (carbonaceous), S-type (silicaceous), and M-type (metallic).

See also: EXTRATERRESTRIAL CATASTROPHE THEORY; NEAR EARTH ASTEROID RENDEZVOUS (NEAR) MISSION.

asteroid belt The region between the orbits of Mars and Jupiter that contains the great majority of

Figure 11. Ham reaches out for an apple after his suborbital flight on January 31, 1961   *(NASA and US Air Force)*

the asteroids or minor planets. These planetoids have periods lying between three and six years and orbit the Sun at distances of 2.2 to 3.3 astronomical units.

See also: ASTEROID.

asteroid detection system (ADS) A proposed planetary defense observation network consisting of multispectral ground-based and space-based sensors for the surveillance, detection, tracking, and characterization of (natural) space objects (i.e., asteroids and comets) that might pose a major threat if they were to collide with Earth. This advanced system also would include a central facility to collect data from all the sensors in the network, maintain a current database of all known space objects, and disseminate collected information to appropriate authorities.

See also: ASTEROID.

asteroid mining The asteroids, especially Earth-crossing asteroids, might serve as "space warehouses" from which future space workers would extract certain critical materials needed in space-based industrial activities and in the construction and operation of large space habitats. On some asteroids scientists expect to find water (trapped), organic compounds, and metals. In time, it may be far more efficient to mine an Earth-crossing asteroid than to lift the very same raw materials from Earth's surface. Therefore, some space visionaries now suggest that asteroid mining could play a major role in the evolution of a permanent human civilization in space.

See also: ASTEROID.

asteroid negation system (ANS) A proposed planetary defense system capable of intercepting any (natural) space object (i.e., an asteroid or comet) that was determined to be a threat to Earth. The system would accomplish this negation task in sufficient time to deflect the space object from its collision course with Earth or else fragment it into smaller pieces that would not pose a major planetary threat. Deflection and/or fragmentation could be accomplished with a variety of means, ranging from the detonation of nuclear explosives to the use of high specific impulse thrusters, kinetic energy projectiles, or directed energy devices.

See also: ASTEROID.

astro- A prefix meaning "star" or "stars" and (by extension) sometimes used as the equivalent of *celestial,* as in *astroengineering* or *astronaut.*

astrobiology The study of living organisms on celestial bodies other than Earth.

See also: EXOBIOLOGY.

astrobleme In planetary science, an impact structure; a geological structure produced by the hypervelocity impact of a meteoroid, comet, or asteroid.

astrochimp(s) The nickname given to the primates used during the early U.S. space program. In the Mercury Project (the first U.S. crewed space program), these astrochimps were used to test space capsule and launch system hardware prior to its commitment to human flight. For example, on January 31, 1961, a 17-kilogram (kg) (37-pound [lb]) chimpanzee, named Ham, was launched from Cape Canaveral by a Redstone rocket on a suborbital flight test of the Mercury Project spacecraft. During this mission, the propulsion system developed more thrust than planned—and the simian space traveler experienced overacceleration. After recovery Ham appeared to be in good physical condition. (See Figure 11.) However, when shown another space capsule, his reactions made it quite clear to his handlers that this particular astrochimp wanted no further role in the space program.

On November 29, 1961, another astrochimp, a 17-kg (37-lb) chimpanzee, named Enos, was launched successfully from Cape Canaveral by an Atlas rocket on the final orbital qualification flight test of the Mercury spacecraft. During the flight, Enos performed psychomotor duties and upon recovery was found to be in excellent physical condition.

See also: MERCURY PROJECT.

astrodynamics The practical application of celestial mechanics, astroballistics, propulsion theory, and allied fields to the problem of planning and directing the trajectories of space vehicles.

astrometry The branch of science concerned with the very precise measurement of the motion and position of celestial objects; a subset or branch of astronomy.

astronaut Literally, "star traveler"; in contemporary U.S. aerospace usage, a person who rides in a space vehicle; a person who travels in outer space. Compare with COSMONAUT.

astronautics 1. The science of space flight. 2. The talent, skill, or activity of operating spacecraft or aerospace vehicles.

astronomical Of or pertaining to astronomy or to observations of celestial objects.

astronomical unit (AU) A unit of distance in astronomy and space technology defined as the "mean" distance between the center of Earth and the center of the Sun—that is, the semimajor axis of Earth's orbit. One AU is equal to 149.6×10^6 kilometers (approximately 92.9 million miles), or 499.01 light-seconds.

astronomy The branch of science focusing on celestial objects, dealing with their size, location, composition, dynamics, origin and so on.
See also: ASTROPHYSICS.

astrophysics Astronomy addresses fundamental questions that have puzzled human beings since our primitive beginnings. What is the nature of the universe? How did it begin, how is it evolving, and what will be its eventual fate? As important as these questions are, there is another motive for astronomical studies. Since the 17th century, when Isaac Newton's studies of celestial mechanics helped him formulate the three basic laws of motion and the universal law of gravitation, the sciences of astronomy and physics have become intertwined. "Astrophysics" can be defined as the study of the nature and physics of stars and star systems. It provides the theoretical framework for understanding astronomical observations. At times astrophysics can be used to predict phenomena such as black holes, before they even have been observed by astronomers. The vast laboratory of outer space makes it possible to investigate large-scale physical processes that cannot be duplicated in a terrestrial laboratory.

Today astrophysics has within its reach the ability to bring about one of the greatest scientific achievements ever—a unified understanding of the total evolutionary scheme of the universe. This remarkable revolution in astrophysics is happening due to the confluence of two streams of technical development: remote sensing and space technology. Through the science of remote sensing, we

have developed sensitive instruments capable of detecting and analyzing radiation across the entire range of the electromagnetic (EM) spectrum. Space technology enables astrophysicists to place these sensitive instruments above Earth's atmosphere, where they can sense electromagnetic signals over nearly the entire spectrum (i.e., from the primordial microwave background radiation of the big bang to the energetic gamma ray emissions associated with compact objects such as neutron stars and black holes). Due to the absorbing nature of Earth's atmosphere, ground-based observatories are restricted to a rather narrow range of observable electromagnetic frequencies.

See also: BIG BANG THEORY; COSMIC BACKGROUND EXPLORER; COSMIC RAYS; GAMMA RAY OBSERVATORY; GAMMA RAY ASTRONOMY; HUBBLE SPACE TELESCOPE; INFRARED ASTRONOMY; ULTRAVIOLET (UV) ASTRONOMY; X-RAY ASTRONOMY.

asymmetric Lacking a mirror-image construction on both sides of a dividing line.

Atlas A family of launch vehicles originally developed by the U.S. Air Force as intercontinental ballistic missiles in the early 1960s. In 1946 the air force awarded a research contract to develop a missile capable of carrying a warhead 9,260 kilometers (km) (some 5,760 miles [mi]). At that time, the only "long-range" rocket in existence was the 320-km-(200-mi-) range German V-2 rocket from World War II. However, because of budget cuts and other government priorities, this missile was not given top priority and pursued by the air force until 1954.

The original Atlas manufacturing cycle began in 1955. On November 28, 1958 (less than 18 months after the first U.S. intercontinental ballistic missile [ICBM] flight), the Atlas performed a full-range flight test, flying more than 10,150 km (6,300 mi) across the South Atlantic Ocean from its launch site at Cape Canaveral Air Force Station, Florida. (See Figure 12.)

The capability of the Atlas for space missions was demonstrated dramatically on December 18 when an Atlas sustainer stage "steered" a communications repeater satellite into orbit. This satellite, Project SCORE (*S*ignal *C*ommunications *O*rbiting *R*elay *E*quipment) broadcast President Dwight O. Eisenhower's prerecorded Christmas message to the world. It was the first time the human voice had been beamed from space.

Figure 12. An Atlas-ABRES missile experiencing prelaunch checkout at Pad 11, Cape Canaveral AFS, Florida (March 1963) *(US Air Force)*

While research and development of the Atlas ICBM continued and the weapon system became operational and was installed in a variety of missile complexes around the country, this vehicle also began to achieve an enviable record as a space booster. In this new role, the Atlas systems were modified as required for many air force and NASA missions.

The "first generation" of Atlas vehicles (including the Atlas E, F, G, H, and Standard Launch Vehicle-3D [SLV-3D]) were all intermediate boosters. They served as launch vehicles in such space program missions as the Mercury Project, Ranger, Mariner, Mariner-Mars, Pioneer, INTELSAT, Fleet Satellite Communications (FLTSATCOM) and the Navstar Global Positioning System (GPS). In fact, the Atlas E and F space boosters were ICBMs that were removed from operational use in 1965 and stored until modified and launched as needed. The Atlas H and SLV-3D were basically the same vehicle, except for the addition of Atlas E guidance system to the Atlas H vehicle and the addition of the Centaur upper-stage inertial guidance system to the SLV-3D. The SLV-3D was stretched and then reidentified as the Atlas G vehicle. The following table summarizes some of the characteristics of the later members of the "first generation" in the Atlas launch vehicle family.

CHARACTERISTICS OF EARLY ATLAS SPACE BOOSTERS

Vehicle Designation:	Atlas E/F	Atlas G	Atlas H
Thrust (at sea level):			
meganewtons	1.744	1.953	1.953
lb-force	392,000	439,000	439,000
Guidance System:	radio	radio	Centaur-inertial
Mass (loaded at launch)[a]			
kilograms	120,200	143,790	130,640
lb-mass	265,000	317,000	288,000
Size:[a]			
length, m (ft)	20.4 (67)	22.0 (72)	20.1 (66)
diameter, m (ft)	3.05 (10)	3.05 (10)	3.05 (10)
engine-cluster cross-section diameter, m (ft)	4.88 (16)	4.88 (16)	4.88 (16)

[a] Not including upper stage and payload.

Source: *Courtesy U.S. Air Force.*

Atlas vehicles have a cluster of three main-stage liquid-propellant rocket engines (two boosters and one sustainer engine) and two small vernier engines, which burn liquid oxygen (LO_2) and kerosene (RP-1). The main engines are ignited on the ground and brought up to approximately full thrust before vehicle launch. The modified Atlas E vehicles, with a total thrust of from 1.725 to 1.744 meganewtons (388,000 to 392,000 pounds-force [lbf]), are capable of boosting an 1,800-kilogram

Typical Missions	Atlas I Fairing		Atlas II Fairing		Atlas IIA Fairing		Atlas IIAS Fairing	
	Medium	Large	Medium	Large	Medium	Large	Medium	Large
Geosynchronous transfer orbit: 167 x 35,788 km (90 x 19,324 nmi) 27.0-deg transfer orbit inclination	2,375 kg 5,240 lb	2,255 kg 4,970 lb	2,950 kg 6,500 lb	2,810 kg 6,200 lb	3,160 kg 6,970 lb	3,045 kg 6,710 lb	3,830 kg 8,450 lb	3,700 kg 8,150 lb
Low earth orbit: 185 x 185 km (100 x 100 nmi) 28.5-deg orbit inclination				6,580 kg 14,500 lb		7,280 kg 16,050 lb		8,640 kg 19,050 lb
Earth escape: C_3=0 km²/sec²	1,635 kg 3,600 lb	1,530 kg 3,380 lb	2,100 kg 4,630 lb	1,900 kg 4,395 lb	2,660 kg 4,980 lb	2,165 kg 4,770 lb	2,795 kg 6,160 lb	2,685 kg 5,920 lb

Figure 13. Configurations and capabilities of contemporary Atlas Launch Vehicle family   *(NASA and Lockheed-Martin Company)*

(4,000-pounds-mass [lbm]) payload to an altitude of about 830 km (515 mi). In a typical launch sequence, all Atlas engines are ignited prior to liftoff. At approximately two minutes into the flight, the two booster engines are jettisoned and the sustainer engine continues to burn until cutoff at approximately 321 seconds into the flight, followed by payload separation at some 346 seconds into the flight. The liquid oxygen–(LO_2) and liquid hydrogen—(LH_2) burning Centaur upper stage often is used with the Atlas launch vehicle.

Newer versions of the Atlas vehicle have been developed to support contemporary government and commercial space transportation needs. (See Figure 13.)

See also: LAUNCH VEHICLE.

Atlas-Centaur class payload A payload with a mass of approximately 1,800 kilograms to 2,000 kilograms (4,000 pounds-mass to 4,400 pounds-mass).

atmosphere 1. In general, gases and suspended solid and liquid materials that are gravitationally bound to the region around a planet or satellite. 2. The breathable environment inside a space capsule, aerospace vehicle, spacecraft, or space station. The cabin atmosphere. 3. A unit of (gas) pressure, representing the pressure exerted by the air on a 29.92 inch (76 cm) column of mercury at sea level at 45 degrees latitude.

$$1 \text{ atm} = 14.7 \text{ lb}_{force}/in^2 = 1.01325 \times 10^5 \text{ N}/m^2 \text{ (pascals)}$$

atm = atmosphere
lb_{force} = pounds-force
in^2 = inches-squared
N = newton
m^2 = meter squared

4. The gaseous envelope surrounding planet Earth. The normal composition of clean, dry atmospheric air near sea level is approximately: nitrogen (N_2), 78%; oxygen (O_2), 21%; argon (Ar), 0.9%; and carbon dioxide (CO_2), 0.03%. In addition to small amounts of other gases (i.e., neon [Ne], xenon [Xe], helium [He], and krypton [K_R]), the atmosphere contains water vapor, dust particles, human-generated pollutant chemicals, bacteria, among other things. Earth's electrically neutral atmosphere is composed of four primary layers. The lowest layer, the one we live in on Earth's surface, is called the *troposhere.* This region extends up to about 16 kilometers (9.94 mi) altitude and is the place within which most of Earth's "weather" occurs. Extending from about 16 km altitude to 48 km (29.8 mi) is the *stratosphere.* The vast majority (some 99%) of the air in Earth's atmosphere is located in these two regions. Above the stratosphere, from approximately 48 km (29.8 mi) to 85 km (52.8 mi) is the *mesosphere.* Finally, the uppermost layer of the atmosphere is called the *thermosphere* (or *ionosphere*), which extends out to approximately 1,000 km (621 mi). The upper thermosphere is also characterized by the presence of electrically charged gases, or plasma. The boundaries of and structure within the ionosphere vary considerably according to solar activity. Finally, overlapping the ionosphere is the *magnetosphere,* which extends from approximately 80 km (49.7 mi) to 65,000 km (40,400 mi) on the side of Earth toward the Sun and trails out more than 300,000 km (186,540 mi) on the side of Earth away from the Sun. The geomagnetic field of Earth plays a dominant role in the behavior of charged particles in the magnetosphere.

See also: EARTH; MAGNETOSPHERE.

atmospheric braking The action of slowing down an object entering the atmosphere of Earth or another planet from space, by using the aerodynamic drag exerted by the atmosphere.

See also: AEROBRAKE.

atmospheric compensation The physical distortion or modification of the components of an optical system to compensate for the distortion of light waves as they pass through the atmosphere and the optical system.

atmospheric drag With respect to Earth-orbiting spacecraft, the retarding force produced on a satellite, aerospace vehicle, or spacecraft by its passage through upper regions of Earth's atmosphere. This retarding force drops off exponentially with altitude and has only a small effect on spacecraft whose perigee is higher than a few hundred kilometers. For spacecraft with lower perigee values, the cumulative effect of atmospheric drag eventually will cause them to reenter the denser regions of Earth's atmosphere (and be destroyed) unless they are provided with an onboard propulsion system that can accomplish periodic reboost.

atmospheric electricity Electrical phenomena (i.e., lightning), regarded collectively, which occur in Earth's atmosphere.

atmospheric entry The penetration of any planetary atmosphere by an object from outer space; specifically, the penetration of Earth's atmosphere by a crewed or uncrewed capsule, aerospace vehicle, or spacecraft. Also called *entry* and sometimes *reentry* (although typically the object is making its initial return or entry after a space flight).

atmospheric heave In ballistic missile defense, raising a large volume of the upper atmosphere to a substantially higher altitude (i.e., hundreds of kilometers) by means of a nuclear detonation within the atmosphere. This could have several different effects on the capability of a missile defense system. For example, nuclear background radiation problems could be worsened substantially for the defense and some directed-energy weapons could be partially neutralized. On the other hand, offensive decoys could become more detectable and offensive targeting could become more difficult.
See also: BALLISTIC MISSILE DEFENSE.

atmospheric pressure The pressure (force per unit area) at any point in a planetary atmosphere due solely to the weight of the atmospheric gases above that point.

atmospheric probe Scientific instruments (usually carried by a space probe) for determining the pressure, composition, and temperature of a planet's atmosphere at different altitudes. For example, the atmospheric probe that was released from the Galileo spacecraft and plunged into the Jovian atmosphere in December 1995.
See also: GALILEO PROJECT.

atmospheric refraction Refraction resulting when a ray of radiant energy passes obliquely through an atmosphere.

atmospheric window A wavelength interval within which a planetary atmosphere readily transmits electromagnetic radiation.
See also: WINDOW.

atom A tiny particle of matter (the smallest part of an element) indivisible by chemical means. An atom is the fundamental building block of the chemical elements. The elements, such as hydrogen, iron, lead, and uranium, differ from each other because they consist of different types of atoms. According to (simplified) contemporary atomic theory, an atom consists of a dense inner core (the nucleus) that contains protons and neutrons and a cloud or swarm of orbiting electrons. Atoms are electrically neutral, with the number of protons being equal to the number of electrons.

atomic bomb A bomb whose energy comes from the fission (splitting) of heavy elements, such as uranium and plutonium. Compare this term with HYDROGEN BOMB.
See also: NUCLEAR WEAPON.

atomic clock A precision device for measuring or standardizing time that is based on periodic vibrations of certain atoms (cesium) or molecules (ammonia). For example, the cesium clock is used in establishing the SI definition of the second.
See also: INTERNATIONAL SYSTEM OF UNITS.

atomic mass The mass of a neutral atom of a nuclide usually expressed in atomic mass units (amu).
See also: ATOMIC MASS UNIT; ATOMIC WEIGHT; MASS NUMBER.

atomic mass unit (amu) One-twelfth ($1/12$) the mass of a neutral atom of the most abundant isotope of carbon, ^{12}C.

atomic number (symbol: Z) The number of protons in the nucleus of an atom and also its positive charge. Each chemical element has its characteristic atomic number. For example, the atomic number for carbon is 6, while the atomic number for uranium is 92.

atomic weapon An explosive weapon in which the energy is produced by nuclear fission or fusion.
See also: NUCLEAR WEAPON.

atomic weight The mass of an atom relative to other atoms. The present-day basis of the scale of atomic weights is carbon; the most common isotope of this element has arbitrarily been assigned an atomic weight of 12. The unit of the scale is $1/12$ the weight of the carbon-12 atom, or roughly the mass of one proton or one neutron. The atomic weight of any element is approximately equal to the total number of protons and neutrons in its nucleus.

atomize To divide a liquid into extremely minute particles, either by impact with a jet of steam or compressed air or by passage through some mechanical device.

attached payload 1. With respect to the space shuttle, any payload that is launched in the orbiter, remains structurally and functionally attached throughout the flight, and is landed in the orbiter. 2. With respect to a space station, a payload located on the base truss outside the pressurized modules.

See also: PAYLOAD.

attached shock wave An oblique or conical shock wave that appears to be in contact with the leading edge of an airfoil or the nose of a body in a supersonic flow field. Also called an *attached shock.*

attack assessment An evaluation of information to determine the potential or actual nature and objectives of an attack for the purposes of providing information for timely decisions.

attenuation The decrease in intensity of a signal, beam, or wave upon passage through a transmitting medium. Attenuation is due to the action of the transmitting medium itself and occurs as a result of absorption of energy and of scattering out of the path of a detector but does not include the reduction due to geometric spreading (i.e., the inverse square of the distance effect). The attenuation process can be described by the equation:

$$I = I_0 \, e^{-\alpha x}$$

where I is the flux (photons or particles per unit area) at a specified distance (x) into the attenuating medium, I_0 is the initial flux, and α is the attenuation coefficient (with units of inverse length) and e is a special mathematical function, the irrational number 2.71828 . . . The expression e^x is called the exponential function.

attitude In general, the position of a body as determined by the inclination of the axes to some frame of reference. In aerospace, the position or orientation of a vehicle (e.g., a spacecraft, shuttle orbiter,

airplane) either in motion or at rest, as determined by the relationship between its axes and a reference line or plane (e.g., the horizon) or a fixed system of reference axes. Attitude often is expressed in terms of *pitch, roll,* and *yaw.*

attitude and articulation control subsystem (AACS) A spacecraft's *attitude,* or orientation in space, must be stabilized and controlled for a variety of reasons, including: to accurately point the spacecraft's high-gain antenna to Earth, to precisely point onboard science experiments for accurate data collection and subsequent interpretation and analysis, to support spacecraft thermal control by carefully managing the heating and cooling effects of sunlight and shadow, and to support the precise execution of propulsive maneuvers so that the spacecraft achieves the correct trajectory and final destination on its mission.

Stabilization can be achieved by spinning the spacecraft, as was done on the *Pioneer 10* and *11* missions to the outer solar system and on the Galileo mission to Jupiter. In this approach, the gyroscopic action of the rotating spacecraft mass is the stabilizing mechanism. Propulsion-subsystem thrusters are fired to make any desired changes in the spacecraft's spin-stabilized attitude.

The spacecraft also can be designed for active three-axis stabilization, as was done on the *Voyager 1* and *2* spacecraft, which explored the outer solar system and beyond. In this method of stabilization, small propulsion subsystem thrusters gently nudge the spacecraft back and forth within a deadband of allowed attitude error. Another method of achieving active three-axis stabilization is to use electrically powered reaction wheels, which are also called *momentum wheels.* These massive wheels are mounted in three orthogonal axes onboard the spacecraft. To rotate the spacecraft in one direction, the proper wheel in the opposite direction is spun. To rotate the vehicle back, the wheel is slowed down. Excessive momentum, which builds up in the system due to internal friction and external forces, occasionally must be removed from the system; this usually is accomplished with propulsive maneuvers.

Either general approach to spacecraft stabilization has basic advantages and disadvantages. Spin-stabilized vehicles provide a continuous "sweeping motion," which is generally desirable for fields and particle instruments, but these types of spacecraft then may require complicated systems to despin antennas or optical instruments that must be pointed at targets in space. Three-axis controlled spacecraft can point antennas and optical instruments precisely (without the necessity for despinning), but these craft then may have to perform rotation maneuvers to use their fields and particles science instruments properly.

The attitude and articulation control subsystem (AACS) computer manages the tasks involved in spacecraft stabilization through its interface equipment. Celestial references and/or onboard gyroscopes provide the necessary attitude reference data. For example, star trackers, star scanners, solar trackers, Sun sensors, and planetary limb trackers might be used (depending on the spacecraft's mission characteristics) to provide celestial reference data. Gyroscopes also are carried onboard the spacecraft for attitude reference when celestial references are not being used. Some spacecraft have been designed to use celestial reference data nearly continuously, they rely on gyroscopes for attitude reference data only during relatively brief maneuver periods when celestial reference is lost. Since gyroscopes are mechanical devices, they precess and drift due to internal friction. Great care must be taken in calibrating these drift rates, the AACS computer should be capable of compensating for them as part of its attitude knowledge-base development during the mission.

The AACS also can control the articulation of a spacecraft's movable appendages, such as high-gain antennas, solar panels, despun components, and optical scan platforms. In many modern spacecraft this is a function for the AACS, because the subsystem keeps track of the spacecraft's attitude and the locations of the Sun and Earth, and it can compute the proper direction to point a specific appendage or articulated component readily. For example, during a planetary flyby encounter, certain optical instruments might need to be kept precisely on target, while the spacecraft's high-gain antenna needs to be pointed to Earth for data transmission.

See also: GALILEO PROJECT; PIONEER 10, 11; SPACECRAFT; VOYAGER.

attitude control 1. The regulation of the attitude of an aircraft, spacecraft, or aerospace vehicle. 2. The device or system that automatically regulates and corrects attitude, especially in a pilotless or robotic vehicle.
See also: ATTITUDE.

attitude jet A jetstream used to correct or change the attitude of an aircraft, spacecraft, or aerospace vehicle; the nozzle that directs this jetstream.
See also: ATTITUDE.

attrition rate In defense, a factor (normally expressed as a percentage) reflecting the degree of loss of personnel or material due to various causes within a specified time.

audible sound Sound containing frequency components lying between 15 hertz (a low rumble) and 20,000 hertz (a shrill, high-pitched whistle)—the hearing limits of the human ear.

audiofrequency range The range of sound wave frequencies to which the human ear is sensitive, approximately 15 hertz (a low rumble) to 20,000 hertz (a shrill whistle). Also called *audiorange.*

aurora Visible glow in a planet's ionosphere produced by interaction of the planet's magnetosphere and particles from the Sun (solar wind). On Earth, the Aurora Borealis (or Northern Lights) and the Aurora Australis (or Southern Lights) are visible manifestations of the intense activity in the geomagnetic field surrounding the planet. Observed and studied since ancient times, true explanation of the aurora awaited the discovery of the trapped radiation belts (also called the VAN ALLEN RADIATION BELTS) surrounding Earth. Disturbances in the geomagnetic field scatter trapped electrons and protons into the upper atmosphere at high latitudes, where they excite the nitrogen and oxygen atoms and molecules. The variety of auroral color is due to mixing of line emissions from discrete excited states of atmospheric gases.
See also: EARTH'S TRAPPED RADIATION BELTS.

autoignition Self-ignition or spontaneous combustion of propellant.
See also: HYPERGOLIC IGNITION.

autoignition temperature The temperature at which combustible materials ignite spontaneously in air.

automated payloads Payloads that are supported by an uncrewed spacecraft capable of operating independently of the space shuttle orbiter vehicle. Automated payloads are detached from the orbiter during the operational phase of their flights.
See also: SPACE TRANSPORTATION SYSTEM.

automatic control Control of devices and equipment, including aerospace vehicles and spacecraft, by automatic means.

automatic pilot Equipment that automatically stabilizes the attitude of a vehicle about its pitch, roll, and yaw axes. Also called *autopilot;* sometimes referred as "George"—as in "let George (the autopilot) fly the vehicle."

automation 1. Mechanization of a process or system to proceed without human intervention. 2. The implementation of processes by automatic means. 3. The branch of science dealing with the theory and construction of self-controlled systems and machines.

auxiliary power unit (APU) A power unit carried on a spacecraft, aerospace vehicle, or aircraft that can be used in addition to the main sources of power on the craft.

auxiliary stage 1. A small propulsion unit that may be used with a payload. One or more of these units may be used to provide the additional velocity required to place a payload in the desired orbit or trajectory. 2. A propulsion system used to provide midcourse trajectory corrections, braking maneuvers, and/or orbital adjustments.

avionics The contraction of *aviation* and *electronics.* The term refers to the application of electronics to systems and equipment used in aeronautics and astronautics.

Avogadro's hypothesis The volume occupied by a mole of gas at a given pressure and temperature is the same for all gases. This hypothesis also can be expressed as: Equal volumes of all gases measured at the same temperature and pressure contain the same number of molecules. This hypothesis was first proposed in 1811 by Count Amedeo Avogadro (1776–1856), an Italian physicist. In a strict sense, it is valid only for ideal or perfect gases.

Avogadro's number (symbol: N_A) The number of molecules per mole of any substance.

$$N_A = 6.022 \times 10^{23} \text{ molecules/mole}$$

Also called the *Avogadro constant.*

axial flow compressor A rotary compressor having interdigitated rows or stages of rotary and stationary blades through which the flow of fluid is substantially parallel to the rotor's axis of rotation. Compare CENTRIFUGAL COMPRESSOR.

axis (plural: axes) 1. A straight line about which a body rotates (axis of rotation) or along which its center of gravity moves (axis of translation). 2. A straight line around which a plane figure may rotate to produce a solid; a line of symmetry. 3. One of a set of reference lines for a coordinate system.

azimuth 1. Horizontal direction or bearing. 2. In navigation, the horizontal direction of a celestial point from a terrestrial point, expressed as the angular distance from a reference direction, usually measured from 0° at the reference direction clockwise through 360 degrees. 3. In astronomy, the direction of a celestial point from a terrestrial point measured clockwise from the north or south point of the meridian plane. 4. In surveying, the horizontal direction of an object measured clockwise from the south point of the meridian plane.

background 1. In general, any effect in a remote sensing system or other monitoring device above which the phenomenon of interest must manifest itself before it can be observed meaningfully. 2. In astronomy, the uniform intensity over a large region of the sky. 3. In environmental science and air pollution control, the concentration of air pollutants in a definite area during a fixed period of time prior to the starting up or on the stoppage of a source of emission under control. In toxic substance monitoring, the average presence in the environment, originally referring to naturally occurring phenomena. Sometimes called *background level.*

background radiation The nuclear (ionizing) radiation occurring in the natural environment, including cosmic rays and radiation from naturally radioactive elements found in the air, the soil, and the human body. Sometimes referred to as *natural radiation background.* The term also may mean ionizing radiation (natural and human-made) that is unrelated to a particular experiment or series of measurements.

backlash 1. Dead space or unwanted movement that results from fabrication and assembly tolerance in linkages; excessive backlash produces poor positional control of the supervised element or error in position instrumentation. 2. The clearance between the tooth spacing of a gear and the tooth thickness of a meshing gear.

backlobe A radiation (radio frequency) lobe whose axis makes an angle of approximately 180 degrees with respect to the axis of the major lobe of the antenna.

backout To undo things or events that already have been done during a launch vehicle countdown, usually in reverse order.

backscattering In general, the scattering of radiation in a direction generally opposite to the direction of the incident radiation. In radar surveillance, that portion of the radar beam scattered directly back toward the source by the terrain surface.

backup 1. A unit or item kept available to replace one that fails to perform satisfactorily. 2. An item or system under development (e.g., a space probe) intended to perform the same general functions as another item or system under development.

backup crew A crew of astronauts or cosmonauts trained to replace the prime crew, if necessary, on a particular space mission.

baffle 1. In the combustion chamber of a liquid rocket engine, an obstruction used to prevent combustion instability by maintaining uniform propellant mixtures and equalizing pressures. 2. In the fuel tank of a liquid rocket system, an obstruction used to prevent sloshing of the propellant. 3. In an optical or multispectral sensor system, a barrier or obstruction used to prevent stray (unwanted) radiation from reaching a sensitive detector element.

ballast 1. With respect to lighter-than-air (LTA) craft, any expendable mass (e.g., water) that can be dropped overboard to enable the airship or balloon to ascend to higher altitudes or to compensate for increased payload mass or lifting gas (e.g., helium) loss. 2. With respect to aerospace flight vehicles and satellites, an inactive (i.e., nonfunctioning) high-density mass used to maintain the system's dynamic stability and overall mass balance.

ballistic body A body free to move, behave, and be modified in appearance, contour, or texture by ambient conditions, substances, or forces, such as by the pressure of gases in a gun, by the rifling or grooves in a gun barrel, by gravity, by temperature, or by air particles. It should be noted that a guided missile or rocket with a self-contained propulsion unit is *not* considered a ballistic body during the period of its propulsion or guidance.

ballistic coefficient An aerospace design parameter that indicates the relative magnitude of inertial and aerodynamic effects and is a measure of an object's ability to penetrate atmospheric resistance. This parameter is used in performance analysis of objects moving through the atmosphere.

ballistic flyby Unpowered flight similar to a bullet's trajectory, governed by gravity and by the body's previously acquired velocity.

ballistic missile A missile that is guided and propelled only during the initial phase of its flight. During the nonpowered, nonguided portion of its flight, it describes a trajectory similar to that of an artillery shell and operates primarily in accordance with the laws of ballistics. Any missile that does not rely on aerodynamic surfaces to produce lift and consequently follows a ballistic trajectory when thrust is terminated. A guided vehicle propelled into space by rocket engines. Thrust is terminated at a predesignated time after which the missile's reentry vehicles are released and follow free-falling (ballistic) trajectories toward their ground targets under the influence of gravity. Much of a reentry vehicle's trajectory will be above Earth's atmosphere. Compare with CRUISE MISSILE and GUIDED MISSILE.

See also: BALLISTIC MISSILE DEFENSE; LAUNCH VEHICLE.

ballistic missile defense (BMD) A defense system that is designed to protect a territory from incoming ballistic missiles. A BMD system usually is conceived of as having several independent layers designed to destroy ballistic missiles or their warheads at any or all points in their trajectory—from launch until just before target impact.

The phases of a typical ballistic missile trajectory are shown in Figure 14. During the boost phase, the rocket engines accelerate the missile and its warhead payload through and out of the atmosphere and provide intense, highly specific observables. A post-boost, or bus deployment, phase occurs next, during which multiple warheads (or perhaps a single warhead) and penetration aids are released from a post-boost vehicle. In the midcourse phase, the warheads and penetration aids travel on trajectories above the atmosphere; they reenter the atmosphere in the terminal phase, where they are affected by atmospheric drag.

An effective ballistic missile defense system capable of engaging the missile attack all along its flight path must perform certain key functions including: (1) promptly and reliably warning of an attack and initiating the defense; (2) continuously tracking all threatening objects from the beginning to the end of their trajectories; (3) efficiently intercepting and destroying the booster or post-boost vehicle; (4) efficiently discriminating between enemy warheads and decoys through filtering of lightweight penetration aids; (5) efficiently and economically intercepting and destroying enemy warheads (reentry vehicles) in the midcourse phase of their flight; (6) intercepting and destroying the enemy warheads (reentry vehicles) at the outer reaches of the atmosphere during the terminal phase of their flight; and (7) effectively coordinating all of the defensive system's components through battle management, communications, and data processing.

Figure 15 presents a concept for ballistic missile defense during the *boost phase* of the enemy's bal-

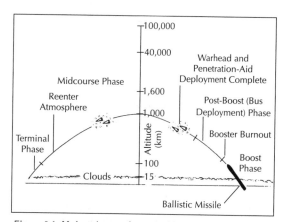

Figure 14. Major phases of a typical ballistic missile flight trajectory *(U.S. Department of Defense)*

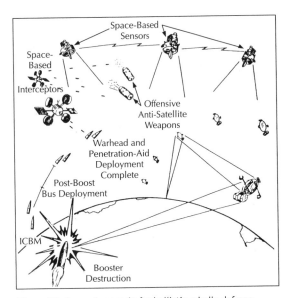

Figure 15. General scenario for ballistic missile defense during the boost phase of a ballistic missile's flight
(U.S. Department of Defense)

listic missile flight. An essential requirement is a global, full-time surveillance capability to detect a ballistic missile attack, to define its destination and intensity, to determine targeted areas, and to provide data to guide boost-phase interceptors and post-boost vehicle tracking systems. Attacks may range from a single or perhaps a few missiles to a massive simultaneous launch. For every enemy booster destroyed during this phase, the number of potentially hostile objects to be identified and sorted out by the remaining elements of a multilayered (or multitiered) ballistic missile defense system will be significantly reduced. An early defensive response also will minimize the numbers of deployed penetration aids. Space-based sensors would be used to detect and define the ballistic missile attack. Space-based interceptors would protect these sensor systems from enemy antisatellite (ASAT) weapons and, as a secondary mission, also would be used to attack the enemy ballistic missiles. For the boost phase defense scenario depicted in Figure 15, nonnuclear, direct-impact projectiles (i.e., kinetic energy weapons) are being used against the enemy's offensive weapons (i.e., ASAT weapons and warheads) while directed-energy weapons (e.g., high-energy lasers) are being used to destroy the enemy's boosters early in the flight trajectory.

Similarly, Figure 16 illustrates a generalized ballistic missile defense scenario that might occur during the *midcourse* phase. Intercept outside the atmosphere during the midcourse phase of a missile attack would require the defense to cope with decoys designed to attract interceptors and to exhaust the defensive forces. However, continuing discrimination of nonthreatening objects and continuing attrition of reentry vehicles would reduce the pressure on the terminal phase missile defense system. Engagement times are longer during the midcourse phase than during other phases of a ballistic missile trajectory. Figure 16 depicts space-based sensors that can discriminate among warheads, decoys, and debris and the interceptors that the defense has committed to the battle. The nonnuclear, direct-impact projectiles race toward warheads that the space-based sensors have identified as credible targets.

Finally, Figure 17 illustrates a ballistic missile defense scenario during the *terminal phase* of the attack. This phase is essentially the final line of defense. Threatening objects include warheads shot at but not destroyed, objects not previously detected, and decoys that have neither been discriminated against nor destroyed. All of these threatening objects must be dealt with by the interceptors of the terminal phase defensive system. An airborne optical adjunct (i.e., airborne sensor plat-

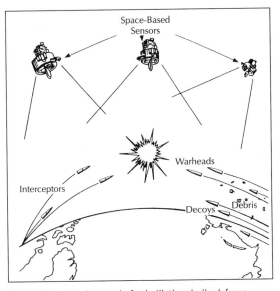

Figure 16. General scenario for ballistic missile defense during the midcourse phase of a ballistic missile's flight
(U.S. Department of Defense)

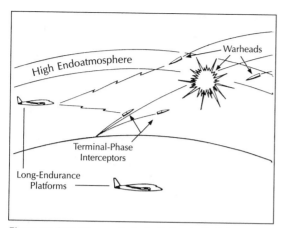

Figure 17. General scenario for ballistic missile defense during the terminal phase of a ballistic missile's flight
(*U.S. Department of Defense*)

form) is depicted here. Surviving enemy reentry vehicles are detected in the late exoatmospheric portion of their flight with sensors onboard the long-endurance (crewed or robotic) aerial platforms. Then terminal defense interceptors, illustrated here as nonnuclear, direct-impact projectiles, are guided to these remaining warheads and destroy them as they travel through the upper portions of the atmosphere.

Previous and contemporary ballistic missile defense studies continue to support the general conclusion that an efficient defense against ballistic missile attacks would most likely require a multilayered or multitiered defensive system. Most likely some missiles (or other objects that are part of the attack) will be able to penetrate any one defensive tier, such that those that have not been intercepted and destroyed at one phase will move on to the next phase. For example, a 10% "leakage" in each of three defensive tiers would amount to an overall leakage of only 0.1% for the defensive system. A single defensive layer that can achieve 90% intercept-and-destroy effectiveness appears to be less complex and costly than a single-layer defensive system required to achieve 99.9% effectiveness. Consequently, scientists and planners involved in designing and developing ballistic missile defense systems consider it far more reasonable to construct a three- or perhaps four-layer defense system with an equivalent effectiveness of 99.9% or better than it is to develop a comparable single-layer ballistic missile defense system. Finally, a multitiered defense system also compli-

cates an attacker's planning because most likely any single method the attacker might use to circumvent the defensive system would not be equally effective for each tier. This compounds the uncertainty enemy planners would have about the effectiveness of any missile attack they might contemplate.

ballistic trajectory The path followed by a body being acted only by gravitational forces and the resistance of the medium through which it passes. A rocket without lifting surfaces describes a ballistic trajectory after its propulsive unit(s) stops operating.

balloon-type rocket A liquid-fuel rocket, such as the Atlas, which requires the pressure of its propellants (or other gases) within to give it structural integrity.
See also: ATLAS.

ball valve A valve in which a ball regulates an opening by rising and falling due to fluid pressure, a spring, or its own weight.

band 1. In physics and spectroscopy, a closely spaced set of spectral lines associated with atomic or molecular energy levels (e.g., an *absorption band*). 2. In communications and radar technology, a frequency band or range of frequencies (e.g., *C-band*, the microwave band in which the wavelengths are at or near 5.6 centimeters).

band-pass filter A wave filter that has a single transmission band extending from a lower cutoff frequency greater than zero to a finite upper cutoff frequency.

bandwidth 1. In general, the number of hertz (cycles per second) between the upper and lower limits of a frequency band. Bandwidth is essentially a measure of the span of frequencies available in a signal or passed by the band-limiting stages of a system. Bandwidth, for example, is a fundamental parameter of any imaging system and determines the ultimate resolution available. 2. In information and communications theory, the data capacity of a communications channel; the range of frequencies that can pass along a communications link. For example, telephone lines carry voice communications at approximately 3 kilohertz bandwidth (3,000 hertz). 3. In antenna theory, the range of frequencies within which an antenna's performance conforms to a specified standard.

bar A unit of pressure in the centimeter-gram-second (cgs) system.

$$1 \text{ bar} = 10^6 \text{ dynes/cm}^2 = 10^5 \text{ newtons/m}^2 \text{ (pascals)} \approx 750 \text{ mmHg}$$

The term *millibar* (symbol: mb) is encountered often in meteorology.

$$1 \text{ millibar (mb)} = 10^{-3} \text{ bar} = 100 \text{ pascals}$$

barbecue mode The slow roll of an aerospace vehicle, such as the space shuttle orbiter, or a spacecraft for the purposes of thermal conditioning. In outer space solar radiation (unattenuated by any atmosphere) is intense on the side of the aerospace vehicle or spacecraft facing the Sun, while the side opposite the Sun becomes extremely cold. This slow rolling, or "barbecue," maneuver helps to equalize the external temperature of the space vehicle.

barn (symbol: b) A unit of area used in expressing nuclear cross sections.

$$1 \text{ barn (b)} = 10^{-24} \text{ cm}^2 = 10^{-28} \text{ m}^2$$

Barnard's star A red dwarf star approximately six light-years from the Sun, making it the fourth nearest star to our solar system. Discovered in 1916 by E. E. Barnard (1857–1923), this star is of popular interest because recent investigations of its "wobbling" motion have hinted at the possible existence of one or more Jupiter-size planets orbiting around it.

See also: EXTRASOLAR PLANETS; STARS.

barrier cooling In rocketry, the use of a controlled mixture ratio near the wall of a combustion chamber to provide a film of low-temperature gases to reduce the severity of gas-side heating of the chamber.

barycenter The center of mass of a system of masses at which point the total mass of the system is assumed to be concentrated. In a system of two particles (i.e., a binary system), the barycenter is located somewhere on a straight line connecting the center of each particle, but closer to the larger mass.

To illustrate the concept, let us consider Earth and the Moon as a binary system of masses. To simplify the discussion, we further assume that the mass of Earth (M_c) (about 6×10^{24} kilograms [kg]) is concentrated at its geometric center and that the mass of the Moon (M_m) (about 7.4×10^{22} kg) is also concentrated at its geometric center. The average distance (d) from the center of Earth to the center of the Moon is approximately 384,400 kilometers (km). The location of the barycenter (X_{BC}) along a line connecting the center of Earth and the center of the Moon is given by the equation: $X_{BC} = [M_m d] / [M_c + M_m]$, where the point X_{BC} is identified with respect to its distance from the center of Earth. Since the ratio of masses of Earth and the Moon is approximately 81 to 1, the barycenter is found at a distance from Earth's center equal to 1/82 of the distance from Earth to the Moon. This is a distance of about 4,700 km (2,920 miles), a point actually located within Earth (since Earth has a radius of about 6,400 kilometers).

See also: EARTH; MOON.

base 1. In mathematics, the number of different symbols in a number system; for example, 2 is the base in the binary system, while 10 is the base in the decimal system. Also, the number that when raised to a specific power has a logarithm equal to that power. For example, if the number 10 is raised to the power 4, it is equal to 10,000; the number 4 is then called the common logarithm of 10,000 to the base 10. 2. In chemistry, any of a large class of compounds that react with acids to form water and a salt. 3. In aerospace, a major facility or central location for extraterrestrial operations, such as a *lunar base*, a *Mars base*, or a *space base*.

base heating In aerospace, the heating of the aft (rear) portion of an aerospace vehicle or spacecraft. For example, as the space shuttle vehicle ascends through the atmosphere, thermal radiation from the expanding main engine and solid rocket exhaust plumes can preferentially heat the aft portion of the vehicle.

baseline In general, any line that serves as the basis for measurement of other lines. Often in aerospace usage, a reference case, such as a *baseline design*, a *baseline schedule*, or a *baseline budget*.

basic research Research directed toward the increase of knowledge, the primary aim being a greater understanding of the subject under study. Compare with APPLIED RESEARCH.

battery An electrochemical energy storage device that serves as a source of direct current or voltage, usually consisting of two or more electrolytic cells that are joined together and function as a single unit. The earliest Soviet and American Earth orbiting spacecraft (e.g., *Sputnik 1* and *Explorer 1*) depended on batteries for all their electric power. In general, however, batteries are acceptable as the sole source of electric power only on spacecraft or probes with missions of very short duration—hours, perhaps days, or at the most weeks in length. Solar photovoltaic arrays are used in combination with rechargeable batteries on the vast majority of today's spacecraft. The rechargeable batteries provide electrical power during "dark times" when the solar arrays cannot view the Sun. For example, the nickel-cadmium battery has been the common energy storage companion for solar cell power supply systems on many spacecraft. Specific energy densities (i.e., energy per unit mass) of about 10 watt-hours/kilogram are common at the 10 to 20% depths of discharge used to provide cycle life. The energy storage subsystem is usually the largest and heaviest part of a solar cell-rechargeable battery space power system.

Storable batteries can be used as the sole power supply for expendable space probes required to

operate in harsh planetary environments. For example, Figure 18 shows a typical high-temperature battery with a service life of about 5 minutes that can operate at a temperature of 430° Celsius. Activated when needed by a pyrotechnic device, this type of high-temperature battery could be used to power a probe briefly functioning in the high-temperature surface environment of Mercury or Venus. Unless extraordinary design features were built into a probe, its instruments and supporting subsystems most likely would succumb to the elevated temperature environment within a short time.

battle management In general, the analysis of data on the state of a battle and decisions regarding weapon aiming and allocation. Subtasks include command and communication, kill assessment, maintaining knowledge of the state and positions of all elements of the defense system, and calculation of target track files. With respect to ballistic missile defense (BMD), the set of instructions and rules and the corresponding hardware controlling the operation of a BMD system. Sensors and interceptors are allocated by the BMD system, and updated battle results are presented to the individuals in command for analysis and (as necessary) human intervention.

See also: BALLISTIC MISSILE DEFENSE.

baud (rate) A unit of signaling speed. The baud rate is the number of electronic signal changes or data symbols that can be transmitted by a communications channel per second. Named after J. M. Baudot (1845–1903), a French telegraph engineer.

beacon A light, group of lights, electronic apparatus, or other type of signaling device that guides, orients, or warns aircraft, spacecraft, or aerospace vehicles in flight. For example, a crash locator beacon emits a distinctive or characteristic signal that can be used by search-and-rescue teams to locate a downed aircraft, aerospace vehicle, or aborted or reentered spacecraft or space probe.

beam A narrow, well-collimated stream of particles (e.g., electrons or protons) or electromagnetic radiation (e.g., gamma ray photons) traveling in a single direction.

Figure 18. Diagram of a typical high-temperature battery with a service life of about five minutes and an operating temperature of 430° Celsius   (NASA)

beam director A system that focuses and points a laser or particle beam in the desired direction.

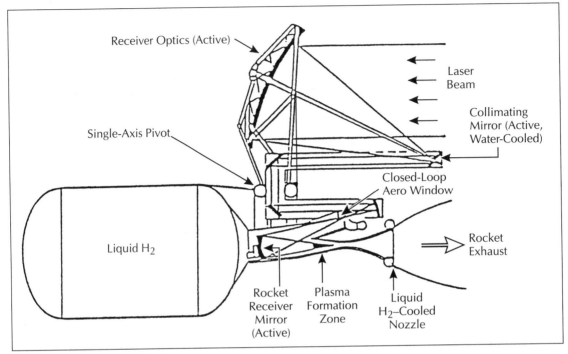

Figure 19. Conceptual laser thermal propulsion system *(NASA)*

beamed energy propulsion An advanced propulsion system concept in which a remote power source (e.g., the Sun or a high-powered laser) supplies thermal energy to the orbital transportation system. Two beamed energy concepts that have been subject to some recent study are *solar thermal propulsion* and *laser thermal propulsion.*

Solar thermal propulsion makes use of the Sun and does not require an onboard power source. Rather, a solar thermal rocket has to carry only the means of capturing solar energy, such as concentrators and mirrors. Then, instead of converting solar energy to electrical energy, as photovoltaic systems do, a solar thermal propulsion system uses the captured sunlight directly, as heat. The solar radiation is collected and focused to heat a propellant, such as hydrogen. The heated propellant is then fed through a conventional converging-diverging nozzle to produce thrust. Recent work on solar thermal thrusters has produced designs capable of using hydrogen propellant at a temperature of 2,700° Kelvin and of producing a thrust of 3.7 newtons with a corresponding propellant exhaust velocity of 7,900 meters per second. Further work is needed to develop very lightweight concentrators and simple yet reliable thrusters before these low-thrust solar thermal rockets can be used to move cargo between various destinations in cislunar space, as, for example, from LOW EARTH ORBIT (LEO) to low lunar orbit (LLO).

Laser thermal propulsion uses a remotely located high-power laser device to beam energy to the orbital transportation system, where it heats a propellant, such as hydrogen. The heated propellant is then discharged through a nozzle to produce thrust. (See Figure 19.) Laser propulsion concepts often are categorized according to the type of remote laser power source, namely continuous wave (CW) or repetitively pulsed (RP) systems. This type of low-thrust advanced orbital propulsion system also would support the transport of cargo between various destinations in cislunar space and possibly even from the surface of the Moon to low lunar orbit.

beam neutralizer A device located at the exit of a particle accelerator that neutralizes the charged ion beam in order to produce a neutral particle beam. Usually this is accomplished by stripping off extra electrons. (Note: A charged particle beam can be accelerated and focused by an accelerator while a neutral particle beam cannot.) This device can be a gas cell or foil, or may even utilize an appropriate laser beam.

beam rider A missile guided to its target by a beam of electromagnetic radiation, such as a radar beam or a laser beam.

becquerel (symbol: Bq) The SI UNIT of radioactivity. One becquerel corresponds to one nuclear transformation (disintegration) per second. Named after the French physicist A. Henri Becquerel (1852–1908), who discovered radioactivity in 1896. This unit is related to the *curie* (the traditional unit for activity) as follows: 1 curie (Ci) = 3.7 x 10^{10} becquerels (Bq).

bel (symbol: B) A logarithmic unit (n) used to express the ratio of two power levels, P_1 and P_2. Therefore, n (bels) = $\log_{10} (P_2/P_1)$. The *decibel* (symbol: dB) is encountered more frequently in physics, acoustics, telecommunications, and electronics, where 10 decibels = 1 bel. This unit is named after the American inventor Alexander Graham Bell (1847–1922). Compare with NEPER.

bell nozzle A nozzle with a circular opening for a throat and an axisymmetric contoured wall downstream of the throat that gives the nozzle a characteristic bell shape.
See also: NOZZLE; ROCKET.

bellows A thin-walled, circumferentially corrugated cylinder that can be elongated or compressed longitudinally and, when integrated into a duct assembly, can accommodate duct movements by deflection of the corrugations (convolutions); also used in tanks to provide positive expulsion of fluid and in fluid flow systems to isolate a regulator or valve or similar component.

bent-pipe communications Aerospace industry jargon for the use of relay stations to achieve non-line-of-sight transmission links.

Bernal sphere A spherical space habitat first proposed by the British physicist and writer J. Desmond Bernal in his 1929 work *The World, the Flesh, and the Devil* in which he boldly speculated about the colonization of outer space. Bernal's concept of spherical space habitats has influenced both early space station designs and more recent space settlement concepts. (See Figure 20.)

Figure 20. Large space settlement concept based on the Bernal sphere *(NASA)*

berthing In general, the joining of two orbiting spacecraft using a manipulator, or other mechanical device, to move one into contact (or very close proximity) with the other at a chosen interface. With respect to the space shuttle, the process of using the remote manipulator system (RMS) to gently bring together an orbital element (e.g., a deployable spacecraft) and the orbiter vehicle—as, for example, the positioning of an orbital element on the repair/maintenance support fixture in the orbiter's cargo bay.

beta decay The radioactive transformation of an atomic nucleus associated with the emission of a beta (β) particle. When a negative beta particle ($^0_{-1}β$) is emitted, a neutron has, in effect, been converted to a proton in the nucleus, thereby increasing the atomic number (Z) by one and leaving the atomic mass number (A) unchanged. In the case of positive beta particle ($^0_{+1}β$) decay, a *positron* (essentially an electron with a positive sign) is emitted from the radioactive nucleus, reflecting a change of a proton into a neutron. In the positive beta decay process, the atomic number of the nucleus is decreased by one, while the atomic mass number remains unchanged.

big bang theory A theory in cosmology concerning the origin of the universe. According to the big bang cosmological model, a very large explosion, also called the "initial singularity," started the space and time of our universe. The universe itself has been expanding ever since. It is currently thought that the big bang event occurred some 15 to 20 billion years ago. Astrophysical observations and discoveries lend support to the big bang model, especially the discovery of the cosmic microwave background (CMB) radiation in 1964.

Actually, there are two general variations of the big bang model. In one, it is assumed that the universe will expand forever. This is called the "open-universe model." The other variation, called the "closed-universe model," assumed that the universe eventually will recollapse—possibly back into another "singularity," or "big crunch," as some cosmologists like to call it.

Following the big bang, as the matter in the universe expanded, it cooled, condensing into galaxies, which in turn gave rise to stars and eventually other celestial objects, such as planets, asteroids, comets, and so on. The radiation released from this ancient explosion has now cooled and can be observed as the cosmic microwave background radiation.

See also: ASTROPHYSICS; COSMIC BACKGROUND EXPLORER.

binary 1. In chemistry, an alloy or compound formed from two elements. 2. In mathematics, a numerical system that uses the base 2. 3. In computer science a circuit or device that can be placed in either of two stable states; for example, either 0 or 1. Also called a *binary cell.*

binary code A code consisting of a combination of entries, each of which can assume only one of two possible values, for example, either 0 or 1. The "word" 00100110 is an example of an eight-bit binary code.

binary digit (bit) The fundamental unit of information (either 0 or 1) in binary notation. A grouping of such bits is needed to represent more complex units of information, such as symbols and letters. One such grouping used in modern computer systems is a sequence of eight bits to make up a more complex unit of information. This sequence of eight bits is called a *byte* (*binary digit eight*).

binary notation A numeric system that uses only two different characters, usually 0 and 1.

Decimal Number	Binary Notation
0	0
1	1
2	10
3	11
4	100
5	101
6	110
7	111
8	1000
9	1001
10	1010

Because the numbers 0 and 1 can be represented easily by the "OFF" and "ON" conditions of an electric circuit, binary notation is widely used in modern digital computers.

binary stars A pair of stars that orbit about their common center of mass. By convention, the star that is nearest the center of mass in a binary star system is called the "primary," while the other (smaller) star of the system is called the "companion." Binary star systems can be classified further as visual binaries, eclipsing binaries, spectroscopic binaries, and astrometric binaries. A new class of binary star systems, called X-ray binaries, was discovered during the 1970s by means of space-based X-ray observations.

See also: STARS; X-RAY ASTRONOMY.

binding energy The minimum energy required to dissociate a nucleus (or system of particles) into its component nucleons (i.e., its neutrons and protons). Also called *total binding energy.* For a particle in a system (i.e., a neutron or proton in a nucleus), the minimum net energy required to remove that particle from its system. Occasionally referred to as the *separation energy.* The *electron binding energy* is that required to remove the electron from an atom or molecule. Nuclear binding energies are on the order of millions of electron volts (MeVs), while chemical binding energies (electron binding energies) are on the order of tens of electron volts (eVs).

bioclean room Any enclosed area where there is control over viable and nonviable particulates in the air with temperature, humidity, and pressure control as required to maintain specified standards. A viable particle is a particle that will reproduce to form observable colonies when placed on a specified culture medium and incubated according to optimum environmental conditions for growth after collection. A nonviable particle will not reproduce to form observable colonies when placed on a specified culture medium and incubated according to optimum environmental conditions for growth after collection. A bioclean room is operated with emphasis on minimizing airborne viable and nonviable particle generation or concentrations to specified levels. Particle size is expressed as the apparent maximum linear dimension or diameter of the particle—usually in microns or micrometers (μ). (A micron is one-millionth of a meter.)

There are three clean room classes based on total (viable and nonviable) particle count with the maximum number of particles per unit volume or horizontal surface area being specified for each class. The "cleanest" or most stringent airborne particulate environment is called a *Class 100 Bioclean Room* (called a *Class 3.5 Room* in SI unit system). In this type of bioclean room, the particle count may not exceed a total of 100 particles per cubic foot (3.5 particles per liter) of a size 0.5 micron and larger; the viable particle count may not exceed 0.1 per cubic foot (0.0035 per liter) with an average value not to exceed 1,200 per square foot (12,900 per square meter) per week on horizontal surfaces. The *Class 10,000 Bioclean Room* (called a *Class 350 Room* in SI unit system) is the next most clean environment, followed by a *Class 100,000 Bioclean Room* (called a *Class 3,500 Room* in the SI unit system). The table summarizes the air cleanliness conditions for each type of clean room.

In aerospace applications, bioclean rooms, or "clean rooms," as they are frequently called, are used to manufacture, assemble, test, disassemble, and repair delicate spacecraft sensor systems, electronic components, and certain mechanical subsystems. Special protective clothing, including gloves, smocks (often called "bunnysuits"), and head and foot coverings are worn by aerospace workers to reduce the level of dust and contamination in clean rooms. A Class 10,000 Clean Room facility is typically the cleanliness level encountered in the assembly and testing of large spacecraft. If a space probe is being prepared for a trip to a planet like Mars, care is also taken in the bioclean room to ensure that "hitchhiking terrestrial microorganisms" are brought to the minimum population levels consistent with planetary quarantine protocols—thereby avoiding the potential of forward contamination of the target alien world.

See also: EXTRATERRESTRIAL CONTAMINATION; INTERNATIONAL SYSTEM OF UNITS.

biogenic elements Those elements generally considered by scientists to be essential for all living systems. Exobiologists usually place primary emphasis on the elements hydrogen (H), carbon (C), nitrogen (N), oxygen (O), sulfur (S), and phosphorous (P). The chemical compounds of major interest are those normally associated with water (H_2O) and with organic chemistry, in which carbon (C) is bonded to itself or to other biogenic elements. Exobiologists also include several "life-essential" elements associated with inorganic chemistry, such

BIOCLEAN ROOM AIR CLEANLINESS LEVELS

Class English System (metric system)	Maximum Number of Particles per Cu Ft 0.5 Micron and Larger (per liter)	Maximum Number of Viable Particles per Cu Ft (per liter)	Average Number of Viable Particles per Sq Ft per Week (per m2 per week)
100	100	0.1	1,200
(3.5)	(3.5)	(0.0035)	(12,900)
10,000	10,000	0.5	6,000
(350)	(350)	(0.0176)	(64,600)
100,000	100,000	2.5	30,000
(3,500)	(3,500)	(0.0884)	(323,000)

Source: NASA.

as iron (Fe), magnesium (Mg), calcium (Ca), sodium (Na), potassium (K), and chlorine (Cl), in this overall grouping, but often these are given secondary emphasis in cosmic evolution studies.

biogeochemical cycle The chemical interactions among the atmosphere, biosphere, hydrosphere, and lithosphere.
See also: GLOBAL CHANGE; MISSION TO PLANET EARTH.

biomass The total dry organic matter or stored energy content of living organisms that is present at a specific time in a defined unit (e.g., community, ecosystem, crop, etc.) on the surface of Earth. The term often refers to vegetation.

bionics The branch of science or engineering that studies and develops systems (especially electromechanical systems) that function in a way resembling or characteristic of living systems.

biopak A container for housing a living organism (e.g., an insect, fish, or small mammal) in a habitable environment and for recording biological activities during space flight.

bioregenerative life support system *See:* LIFE SUPPORT SYSTEM.

biosensor A sensor used to provide information about a life process. Developments in miniaturization and information technologies are making possible biosensors that are only a few thousandths of a centimeter wide. Smaller biosensors have two distinct advantages: (1) they can be placed in areas that were previously inaccessible, and (2) they are fast since life process measurements can be made in situ (e.g., in the human being or in the field) instead of at a central laboratory. New generations of biosensors will take advantage of their common heritage with information technology to integrate logic functions into the same tiny package with the biosensors. Integrating logic with sensors can result in more useful devices. For example, a glucose sensor with integrated logic functions might be designed to respond differently to measured blood sugar levels at different times of the day.

biosphere The life zone of a planetary body; for example, the part of Earth and its atmosphere inhabited by living organisms.
See also: GLOBAL CHANGE.

biota The fauna and flora (animal and plant life) of a given area.

biotelemetry The remote measurement and evaluation of life functions. For example, medical specialists at mission control can monitor the heartbeat and respiration rate of an astronaut during a strenuous extravehicular activity. Data from biosensors attached to the astronaut are telemetered back to Earth for purposes of monitoring and evaluation.

bipropellant rocket A rocket using two unmixed or uncombined chemical propellants (a fuel and an oxidizer), which are kept separate until mixing in the combustion chamber.
See also: PROPELLANT; ROCKET.

bipropellant valve A valve incorporating both fuel and oxidizer valving units driven by a common actuator.

bird Aerospace jargon for a rocket, missile, satellite, or spacecraft.

birth-to-death tracking In ballistic missile defense, the ability to track and its payload (e.g., satellites, reentry vehicles, and/or decoys that simulate these objects) from launch until each object is intercepted and destroyed or completes its mission (i.e., impacting on a target or deploying a postboost vehicle).
See also: BALLISTIC MISSILE DEFENSE.

bistatic radar A radar system that has transmitters and receivers at two separate locations; this is a special case of multistatic radar. The reasons for this separation may include enhanced survivability and the ability to overcome the countermeasure of retroreflectors.

bit A binary digit, the basic unit of information (either 0 or 1) in binary notation.
See also: BINARY DIGIT; BINARY NOTATION.

blackbody A perfect emitter and perfect absorber of electromagnetic radiation. It is capable of radiating at all frequencies and of absorbing incident radiant energy at all frequencies. The radiant energy emitted by a blackbody, called *blackbody radiation*, is a function only of its temperature. The physical laws describing the behavior and properties of a blackbody come from equilibrium thermodynamics.

See also: RADIATION LAWS.

black holes Theorized gravitationally collapsed masses from which nothing—light, matter, or any other kind of signal—can escape. Scientists generally speculate today that a black hole is the natural end product when a giant star dies and collapses. If the star has three or more solar masses left after exhausting its nuclear fuels (a solar mass is a unit of measure equivalent to the mass of our own Sun), then it can become a black hole. As with the formation of a white dwarf or a NEUTRON STAR, the collapsing giant star's density and gravity increase with contraction. However, in this case, because of the large mass involved, the gravity of the collapsing star becomes too strong for even neutrons to resist, and an incredibly dense point mass, or *singularity,* is formed. Therefore, a black hole is essentially a singularity surrounded by an event region in which the gravity is so strong that absolutely nothing can escape. When a giant star has collapsed to a dimension called the *Schwarzschild radius,* its gravitational escape velocity is equal to the speed of light. At this point, not even light itself can escape from the black hole. The Schwarzschild radius is sometimes called the *event horizon,* or boundary of no return, for a black hole.

See also: STARS.

blackout 1. In communications, a fadeout, due to environmental factors, of radio and telemetry transmission between ground stations and aerospace vehicles traveling at high speeds in the atmosphere. It is caused by attenuation of the transmission signal as it passes through the ionized boundary layer (plasma sheath) and shockwave regions generated by the high-velocity vehicle. 2. In defense, the disabling of radar by means of a nuclear explosion. The intense electromagnetic energy released generates a large background that obscures signals and renders many types of radar useless for minutes or longer. 3. In aerospace medicine, a physical condition in which vision is temporarily obscured by a blackness, accompanied by a dullness of certain other senses. This is brought on by decreased blood pressure in the head and a consequent lack of oxygen. The condition may occur when pulling out of a high-speed dive in a plane.

blade 1. One of a set of slatlike objects rigidly fixed to a rotatable shaft, each slat being carefully shaped as an airfoil such that (a) rotation of the shaft in a fluid creates a flow of fluid, or (b) fluid flow impinging on the blades rotates the shaft. 2. A flat plate used to adjust flow in a blade valve.

blade valve 1. (rotary) The valve that controls flow by means of a flat plate that is rotated transversely in a slotted chamber between upstream and downstream lines. 2. (slide) The valve that controls flow by means of a flat plate that slides transversely in a slotted chamber between upstream and downstream lines.

blast effect Destruction of or damage to structures and personnel by the force of an explosion on or above the surface of the ground. Blast effect may be contrasted with the cratering and groundshock effects of a projectile or charge that goes off beneath the surface.

blastoff Aerospace jargon used to describe the liftoff of a rocket or launch vehicle.

bleed 1. The continuous flow of a gas through a pilot valve. 2. To remove or draw off fluid from a system.

blinding Destroying elements of an optical sensor by overloading them with electromagnetic (optical) radiation.

blockhouse (*also written as* **block house**) A reinforced-concrete structure, often built underground or partly underground, and sometimes dome-shaped, to provide protection against blast, heat, or explosion during rocket launchings or related activities; specifically, a launch site structure that houses electronic control instruments used in launching a rocket.

blowdown system A closed propellant/pressurant system that decays in ullage pressure level as the propellant is consumed and ullage volume is increased.

blueshift Electromagnetic radiation from a moving celestial body or object is called "blueshifted" when spectral lines in the visible part of the spectrum appear shifted toward the blue (higher-frequency, shorter-wavelength) part of the spectrum.

This occurs when the object being observed is approaching the observer. Compare this term with REDSHIFT.

See also: DOPPLER SHIFT.

boattail The aft (rear) end of a rocket containing the propulsion system and its interface with vehicle tankage.

boiloff The vaporization (and loss) of a cryogenic propellant, such as liquid oxygen or liquid hydrogen, as the temperature of the propellant mass rises in the tank of a rocket being readied for launch.

bolide A brilliant meteor, especially one that explodes into fragments near the end of its trajectory in Earth's atmosphere.

bolometer A sensitive instrument that measures the intensity of incident radiant (thermal) energy, usually by means of a thermally sensitive electrical resistor. The change in electrical resistance is an indication of the amount of radiant energy reaching the exposed material.

Boltzmann constant (symbol: k) The ratio of the universal gas constant to Avogadro's number. It is equal to 1.381×10^{-23} joules/degree Kelvin.

Boolean algebra A form of algebra, based on symbolic logic, developed by George Boole (1815–64), an English mathematician. It is based on the concept that logical propositions can be treated as two-state variables (i.e., TRUE or FALSE) and that relationships between these two-state variables can be described with a logical operator, such as AND, OR, and NOT. Boolean algebra can be used in modern digital computers to solve problems and to process information.

See also: BINARY NOTATION.

boost 1. To launch or to push along during a portion of flight, as to boost a ramjet to flight speed by means of a rocket, or a spacecraft or rocket vehicle boosted to altitude with a (booster) rocket. 2. The first portion of a ballistic missile trajectory. 3. Additional power, pressure, or force supplied by a booster engine; as, for example, a hydraulic boost, or the extra propulsion given a flying vehicle during liftoff, climb, or another phase of its flight as with a booster engine. 4. To supercharge.

booster 1. The rocket that places a ballistic missile in its trajectory toward a target or that launches a satellite or spacecraft into orbit. 2. An auxiliary or initial propulsion system that travels with a missile or aircraft and that may or may not separate from the parent craft when its impulse has been delivered. A booster system may contain, or consist of, one or more units. 3. A high-explosive element sufficiently sensitive as to be actuated by small explosive elements in a fuse or primer and powerful enough to cause detonation of the main explosive charge.

booster clustering Locating boosters relatively near one another (typically within hundreds of kilometers) in order to force a space-based ballistic missile defense (BMD) system to a higher absentee ratio and, therefore, to increase the required number of space-based interceptors.

See also: BALLISTIC MISSILE DEFENSE.

booster decoy A rocket that would imitate the early phase of booster plume and trajectory in order to draw fire from an opponent's ballistic missile defense (BMD) system but that would actually not be an armed (i.e., warhead-equipped) intercontinental ballistic missile (ICBM). A booster decoy would cost substantially less than a fully equipped ICBM.

See also: BALLISTIC MISSILE DEFENSE.

booster engine An engine, especially a booster rocket, that adds its thrust to the thrust of a sustainer engine.

booster pump A pump in a fuel system, hydraulic system, or the like, used to provide additional or auxiliary pressure when needed or to provide an initial pressure differential before entering a main pump, as in pumping hydrogen near the boiling point.

booster rocket 1. A rocket motor, either solid or liquid propellant, which assists the main propulsive system or sustainer engine of a rocket or aerospace vehicle in some phase of its flight. 2. A rocket used to set a vehicle in motion before another engine takes over. In this sense, the term "launch vehicle" is preferred.

See also: LAUNCH VEHICLE.

booster separation motor (BSM) The small, solid-fueled booster separation motors that translate, or

nother burning surface at the time when
ing surface undergoes a major change.
o: ROCKET; SOLID-PROPELLANT ROCKET.

1. (in aerospace technology) The vaporiza-
 disintegration of a satellite, spacecraft, or
 r any of their components by aerodynamic
upon entry into a planetary atmosphere. 2.
ear energy technology) A measure of reac-
consumption. It can be expressed as (a) the
age of fuel atoms that have undergone fis-
 r (b) the amount of energy produced per
unit of fuel in the reactor (e.g.: megawatt-
 r metric ton (tonne) [MWd/t]).

disk Passive physical barrier in a fluid sys-
at blocks the flow of fluid until ruptured by
ive) fluid pressure.

pressure Fluid pressure at which a pressur-
component will rupture. For example, the
pressure at which a burst disk will rupture.

test Pressure test of a component to rupture
termine whether the component can with-
the calculated burst pressure.

The rocket-propelled final stage of an inter-
nental ballistic missile (ICBM) that, after

---

booster burnout, places warheads and (possibly)
decoys on ballistic paths toward their targets. Also
called the *post-boost vehicle (PBV)*.
See also: BALLISTIC MISSILE DEFENSE.

bus deployment phase In ballistic missile defense
(BMD), the portion of a missile flight during which
multiple warheads are deployed on different paths
to different targets. The warheads on a single intercontinental ballistic missile (ICBM) are carried on a
platform, called the *bus* (or *post-boost vehicle*), which
has a small rocket motors to move the bus slightly
from its original flight path. This phase is also
called the *post-boost phase*.
See also: BALLISTIC MISSILE DEFENSE.

butterfly valve Valve constructed to close off or
throttle flow by rotation of a circular disk around a
transverse axis within the flow passage.

byte (*binary digit eight*) A basic unit of information or data consisting of eight binary digits (bits).
The information storage capacity of a computer
system often is defined in terms of kilobytes (kb),
megabytes (Mb), and even gigabytes (Gb). One
kilobyte corresponds to 2^{10} or 1,024 bytes, while 1
megabyte corresponds to 2^{20} or 1,048,576 bytes.

---

move, the space shuttle solid rocket boosters away
from the orbiter's still-thrusting main engines and
the external tank.
See also: SPACE TRANSPORTATION SYSTEM.

boostglide vehicle An aerospace vehicle (part aircraft, part spacecraft) designed to fly to the limits
of the sensible atmosphere, then to be boosted by
rockets into outer space, returning to Earth by gliding under aerodynamic control.

boost phase In general, that portion of the flight of
a ballistic missile or launch vehicle during which
the booster and sustainer engines operate. In ballistic missile defense (BMD), the first portion of a
ballistic missile trajectory during which it is being
powered by its engines. During this period, which
typically lasts from three to five minutes for an
intercontinental ballistic missile (ICBM), the missile reaches an altitude of about 200 kilometers
whereupon powered flight ends and the ICBM
begins to dispense its reentry vehicles. (The other
portions of the missile flight, including the midcourse and reentry phases, take up the remainder
of an ICBM's flight time of about 25 to 30 minutes.)
See also: BALLISTIC MISSILE DEFENSE.

bootstrap Refers to a self-generating or self-sustaining process. An example in aerospace technology would be the operation of a liquid propellant
rocket engine in which (during main-stage operation) the gas generator is fed by the main propellants pumped by the turbopump, and the turbopump (in turn) is driven by hot gases from the generator system. Of course, the operation of such a
system must be started by outside power or propellant sources. However, when its operation is no
longer dependent on these external sources, the
rocket engine is said to be in "bootstrap" operation.
Similarly, in computer science, bootstrap refers to a
sequence of commands or instructions the execution of which causes additional commands or
instructions to be loaded and executed until the
desired computer program is completely loaded in
storage.

borescope An arrangement of tiny mirrors or fiber
optic materials that makes possible visible inspection of otherwise inaccessible locations.

boundary layer The layer of fluid in the immediate vicinity of a bounding surface; in fluid mechan-

---

ics, the layer of fluid affected primarily by the viscosity of the fluid. This term refers ambiguously to
the laminar boundary layer, the turbulent boundary layer, the planetary boundary layer, or the surface boundary layer. In aerodymanics, the boundary layer thickness often is measured from the surface to a point at which the air flow has 99% of the
free stream velocity.

bow shock 1. A shock wave in front of a body,
such as an aerospace vehicle or an airfoil. 2. The
interface formed where the electrically charged
solar wind encounters an obstacle in space, such as
a planet's magnetic field or atmosphere.
See also: MAGNETOSPHERE.

Boyle's law The empirical generalization that for
an ideal or perfect gas, the product of pressure (p)
and volume (V) is constant in an isothermal (i.e.,
constant temperature) process:

$$pV = \text{constant}$$

This ideal gas relationship was first observed in
1662 by the Irish physicist Robert Boyle (1627–91).
It is sometimes referred to as the *Boyle-Mariotte Law*
or *Mariotte's law*, after E. Mariotte, who discovered
this relationship independently in 1676.

braking ellipses A series of ellipses, decreasing in
size due to aerodynamic drag, followed by a spacecraft in entering a planetary atmosphere.
See also: AEROBRAKE.

Brayton cycle A thermodynamic cycle representing the idealized behavior of a gaseous working
fluid in a turbine form of heat engine. The idealized Brayton cycle is described in Figure 21. In this
description, each stage of the thermodynamic
process is assumed to have been completed before
the next stage is initiated. However, in an actual
Brayton cycle engine, there is a gradual rather than
a sharp transition from one stage to the next; consequently, the sharp points in this idealized figure
actually would be rounded off. This cycle, developed by the American engineer George Brayton
(1830–92), can be either a closed cycle (in which the
working gas is constantly recycled) or an open
cycle (in which the working gas, like air, passes
through the system just once). Figure 22 depicts a
closed Brayton cycle system, using either nuclear
or solar energy as the heat source, which is suitable
for space-based applications. In this system, power

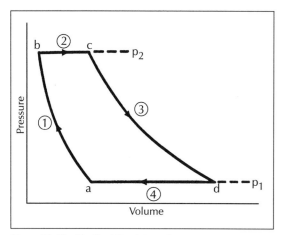

Figure 21. The idealized Brayton cycle *(US Department of Energy)*

from the gas-driven turbine is used to compress a working gas (e.g., helium), which then is heated by either solar or nuclear energy to increase its pressure. After passing through the turbine, the gas is cooled in a heat exchanger and then recycled through the compressor. In this system, the working fluid remains gaseous throughout.

breadboard An assembly of preliminary circuits or parts used to prove the feasibility of a device, circuit, system, or principle without regard to the final configuration or packaging of the parts.

breakaway disconnect Separable connector that is disengaged by the separation force as the launch vehicle rises from the launch pad or as a stage separates from a lower stage. Also called a *rise-off* or *staging disconnect*.

breakoff phenomenon The feeling of isolation that sometimes occurs during high-altitude flight or spaceflight. The traveler can feel totally separated and detached from Earth and human society. Also called the *breakaway phenomenon* and the *Shimanagashi syndrome*.

bremsstrahlung (German word meaning: breaking radiation) Electromagnetic radiation emitted as photons (X rays) when a fast-moving charged particle (usually an electron) loses energy upon being accelerated and deflected by the electric field surrounding a positively charged atomic nucleus. X rays produced in ordinary X-ray machines are an example of bremsstrahlung.

brennschluss (German word meaning: combustion termination) The cessation of burning in a rocket, resulting from consumption of the propellants, from deliberate shutoff, or from other causes; the time at which this cessation occurs.

bridgewire Resistance wire, attached to the leads of an electroexplosive device, whose function is to convert the electrical firing signal into thermal energy adequate to ignite the prime charge of an igniter.

brightness In BALLISTIC MISSILE DEFENSE (BMD), the amount of power that can be delivered on a target per unit solid angle by a directed energy weapon.

Brinell hardness A scale for measuring the hardness of metals. Indentation hardness is determined by pressing a hardened-steel sphere into the test material under a specified load for a specified time; the diameter of the impression produced is an index (called the *Brinell number*) to the hardness of the material. Developed by the Swedish scientist J. A. Brinell (1849–1925).

British thermal unit (BTU) A unit quantity of energy, especially thermal energy (heat). Defined as the amount of thermal energy (heat) needed to increase the temperature of 1 pound of water 1 degree Fahrenheit (F) at normal atmospheric pressure. In general, the initial temperature of the water is specified as 39° F and the final temperature as 40° F—a physical condition where water has its maximum density.

$$1 \text{ BTU} = 1055 \text{ joules}$$

brittle failure Rupture of structural material that is not preceded by appreciable deformation of the material.

buffeting The beating of an aerodynamic structure or surface by unsteady flow, gusts, and the like; the irregular shaking or oscillation of a vehicle component owing to turbulent air or separated flow.

bug An error in a computer program. The process of removing this error often is called *debugging*.

bulkhead A dividing wall in a rocket, spacecraft, or aircraft fuselage, at right angles to the longitudinal axis of the structure, that serves to strengthen, divide, or help shape the structure. A bulkhead sometimes is designed to withstand pressure differences.

burble A separation flow past a body; th resulting from this. operating at an ang angle of maximum lif an increase of drag. *See a*

burn In aerospace ope et engine. For examp space shuttle's orbital r engines would mean th tle flight that the OMS e *burn time* is simply the le

burning surface The su grain that is not restric given time during propel

burnout The point in tim tory when combustion of is terminated—usually as propellants.

burnout angle The angle l cal and the velocity vector (i.e., at burnout).

burnout velocity The veloc sile, rocket, or aerospace veh of thrust (i.e., at burnout).

burn rate Literally, the rate pellant burns—that is, the r burning propellant surface, p surface, at a specified pressure ture; with respect to solid prop the rate at which the web dec during rocket motor operation. imum thickness of a solid prop from the initial ignition surfac case wall or to the intersection (surface at the time when the bur riences a major change. Also call *See also:* ROCKET; SOLID-PROPELL

burn time In general, the lengt period for a rocket engine. For a rocket, the interval from attainme initial fraction of maximum thrust to web burnout. The web is the mir of a solid propellant rocket grain surface to the insulated case wall or

burnup tion of the bur *See a* **burnup** tion an rocket heating (in nu tor fue percen sion, weigh days

burst tem th (exce

burst ized fluid

burs to d stan

bus con

Figure 22. The closed Brayton cycle (suitable for applications in outer space)   *(NASA)*

calendar day By convention, the time interval from midnight to midnight. The calendar day is 24 hours of mean solar time in length and coincides with the civil day unless a time change occurs during that day.

calendar year The time interval that is used as the basis for an annual calendar. For example, the *Gregorian calendar year* contains an average of 365.2425 days, so that each calendar year contains 365 days, with an extra day being added every fourth calendar year to make a *leap year* (which contains 366 days).

calibration The process of comparing measurements made by an instrument with a standard or set of reference data.

calorie (symbol: cal) A unit of thermal energy originally defined as the amount of heat required to raise 1 gram of water 1° Celsius (C). Sometimes referred to as the gram-calorie or "small" calorie, it is a unit in the centimeter-gram-second (cgs) system and is related to the joule (a unit of energy in the SI system) as follows: 1 calorie = 4.1868 joules.

In metabolism studies, physiologists use a unit called the kilocalorie (or kilogram-calorie). This "large" calorie is equal to 1,000 calories (as defined above). The word "calorie" derives from a former thermodynamics theory popular in the 1780s and 1790s in France. This theory, called *caloric theory,* tried to explain the nature of thermal energy or heat flow by assuming that heat was a weightless fluid—named *caloric.* Precise thermodynamic experiments performed by James Prescott Joule (1818–89) in the 19th century, which quantitatively demonstrated that heat was actually a form of energy in transition similar to mechanical work, caused the abandonment of the caloric "fluid" theory of heat.

See also: BRITISH THERMAL UNIT; INTERNATIONAL SYSTEM OF UNITS; JOULE.

calorimeter A device in or with which precise measurements of thermal energy (heat) flow can be made.

camber Curvature of the mean line on an airfoil; the distance from the point of greatest curvature to the chord.

canard 1. Pertaining to an aerodynamic vehicle in which the horizontal surfaces used for trim and control are placed forward of the main lifting surface. 2. The horizontal trim and control surfaces in such an arrangement.

candela (symbol: Cd) The SI UNIT of luminous intensity. It is defined as the luminous intensity in a given direction of a source that emits monochromatic radiation at a frequency of 540 x 10^{12} hertz and whose radiant intensity in that direction is 1/683 watt per steradian. The physical basis for this unit is the luminous intensity of a BLACKBODY radiator at a temperature of 2046° Kelvin (the temperature at which molten platinum solidifies).

See also: LUMEN.

cannibalize In aerospace jargon, the process of removing serviceable parts from one item of equipment or system in order to install them on another item of equipment or system.

Figure 23. A *Titan 34D* space launch vehicle is shown ready for launch from Complex 40 at Cape Canaveral AFS, Florida (circa 1982). Other portions of the air force's Integrated Transfer Launch Facility (ITLF) appear in the background.   *(Courtesy of U.S. Air Force and Lockheed-Martin Company)*

Cape Canaveral Air Force Station (CCAFS) Cape Canaveral Air Force Station, located on the Atlantic Ocean on Florida's east central coast, has been the scene of more than 3,000 rocket launches since 1950. It is the first station in the 16,000-kilometer (km) (10,000-mile-[mi]) long Eastern Range. Together with Patrick Air Force Base (some 32 km [20 miles] to the south), CCAFS forms a complex that is the center for the Department of Defense launch operations on the East Coast of the United States. The station covers a 65-square-km (about 25-square-mi) area. Much of the land is now inhabited by large populations of animals, including deer, alligators, and wild boar. The nerve center for CCAFS and the entire Eastern Range is the range control center (RCC) from which all launches, as well as the status of range resources, are monitored. The range safety function also is performed in the range control center.

Active launch sites include space launch complexes 40 and 41 in the Integrated Transfer Launch Facility (ITLF) where preparation and launch of the Titan vehicle occurs. (See Figure 23.) Delta boosters are processed and launched from space complexes 17A and 17B, and Atlas vehicles are launched from complexes 36A and 36B. Space launch complex 20 is used for suborbital launches, and weather (meteorological sounding) rockets are launched from the Meteorological Rocket Launch Facility. Department of Defense satellites are prepared for launch from two facilities: the Satellite Processing and Integration Facility and the Navstar Processing Facility.

capillary A tube or pipe of very narrow diameter. A fluid, such as water, will rise or move through a capillary as a result of the fluid's surface tension. This process is called *capillarity*. On Earth, for example, capillarity is a very important process in living plants, since it is responsible for the transport of water throughout the plant against the forces of terrestrial gravity.

See also: HEAT PIPE.

capital satellite A highly valued or costly satellite, as distinct from an expensive decoy satellite.

capsule 1. In general, a boxlike container, component, or unit that often is sealed. 2. A small, sealed, pressurized cabin that contains an acceptable environment for human crew, animals, or sensitive equipment during extremely high-altitude flight, space flight, or emergency escape. As these pressurized cabins became larger, such as the Apollo capsule, the term "spacecraft" replaced the term "capsule" in aerospace use. 3. An enclosed container carried on a rocket or spacecraft, which supports and safely transports a payload, experiment, or instrument intended for recovery after flight.

captive firing Test firing of a propulsion system, in which the engine is operated at full or partial thrust while restrained in a test stand; the system is completely instrumented to obtain data to verify design and demonstrate performance.

capture 1. In orbital mechanics, the process by which the central force field of a planet or star overcomes by gravitational attraction the velocity of a passing celestial object (e.g., comet, tiny planetoid, etc.) or spacecraft and brings that body under the control of the central force field. 2. In aerospace operations, that moment during the rendezvous and docking of two spacecraft when the capture mechanism engages and locks the two orbiting vehicles together. 3. In space shuttle operations, the event of the remote manipulator system (RMS) and effector making contact with and firmly attaching to a payload grappling fixture. A payload is considered *captured* at any time it is firmly attached to the remote manipulator system. 4. In nuclear physics, a process in which an atomic or a nuclear system acquires an additional particle; for example, the capture of electrons by positive ions, or the capture of electrons or neutrons by nuclei.

carbon dioxide (symbol: CO$_2$) A colorless, odorless noncombustible gas present in Earth's atmosphere. Carbon dioxide (CO$_2$) is formed by the combustion of carbon and carbon compounds (e.g., fossil fuels, wood, and alcohol), by respiration, and by the gradual oxidation of organic matter in the soil. Carbon dioxide is removed from the atmosphere by green plants (during photosynthesis) and by absorption in the oceans. Since it is a *greenhouse gas*, the increasing presence of CO$_2$ in Earth's atmosphere could have significant environmental consequences, such as global warming. The preindustrial revolution atmospheric concentration of CO$_2$ is estimated to be about 275 parts per million by volume (ppmv). Environmental scientists now predict that if current trends in the rise in atmospheric CO$_2$ concentration continue (currently about 340 to 350 ppmv), then sometime after the middle part of the next century, the atmospheric concentration of CO_2 will reach *twice* its preindustrial revolution value, perhaps severely altering Earth's environment through global warming, polar cap melting, and increased desertification.

See also: GLOBAL CHANGE; MISSION TO PLANET EARTH.

cargo The total complement of payloads (one or more) on any one space shuttle flight. Cargo includes everything contained in the *orbiter cargo bay* plus other equipment, hardware, and consumables located elsewhere in the orbiter vehicle that are unique to the user and are not carried as part of the basic orbiter payload support.

See also: CARGO BAY.

cargo bay The unpressurized midpart of the space shuttle orbiter vehicle fuselage behind the cabin aft (rear) bulkhead where most payloads are carried. Its maximum usable payload envelope is 18.3 meters (m) (60 feet [ft]) long and 4.6 m (15 ft) in diameter. Hinged doors extend the full length of the cargo bay.

See also: SPACE TRANSPORTATION SYSTEM.

Carnot cycle An idealized reversible thermodynamic cycle for a theoretical heat engine, first postulated in 1824 by the French engineer Nicolas Sadi Carnot (1746–1832). As shown in Figure 24, the Carnot cycle consists of two adiabatic (no energy transfer as heat) stages, alternating with two isothermal (constant temperature) stages. In stage 1, an ideal working fluid experiences adiabatic compression along path *ab*. Since no thermal energy (heat) is allowed to enter or leave the system, the mechanical work of compression causes the temperature of the working fluid to increase from T_1 (the sink temperature) to T_2 (the source temperature). During stage 2 of the Carnot cycle, the working fluid experiences isothermal (constant temperature) expansion. While the working fluid expands in traveling along path *bc*, thermal energy (heat) is transferred to it from the source at temperature T_2. Then in traveling along path *cd* during stage 3, the working fluid undergoes adiabatic expansion. Travel along this path essentially completes "power stroke" of the cycle, and the work of expansion causes the temperature of the working fluid to fall from T_2 to T_1. Finally, in stage 4, the working fluid undergoes isothermal compression while traveling along path *da*. Mechanical work is

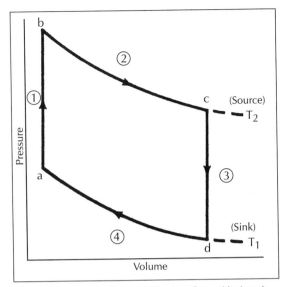

Figure 24. Pressure-volume relationships for an ideal working fluid undergoing the four stages of the Carnot cycle—an ideal, reversible heat engine cycle   *(Drawing courtesy of U.S. Department of Energy)*

performed on the working fluid and an equivalent amount of heat is rejected to the sink (environment), which is at the lower temperature, T_1. The working fluid is now back to its initial state and is ready to repeat the cycle again.

The thermal efficiency (η_{th}) of the Carnot cycle is given by the expression:

$$\eta_{th} = 1 - T_1/T_2$$

where T_1 is the sink (lower) temperature and T_2 is the source (upper) temperature expressed on an absolute scale (i.e., temperature in degrees Kelvin or Rankine). The thermal efficiency of the Carnot cycle is the best possible efficiency of any heat engine operating between temperatures T_1 and T_2. This fact is sometimes referred to as the *Carnot principle*. Therefore, for maximum efficiency in a reversible heat engine, the source temperature (T_2) should be as high as possible (within the temperature limits of the materials involved), while the sink or environmental reservoir temperature (T_1) should be as low as possible. Heat engines operating on Earth must reject thermal energy to the surrounding terrestrial environment; therefore, T_1 typically is limited to about 300 °Kelvin (K) (depending on the local environmental conditions). Heat engines operating in space have the opportunity (depending on radiator design) to reject thermal energy to the coldest regions of outer space (about 4° K). Although the Carnot cycle is a postulated, idealized cycle, it is very useful in understanding the performance limits of real heat engines that operate using somewhat less than idealized Brayton or Rankine cycles.

See also: BRAYTON CYCLE; HEAT ENGINE; RANKINE CYCLE; STIRLING CYCLE.

carrier 1. In electronics, a charge carrier; the mobile conduction electron or hole in a semiconductor. 2. In telecommunications, a carrier wave; the electromagnetic wave suitable for carrying information by making small changes in (i.e., modulating) either its frequency or its amplitude. 3. In nuclear technology, a carrier substance; a stable isotope or normal (nonradioactive) element to which radioactive atoms of the same element can be added to obtain a quantity of radioactive mixture sufficient for handling, or to produce a radioactive mixture that will undergo the same physical, chemical, or biological reaction as the stable isotope. 4. In aerospace technology, a payload carrier; for example, in the Space Transportation System, those payload-carrying flight elements not including the space shuttle orbiter vehicle itself, specifically the Spacelab and the Inertial Upper Stage.

carrier vehicle (CV) In ballistic missile defense (BMD), an Earth-orbiting space platform whose principal function is to house the space-based interceptors in a protective environment prior to use.

See also: BALLISTIC MISSILE DEFENSE.

carrier wave (CW) In telecommunications, an electromagnetic wave intended for modulation. This wave is transmitted at a specified frequency and amplitude. Information then is superimposed on this carrier wave by making small changes in (i.e., modulating) either its frequency or its amplitude.

cartesian coordinates A coordinate system in which locations of points in space are expressed by reference to three mutually perpendicular planes, called *coordinate planes.* The three planes intersect in three straight lines called *coordinate axes.*

case 1. In general, the outer portion of a metallic material. 2. In rocketry, the structural envelope for the solid propellant in a solid-propellant rocket motor.

case bonding Cementing of the solid propellant to the motor case through the insulation by use of a thin layer of adhesive (the liner).

See also: ROCKET; SOLID-PROPELLANT ROCKET.

casing The part of a pump's housing that surrounds the impeller, a device in a pump that imparts motion to a fluid.

Cassegrain telescope A compound reflecting telescope in which a small hyperboloidal mirror reflects the convergent beam from the paraboloidal primary mirror through a hole in the primary mirror to an eyepiece in back of the primary mirror. Designed by the Frenchman Guillaume Cassegrain in 1672. Also called a *Cassegrainian telescope.*

See also: TELESCOPE.

Cassini mission The Cassini mission was launched successfully by a Titan IV-Centaur vehicle on October 15, 1997, on a joint NASA and European Space Agency (ESA) project to Saturn, its major moon Titan, and its complex system of other moons. The Cassini orbiter spacecraft's mission consists of delivering a probe, called Huygens (provided by ESA), to Titan and then remaining in orbit around Saturn for detailed studies of the planet and its rings and satellites. (See Figure 25.) The principal objectives of this mission are to: (1) determine the three-dimensional structure and dynamical behavior of the rings; (2) determine the composition of the satellite surfaces and the geological history of each object; (3) determine the nature and origin of the dark material on Iapetus' leading hemisphere; (4) measure the three-dimensional structure and dynamical behavior of the Saturnian magnetosphere; (5) study the dynamical behavior of Saturn's atmosphere at cloud level; (6) study the time variability of Titan's clouds and hazes; and (7) characterize Titan's surface on a regional scale. The Cassini spacecraft's instrumentation consists of: a radar mapper, a charge-coupled-device (CCD) imaging system, a visual/infrared mapping spectrometer, a composite infrared spectrograph, a cosmic dust analyzer, radio and plasma wave experiments, an ultraviolet imaging spectrograph, a magnetospheric imaging instrument, a magnetometer, and an ion/neutral mass spectrometer. Telemetry from the communications antenna will be used to make observations of the atmospheres of Titan and Saturn and to measure the gravity fields of the planet and its satellites. The spacecraft is named in honor of the Italian-born French astronomer Giovanni Domenico Cassini (1625–1712), who was the first director of the Royal Observatory in Paris.

The Cassini mission is taking a similar tour of the solar system as did the Galileo mission—namely the Venus-Venus-Earth-Jupiter Gravity Assist (VVEJGA) trajectory. As currently planned, the Cassini spacecraft will arrive in the Saturnian system in June 2004. Shortly after entering orbit around Saturn, the Huygens probe will separate from the Cassini orbiter spacecraft and begin its entry into the atmosphere of Titan. This atmospheric probe carries six science instruments. Should it survive impact with the surface of Titan, it may even be able to transmit some science data from the surface. The Huygens probe is sponsored by the European Space Agency and is named after the Dutch physicist and astronomer Christiaan Huygens (1629–95), who first described the nature of Saturn's rings and discovered its major moon, Titan. The Cassini spacecraft, which receives its electric power (over 625 watts projected at end of mission) from three radioisotope thermoelectric generators (RTGs), is then expected to make at least 30 loose elliptical orbits of Saturn, with each orbit being optimized for a different set of Saturnian system observations.

See also: GALILEO PROJECT; SATURN.

catalysis A chemical reaction caused by a substance that itself does not enter into the chemical reaction or is not changed by the reaction.

catalyst A substance that changes (increases) the rate of a chemical reaction without being consumed or changed by the reaction. A *negative catalyst* is a substance that retards a chemical reaction.

Figure 25. Cassini spacecraft line drawing (shown in interplanetary flight configuration)   *(Drawing courtesy of NASA/JPL)*

catapult A power-activated device that provides an auxiliary source of thrust to a missile or aircraft; it combines the functions of directing and accelerating the missile during its travel on the catapult and serves the same functions for a missile as does a gun tube for a shell.

cathode The negative electrode in an electron (discharge) tube or electrolytic cell through which a primary stream of electrons enters a system. Compare with ANODE.

cathode ray tube (CRT) A vacuum tube that permits the visual observation of electrical signals. The cathode ray tube consists essentially of an electron gun that produces a concentrated electron beam (i.e., the cathode rays), a grid to control the beam intensity and therefore the display's brightness, and a phosphorescent coating (phosphor) on the back of a viewing screen to convert the electron beam into visible light. The excitation of the phosphorescent coating produces light, the intensity of which is controlled by regulating the flow of electrons. Deflection of the electron beam is achieved either electromagnetically (by currents in coils around the tube) or electrostatically (by voltages on internal deflection plates). In general, electrostatic deflection is used when high-frequency waves are to be displayed, whereas electromagnetic deflection is used when high-velocity electron beams are needed to give a bright display, as, for example, in radar screens and television screens.

Cauchy number A nondimensional number arising in the study of elastic properties of a fluid. It is expressed as the ratio of inertial force to elastic force and may be written as: $(U^2 \rho)/E$, where U is a characteristic velocity, ρ is the density, and E the modulus of elasticity of the fluid. It is the square of the Mach number (i.e., M^2). Named in honor of the French mathematician Augustin Louis Cauchy (1789–1857), who studied elasticity.

caution (light) In aerospace operations, any out-of-limit condition or malfunction of a system that affects primary mission objectives or could result in loss of a space vehicle or system—if not responded to in time.

caution period In aerospace launch operations, a time period when nonessential personnel must be evacuated from an area because of a hazardous condition or operation, such as fueling the launch vehicle.

cavitating venturi Convergent-divergent constriction in a fluid line that produces cavitation at its throat; because of the cavitation effects, flow of the liquid in the line is a function only of the pressure upstream of the constriction—even though the downstream pressure varies.

cavitation The formation of bubbles (or cavities) in a fluid (liquid) that occurs whenever the static pressure at any point in the fluid becomes less than the fluid vapor pressure. In the flow of a liquid, the lowest pressure reached is the vapor pressure. If the fluid velocity is further increased, the flow condition changes and cavities are formed. The formation of these cavities (or vapor regions) alters the fluid flow path and therefore the performance of hydraulic machinery and devices, such as pumps. The collapse of these bubbles in downstream regions of high pressure creates local pressure forces that may result in pitting or deformation of any solid surface near the cavity at the time of collapse. Cavitation effects are most noticeable with high-speed hydraulic machinery, such as a liquid propellant rocket engine's turbopumps.

celestial Of or pertaining to the heavens.

celestial body Any aggregation of matter in space constituting a unit for astronomical study, such as the Sun, Moon, a planet, comet, asteroid, star, nebula, and so on. Also called a *heavenly body*.

celestial guidance The guidance of a missile or other aerospace vehicle by reference to celestial bodies.
See also: GUIDANCE SYSTEM.

celestial-inertial guidance The process of directing the movements of an aerospace vehicle or spacecraft, especially in the selection of a flight path, by an inertial guidance system that also receives inputs from observations of celestial bodies.
See also: GUIDANCE SYSTEM.

celestial mechanics The branch of science that investigates the dynamic relationships among bodies of the solar system and deals with the relative motions of celestial bodies under the influence of gravitational fields.
See also: ORBITS OF OBJECTS IN SPACE.

celestial navigation The process of directing an aircraft, aerospace vehicle, or spacecraft from one point to another by reference to celestial bodies of known coordinates. Celestial navigation usually refers to the process as accomplished by a human operator. The same process accomplished automatically by a machine usually is called *celestial guidance* or sometimes *automatic celestial navigation*.

See also: GUIDANCE SYSTEM.

Celsius temperature scale (° C) A relative temperature scale in which the fixed points are water in equilibrium with ice (O° C) and water in equilibrium with steam at standard pressure (100° C). This scale is divided into 100 degrees. Named after the Swedish scientist Anders Celsius (1701–1744). Formerly called the *centigrade scale.* Since 1948 by international agreement, the term "degree Celsius" has replaced the term "degree centigrade" in technical literature.

See also: ABSOLUTE TEMPERATURE SCALE.

Centaur A versatile and powerful rocket, originally developed by the United States Department of Defense in the late 1950s as an upper stage vehicle for the Atlas booster. The Centaur vehicle was conceived by Dr. Krafft Ehricke, who then directed its development while at General Dynamics. It was the first U.S. rocket vehicle to use liquid hydrogen as a propellant. The Centaur successfully served on a variety of important Department of Defense and NASA space missions, where heavier payload and/or demanding mission requirements necessitated the use of a more energetic upper stage.

See also: LAUNCH VEHICLE.

centaurs Outer solar system objects, such as Chiron, which exhibit a dual comet/asteroid nature. This group of objects has been named after the centaurs in Greek mythology, a race of half-man/half-horse beings.

See also: CHIRON.

centi- (symbol: c) The prefix in the SI unit system that denotes one hundredth (1/100).

See also: INTERNATIONAL SYSTEM OF UNITS.

centigrade temperature scale (° C) An obsolete name for the relative temperature scale that sets 0° at the temperature of water and ice in equilibrium and 100° at the boiling point of water (under normal atmospheric pressure). Since 1948 by interna-

tional agreement, this relative temperature scale has been called the *Celsius temperature scale.*

See also: CELSIUS TEMPERATURE SCALE.

centimeter (cm) One hundredth of a meter (i.e., 0.01 meter).

2.54 cm = 1 inch (US) (exactly)

centimeter-gram-second system (cgs-system) A system of units based on the centimeter (cm) as the unit of length, the gram (g) as the unit of mass, and the second (s) as the unit of time. In the great majority of contemporary technical literature, the cgs-system has been superseded by SI units.

See also: INTERNATIONAL SYSTEM OF UNITS; SI UNITS.

center-of-gravity For a rigid body, that point about which the resultant of the gravitational torques of all the particles of the body is zero. If the mass of a rigid body can be considered as concentrated at a central point, called the CENTER-OF-MASS, then the "weight" of this body (i.e., its response to a gravitational field) also may be considered concentrated at this point, such that the center-of-mass is also the center-of-gravity.

center-of-mass That point in a given body, or in a system of two or more bodies acting together in respect to another body (e.g., the Earth-Moon system orbiting around the Sun), which represents the mean position of matter in the bodies or system of bodies. Also called *barycenter.*

central force A force that for the purposes of computation can be considered to be concentrated at one central point with its intensity at any other point being a function of the distance from the central point. For example, gravitation is considered as a central force in CELESTIAL MECHANICS.

central processing unit (CPU) The computational and control unit of a computer—the device that functions as the "brain" of a computer system. The central processing unit (CPU) interprets and executes instructions and transfers information within the computer. Microprocessors, which have made possible the personal computer "revolution," contain single-chip CPUs, while the CPUs in large mainframe computers and many early minicomputers contain numerous circuit boards (each packed full of integrated circuits).

centrifugal compressor A compressor having one or more vaned rotary impellers that accelerate the incoming fluid radially outward into a diffuser, compressing the fluid by centrifugal force. Sometimes called a *centrifugal-flow compressor*. Compare AXIAL FLOW COMPRESSOR.

centrifuge 1. A device that swings material around in a circle. The centrifugal force on this material can be made to equal many g's (i.e., multiples of the acceleration of gravity found on the surface of Earth). A high-speed centrifuge can separate materials, such as cells in a liquid, by taking advantage of the density difference of each type of cell. 2. A large motor-driven apparatus with a long arm at the end of which human and animal subjects or delicate equipment can be revolved and rotated at various speeds to simulate (quite accurately) the prolonged, high-g acceleration environments encountered in modern aircraft, aerospace vehicles, or spacecraft.

centripetal force The force acting upon a body that causes it to move in a circular path. Consider an object of mass (m), moving at constant speed (v) in a circular path, the radius of which is (r). From Newton's laws of motion, the magnitude of this force is: mv^2/r and it is directed inward toward the center of the circle—thus the name "centripetal" force.

See also: CENTRIFUGAL FORCE; NEWTON'S LAWS OF MOTION.

Cepheid variable One of a group of very bright, supergiant stars that pulsate periodically in brightness.

See also: STARS.

Cerenkov radiation Electromagnetic radiation (usually bluish light) emitted when high-energy charged particles pass through a transparent medium at a velocity greater than the velocity of light in that material. This phenomenon can be seen, for example, as a blue glow in the water around the

Figure 26. The crew members for the ill-fated 51-L mission (left to right): Payload Specialist Christa McAuliffe, Payload Specialist Gregory Jarvis, Mission Specialist Judith Resnik, Commander Francis R. Scobee, Mission Specialist Ronald E. McNair, Pilot Michael J. Smith, and Mission Specialist Ellison Onizuka *(Courtesy of NASA)*

spent (irradiated) fuel elements in a reactor cooling pool. Named in honor of the Russian scientist Pavel Cerenkov, (also spelled Cherenkov; 1904–90) who first explained the origin of this light in 1934.

CETI An acronym that stands for "communication with extraterrestrial intelligence." Compare with *SETI*.
See also: SEARCH FOR EXTRATERRESTRIAL INTELLIGENCE.

chaff Radar confusion reflectors, which consist of thin, narrow metallic strips of various lengths and frequency responses; usually dropped from aircraft or expelled from shells, rockets, or spacecraft as a radar countermeasure.

chain of command The succession of commanding officers from a superior to a subordinate through which command is exercised.

chain reaction A reaction that stimulates its own repetition. In nuclear physics, a *fission chain reaction* starts when a fissile nucleus (such as uranium-235 or plutonium-239) absorbs a neutron and splits, or "fissions," releasing additional neutrons. A fission chain reaction is self-sustaining when the number of neutrons released in a given time equals or exceeds the number of neutrons lost by escape from the system or by nonfission (parasitic) capture.
See also: FISSION (NUCLEAR).

Challenger accident The orbiter *Challenger* lifted off Pad B, Complex 39, at the Kennedy Space Center (KSC) in Florida at 11:38 A.M. on the morning of January 28, 1986, as part of shuttle mission 51-L. At just under 74 seconds into the flight, an explosion occurred that caused the loss of the vehicle and its entire crew, consisting of Francis R. (Dick) Scobee (Commander), Michael John Smith (Pilot), Ellison S. Onizuka (Mission Specialist One), Judith Arlene Resnik (Mission Specialist Two), Ronald Erwin McNair (Mission Specialist Three), S. Christa McAuliffe (Payload Specialist One), and Gregory Bruce Jarvis (Payload Specialist Two). (See Figure 26.) Christa McAuliffe was a schoolteacher from New Hampshire (flying the shuttle as part of NASA's Teacher-in-Space program), and Gregory Jarvis was an engineer representing the Hughes Aircraft Company. The other five were members of NASA's astronaut corps.
See also: SPACE TRANSPORTATION SYSTEM.

chamber filling interval Time period from complete ignition of the solid-propellant grain to achievement of equilibrium burning pressure.
See also: SOLID-PROPELLANT ROCKET.

chamber pressure (symbol: P_c) The pressure of gases within the combustion chamber of a rocket engine.
See also: ROCKET.

chamber volume (symbol: V_c The volume of a rocket's combustion chamber, including the convergent portion of the nozzle up to the throat.
See also: ROCKET.

change detection The practice in remote sensing applications of comparing two digitized images of the same scene that have been acquired at different times. By comparing the intensity differences (either graytone or natural color differences) between corresponding pixels in the time-separated images of the scene, interesting information concerning change and activity (i.e., vegetation growth, urban sprawl, migrating environmental stress in crops, etc.) can be detected quickly in a semiautomated, quasi-empirical fashion.
See also: REMOTE SENSING.

channel construction Use of machined grooves in the wall of the nozzle or combustion chamber of a rocket to form coolant passages.
See also: ROCKET.

characteristic chamber length (symbol: L^*) The length of a straight cylindrical tube (with no converging section) having the same volume as the chamber a rocket engine would have if it had no converging section. By convention in rocketry, the combustion CHAMBER VOLUME (V_c) is considered to include all the volume up to the throat area of the nozzle.
See also: ROCKET.

characteristic exhaust velocity (symbol: c*) Of a rocket engine, a descriptive parameter,

$$c^* = V_e / C_F$$

where V_e is the effective exhaust velocity and C_F is the thrust coefficient. Also called *characteristic velocity*.

characterization 1. In general, definition of the total functional capability of a component system. 2. In rocketry, definition of physical or chemical properties of a material in relation to its application or use in a propellant formulation or rocket motor.

charge coupled device (CCD) A versatile solid-state electronic device that consists of a regular array of light-(electromagnetic radiation) sensitive elements that emit electrons when exposed to light. This emitted charge is then collected by attached electronic circuits, and the resulting information is analyzed. CCDs are used as the sensor (i.e., light-detecting element) in solid-state cameras, telescopes, and the like.

charged particle An ion; an elementary particle that carries a positive or negative electric charge (e.g., an electron, a proton, or an alpha particle).

charged particle detector A device that counts and/or measures the energy of charged particles; frequently found as part of the scientific instrument payload on planetary flyby and deep-space exploration missions.

Charon The moon of Pluto. It has an approximate diameter of 1,200 kilometers, a sidereal period of 6.388 days, and orbits at a mean distance of 20,000 kilometers from planet.
See also: PLUTO.

charring ablator An ablation material characterized by the formation of a carbonaceous layer at the heated surface that impedes thermal energy (heat) flow into the material by virtue of its insulating and radiation heat transfer characteristics.
See also: ABLATION.

chase pilot A pilot who flies in an escort airplane advising a pilot who is making a check, training, or research flight in another craft.

chaser spacecraft During orbital rendezvous and docking/berthing operations, the spacecraft or aerospace vehicle that performs the maneuvers in rendezvous and proximity operations.

chatter Uncontrolled rapid seating and unseating of a flow-control device, usually at low-flow conditions.

check flight 1. A flight made to check or test the performance of an aircraft, aerospace vehicle, rocket or spacecraft, or a piece of equipment or component; or to obtain measurements or other data on performance; a test flight. 2. A familiarization flight in an aircraft or aerospace vehicle, or flight in which a pilot or other crew members are tested for proficiency.

checkout 1. A sequence of actions taken to test a system or device as to its readiness for incorporation into a new phase of use, or for the performance of its intended use. 2. The sequence of steps taken to familiarize a person with the operation of an airplane, aerospace vehicle, or other piece of aerospace equipment. 3. A sequence of functional, operational, and calibrational tests to determine the condition and status of a weapon system or element thereof.

check valve Flow-control device that allows flow in one direction only.

chemical energy Energy liberated or absorbed in the process of a chemical reaction. In such a reaction, energy losses or gains usually involve only the outermost electrons of the atoms or ions of the system undergoing change; here a chemical bond of some type is established or broken without disrupting the original atomic or ionic identities of the constituents. Chemical changes, according to the nature of the substance entering into the change, may be induced by thermal (thermochemical), light (photochemical), or electric (electrochemical) energies.

chemical fuel A fuel that depends on an oxidizer for combustion or the development of thrust, such as liquid or solid rocket fuel or internal-combustion-engine fuel; as distinguished from nuclear fuel (i.e., uranium-235).

chemical laser A laser that uses chemical reactions to pump energy into a lasting medium, thereby creating the inverted state population needed for lasing. An example of a high-power chemical laser is the hydrogen fluoride (HF) laser—a laser in which a hydrogen-fluorine reaction produces lasing in a hydrogen-fluoride medium.

chemical pressurization The pressurization of propellant tanks in a rocket by means of high-pressure gases developed by the combustion of a fuel and oxidizer or by the decomposition of a substance.

chemical rocket A rocket that uses chemical fuel, that is, fuel that requires an oxidizer for combustion. The chemical fuel can be either solid propellant or liquid propellant.

See also: ROCKET.

chemiluminescence Any luminescence produced by chemical action.

chemisorption The binding of a liquid or gas on the surface or in the interior of a solid by chemical bonds or forces.

Cheyenne Mountain Air Station A hollowed-out mountain in the Colorado Rockies is the location of the U.S. nerve center that would sound the first alarm of an attack against North America. Cheyenne Mountain Air Station, Colorado, located near Colorado Springs, shields North American Aerospace Defense Command (NORAD) and United States Space Command warning and surveillance centers that keep watch on foreign aircraft, missiles, and space systems that could threaten the United States and Canada.

The early-warning function was moved from a vulnerable aboveground building in Colorado Springs to the granite-shielded security of Cheyenne Mountain in the mid-1960s. The heart of the underground complex is the NORAD command center, which began operations inside Cheyenne Mountain in 1966. Within the command center, the NORAD/U.S. Space Command commander-in-chief and his/her battle staff can receive immediate warning and surveillance information from a worldwide system of ground-based sensors and orbiting satellites. Computers in the command center translate and display the information on maps of North America and the world to give the battle staff a realistic picture of current situations.

Sharing the mountain complex with the men and women of the NORAD command center are members of the U.S. Space Command, Air Force Space Command, Air Weather Service, and the Federal Emergency Management Agency (FEMA). The U.S. Civil Defense National Warning Center, located next to the NORAD command center, also uses the mountain's communications system to receive and transmit warning data. This center is responsible for warning the civilian populace of North America.

In addition, present and future orbital paths of space systems (including defunct space systems or space debris) can be projected on computer screens. Superimposed on a world background map, a satellite's (or space object's) ground traces tell where the space vehicle will be several hours in the future.

For more than 30 years, the crews operating the missile warning center inside Cheyenne Mountain have maintained an early-warning trip line to give North American military and national leaders advance warning of an incoming ballistic missile attack. However, during the Gulf War, American and allied forces faced the threat of theater ballistic missiles, such as Iraqi-launched Scud missiles. These theater ballistic missiles have relatively short flight times (about 8 to 10 minutes) from launch to target impact. Any warning that could be provided by the Cheyenne Mountain complex was, therefore, considered extremely important in avoiding casualties and in alerting terminal defense systems, such as Patriot missile batteries.

Consequently, since the Gulf War, the ballistic missile warning mission has evolved beyond searching for incoming "Soviet" intercontinental ballistic missiles (ICBMs). Now Cheyenne Mountain's advanced early-warning "eyes" (including eight phased-array radar complexes, a constellation of Defense Support Program [DSP] satellites, and satellite ground stations) also look for shorter-range tactical missiles. It's current mission of vigilance includes Europe, other overseas theaters plus North America. Theater commanders around the world have shown interest in the (theater) missile warning the center provides due to the short flight times of these missiles. In contrast, land- (silo) based and sea- and air-launched strategic missiles take longer to reach their targets (about 15 to 30 minutes or more from launch to target impact).

See also: BALLISTIC MISSILE DEFENSE; DEFENSE SUPPORT PROGRAM.

chilldown Cooling of all or part of a cryogenic engine system from ambient temperature to cryogenic temperature by circulating cryogenic fluid through the system prior to engine start.

chilling effect The lowering of Earth's global temperature because of increased particles in the atmosphere (e.g., volcanic ash) that block incoming solar radiation. Compare with GREENHOUSE EFFECT.

Chiron An unusual celestial object which was discovered in 1977. Its highly perturbed, "chaotic" orbit lies almost entirely between the planets Saturn and Uranus. Chiron is unusual because it has a detectable COMA, indicating that it is a cometary body, but it is over 50,000 times the characteristic volume of a comet and is of a size more commensurate with a large asteroid (which it was first assumed to be). In addition, its curious orbit is unstable on time scales of a million years, indicating to astronomers and space scientists that it has not been in its current orbit long. Chiron was the first of four bodies discovered to date with similar orbits and properties. These bodies have been designated *centaurs,* in recognition of their dual comet/asteroid nature. In Greek mythology, the centaurs were a race of half-man/half-horse beings, and Chiron the Centaur (for whom this particular celestial object is named) was the wisest of the centaurs—the tutor of Hercules and Achilles. Scientists are now speculating that the astonomical centaurs, including Chiron, may have escaped from the Kuiper belt, a disk of celestial objects assumed to be orbiting beyond Neptune.

Chiron's highly elliptical (eccentricity = 0.383) 50.7-year orbit has a semimajor axis of 13.7 astronomical unit (AU), a perihelion of 8.46 AU, and an aphelion of about 19 AU. As a point of comparison, Saturn orbits the Sun at approximately 9.54 AU, while Uranus orbits at 19.18 AU. Chiron is estimated to have a diameter of between 148 and 208 kilometers (km) and a rotational period of about 5.9 hours. A gas and dust coma that varies with time in both size and brightness has been observed about Chiron's nucleus. The diameter of this coma has been measured to reach almost 2 million km on occasion. In addition, a gravitationally bound "dust atmosphere" appears to be suspended in the inner 1,200 km of the coma.

choked flow Flow in a duct or passage such that the flow upstream of a certain critical section cannot be increased by a reduction of downstream pressure.

chord line A straight line through the centers of curvature of the leading and trailing edges of an airfoil section. This line generally is used as a reference line from which the ordinates and angles of an airfoil are measured.

See also: AIRFOIL; WING.

chromosphere The region of the solar atmosphere located between the photosphere (i.e., the apparent solar surface) and the base of the corona. It is the source of solar prominences.

See also: SUN.

chronic radiation dose A dose of ionizing radiation received either continuously or intermittently over a prolonged period of time. Compare with ACUTE RADIATION DOSE.

chuffing The characteristic of some rockets to burn intermittently and with an irregular noise.

chugging 1. A form of combustion instability in a rocket engine (especially a liquid-propellant rocket engine), characterized by a pulsing operation at a fairly low frequency; sometimes defined as occurring between particular frequency limits. 2. The noise made in this kind of combustion.

circadian rhythms An organism's day/night cycle of living; a regular change in physiological function occurring in approximately 24-hour cycles.

circle of equal probability (CEP) In missilry, a measure of the accuracy with which a rocket or missile can be guided; a radius of the circle at a specific distance in which 50% of the reliable shots land. Sometimes called *circular error probable.*

circuit 1. In general, a network providing one or more closed paths. 2. In electronics, a closed path that can carry an electrical current; a combination of electrical components interconnected in a conductive path (or series of conductive paths) that can perform a particular task (or series of tasks). 3. In aerospace operations, the communication link between crewed spacecraft and ground stations. Some circuits are dedicated specifically to voice, television, or telemetry communications. In this context, also called a *communication channel.*

circuit board A flat piece of insulating material (e.g., phenolic resin) upon which electrical components are mounted. Thin copper foil patterns are used to connect the electrical components. If the copper foil pattern is produced on the board by a printing process (e.g., photolithography), then the device is called a *printed circuit board.*

circularize To change an elliptical orbit into a circular one, usually by firing a rocket motor when the space vehicle is at apogee.

See also: APOGEE; APOGEE MOTOR.

circular velocity At any specific distance from the primary (i.e., central body), the orbital velocity required to maintain a constant-radius orbit.

circulation The flow of a fluid through a given area or volume.

circumferential seal Seal composed of a continuous ring or of one or more segmented rings whose sealing surface is parallel to the centerline of the flow passage. Also called *radial seal.*

circumlunar Around the Moon; a term generally applied to trajectories.

circumsolar space Around the Sun; heliocentric (Sun-centered) space.

circumstellar Around a star—as opposed to *interstellar,* between the stars.

cislunar Generally, in or pertaining to the region of outer space between Earth and the Moon. By convention, the outer limit of cislunar space is considered to be the outer limit (from the Moon) of its sphere of gravitational influence. The term originates from the Latin word *cis* meaning "on this side" and *lunar*—or simply "on this side of the Moon."

clean room A controlled work environment in which dust, temperature, and humidity are controlled as necessary for the fabrication, assembly, and/or testing of critical components.

See also: BIOCLEAN ROOM.

Clementine A joint project between the Department of Defense (Strategic Defense Initiative Organization [SDIO]) and NASA. The objective of the mission, also called the *Deep Space Program Science Experiment,* was to test sensors and spacecraft components under extended exposure to the space environment and to make scientific observations of the Moon and the near-Earth asteroid 1620 Geographos. The observations included imaging at various wavelengths including ultraviolet (UV) and infrared (IR), laser altimetry, and charged particle measurements. Clementine was launched on January 25, 1994, from Vandenburg Air Force Base in California aboard a Titan II-G rocket. After two Earth flybys, lunar insertion was achieved on February 21, 1994. Lunar mapping took place over approximately two months, in two parts. The first part consisted of a five-hour elliptical polar orbit with a perilune of about 400 kilometers (249 miles) at 28 degrees south latitude. After one month of mapping, the orbit was rotated to a perilune of 29 degrees north latitude, where it remained for one more month. After leaving lunar orbit, a malfunction in one of the onboard computers occurred on May 7, 1994. This malfunction caused a thruster to fire until it had used up all its propellant, leaving the spacecraft spinning at about 80 revolutions per minute (RPM) with no spin control. This made the planned continuation of the mission, a flyby of the asteroid 1620 Geographos, impossible. The spacecraft remained in geocentric orbit and continued testing the spacecraft components until the end of mission.

clevis A fitting with a U-shaped end for attachment to the end of a pipe or rod.

climate The statistical collection and representation of the weather conditions for a particular area during a specified time interval, usually decades, together with a description of the state of the external system or boundary conditions. The properties that characterize the climate are: thermal (temperatures of the surface air, water, land and ice); kinetic (wind and ocean curents, together with associated vertical motions and the motions of air masses, aqueous humidity, cloudiness and cloud water content, groundwater, lakes and water content of snow on land and sea ice); and static (pressure and density of the atmosphere and ocean, composition of the dry air, salinity of the oceans, and the geometric boundaries and physical constants of the system). These properties are interconnected by the various physical processes such as precipitation, evaporation, infrared radiation, convection, advection, and turbulence.

See also: GLOBAL CHANGE.

climate change The long-term fluctuations in temperature, precipitation, wind, and all other aspects of Earth's climate. External processes, such as solar-irradiance variations, variations of Earth's orbital parameters (e.g., eccentricity, precession, and inclination), lithosphere motions, and volcanic activity, are factors in climatic variation. Internal variations of the climate system also produce fluctuations of sufficient magnitude and variability to explain observed climate change through the feedback processes that interrelate the components of the climate system.
See also: GLOBAL CHANGE.

clock An electronic circuit, often an integrated circuit, that produces high-frequency timing signals. A common application is synchronization of the operations performed by a computer or microprocessor-based system. Typical clock rates in microprocessor circuits are in the megahertz range, with 1 megahertz (1 MHz) corresponding to 1 million cycles per second (10^6 cps). A *spacecraft clock* is usually part of the command and data handling subsystem. It meters the passing time during the life of the spacecraft and regulates nearly all activity within the spacecraft. It may be very simple (e.g., incrementing every second and bumping its value up by one), or it may be much more complex (with several main and subordinate fields of increasing resolution). In aerospace operations, many types of commands that are uplinked to the spacecraft are set to begin execution at specific spacecraft clock counts. In downlinked telemetry, spacecraft clock counts (which indicate the time a telemetry frame was created) are included with engineering and science data to facilitate processing, distribution, and analysis.

clone 1. In general, an object that is an exact replica or copy of another. 2. In computer technology, a computer system, microprocessor, or peripheral device that is an "act-like" and "look-alike" version of original (usually more expensive) equipment being replicated or imitated. 3. In genetic engineering, a living organism (e.g., plant or animal) descended asexually (i.e., without recourse to the normal reproduction process) from a single ancestor.

closed ecological life support system (CELSS) A system that provides for the maintenance of life in an isolated living chamber or facility through complete reuse of the materials available within the chamber or facility. This is accomplished, in particular, by means of a cycle in which exhaled carbon dioxide, urine, and other waste matter are converted chemically or by photosynthesis into oxygen, water, and food. On a grand (macroscopic) scale, the planet Earth itself is a closed ecological system; on a more modest scale, a "self-sufficient" space base or space settlement also would represent another example of a closed ecological system. In this case, however, the degree of "closure" for the space base or space settlement would be determined by the amount of makeup materials that had to be supplied from Earth.

Material recycling in a life support system can be based on physical and chemical processes, can be biological in nature, or can be a combination of both. Chemical and physical systems are designed more easily than biological systems, but provide little flexibility or adaptability to changing needs. A life support system based solely on physical and chemical methods also would be limited because it would still require resupply of food and some means of waste disposal. A *bioregenerative* life support system incorporates biological components in the creation, purification, and renewal of life support elements. Plants and algae are used in food production, water purification, and oxygen release. While the interactions of the biomass with the environment are very complex and dynamic, creating a fully closed ecological system—one that needs no resupply of materials (although energy can cross its boundaries, as does sunlight into Earth's biosphere)—appears possible and even essential for future, permanently inhabited human bases and settlements within the solar system. Life scientists call a human-made closed ecological system that involves a combination of chemical, physical, and biological processes a *closed ecological life support system* (CELSS). This type of closed ecological system is sometimes called a *controlled ecological life support system.*

closed loop Term applied to an electrical or mechanical system in which the output is compared with the input (command) signal, and any discrepancy between the two results in corrective action by the system elements.

closed-loop RF check In aerospace launch operations, the radio frequency (RF) check of the command destruct system without open-air RF transmission. This is generally accomplished by hard-line from the transmitter to the receiver.

See also: COMMAND DESTRUCT SIGNAL.

closed-loop telemetry 1. A telemetry system that is used as the indicating portion of a remote-control system. 2. A system used to check out test vehicle or telemetry performance without radiation of radio-frequency (RF) energy.

closed respiratory gas system A completely self-contained system within a sealed cabin, capsule, spacecraft, or space station that will provide adequate oxygen for breathing, maintain adequate cabin pressure, and absorb the exhaled carbon dioxide (CO_2) and water vapor.

closed system 1. In thermodynamics, a system in which no transfer of mass takes place across its boundaries. Compare with OPEN SYSTEM. 2. A closed ecological system. *See also:* CLOSED ECOLOGICAL LIFE SUPPORT SYSTEM. 3. In mathematics, a system of differential equations and supplementary conditions such that the values of all the unknowns (dependent variables) of the system are mathematically determined for all values of the independent variables (usually space and time) to which the system applies. 4. A system that constitutes a feedback loop so that the inputs and controls depend on the resulting output.

close encounter (CE) An interaction with an unidentified flying object (UFO).

See also: UNIDENTIFIED FLYING OBJECT.

closest approach 1. The point in time and space when two planets or other celestial bodies are nearest to each other as they orbit about the Sun or other primary. 2. The point in time and space when a scientific spacecraft on a flyby encounter trajectory is nearest the target celestial object. 3. The place or time of such an event.

closing rate The speed at which two bodies approach each other—as, for example, two spacecraft "closing" for an orbital rendezvous and/or docking operation.

cloud albedo Reflectivity that varies from less than 10% to more than 90% of the incoming sunlight (insolation) and depends on drop sizes, liquid water content, water vapor content, thickness of the cloud, and the Sun's zenith angle. The smaller the drops and the greater the liquid water content, the greater the cloud albedo, if all other factors are the same.

cloud feedback The coupling between cloudiness and surface air temperature in which a change in surface temperature could lead to a change in clouds, which then could amplify or diminish the initial temperature perturbation. For example, an increase in surface air temperature could increase the evaporation; this in turn might increase the extent of cloud cover. Increased cloud cover would reduce the solar radiation (insolation) reaching Earth's surface, thereby lowering the surface temperature. This is actually an example of *negative feedback* and does not include the effects of long-wavelength (thermal infrared) radiation or the advection in the oceans and the atmosphere, which also must be considered in the overall relationship of the climate system.

cluster Two or more rocket motors bound together so as to function as one propulsion unit.

See also: ROCKET.

cluster of galaxies An accumulation of galaxies. These galactic clusters can occur with just a few members (say 10 to 100), such as the *Local Group*, of which the Milky Way Galaxy is a part, or they can occur in great groupings involving thousands of galaxies. Clusters of galaxies are gravitationally bound systems of galaxies within a few million light-years of each other. When observed optically, these clusters are dominated by the (visible) light emission from individual galaxies, but when viewed in the X-ray region of the electromagnetic spectrum, most of their X-ray emission appears to come from hot gas between the galaxies. In fact, scientists now think that there is about as much of this hot gaseous material between the galaxies in a cluster as there is matter in the galaxies themselves.

See also: GALAXY.

coasting flight In rocketry, the flight of a rocket between burnout or thrust cutoff of one stage and ignition of another, or between burnout and summit altitude or maximum horizontal range.

coated optics Optical elements (lenses, prisms, etc.) that have their surfaces covered with a thin transparent film to minimize light loss due to reflection.

coating A thin layer of solidified material that adheres to the surface of an object and provides protection, decoration, or some other functional task (e.g., radar signature suppression).

coaxial cable A cable or form of waveguide consisting of two concentric conductors—a central wire inside of and insulated from a grounded cylindrical braided wire shield. This braided wire shield minimizes radiofrequency and electrical interference. Sometimes called *coax cable* or simply *coax*.

coaxial injector Type of liquid rocket engine injector in which one propellant surrounds the other at each injection point.

coefficient 1. A constant in an algebraic equation. For example, in the equation

$$y = mx + 10$$

m is called the coefficient of x, while x and y are variables. 2. A number indicating the amount of some change under certain physical specified conditions, usually expressed as a ratio. For example, the *coefficient of linear expansion* of a substance is defined as the ratio of its change in length to the original length for a unit change of temperature from some standard.

coherence 1. The matching, in space (transverse coherence) or time (temporal coherence), of the wave structure of different parallel rays of a single frequency of electromagnetic radiation. This results in the mutual reinforcement of the energy of these different components of a larger beam. Properly designed lasers and radar systems produce coherent radiation. 2. The process of having a spacecraft telecommunications subsystem generate a downlink signal that is phase-coherent to the uplink signal it receives. The resulting spacecraft downlink signal, based on and coherent with an uplink signal, has extraordinary high frequency stability and can be used for precisely tracking the spacecraft and for carrying out science experiments.

coherent light The physical state in which light waves are in phase over the time period of interest.

Light travels in discrete bundles of energy, called *photons*. Each photon may be treated like an ocean wave. If all the waves are in phase, they are said to be coherent. When light is coherent, the effects of each photon build on top of the others. A laser produces coherent light and therefore can concentrate energy.

coined groove A narrow channel or depression stamped in a burst disk to provide localized thinning of material in a desired pattern.
  See also: BURST DISK.

coinvestigator A scientist working with the *principal investigator* (PI) on a space sciences experiment or an aerospace technology demonstration.

cold body An object at or near low ambient temperature. The object would appear "cold" when viewed in thermal infrared (long-wavelength) portion of the electromagnetic spectrum.

cold flow 1. Term applied to a test of a rocket engine in which fluid (propellant) is allowed to flow through the test configuration without the engine being started. 2. Permanent deformation of material caused by a compressive load that is less than the load necessary for the material to give way under pressure (i.e., yield); some time is required to obtain a cold flow.

cold-flow test A test of a liquid rocket engine without firing (igniting) it to check or verify the efficiency of a propulsion subsystem, providing for the conditioning and flow of propellants—including tank pressurization, propellant loading, and propellant feeding.

coldsoak The exposure of a system or equipment to low temperature for a long period of time to ensure that its temperature is lowered to that of the surrounding atmosphere or operational environment.

cold war The ideological conflict between the United States and the former Soviet Union from approximately 1946 to 1989, involving rivalry, mistrust, and hostility just short of overt military action. The tearing down of the Berlin Wall in November 1989 generally is considered as the (symbolic) end of the cold war period.

cold working Deforming metal plastically at a temperature lower than the recrystallization temperature.

colloidal system An intimate mixture of two substances one of which, called the dispersed phase (or colloid), is uniformly distributed in a finely divided state through the second substance, called the continuous phase or dispersion medium. The continuous phase may be a gas, a liquid, or a solid, and the dispersed phase material has very small dimensions, typically 10^{-9} to 10^{-6} meters.

column In a structure, a body whose function is to carry compression loads to its longest dimension.

coma 1. The gaseous envelope that surrounds the nucleus of a comet. *See also:* COMET. 2. In an optical system, a result of spherical aberration in which a point source of light (not on axis) has a blurred, comet-shaped image. *See also:* ABERRATION.

Combined Release and Radiation Effects Satellite (CRRES) A joint Department of Defense (Air Force)/NASA spacecraft launched into a geosynchronous transfer orbit (GTO) by a Delta rocket on July 25, 1990. As part of the CRRES program, the air force SPACERAD (Space Radiation Effects) project investigated the radiation environment of the inner and outer radiation belts and measured radiation effects on state-of-the-art microelectronic devices. Other magnetospheric, ionospheric, and cosmic ray experiments were included onboard CRRES. The NASA chemical release project used the release of chemicals from onboard canisters at low altitudes near dawn and dusk perigee times and at high altitudes near local midnight. The chemical releases were monitored with optical and radar instrumentation by ground-based observers to measure the bulk properties and movement of the expanding clouds of photoionized plasma along magnetic field lines after the releases occurred. Contact with the CRRES spacecraft was lost on October 2, 1991, and was assumed to be due to onboard battery failure.

combined stresses Stresses resulting from simultaneous action of all loads to which a structure is subject.

combustion Burning, or rapid oxidation, accompanied by the release of energy in the form of heat and light. The combustion of hydrogen, however, emits radiation outside of the visible spectrum—making a "hydrogen flame" essentially invisible to the naked eye.

combustion chamber Any chamber for the combustion of fuel; specifically, that part of the rocket engine in which the combustion of propellants takes place at high pressure. Sometimes called the *firing chamber* or simply *chamber*.
See also: ROCKET.

combustion devices Devices located in those portions of a liquid-propellant rocket engine where controlled combustion, or burning, of the liquid fuel and oxidizer occur. Typical components in this group include: the ignition system, the preburners, the main injector, the main combustion chamber, and the nozzle assembly.
See also: ROCKET.

combustion efficiency The efficiency with which rocket fuel is burned, often expressed as the ratio of the actual energy released by the combustion of a unit mass of fuel to the potential chemical energy stored in a unit mass of fuel.
See also: ROCKET.

combustion instability Unsteadiness or abnormality in the combustion of fuel, as may occur in a rocket engine.
See also: ROCKET.

combustion product Gaseous or solid materials produced during the burning (oxidation) of a fuel or combustible substance.

comet A dirty ice "rock" orbiting the solar system that the Sun causes to vaporize, glow visibly, and stream out a long, luminous tail. Comets generally are regarded as samples of primordial material from which the planets were formed billions of years ago. The comet's nucleus is a type of dirty ice ball, consisting of frozen gases and dust. As the comet approaches the Sun from the frigid regions of deep space, the Sun's radiation causes these ices to sublime (vaporize), and the resultant vapors form an atmosphere or "coma" with a diameter that may reach 100,000 kilometers (km). However, cometary nuclei have diameters of only a few tens of kilometers. Ions produced in the coma are affected by the charged particles in the solar wind, while dust particles liberated from the comet's nucleus are impelled in a direction away from the Sun by the pressure of the solar wind.

As a result of the highly successful international efforts in 1986 to explore Comet Halley, scientists have been able to confirm their postulated dirty ice "rock" model of a comet's nucleus. The Halley nucleus is a discrete, single "peanut-shaped" body (some 16 x 8 x 7.5 km in dimension). A very low albedo (about 0.05), dark dust layer covers the nucleus. The total gas production rate from the comet's nucleus at the time of the *Giotto* spacecraft's flyby encounter (March 14, 1986) was observed as 6.9 x 10^{29} molecules per second, of which 5.5 x 10^{29} molecules per second were water vapor. This observation means that 80 to 90% of the comet's nucleus consists of water ice and dust. Other "parent" molecules detected in the nucleus include carbon dioxide (CO_2), ammonia (NH_3), and methane (CH_4).

Many comets are believed to originate far from the Sun in the Oort Cloud, which is thought to extend out to the limits of the Sun's gravitational attraction, creating a sphere with a radius of between 60,000 and 80,000 astronomical units (AUs). This cloud, first described by the Dutch astronomer Jan Hendrik Oort (1900–92), is thought to contain billions of comets, whose total mass is estimated to be roughly equal to the mass of Earth. Small numbers of these comets constantly enter the planetary regions of the solar system, possibly through the gravitational perturbations caused by neighboring stars or other "chaotic" phenomena. Once a comet approaches the solar system, it is also subject to the gravitational influences of the major planets, especially Jupiter, and the comet eventually may achieve a quasi-stable orbit within the solar system. By convention, comet orbital periods are divided into two classes: *long-period comets* (which have orbital periods in excess of 200 years) and *short-period comets* (which have periods less than 200 years).

The chance of any particular "new" comet being captured in a short-period orbit is quite small. Most of these cosmic wanderers, after briefly visiting the planetary portion of the solar system, simply return to the Oort Cloud—possibly to loop back into the solar system again eons later. Or else they are ejected into interstellar space along hyperbolic orbits. Sometimes, however, a comet falls into the Sun. One such event was observed by instruments on a spacecraft in August 1979. Other comets simply break up because of gravitational (tidal) forces or possible outbursts of gases from within. When a comet's volatile materials are exhausted or when its nucleus is totally covered with nonvolatile substances, it becomes an "inactive" comet. Some space scientists think that an inactive comet may become a "dark asteroid," such as those in the Apollo asteroid group, or else simply disintegrate into meteoroids. Finally, on very rare occasions a comet may collide with a planetary body in the solar system, an event with the potential of causing a cosmic catastrophe.

In July 1994, 20-km-diameter or so chunks of Comet Shoemaker-Levy 9 plowed into the southern hemisphere of Jupiter. These cometary fragments collectively deposited the energy equivalent of about 40 million megatons of TNT. Scientists, using a variety of space-based and Earth-based observatories, detected plumes of hot, dark material rising higher than 1,000 km above the visible Jovian cloud tops. These plumes emerged from the holes punched in the Jovian atmosphere by the exploding comet fragments.

See also: GIOTTO SPACECRAFT, KUIPER BELT.

command A signal that initiates or triggers an action in the device that receives the signal. In computer operations, also called an *instruction*.

command and control system The facilities, equipment, communications, procedures, and personnel essential to a commander for planning, directing, and controlling operations of assigned forces pursuant to the missions assigned.

command destruct signal A signal used to intentionally activate the self-destruct system in a missile or rocket; usually sent when the missile or rocket behaves in an erratic manner and/or veers off the intended flight path, endangering people and property outside the rocket range boundaries.

See also: ABORT.

commander In aerospace operations involving human spaceflight, the crew person who has ultimate responsibility for the safety of the personnel onboard the spacecraft or aerospace vehicle and has authority throughout the flight to deviate from the flight/mission plan, procedures, and personnel assignments as necessary to preserve crew safety or vehicle integrity.

command guidance A guidance system wherein information (including the latest data/intelligence about a target) is transmitted to the in-flight missile from an outside source, causing the missile to traverse a directed flight path.

See also: GUIDANCE SYSTEM.

command module (CM) The part of the Apollo spacecraft in which the astronauts lived and worked; it remained attached to the service module (SM) until reentry into Earth's atmosphere, when the SM was jettisoned and the command module (CM) brought the lunar astronauts back safely to the surface of Earth.

See also: APOLLO PROJECT.

command system In aerospace range operations, the combination of onboard flight termination system and the ground transmitter that sends the arm and destruct commands.

See also: COMMAND DESTRUCT SIGNAL.

commonality The use of the same or similar hardware and software throughout an aerospace vehicle, spacecraft or space station program to accomplish the same function with the primary objective of reducing costs.

common item An item of supply used in two or more systems, subsystems, or pieces of support equipment, including related components and spares.

common failure mode Refers to a type of system failure in which diverse components are disabled by the same single cause.

communications satellite An orbiting spacecraft, which relays signals between two (or more) communications stations. There are two general types: the *active communications satellite*, which is a satellite that receives, regulates, and retransmits signals between stations, and the *passive communications satellite*, which simply reflects signals between stations. The active communications satellite is the type used to create today's global communication infrastructure. Communication is the most successful commercial space enterprise yet achieved. Of the hundreds of communications satellites sent into orbit over the past 35 or so years, about 150 are still operational—with newer, more capable spacecraft joining the international inventory each year.

The concept of the communications satellite can be traced back to the British space visionary and author Arthur C. Clarke, who in 1945, published a short article entitled: "Extra-Terrestrial Relays." In this article, Clarke described the use of manned satellites in 24-hour orbits high above the world's landmasses to distribute television programs. This idea was essentially unnoticed until the early 1960s, when the U.S. Department of Defense began to pursue active communication satellites (e.g., the ADVENT communications satellite program, which was canceled in 1962 due to spacecraft complexity and cost overruns), while initially NASA (under congressional direction) was confined to passive communication satellites. NASA's *Echo 1* and 2 satellites (launched on August 12, 1960 and January 25, 1964 respectively) were large metallized balloons that served as passive reflectors of radio signals. Passive communications satellites, however, proved to be unattractive for commercial use because the reflected signal is so weak. Then, in 1960, AT&T filed with the Federal Communications Commission (FCC) for permission to launch an experimental communications satellite with a view to rapidly developing and implementing an operational system. AT&T's *Telstar I* was launched on July 10, 1962 and was followed by *Telstar II* on May 7, 1963. These privately financed spacecraft (launched with NASA's assistance on a cost-reimbursable basis) were prototypes for a planned constellation of 50 medium-orbit satellites that AT&T was planning to put in place. When the U.S. Government decided to give the monopoly on satellite communications to the Communications Satellite Corporation (COMSAT), which was formed as a result of the Communications Satellite Act of 1962, AT&T's satellite project was halted.

By the middle of 1961, NASA decided to build an medium-orbit (6,400 kilometer [km] [4,000 mile (mi)] altitude) active communications satellite, called Relay. Unlike the previous Echo satellites, which were passive, Relay was an active satellite (like all the communications satellites that followed) that received a radio signal from the ground and retransmitted it back to another location on Earth. *Relay 1* was launched on December 13, 1962; *Relay 2* followed on January 21, 1964. The traveling-wave-tube (TWT) was the key power amplifying device in the Relay satellite. This device, improved with time, has become a basic component in modern communications satellites.

In the *Relay 1* satellite, the early TWT had a mass of 1.6 kilograms (3.5 pounds) and produced a minimum radio frequency (rf) output of 11 watts at a gain of 33 decibels (dB) over the 4050 to 4250 megahertz band with an overall efficiency of at least 21%.

In 1961 NASA also pursued the development of an experimental 24-hour orbit (geosynchronous) communications satellite, called Syncom. The Syncom project objective was to demonstrate the technology for synchronous-orbit communications satellites. A synchronous orbit (also called geosynchronous Earth orbit, or GEO) is one in which the satellite makes one orbit per day. Since Earth rotates once a day and the satellite goes around Earth at the same angular rate, the satellite hovers over the same area of the Earth's surface all the time. The altitude of a synchronous orbit is 35,784 kilometers (22,235 miles). At lower altitudes, satellites orbit Earth more than once per day. About 42% of Earth's surface is visible from a synchronous orbit. Therefore, with three properly placed satellites, the entire globe is covered. The idea for synchronous communications was invented by Arthur C. Clarke in 1945, but the first spacecraft to synchronous orbit, *Syncom I,* was not launched until February 14, 1963. Unfortunately, when the apogee kick motor (which is used to circularize a satellite's orbit) was fired, the spacecraft apparently suffered some type of catastrophic communications failure and fell silent. Telescopic observations later confirmed that the "silent" satellite was, nonetheless, in an appropriate orbit of nearly 24 hours at a 33 degree inclination.

A key advantage of the synchronous orbit communications satellite is that a ground station has a much easier tracking and antenna-pointing job because the satellite is always in view. For lower-altitude orbits, the spacecraft must be acquired as it comes into view above one horizon, then it must be tracked across the sky with the antenna slewing over to the opposite horizon, where the spacecraft disappears until its next pass. To cover a satellite continuously, ground stations would have to be distributed around the globe so that the satellite rises over the viewing horizon of one ground station as it sets for another station.

A particular type of synchronous orbit is the geostationary orbit. In this synchronous orbit around the equator, the satellite appears stationary over a point on the surface. This type of orbit was first demonstrated by the *Syncom 3* spacecraft. The *Syncom 2* spacecraft was placed in an orbit that was inclined 33 degrees to the equator so that it appeared to move 33 degrees north and 33 degrees south in a figure-eight path over a 24-hour period as observed from the ground.

Syncom 1 was launched on February 14, 1963 into a nearly synchronous orbit but failed during the apogee motor burn. The most likely cause was determined to be a failure of the high-pressure nitrogen tank. The Syncom spacecraft had two separate attitude-control jet propellants: nitrogen and hydrogen peroxide. One of the objectives of NASA's Syncom program was to demonstrate attitude control for antenna pointing and stationkeeping. After improvements in the nitrogen tank design were incorporated into it, *Syncom 2* was launched on July 26, 1963. It was a success and the satellite transmitted data, telephone, pioneering facsimile (fax), and video signals. Finally, the NASA *Syncom 3* spacecraft was launched successfully on August 19, 1964 into a geostationary orbit. It had the addition of a wideband channel for television and provided "live" coverage of the 1964 Olympic Games, which were being held in Tokyo. Both the *Syncom 2* and *Syncom 3* spacecraft were turned over to the Department of Defense in April 1965, and they were finally retired (turned off) in April 1969. It is important to recognize that in the early 1960s just reaching a synchronous orbit was a challenge. A major goal of the successful Syncom program was just to show that a synchronous satellite was possible.

Syncom led to the development of the *Early Bird I* commercial communications spacecraft as well as the Application Technology Satellite (ATS) series of NASA research satellites. By 1964 COMSAT had chosen the 24-hour-orbit (geosynchronous) satellite offered by the Hughes Aircraft Company for its first two commercial systems. On April 6, 1965 COMSAT's first spacecraft, *Early Bird I,* was launched successfully from Cape Canaveral. The era of the global village linked instantaneously by commercial communications satellites had begun! By that time communications Earth stations already existed in the United Kingdom, France, Germany, Italy, Brazil, and Japan. On August 20, 1964 agreements were signed that created the International Telecommunications Satellite Organization (INTELSAT). The *INTELSAT II* series of communication satellites was a slightly more capable and longer-lived version of the Early Bird satellite. The *INTELSAT III* series was the first to provide Indian Ocean coverage, thereby completing the global network.

In 1972 Telesat Canada launched the world's first domestic communications satellite, called ANIK. This satellite series served the vast Canadian continental area. On April 13, 1974 the first U.S. domestic communications satellite, Western Union's *WESTAR I*, was launched. In February 1976 COMSAT launched a new type of communications satellite, MARISAT, to provide mobile services to the U.S. Navy and other maritime customers. The U.N. International Maritime Organization sponsored the establishment of the International Maritime Satellite Organization (INMARSAT) in 1979; after leasing transponders on available satellites in the 1980s, eventually launched its own communications satellites, INMARSAT II F–1, starting in late 1990.

Much of the basic technology for communications satellites existed in 1960 at the beginning of the space age. But many improvements have been made to the global fleets of communication satellites that have entered service in the 1970s, 1980s, and 1990s. (See Figure 27.) Today new demands for personal communication systems are focusing attention on systems of small communication satellites in low Earth orbits, orbits significantly lower than those used by the Telestar or Relay satellites in the early 1960s. Typically, companies seeking to offer innovative global communications services to cellular telephone customers are planning to place constellations of 50 to 70 small satellites in polar orbit at altitudes of about 650 km (400 mi). (A typical constellation might involve 10 to 11 satellites in each of several orbital planes.)

Today fiber optics represent the major market challenge to the communications satellite. Where optical fiber cable systems are available, they offer a less expensive communications solution because of their wide bandwidth. However, satellites will still maintain a niche in providing communications services where running fiber optics is simply too expensive and in mobile applications (such as ships at sea). At present, satellites still maintain two distinct advantages over fiber optic cable: They are more reliable and they can be used point-to-multipoint (broadcasting). Recently, however, direct broadcast television delivery by satellite has made inroads into the home-television market, since providing fiber optic lines to individual homes is still an expensive undertaking.

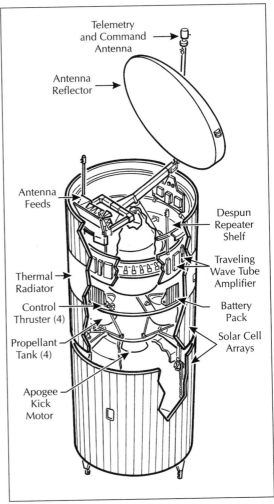

Figure 27. Cutaway diagram of a modern communications satellite —here the Hughes 376 spacecraft configuration. On orbit, this 2.13-m (7-ft.) diameter satellite extends to a full vertical configuration (as shown) of about 6.7 m (22 ft). Numerous versions of this commercial communications satellite have been placed into service in geosynchronous orbit. *(Drawing courtesy of Hughes Aircraft Company)*

companion body   A nose cone, last-stage rocket, or other body that orbits Earth along with the satellite or spacecraft.

See also: SPACE DEBRIS.

compatibility   An aerospace engineering characteristic applied to a major subsystem that indicates that it functions well in the overall system; also, an aerospace system is said to have *good compatibility* when all the various subsystems work well together.

complex Aerospace jargon for *launch complex;* for example, Complex 39A at the NASA Kennedy Space Center.

component An assembly or any combination of parts, subassemblies, and assemblies mounted together in manufacture, assembly, maintenance, or rebuild. A component usually has a specified function and can be installed or replaced only as a whole.

component life The period of acceptable usage after which the likelihood of failure sharply increases and before which the components are removed in the interests of reliability of operation.

composite materials Structural materials of metals, ceramics, or plastics with built-in strengthening agents that may be in the form of filaments, foils, powders, or flakes of a different compatible material.

composite propellant A solid-rocket propellant consisting of a fuel (typically organic resins or plastics) and an oxidizer (i.e., nitrates or perchlorates) intimately mixed in a continuous solid phase. Neither the fuel nor the oxidizer would burn without the presence of the other.
See also: ROCKET.

compressed liquid In thermodynamics, a liquid that exists at a pressure greater than the saturation pressure for its temperature or at a temperature lower than the saturation temperature corresponding to its pressure. Also called a *subcooled liquid.*

compressibility The physical property of a substance, such as air, whereby its density (mass per unit volume) increases with increasing pressure (force per unit area). Compressibility effects (such as buffeting, shifts in trim, etc.) become pronounced when an aircraft or aerospace vehicle undergoes high speed (i.e., transsonic or supersonic) flight in the air.

compressible flow In fluid mechanics, flow in which density changes in the fluid cannot be neglected.

compression chamber A sturdy chamber in which the air pressure can be raised to two or more atmospheres.

compressor A device for compressing air or other fluid. Compressors can be distinguished by the manner in which they handle the fluid being compressed, such as an *axial-flow compressor, centrifugal compressor, single-entry compressor,* and *supersonic compressor.* Compressors also can be identified by the number of stages they possess, such as *single-stage compressor* or *multistage compressor.*

compressor blade Either a rotor blade or a stator blade in an axial-flow compressor.

Compton effect Scattering of high-energy photons (either X rays or gamma rays) by free electrons. In this process the electron gains energy and recoils, and the scattered photon loses some of its energy (which has been transferred to the scattered electron) and increases in wavelength. First observed in 1923 by the American physicist A. H. Compton (1892–1962).
See also: GAMMA RAYS; X-RAY.

Compton Observatory An Earth-orbiting gamma ray observatory.
See also: GAMMA RAY OBSERVATORY.

concave lens (or mirror) A lens or mirror with an inward curvature.

concentration For a solution, the quantity of dissolved substance per unit quantity of solvent. Concentration can be expressed in several ways. The *mass concentration,* for example, is defined as the mass of solute per unit volume of solvent and has as typical units (i.e., kilograms per cubic meter [kg/m^3] or grams per cubic centimeter [g/cm^3]). The *molal concentration,* on the other hand, is defined as the amount of substance dissolved per unit mass of substance and has the units mol/kg (i.e., moles per kilogram).

concept A notion or statement of an idea, expressing how something might be done or accomplished, that may lead to an accepted procedure.

condensation The phase change process by which a vapor becomes a liquid. The opposite of *evaporation.*

condensation cloud A mist or fog of minute water droplets that temporarily surround the fireball following a nuclear detonation in a comparatively humid atmosphere. The expansion of the air in the negative phase of the blast wave from the explosion results in a lowering of the air temperature, so that condensation of water vapor present in the air occurs and a cloud forms. The cloud is soon dispelled when the pressure returns to normal and the air warms up again.

condensation trail A visible cloud streak, usually brilliantly white in color, that trails behind a missile or other vehicle in flight under certain conditions. There are three general types of condensation trails: the *aerodynamic* type, caused by reduced pressure of the air in certain areas as it flows past the missile or aircraft; the *convection* type, caused by the rising of air warmed by an engine; and the *engine-exhaust* (or exhaust-moisture) type, formed by the ejection of water vapor into a cold atmosphere. Also called a *contrail* or *vapor trail*.

conductance (symbol: G) The reciprocal of electrical resistance (for a direct current circuit); generally measured in siemens (S), the SI UNIT of electrical conductance; previously measured in *mho* ("ohm" spelled backward) or reciprocal ohm.

conduction (thermal) The transport of thermal energy (heat) through a body by means of a temperature gradient (i.e., from a region of high temperature to a region of lower temperature). In solids and liquid metals, conduction heat transport generally is accomplished by the migration of rapidly moving electrons; in gases and most liquids, conduction heat transfer is accomplished by atomic or molecular collisions.

conduction band The range of electron energies in a solid in which electrons can move freely under the influence of an electric field. The conduction band is the highest occupied band in metals; in semiconductor materials, the conduction band is a vacant band of higher energy than the valence band.

conductivity 1. In general, the ability to transmit, as electricity, thermal energy, sound and so on. 2. *Thermal conductivity* is a measure of a substance's ability to transport (via conduction) thermal energy (heat). Typical SI UNITS are joules per second per degree Kelvin per meter ($J\ s^{-1}\ m^{-1}$). Metals, such as copper and silver, have high values of thermal conductivity. 3. *Electrical conductivity* is a measure of a

substance's ability to transport electric charge. It is the reciprocal of the material's resistivity. Electrical conductivity is generally expressed by the SI units siemens per meter ($S\ m^{-1}$). Metals, such as copper and silver, also have high values of electrical conductivity.

conductor A general term describing a conducting medium; a substance that transmits electricity, thermal energy (heat), sound, and so on.
  See also: CONDUCTIVITY.

cone A geometric configuration having a circular bottom and sides tapering off to an apex (as in *nose cone*).
  See also: CONIC.

configuration 1. In general, the relative position or disposition of various things, or the pattern so formed. 2. A particular version of an aerospace vehicle, aircraft, missile, or rocket; as, for example, the Atlas-D configuration. 3. The requirements, design, and implementation that define a particular version of a system or system component. 4. The functional and/or physical characteristics of hardware/software as set forth in technical documentation and achieved in a product.

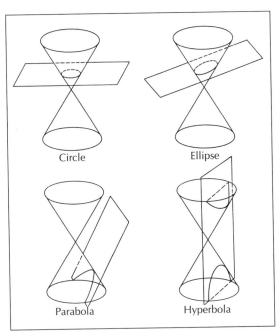

Figure 28. The basic conic sections   *(Drawing courtesy of NASA)*

configuration control Systematic evaluation, co-ordination, approval (or disapproval) of all changes to a baseline configuration.

See also: CONFIGURATION.

confluence The flowing together of two or more streams; specifically, the rate at which an adjacent flow is converging along an axis oriented normal to that flow. Compare CONVERGENCE.

conic A curve formed by the intersection of a plane and a right circular cone. Also called *conic section.* The conic sections are the *ellipse,* the *parabola,* and the *hyperbola*—all curves that describe the paths of bodies moving in space. The *circle* is a special case of the ellipse, an ellipse with an eccentricity of zero. (See Figure 28.)

conjunction The alignment of two objects in the solar system so that they have the same celestial longitude as seen from Earth. A planet is at a *superior conjunction* if the Sun lies between it and Earth; the planet Venus or Mercury is at an *inferior conjunction* when either lies between the Sun and Earth.

connector Mechanical device for joining or fastening together two or more similar parts, such as lines or tubes in a fluid system or wires in an electrical system.

conservation of angular momentum The principle of physics that states that absolute angular momentum is a property which cannot be created or destroyed but can only be transferred from one physical system to another through the action of a net torque on the system. As a consequence, the absolute angular momentum of an isolated physical system remains constant.

conservation of charge A principle of physics that states that for an isolated system, the total net charge is a constant; that is, charge can neither be created nor destroyed.

conservation of energy The principle of physics that states that the total energy of an isolated system remains constant if no interconversion of mass and energy takes place within the system. Also called the *First Law of Thermodynamics.*

conservation of mass The principle of classical (Newtonian) physics that states that mass can nei-ther be created nor destroyed but only transferred from one volume to another.

See also: CONSERVATION OF MASS AND ENERGY.

conservation of mass and energy From special relativity and Einstein's famous mass-energy equivalence formula ($E = \Delta m\ c^2$), this conservation principle states that for an isolated system, the sum of the mass and energy remains constant, although interconversion of mass and energy can occur within the system.

conservation of momentum The principle of physics that states that in the absence of external forces, absolute momentum is a property that cannot be created or destroyed.

See also: NEWTON'S LAWS OF MOTION.

conservation principle A principle or law of physics that states that the total quantity or magnitude of a certain physical property of a system (e.g., mass, charge, or momentum) remains unchanged even though there may be exchanges of that property between components within the system. Scientists consider such conservation principles to be universally true; so, for example, the conservation of momentum principle applies both on Earth as well as on Mars.

console An array of controls, indicators, and display devices for the monitoring and control of a particular sequence of actions, as in the prelaunch checkout of a missile, a countdown action, or a launch procedure. A console usually is designed around desklike arrays. It permits the operator to monitor and control different activating devices, data recording instruments, or event sequences. During a space mission, it is the place from which to issue commands or retrieve and display information concerning an aerospace vehicle (i.e., space shuttle orbiter), a payload, an Earth-orbiting spacecraft, or an interplanetary probe. Clusters of consoles (each assigned to specific monitoring and control tasks) usually are found at a mission control center. Depending on the nature and duration of the space mission, a console may be monitored continuously by a human being or only intermittently.

constant 1. A quantity whose numerical value always remains the same. 2. A component in an algebraic equation that expresses a relationship between variables but does not change its own value. For example, in the equation $y^2 = m x$, the components x and y are variables, while the component m is a constant. 3. A *fundamental* constant is a parameter believed by scientists to be the same throughout the universe. For example, the gravitational constant (G) (which appears in Newton's law of gravitation) is generally considered by scientists to be a universal constant and has a numerical value of 6.6726×10^{-11} N[newtons] m^2 kg^{-2}.

constellation 1. In astronomy, an easily identifiable configuration of the brightest stars in a moderately small region of the night sky. Originally these constellations, such as Orion the Hunter, were named by ancient astronomers after the heroes and creatures from various mythologies. Today each constellation has a Latin name; for example, Ursa Major (the Great Bear). 2. The number and orbital disposition of a set of satellites, such as the *constellation* of global positioning satellites. 3. In BALLISTIC MISSILE DEFENSE (BMD) studies, the number and orbital disposition of a set of space-based weapons forming part of a defensive system.

constellation size The number of defensive weapon satellites placed in orbit around Earth as part of a BALLISTIC MISSILE DEFENSE (BMD) system.

constrained threat A situation where opponents are limited in the number of warheads or types of missiles they can maintain, for example, by arms control agreements.

consumption rate The average quantity of an item consumed or expended during a given time interval, expressed in quantities by the most appropriate unit of measurement per applicable stated basis. For example, on a 300-day-duration human mission to the planet Mars, each crew member might consume an average of 2 kilograms of food each day (24-hour period). The food consumption rate for this mission could then be expressed as: 2 kg/(day-crew member).

continuously crewed spacecraft A spacecraft that has accommodations for continuous habitation during its mission. Sometimes called a *continuously manned spacecraft*.

continuously habitable zone (CHZ) The region around a star in which a planet can maintain appropriate conditions for the existence of life (including the retention of significant amounts of liquid water) for a period sufficient to allow the emergence of life.

continuous-wave (CW) laser A laser system in which the coherent light is generated continuously rather than at fixed time intervals. Also called a *CW laser*.

continuous wave (CW) radar A family of radar systems that transmits either modulated or unmodulated continuous waves. The simplest form of this type of radar system transmits a single frequency and detects moving targets by means of the DOPPLER EFFECT.

continuum That which is continuous; having no discrete parts. A continuous series of components or elements, such as the thermal radiation *background continuum* of a spectrogram.

contraction ratio For a rocket engine, the ratio of the area of the combustion chamber at its maximum diameter to the area of the nozzle throat.
  See also: ROCKET.

contrail A long, narrow cloud (usually bright white) produced by high-flying aircraft and missiles in the upper atmosphere.
  See also: CONDENSATION TRAIL.

contravane A vane that reverses or neutralizes rotation of a flow. Also called a *countervane*.

control 1. A lever, switch, cable, pushbutton, knob, or other device by means of which direction, regulation, or restraint is exercised over something. 2. In plural (*controls*), a system or assembly of devices (e.g., levers, gears, cables, valves, etc.) used to control the attitude, direction, movement, speed, or thrust level of an aircraft, aerospace vehicle, rocket, or spacecraft. 3. Sometimes capitalized as in *Mission Control*, to specify an organization or activity that directs and regulates a particular space flight or mission. 4. Specifically, to direct the movements of an aircraft, aerospace vehicle, or rocket with particular references to change in attitude and speed.

controllability The capability of an aircraft, rocket, or aerospace vehicle to respond to control, especially in direction and attitude.

controller In general, a device that converts an input signal from the controlled variable (temperature, pressure, fluid level, or fluid flow rate) to a valve actuator input (pneumatic, hydraulic, electrical, or mechanical) to vary the valve position to provide the required correction of the controlled variable.

control mass In thermodynamics, the mass inside a closed system; for example, the working fluid inside a sealed piston-cylinder system.

control rocket A vernier rocket, retrorocket, or other such low-thrust rocket, used to change the attitude of, to guide, or to make small changes in the velocity of a rocket, aerospace vehicle, or spacecraft.

control system (missile) A system that serves to maintain attitude stability and to correct deflections.
See also: GUIDANCE SYSTEM.

control vane A movable vane used for control; especially a movable air vane or exhaust jet vane on a rocket, used to control flight attitude.

control volume In thermodynamics, a defined region in space across the boundaries of which matter and energy can flow.

convection 1. In heat transfer, mass motions within a fluid resulting in the transport and mixing of the properties of that fluid. The up-and-down drafts in a fluid heated from below in a gravitational environment. Because the density of the heated fluid is lowered, the warmer fluid rises (natural convection); after cooling, the density of the fluid increases, and it tends to sink. Compare to CONDUCTION and RADIATION. 2. In planetary science, atmospheric or oceanic motions that are predominately vertical and that result in the vertical transport and mixing of atmospheric or oceanic properties. Because the most striking meteorological features result if atmospheric convective motion occurs in conjunction with the rising current of air (i.e., updrafts), convection sometimes is used to imply only upward vertical motion.

convergence 1. The quasi-horizontal flow of a fluid toward a common destination from different directions. When waters of different origins come

together at a point along a line (the convergence line), the denser water from one side sinks under the lighter water from the other side. The ocean convergence lines are the polar, subtropical, tropical, and equatorial. 2. In mathematics, the property of a sequence or series of numbers or functions that ensures that it will approach a definite finite limit. For example, a series representation of a mathematical function exhibits convergence if the sum of the terms of the series approaches the value of the function more closely as more terms of the series are used. Similarly, the sequence:

$$1/2, 2/3, 3/4, 4/5, 5/6, 6/7, 7/8\ldots$$

is convergent with the limit point at "1". 3. A decrease in area or volume; as, for example, the converging section of a rocket nozzle.

converging-diverging (CD) nozzle In a supersonic converging-diverging nozzle, the velocity of the fluid upstream of the nozzle throat is subsonic (i.e., the Mach Number [M] < 1), reaches sonic velocity at the throat of the nozzle (M = 1), and is then expanded to supersonic velocity (M > 1) downstream of the nozzle throat region by the diverging section of the nozzle.

convex lens (or mirror) A lens or mirror with an outward curvature. Compare CONCAVE LENS.

cook-off The deflagration or detonation of ordnance by the absorption of thermal energy (heat) from its environment.

coolant 1. In general, a gas or liquid used to remove thermal energy (heat) from some device or system, as, for example, a rocket's combustion chamber or nozzle throat wall. 2. Specifically, a substance (liquid or gas) circulated through the core of a nuclear reactor to remove or transfer thermal energy (heat). Common coolants are water, air, carbon dioxide (CO_2), liquid sodium (Na), and sodium-potassium alloy (NaK).

coolant tube In astronautical engineering, relatively small-diameter thin-walled conduit attached to or forming the wall of a regeneratively cooled combustion chamber or nozzle and carrying propellant to cool the wall.

cooperative target In aerospace operations, a three-axis stabilized orbiting object (e.g., a payload platform or spacecraft) that has enhanced electro-magnetic reflection or signal characteristics to facilitate rendezvous and docking/capture operations by a chaser spacecraft.

coordinates Linear or angular quantities that designate the position that a point occupies in a given reference frame or system. Also used as a general term to designate the particular kind of reference frame or system, such as *plane rectangular coordinates* or *spherical coordinates.*

Copernicus A well-known lunar impact crater about 90 kilometers (56 miles) in diameter and possessing a well-defined ejecta blanket with long rays; named for the famous Polish astronomer Nicolaus Copernicus (1473–1543).
See also: MOON.

Copernicus **(spacecraft)** NASA's *Copernicus* spacecraft was launched on August 21, 1972. This mission was the third in the Orbiting Astronomical Observatory (OAO) program and the second successful spacecraft to observe the celestial sphere from above Earth's atmosphere. An ultraviolet (UV) telescope with a spectrometer measured high-resolution spectra of stars, galaxies, and planets with the main emphasis being placed on the determination of interstellar absorption lines. Three X-ray telescopes and a collimated proportional counter provided measurements of celestial X-ray sources and interstellar absorption between 1 and 100 angstroms (Å) wavelength. Also called the Orbiting Astronomical Observatory-3 (OAO-3), its observational mission life extended from August 1972 through February 1981—some nine and one-half years. The spacecraft was named in honor of the famous Polish astronomer Nicolaus Copernicus (1473–1543).

coriolis effect(s) 1. The physiological effects (e.g., nausea, vertigo, dizziness, etc.) felt by a person moving radially in a rotating system, such as a rotating space station. 2. The tendency for an object moving above Earth (e.g., a missile in flight) to turn to the right in the Northern Hemisphere and to the left in the Southern Hemisphere relative to Earth's surface. This effect arises because Earth rotates and is not, therefore, an inertial reference frame.

corona The outermost region of the solar atmosphere, consisting of low-density clouds of hot gases and ionized materials.
See also: SUN.

Corporal An early medium-range (about 120-kilometer [75-mile]) liquid-propellant, surface-to-surface guided missile developed and deployed by the U.S. Army.

corpuscular Consisting of minute particles.

corrective action In aerospace operations, action taken to preclude occurrence of an identified hazard or to prevent recurrence of a problem.

corrosion The dissolving and wearing away of metal caused by a chemical or electrochemical reaction with its environment.

cosmic Of or pertaining to the universe, especially that part outside Earth's atmosphere. This term is used frequently in the Soviet and later Russian space program as equivalent to "space" or "astro-," as in cosmic rocket, cosmonaut, cosmic station.

Cosmic Background Explorer **(**COBE**)** NASA's *Cosmic Background Explorer* (*COBE*) spacecraft was launched successfully from Vandenberg Air Force Base, California, by an expendable Delta rocket on November 18, 1989. The 2,268 kilogram (kg) (5,000 pounds-mass [lbm]) spacecraft was placed in a 900-kilometer (559-mile), 99-degree inclination (polar) orbit, passing from pole to pole along Earth's terminator (the line between night and day on a planet or moon) to protect its sensitive instruments from the heat and light of the Sun and to prevent the spacecraft's instruments from pointing at the Sun or Earth.

COBE's mission was to study some of the most basic questions in astrophysics and cosmology. What was the nature of the primeval explosion (often called the "big bang") that started the expanding universe? What started the formation of the galaxies? What caused galaxies to be arranged in giant clusters with vast unbroken voids in between? The *COBE* spacecraft carried three instruments: a far infrared absolute spectrophotometer (FIRAS) to compare the spectrum of the cosmic microwave background radiation with a precise BLACKBODY; a differential microwave radiometer (DMR) to map the cosmic radiation precisely; and a diffuse infrared background experiment (DIRBE) to search for the cosmic infrared background radiation.

The cosmic microwave background (CMB) spectrum was measured by the FIRAS instrument with a precision of 0.03%, and the resulting CMB temperature was found to be 2.726 +/- 0.010 Kelvin, over the wavelength range from 0.5 to 5 millimeters. The FIRAS ceased to operate when the *COBE* supply of liquid helium was depleted on September 21, 1990.

See also: ASTROPHYSICS; BIG BANG THEORY.

cosmic dust Fine microscopic particles drifting in outer space.

See also: INTERPLANETARY DUST.

cosmic rays Atomic particles (mostly bare atomic nuclei) that have been accelerated to very high velocities and carry great amounts of energy. Cosmic rays move through space at speeds just below the speed of light. They carry an electric charge and spiral along the weak lines of magnetic force that permeate the galaxy. Although discovered over 50 years ago, their origin still remains a mystery. Scientists currently believe they are galactic in origin, but some cosmic rays (especially the most energetic) actually may originate from outside the Milky Way galaxy, making them tiny pieces of extragalactic material.

Galactic cosmic rays represent a unique sample of material from outside the solar system. Although hydrogen nuclei (i.e., protons) make up the highest proportion of the cosmic ray population (approximately 85%), these particles also range over the entire periodic table of elements, from hydrogen through uranium, and include electrons and positrons. Galactic cosmic rays bring astrophysicists direct evidence of processes such as nucleosynthesis and particle acceleration that occur as a result of explosive processes in stars throughout the galaxy.

Solar cosmic rays consist of protons, alpha particles, and other energetic atomic particles ejected from the Sun during solar flares events. Solar cosmic rays are generally lower in energy than galactic cosmic rays.

See also: ASTROPHYSICS.

Cosmic Ray Satellite-B (COS-B) A satellite developed by the European Space Agency (ESA) to study extraterrestrial gamma radiation in the 25

million electron volts (MeV) to 1 billion electron volts (GeV) range from a highly elliptical Earth orbit of approximately 100,000 kilometers (km) apogee, 350 km perigee, and near-polar inclination. It was launched on August 9, 1975 by a Delta rocket that NASA provided to ESA on a fully reimbursable basis.

See also: EUROPEAN SPACE AGENCY.

cosmodrome In the Soviet and later Russian space program, a place that launches space vehicles and rockets. The three main cosmodromes in the Russian space program are: the Plesetsk Cosmodrome, which is situated south of Archangel in the northwest corner of Russia; the Kapustin Yar Cosmodrome, on the banks of the Volga River southeast of Moscow; and the first and main cosmodrome (the site which launched *Sputnik 1*), the Baikonur Cosmodrome, located just east of the Aral Sea in Kazakstan (now an independent country). The Baikonur Cosmodrome has also been referred to as *Tyuratam*.

cosmology The study of the origin, evolution, and structure of the universe. Astrophysical discoveries in recent years tend to support the big bang theory of cosmology—a theory stating that about 15 to 20 billion (10^9) years ago, the universe began in a great explosion (sometimes called the "initial singularity") and has been expanding ever since. For example, the 1964 discovery of the 2.7° Kelvin cosmic microwave background radiation with a radio telescope provided the initial observational evidence that there was a very hot phase early in the

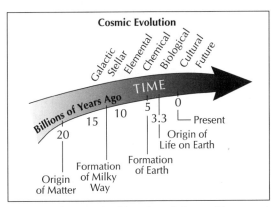

Figure 29. The scenario of *cosmic evolution* provides a grand synthesis for the long series of alterations of matter that have given rise to our galaxy, our Sun, our planet, and ourselves. *(Diagram courtesy of NASA)*

history of the universe. The history of the universe can be considered to follow a more or less linear time scale. This approach, sometimes called the scenario of *cosmic evolution,* links the development of the galaxies, stars, heavy elements, life, intelligence, technology, and the future. (See Figure 29.)

See also: ASTROPHYSICS; "BIG BANG" THEORY; COSMIC BACKGROUND EXPLORER.

cosmonaut The name used by Russia (formerly the Soviet Union) for its space travelers or "astronauts."

Cosmos The general name applied to a large variety of Soviet and later Russian spacecraft, ranging from military satellites to scientific spacecraft investigating the upper atmosphere of Earth. *Cosmos 1* was launched in March 1962; since then well over 2,000 Cosmos satellites have been sent into space. Also called *Kosmos.*

cost-exchange ratio In the context of ballistic missile defense (BMD), the ratio of the cost of an item to the defense to the cost of an equal and opposing item to the offense. For example, the cost-exchange ratio of a terminal defense system would be the cost to the defense of the number of rockets (plus the prorated cost of support sensors) needed to kill one incoming warhead compared to the cost to the offense of putting that warhead and associated decoys in the terminal phase of flight.

See also: BALLISTIC MISSILE DEFENSE.

coulomb (symbol: C) The SI UNIT of electric charge. The quantity of electric charge transported in one second by a current of one ampere. Named after the French physicist Charles de Coulomb (1736–1806).

count 1. In aerospace operations, to proceed from one point in a countdown to another, normally by calling a number to signify the point reached; to proceed in a countdown, as in *T minus 20 seconds and counting.* 2. With respect to the detection of ionizing radiation, one pulse of current or voltage from a detector, indicating the passage of a photon or particle through the detector.

countdown The step-by-step process leading to initiation of missile or aerospace vehicle testing, launching, and firing. It is performed in accordance with a predesignated time schedule; inverse count-

ing generally is performed during the process, with zero being the go or activate time.

counterattack Attack by part or all of a defending force against an attacking enemy force, for such specific purposes as regaining lost ground or cutting off or destroying enemy advance units, and with the general objective of denying to the enemy the attainment of his/her purpose in attacking.

counter-countermeasures Measures taken by the defense to defeat offensive countermeasures.

counterforce operations Those space or transatmospheric activities aimed at opposing or defending against threatening force anywhere on the planet or in a region of space. Although counterforce activities generally are viewed as defensive, they do not preclude defense by offensive action. Counterforce activities include the use of information and weather as weapons, and extend to defense against nonhuman threats to the security of the nation and the people of Earth (e.g., a small asteroid on a collision course).

countermeasures A tactic used by the offense to oppose defensive measures or by the defense to oppose offensive measures. Nondestructive countermeasures are those intended to nullify the capability of the opposing system by means other than direct attack. Defense suppression countermeasures include means of attacking defensive system elements.

counterpermeation A pressurant (i.e., an inert gas, such as nitrogen) often is used in a rocket's propellant tank to provide the pressure necessary to displace the liquid propellant from the tank and drive it (as a liquid) into the rocket's combustion chamber. Permeation occurs when the inert gas (pressurant) flows from its storage compartment through a porous (i.e., permeable) membrane and interacts with the liquid propellant in the tank. *Counterpermeation* involves the reverse process—that is, the simultaneous (and undesirable) migration of vaporized propellant and inert pressurant back across the permeable membrane into the pressurant's storage compartment. This can occur when the liquid propellant in a rocket's fuel or oxidizer tank becomes heated (possibly due to a loss of the tank's insulation and/or the excessive aerodynamic heating of the tank's surface during launch ascent). Some of the heated liquid propellant will then vaporize. Depending on the amount of heating, the type of propellant, and the overall design of the propellant tank, the propellant's vapor pressure eventually could exceed the pressure of the pressurant and counterpermeation will occur.

See also: PROPELLANT; ROCKET.

coupling 1. In general, a device for joining adjacent ends or parts of electrical, hydraulic, or mechanical equipment; a device that permits energy transfer from one electrical circuit to another, or from one mechanical system to another. 2. A mechanical device that fastens together two parts of a turbopump shaft or connects the shaft to other components of the turbopump. 3. A separable connector in a fluid system line or duct.

course 1. The line of flight taken by a rocket, aircraft, or aerospace vehicle. 2. A predetermined or intended route; a direction to be followed that is measured with respect to a geographic reference direction.

cracking 1. The presence of relatively large cracks extending into the interior of a structure, usually caused by overstressing the structural material. 2. The act of opening (a small amount) a flow-control device to allow the flow of fluid, as in *cracking a valve.* 3. In chemical engineering, thermal decomposition of heavy (complex) hydrocarbons into lighter and simpler hydrocarbons and other products.

craft Any vehicle or device designed to fly through air or space; an aircraft or spacecraft.

crater 1. A bowl-shaped topographic depression with steep slopes; a volcanic orifice. Craters are formed naturally by two general processes: *impact* (as from an asteroid or meteoroid) and *eruptive* (as from a volcanic eruption). 2. The pit, depression, or cavity formed in the surface of Earth by an explosion (chemical explosives or nuclear). It may range from saucer-shaped to conical, depending largely on the depth of burst. 3. The depression resulting from high-speed solid-particle impacts on a rigid material as, for example, a meteoroid or space debris particle impact on the skin of a spacecraft.

creep The slow (but continuous) permanent deformation of material caused by a constant tensile or compressive load that is less than the load necessary for the material to give way under pressure (i.e., to yield); some time is required to induce creep, and the process is accelerated at elevated temperatures.

crevice corrosion Corrosion that occurs in a narrow, relatively deep opening where two similar surfaces meet and trap a reactive fluid that acts as an electrolyte; corrosion occurs because of the concentration gradient of the reactive species established within the trapped fluid.

crew activity planning The analysis and development of activities to be performed in space flight by the human crew, resulting in a timeline of these activities together with the necessary procedures and crew reference data to accomplish flight objectives.

crew module A three-section pressurized working, living, and stowage compartment in the forward portion of the space shuttle orbiter vehicle. It consists of the flight deck, the middeck/equipment bay, and an airlock.

See also: SPACE TRANSPORTATION SYSTEM.

crew-tended spacecraft A spacecraft that has accommodations for only temporary habitation during its mission. Sometimes called a *man-tended spacecraft.* Compare with CONTINUOUSLY CREWED SPACECRAFT.

critical assembly An assembly of sufficient fissile material (such as uranium-235) and moderator to sustain a fission chain reaction at a very low power level. This configuration permits study of the behavior of the components of the assembly for various fissile materials in different geometrical arrangements. Compare with NUCLEAR REACTOR.

critical diameter A diameter of a solid rocket motor such that it can sustain a detonation.

critical hold/scrub point In aerospace operations, that time in the countdown when an unplanned hold normally would be expected to cause a scrubbed launch attempt.

critical ignition pressure Pressure below which propellants cannot be ignited.

criticality The state of a nuclear reactor when it is sustaining a fission chain reaction.
See also: NUCLEAR REACTOR.

critical mass The minimum amount of fissile material capable of supporting a fission chain reaction under precisely specified conditions.

critical path In planning for and managing an aerospace project, that particular sequence of activities or events that has the greatest negative slack or the least positive slack (leeway). A successful project manager will pay particular attention to the activities or events on this critical path.

critical point A fluid's critical point occurs at the highest temperature where liquid and vapor phases can coexist. Above this temperature the fluid, no matter what its density, can have only one phase. In thermodynamics, the critical point is represented as the termination point of the liquid-vapor coexistence line in the pressure-temperature diagram for a particular substance. (See Figure 30.)

critical pressure 1. In thermodynamics, the pressure of a fluid at the critical point—that is, the highest pressure under which the liquid and gaseous phases of a substance can coexist. 2. In rocketry, the pressure in the nozzle throat for which the isentropic (constant entropy) mass-flow rate is a maximum.

critical speed (symbol: V*) The flow velocity (V*) at which the Mach number (M) is unity. It is used

as a convenient reference velocity in the basic equations of high-speed, compressible fluid flow.
See also: MACH NUMBER.

critical temperature The temperature above which a substance cannot exist in a liquid state, regardless of the pressure.
See also: CRITICAL POINT.

critical velocity In rocketry, the speed of sound at conditions prevailing at the nozzle throat. Also called the *throat velocity* and *critical throat velocity.*
See also: ROCKET.

cross section (common symbol: σ [sigma]) 1. In general, the area of a plane surface that is formed when a solid is cut; often this cut is made at right angles to the longest axis of the solid object. 2. In aerospace engineering, the physical (geometric) area presented by an aircraft, aerospace vehicle, or missile system; the frontal (or "head-on") cross section is the surface area that would be observed if the vehicle was flying directly toward the observer. 3. In aerospace operations, the apparent surface area of an aircraft, aerospace vehicle, rocket, or spacecraft that can be detected by a remote sensing system; for example, an aircraft's *radar cross section.* Stealth (low-observables) technology now is being used to reduce a military aircraft's radar cross section. 4. In physics, a measure of the probability that a nuclear reaction will occur. Usually measured in *barns,* it is the apparent (or effective) area presented by a target nucleus (or particle) to an oncoming particle or other nuclear radiation, such as a gamma ray photon.
See also: BARN.

cruise missile A guided missile traveling within the atmosphere at aircraft speeds and, usually, low altitude whose trajectory is preprogrammed. It is capable of achieving high accuracy in striking a distant target. It is maneuverable during flight, is constantly propelled, and, therefore, does not follow a ballistic trajectory. Cruise missiles may be armed with nuclear weapons or with conventional warheads (i.e., high explosives).
See also: TOMAHAWK.

cruise phase In space flight operations involving a scientific spacecraft, the *cruise phase* is bounded at the beginning by the launch phase and at the end

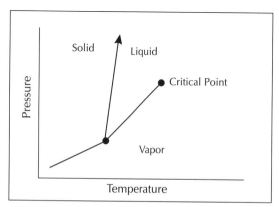

Figure 30. The pressure-temperature diagram for a typical thermodynamic substance. The critical point appears as the termination point of the liquid-vapor coexistence line.
(Courtesy of NASA)

by the encounter phase. After launch the scientific spacecraft is commanded to configure itself for cruise. Appendages that might have been stowed for launch (e.g., an antenna system) can now be deployed either fully or to some intermediate cruise position. Telemetry is analyzed to determine the state of health of the spacecraft and to determine how well it survived the launch. The trajectory is fine-tuned to prepare the spacecraft for its scientific encounter mission. During the cruise phase, ground system upgrades can be made and appropriate tests conducted, spacecraft flight software modifications can be implemented and also tested by the space flight operations facility. Finally, as the spacecraft nears its celestial target, scientific instruments are powered on (if necessary) and calibrated.

crust Outermost, and least dense, solid layer of a planet.

cryogenic Fluids or conditions at low temperatures, usually below -150° Celsius (123° Kelvin).

cryogenic liquid Liquified gas at very low temperature, such as liquid oxygen (LO$_2$ or LOX), liquid hydrogen (LH$_2$), liquid nitrogen, or liquid argon.

cryogenics The branch of science dealing with very low temperatures, applications of these low-temperature environments, and methods of producing them. This science may be concerned with practical engineering problems, such as producing, transporting, and storing the metric ton quantities of liquid oxygen (LO$_2$) or liquid hydrogen (LH$_2$) needed as chemical rocket propellants; or it may help a physicist investigate some basic properties of matter at extremely low temperatures. Cryogenic researchers work with temperature environments down to one-millionth of a degree Kelvin (10^{-6} K)—essentially at the physical threshold of absolute zero.

cryogenic materials Metals and alloys that are usable in systems or structures operating at very low temperatures. These materials usually possess improved physical properties at such temperatures.

cryogenic propellant A rocket fuel, oxidizer, or propulsion fluid that is liquid only at very low tem-

peratures. Liquid hydrogen (LH$_2$) and liquid oxygen (LO$_2$) are examples of cryogenic propellants.

cryogenic pump A pump that uses CRYOPUMPING to create a vacuum.
See also: CRYOPUMP.

cryogenic seal A seal that must function effectively at temperatures below about -150° Celsius (123° Kelvin).

cryogenic system A system in which the temperature falls below -150° Celsius (123° Kelvin).

cryogenic temperature Generally, temperatures below -150° Celsius (C) (123° Kelvin [K]); sometimes the boiling point of liquid nitrogen (LN$_2$), namely -195° C (77.4° K), is used as the "cryogenic temperature" threshold; in other instances, the temperature associated with the boiling point of liquid helium (LHe), namely -269° C (4.2° K), is considered as the threshold of the cryogenic temperature regime.

cryopump An exposed surface refrigerated to cryogenic temperature for the purpose of pumping gases in a vacuum chamber by condensing the residual chamber gases and maintaining the condensate at a temperature such that the equilibrium vapor pressure is equal to or less than the desired ultimate pressure in the chamber.
See also: CRYOPUMPING.

cryopumping The process of removing gases from an enclosure by condensing the gases on surfaces at cryogenic temperatures.

cryosphere The portion of Earth's climate system consisting of the world's ice masses and snow deposits. These include the continental ice sheets, mountain glaciers, sea ice, surface snow cover, and lake and river ice. Changes is snow cover on the land surfaces generally are seasonal and closely tied to the mechanics of atmospheric circulation. The glaciers and ice sheets are closely related to the global hydrologic cycle and to variations of sea level. Glaciers and ice sheets typically change volume and extent over periods ranging from hundreds to millions of years.
See also: GLOBAL CHANGE.

cryptologic Of or pertaining to CRYPTOLOGY.

cryptology The science of hidden, disguised, or encrypted communications. It embraces the fields of communications security and communications intelligence.

crystal A solid composed of atoms, ions, or molecules arranged in a regular repetitive pattern. The shape of the crystal is related to this pattern.

curie (symbol: C or Ci) The traditional unit used to describe the intensity of radioactivity of a sample of material. One curie is equal to 3.7×10^{10} disintegrations per second. (This is approximately the rate of decay of one gram of radium). Named after the Curies, Pierre and Marie, who discovered radium in 1898.
See also: BECQUEREL.

Curie point The temperature above which a ferromagnetic material (e.g., iron or nickel) becomes substantially nonmagnetic.

current (symbol: I) The flow of electric charge through a conductor. The ampere (symbol: A) is the SI UNIT of electric current.
See also: INTERNATIONAL SYSTEM OF UNITS.

cutoff (or cut-off) 1. An act or instance of shutting something off; specifically, in rocketry, an act or instance of shutting off the propellant flow in a rocket, or of stopping the combustion of the propellant. Compare with BURNOUT. 2. Something that shuts off or is used to shut off (e.g., a fuel cutoff valve). 3. Limiting or bounding, as, for example, in *cutoff frequency.*

cutoff velocity The velocity attained by a missile or rocket at the point of cutoff.

cycle Any repetitive series of operations or events; the complete sequence of values of a periodic quantity that occur during a period—for example,

one complete wave. The *period* is the duration of one cycle, while the *frequency* is the rate of repetition of a cycle. The *hertz (Hz)* is the SI unit of frequency; and 1 hertz equals 1 cycle per second.
See also: INTERNATIONAL SYSTEM OF UNITS.

cycle life The number of times a unit may be operated (e.g., opened and closed) and still perform within acceptable limits.

cyclic vibration Vibration mode, induced by rough combustion in a rocket engine, that periodically produces severe g-loads at one dominant frequency.
See also: G; G-FORCE.

cylindrical coordinates A system of curvilinear coordinates in which the position of a point in space is determined by (a) its perpendicular distance from a given line; (b) its distance from a selected reference plane perpendicular to this line; and (c) its angular distance from a selected reference line when projected onto this plane. The coordinates thus form the elements of a cylinder and by convention are written r, θ, and z, where r is the radial distance from the cylinder's axis z and θ is the angular position from a reference line in a cylindrical cross section normal to z. Also called *polar coordinates.*

The relationships between the cylindrical coordinates and the rectangular Cartesian coordinates (x,y,z) are:

$$x = r \cos \theta; \; y = r \sin \theta; \; z = z$$

cylindrical grain A solid-propellant grain in which the internal cross section is a circle.
See also: ROCKET.

cynthion Combining form pertaining to the Moon. For example, *apocynthion* corresponds to apogee.

Dalton law The empirical generalization that a mixture of ideal (perfect) gases would have a pressure equal to the sum of the partial pressures that each of the ideal gases would have as the sole component with the same volume and temperature, providing there is no chemical interaction. Also called the *law of partial pressure.*

damping The suppression of oscillations usually because energy is being expended by the oscillating system to overcome friction or other types of resistive forces.

danger period In aerospace operations, a time period when all personnel must leave some particular area because of a hazardous condition or operation.

dark nebula A cloud of interstellar dust and gas sufficiently dense and thick so that the light from more distant stars and celestial objects is obscured. The Horsehead Nebula (NGC 2024) in Orion is an example of a dark nebula.
See also: NEBULA.

dart configuration A configuration of an aerodynamic vehicle in which the control surfaces are at the tail of the vehicle. Compare with CANARD.

data 1. The plural of *datum*—a single piece of information, a fact. 2. A general term for numbers, digits, characters, and symbols that are accepted, stored, and processed by a computer. When such data become meaningful, then the data components become *information*. 3. Representation of facts, concepts, or instructions in a formalized manner suitable for communication, interpreta-

tion, or processing by humans or by automatic means. Any representations such as characters or analog quantities to which meaning is or might be assigned.

database A collection of interrelated or independent data items stored together to serve one or more applications.

data fusion The technique in which multivariate data from multiple sources are retrieved and processed as a single, unified entity. A significant set of a priori databases is crucial to the effective functioning of the data fusion process. For example, this technique might be used in supporting the development of an evolving "world model" for a robotic lunar rover, which is teleoperated from a control station on Earth. Inputs from the robot vehicle's sensors would be blended, or "fused," with existing lunar environment databases to support a more intelligent exploration strategy and more efficient field operations.

data handling subsystem The onboard computer responsible for the overall management of a spacecraft's activity is usually the same computer that maintains timing; interprets commands from Earth; collects, processes, and formats the telemetry data that is to be returned to Earth; and manages high-level fault protection and saving routines. This spacecraft computer often is referred to as the command and data handling subsystem.

data link 1. The means of connecting one location to another for the purpose of transmitting and receiving data. 2. A communications link suitable for the transmission of data. 3. Any communications channel used to transmit data from a sensor to a computer, a readout device, or a storage device.

data point 1. A unit of fundamental information obtained through the processing of raw data. 2. A value plotted on a chart. 3. A pair of values, such as a measurement and the time the measurement was taken. For example, during a rocket engine test the thrust was measured as "x" newtons at time "t." The corresponding pair of numeric values, "x" and "t," represents a data point that then could appear as a value plotted on a chart that describes engine thrust as a function of time.

data processing (DP) A general term describing the systematic application of procedures—electrical, mechanical, optical, computational, and so on—whereby data are changed from one form to another. Sometimes used to describe the overall work performed by computers. Also called *automatic data processing* (*ADP*) and *electronic data processing* (*EDP*).

data reduction The transformation of raw or observed data into more compact, ordered, or useful information.

data smoothing The mathematical process of fitting a smooth curve to a dispersed set of data points.

datum 1. A single unit of information; the singular of *data*. 2. Any numerical or geometrical quantity or set of such quantities that may serve as reference or base for other quantities. Where the concept is geometric, the preferred plural form is *datums*—as in *two geodetic datums have been employed.*

datum line Any line that can serve as a reference or base for the measurement of other quantities.

datum plane A plane from which angular or linear measurements are reckoned. Also called *reference plane.*

datum point Any point that can serve as a reference or base for the measurement of other quantities.

dazzling The temporary blinding of a sensor by overloading it with an intense signal of electromagnetic radiation, as, for example, from a laser.

deadband In general, an intentional feature in a guidance and control system that prevents a flight-path error from being corrected until that error exceeds a specified magnitude. With respect to the space shuttle orbiter vehicle, that attitude and rate control region in which no orbiter reaction control subsystem (RCS) or vernier correction forces are being generated.

dead spot In a control system, a region about the neutral control position where small movements of the actuator do not produce any response in the system.

debond Localized failure of adhesive at the interface of two components cemented together.

deboost A retrograde burn or braking maneuver, which lowers the altitude of an orbiting spacecraft.

debris 1. In general, human-made materials, components, and extinct or nonfunctioning spacecraft orbiting Earth. *See also:* SPACE DEBRIS. 2. In ballistic missile defense (BMD), large quantities of relatively small particles. Debris might be used as an intentional defense suppression measure; debris also is generated when objects in space are destroyed. *See also:* BALLISTIC MISSILE DEFENSE.

debug To isolate and remove malfunctions from a hardware system, subsystem, or component; to correct mistakes in computer software.

decade 1. A group or series of ten; for example, a period of ten years. 2. The interval between any two quantities having the ratio 10:1.

decay (orbital) The gradual lessening of both the apogee (maximum distance) and perigee (minimum distance) of an orbiting object from its primary (i.e., the body around which it revolves). The orbital decay process for artificial Earth satellites and pieces of space debris often results in their ultimate fiery plunge back into the denser regions of Earth's atmosphere.
See also: ORBITS OF OBJECTS IN SPACE.

decay (radioactive) The spontaneous transformation of one radionuclide into a different nuclide or into a different energy state of the same nuclide. The process results in a decrease, with time, of the number of original radioactive atoms in a sample. It often involves the emission from the nucleus of alpha particles, beta particles, or gamma rays; for heavy radionuclides, the decay process also might include spontaneous fission.

decay heat The thermal energy (heat) released by the decay of radionuclides.

decay time 1. In nuclear physics, the time required for a radioactive substance to decay to a stable state. 2. In aerospace operations, the approximate lifetime of an orbiting object in a nonstable orbit. The decay time reflects the tendency of a satellite (or piece of space debris) to lose orbital velocity due to the influences of atmospheric drag and gravitational forces. A decaying object eventually impacts the surface of Earth (or other planet) or else burns up in the planet's atmosphere. The decay time often is measured in terms of revolutions per day per day (rev/day/day).

deceleration The act or process of moving, or causing to move, with decreasing speed; negative acceleration.

deceleration parachute A parachute attached to a craft and deployed to slow the craft, especially during landing. Also called a *drogue parachute*.
See also: DROGUE PARACHUTE.

deci- (symbol: d) A prefix meaning multiplied by one-tenth (10^{-1}); for example, *decibel*.

decibel (symbol: dB) 1. One-tenth of a bel. 2. A dimensionless measure of the ratio of two powers, sound intensities, or voltages. It is equal to ten times the common logarithm (i.e., the logarithm to the base 10) of the power ratio, P_2/P_1. Namely,

$$n \text{ (decibels)} = 10 \log_{10} (P_2/P_1)$$

Since the bel (B) is an exceptionally large unit, the decibel is encountered frequently in physics and engineering.

decimal digit One of the ten digits used in decimal notation; namely, 0, 1, 2, 3, 4, 5, 6, 7, 8, or 9.

decimal notation The system of numeration that uses the ten decimal digits as various coefficients of the power of 10. For example, the number 426.21

represents the number $(4 \times 10^2) + (2 \times 10^1) + (6 \times 10^0) + (2 \times 10^{-1}) + (1 \times 10^{-2})$. Compare with BINARY NOTATION.

decimal point The base point in decimal notation, usually expressed by a period (.), although a comma (,) or a point midheight of the digits (·) is sometimes used. For example, the expressions

426.21   426,21   426·21

may all be encountered in the technical literature, but the first format (namely, 426.21) is the most common.

decoy 1. In general, an object or phenomenon that is intended to deceive enemy surveillance devices or mislead enemy evaluation of the threat. 2. In ballistic missile defense (BMD), a device that is constructed to look and behave like a nuclear-weapon-carrying warhead, but that is far less costly, much less massive, and can be deployed in large numbers to complicate defenses.
See also: BALLISTIC MISSILE DEFENSE.

decrement A decrease in the value of a variable. Compare INCREMENT.

dedicated Serving a single function; for example, a *dedicated* battery is a power source serving a single load, such as a special ordnance circuit.

deep space The region of outer space at altitudes greater than 5,600 kilometers (approximately 3,500 miles) above Earth's surface.

Deep Space Communications Complex (DSCC) One of three NASA Deep Space Network (DSN) tracking sites at Goldstone, California; Madrid, Spain; and Canberra, Australia. These facilities are approximately equally spaced around Earth for continuous tracking of deep space vehicles.
See also: DEEP SPACE NETWORK.

Deep Space Network (DSN) The NASA Deep Space Network (DSN) is a worldwide system for tracking, navigating, and communicating with uncrewed interplanetary spacecraft, probes, and planetary landers. This global network of antennas serves as the radio communications link to distant interplanetary spacecraft and probes, transmitting instructions to them and receiving the data they return to Earth from deep space.

Operated by the Jet Propulsion Laboratory (JPL), the DSN evolved from tracking and data recovery techniques developed during the conduct of missile work for the U.S. Army and has become a vital element in every space exploration project. For example, in 1958 JPL established a three-station network of receiving stations to gather data from the first U.S. satellite, *Explorer 1.*

The Deep Space Network uses high-sensitivity, large antennas (typically 64-meter [m] [210-feet (ft)] and improved 70-m [230-ft] diameter devices), low-noise receivers and high-power transmitters at locations strategically positioned on three continents (North America, Europe, and Australia). The three Deep Space Communications Complexes (DSCCs) of the DSN are located at Goldstone, California (in the Mojave Desert of Southern California); near Madrid, Spain; and near Canberra, Australia. These locations are approximately 120 degrees longitude apart around Earth, so that the DSN can maintain essentially continuous contact with spacecraft in deep space (as Earth rotates on its axis). Thus, as one antenna dish loses contact due to Earth's rotation, another one takes over the task of receiving data from and sending commands to the interplanetary spacecraft.

Since its creation, the DSN has provided telecommunications support for numerous space exploration projects. The network is also a scientific instrument and has been used for many interesting astronomical activities, including: monitoring natural radio sources (such as pulsars and quasars); radar studies of planetary surfaces and the Saturnian ring system; celestial mechanics experiments; lunar gravity experiments; and Earth physics experiments.

deep space probe A spacecraft designed for exploring *deep space,* especially to the vicinity of the Moon and beyond. A deep space probe with a specific mission may be referred to as a "lunar probe," "Mars probe," "outer planet probe," "solar probe," and so on.

Defense Meteorological Satellite Program (DMSP) A program consisting of a series of Department of Defense (DoD) spacecraft that have collected weather data for U.S. military operations for more than two decades with command and control support from Air Force Space Command. Two operational DMSP Block 5D-2 spacecraft orbit Earth at an altitude of about 832 kilometers (km)

(516 miles [mi]) and scan an area 2,900 km (1,800 mi) wide. Each system covers Earth in approximately 12 hours. Using their primary sensor, called the *Operational Linescan System (OLS),* these military weather satellites take visual and infrared imagery of cloud cover. Military weather forecasters use this imagery to detect developing weather patterns anywhere in the world. It helps in identifying, locating, and determining the severity of thunderstorms, hurricanes, and typhoons.

Besides the Operational Linescan System, DMSP satellites have sensors that measure atmospheric moisture and temperature levels, X rays, and electrons that cause auroras. These satellites also can locate and determine the intensity of auroras, which are electromagnetic phenomena that can interfere with radar system operations and long-range electromagnetic wave communications. The Block 5D-2 series spacecraft were launched from Vandenberg Air Force Base, California, starting in December 1982. Newer generations of this spacecraft have many improvements over early DMSP models, including more sensors with increased capabilities and a longer life span.

Each DMSP spacecraft is placed in a *sun-synchronous* polar orbit at a nominal altitude of 832 km (516 mi). A sun-synchronous orbit is a special polar orbit that allows a satellite's sensors to maintain a fixed relation to the Sun—a feature that is especially useful for meteorological satellites. Each day a satellite in sun-synchronous orbit passes over a certain area on Earth at the same local time. One way to characterize sun-synchronous orbits is by the time the satellites cross the equator. Equator crossings (called "nodes") occur at the same local time each day, with the descending crossings occurring 12 hours (local time) from the ascending crossings. The terms "AM" and "PM" polar orbiters denote satellites with morning and afternoon equator crossings, respectively. The most recent Block 5D-2 DMSP spacecraft measured 3.64 meters (m) (11.9 feet [ft]) long by 1.21 m (3.97 ft) in diameter with an on-orbit mass of 830 kilograms (1,830 pounds-mass [lbm]). Current design life is about four years.

See also: WEATHER SATELLITE.

Defense Satellite Communications System (DSCS) The Defense Satellite Communications System is an important part of the comprehensive plan to meet U.S. military communications needs. Currently, seven Phase II and five Phase III DSCS satellites orbit Earth at an altitude of 37,400 kilometers (23,230 miles). The satellites are super-high-frequency systems capable of providing worldwide secure voice and data transmission. The system is used for high-priority communications, such as the exchange of wartime information between defense officials and battlefield commanders. The military also uses DSCS to transmit space operations and early-warning data to various systems and users.

The first of the operational Phase II DSCS systems was launched in 1971. Their two-dish antennas concentrate electronic beams on small areas of Earth's surface but have limited adaptability in comparison to the newer Phase III satellites. The air force began launching the more advanced Phase III satellites in 1982. This system is built with a single, multiple-beam antenna that provides more flexible coverage than its predecessors. The single steerable dish antenna of the DSCS Phase III system provides an increased power spot beam that can be tailored to suit the needs of different (antenna) size user terminals. Phase III satellites can resist jamming and are expected to operate twice as long as Phase II satellites. Military users on the ground, at sea, or in the air can receive DSCS communications.

The Phase II DSCS has a mass of 610 kilograms (kg) (1,350 pounds-mass [lbm]) and a design life of five years. Its cylindrical body is 2.74 meters (m) (9 feet [ft]) in diameter and 3.96 m (13 ft) high with the antennas deployed. The Phase III DSCS has a mass of 1,170 kg (2,580 lbm) and a design life of ten years. Its rectangular body is 1.83 m (6 ft) by 1.83 m (6 ft) by 2.13 m (7 ft) in a stowed configuration and reaches an 11.6 m (38-ft) span with its solar arrays deployed on orbit.

Defense Support Program (DSP) Air Force Space Command–operated Defense Support Program satellites are a key part of North America's early-warning systems. In their 35,400 kilometer-plus (22,000 mile-plus) geosynchronous orbits, DSP satellites help protect the United States and its allies by detecting missile launches, space launches, and nuclear detonations. Air Force units at Peterson Air Force Base, Colorado operate DSP satellites and report warning information, via communications links, to the North American Aerospace Defense Command (NORAD) and U.S. Space Command early-warning centers within Cheyenne Mountain, located near Colorado Springs, Colorado. These centers immediately forward data to various agencies and areas of operations around the world. DSP satellites use an infrared sensor to detect heat from missile and booster plumes against Earth's background signal.

The program started with the first launch of a DSP satellite in the early 1970s. Since that time, DSP satellites have provided an uninterrupted early-warning capability. For example, the program's effectiveness was proven during the Persian Gulf conflict, which took place from August 1990 through February 1991. During Operation Desert Storm, DSP detected the launch of Iraqi Scud missiles and provided timely warning to civilian populations and United Nations coalition forces in Israel and Saudi Arabia.

Developments in the DSP have enabled it to provide accurate, reliable data in the face of tougher mission requirements, such as greater numbers of targets, smaller signature targets, and advanced countermeasures. Through five upgrade programs, DSP satellites have exceeded their design lives by some 30%. As the satellite's capabilities have grown, so has its mass and power levels. In the early years, the DSP satellite had a mass of about 900 kilograms (kg) (2,000 pounds-mass [lbm]) and its solar paddles generated 400 watts of electric energy. New-generation DSP satellites have a mass of approximately 2,270 kg (5,000 lbm) and improved solar panels that generate more than 1,400 watts of electric energy. The newer DSP satellites are about 6.7 meters (m) (22 feet [ft]) in diameter and 10 m (32.8 ft) high with the solar paddles deployed.

Other space technology developments in the program have led to techniques that have benefited other Department of Defense (DoD) satellite systems. For example, the addition of a reaction wheel removed unwanted orbital momentum from DSP vehicles. The spinning motion of this reaction wheel serves as a countering force on the satellite's movements. This *zero-sum momentum* approach permits precise orbit control with a minimum expenditure of attitude control fuel. As a result of DSP experience, reaction wheels have been added to other DoD space systems, including the Defense Meteorological Satellite Program (DMSP), the Navstar Global Positioning System (GPS), and Defense Satellite Communication System (DSCS) satellites.

defense suppression The act of destroying the elements of an enemy's defensive system.

defensive satellite (DSAT) weapon A proposed space-based weapon system that is intended to defend other orbiting satellites by destroying attacking antisatellite (ASAT) weapons.

deflagration A very rapid combustion process in which large quantities of gas and (thermal) energy are released. It is sometimes accompanied by flame, sparks, or spattering of burning particles. Although a deflagration can be classed as an explosion, the term generally implies the burning process of a substance with self-contained oxygen in which the reaction zone advances into the unreacted material at less than sonic velocity.

deflector A plate or baffle that diverts something in its movement or flow, as: (a) a plate that projects into the airstream on the underside of an airfoil to divert the airflow into a slot; (b) a conelike device placed or fastened on the launch site beneath a vertically launched rocket to deflect the exhaust gases to the sides; (c) any of several different devices used on jet engines to reverse or divert the exhaust gases; (d) a baffle to deflect and mingle fluids prior to combustion.

deformation An alteration of shape brought about by pressure or stress.

degassing The deliberate removal of gas from a material, usually by application of thermal energy (heat) under high-vacuum conditions.

degree (usual symbol: °) A term that has commonly been used to express units of certain physical quantities, such as angles and temperatures. The ancient Babylonians are believed to be the first people to have subdivided the circle into 360 parts, or "degrees," thereby establishing the use of the degree in mathematics as a unit of angular measurement.

degrees of freedom (DOF) A mode of motion, either angular or linear, with respect to a coordinate system, independent of any other mode. A body in motion has six possible degrees of freedom, three linear (sometimes called: X-, Y- and Z-motion with reference to linear [axial]) movements in the Cartesian coordinate system) and three angular (sometimes called: pitch, yaw, and roll with reference to angular movements).

Deimos The tiny outer moon of Mars discovered by Asaph Hall in 1877 and named after Δειμος, a son of Ares (Mars in Roman mythology) whose name means *panic*. Deimos is a dark body that appears to be composed of *C-type surface materials* similar to the C-type (carbonaceous chondrite) asteroids that exits in the outer asteroid belt. The irregularly shaped Deimos has a mean diameter of approximately 12 kilometers (km), a period of rotation of 1.2625 days, and orbits Mars at a mean distance of 23,480 km. This tiny moon has a mass of about 1.8×10^{15} kilograms and a mean density of 1.7 grams/centigrams^3. The escape velocity needed to leave this "natural Martian space station" is only 0.0057 km/second.
See also: MARS; PHOBOS.

de Laval nozzle A converging-diverging nozzle used in certain rockets. Named after Dr. Carl Gustaf Patrik de Laval (1845–1913), a Swedish engineer.
See also: ROCKET.

delay The time displacement (or equivalent distance) of some characteristic of a wave relative to the same characteristic of a reference wave—that is, the difference in phase between a reference wave and an actual wave.

delayer In rocketry, a substance mixed in with solid rocket propellants to decrease the rate of combustion.

Delta (launch vehicle) A family of two- or three-stage liquid-propellant, expendable launch vehicles (ELVs) that uses multiple strap-on boosters in several configurations. The Delta launch vehicle family began in 1959 when NASA awarded a contract to Douglas Aircraft Company (now part of Boeing Corp.) to produce and integrate 12 space launch vehicles. The early Delta vehicle used components from the U.S. Air Force's Thor intermediate-range ballistic missile (IRBM) as its first stage and the U.S. Navy's Vanguard launch vehicle as its second stage. The first Delta vehicle launched from Cape Canaveral Air Force Station successfully placed the *Echo 1* communications relay satellite (a large inflatable sphere) into orbit on May 13, 1960. The original Delta booster was 17 meters (m) (56 feet [ft]) long and 2.4 m (8 ft) in diameter. It used one Rocketdyne MB-3 Block II engine (also called the LR-79-NA11 engine) and burned liquid oxygen been converted into binary notation. Compare ANALOG COMPUTER.

digital image processing Computer processing of the digital number (DN) values assigned to each pixel in an image. For example, all pixels in a particular image with a digital number value within a certain range might be assigned a special "color" or might be changed in value some arbitrary amount to ease the process of image interpretation by a human analyst. Furthermore, two images of the same scene taken at different times or at different wavelengths might have the digital number values of corresponding pixels computer manipulated (e.g., subtracted) to bring out some special features. This is a digital image processing technique called differencing or *change detection.*

See also: REMOTE SENSING.

digital transmission A technique in telecommunications that sends the signal in the form of one of a discrete number of codes (e.g., in binary code, either 0 or 1). The information content of the signal is concerned with discrete states of this signal, such as the presence or absence of voltage or a contact in a closed or open position.

digitize To express an analog measurement in discrete units, such as a series of binary digits. For example, an image or photograph can be scanned and *digitized* by converting lines and shading (or color) into combinations of appropriate digital values for each pixel in the image or photograph.

dipole A system composed of two equal but opposite electric charges that are separated but still relatively close together. The *dipole moment* (μ) is defined as the product of one of the charges and the distance between them. Some molecules, called *dipole molecules,* have effective centers of positive and negative charge that are permanently separated.

dipole antenna A half-wave (dipole) antenna typically consists of two straight, conducting metal rods each one-quarter of a wavelength long that are connected to an alternating voltage source. The electric field lines associated with this antenna configuration resemble those of an electric dipole. (An electric dipole consists of a pair of opposite electric charges [+q and -q] separated by a distance [d].) The dipole antenna is commonly used to transmit

(or receive) radio-frequency signals below 30 megahertz (MHz).

direct ascent nonnuclear antisatellite (DANNASAT) weapon A ground-based rocket with a homing, nonnuclear warhead designed to destroy enemy satellites.

direct ascent nuclear antisatellite (DANASAT) weapon A ground-based rocket with a nuclear warhead designed to destroy enemy satellites.

direct broadcast satellite (DBS) A class of communications satellite, usually placed in geostationary orbit around Earth, which receives broadcast signals (i.e., television programs) from points of origin on Earth and then amplifies and retransmits these signals to individual end users throughout some wide area or specific region. Many households in the United States now receive their television programs directly from space. A hundred or more channels of television signals are sent through a DBS and then are received by small (less than 0.5 meter diameter) satellite dishes placed inconspicuously on the roofs of private homes and businesses.

See also: COMMUNICATIONS SATELLITE.

direct conversion In thermodynamics, the conversion of thermal energy (heat) or other forms of energy into electrical energy without intermediate conversion into mechanical work—that is, without the use of moving components as found in a conventional electric generator system. The main approaches for converting heat directly into electricity include: *thermoelectric* conversion, *thermionic* conversion, and *magnetohydrodynamic* conversion. Solar energy also can be directly converted into electrical energy by means of solar cells (*photovoltaic* conversion), and chemical energy can be directly converted into electrical energy in batteries and fuel cells.

See also: BATTERY; FUEL CELL; MAGNETOHYDRODYNAMIC CONVERTER; SOLAR CELL; THERMIONIC CONVERSION; THERMOELECTRIC CONVERSION.

directed energy Energy in the form of elementary atomic particles, tiny pellets (i.e., kinetic energy weapon devices), or focused beams of electromagnetic radiation (e.g., laser or microwave beams) that can be sent long distances at, or nearly at, the speed of light.

directed energy weapon (DEW) A device that uses a tightly focused beam of very intense energy, either in the form of electromagnetic radiation (e.g., light from a laser) or in the form of elementary atomic particles, to kill its target. The DEW device delivers this lethal amount of energy at or near the speed of light. Also called a *speed-of-light weapon*.

directional antenna An antenna that radiates or receives radio-frequency (RF) signals more efficiently in some directions than in others. A group of antennas arranged for this purpose is called an *antenna array*. Sometimes called a *directive antenna* or a *directional aerial*.

direct readout The capability that allows ground stations to collect and interpret the data messages that are transmitted from satellites.

disarming In aerospace operations, the normal method of returning ordnance systems or components to a safe status.

disc (of galaxy) The flat disc-shaped region of a galaxy, which contains most of its stars and upon which a spiral pattern often is superimposed.
See also: GALAXY.

disconnect Short for quick-disconnect—a separable connector characterized by two separable halves, an interface seal, and, usually, a latch-release locking mechanism; it can be separated without the use of tools in a very short time.

discrete Composed of distinct elements.

discrimination In ballistic missile defense (BMD), the ability of a defensive surveillance system to differentiate decoys or other nonthreatening objects from targets, such as a threatening booster rocket, postboost vehicle, or reentry vehicle.
See also: BALLISTIC MISSILE DEFENSE.

dish Aerospace jargon used to describe a parabolic radio or radar antenna, whose shape is roughly that of a large soup bowl.

disk 1. In astronomy, the visible surface of the Sun (or any other celestial body) projected against the sky. 2. In computer technology, a round, flat flexible (*floppy*) or rigid (*hard*) piece of material, magnetically coated to store digital (binary) data that can be electronically added, recalled, and edited, or deleted.

dispersal Relocation of aerospace forces for the purpose of increasing their survivability.

dispersion 1. The spreading or separation of forces that usually are concentrated in limited areas to reduce vulnerability. 2. A scattered pattern of hits around the mean point of impact of bombs, projectiles, and missile warheads dropped or fired under identical conditions. 3. In chemical warfare (CW) or biological warfare (BW) operations, the dissemination of CW or BW agents in liquid or aerosol form. 4. In optics, the separation of (mixed-wavelength) light rays into their component colors by passage through a diffraction grating or prism. 5. In rocketry, deviation from a prescribed flight path; specifically, circular dispersion. 6. In statistics, a measure of the scatter of data points around a mean value or around a regression curve. 7. In materials science, a scattering of very fine particles (i.e., ceramics) within the body of a metallic material, usually resulting in an overall strengthening of the composite material.

distortion 1. In general, the failure of a system (typically optical or electronic) to transmit or reproduce the characteristics of an input signal with exactness in the output signal. 2. An undesired changed in the dimensions or shape of a structure; for example, the *distortion* of a cryogenic propellant tank because of extreme temperature gradients.

distributed architecture A system design whose primary functions are dispersed and repeated in numerous nodes at diverse locations. Each node has a large amount of autonomy. This has the effect of increasing the survivability of the system, since the loss of a few nodes will not cause the system to fail catastrophically. It may, however, cause redundant actions and therefore require more system elements than a more efficient architecture. The term often is used in the context of BALLISTIC MISSILE DEFENSE (BMD).

distributed battle management A battle management system that relies on a distributed architecture with numerous, largely autonomous nodes.

diurnal Having a period of, occurring in, or related to a day; daily.

docking In general, the act of joining two spacecraft by independently maneuvering one into contact with the other at a chosen interface. More specifically, the process of sealing two crewed spacecraft together in orbit with latches and sealing rings so that two hatches can be opened between them without losing cabin pressure to permit crew members to move from one spacecraft to the other.

docking interface The area of contact between two docking mechanisms.

docking mechanism A mechanism that performs functions to connect one spacecraft to another in a docking operation.

docking module A structural element that provides a support and attachment interface between a docking mechanism and a spacecraft. For example, the special component added to the U.S. Apollo spacecraft so that it could be joined with the Russian Soyuz spacecraft in the Apollo-Soyuz Test Project; or the component carried in the cargo bay of the U.S. space shuttle so that it could be joined with the Russian Mir space station.
See also: APOLLO-SOYUZ TEST PROJECT; DOCKING.

doffing Act of removing apparel or equipment, such as a spacesuit.

dogleg A directional turn made in the launch trajectory to produce a more favorable orbit inclination or to avoid passing over a populated (no-fly) region.

donning Act of putting on apparel or equipment, such as a spacesuit.

Doppler effect The phenomenon evidenced by the change in the observed frequency of a sound or radio wave caused by a time rate of change in the effective length of the path of travel between the source and the point of observation.
See also: DOPPLER SHIFT.

Doppler imaging The use of radar or laser radar (ladar) to produce reflected Doppler-shifted electromagnetic signals from different parts of an object. This technique can provide an image of the object if it is spinning or tumbling. Since the DOPPLER SHIFT depends on the velocity of the object

with respect to the observer, reflections from those parts of the object receding from the observer will have different shifts from those moving toward the observer.

Doppler radar Any form of radar that detects motion relative to a reflecting surface by measuring the frequency shift of reflected electromagnetic energy due to the motion of the observer or of the reflecting surface. A Doppler radar system can differentiate between fixed and moving targets by detecting the apparent change in frequency of the reflected electromagnetic wave due to motion of the target.

Doppler shift The change in (apparent) frequency and wavelength of a source due to the relative motion of the source and an observer. If the source is approaching the observer, the observed frequency is higher and the observed wavelength is shorter. This change to shorter wavelengths often is called the *blueshift*. If, on the other hand, the source is moving away from the observer, the observed frequency will be lower and the wavelength will be longer. This change to longer wavelengths is called the *redshift*, since for a visible light source this would mean a shift to the longer-wavelength, or red, portion of the visible spectrum.

dose In radiation protection, a general term describing the amount of energy delivered to a given volume of matter, a particular body organ, or a person (i.e., a *wholebody dose*) by ionizing radiation.
See also: ABSORBED DOSE.

dose equivalent (symbol: H) In radiation protection, the product of absorbed dose (D), quality factor (QF), and any other modifying factors used to characterize and evaluate the biological effects of ionizing radiation doses received by human beings (or other living creatures). The traditional unit of dose equivalent is the *rem* (an acronym for *r*oentgen *e*quivalent *m*an). The *sievert* (*Sv*) is the SI special unit for dose equivalent. These units are related as follows:

$$100 \text{ rem} = 1 \text{ sievert (Sv)}$$

See also: INTERNATIONAL SYSTEM OF UNITS.

dose rate The amount of ionizing radiation delivered per unit time—that is, the radiation dose per unit time.

dosimetry The measurement of radiation doses. The term applies to both the devices used (i.e., *dosimeters*) and to the measurement techniques involved.

double-base propellant A solid rocket propellant using two unstable compounds, such as nitrocellulose and nitroglycerin. The unstable compounds used in a double-base propellant contain enough chemically bonded oxidizer material and do not require a separate oxidizer to sustain combustion.

double-entry compressor A centrifugal compressor that takes in air or other fluid on both sides of the impeller (a device that imparts motion to a fluid), with vanes on each side to accelerate the working fluid into the diffuser. The double-entry compressor is not a multistage compressor.

downcomer 1. Vertical feedline that conveys fluid from a higher to a lower location on a vehicle. 2. Coolant tube in which coolant flows in the same direction as the exhaust gas.

downlink In general, a signal from a higher physical elevation to a lower physical elevation; for example, a signal received from a spacecraft.
See also: TELECOMMUNICATIONS.

downrange At a location or in a direction away from the launch site but along the intended flight path of a missile or rocket being tested on the range. For example, Ascension Island in the South Atlantic Ocean is far *downrange* from the launch sites at Cape Canaveral Air Force Station in Florida.

downtime A period during which equipment is not operating; this outage can be due to planned maintenance or unplanned component failure.

downweight Landing weight; specifically space shuttle (STS—Space Transmittal System) payloads and all items required by specific payloads.

drag (symbol: D) 1. A retarding force acting upon a body in motion through a fluid, parallel to the direction of motion of the body. It is a component of the total forces acting on the body. 2. Atmospheric resistance to the orbital motion of a spacecraft. The effect of atmospheric drag is to cause the satellite's orbit to "decay," or spiral downward. A satellite of very high mass, very low cross-sectional area, and in very high orbit will not be affected greatly by drag. However, a high cross-sectional area satellite of low mass in a low-altitude orbit will be affected very strongly by drag. For Earth orbits above about 200 kilometers (124 miles), the satellite's altitude decreases very slowly due to drag; but below 150 kilometers (93.2 miles), the orbit decays very rapidly. In fact, at lower orbital altitudes, drag is the major space environment condition affecting satellite lifetime. For example, the abandoned U.S. Skylab space station came crashing back to Earth in July 1979 due to relentless action of atmospheric drag.

drag coefficient (C^D) A coefficient representing the drag on a given airfoil or other aerodynamic body.

drag parachute 1. A drogue parachute. 2. Any of several types of parachutes attached to high-performance aircraft or aerospace vehicles that can be deployed, usually during landings, to decrease speed and also, under certain flight conditions, to control and stabilize the vehicle.

drift 1. In ballistics, a shift in projectile direction due to gyroscopic action that results from gravitational and atmospherically induced torques on the spinning projectile. 2. The lateral divergence from the prescribed flight path of an aircraft, rocket, or aerospace vehicle, due primarily to the effect of crosswind. 3. The angular deviation of the spin axis of a gyro from a fixed reference in space. 4. A slow change in frequency of a radio transmitter. 5. A gradual movement in one direction of an instrument's pointer. 6. With respect to semiconductor materials, the movement of carriers (i.e., holes and electrons) in an electric field. Also called *drift mobility* or *carrier mobility*.

drift rate The amount of DRIFT per unit time. Drift rate has many specific meanings in different fields. The type of drift rate always should be specified.

drogue A spacecraft docking receptacle that captures the probe of another spacecraft. The device usually is shaped like a funnel or cone and serves as the "female"-type connector into which the probe ("male"-type connector) fits.

drogue parachute A small parachute used specifically to pull a larger parachute out of stowage; a small parachute used to slow down a descending space capsule, aerospace vehicle, or high-performance airplane.

drogue recovery A type of recovery system used for space capsules after initial atmospheric entry, involving the deployment of one or more small parachutes to diminish speed, to reduce aerodynamic heating, and to stabilize the vehicle so that larger recovery parachutes can be deployed safely at lower altitudes without too great an opening shock.

drone 1. In general, a mechanism or vehicle that can operate without direct human guidance. 2. In aerospace, an uncrewed air vehicle that is controlled remotely or automatically. Drones often are used as test targets for missile and fighter aircraft weapon systems.

drop tower A tall tower (about 90 meters [294 feet] high or more) in which experimental packages are carefully dropped under "free-fall" conditions. A well-designed drop tower can provide low-gravity conditions for about 3 to 5 seconds—enough time to perform useful preliminary experiments simulating (briefly) the microgravity or weightlessness conditions encountered in an orbiting spacecraft. A catch tube system at the bottom of the drop tower decelerates and recovers the experimental package. Also called a *low-gravity drop tower* and a *drop tube*. *See also:* MICROGRAVITY.

dry cycle Operation of a valve or similar component without propellant or test fluid in the flow passages.

dry emplacement A launch site or emplacement that has no provision for water cooling (of the pad) during launch operations. Compare WET EMPLACEMENT.

dry-film lubricant Material that reduces rolling or sliding friction between mating surfaces by coating one or both of the surfaces with a slippery film, often permanently bonded to the surface; also called *solid lubricant.*

dry run In aerospace operations, a practice exercise or rehearsal for a specific mission task or launch operation; a practice launch without propellant loaded in the rocket vehicle.

dry weight The weight of a missile or rocket vehicle without its fuel. This term, especially appropriate for liquid-propellant rockets, sometimes is considered to include the payload.

dual propellant loading An aerospace operation involving the transfer of both fuel and oxidizer.

duct A tube or passage that confines and conducts a fluid; for example, a passage for the flow of air to the compressor of a gas turbine.

ducted fan A fan enclosed in a duct.

ductile failure Rupture of structural material after plastic deformation; also, unacceptable dimensional change without fracture.

duct propulsion A means of propelling a vehicle by ducting a surrounding fluid through an engine, adding momentum to it by mechanical or thermal means, and ejecting the fluid to obtain a reactive force. Compare ROCKET PROPULSION.

dud An explosive munition that has not been armed as intended or that has failed to explode after being armed.

dudding The process of permanently degrading an electroexplosive device initiator to a state where it cannot perform its intended (designed) function.

dune In planetary geology, a low hill or bank of drifted sand.

duplexer A device that permits a single antenna system to be used for both transmitting and receiving. (Should not be confused with *diplexer*—a device that permits an antenna to be used simultaneously or separately by two transmitters.)

dust detector A direct-sensing science instrument that measures the velocity, mass (typical range 10^{-16} g to 10^{-6} g), flight direction, charge (if any), and number of dust particles striking the instrument, carried by some spacecraft.

duty cycle In general, the percentage of time a system is functioning; for example, in the case of a pulsed radar system, the pulse repetition rate times the pulse width—or, simply, the percentage of time the radar is transmitting.

dwarf galaxy A small, often elliptical galaxy containing a million (10^6) to perhaps a billion (10^9) stars. The Magellanic Clouds, our nearest galactic neighbors, are examples of dwarf galaxies.

See also: GALAXY; MAGELLANIC CLOUDS.

Dynamic Isotope Power System (DIPS) A proposed device for producing electric power for spacecraft and planetary rover systems that uses the thermal energy (heat) generated by a quantity of radioactive material (i.e., the radioisotope plutonium-238) as a power source and then converts this thermal energy to electric energy by means of a dynamic heat engine (e.g., a closed Brayton cycle).

See also: SPACE NUCLEAR POWER.

dynamic load A load imposed by dynamic action, as distinguished from a static load. Specifically with respect to aircraft, aerospace vehicles, and rockets, a load due to an acceleration of the craft, as imposed by wind gusts during atmospheric flight, by maneuvering, by landing, by firing rockets, and so on.

dynamic load factor A multiplying factor applied to the maximum static load (rated load) that is used to account for load increase caused by inertial loads encountered during handling (i.e., lifting, rotating, transportation, etc.). Typically, in aerospace operations, a minimum dynamic load factor of 1.5 is used in performing safety analyses involving mechanical handling equipment (MHE) and mechanical ground support equipment (MGSE).

dynamic model A scale model of a system, such as a rocket, spacecraft, or aircraft, that has its linear dimensions, mass, and moments of inertia reproduced in proportion to the original system.

dynamic pressure (common symbol: Q or q) 1. The pressure exerted by a fluid, such as air, by virtue of its motion; it is equal to $1/2 \, \rho \, V^2$, where ρ is the density and V is the velocity of the fluid. 2. The pressure exerted on a body by virtue of its motion through a fluid, as, for example, the pressure exerted on a rocket vehicle as it flies through the atmosphere. The condition of maximum dynamic pressure experienced by an ascending rocket vehicle is often called *max-Q*.

dynamic reconfiguration A means whereby a battle management system can change its condition during a battle to respond to changing circumstances, such as the destruction of some defensive system components.

dynamics The branch of science that studies the motion of bodies under the influence of forces, especially forces that originate outside the body under consideration.

dynamic seal A mechanical device used to minimize leakage of fluid from the flow-stream region of a fluid-system component when there is relative motion of the sealing interfaces.

dynamic similarity The relationship that exists between a scale model and a prototype (full-scale) vehicle when, by virtue of the proportionalities between their geometric dimensions and mass distributions or elastic characteristics, the motion of the model is in some respect (i.e., linear velocity, acceleration, vibration, or flutter) similar to the motion of the prototype vehicle. Also refers to the similarity between fluid flows around a scale model (as perhaps in a wind tunnel) and the flow conditions experienced by a full-scale prototype vehicle during atmospheric flight.

dynamic stability The characteristics of a body, such as an aircraft, spacecraft, or aerospace vehicle, that causes it, when disturbed from an original state of steady flight or motion, to damp the oscillations induced by the disturbance and gradually return to its original state.

Dyna-Soar (*Dyna*mic *Soar*ing) An early U.S. Air Force space project involving a manned, "boost-glide" orbital vehicle that was to be launched into orbit by an expendable rocket, perform its military mission, and then return to Earth using its wings to glide through the atmosphere during reentry (in a manner similar to today's space shuttle orbiter). Begun in 1958, Dyna-Soar was canceled in 1963 in favor of the civilian (NASA) manned space flight program (i.e., the Mercury, Gemini and Apollo projects) before it ever became operational. Also called the *X-20 Project*.

See also: APOLLO PROJECT; GEMINI PROJECT; MERCURY PROJECT; X-20.

dyne (symbol: d) A unit of force in the centimeter-gram-second (c.g.s.) system equal to the force required to accelerate a one-gram mass one centimeter per second per second; that is, 1 dyne = 1 gm-cm/sec^2. Compare NEWTON.

dysbarism A general aerospace medicine term describing a variety of symptoms within the human body caused by the existence of a pressure differential between the total ambient pressure and the total pressure of dissolved and free gases within the body tissues, fluids, and cavities. For example, increased ambient pressure, as accompanies a descent from higher altitudes, might cause painful distention of the eardrums.

early warning satellite A military spacecraft that has the primary mission of detecting and reporting the launch or approach of unknown weapons or weapon systems. For example, a hostile missile launch might be detected and reported through the use of special infrared (IR) sensors onboard this type of surveillance satellite.

See also: DEFENSE SUPPORT PROGRAM.

Earth Earth is the third planet from the Sun and the fifth largest in the solar system. Our planet circles its parent star at an average distance of 149.6 million kilometers (93 million miles). Earth is the only planetary body in the solar system currently known to support life. The table presents some of the physical and dynamic properties of Earth as a planet in the solar system.

From space, our planet is characterized by its blue waters and white clouds, which cover a major portion of it. Earth is surrounded by an ocean of air, consisting of 78% nitrogen and 21% oxygen; the remainder is argon, neon, and other gases. The standard atmospheric pressure at sea level is 101,325 newtons per square meter (14.7 pounds per square inch). Surface temperatures range from a maximum of about 60° Celsius (C) (140° Fahrenheit [F]) in desert regions along the equator to a minimum of minus 90° C (minus 130° F) in the frigid polar regions. In between, however, surface temperatures are generally much more benign.

Earth's rapid spin and molten nickel-iron core give rise to an extensive magnetic field. This magnetic field, together with the atmosphere, shields us from nearly all of the harmful charged-particle and ultraviolet radiation coming from the Sun and cosmic sources. Furthermore, most meteors burn up in Earth's protective atmosphere before they can strike the surface. Earth's nearest celestial neighbor, the Moon, is its only natural satellite.

DYNAMIC AND PHYSICAL PROPERTIES OF THE PLANET EARTH	
Radius	
Equatorial	6,378 km
Polar	6,357 km
Mass	5.98×10^{24} kg
Density (average)	5.52 g/cm³
Surface area	5.1×10^{14} m²
Volume	1.08×10^{21} m³
Distance from the Sun (average)	1.496×10^8 km (1 AU)
Eccentricity	0.01673
Orbital period (sidereal)	365.256 days
Period of rotation (sidereal)	23.934 hours
Inclination of equator	23.45 degrees
Mean orbital velocity	29.78 km/sec
Acceleration of gravity, g (sea level)	9.807 m/sec²
Solar flux at Earth (above atmosphere)	$1,371 \pm 5$ watts/m²
Planetary energy fluxes (approximate)	
Solar	10^{17} watts
Geothermal	2.5×10^{13} watts
Tidal friction	3.4×10^{12} watts
Human-made	
Coal-burning	3.06×10^{12} watts
Natural gas-burning	2.00×10^{12} watts
Oil-burning	3.82×10^{12} watts
Nuclear power	0.49×10^{12} watts
Hydroelectric	0.69×10^{12} watts
Total human-made	10.06×10^{12} watts
Number of natural satellites	1 (the Moon)

See also: EARTH'S TRAPPED RADIATION BELTS; GLOBAL
CHANGE; MISSION TO PLANET EARTH; MOON.

Earth-based telescope A telescope located on the
surface of Earth. Compare with the HUBBLE SPACE
TELESCOPE.

Earth-crossing asteroid (ECA) An asteroid whose
orbit now crosses Earth's orbit or will at some time
in the future cross Earth's orbit, as its orbital path
evolves under the influence of perturbations from
Jupiter and the other planets.

See also: ASTEROID.

Earthlike planet An extrasolar planet that is located in an ecosphere and has planetary environmental conditions that resemble the terrestrial biosphere—especially a suitable atmosphere, a temper-

ature range that permits the retention of large
quantities of liquid water on the planet's surface,
and a sufficient quantity of energy striking the
planet's surface from the parent star. These suitable
environmental conditions could permit the chemical evolution and the development of carbon-
based life as we know it on Earth. The planet also
should have a mass somewhat greater than 0.4
Earth masses (to permit the production and retention of a breathable atmosphere) but less than
about 2.4 Earth masses (to avoid excessive surface
gravity conditions).

Earth-observing satellite An Earth-orbiting spacecraft that has a specialized collection of sensors
capable of monitoring important environmental
variables. Data from these satellites help meet the
needs of multidisciplinary Earth system science.

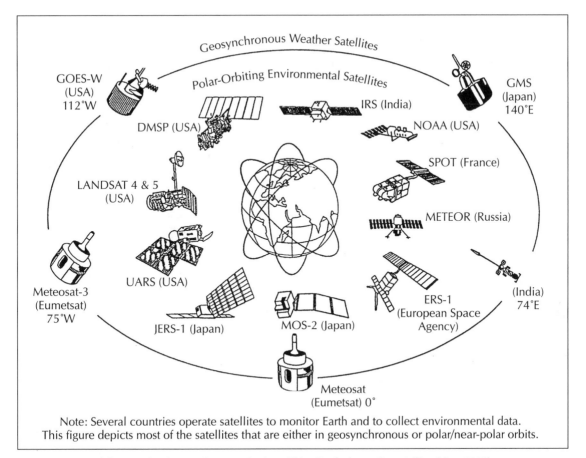

Note: Several countries operate satellites to monitor Earth and to collect environmental data.
This figure depicts most of the satellites that are either in geosynchronous or polar/near-polar orbits.

Figure 32. Some of the operational geostationary and polar-orbiting Earth observation satellites (circa 1994) *(Illustration courtesy of U.S. Congress, Office of Technology Assessment [OTA])*

Two types of orbit generally are selected for these spacecraft: either *geostationary orbit,* which provides a simultaneous "big picture" view of an entire hemisphere, or *polar orbit,* which provides a closer synoptic view of Earth, including some of its more difficult to monitor locations (such as the Arctic and Antarctic). Also called an *environmental satellite* or a *green satellite.* (See Figure 32.)

Some of the environmental variables of interest to an Earth-observing satellite include: (1) cloud properties; (2) the energy exchange between Earth and space; (3) surface temperature; (4) the structure, composition, and dynamics of the atmosphere, winds, lightning, and precipitation (rainfall); (5) the accumulation and ablation (melting) of snow; (6) biological activity on land and in near-surface waters; (7) circulation patterns of the oceans; (8) the exchange of energy, momentum, and gases between Earth's surface and its atmosphere; (9) the structure and motion of sea ice and the growth, melting and flow rates of glaciers; (10) the mineral composition of exposed soils and rocks; (11) the changes in stress and surface elevation around global faults; and (12) the input of radiant energy and energetic particles to the Earth from the Sun. Of course, no one satellite monitors all of these environmental variables. Instead, different types of satellite-derived, Earth observation data now are being shared internationally by government agencies and scientists concerned with modeling and protecting the planet's fragile environment.

See also: GLOBAL CHANGE; MISSION TO PLANET EARTH; REMOTE SENSING; WEATHER SATELLITE.

Earth Observing System (EOS) In 1991 NASA began a global-scale examination of Earth to study the interaction of all the environmental components—air, water, land, life—that make up the Earth system. This global monitoring program, called *Mission to Planet Earth* (MTPE), is a long-term coordinated research effort to study Earth as a global environmental system. MTPE is using the unique perspective available from space to allow us to better understand environmental changes and to help distinguish between natural and human-induced (anthropogenic) changes. As currently structured, Phase I of MTPE involves free-flying environmental satellites, such as the *Upper Atmosphere Research Satellite* (*UARS*) and certain space shuttle missions. These space missions are complemented by airborne and ground-based environmental studies.

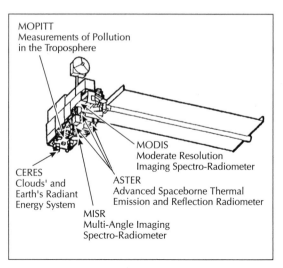

Figure 33. The *EOS-A* satellite and some of its environmental instruments *(Drawing: U.S. Congress, Office of Technology Assessment (OTA); Lockheed-Martin Aerospace)*

Phase II of MTPE begins at the end of the century with the launch of the first Earth Observing System (EOS) satellite, now designated *Earth Observing System-A* or *EOS-A,* for short. The primary goal of the *EOS-A* satellite is to provide a suite of measurements related to potential global warming and other critical aspects of global change. Specific observations include Earth's radiation balance, atmospheric circulation, air-sea interaction, biological productivity, and land surface properties (See Figure 33.) As now planned, the *EOS-A* instruments will constitute a minimum set of synergistic sensors capable of making simultaneous observations of related environmental variables. Simultaneity is essential for scientists studying Earth as an integrated system. It permits cross-calibration of instruments and avoids the adverse impact that rapid atmospheric and illumination (i.e., sunlight levels) changes can have on measurements.

See also: GLOBAL CHANGE; MISSION TO PLANET EARTH; REMOTE SENSING.

Earth radiation budget (ERB) The Earth radiation budget is perhaps the most fundamental quantity influencing Earth's climate. The ERB components include the incoming solar radiation; the solar radiation reflected back to space by the clouds, the atmosphere, and Earth's surface; and the long-wavelength thermal radiation emitted by Earth's surface and its atmosphere. The latitudinal variations of Earth's radiation budget are the ultimate driving force for the atmospheric and oceanic circulations and the resulting planetary climate.

See also: GLOBAL CHANGE; MISSION TO PLANET EARTH.

Earth satellite An artificial (human-made) object placed in orbit around the planet Earth.

earthshine A spacecraft or space vehicle in orbit around Earth is illuminated by both sunlight and "earthshine." Earthshine consists of sunlight (0.4- to 0.7-micrometer wavelength radiation, or visible light) reflected by Earth and thermal radiation (typically 10.6-micrometer wavelength infrared radiation) emitted by Earth's surface and atmosphere.

Earth's trapped radiation belts The magnetosphere is a region around Earth through which the solar wind cannot penetrate because of the terrestrial magnetic field. Inside the magnetosphere are two belts or zones of very energetic atomic particles (mainly electrons and protons) that are trapped in Earth's magnetic field hundreds of kilometers above the atmosphere. These belts were discovered by Professor James Van Allen of the University of Iowa and his colleagues in 1958. Van Allen made the discovery using simple atomic radiation detectors placed onboard *Explorer 1,* the first American satellite.

The two major trapped radiation belts form a doughnut-shaped region around Earth from about 320 to 32,400 kilometers (200 to 20,000 miles) above the equator (depending on solar activity). Energetic protons and electrons are trapped in these belts. The inner Van Allen belt contains both energetic protons (major constituent) and electrons that were captured from the solar wind or were created in nuclear collision reactions between energetic cosmic ray particles and atoms in Earth's upper atmosphere. The outer Van Allen belt contains mostly energetic electrons that have been captured from the solar wind.

Spacecraft and space stations operating in Earth's trapped radiation belts are subject to the damaging effects of ionizing radiation from charged atomic particles. These particles include protons, electrons, alpha particles (helium nuclei), and heavier atomic nuclei. Their damaging effects include degradation of material properties and

component performance, often resulting in reduced capabilities or even failure of spacecraft systems and experiments. For example, solar cells used to provide electric power for spacecraft often are severely damaged by passage through the Van Allen belts. Earth's trapped radiation belts also represent a very hazardous environment for human beings traveling in space.

Radiation damage from Earth's trapped radiation belts can be reduced significantly by designing spacecraft and space stations with proper radiation shielding. Often crew compartments and sensitive equipment can be located in regions shielded by other spacecraft equipment that is less sensitive to the influence of ionizing radiation. Radiation damage also can be limited by selecting mission orbits and trajectories that avoid long periods of operation where the radiation belts have their highest charged-particle populations. For example, for a spacecraft or space station in low Earth orbit, this would mean avoiding the South Atlantic Anomaly and, of course, the Van Allen Belts themselves.

See also: EXPLORER 1; MAGNETOSPHERE; SOLAR WIND; SOUTH ATLANTIC ANOMALY.

eccentricity (symbol: e) A measure of the ovalness of an orbit. For example, when e = 0, the orbit is a circle; when e = 0.9, the orbit is a long, thin ellipse. (See Figure 34.)

The eccentricity (e) of an ellipse can be computed by the formula:

$$e = \sqrt{[1 - b^2/a^2]}$$

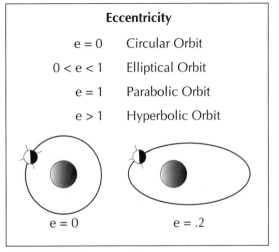

Eccentricity	
e = 0	Circular Orbit
0 < e < 1	Elliptical Orbit
e = 1	Parabolic Orbit
e > 1	Hyperbolic Orbit

e = 0   e = .2

Figure 34. Eccentricity   *(Drawing courtesy of NASA)*

where a is the semimajor axis and b is the semiminor axis.

See also: KEPLERIAN ELEMENTS; ORBITS OF OBJECTS IN SPACE.

eccentric orbit An orbit that deviates from a circle, thus forming an ellipse.

See also: ORBITS OF OBJECTS IN SPACE.

Echo satellite A large, inflatable passive communications-relay satellite from which radio signals from one point on Earth could be bounced off and received by another location on Earth. NASA's *Echo 1*, the world's first passive communications-relay satellite, was launched successfully from Cape Canaveral Air Force Station on August 12, 1960.

eclipse 1. The reduction in visibility or the disappearance of a nonluminous body by passing into the shadow cast by another nonluminous body. 2. The apparent cutting off, wholly or partially, of the light from a luminous body by a dark (nonluminous) body coming between it and the observer.

The first type of eclipse is exemplified by a *lunar eclipse,* which occurs when the Moon passes through the shadow cast by Earth or when a satellite passes through the shadow cast by its planet; when a satellite passes directly behind its planet, an *occultation* is said to occur. The second type of eclipse is exemplified by a *solar eclipse,* which occurs when the Moon passes between the Sun and Earth.

ecliptic plane The plane of the orbit of Earth in its annual motion around the Sun.

ecological system A habitable environment, either created artificially (as in a crewed space vehicle) or occurring naturally (i.e., the environment on the surface of Earth), in which human beings, animals, and/or other organisms can live in mutual relationship with one another and the environment. Under ideal circumstances, the environment furnishes the sustenance for life, and the resulting waste products revert or cycle back into the environment to be used again for the continuous support of life. The interacting system of a biological community and its nonliving environmental surroundings. Also called *ecosystem.*

See also: CLOSED ECOLOGICAL LIFE SUPPORT SYSTEM.

ecology The study of the relationship of living things to one another and their environment. Remote-sensing data provided by Earth-orbiting satellites are of great value to scientists in their efforts to study and monitor the complex relationships taking place in Earth's ecosphere.

See also: GLOBAL CHANGE; MISSION TO PLANET EARTH; REMOTE SENSING.

effector 1. In aerospace engineering, any device used to maneuver a rocket in flight, such as an aerodynamic surface, a gimbaled motor, or a control jet. 2. In robotics, the portion of a manipulator that causes the desired action, such as gripping or positioning.

efficiency (symbol: η) In general, the ratio of useful output of some physical quantity to its total input. In thermodynamics, the ratio of energy output to energy input. For a heat engine, the thermal efficiency ($\eta_{thermal}$) is defined as the ratio of the work (mechanical energy) out to thermal energy (heat) input.

egads button Early aerospace jargon used to describe a control panel button used by the range safety officer to initiate destruction of a rocket vehicle in flight, if its course (as plotted during flight) went beyond the destruct line. *Egads* is an acronym for *e*lectronic *g*round *a*utomatic *d*estruct sequencer.

See also: ABORT.

ejection capsule 1. In an aircraft, aerospace vehicle, or crewed spacecraft, a detachable compartment serving as a cockpit or cabin, which may be ejected as a unit and parachuted to the ground. 2. In a satellite, probe, or uncrewed spacecraft, a boxlike unit (usually containing records of observed data or experimental samples) that may be ejected and returned to Earth by a parachute or other deceleration device.

ejector A device consisting of a nozzle, a mixing tube, and a diffuser that uses the kinetic energy of a fluid stream to pump another fluid from a low-pressure region by direct mixing and ejecting both streams.

elasticity The ability of a body that has been deformed by an applied force to return to its original shape when the force is removed.

elasticizer An elastic substance or fuel used in solid rocket propellant to prevent cracking of the propellant grain and to bind it to the combustion-chamber case.

elastic limit The maximum stress that can be applied to a body without producing permanent deformation.

elastomer Rubberlike, polymeric material that can be deformed by a force and then regain its original shape after the force has been removed.

electrical Involving the flow of electricity in a conductor. Compare ELECTRONIC.

electrical delay In aerospace engineering and robotics, the time period from the initial electrical signal to the first motion of the activated part.

electric field A region in which a charged particle experiences an electrical force, usually because of a distribution of other electric charges or varying magnetic field.

electric field strength (symbol: E) The electrical force exerted on a unit positive charge at a given point in space. Electric field strength typically is expressed in volts per meter.

electricity Flow of energy due to the motion of electric charges; any physical effect that results from the existence of moving or stationary electric charges (e.g., *static electricity, lightning*).

electric potential (symbol: V) The work done in moving a unit positive charge from infinity to the point in an electric field whose potential is being specified. The unit of electric potential is the volt. For example, if 1 joule is required to transfer a charge of 1 coulomb, then the electric potential is 1 volt.

electric propulsion The electric rocket engine is a device that converts electric power into a forward-directed force or thrust by accelerating an ionized propellant (i.e., mercury, cesium, argon, or xenon) to a very high exhaust velocity. The concept for an electric rocket is not new. In 1906 Dr. Robert Goddard (the famous American rocket scientist) suggested that the exhaust velocity limit encountered with chemical rocket propellants might be overcome if electrically charged particles could be used as a rocket's reaction mass. This technical suggestion often is regarded as the birth of the electric propulsion concept. The basic electric propulsion system consists of three main components: (1) some type of electric thruster that accelerates the ionized propellant; (2) a suitable propellant that can be ionized and accelerated; and (3) a source of electric power. The acceleration of electrically charged particles requires a large quantity of electric power.

The needed power source could be self-contained, such as a space nuclear reactor, or it might involve the use of solar energy by photovoltaic or solar thermal conversion techniques. Electric propulsion systems using a nuclear reactor power supply are called *nuclear electric propulsion* (*NEP*) systems, while those using a solar energy power supply are called *solar electric propulsion* (*SEP*) systems. Within the orbit of Mars, both NEP and SEP systems can be considered, but past Mars and especially for deep-space missions to the edges of the solar system and beyond, only nuclear electric propulsion systems can be considered because the amount of solar energy available for collection and conversion falls off according to the inverse square law, that is, as one over the distance from the Sun squared $[1/(distance)^2]$.

There are three general types of electric rocket engine: *electrothermal, electromagnetic,* and *electrostatic*. In the basic *electrothermal rocket*, electric power is used to heat the propellant (e.g., ammonia) to a high temperature, which is then expanded through a nozzle to produce thrust. (See Figure 35.) Propellant heating may be accomplished by flowing the propellant gas through an electric arc (this type of electric engine is called an *arc jet engine*) or by flowing the propellant gas over surfaces heated with electricity. Although the *arc jet engine* can achieve exhaust velocities higher than those of chemical rockets, the dissociation of propellant gas molecules creates an upper limit on how much energy can be added to the propellant. In addition, other factors, such as erosion caused by the electric arc itself and material failure at high temperatures, establish further limits on the arc jet engine. Because of these limitations, arc jet engines appear more suitable for a role in orbital transfer vehicle propulsion and large spacecraft stationkeeping than as the electric propulsion system for deep-space exploration missions.

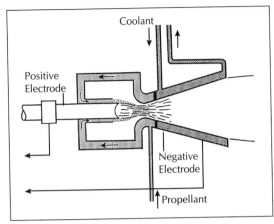

Figure 35. Basic components of an electrothermal rocket
(*Drawing courtesy of NASA*)

The second major type of electric rocket engine is the *electromagnetic engine* or *plasma rocket engine.* (See Figure 36.) In this type of engine, the propellant gas is ionized to form a plasma, which is then accelerated rearward by the action of electric and magnetic fields. The *magnetoplasmadynamic (MPD)* engine can operate in either a steady state or a pulse mode. A high-power (approximately 1 megawatt-electric) steady-state MPD, using either argon or hydrogen as its propellant, is an attractive option for an electric propulsion orbital transfer vehicle (OTV).

The third major type of electric rocket engine is the *electrostatic rocket engine* or *ion rocket engine.* (See Figure 37.) As in the plasma rocket engine, propellant atoms (i.e., cesium, mercury, argon, or xenon)

are ionized by removing an electron from each atom. In the electrostatic engine, however, the electrons are removed entirely from the ionization region at the same rate as ions are accelerated rearward. The propellant ions are accelerated by an imposed electric field to a very high exhaust velocity. The electrons removed in the ionizer from the propellant atoms are also ejected from the spacecraft, usually by being injected into the ion exhaust beam. This helps neutralize the accumulated positive electric charge in the exhaust beam and maintains the ionizer in the electrostatic rocket at a high voltage potential.

In 1970 two 15-centimeter (cm) (diameter) mercury-propellant ion thrusters were tested successfully in space onboard the *SERT 2* (*Space Electric Rocket Test-2*) spacecraft, which was placed in a 1,000-kilometer (620-mile) altitude sun-synchronous, polar orbit. Each of these ion thrusters provided a maximum thrust of about 26.7 millinewton (6 millipound-force). (A milli- is 10^{-3}.) The extended operation of the two thrusters demonstrated long-term ion thruster performance in the near Earth orbital environment but also introduced the problem of "sputtering." Sputtering involved the buildup of molecular metal (mercury) contaminants on the solar arrays of the *SERT 2* spacecraft as a result of ion thruster exhaust plume contamination. Thruster experimentation was terminated in 1981 when the mercury propellant supply was exhausted.

Recently the principal focus of the U.S. electric propulsion technology program has been the J-series 30-cm mercury ion thruster. This type of electric rocket represents reasonably mature technology. However, because of the potential for pollution

Figure 36. The fundamental components of an electromagnetic or plasma rocket engine   (*Drawing courtesy of NASA*)

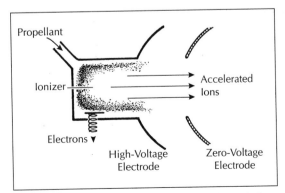

Figure 37. The fundamental components of an electrostatic or ion rocket engine   (*Drawing courtesy of NASA*)

and contamination (i.e., sputtering phenomenon), mercury may not be an acceptable propellant for future heavy orbital transfer vehicle traffic operating from low Earth orbit to destinations in CISLUNAR space. Therefore, ion thrusters now are being developed that use argon or xenon as the propellant. Because of its potential for providing very high exhaust velocities (typically 10^5 meters per second [10^5 m/s]) and very high efficiency, ion propulsion appears well suited for interplanetary and deep-space exploration missions.

Space visionaries, starting with Robert Goddard in 1906, have recognized the special role electric propulsion could play in the conquest of space—namely, high-performance missions starting in a low gravity field (such as Earth orbit or lunar orbit) and the vacuum of free space. In comparison to high-thrust, short-duration-burn chemical engines, electric propulsion systems are inherently low-thrust, high-specific-impulse rocket engines with fuel efficiencies two to ten times greater than the propulsion efficiencies achieved using chemical propellants. Electric rockets work continuously for long periods, smoothly changing a spacecraft's trajectory. For missions to the outer solar system, the continuous acceleration provided by an electric propulsion thruster can yield shorter trip times and/or deliver higher-mass scientific payloads than those delivered by chemical rockets.

See also: ROCKET PROPULSION; SPACE NUCLEAR POWER; SPACE NUCLEAR PROPULSION.

electrode A conductor (terminal) at which electricity passes from one medium into another. The positive electrode is called the *anode;* the negative electrode is called the *cathode.* In semiconductor devices, an element that performs one or more of the functions of emitting or collecting electrons or holes, or of controlling their movements by an electric field. In electron tubes, a conducting element that performs one or more of the functions of emitting, collecting, or controlling the movements of electrons or ions usually by means of an electromagnetic field.

electroexplosive device (EED) A pyrotechnic device in which electrically insulated terminals are in contact with, or adjacent to, a material mixture that reacts chemically (often explosively) when the required electrical energy level is discharged through the terminals. Explosive stage separation devices and missile self-destruct packages (for

Figure 38. A basic electrolytic cell   *(Department of Energy [DOE])*

vehicles that have departed from an acceptable flight trajectory) are examples of EEDs used in aerospace applications.

electrolysis In general, a chemical reaction produced by the passage of an electric current through an electrolyte. Specifically, the process of splitting water into hydrogen and oxygen by means of a direct electric current. As shown in Figure 38, a basic electrolysis cell consists of two electrodes immersed in an aqueous conducting solution called an *electrolyte.* A source of direct current (dc) voltage is applied to the electrodes so that an electric current flows through the electrolyte from the anode (positive electrode) to the cathode (negative electrode). As a result, the water in the electrolyte solution is decomposed into hydrogen gas (H_2), which is released at the cathode, and oxygen gas (O_2), which is released at the anode. Although only the water is split, an electrolyte (i.e., potassium hydroxide) is needed because water itself is a very poor conductor of electricity.

See also: FUEL CELL; HYDROGEN.

electromagnetic Having both electric and magnetic properties; pertaining to magnetism produced or associated with electricity.

electromagnetic (EM) communications In aerospace, the technology involving the development and production of a variety of telecommunication equipment used for electromagnetic transmission of information over any media. The information may be analog or digital, ranging in bandwidth from a single voice or data channel to video or multiplexed channels occupying hundreds of megahertz. Included are onboard satellite communication equipment and laser communication techniques capable of automatically acquiring and tracking signals and maintaining communications through atmospheric and exoatmospheric media.

electromagnetic (EM) gun A gun in which the projectile is accelerated by electromagnetic forces rather than by a chemical explosion as in a conventional gun.

electromagnetic (EM) launcher A device that can accelerate an object to high velocities using the electromotive force produced by a large current in a transverse magnetic field.

electromagnetic pulse (EMP) A large pulse of electromagnetic radiation, effectively reaching out to distances of hundreds of kilometers or more; caused by the interactions of gamma rays from a high-altitude nuclear explosion with atoms in the upper atmosphere. The resulting electromagnetic fields may couple with electrical and electronic systems to produce damaging current and voltage surges. EMP also can be created by nonnuclear means.

electromagnetic radiation (EMR) Radiation made up of oscillating electric and magnetic fields and propagated with the speed of light. Includes (in order of decreasing frequency) gamma radiation, X rays, ultraviolet, visible, and infrared (IR) radiation, and radar and radio waves.

See also: ELECTROMAGNETIC SPECTRUM.

electromagnetic (EM) spectrum When sunlight passes through a prism, it throws a rainbowlike array of colors onto a surface. This display of colors is called the *visible spectrum*. It represents an arrangement in order of wavelength of the narrow band of electromagnetic (EM) radiation to which the human eye is sensitive.

The electromagnetic spectrum comprises the entire range of wavelengths of electromagnetic radiation, from the shortest-wavelength gamma rays to the longest-wavelength radiowaves. (See Figure 39.) The entire EM spectrum includes much more than meets the eye.

As shown in the figure, the names applied to the various regions of the EM spectrum are (going from shortest to longest wavelength) gamma ray, X ray, ultraviolet (UV), visible, infrared (IR) and radio. EM radiation travels at the speed of light (i.e., about 300,000 kilometers per second [~ 186,400 miles per second]) and is the basic mechanism for energy transfer through the vacuum of outer space.

One of the most interesting discoveries of 20th-century physics is the dual nature of electromagnetic radiation. Under some conditions electromagnetic radiation behaves like a wave, while under other conditions it behaves like a stream of particles, called *photons*. The tiny amount of energy carried by a photon is called a *quantum of energy* (plural: quanta). The word "quantum" comes to us from the Latin language and means "little bundle."

The shorter the wavelength, the more energy is carried by a particular form of EM radiation. All things in the universe emit, reflect, and absorb electromagnetic radiation in their own distinctive ways. The way an object does this provides scien-

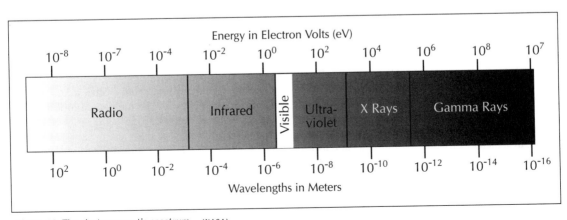

Figure 39. The electromagnetic spectrum *(NASA)*

tists with special characteristics, or a signature, that can be detected by remote sensing instruments. For example, the spectrogram shows bright lines for emission or reflection and dark lines for absorption at selected EM wavelengths. Analyses of the positions and line patterns found in a spectrogram can provide information about the object's composition, surface temperature, density, age, motion, and distance.

For centuries, astronomers have used spectral analyses to learn about distant extraterrestrial phenomena. But up until the space age, they were limited in their view of the universe by the Earth's atmosphere, which filters out most of the EM radiation from the rest of the cosmos. In fact, ground-based astronomers are limited to just the visible portion of the EM spectrum and tiny portions of the infrared, radio, and ultraviolet regions. Space-based observatories now allow us to examine the universe in all portions of the EM spectrum. We now have examined the cosmos in the infrared, ultraviolet, X-ray, and gamma ray portions of the EM spectrum and have made startling discoveries. We also have developed sophisticated remote sensing instruments to look back on Earth in many regions of the electromagnetic spectrum, providing powerful tools for a more careful management of the terrestrial biosphere.

See also: REMOTE SENSING.

electromotive force (emf) The characteristic of an electrical energy source that enables a current to flow in a circuit. It is the sum (algebraic) of the potential differences acting in an electric circuit. The emf (typical unit: volts) is measured by the energy liberated when a unit electric charge passes completely around the circuit.

electron (symbol: e) A stable elementary particle with a unit negative electrical charge (1.602 x 10^{-19} coulomb) and a rest mass (m_e) of 1/1837 that of a proton (namely, 9.109 x 10^{-31} kilogram). Electrons surround the positively charged nucleus and determine the chemical properties of the atom. Positively charged electrons, or *positrons*, also exist. Electrons were first discovered in the late 1890s by the British scientist Sir J. J. Thomson (1856–1940).

electronic Of or pertaining to any of the large number and wide variety of devices that involve the generation, transmission, use, or control of electricity.

electronics The branch of physics dealing with the understanding, design, and application of devices based on the conduction of electricity through a vacuum, gas, or semiconductor. Although this term originated with vacuum (electron) tube applications, modern electronics is concerned primarily with semiconductor devices.

electron volt (eV) A unit of energy equivalent to the energy gained by an electron when it experiences a potential difference of one volt. Larger multiple units of the electron volt are encountered frequently—as, for example: *keV* for thousand (or kilo-) electron volts (10^3 eV); *MeV* for million (or mega-) electron volts (10^6 eV); and *GeV* for billion (or giga-) electron volts (10^9 eV).

$$1 \text{ electron volt} = 1.602 \times 10^{-19} \text{ joules}$$

electro-optical countermeasures Countermeasures designed to confuse the sensors of an adversary by jamming, blinding, or dazzling, or by reducing the radiations and reflections produced by one's own assets, or by using decoy targets in conjunction with real targets.

electro-optics The interaction between optics and electronics leading to the transformation of electrical energy into light, or vice versa, with the use of an optical device.

element A chemical substance that cannot be divided or decomposed into simpler substances by chemical means. A substance whose atoms all have the same number of protons (atomic number, Z) and electrons. There are 92 naturally occurring elements, and over 10 humanmade or transuranium elements, such as plutonium (atomic number 94).

element set Specific information used to define and locate a particular satellite or orbiting object. Also called *Keplerian elements*.

See also: KEPLERIAN ELEMENTS; ORBITS OF OBJECTS IN SPACE.

ellipse A smooth, oval curve accurately fitted by the orbit of a satellite around a much larger mass. Specifically, a plane curve constituting the locus of all points the sum of whose distances from two fixed points (called *focuses* or *foci*) is constant; an elongated circle. The orbits of planets, satellites, planetoids, and comets are ellipses; the center of attraction (i.e., the primary) is at one focus.

See also: ORBITS OF OBJECTS IN SPACE.

elliptical orbit A noncircular Keplerian orbit.

See also: ORBITS OF OBJECTS IN SPACE.

emergency In aerospace operations, any condition that can result in crew injury or threat to life and requires immediate corrective action, including predetermined crew response.

emission In electromagnetic radiation, the process by which a body emits electromagnetic radiation as a consequence of its temperature. 2. In electric propulsion and energy conversion, the sending out of charged particles from a surface generating these particles, such as the emission of ions from an ionizing source in an ion engine. 3. In environmental science, materials (often pollutants), such as gases, particles, vapors, and chemical compounds, discharged into the atmosphere from industrial facilities, residential chimneys, motor vehicle tailpipes, and locomotive or aircraft exhaust systems.

See also: ELECTRIC PROPULSION; ELECTROMAGNETIC RADIATION; REMOTE SENSING; THERMIONIC CONVERSION.

emission line A very small range of wavelengths (or frequencies) in the electromagnetic spectrum within which radiant energy is being emitted by a radiating substance. For example, the small band of wavelengths emitted by a low-density gas when it glows. The pattern of several emission lines is characteristic of the gas and is called the *emission spectrum.* Each radiating substance has a unique, characteristic emission spectrum.

emission spectroscopy Analytical spectroscopic methods that use the characteristic electromagnetic radiation emitted when materials are subjected to thermal or electrical sources for purposes of identification. These thermal or electrical sources excite the molecules or atoms in the sample of material to energy levels above the ground state. As the molecules or atoms return from these higher energy states, electromagnetic radiation is emitted in discrete, characteristic wavelengths or emission lines. The pattern and intensity of these emission lines creates a unique emission spectrum, which enables the analyst to identify the substance.

emissivity (symbol: e or ε) The ratio of the radiant flux per unit area (sometimes called *emittance, E)* emitted by a body's surface at a specified wavelength (λ) and temperature (T) to the radiant flux per unit area emitted by a BLACKBODY radiator at the same temperature and under the same conditions. The greatest value that an emissivity may have is unity (1)—the emissivity value for a blackbody radiator—while the least value for an emissivity is zero (0).

See also: STEFAN-BOLTZMANN LAW.

emittance (symbol: E) The radiant flux per unit area emitted by a body. *Spectral emittance* refers to emittance measured at a specified wavelength (λ).

See also: EMISSIVITY.

encounter A close flyby or rendezvous of a spacecraft with a target body.

end effector In robotics, the tool or "hand" at the end of a robotic arm or manipulator. This is the gripper, actuator, or mechanical device by which objects are physically grasped or acted upon.

endoatmospheric Within Earth's atmosphere, generally considered to be at altitudes below 100 kilometers (62 miles).

endoatmospheric interceptor In aerospace defense, an interceptor rocket that attacks incoming reentry vehicles during their terminal flight phase within Earth's atmosphere.

See also: BALLISTIC MISSILE DEFENSE.

endothermic reaction In thermodynamics, a reaction in which thermal energy (heat) is absorbed from the surroundings; a reaction to which heat must be provided. Compare EXOTHERMIC REACTION.

end-to-end test In aerospace safety operations, a full-up (i.e., complete) systems test of the ground and flight system's flight-termination (abort) subsystem with the destruct initiators disconnected.

"energetic" propellants 1. Liquid propellants that contribute energy to the exhaust gas through exothermal decomposition prior to oxidation reactions. 2. Solid propellant with added ingredients that raise energy output above the norm for that class of propellant.

energy (symbol: E) In general, the capacity to do work. Work is done when an object is moved by a force through a distance or when a moving object is accelerated. Energy can be manifested in many different forms, such as mechanical, thermal, chemical, electrical, and nuclear. The First Law of Thermodynamics states that energy is conserved, that is, it can neither be created nor destroyed, but simply changes form (including mass-energy transformations, in which matter is transformed into energy according to Einstein's formula $E = \Delta m\, c^2$). Typical units of energy are the joule (SI unit system) and the British thermal unit (Btu).

Potential energy arises from the position, state, or configuration of a body (or system). *Kinetic energy* is energy associated with a moving object. For example, in classical physics, a body of mass (m) moving at a velocity) (V) has a kinetic energy of: $E_{kinetic} = {}^1/_2\, (m\, V^2)$. In thermodynamics, the concept of *internal energy* is used to provide a macroscopic description of the energy within an object due to the microscopic behavior of molecules and atoms. Similarly, in thermodynamic analyses, *heat* or *thermal energy* is treated as disorganized energy in transit, while *work* is treated as organized energy in transit. Thermodynamically, a system never stores work or heat, since these are perceived as transitory energy transfer phenomena, which cease once a particular process has been completed.

Nuclear energy involves liberation of energy as a result of processes in the atomic nucleus, which often involve the transformations of small quantities of matter. *Solar energy* involves the Sun's electromagnetic energy output; while *geothermal energy* involves the thermal energy within Earth as a result of its molten core and the decay of certain radioactive nuclei in its crust.

energy conversion efficiency In rocketry, the efficiency with which a nozzle converts the energy of the working substance (i.e., the propellant) into kinetic energy. This can be expressed as the ratio of the kinetic energy of the jet leaving the nozzle to the kinetic energy of an ideal (hypothetical) jet leaving an ideal nozzle using the same working substance at the same initial state and under the same conditions of velocity and expansion.

energy management In aerospace operations and rocketry, the monitoring of fuel expenditure for the purposes of flight control and navigation.

energy release system The portion of a solid rocket fuel igniter that provides the thermal energy (heat) necessary to ignite the solid propellant and raise it to a self-sustaining combustion level.

energy satellite A very large space structure assembled in Earth orbit that takes advantage of the nearly continuous availability of sunlight to provide useful energy to a terrestrial power grid. As proposed most frequently, these large energy satellites would be located in geosynchronous orbit, where they would gather incoming sunlight (solar energy) and then convert it into electric energy by photovoltaic or solar-thermal conversion techniques. The electric energy then would be transmitted to power grids on Earth or to other energy consumption locations in CISLUNAR space (e.g., a space-based manufacturing center) by beams of microwave or laser radiation.

See also: SATELLITE POWER SYSTEM.

engagement time The amount of time that a weapon platform takes to negate (i.e., destroy or incapacitate) a given target. This includes not only firing at the target but all other necessary weapon functions involved that are unique to that particular target.

engine A machine or thermodynamic device that converts energy, especially thermal energy (heat), into useful work.

See also: ENERGY; HEAT ENGINE; ROCKET ENGINE.

engine bell The conical thrust chamber enclosure, or nozzle, of a rocket engine. It is located behind the combustion chamber.

See also: ROCKET ENGINE.

engine control Any control device for regulating the power level or speed of an engine, such as the throttle, mixture control, manifold-pressure regulator, fuel-pressure control, and supercharger control.

See also: ROCKET ENGINE.

engine cut-off The specific time when a rocket engine is shut down during a flight. In the case of the space shuttle, for example, this time is referred to as MECO, or "main engine cut-off." Sometimes called *burnout*.

See also: ROCKET.

engine mount A structure used for attaching an engine to a vehicle.
See also: ROCKET.

engine spray The part of a launch pad deluge system that cools a rocket engine and its exhaust during launch, thereby preventing thermal damage to the launch vehicle and the launch pad structure.

enthalpy (symbol: H, h) A property of a thermodynamic system defined as:

$$H = U + pV$$

where H is the total enthalpy (joules), U is the total internal energy (joules), p is pressure (pascals), and V is volume (cubic meters). In many thermodynamic problems, the enthalpy function does not lend itself to a specific physical interpretation although it does have the dimension of energy (joules or British thermal units [BTUs]) or, as an intrinsic property (symbol: h), the dimensions of energy per unit mass (joules/kg or BTU/lb_{mass}). However, since U and the product (pV) appear together in many thermodynamic analyses, the enthalpy function is often an advantageous property to describe a particular process.

entropy (symbol: S, s) 1. A measure of the extent to which the energy of a system is unavailable. A mathematically defined thermodynamic function of state, the increase in which gives a measure of the energy of a system that has ceased to be available for work during a certain process:

$$ds = [dq/T]_{REV}$$

where s is specific entropy (joules/kg-°K), T is absolute temperature (°Kelvin), and q is thermal energy (heat) input per unit mass (joules/kg), for reversible processes. 2. A simplified statistical thermodynamics definition of entropy as a disorder or uncertainty indicator, based on the work of the American scientist Josiah Willard Gibbs (1839–1903), is:

$$s = - k \, \Sigma \, p_i \ln p_i$$

where k is the Boltzmann constant and p_i is the probability of the *i*th quantum state of the system. 3. In communication theory, the average information content (nonredundant) of an object.
See also: SECOND LAW OF THERMODYNAMICS; THIRD LAW OF THERMODYNAMICS.

entry Region of the thrust chamber where the contour of the chamber converges to the nozzle throat area.
See also: ROCKET ENGINE.

entry corridor The acceptable range of flight-path angles for an aerospace vehicle or space probe to enter a planetary atmosphere and safely reach the surface or a predetermined altitude in the planet's atmosphere at which parachutes or other soft-landing assistance devices would be employed. If the flight-path angle is too steep (i.e., greater than the entry corridor range), the aerospace vehicle or probe would encounter excessive aerodynamic heating as it plunged into the thickening atmosphere and burn up. If the flight path angle is too shallow (i.e., less than the entry corridor range), the vehicle or probe would bounce off the atmosphere, much like a smooth pebble skipping across a pond, and go past the target planet back into outer space. For example, a space shuttle orbiter undergoes its gliding atmospheric entry at an initial velocity of about 7.5 kilometers per second (4.66 miles per second). The flight-path angle is typically -1.2 degrees at the entry interface altitude of 122 kilometers (75.8 miles).
See also: SPACE TRANSPORTATION SYSTEM.

envelope 1. In aerospace engineering, the external boundary defining the limits on the dimensions of the component, subsystem, or system. 2. In aerospace operations, the bounds within which a certain aerospace vehicle, spacecraft, or probe can operate—for example, a *flight envelope*. 3. In mathematics, a curve that bounds the values that a variable can assume.

environment An external condition, or the sum of such conditions, in which a piece of equipment, a living organism, or a system operates; for example, *vibration environment, temperature environment, radiation environment,* or *space environment*. Environments can be natural or human-engineered (artificial) and often are specified by a range of values.

environmental chamber A test chamber in which temperature, pressure, fluid content and composition, humidity, noise, and movement can be controlled so as to simulate the different operational environments that an aerospace component, subsystem, or system might be required to perform in.

eolian Pertaining to, carried by, or caused by the wind. For example, *eolian sand dunes* on the surface of Mars.

ephemeris A collection of data about the predicted positions (or apparent positions) of celestial objects, including artificial satellites, at various times in the future. A satellite ephemeris might contain the orbital elements of satellites and their predicted changes.
See also: ORBITS OF OBJECTS IN SPACE.

equation of state (EOS) An equation relating the thermodynamic temperature (T), pressure (p), and volume (V) for an amount of substance (n) in thermodynamic equilibrium. A large number of such equations have been developed. Of these, perhaps the simplest and most widely known is the *ideal* or *perfect gas* equation of state:

$$p V = n \Re T$$

where $\Re$ is the universal gas constant, which has a value of 8314.5 joules per kilogram-mole per degree Kelvin [J/(kmol-°K)].

equations of motion A set of equations that gives information regarding the motion of a body or of a point in space as a function of time when initial position and initial velocity are known.
See also: NEWTON'S LAWS OF MOTION.

equator An imaginary circle around a celestial body that is everywhere equidistant (90 degrees) from the poles, defining the boundary between the Northern and Southern Hemisphere.

equatorial bulge The excess of a planet's equatorial diameter over the polar diameter.

equatorial orbit An orbit with an inclination of zero degrees. The plane of an equatorial orbit contains the equator of the primary body.

equatorial satellite A satellite whose orbital plane coincides, or nearly coincides, with the equatorial plane of the primary body.

equilibrium The state of a thermodynamic system in which there are no net changes—that is, a system in which forces, reactions, energy flows, and transitions balance each other out. For example, the state within a gas in which reactions between com-ponents are proceeding equally in the forward and backward direction so that the relative concentrations of the components would not change with time.

equilibrium composition In rocketry, the chemical composition that the exhaust gas would attain, if given sufficient time for the reactants to achieve chemical balance.

erector A vehicle used to support a rocket for transportation and to place the rocket in an upright position within a gantry.

erg The unit of energy or work in the centimeter-gram-second (c.g.s.) unit system. An erg is the work performed by a force of 1 dyne acting through a distance of 1 centimeter.

$$1 \text{ erg} = 10^{-7} \text{ joule}$$

ergometer A bicyclelike instrument used for measuring muscular work and for exercising "in place." Astronauts and cosmonauts use specially designed ergometers to exercise while on extended orbital flights.

ergonomics That portion of human factors engineering that is concerned with people-machine interfaces and studies the relationship between workers and their working environment.

erosion 1. In general, the progressive loss of original material from a solid due to the mechanical interaction between that surface and a fluid or the impingement of liquid droplets or solid particles. 2. In geology, the collective group of processes whereby rock material is removed and transported. The four major agents of erosion are: running water, wind, glacial ice, and gravity. 3. In environmental science, the wearing away of the land surface by wind and water. Erosion occurs naturally from weather or runoff but can be intensified by land-clearing practices associated with farming, residential or industrial development, road-building, or timber-cutting.

erosive burning The increased burning of solid propellant that results from the scouring influence of combustion products moving at high velocity over the burning surface.
See also: ROCKET.

error 1. In science and mathematics, the difference or discrepancy between a true or theoretically correct value and an observed, computed, or measured value. 2. In computer science and applications, any incorrect step, process, procedure, or result. 3. In human factors engineering, a mistake; a crewperson's act of omission or commission that leads to undesirable consequences or results.

ERS-1 (European Remote Sensing-I satellite) The European Space Agency's *ERS-1* satellite was put into orbit in July 1991 by an Ariane launcher. It weighs well over 2 tonnes and fully deployed on orbit it is almost 12 meters long. *ERS-1* circles Earth once every 100 minutes at an altitude of 780 kilometers. Its payload consists essentially of two specialized radars plus an infrared sensor. Day and night, it has been using these instruments to survey the structure of our planet's surface, taking radar images that reveal important details and monitor changes. Data from *ERS-1* has helped scientists watch shorelines, ocean currents, and the sea surface, monitor the growth of crops and vegetation, survey and map the polar icecaps and drift ice, and even detect oil spills at sea.

See also: EUROPEAN SPACE AGENCY; REMOTE SENSING.

escape rocket A small rocket engine attached to the leading end of an escape tower, which is used to provide additional thrust to the crew capsule to obtain separation of this capsule from the expendable booster vehicle in the event of a launch pad abort or emergency.

See also: MERCURY PROJECT.

escape tower A trestle tower placed on top of a crew (space) capsule, which during liftoff connects the capsule to the escape rocket. After a successful liftoff and ascent, the escape tower and escape rocket are separated from the capsule.

See also: ESCAPE ROCKET; MERCURY PROJECT.

escape velocity (symbol: V_e) The minimum velocity needed by a object to climb out of the gravity well (overcome the gravitational attraction) of a celestial body. From classical Newtonian mechanics, the escape velocity from the surface of a celestial body of mass (M) and radius (R) is given by the equation:

$$V_e = \sqrt{(2\,G\,M)/R}$$

where G is the universal constant of gravitation

ESCAPE VELOCITY FOR VARIOUS OBJECTS IN THE SOLAR SYSTEM

Celestial Body	Escape Velocity (V_e) (km/sec)
Earth	11.2
Moon	2.4
Mercury	4.3
Venus	10.4
Mars	5.0
Jupiter	~ 61
Saturn	~ 36
Uranus	~ 21
Neptune	~ 24
Pluto	~ 1
Sun	~618

Source: Developed by the author, based on NASA and other astrophysical data.

$(6.672 \times 10^{-11}\ \text{N} - \text{m}^2/\text{kg}^2)$

M is the mass of the celestial object (kg), N is Newton (unit of force in the SI system), and R is the radius of the celestial object (m). The table presents the escape velocity for various objects in the solar system (or an estimated equivalent V_e for those celestial bodies that do not possess a readily identifiable solid surface, such as the giant outer planets and the Sun).

Europa One of the Galilean moons of Jupiter. This smooth-surfaced moon has a diameter of 3,138 kilometers (km), a sidereal period of 3.551 days, and orbits Jupiter at a mean distance of 670,900 km.

See also: JUPITER.

European Space Agency (ESA) In 1975 the European Space Agency, or ESA, was formed out of, and took over the obligations and rights of, the two earlier European space organizations: the European Space Research Organization (ESRO) and the European Organization for the Development and Construction of Space Vehicle Launchers (ELDO). Current member states are: Austria, Belgium, Denmark, Finland, France, Germany, Ireland, Italy, the Netherlands, Norway, Spain, Sweden, Switzerland, and the United Kingdom. Canada is a cooperating state. ESA is an international organization whose task is "to provide for and to promote, for exclusively peaceful purposes, cooperation among European states in space research and technology and their space applications."

Today ESA's involvement spans the fields of space science, Earth observation, telecommunications, space segment technologies (including orbital stations and platforms), ground infrastructures and space transportation systems, as well as basic research in microgravity. ESA has its headquarters in Paris, France, a number of other establishments within Europe (ESTEC, ESOC, ESRIN, and EAC), a launch base at Kourou in French Guiana, and a liaison office in Washington, D.C.

Located in Noordwijk, the Netherlands, ESTEC (the European Space Research and Technology Center) is the technical heart of ESA and its biggest establishment. ESOC, the European Space Operations Center in Darmstadt, Germany, monitors and controls orbiting ESA spacecraft, from the moment of launch and throughout their mission. ESRIN (European Space Research Institute located at Frascati, south of Rome, Italy) is involved with ESA's Earth observation program. Finally, EAC, the European Astronaut Center at Cologne in Germany, is the latest of the agency's establishments and has the task of selecting and training men and women who will participate in crewed missions onboard orbiting space stations. ESA has its own corps of astronauts. They have participated on U.S. space shuttle missions involving Spacelab and they have also flown on-board the Russian Mir Space Station as part of a EuroMir mission program.

The driving force behind the decision of European governments to coordinate and pool their efforts in joint space endeavors was, quite simply, economics. No individual European county could afford to individually sponsor a complete range of space projects and all the necessary infrastructure—although some countries, such as France, still maintain thriving national space programs in addition to participation in ESA.

See also: CASSINI MISSION; ERS-1; GIOTTO SPACECRAFT; SPACELAB; ULYSSES MISSION.

European X-Ray Observatory Satellite (EXOSAT)
A European Space Agency (ESA) science mission successfully launched in 1983 to observe white dwarfs, neutron stars, black holes, and other interesting astronomical phenomena through their X-ray emissions. The mission lasted until 1986.

See also: EUROPEAN SPACE AGENCY; X-RAY ASTRONOMY.

eutectic A mixture of two materials that has a lower melting point than either material alone. When the molten mixture solidifies, one material freezes in a regular pattern throughout the other.

evaporation The physical process by which a liquid is transformed to the gaseous state (i.e., the vapor phase) at a temperature below the boiling point of the liquid. Compare with SUBLIMATION.

evaporation rate 1. In thermodynamics, the mass of material evaporated per unit time per unit surface area of a liquid or liquid-saturated porous solid. 2. In physics and chemistry, the number of atoms or molecules of a given substance evaporated per second per unit surface area (typically per centimeters squared [cm^2]) from the free surface of the condensed phase.

evaporative cooling An air-cooling technique that takes advantage of the temperature drop caused by the evaporation of water from a moist surface. This technique works reasonably well with dry (i.e., low-humidity) air.

evaporative freezing Freezing that can occur when a liquid is injected or leaks into a hard vacuum and expands to pressures below the triple point of the substance. The triple point is the temperature and pressure at which the solid, liquid, and gaseous (vapor) phases of a substance can exist simultaneously in equilibrium.

evapotranspiration The loss (discharge) of water from Earth's surface to its atmosphere by evaporation from bodies of water or other surfaces (e.g., the soil) and by transpiration from plants.

excited state The state of a molecule, atom, electron, or nucleus when it possesses more than its normal (i.e., ground state) energy. Excess nuclear energy often is released as a gamma ray. Excess molecular energy may appear as thermal energy (heat) or fluorescence. Compare this term with GROUND STATE.

exhaust plume Hot gas ejected from the thrust chamber of a rocket engine. The plume expands as a launch vehicle ascends through Earth's atmosphere, exposing the engine and the vehicle (especially the aft portion) to a greater thermal radiation area.

exhaust plume blowback A condition in which ambient (atmospheric) pressure drives the nozzle exhaust gases forward, over the rocket motor and its attachments.

exhaust stream The stream of gaseous, atomic, or radiant particles that emit from the nozzle of a rocket or other reaction engine.

exhaust velocity The velocity (relative to the rocket) of the gases and particles that exit through the nozzle of a rocket motor.
See also: ROCKET.

exit The aft end of the divergent portion of a rocket nozzle; the plane at which the exhaust gases leave the nozzle. Also called *exit plane.*
See also: NOZZLE; ROCKET.

exit pressure Pressure of the exhaust gas as it leaves a rocket's nozzle; gas pressure at the exit plane of a nozzle.
See also: NOZZLE; ROCKET.

exoatmospheric Outside Earth's atmosphere, generally considered as occurring at altitudes above 100 kilometers (62 miles).

exoatmospheric interceptor In ballistic missile defense (BMD), an interceptor rocket that destroys incoming reentry vehicles above Earth's atmosphere during the late midcourse phase of their flight path.
See also: BALLISTIC MISSILE DEFENSE.

exobiology The multidisciplinary field that involves the study of extraterrestrial environments for living organisms, the recognition of evidence of the possible existence of life in these environments, and the study of any nonterrestrial (i.e., extraterrestrial) life-forms that may be encountered. The challenges of exobiology are being approached from several different directions. First, material samples from alien worlds in our solar system can be obtained for study on Earth, as was accomplished during the Apollo lunar expeditions (1969–1972); or such samples can be studied on the spot by robot explorers, as was accomplished by the Viking Landers (1976). Lunar rock and soil samples have not revealed any traces of life, while the biological results of the Viking Lander experiments involving Martian soils are still unclear and subject to debate.

A second major approach in exobiology involves conducting experiments in terrestrial or space laboratories that attempt either to simulate the primeval conditions that led to the formation of life on Earth and extrapolate these results to other planetary environments or to study the response of terrestrial organisms under environmental conditions found on other worlds.

A third general approach in exobiology involves an attempt to communicate with, or at least listen for signals from, other intelligent life-forms within our galaxy. This effort often is called the search for extraterrestrial intelligence (or SETI, for short). Contemporary SETI activities throughout the world have as their principal aim to listen for evidence of extraterrestrial radio signals generated by intelligent alien civilizations. Also called astrobiology.
See also: APOLLO PROJECT; SEARCH FOR EXTRATERRESTRIAL INTELLIGENCE; VIKING PROJECT.

exoskeleton In robotics, the external supporting structure of a machine, especially an anthropomorphic device. Certain hard-shelled space suits and deep-sea diver suits sometimes are called exoskeletons. The term derives from a biological description of the rigid external covering found in certain animals, such as mollusks. The exoskeleton supports the animal's body and provides attachment points for its muscles.

exosphere The outermost region of Earth's atmosphere. Sometimes called the *region of escape.*
See also: ATMOSPHERE.

exothermic reaction A chemical or physical reaction in which thermal energy (heat) is released into the surroundings. Compare with ENDOTHERMIC REACTION.

exotic fuel Any rocket fuel considered to be unusual, such as a boron-based fuel.

expandable space structure A structure that can be packaged in a small volume for launch and then erected to its full size and shape outside Earth's atmosphere.
See also: SPACE CONSTRUCTION.

expanded launch danger area The land area immediately beyond and surrounding the *launch danger area* where the danger (during a particular launch operation) may be sufficient to preclude the exposure of all nonessential personnel. Normally this expanded safety area is applied to the first few launches of a new missile or rocket vehicle.

See also: LAUNCH DANGER AREA; LAUNCH DANGER ZONE.

expansion geometry The contour of a rocket nozzle, from the throat to the exit plane.

See also: NOZZLE; ROCKET.

expansion ratio (symbol: ε) For a converging-diverging (de Laval-type) rocket nozzle, the expansion ratio (ε) is defined as the ratio of the exit plane area (A_{exit}) to the throat area (A_{throat}). Also called *nozzle area expansion ratio.*

$$\varepsilon = A_{exit} / A_{throat}$$

See also: NOZZLE; ROCKET.

expendable launch vehicle (ELV) A ground-launched propulsion vehicle, capable of placing a payload into Earth orbit or Earth-escape trajectory, whose various stages are not designed for or intended for recovery and/or reuse. The U.S. Atlas, Delta, Titan, and Scout rockets are examples of expendable launch vehicles.

See also: LAUNCH VEHICLE.

experiment The system of hardware, software, and procedures for performing a scientific investigation that is undertaken to discover unknown phenomena, establish the basis of known physical laws, or evaluate the feasibility of a process, application, or piece of equipment.

experimental vehicle (symbol: X) An aircraft, missile, or aerospace vehicle in the research, development, and testing portion of its life cycle and not yet approved for operational use. Often designated by the symbol X.

See also: X-1; X-15; X-33; X-34.

exploding bridgewire (EBW) An initiator consisting of a small-diameter wire that explodes when high voltage is applied; used to ignite small retro-rockets, stage separation rockets, and explosive bolt devices.

exploding galaxies Violent, very energetic explosions centered in certain galactic nuclei where the total mass of ejected material is comparable to the mass of some 5 million average-size stars. Jets of gas 1,000 light-years long are also typical.

See also: GALAXY.

Explorer I The first U.S. Earth satellite. (See Figure 40.) *Explorer I* was launched successfully from Cape Canaveral Air Force Station on January 31, 1958 by a Juno I four-stage configuration of the Jupiter C launch vehicle. It was a joint project of the Army Ballistic Missile Agency (ABMA) and the Jet Propulsion Laboratory (JPL). ABMA supplied the Jupiter C launch vehicle, while JPL supplied the fourth stage rocket and the satellite itself. Dr. James Van Allen of the State University of Iowa provided the instruments, which detected the inner of Earth's two major trapped radiation belts for the first time. *Explorer I* measured three phenomena: cosmic ray and radiation levels, the temperature in the spacecraft, and the frequency of collisions with

Figure 40. Jubilant team leaders (from left to right) Dr. Pickering (JPL), Dr. Van Allen (State Univ. of Iowa), and Dr. von Braun (ABMA) hold aloft a model of the *Explorer I* spacecraft and its solid-rocket final stage. The first U.S. Earth satellite was successfully launched on January 31, 1958. *(NASA—Photo # 78-H-136)*

micrometeorites. There was no provision for data storage, and therefore the satellite transmitted information continuously. Earth's trapped radiation belts, discovered by the *Explorer I,* are called the *Van Allen Belts* in honor of Dr. Van Allen.

Explorer satellites The name "Explorer" has been used by NASA to designate a large series of scientific satellites used to "explore the unknown." Explorer spacecraft were used by NASA since 1958 to study: (1) Earth's atmosphere and ionosphere; (2) the magnetosphere and interplanetary space; (3) astronomical and astrophysical phenomena; and (4) Earth's shape, magnetic field, and surface. Many of the Explorer satellites had project names that were used before they were orbited and then were replaced by Explorer designations once they were placed in orbit. Other Explorer satellites, especially the early ones, were known before launch and after achieving orbit simply by their numerical designations. A brief (but not all inclusive) listing will help illustrate the great variety of important scientific missions performed by these satellites: Aeronomy Explorer, Air Density Explorer, Interplanetary Monitoring Platform (IMP), Ionosphere Explorer, Meteoroid Technology Satellite (MTS), Radio Astronomy Explorer (RAE), Solar Explorer, and Small Astronomy Satellite (SAS).

Geodetic Satellites (GEOS) also were called *Geodetic Explorer Satellites.* For example, GEOS 1 (*Explorer 29,* launched on November 6, 1965) and GEOS 2 (*Explorer 36,* launched on January 11, 1968) refined our knowledge of Earth's shape and gravity field. SAS-A, an X-ray Astronomy Explorer, became *Explorer 42* when launched on December 12, 1970 by an Italian launch crew from the San Marco platform off the coast of Kenya, Africa. Because it was launched on Kenya's Independence Day, this small spacecraft was also called *Uhuru* (the Swahili word for "Freedom"). It successfully mapped the universe in X-ray wavelengths for four years, discovering X-ray pulsars and providing preliminary evidence of the existence of black holes.

See also: EXPLORER-I.

explosion (chemical) The rapid production of a large quantity of hot gas due to very energetic chemical reactions that release thermal energy (heat) and cause a sudden increase in pressure. The volume of this hot gas is much larger than the original volume of the chemical substance that caused the explosion. Trinitrotoluene (TNT) is an example of an explosive chemical substance.

explosion-proof apparatus An apparatus enclosed in a special protective case that is capable of: withstanding an explosion of a specific gas or vapor that may occur within it; or preventing the ignition of a specified gas or vapor surrounding the enclosure by internal sparks, flashes, or explosions of the gas or vapor within. Also an apparatus that operates at such an external temperature that a surrounding flammable atmosphere will not be ignited.

explosive A substance or mixture of substances (i.e., trinitrotoluene (TNT) or gunpowder) that can undergo a rapid chemical change without an outside supply of oxygen and with the release of large quantities of energy—generally accompanied by the evolution of a large volume of hot gases.

explosive-activated device (EAD) An electrically initiated pyrotechnic device, such as an explosive bolt. Used to separate rocket stages or to separate a spacecraft from its rocket vehicle.

explosive bolt A bolt incorporating an explosive charge that can be detonated on command (usually by an electrical signal or pulse), thereby destroying the bolt and releasing pieces of aerospace equipment it was retaining. Explosive bolts and spring-loaded mechanisms can be used to quickly separate launch vehicle stages or a spacecraft from its propulsion system.

explosive decompression A very rapid reduction of air pressure inside the pressurized portion (i.e., crew compartment) of an aircraft, aerospace vehicle, or spacecraft. For example, collision with a large piece of space debris might puncture the wall of one of the pressurized modules on a space station, causing an explosive decompression situation within that module. Air locks would activate, sealing off the stricken portion of the pressurized space habitat.

explosive train An arrangement of explosive or combustible elements used to perform an end function or to transfer energy to perform an end function. When an explosive train is used to transfer energy from one point, such as a safe and arm (S&A) detonator, to an end function, such as a solid

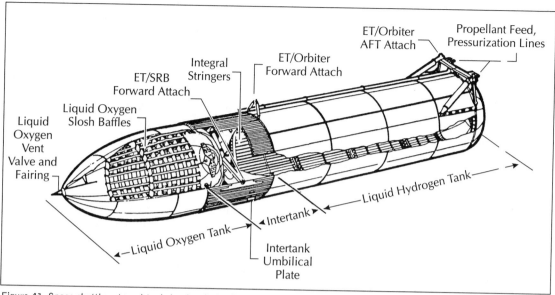

Figure 41. Space shuttle external tank (major design features) *(NASA)*

rocket motor igniter, the device may be called an *explosive transfer assembly (ETA)* or an *energy transfer system (ETS)*.

explosive valve A valve having a small explosive charge that, when detonated, provides high-pressure gas to change the valve position. Also known as a *squib valve.*

exponent The number or symbol that represents the power to which another number or algebraic expression is raised. For example, in the expression 10^4, the exponent "4" indicates that the number "10" is being raised to the 4th power—that is, $10^4 = 10\cdot10\cdot10\cdot10 = 10,000$. Similarly, in the expression $(ab)^2$, the exponent "2" indicates that the algebraic product (ab) is being raised to the 2nd power or being "squared"—that is, $(ab)^2 = (ab)\cdot(ab) = a^2b^2$.

exposure suit A garment designed to protect a person from a harmful natural environment, such as frigid water.

external tank (ET) The large tank that contains the propellants for the three space shuttle main engines (SSMEs) and forms the structural backbone of the space shuttle flight system in the launch configuration. At liftoff, the external tank absorbs the total 28,580-kilonewton (6,425,000-

pounds-force [lbf]) thrust loads of the three main engines and the two solid rocket boosters (SRBs). When these SRBs separate at an altitude of approximately 44 kilometers (km) (27 miles [mi]), the orbiter vehicle, with the main engines still burning, carries the ET piggyback to near orbital velocity. Then, at an altitude of approximately 113 km (70 mi), some 8.5 minutes into the flight, the now nearly empty tank separates from the orbiter and falls in a preplanned trajectory into a remote area of the Indian Ocean. The ET is the only major expendable element of the space shuttle.

The three main components of the ET are an oxygen tank (located in the forward position), a hydrogen tank (located in the aft position), and a collarlike intertank, which connects the two propellant tanks, houses instrumentation and processing equipment, and provides the attachment structure for the forward end of the solid rocket boosters. In June 1998, a lighter version of the external tank entered service. Made of a special lightweight material called aluminum lithium, the new tank has a mass of approximately 26,300 kilograms (kg) [58,000 pounds-mass (lbm)]—about 3,400 kg (7,500 lbm) less mass than the previous version. The reduced tank mass means heavier payloads can be carried into orbit by the space shuttle. (See Figure 41.)

See also: SPACE TRANSPORTATION SYSTEM.

extragalactic Occurring, located, or originating beyond our galaxy (the Milky Way); typically, farther than 100,000 light-years distant.

extragalactic astronomy A branch of astronomy that started around 1930 that studies everything in the universe outside of our galaxy, the Milky Way.

extrasolar Occurring, located, or originating outside of our solar system; as, for example, extrasolar planets.

extrasolar planets Planets that belong to a star other than the Sun.

extraterrestrial (ET) Refers to something that occurs, is located, or originates outside of the planet Earth and its atmosphere.

extraterrestrial catastrophe theory The postulation by some scientists that a large asteroid (or possibly a comet) struck ancient Earth some 65 million years ago and that this cosmic collision produced severe environmental consequences that annihilated about 90% of all animal species then living, including the dinosaurs. Today space scientists recognize the possibility that an asteroid or comet could strike Earth and that this type of collision could trigger a global catastrophe. One current estimate suggests that Earth should experience at least one collision with an "Earth-crossing" asteroid (of 1 kilometer diameter size or greater) every 300,000 years or so. This type of threat from space now is considered quite real (from a long-term perspective). For example, on May 22, 1989 a small "Earth-crossing" asteroid, called 1989FC, passed within 690,000 kilometers (only 0.0046 astronomical units) of our planet. Cosmic impact specialists have estimated that if a small asteroid of this type (about 200 to 400 meters in diameter) experiences a straight-in collision with Earth at a relative velocity of some 16 kilometers per second, it would impact with an explosive force of some 400 to 2,000 megatons. (A megaton is the energy of an explosion that is equivalent to one million tons of TNT.) Furthermore, if an asteroid even this small were to hit a terrestrial landmass (instead of impacting in water), it would form a crater about 4 to 7 kilometers across and throw tons of dirt, dust, and debris into the atmosphere.

See also: ASTEROID; COMET.

extraterrestrial contamination In general, the contamination of one world by life-forms, especially microorganisms, from another world. Using Earth and its biosphere as a reference, this planetary-contamination process is called *forward contamination* if an extraterrestrial sample or the alien world itself is contaminated by contact with terrestrial organisms; and *back contamination* if alien organisms are released into Earth's biosphere. An alien species probably would not survive when introduced into a new ecological system, because it would be unable to compete with native species that are better adapted to the particular environment. It is possible, however, that some alien species might thrive, because the new environment is very suitable and indigenous life-forms are unable to defend themselves successfully against these alien invaders. This might very well cause a permanent disruption of the host ecosphere, with severe biological and environmental consequences.

At the start of the space age, scientists were aware of the potential extraterrestrial contamination problem in either direction. Quarantine protocols (procedures) were established to avoid the forward contamination of other worlds in our solar system by outbound robot spacecraft as well as the potential back contamination of the terrestrial biosphere when lunar samples were returned to Earth as part of the Apollo Project.

During the Apollo Project, no evidence was discovered that native alien life was then present or ever existed on the Moon. Consequently, after the first few Apollo expeditions the concern for back contamination was dropped. However, to preserve the scientific value of the pristine lunar samples, they were and still are being carefully protected from contamination by Earth's environment at the Lunar Receiving Laboratory (LRL) at the Johnson Space Center in Texas.

As scientists now plan to return samples from Mars and other worlds in our solar system using robot space systems, the issue of potential contamination of the terrestrial biosphere must be addressed again. There are three fundamental approaches toward avoiding back contamination. First, the samples could be sterilized while en route back to Earth from the alien world. Second, they could be retrieved carefully and then placed directly in quarantine in a remotely located, maximum-confinement facility on Earth while scientists examine them closely. Third, the pristine (nonsterilized) samples initially could be subjected to a preliminary hazard analysis (called the *extraterrestrial protocol tests*) in an orbiting quarantine facility before they are allowed to enter the terrestrial biosphere.

extraterrestrial life Life-forms that may have evolved independent of and now exist outside of the terrestrial biosphere.
See also: EXOBIOLOGY.

extraterrestrial resources The resources to be found in space that could be used to help support an extended human presence and eventually become the physical basis for a thriving solar system–level civilization. These resources include unlimited solar energy, a full range of raw materials (from the Moon, asteroids, comets, Mars, numerous moons of outer planets, etc.), and an environment that is both special (e.g., access to high vacuum, microgravity, physical isolation from terrestrial biosphere) and reasonably predictable.

extravehicular activity (EVA) Extravehicular activity, or EVA, may be defined as the activities

Figure 42. Astronaut Foale, extended on the Remote Manipulator System, prepares to grab Spartan 204, while astronaut Harris (right) looks on during an EVA in the Orbiter *Discovery*'s cargo bay. *(STS-63 mission, February, 1995). (NASA)*

conducted in space by an astronaut or cosmonaut outside the protective environment of his/her spacecraft, aerospace vehicle, or space station. In the U.S. space program, the first EVA was performed by Astronaut Edward H. White II on June 3, 1965 when he left the protective environment of his *Gemini IV* space capsule and ventured into space (while constrained by an umbilical tether). Since that historic demonstration, EVA has been used successfully during a variety of American and Russian space missions to make critical repairs, perform inspections, help capture and refurbish failed satellites, clean optical surfaces, deploy equipment, and retrieve experiments. The term "EVA," as applied the space shuttle, includes all activities for which crew members don their spacesuits and life support systems and then exit the orbiter vehicle's crew cabin to perform operations internal or external to the cargo bay. (See Figure 42.)

See also: SPACESUIT.

extreme ultraviolet (EUV) The region of the electromagnetic spectrum corresponding to wavelengths between 10 and 100 nanometers (100 and 1,000 angstroms).

See also: ELECTROMAGNETIC SPECTRUM.

Extreme Ultraviolet Explorer NASA's 70th Explorer-class satellite launched from Cape Canaveral Air Force Station in 1992 into a 525-kilometer (328-mile) Earth orbit. It provided astronomers with a view of the relatively unexplored region of the electromagnetic spectrum—the extreme ultraviolet (EUV) region (i.e., 10 to 100 nanometers wavelength). It gathered important data about sources of EUV radiation within the "Local Bubble"—a hot, low-density region of the Milky Way galaxy (including our Sun) that is the result of a supernova explosion some 100,000 years ago. Interesting EUV sources include white dwarf stars and binary star systems in which one star is siphoning material from the outer atmosphere of its companion.

eyeballs in, eyeballs out Aerospace jargon, derived from test pilots and used to describe the acceleration experienced by an astronaut or cosmonaut at liftoff or when the retrorockets fire. The experience at liftoff is "eyeballs in" (positive g because of vehicle acceleration), while the experience when the retrorockets fire is "eyeballs out" (negative g because of space capsule or aerospace vehicle deceleration).

Fahrenheit (symbol: F) A relative temperature scale with the freezing point of water (at atmospheric pressure) given a value of 32° Fahrenheit and the boiling point of water (at atmospheric pressure) assigned the value of 212° Fahrenheit.

fail-operational The ability of an aerospace system to sustain a failure and retain full operational capability for safe mission continuation.

fail-safe 1. Term for philosophy in the design of aerospace system hardware that seeks to avoid the compounding of failures; fail-safe design provisions ensure that the component (e.g., a valve element in the liquid-fuel rocket propulsion system) will move to a predetermined "SAFE" position if electric, pneumatic, or hydraulic power is lost. 2. The ability of an aerospace system to sustain a failure and retain the capability to terminate the mission successfully. For ground support equipment (GSE), the ability to sustain a failure without causing loss of space vehicle systems or loss of personnel capability.

fail-safe device A device used to minimize risk in case of a malfunction or abort of a system. It usually involves an automatic mechanism that makes the system cease operation whenever a failure in a critical component or subsystem is detected or whenever abnormal operating conditions are experienced. One of the most common examples of a fail-safe device is the electric fuse.

fail-safe system(s) System(s) used in aerospace operations to minimize risk in case of malfunction.

fairing A structural component of a rocket or aerospace vehicle designed to reduce drag or air resistance by smoothing out nonstreamlined objects or sections.

Falcon An air-to-air guided missile (AAGM) that can be carried either internally or externally on interceptor aircraft.

fallaway section A section of a launch vehicle or rocket that is cast off and separates from the vehicle during flight, especially a section that falls back to Earth.

farad (symbol: F) The SI UNIT of electrical capacitance. It is defined as the capacitance of a capacitor whose plates have a potential difference of one volt when charged by a quantity of electricity equal to one coulomb. This unit is named after the 19th century British scientist Michael Faraday (1791–1867), who was a pioneer in the field of electromagnetism. Since the farad is too large a unit for typical applications, submultiples—such as the *microfarad* (10^{-6}F), the *nanofarad* (10^{-9}F), and the *picofarad* (10^{-12}F)—are encountered frequently.

farside The side of the Moon that never faces Earth.
See also: MOON.

fast-burn booster A ballistic missile that can burn out much more quickly than current versions, possibly before exiting the atmosphere entirely. Such a rapid booster burnout complicates a boost-phase ballistic missile defense (BMD) system.
See also: BALLISTIC MISSILE DEFENSE.

fatigue 1. A weakening or deterioration of metal or other material occurring under load, especially under repeated cyclic or continued loading. Self-explanatory compounds of this term include: *fatigue crack, fatigue failure, fatigue load, fatigue resistance,* and *fatigue test.* 2. The state of the human organism after exposure to any type of physical or psychological stress, as, for example, *pilot fatigue.*

fatigue life Number of cycles of stress, under stated test condition, that can be sustained by a material prior to failure.

fatigue strength The maximum stress that can be sustained for a specified number of cycles without failure, the stress being completely reversed within each cycle unless otherwise stated.

fault tolerance The capability of an aerospace system to function despite one or more critical failures; usually achieved by use of redundant circuits or functions and/or reconfigurable components.

feasibility study A study to determine whether an aerospace mission plan is within the capacity of the resources and/or technologies that can be made available—for example, a NASA feasibility study involving a robotic soil sample return mission to the surface of Mars.

feedback 1. The return of a portion of the output of a device to the input. *Positive feedback* adds to the input; *negative feedback* subtracts from the input. 2. Information concerning results or progress returned to an originating source. 3. In aeronautics, the transmittal of forces initiated by aerodynamic action on control surfaces or rotor blades to the cockpit controls.

femto- (symbol: f) The SI prefix for 10^{-15}. This prefix is used to designate very small quantities, such as a *femtosecond (fs)*, which corresponds to 10^{-15} second—a very brief flash of time.

ferret In defense, a vehicle (i.e., an aircraft or satellite) especially equipped for the detection, location, recording, and analyzing of electromagnetic radiation.

ferry flight An (in-the-atmosphere) flight of a space shuttle orbiter mated on top of the Boeing 747 shuttle carrier aircraft.
See also: SPACE TRANSPORTATION SYSTEM (STS).

fiducial mark A symbol or collimating mark used as a reference.

field 1. In physics, a region in which an object experiences a *force* due to the presence of other objects (i.e., a *gravitational field*) or due to the presence of certain phenomena, such as a *magnetic field* and/or *electric field.* 2. In information and science, the smallest unit of data in a record. 3. In remote sensing, the field of view of a sensor.

field of view (FOV) The area or solid angle that can be viewed through or scanned by an optical instrument.

film badge A "badgelike" packet of ionizing radiation-sensitive materials (including certain types of photographic film) used for measuring and permanently recording the radiation dosage a person has received. An astronaut or cosmonaut often wears a film badge during spaceflight to record his/her exposure to the space radiation environment.

film cooling The cooling of a body or surface, such as the inner surface of a rocket's combustion chamber, by maintaining a thin fluid layer over the affected area.

filter 1. A thin layer of selective material placed in front of a detector that lets through only a selected color (e.g., a blue-light filter for a photometer), group of electromagnetic radiation wavelengths (e.g., thermal infrared band radiation between 10 and 11 micrometers wavelength), group of photon energies (e.g., gamma rays with energies between 1.0 and 1.1 MeV [million electron volts]), or a desired (often narrow) range of particle energies (e.g., solar protons between 2.0 and 2.2 MeV). Narrow-band filters for can be quite selective, passing radiation only in a very narrow region of the electromagnetic spectrum—for example, a 427.8 nanometer (4278 Å) wavelength narrow-band optical filter. Other radiation filters are reasonably broad—for example, a filter that passes an entire "color" in the visible spectrum (i.e., blue-light filter or a red-light filter). 2. A device that removes suspended particulate matter from a liquid or a gas. This removal process is accomplished by forcing the fluid (with the suspended matter) through a permeable material (i.e., one that has many tiny holes or pores). The permeable material retains the solid matter while permitting the passage of the fluid that has now been "filtered" to some level of purity. 3. In electronics, a device that transmits only part of the incident electromagnetic energy and thereby may change its spectral distribution. *High-pass filters* transmit energy above a certain frequency, while *low-pass filters* transmit energy below a certain frequency. *Band-pass filters* transmit energy within a certain frequency band, while *band-stop filters* transmit only energy outside a specific frequency band.

fin 1. In aeronautics, a fixed or adjustable airfoil attached longitudinally to an aircraft, missile, rocket, or similar body to provide a stabilizing effect. 2. In heat transfer, a projecting flat plate or structure that facilitates thermal energy transfer, such as a *cooling fin*.

fire 1. In chemistry, the persistent and rapid reaction that liberates thermal energy (heat) and produces light; the combination of a combustible substance with oxygen that releases thermal energy (i.e., the *exothermic* process involving oxygen and a combustible substance). 2. In aerospace operations, a term meaning to ignite a rocket engine or to launch a rocket vehicle. 3. To detonate the main explosive charge by means of a firing system. 4. In military operations, the command given to discharge a weapon or weapons.

Firebee A remotely controlled target drone that is powered by a turbojet engine. It achieves high subsonic speeds and is designed to be ground-launched or air-launched. The Firebee is used to test, train, and evaluate weapon systems employing surface-to-air and air-to-air missiles. Also called the *BQM-34*.

First Law of Thermodynamics The principle of conservation of energy. For a control mass (i.e., a thermodynamic system of specified matter), the first law can be written in the form of an energy balance:

$$\text{Energy Output - Energy Input = Change in Energy Storage}$$
$$W - Q = \Delta E_{storage}$$

where W is the amount of energy transferred out of the control mass as work, Q is the amount of energy transferred into the control mass as heat (thermal energy), and $\Delta E_{storage}$ is the change (increase

or decrease) in energy of the control mass (i.e., $E_{final} - E_{initial}$). In thermodynamics, the use of an energy balance often is referred to as a *first-law analysis*.

See also: THERMODYNAMICS.

first strike The first offensive move of a war. (This term often is associated with nuclear operations.)

fissile material While sometimes used as a synonym for *fissionable material*, this term has a more restricted meaning, namely, any material fissionable (i.e., capable of undergoing *fission*) by neutrons of all energies, including (and especially) thermal (slow) neutrons as well as fast neutrons. Uranium-235 ($^{235}_{92}U$), uranium-233 ($^{233}_{92}U$), and plutonium-239 ($^{239}_{94}Pu$) are fissile.

See also: FISSION (NUCLEAR).

fission (nuclear) In nuclear fission, the nucleus of a heavy element, such as uranium (U) or plutonium (Pu), is bombarded by a neutron, which it absorbs. The resulting compound nucleus is unstable and soon breaks apart, or "fissions," forming two lighter nuclei (called *fission products*) and releasing additional neutrons. In a properly designed nuclear reactor, these fission neutrons are used to sustain the fission process in a controlled chain reaction. The nuclear fission process is accompanied by the release of a large amount of energy, typically 200 million electron volts per reaction. Much of this energy appears as the kinetic (or motion) energy of the fission product nuclei, which is then converted to thermal energy (or heat) as the fission products slow down in the reactor fuel material. This thermal energy is removed from the reactor core and used to generate electricity or as process heat.

Because the fission process is accompanied by the instantaneous liberation of neutrons, it is also possible to produce an exponentially diverging (growing) fission chain reaction that is accompanied by the very rapid release of large amounts of energy. As a result, a few kilograms of fissionable material can be made to liberate, within a very small fraction of a second, as much energy as the explosion of many thousands of tons of TNT. This is the basic principle of nuclear fission weapons.

Energy is released during the nuclear fission process because the total mass of the fission products and neutrons after the reaction is less than the total mass of the original neutron and the heavy nucleus that absorbed it. From Einstein's famous mass-energy equivalence relationship, $E = mc^2$, the energy release is equal to the tiny amount of mass that has disappeared multiplied by the square of the speed of light.

Nuclear fission can occur spontaneously in heavy elements but usually is caused when these nuclei absorb neutrons. In some circumstances, nuclear fission also may be induced by very energetic gamma rays (in a process called *photofission*) and by extremely energetic (GeV-class, that is, billion-electron-volt-class) charged particles.

The most important fissionable (or fissile) materials are uranium-235, uranium-233, and plutonium-239.

See also: SPACE NUCLEAR POWER; SPACE NUCLEAR PROPULSION.

fission products Medium-mass nuclei (fission fragments) formed by the splitting or fission of heavy nuclei, such as uranium-235 or plutonium-239. Also, the nuclides formed by the radioactive decay of the primary fission products.

See also: FISSION (NUCLEAR).

fixed-area exhaust nozzle An exhaust nozzle exit that remains constant in area.

fixed satellite An Earth satellite that orbits from west to east at such speed as to remain constantly over a given place on Earth's equator.

See also: GEOSTATIONARY EARTH ORBIT.

flame bucket A deep, cavelike construction built beneath a launch pad. It is open at the top to receive the hot gases from the rocket or missile positioned above it and is also open on one to three sides below, with a thick metal fourth side bent toward the open side(s) so as to deflect the exhausting gases.

See also: FLAME DEFLECTOR.

flame deflector 1. In a vertical launch pad, any of the obstructions of various designs that intercept the hot exhaust gases of the rocket engine(s), thereby deflecting them away from the launch pad structure or the ground. The flame deflector may be a relatively small device fixed to the top surface of the launch pad, or it may be a heavily constructed piece of metal mounted as a side and bottom of a flame bucket. In the latter case, the flame deflector also may be perforated with numerous

holes connected with a source of water. During thrust buildup and the beginning of launch, a deluge of water pours from the holes in such a deflector to keep it from melting. 2. In a captive (hot) test of a rocket engine, an elbow in the exhaust conduit or flame bucket that deflects the flame into the open.

flame spreading interval Time period from first ignition of the solid-propellant grain to the ignition of the entire grain surface.

flammability The relative ease of ignition of a material; also, the ability of a material to sustain combustion.

flare A bright eruption from the Sun's chromosphere. Solar flares may appear within minutes and fade within an hour—or else linger for days. They cover a wide range of intensity and size. Flares can cause ionospheric disturbances and telecommunications (radio) fadeouts on Earth. Solar flares also represent a major ionizing radiation hazard to astronauts or cosmonauts walking on the lunar surface or traveling through interplanetary space (i.e., traveling outside the relative protection of Earth's magnetosphere).

See also: SUN.

fleet ballistic missile submarine A nuclear-powered submarine designed to deliver ballistic missile attacks against assigned targets from either a submerged or surface condition. Also designated by the U.S. Navy as *SSBN*.

Fleet Satellite Communications (FLTSATCOM) System A geostationary orbit military system designed to provide a near-global, operational satellite communications network to support high-priority communications requirements of the U.S. Navy and Air Force.

flexible hose Pliant conduit consisting of a flexible inner core of convoluted metal or plastic tubing and an outer braided wire sleeve that is attached to fixed ends to prevent buckling and separation when the core is pressurized.

flexible joint (flexible section) Nonrigid connector such as metal bellows, flexible hose, or ball-joint assembly that joins two duct sections and permits relative motion between the ducts in one or more planes; includes both the flexible member and the restraint linkage.

flexible response The capability of aerospace forces for effective reaction to any enemy threat or attack with actions appropriate and adaptable to the existing circumstances.

flexible spacecraft A space vehicle (usually a space structure or rotating satellite) whose surfaces and/or appendages may be subject to and can sustain elastic flexural deformations (vibrations).

flight The movement of an object through the atmosphere or through space, sustained by aerodynamic, aerostatic, or reaction forces or by orbital speed; especially, the movement of a human-operated or human-controlled device, such as a rocket, space probe, aerospace vehicle, or aircraft, as in *space flight, high-altitude flight,* or *high-speed flight.*

flight acceptance test(s) The environmental and other tests that spacecraft, subsystems, components, or experiments scheduled for space flight must pass before launch. These tests are planned to approximate anticipated environmental and operational conditions and have the purpose of detecting flaws in material and workmanship.

flight characteristics Flight performance qualities exhibited by an aircraft, missile, rocket, or aerospace vehicle, such as a tendency to stall or to yaw or an ability to remain stable at certain speeds.

flight control room The facility used by the flight control team for direct support of a space shuttle flight from prelaunch countdown through landing rollout.
See also: SPACE TRANSPORTATION SYSTEM (STS).

flight control team Personnel in the Mission Control Center (MCC) on duty to provide support for the duration of each space shuttle flight. The team is composed of the dedicated flight control room teams and the multipurpose support room personnel.
See also: MISSION CONTROL CENTER; SPACE TRANSPORTATION SYSTEM.

flight crew In general, any personnel onboard an aerospace vehicle, space station, or interplanetary spacecraft. With respect to the space shuttle, any personnel engaged in flying the orbiter and/or managing resources onboard (e.g., the commander, pilot, mission specialist).

flight deck A portion of the crew station module of the space shuttle orbiter vehicle.
See also: SPACE TRANSPORTATION SYSTEM.

flight-dependent training With respect to space shuttle operations, the preparation of a mission specialist or payload specialist for a specific flight. Part of the training involves integrated simulations with the rest of the shuttle flight crew and ground support teams.
See also: SPACE TRANSPORTATION SYSTEM.

flight design In general, the detailed trajectory and consumables analysis to help plan a crewed space mission. With respect to the Space Transportation System (STS), the analysis of trajectory, consumables, attitude and pointing, and navigation necessary to support the planning of a space shuttle flight.

flight envelopes The performance bounds within which a certain flight system can operate; especially a graphic representation of these bounds showing the interrelationships of operational parameters.

flight operations Collective term for ground support operations by flight crew or support personnel in preparation for space flight; also, the tasks performed by the astronaut crew during flight.

flight path The line connecting the successive positions occupied, or to be occupied, by an aircraft, missile, or space vehicle as it moves through the atmosphere or outer space.

flight readiness firing A short-duration test operation of a rocket consisting of the complete firing of the liquid-propellant engines while the vehicle is restrained at the launch pad. This test is conducted to verify the readiness of the rocket system for a flight test or operational mission.

flight simulation An aerospace training session in which the flight crew and/or ground operations support personnel practice a portion (or all) of a crewed flight.

flight simulator A training device (often highly computer interactive) that can replicate certain conditions of flight or flight operations. With the arrival of high-resolution graphic displays and virtual reality technologies, a high-fidelity simulator sometimes is referred to as "the real world in a box."

flight test Test of an aircraft, rocket, missile, or other type of aerospace vehicle by actual flight or launching. Flight tests are planned to achieve specific test objectives and to gain operational information.

flight test vehicle A rocket, missile, aircraft, or aerospace vehicle used for conducting flight tests. These flight tests can involve either the vehicle's own capabilities or the capabilities of equipment carried onboard the vehicle.

flight unit A spacecraft that is undergoing or has passed *flight acceptance tests* (i.e., environmental and other tests) that qualify it for launch and space flight.
   See also: FLIGHT ACCEPTANCE TEST(S).

flow-to-close valve Valve in which the flow direction and forces acting on the valving element provide a closing force.

flow-to-open valve Valve in which the flow direction and forces acting on the valving element provide an opening force.

flow work In thermodynamics, the amount of work associated with the expansion or compression of a flowing fluid.

fluence In ballistic missile defense (BMD), the amount of energy per unit area delivered by a high-energy laser on target.
   See also: BALLISTIC MISSILE DEFENSE.

fluid A substance that, when in static equilibrium, cannot sustain a shear stress. A *perfect* or *ideal* fluid is one that has zero viscosity—that is, it offers no resistance to shape change. Actual fluids only approximate this behavior. The term "fluid" is used to refer to both liquids and gases.

fluid-cooled Term applied to a rocket's thrust chamber or nozzle whose walls are cooled by fluid supplied from an external source, as in *regenerative cooling, transpiration cooling,* or *film cooling.*

fluid-film bearing Type of bearing in which separation of the bearing and journal depends on the shearing of a lubricating film in the clearance region between the parts; viscous forces within the fluid support the bearing load.

fluid interface Common boundary of two or more surfaces exposed to a fluid (e.g., mating flanges of a duct) or the interface between a fluid and its containing device (e.g., a tube wall).

fluid management The isolation and separation of liquids from gas in a storage vessel that operates in a reduced- or zero-gravity environment.

fluid mechanics The major branch of science that deals with the behavior of fluids (both gases and liquids) at rest (*fluid statics*) and in motion (*fluid dynamics*). This scientific field has many subbranches and important applications, including: aerodynamics (the motion of gases, including air), hydrostatics (liquids at rest), and hydrodynamics (the motion of liquids, including water).

fluid-solid interaction The interaction of a rigid or elastic structure with an incompressible or compressible fluid. Airblast loading, acoustic interaction, aeroelasticity, and hydroelasticity are examples of such interactions.

fluorescence Many substances can absorb energy (as for example, from X rays, ultraviolet light, or radioactive particles) and immediately emit this absorbed ("excitation") energy as an electromagnetic photon of visible light. This light-emitting process is called fluorescence; the emitting substances are said to be *fluorescent.*

flux (symbol: ϕ) 1. In general, the rate of transport or flow of some quantity per unit area; often used in reference to the flow of some form of energy. 2. Specifically, *neutron flux* is defined as the number of neutrons passing through one square centimeter of a given target in one second. For a well-collimated beam of monoenergetic neutrons, the neutron flux can be expressed as $\phi_n = nv$, where n equals the number of neutrons per cubic centimeter and v equals the neutron velocity (cm/sec). Therefore, the neutron flux (ϕ_n) has the units neutrons/(cm²-sec).

flyby An interplanetary or deep-space mission in which the *flyby spacecraft* passes close to its celestial target (i.e., a distant planet, moon, asteroid, or comet) but does not impact the target or go into orbit around it. Flyby spacecraft follow a continuous trajectory, never to be captured into a planetary orbit. Once the spacecraft has flown past its target (often after years of travel through deep space), it cannot return to recover lost data. So flyby operations often are planned years in advance of the encounter and refined and practiced in the months prior to the encounter date. Flyby operations are conveniently divided into four phases: *observatory phase, far-encounter phase, near-encounter phase,* and *postencounter phase.*

The *observatory phase* of a flyby mission is defined as the period when the celestial target can be better resolved in the spacecraft's optical instruments than it can from Earth-based instruments. The phase generally begins a few months prior to the date of the actual planetary flyby. During this phase the spacecraft is completely involved in making observations of its target, and ground resources become completely operational in support of the upcoming encounter. The *far-encounter phase* includes time when the full disc of the target planet (or other celestial object) can no longer fit within the field of view of the spacecraft's instruments. Observations during this phase are designed to accommodate parts of the planet (e.g., a polar region, an interesting wide-expanse cloud feature such as Jupiter's Red Spot, etc.) rather than the entire planetary disc, and to take advantage of the higher resolution available. The *near-encounter phase* includes the period of closest approach to the target. It is characterized by intensely active observations by all of the spacecraft's science experiments. This phase of the flyby mission provides scientists the opportunity to obtain the highest resolution data about the target. Finally, the *post encounter phase* begins when the near-encounter phase is completed, and the spacecraft is receding from the target. This phase is characterized by day-after-day observations of a diminishing, thin crescent of the planet just encountered. It provides an opportunity to make extensive observations of the night side of the planet. After the postencounter phase is over, the spacecraft stops observing the target and returns to the less intense activities of its interplanetary cruise phase—a phase in which scientific instruments are powered down and navigational corrections made to prepare the spacecraft for an encounter with another celestial object of opportunity or for a final journey of no return into deep space. Some scientific experiments, usually concern-

ing the properties of interplanetary space, can be performed in this cruise phase.

See also: PIONEER 10, 11; VOYAGER.

flying test bed A rocket, aerospace vehicle, aircraft, or other flying vehicle used to carry objects or devices being flight tested.

flywheel A massive, rotating wheel that can store energy as kinetic (or motion) energy as its rate of rotation is increased; energy then can be removed from this system by decreasing the rate of rotation of the wheel. An advanced-design flywheel energy storage system has been suggested for lunar surface base applications. During the lunar daytime, solar energy would be converted into electricity using Stirling-cycle heat engines. This electricity would be used for lunar base needs as well as for spinning up several very large flywheels. Excess thermal energy (heat) in the system would be transported away to a radiator by a configuration of heat pipes. During the long lunar nighttime, energy would be extracted from the flywheels and converted into electricity for the surface base.

focal length (common symbol: f) The distance between the center of a lens or mirror to the focus or focal point.

focal plane The plane, perpendicular to the optical axis of the lens, in which images of points in the object field of the lens are focused.

folded optics Any optical system containing reflecting components for the purpose of reducing the physical length of the system or changing the path of the optical axis.

foot (symbol: ft) A unit of length in the traditional (foot-pound-second [fps]), or English, unit system equal to one-third of a yard. The foot is now defined as equal to 0.3048 meter.

foot-pound (force) (symbol: ft-lb$_{force}$) A unit of work (energy) in the traditional (foot-pound-second [fps]), or English, unit system equal to the work required when a 1-pound weight (i.e., a 1-pound mass at sea level on Earth under the influence of gravity) is raised 1 foot (in height). The foot-pound (force) is now defined as equal to:

$$1 \text{ foot-pound force (lbf)} = 1.3558 \text{ joules}$$

footprint An area within which a spacecraft or reentry vehicle is intended to land.

force (symbol: F) In physics, the cause of the acceleration of material objects measured by the rate of change of momentum produced on a free body. For a body of constant mass (m) traveling at a velocity (v), the momentum is (m·v). The force (F) is given by:

$$F = d(mv)/dt = m \, dv/dt = ma$$
(Newton's 2nd Law of Motion)

where a is the acceleration. The *newton* (symbol: N) is the SI unit of force. Forces between bodies occur in equal and opposite reaction pairs.
    See also: NEWTON'S LAWS OF MOTION.

forced-separation disconnect Separable connector that is disengaged by explosive, hydraulic, or pneumatic pressure.

forced vibration An oscillation of a system in which the response is imposed by the excitation. If the excitation is periodic and continuing, the oscillation is steady state.

forcing function Vibration or alternating stress that imposes an oscillation on a system.

four-dimensional Involving *space-time;* that is, three spatial dimensions (e.g., x, y, and z) plus the dimension of time (t).

Fourier number A dimensionless number used in heat transfer. It is defined as: $[kt] / [c_p \, \rho \, l^2]$, where k is thermal conductivity, t is time, c_p is specific heat at constant pressure, ρ is mass density, and l is a characteristic length. Encountered in unsteady heat transfer problems. Named in honor of the French mathematician Jean Baptiste Joseph Fourier (1768–1830).

Fourier's law (of heat conduction) A fundamental physical principle that states that when a temperature gradient ($\delta T/\delta x$) exists in a body, there is thermal energy transfer through the body from the region of high temperature to the region of low temperature. In its most simple form (i.e., steady-state, one-dimensional heat transfer with uniform thermophysical properties except for the temperature gradient), Fourier's law can be written as:

$$q = -k \, A \, [\partial T/\partial x]$$

where q is the thermal energy transfer rate through the body (e.g., joules/-sec), k is the thermal conductivity e.g., joules per meter per degree Kelvin per second (J/m-K-s), A is the area in square meters (m^2) through which thermal energy is being transferred, and $\partial T/\partial x$ is the temperature gradient (degrees Kelvin per meter [K/m]). The minus sign (-) is used on the right side of the above expression to fulfill the requirements of the Second Law of Thermodynamics, indicating that heat (thermal energy) flows naturally from a higher-temperature region to a low-temperature region. Note also that the heat transfer rate (q) can be expressed in watts (W), where 1 watt = 1 joule/second. This law is named after the French mathematician Jean Baptiste Joseph Fourier (1768–1830).

four-way valve A valve having four controlled working passages such that there are two simultaneous flow paths through the valve; commonly used to control double-acting actuators.

fractal In general, any irregular shape, such as a snowflake, that is not normally described in geometry. In computer graphics, a surrealistic landscape or branching form created through mathematical formulas. Fractal mathematics plays a significant role in chaos theory.

fractional orbit bombardment system (FOBS) A potential method of delivering a warhead from a partial satellite orbit and therefore approaching a target on Earth from any direction with very little (if any) warning time.

fracture toughness Capability of a material to resist brittle failure.

fragment clouds Clusters of small objects placed in front of a target in space. This concept has been proposed as a relatively simple way to destroy a target.
    See also: BALLISTIC MISSILE DEFENSE.

fratricide The destructive effect of the earlier-detonating weapons in a barrage on those weapons that arrive later.

free electron laser (FEL) A multifrequency (multiwavelength) laser that achieves optical radiation amplification by a beam of (accelerator-produced) free electrons passing through a vacuum in a transverse periodic magnetic field. This laser technique differs from conventional lasers in which the oscillating electrons are bound to atoms and molecules and therefore produce optical radiation of a specific, characteristic wavelength.

free energy (symbol: ΔG) In thermodynamics, the Gibb's function (G) is defined as:

$$G = H - TS$$

where H is the total ENTHALPY, T is the absolute temperature, and S is the total ENTROPY. The change in the Gibb's function, ΔG, is sometimes called the *free energy* change for a chemical reaction and is useful for indicating the conditions under which a chemical reaction might occur. For example, if ΔG is negative, the chemical reaction will proceed to equilibrium spontaneously, while if ΔG is positive, energy must be supplied if the reaction is to proceed.
See also: THERMODYNAMICS.

free fall The unimpeded fall of an object in a gravitational field. For example, an elevator car whose cable has snapped; the plunge of a skydiver before his/her chute has been opened; or the fall back to Earth of a sounding rocket and its payload (after thrust termination and maximum altitude has been achieved) that is not retarded by a parachute or braking device.
See also: MICROGRAVITY.

free flight Unconstrained or unassisted flight, as: the flight of a rocket after consumption of its propellant or after motor shutoff; the flight of an unguided projectile.

free-flyer Any payload that can be detached from the space shuttle orbiter during the operational phase of that payload and is capable of independent operations.

free rocket A rocket not subject to guidance or control in flight.

free stream The stream of fluid outside the region influenced by a body immersed in the fluid.

frequency (common symbol: f or ν) In general, the rate of repetition of a recurring or regular

event; for example, the number of vibrations of a system per second or the number of cycles of a wave per second. For electromagnetic radiation, the frequency (ν) of a quantum packet of energy (i.e., a photon) is given by: $\nu = E/h$, where E is the photon energy and *h* is the Planck constant. The SI UNIT of frequency is the *hertz (Hz)*, which is defined as 1 cycle per second.

frequency modulation (FM) An information transfer technique used in telecommunications in which the frequency of the carrier wave is modulated (i.e., increased or decreased) as the signal (to be transferred) increases or decreases in value but the amplitude of the carrier wave remains constant. Specifically, angle modulation of a sine carrier wave in which the instantaneous frequency of the modulated wave differs from the carrier frequency by an amount proportional to the instantaneous value of the modulating wave.

Fresnel lens A thin lens constructed with stepped setbacks so as to have the optical properties of a much thicker lens.

friability The tendency of a crystalline structure to crumble.

friction The force that resists the relative motion of one body (or surface) rolling, sliding, or flowing over another body (or surface) with which it is in contact.

frontal attack 1. An offensive maneuver in which the main action is directed against the front of the enemy forces. 2. In aerospace intercept operations, an attack by an interceptor vehicle that terminates with a heading crossing angle greater than 135 degrees.

Froude number (symbol: Fr) In fluid dynamics, a nondimensional number defined as the ratio of inertia force to gravity force.

$$\text{Froude (Fr) number} = \frac{\text{inertia force}}{\text{gravity force}} = \frac{V^2}{g\, l^*}$$

where V is the velocity of the fluid, g is the acceleration of gravity, and l^* is a characteristic length.

frozen composition Exhaust gas chemical composition that does not change during expansion in the rocket's nozzle.

frustration threshold The point at which an individual feels or shows frustration over his/her inability to achieve an objective.

fuel 1. Any substance used to liberate thermal energy, either by chemical or nuclear reaction; a substance that might be used, for example, in a heat engine or a rocket engine. When discussing a liquid-propellant rocket engine, ordinarily the *fuel* (a propellant chemical such as kerosene) is distinguished from the *oxidizer* (e.g., liquid oxygen, or LOX) when these two are stored separately. 2. In nuclear technology, the term "fuel" applies to the fissionable (or fissile) material used to produce energy in a nuclear reactor. Uranium-235 is an example of nuclear reactor fuel.

fuel binder A continuous-phase substance that contributes the principal structural condition to solid propellant but does not contain any oxidizing element, either in solution or chemically bonded.

fuel cell A device that converts chemical energy directly into electrical energy by reacting with continuously supplied chemicals. The reaction is between a fuel (e.g., hydrogen) and an oxidant (e.g., oxygen—often taken from the air). It is a noncombustible reaction promoted by a catalyst. (See Figure 43.)

In many fuel cells, hydrogen is the active material at the negative electrode and oxygen is the active material at the positive electrode. Since

Figure 43. Components of a simple hydrogen-oxygen fuel cell
(Diagram courtesy of US Dept. of Energy)

hydrogen and oxygen often are used as gases in fuel cells, a typical cell requires a solid electrical conductor to serve as a current collector and to provide a terminal at each electrode. This solid electrode material is generally porous and provides a large number of sites where the gas, the electrolyte, and the electrode are in contact. The cell's electrochemical reactions occur at these sites. The reactions are normally very slow, so often a catalyst is included in the electrode to expedite processes.

One of the best electrochemical catalysts is finely divided platinum or platinumlike metal deposited on or incorporated with the porous electrode material. The very small catalyst particles provide a very large number of active sites at which the cell's electrochemical reactions can occur at a fairly rapid pace. This catalyst will gradually lose its ability during the overall lifetime of a fuel cell.

The electrochemical reaction in a hydrogen-oxygen fuel cell is the exact opposite of the electrolysis of water. The number of fuel cells determines the voltage, just as the number of battery cells determines a battery's voltage. The concept of using an electrochemical process to generate and store electrical energy in flashlight batteries is familiar to most people. In a flashlight battery, the chemical energy is stored inside the cell, whereas in a fuel cell, the chemical energy is stored outside the cell. Fuel cells will produce electricity as long as the fuel and the oxidant are supplied.

The idea of deriving electrical energy directly from oxidizable fuels has attracted attention for many years because this method enables electricity to be provided without heat engine or mechanical devices. It is possible to achieve very high conversion efficiencies using such fuel cells. Some key advantages of fuel cells in electric energy production include: (1) low noise and low pollution emissions, (2) reliability and long life due to the absence of moving parts, and (3) high energy conversion efficiency. Fuel cells have been used in many aerospace applications including electric power generation on the space shuttle orbiter. A hydrogen oxygen regenerative fuel cell (RFC) has been suggested for use on the lunar surface to support base power and life support system needs. This regenerative fuel cell system would use electricity supplied from the Sun (via solar cells) to electrolyze water into hydrogen and oxygen, which would be stored in tanks. These gases then would be used in a hydrogen-oxygen fuel cell to generate electricity (especially during the long lunar night) and produce water as a by-product. This by-product water then would be used in various life support operations, collected, and then recycled through the electrolyzer. The specific energy density for such a system is approximately 20 watt-hours/kilogram (20 Whr/kg) and an anticipated system lifetime of between five and seven years.

fuel consumption The mass rate of fuel use (typically kg/sec or lb_{mass}/sec) by a rocket engine or power plant.

fuel shutoff The termination of the flow of liquid fuel into a rocket's combustion chamber; or the process of stopping the combustion (burning) of a solid rocket fuel. The event or time marking this particular action. Compare this term with CUTOFF.

functional kill The destruction of a target by disabling vital components in a way not immediately detectable but nevertheless able to prevent the target from functioning properly. For example, the destruction of electronics components in a guidance system of a hostile missile by a space-based neutral particle beam (NPB) weapon system.

See also: BALLISTIC MISSILE DEFENSE.

fuse Igniting device consisting of a detonating or deflagrating train for the propagation of ignition energy.

fuselage The central part of an aircraft or aerospace vehicle that accommodates crew, passengers, payload, or cargo.

fusion (nuclear) In nuclear fusion, lighter atomic nuclei are joined together, or fused, to form a heavy nucleus. For example, the fusion of deuterium (D) with tritium (T), both isotopes of the element hydrogen, results in the formation of a helium (He) nucleus and a neutron (n). Because the total mass of the fusion products is less than the total mass of the reactants (i.e., the original deuterium and tritium nuclei), a tiny amount of mass has disappeared, and the equivalent amount of energy is released in accordance with Einstein's mass-energy equivalence formula, $E = m c^2$. This fusion energy then appears as the kinetic (motion) energy of the reaction products. When isotopes of elements lighter than iron (Fe) fuse together, some energy is liberated. Energy must be added to any fusion reaction involving elements heavier than iron.

The Sun is our oldest sources of fusion energy, the very mainstay of all terrestrial life. The energy of the Sun and other stars comes from thermonuclear-fusion reactions. Fusion reactions brought about by means of very high temperature are called *thermonuclear reactions*. The actual temperature required to join, or fuse, two atomic nuclei depends on the nuclei and the particular fusion reaction involved. (Remember, the two nuclei being joined must have enough energy to overcome Coulombic, or "like-electric charge," repulsion.) In stellar interiors, fusion occurs at temperatures of tens of millions of degrees Kelvin (K). When we try to develop useful controlled thermonuclear reactions (CTR) here on Earth, reaction temperatures of 50 million to 100 million° K are necessary.

Table 1.
SINGLE-STEP FUSION REACTIONS USEFUL IN POWER
AND PROPULSION SYSTEMS

Nomenclature	Thermonuclear Reaction	Energy Released Per Reaction (MeV) [Q Value]	Threshold Plasma Temperature (keV)[a]
(D-T)	${}_1^2D + {}_1^3T \rightarrow {}_2^4He + {}_0^1n$	17.6	10
(D-D)	${}_1^2D + {}_1^2D \rightarrow {}_2^3He + {}_0^1n$	3.2	50
	${}_1^2D + {}_1^2D \rightarrow {}_1^3T + {}_1^1P$	4.0	50
(D-³He)	${}_1^2D + {}_2^3He \rightarrow {}_2^4He + {}_1^1p$	18.3	100
(¹¹B-p)	${}_5^{11}B + {}_1^1p \rightarrow 3({}_2^4He)$	8.7	300

[a]10 keV = 100 million degrees Kelvin.
Note: D is deuterium; T is tritium; He is helium; n is neutron; p is proton; B is boron.

Table 1 describes the major single-step thermonuclear reactions that are potentially useful in controlled fusion reactions for power and propulsion applications. Large space settlements and human-made "miniplanets" eventually might be powered by such CTR processes, while robotic interstellar probes and giant inhabited "space arks" could use fusion for both power and propulsion. Helium-3 is a rare helium isotope. Some space visionaries have proposed mining the Jovian atmosphere or the lunar surface for helium-3 to fuel our first interstellar probes or to help resolve Earth's long-term energy needs.

At present, immense technical difficulties prevent our effective use of controlled fusion as a terrestrial or space energy source. The key problem is that the fusion gas mixture must be heated to tens of millions of degrees K and held together for a long enough time for the fusion reaction to occur. For example, a deuterium-tritium gas mixture must be heated to at least 50 million° K—and this is considered the easiest controlled fusion reaction to achieve. At 50 million degrees, any physical material used to confine these fusion gases would disintegrate, and the vaporized wall materials would then "cool" the fusion gas mixture, quenching the reaction.

There are three general approaches to confining these hot fusion gases, or plasmas: gravitational confinement, magnetic confinement, and inertial confinement.

Because of their large masses, the Sun and other stars are able to hold the reacting fusion gases together by gravitational confinement. Interior temperatures in stars reach tens of millions of degrees K and use complete thermonuclear-fusion cycles to generate their vast quantities of energy. For main sequence stars similar to or cooler than our Sun (about 10 million° K), the proton-proton cycle, shown in Table 2, is believed to be the principal energy-liberating mechanism. The overall effect of the proton-proton stellar fusion cycle is the conversion of hydrogen into helium. Stars hotter than our Sun (i.e., those with interior temperatures of 10 million° K and higher) release energy through the carbon cycle, shown in Table 3. The overall effect of this cycle is again the conversion of hydrogen into helium, but this time with carbon (the carbon-12 isotope) serving as a catalyst.

Scientists have attempted to achieve controlled fusion through two basic techniques: magnetic-confinement fusion (MCF) and inertial-confinement fusion (ICF). In the magnetic confinement approach, strong magnetic fields are used to "bottle up," or hold, the intensely hot plasmas needed to make the various single-step fusion reactions occur. In the inertial-confinement approach, pulses of laser light, energetic electrons, or heavy ions are used to very rapidly compress and heat small spherical targets of fusion material. This rapid compression and heating of an ICF target allows the conditions supporting fusion to be reached in the interior of the pellet—before it blows itself apart.

Although many difficult technical issues remain to be resolved before we can achieve controlled fusion, it promises to provide an essentially limitless terrestrial energy supply and represents a powerful technology in the full exploration and settlement of our solar system and regions beyond.

In sharp contrast to previous and current scientific attempts at controlled nuclear fusion for

---

Table 2.
MAIN THERMONUCLEAR REACTIONS IN THE PROTON-PROTON CYCLE

$${}^{1}_{1}H + {}^{1}_{1}H \rightarrow {}^{2}_{1}D + e^{+} + \upsilon$$
$${}^{2}_{1}D + {}^{1}_{1}H \rightarrow {}^{3}_{2}He + \gamma$$
$${}^{3}_{2}He + {}^{3}_{2}He \rightarrow {}^{4}_{2}He + {}^{1}_{1}H + {}^{1}_{1}H$$

Note: ${}^{1}_{1}H$ is a hydrogen nucleus (that is, a proton, ${}^{1}_{1}p$); ${}^{2}_{1}D$ is deuterium (an isotope of hydrogen); ${}^{3}_{2}He$ is helium -3 (a rare isotope of helium); ${}^{4}_{2}He$ is the main (stable) isotope of helium; υ is a neutrino; ε^{+} is a positron; γ is a gamma ray.

Table 3.
MAJOR THERMONUCLEAR REACTIONS IN THE CARBON CYCLE

$${}^{12}_{6}C + {}^{1}_{1}H \rightarrow {}^{13}_{7}N + \gamma$$
$${}^{13}_{7}N \rightarrow + {}^{13}_{6}C\ e^{+} + \upsilon \quad \text{(radioactive decay)}$$
$${}^{1}_{1}H + {}^{13}_{6}C \rightarrow {}^{14}_{7}N + \gamma$$
$${}^{1}_{1}H + {}^{14}_{7}N \rightarrow {}^{15}_{8}O + \gamma$$
$${}^{15}_{8}O \rightarrow + {}^{15}_{7}N\ e^{+} + \upsilon \quad \text{(radioactive decay)}$$
$${}^{1}_{1}H + {}^{15}_{7}N \rightarrow {}^{12}_{6}C + {}^{4}_{2}He$$

Note: g is a gamma ray; u is a neutrino; e+ is a positron.

power and propulsion applications, since the early 1950s nuclear weapon designers have been able to harness (however briefly) certain fusion reactions in advanced weapon systems called *thermonuclear weapons*. In these types of nuclear weapons, the energy of a fission bomb is used to create the conditions necessary to achieve (for a brief moment) a significant number of fusion reactions of either the deuterium-tritium (D-T) or deuterium-deuterium (D-D) kind. Very powerful modern thermonuclear weapons have been designed and demonstrated with total explosive yields from a few hundred kilotons to the multimegaton range. (Ton here refers to the explosive equivalent of 1,000 kilograms (kg) [a 2,000 pounds-mass (lbm)] of the chemical high explosive trinitrotoluene, or TNT.)

See also: INTERSTELLAR TRAVEL; STARS; SUN.

fusion weapon A nuclear weapon that uses the energy of fusion; a thermonuclear weapon or "hydrogen" bomb.

g The symbol used for the acceleration due to gravity. For example, at sea level on Earth the acceleration due to gravity is approximately 9.8 meters per second-squared (32.2 feet per second-squared)—that is, "one g." This term is used as a unit of stress for bodies experiencing acceleration. When a spacecraft or aerospace vehicle is accelerated during launch, everything inside it experiences a force that may be as high as several gs.

gage pressure (symbol: p_G) In engineering, a term used to indicate the difference between atmospheric pressure (p_{ATMOS}) and absolute pressure (p_{ABS}).

gain 1. An increase or amplification. 2. In electrical engineering, this term is used to describe the ability of an electronic device to increase the magnitude of an electrical input parameter. For example, the gain of a power amplifier is defined as the ratio of the output power to the input power. Gain usually is expressed in decibels. 3. In signal processing, gain is used to denote an increase in signal power in transmission from one point to another. 4. In radar technology, there are two frequently encountered general uses of this term: (a) *antenna gain*, or gain factor, which is defined as the power transmitted along the radar beam axis to that of an isotropic radiator transmitting the same total power; and (b) *receiver gain*, which is the amplification given to an incoming radar signal by the receiver.

gal (derived from: *Galileo*) A unit of acceleration equal to 10^{-2} meter per second-squared (or 1 centimeter per second-squared). The name was chosen to honor Galileo Galilei (1564–1642), the famous

Italian scientist who conducted early experiments involving the acceleration of gravity. The gal and the "milligal" (1000 milligal = 1 gal) often are encountered in geological survey work, where tiny differences in the acceleration due to gravity at Earth's surface are important.

galactic Of or pertaining to a galaxy, such as the Milky Way galaxy.

galactic cluster A diffuse collection of from ten to perhaps several hundred stars, loosely held together by gravitational forces. Also called an *open cluster*.
See also: GLOBULAR CLUSTER.

galactic cosmic rays (GCRs) Very energetic atomic particles that originate outside the solar system and generally are believed to come from within our Milky Way Galaxy.
See also: COSMIC RAYS.

galaxy A very large accumulation of from 10^6 to 10^{12} stars. Galaxies—or "island universes," as they are sometimes called—come in a variety of shapes and sizes. They range from dwarf galaxies, such as the Magellanic Clouds, to giant spiral galaxies, such as the Andromeda Galaxy. Astronomers usually classify galaxies as elliptical, spiral (or barred spiral), or irregular. Galaxies are typically tens to hundreds of thousands of light-years across, and the distance between neighboring galaxies is generally a few million light-years. For example, the Andromeda Galaxy is approximately 130,000 light-years in diameter and about 2.2 million light-years away.

Galilean satellites The four largest and brightest satellites of the planet, Jupiter: Io, Europa,

Ganymede, and Callisto. These major Jovian moons were discovered by the famous Italian scientist Galileo Galilei in 1610.

See also: JUPITER.

Galileo Project NASA's Galileo spacecraft was launched into Earth orbit on board the space shuttle *Atlantis* on October 18, 1989. An inertial upper stage (IUS) boosted the spacecraft from low Earth orbit into its interplanetary trajectory. Its six-year journey to Jupiter used a Venus-Earth-Earth Gravity Assist (VEEGA) trajectory that provided the spacecraft sufficient energy to reach the giant planet in December 1995. The Galileo mission included a 2,668-kilogram (kg) (5,883 pounds-mass [lbm]) orbiter spacecraft and a 335-kg (740-lbm) atmospheric probe, which was released about 150 days before arrival at Jupiter and successfully entered Jupiter's atmosphere on December 7, 1995. The probe then relayed data obtained during its 57-minute descent mission back to the Galileo orbiter, which was more than 209,000 kilometers (km) (130,000 miles [mi]) overhead, for storage and transmission back to Earth. The Galileo orbiter spacecraft, powered by two plutonium-238 fueled, radioisotope thermoelectric generator (RTG) units, is now engaged in a mission to study Jupiter and its moons.

The Galileo atmospheric probe detected extremely strong winds and very intense turbulence during its descent through Jupiter's thick atmosphere. These data provided space scientists preliminary evidence that the energy source driving much of Jupiter's distinctive circulation phenomena is probably heat (thermal energy) escaping from the deep interior of the planet. The successful probe also discovered an intense new radiation belt about 50,000 km (31,000 mi) above Jupiter's cloud tops. Following probe parachute deployment, six science instruments on the Galileo probe collected data throughout 156 km (97 mi) of the descent. During that time, the probe endured severe winds, periods of intense cold and heat, and strong turbulence. The extreme temperatures and pressures of the Jovian environment eventually caused the probe communications subsystem to terminate transmission operations.

The Galileo orbiter spacecraft is now injected into a highly elliptical orbit around Jupiter and is studying the giant planet, the four major Jovian moons (Io, Europa, Ganymede, and Callisto), and Jupiter's magnetosphere. The orbiter is using Jovian satellite gravity assists to fly a series of ever-changing elliptical paths through a broad region of Jupiter's environment, including at least one pass deep into the Jovian magnetotail, a region not previously studied.

During its long journey through interplanetary space, the Galileo spacecraft survived the failure of its high-gain antenna to unfurl properly (in April 1991) and problems with a tape recorder and a stuck fuel valve. On October 29, 1991 the spacecraft completed the first-ever flyby of an asteroid (called Gaspra); in August 1993 it flew past the asteroid Ida and took images showing a tiny moon (now called Dactyl) orbiting this asteroid. Finally, the spacecraft was the only scientific instrument to have a direct view of the collision of the Comet Shoemaker-Levy 9 with Jupiter (in July 1994). The Galileo spacecraft is named in honor of the Italian Renaissance scientist Galileo Galilei, who discovered Jupiter's major moons in 1610.

See also: JUPITER.

gallon (or imperial gallon; symbol: gal) A unit of volume in the foot-pound-second British imperial units system. The imperial gallon is defined as the volume occupied by precisely 10 pounds (mass) of distilled water that has a density of 0.998859 gram per milliliter in air at a density of 0.001217 gram per milliliter. The imperial gallon is somewhat larger than the gallon used in the United States.

1 imperial gallon = 1.20094 U.S. gallons = 4.5460 liters

or

1 U.S. gallon = 0.83268 imperial gallon = 3.7854 liters

gamma ray astronomy Astronomy based on the detection of gamma rays. Gamma ray astronomy reveals the explosive, high-energy processes associated with such celestial phenomena as supernovae, exploding galaxies, quasars, pulsars, and suspected black holes. This field of astronomy is especially significant because the gamma rays being observed by spacecraft orbiting Earth might have traveled across our entire galaxy, or perhaps even across most of the universe, without suffering appreciable line-of-sight alteration or loss of energy. Consequently, these energetic gamma rays reach our solar system with essentially the same characteristics, including directional and temporal features, as they started with at their sources. Gamma ray astronomy can provide important information on astrophysical phenomena not observable at other wavelengths in the electromagnetic spectrum and on spectacularly energetic events (e.g., matter-antimatter annihilation) that may have occurred far back in the evolutionary history of the universe.

See also: GAMMA RAYS; GAMMA RAY OBSERVATORY.

Gamma Ray Observatory (GRO) NASA's Compton Gamma Ray Observatory was deployed successfully by the space shuttle *Atlantis* on April 7, 1991 during Shuttle Mission STS-37 in low Earth orbit and then boosted to a higher circular orbit. This large spacecraft carries a variety of sensitive instruments designed to detect gamma rays over an extensive range of energies. The GRO is an extremely powerful tool for investigating some of the most puzzling mysteries in the universe, including gamma ray bursts, pulsars, quasars, and active galaxies. The Gamma Ray Observatory has four major instruments: the Burst and Transient Source Experiment (BATSE), the Imaging Compton Telescope (COMPTEL), the Oriented Scintillation Spectrometer Experiment (OSSE), and the Energetic Gamma Ray Experiment Telescope (EGRET). Space scientists and astronomers are now using data from the GRO to achieve the following objectives: (1) to study dynamic evolutionary forces in compact objects such as neutron stars and black holes; (2) to search for evidence of nucleosynthesis (the process of creating heavy elements in violent, supernova explosions); (3) to study gamma ray–emitting objects whose nature is not now understood; (4) to conduct a gamma ray emission survey of our own galaxy; (5) to study the nature of other galaxies in the energetic realm of gamma rays; and (6) to conduct a search for possible primordial black hole emissions. Also called the *NASA Compton Gamma Ray Observatory.*

gamma rays (symbol: γ) High-energy, very-short-wavelength packets or quanta of electromagnetic radiation. Gamma ray photons are similar to X rays, except that they are usually more energetic and originate from processes and transitions within the atomic nucleus. Gamma rays typically have energies between 10,000 electron volts and 10 million electron volts (i.e., between 10 keV and 10 MeV) with correspondingly short wavelengths and high frequencies. The processes associated with gamma ray emissions in astrophysical phenomena include: (1) the decay of radioactive nuclei, (2) cos-

mic ray interactions, (3) curvature radiation in extremely strong magnetic fields, and (4) matter-antimatter annihilation. Gamma rays are very penetrating and are best stopped or shielded against by dense materials, such as lead or tungsten. Sometimes called *gamma radiation.*

See also: GAMMA RAY ASTRONOMY, GAMMA RAY OBSERVATORY.

gantry A frame that spans over something, such as an elevated platform that runs astride a work area, supported by wheels on each side. Specifically, the term is short for *gantry crane* or *gantry scaffold.*

gantry crane A large crane mounted on a platform that usually runs back and forth on parallel tracks astride a work area. Often shortened to *gantry.*

gantry scaffold A massive scaffolding structure mounted on a bridge or platform supported by a pair of towers or trestles that normally run back and forth on parallel tracks. This structure is used to assemble and/or service a large rocket vehicle as the rocket rests on its launch pad. The term often is shortened to *gantry.* The term "service tower" also is used.

gas The state of matter in which the molecules are practically unrestricted by intermolecular forces so that the molecules are free to occupy any space within an enclosure.

See also: IDEAL GAS.

gas cap The gas immediately in front of a body (such as a reentry vehicle or meteor) as it travels through a planetary atmosphere. This region of atmospheric gas is compressed and adiabatically heated, often to incandescence.

gas chromatograph An instrument for organic chemical analysis used to identify gases and volatile molecular species through their residence times in adsorption columns of various lengths, diameters, and materials. In an instrument called the gas chromatograph-mass spectrometer (GCMS), a gas chromatograph is used to separate a mixture into its basic components, which are then fed directly into a mass spectrometer for a determination of the relative abundances of these components.

gas constant (symbol: R_u) The constant factor in the equation of state for an ideal (perfect) gas. The universal gas constant is

R_u = 8.315 joules per mole per degree Kelvin [J/(mol-°K)]

The gas constant for a particular, nonideal gas is called the *specific gas constant* (symbol: R_{sp}) and is related to the universal gas constant as follows:

$R_{sp} = R_u/M$ where M is the molecular weight of the particular gas.

See also: IDEAL GAS.

gas distributor A passive device that determines the flow pattern of the gas entering an ullage space. The term "ullage" refers to the amount that a container, such as a propellant tank, lacks of being full.

gas generator 1. An assemblage of parts similar to a small rocket engine in which a propellant is burned to provide hot exhaust gases. These hot gases are then used to: (1) drive the turbine in the turbopump assembly of a rocket vehicle, or (2) pressurize liquid propellants, or (3) provide thrust by exhausting through a nozzle. 2. A device used in a laboratory to generate gases, such as hydrogen and oxygen from water.

gasket A preformed deformable part designed to be placed between two adjoining, relatively static parts to prevent the leakage of liquid or gas between the parts.

gas laws The thermodynamic laws applying to the behavior of ideal (perfect) gases.
See also: IDEAL GAS.

gas scrubbing The process of contacting a gaseous mixture with a liquid for the purpose of removing gaseous contaminants or entrained liquids or solids.

gas-solid interactions The effects of the impingement of gases (and tiny particles) on solid surfaces in various environments.

gas solubility The capability of a given gas to dissolve in a given fluid under specified thermophysical conditions.

gas turbine A heat engine that uses high-temperature, high-pressure gas as a working fluid. Its operation approximates the ideal *Brayton cycle,* and a

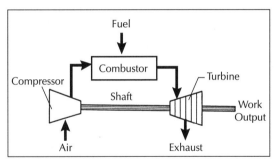

Figure 44. The major components of an open-cycle gas turbine heat engine *(Diagram courtesy of U.S. Department of Energy)*

portion of the energy content of the gaseous working fluid is converted directly into work (i.e., rotating shaft action). Often the hot gases for operation of a gas turbine are obtained by the combustion of a fuel in air. These types of gas turbines are also called *combustion turbines.* The simplest combustion gas turbine heat engine is the open cycle system, which has three major components: the compressor, the combustion chamber (or combustor), and the gas turbine itself. (See Figure 44.) The compressor and turbine usually are mounted on the same shaft, so that a portion of the mechanical ("shaft") work produced by the turbine can be used to drive the compressor.
See also: BRAYTON CYCLE.

gauss (symbol: G or Gs) In the centimeter-gram-second (cgs) unit system, the unit of magnetic flux density. Earth's magnetic field at the planet's surface is on the average 0.3 to 0.6 gauss.

1 gauss = 10^{-4} tesla

Gaussian distribution In statistics, a *normal* distribution. A normal distribution is represented by a "bell-shaped" curve that is symmetrical about the mean value $\bar{x}$, which represents the most probable value in the distribution.

Geiger counter A nuclear radiation detection and measurement instrument. It contains a gas-filled tube containing electrodes between which there is an electrical voltage but no current flowing. When ionizing radiation passes through the tube, a short, intense pulse of current passes from the negative electrode to the positive electrode and is measured or counted. The number of pulses per second mea-

SUMMARY OF GEMINI PROJECT MISSIONS

Mission	Date(s) Recovery Ship	Crew	Ground Elapsed Time (GET) Hr:min	Remarks
Gemini 3 (Molly Brown)	March 23, 1965 Intrepid (A)	USAF Maj. Virgil I. Grissom Navy Lt. Comdr. John W. Young	4:53	3 orbits
Gemini 4	June 3-7, 1965 Wasp (A)	USAF Majors James A. McDivitt and Edward H. White, II	97:56	62 orbits:first U.S. EVA (White)
Gemini 5	Aug. 21-29, 1965 Lake Champlain (A)	USAF Lt. Col. L. Gordon Cooper Navy Lt. Comdr. Charles Conrad, Jr.	190:55	120 orbits
Gemini 7	Dec. 4-18, 1965 Wasp (A)	USAF Lt. Col. Frank Borman Navy Comdr. James A. Lovell, Jr.	330:35	Longest Gemini flight; rendezvous target for Gemini 6; 206 orbits
Gemini 6	Dec. 15-16, 1965 Wasp (A)	Navy Capt. Walter M. Schirra, Jr. USAF Maj. Thomas P. Stafford	25:51	Rendezvoused within 1 ft of Gemini 7; 16 orbits
Gemini 8	Mar. 16, 1966 L. F. Mason (P)	Civilian Neil A. Armstrong USAF Maj. David R. Scott	10:41	Docked with unmanned Agena 8; 7 orbits
Gemini 9A	June 3-6, 1966 Wasp (A)	USAF Lt. Col. Thomas P. Stafford Navy Lt. Comdr. Eugene A. Cernan	72:21	Rendezvous (3) with Agena 9; one EVA; 44 orbits
Gemini 10	July 18-21, 1966 Guadalcanal (A)	Navy Comdr. John W. Young USAF Maj. Michael Collins	70:47	Docked with Agena 10; rendezvoused with Agena 8; two EVAs; 43 orbits
Gemini 11	Sept. 12-15, 1966 Guam (A)	Navy Comdr. Charles Conrad, Jr. Navy Lt. Comdr. Richard F. Gordon, Jr.	71:17	Docked with Agena 11 twice; first tethered flights; two EVAs; highest altitude in Gemini program; 853 miles; 44 orbits
Gemini 12	Nov. 11-15, 1966 Wasp (A)	Navy Capt. James A. Lovell, Jr. USAF Maj. Edwin E. Aldrin, Jr.	94:35	Three EVAs total 5 hrs. 30 min.; 59 orbits

Note: A = Atlantic Ocean
      P = Pacific Ocean
      EVA = Extravehicular Activity

Source: NASA.

sures the intensity of the radiation. This instrument is also called a *Geiger-Müller counter* and is named for Hans Geiger and W. Müller who developed it in the 1920s.

Gemini Project The Gemini Project (1964–1966) was the second U.S. crewed space program and the

beginning of sophisticated human space flight. It expanded and refined the scientific and technological endeavors of the Mercury Project and prepared the way for the more sophisticated Apollo Project, which carried U.S. astronauts to the lunar surface. The Gemini Project added a second crew member and a maneuverable spacecraft. New objectives included rendezvous and docking techniques with orbiting spacecraft and extravehicular "walks in space." In all, ten two-person launches occurred, successfully placing 20 astronauts in orbit and returning them safely to Earth. The table summarizes the Gemini Project flights.

See also: APOLLO PROJECT; MERCURY PROJECT.

general relativity The theory of gravity and the nature of gravitational forces as expounded by Albert Einstein (1879—1955).

See also: RELATIVITY.

generation In any technological development, such as of a missile, aerospace vehicle, or spacecraft, a period that is marked by features or performances not existing in a previous period of development or production. For example, the *third generation* of rockets using hydrogen and oxygen as liquid propellants.

geo- A prefix meaning the planet *Earth;* as in *geology* and *geophysics.*

geocentric Relative to Earth as a center; measured from the center of Earth.

geodesy In general, the science of determining the exact size and shape of bodies in our solar system and of the distribution of mass within these bodies. Specifically, the science that deals mathematically with the size and shape of Earth, Earth's external gravity field, and with surveys of such precision that the overall size and shape of Earth must be taken into consideration.

geodetic Pertaining to GEODESY, the science that deals with the size and shape of Earth.

geographic information system (GIS) A computer-assisted system that acquires, stores, manipulates, compares, and displays geographic data, often including multispectral imagery data sets from Earth-observation spacecraft.

geoid The figure of Earth as defined by the geopotential surface that most nearly coincides with mean sea level over the entire surface of Earth.

geomagnetic storm Sudden worldwide fluctuations in Earth's magnetic field, associated with solar flare-generated shock waves that propagate from the Sun to Earth. Geomagnetic storms may significantly alter ionospheric current densities over large portions of the middle- and high-latitude regions of Earth, impacting high-frequency (HF) systems. During a solar storm, large numbers of particles are dumped into the high-altitude atmosphere. These particles produce heating effects (especially near the auroral zone), which then alter the near-Earth-space atmospheric densities from about 100 kilometers (62.1 mi) out to about 1,000 kilometers, impacting the operation of spacecraft orbiting Earth at altitudes below 1,000 kilometers. Polar-orbiting spacecraft can be especially impacted, as, for example, by an increase in atmospheric drag.

geophysics The branch of science dealing with Earth and its environment—that is, the solid Earth itself, the hydrosphere (oceans and seas), the atmosphere, and (by extension) near-Earth space. Classically, geophysics has been concerned primarily with physical phenomena occurring at and below the surface of Earth. This traditional emphasis gave rise to such companion disciplines as geology, physical oceanography, seismology, hydrology, and geodesy. With the advent of the space age, the trend has been to extend the scope of geophysics to include meteorology, geomagnetism, astrophysics, and other sciences concerned with the physical nature of the universe.

geoprobe A rocket vehicle designed to explore outer space near Earth at a distance of more than 6,440 kilometers (km) (4,000 miles) from Earth's surface. By convention, rocket vehicles operating lower than 6,440 km are called *sounding rockets.*

geosphere The solid (*lithosphere*) and liquid (*hydrosphere*) portions of Earth. Above the geosphere lies the *atmosphere,* at the interface between these two regions is found almost all of the *biosphere,* or zone of life.

geostationary Earth orbit (GEO) An orbit at an altitude of 35,900 kilometers (km) (22,310 miles) above Earth's equator (or 42,400 km [26,350 miles]) from Earth's center in which a satellite or spacecraft revolves around Earth at the same rate at which Earth rotates on its axis (namely, 23 hours, 56 minutes, and 4.1 seconds). If the orbit is circular and lies in the equatorial plane, the satellite, when observed from Earth, will appear to be stationary (or geostationary) over a given point on Earth's surface. If the satellite's orbit is inclined to the equatorial plane, then the satellite, when observed from Earth's surface, will appear to trace out a figure-of-eight path every 24 hours. Geostationary Earth orbit is a very useful location for global communication satellites, surveillance satellites, and certain meteorological and environmental monitoring satellites. Compare with: GEOSYNCHRONOUS ORBIT; SYNCHRONOUS ORBIT.

Geostationary Operational Environmental Satellite (GOES) GOES weather satellites maintain orbital positions over the same Earth location along the equator at about 36,000 kilometers (22,300 miles) above Earth, giving them the ability to make continuous observations of weather patterns over and near the United States. Operated by the U.S. National Oceanic and Atmospheric Administration (NOAA), these satellites provide both visible light and infrared images of cloud patterns as well as "soundings," or indirect measurements, of the temperature and humidity throughout the atmosphere. NOAA has been operating GOES satellites since 1974. Data from these spacecraft provide input for the forecasting responsibilities of the National Weather Service. Among other applications, the GOES data assist in monitoring

storms and provide advance warning of emerging severe weather. The geostationary vantage point of GOES satellites permits the observation of large-scale weather events, which is required for forecasting small-scale events. (See Figure 45.)

See also: WEATHER SATELLITE.

geosynchronous orbit (GEO) An orbit of Earth, in which the satellite or space platform has a period precisely equal to the period of Earth's rotation on its axis, namely 23 hours, 56 minutes, and 4.1 seconds. A satellite placed in such an orbit (approximately 35,900 kilometers [22,310 miles] altitude above the equator) revolves around Earth once per day, maintaining the same position relative to the surface of Earth.

See also: GEOSTATIONARY EARTH ORBIT; SYNCHRONOUS ORBIT.

get To remove gas from a vacuum system or device by sorption.

Get Away Special (GAS) The popular name given to the NASA Self-Contained Payload Program, a program intended to fly small payloads (i.e., those with a mass of 90 kilograms [200 lb$_m$] or less) for both public and private groups in self-contained canisters on a space-available basis in the cargo bay

Figure 45. Major components of a future generation of GOES satellites, called GOES-Next *(Drawing courtesy of NASA)*

of the space shuttle. Depending on the features of the GAS canister used, a GAS payload could experience prolonged microgravity, be exposed to the space environment, or even be ejected into space. The "self-contained" nature of the program requires that the small payload provide all its own power and data recording capabilities, since these services are not provided to the GAS canister by the space shuttle orbiter. However, an astronaut can provide simple on-off commands to the GAS canister (via a handheld control panel) once Earth orbit is achieved and the shuttle's cargo bay doors are opened.

See also: SPACE TRANSPORTATION SYSTEM (STS).

getter A material that is included in a vacuum system or device for removing gas by sorption.

geysering The accumulation of gas in a line and the subsequent expulsion of liquid from the line by a gas bubble.

g-force An inertial force usually expressed in multiples of terrestrial gravity.
See also: G.

giant planets In our solar system, the large, gaseous outer planets: Jupiter, Saturn, Uranus, and Neptune.

gibbous A term used to describe a phase of a moon or planet when more than half, but not all, of the illuminated disk can be viewed by the observer.

Gibbs function (symbol: G) A mathematically defined thermodynamic function of state that is constant during a reversible isobaric-isothermal process. In symbols the specific Gibbs function (symbol: g) is

$$g = h - Ts$$

where h is specific ENTHALPY; s is specific ENTROPY; and T is ABSOLUTE TEMPERATURE. Also called *Gibbs free energy, thermodynamic potential.* Compare HELMHOLTZ FUNCTION.

giga- (symbol: G) A prefix meaning multiplied by 10^9.

gigabit A quantity of binary notation data equivalent to one billion (10^9) bits.

gigabyte (symbol: GB) An amount of information (computer data) equivalent to one billion (10^9) bytes.

gigahertz (symbol: GHz) One billion cycles per second, or 10^9 hertz. The proposed satellite power system (SPS), which would beam microwave energy back to receiver stations on Earth, would operate at 2.45 gigahertz; home microwave ovens also operate at gigahertz frequencies.

gigawatt (symbol: GW) One billion watts, or 10^9 W. A gigawatt is a very large amount of power. For example, a modern nuclear reactor powerplant typically has a thermal power level of about 3,000 megawatts (MW) or 3 gigawatts (GW).

gimbal 1. A device, on which an engine or other object may be mounted, that has two mutually perpendicular and intersecting axes of rotation and therefore provides free angular movement in two directions. 2. In a gyroscope, a support that provides the spin axis with a degree of freedom. 3. To move a reaction engine about on a gimbal so as to obtain pitching and yawing correction moments. 4. To mount something on a gimbal.

gimbaled motor A rocket engine mounted on a gimbal.

***Giotto* spacecraft** The European Space Agency's (ESA's) first deep-space spacecraft, *Giotto,* was launched on July 2, 1985 from the agency's Kourou, French Guiana, launch site by an Ariane-1 rocket. It successfully encountered the nucleus of Halley's Comet in mid-March 1986, as the spacecraft streaked within 600 kilometers (km) on the sunward side of the comet's nucleus at a relative encounter velocity of 68.4 km per second. Despite the hazardous cometary dust and particle environment, the spacecraft survived this encounter. All its experiments performed very well and returned a great deal of scientific information. The most important of these, perhaps, was the first clear identification of the cometary nucleus. *Giotto's* camera recorded many images and gave scientists a unique opportunity to determine the shape and material composition of Comet Halley's nucleus.

Though damaged by multiple particle impacts, *Giotto* successfully carried on with its Halley encounter mission. Upon completion of the Halley encounter, the spacecraft was put in a "quiet," or hibernation, mode, while it continued to travel in deep space. It was reactivated in February 1990 for a new task—this time to observe the Comet Grigg-Skjellerup. On July 10, 1992 the *Giotto* spacecraft passed within about 200 km of Comet Grigg-Skjellerup. Once again good-quality scientific data were acquired during this second comet encounter, an activity often called the Giotto Extended Mission (GEM). The spacecraft is now in hibernation awaiting reactivation for possible scientific activities in 1999 and beyond.

This highly successful ESA spacecraft was named *Giotto* after the famous Italian painter Giotto di Bondone (1266–1337), who apparently witnessed the 1301 passage of Comet Halley and then included the first "scientific" representation of this comet in his famous fresco, *Adoration of the Magi*, which can be found in the Scrovegni Chapel in Padua, Italy.

See also: COMET; EUROPEAN SPACE AGENCY.

glide 1. A controlled descent by a heavier-than-air aeronautical or aerospace vehicle under little or no engine thrust in which forward motion is maintained by gravity and vertical descent is maintained by lift forces. 2. A descending flight path of a glide, such as a shallow *glide.* 3. To descend in a *glide.*

glide path The flight path (seen from the side) of an aeronautical or aerospace vehicle in a GLIDE.

glider A fixed-wing aircraft specially designed to GLIDE, or to glide and soar. This type of aircraft ordinarily has no powerplant.

glide ratio The ratio of the horizontal distance traveled to the vertical distance descended in a GLIDE. Also called *gliding ratio.*

glitch A minor problem, malfunction, or difficulty.

global change Earth's environment has been subject to great change over eons. Many of these changes have occurred quite slowly, requiring numerous millennia to achieve their full impact and effect. However, other global changes have occurred relatively rapidly over time periods as short as a few decades or less. These global changes appear in response to such phenomena as the migration of continents, the building and erosion

of mountains, changes in the Sun's energy output or variations in Earth's orbital parameters, the reorganization of oceans, and even the catastrophic impact of a large asteroid or comet. Such natural phenomena lead to planetary changes on local, regional, and global scales, including a succession of warm and cool climate epochs, new distributions of tropical rain forests and rich grasslands, the appearance and disappearance of large deserts and marshlands, the advances and retreats of great ice sheets (glaciers), the rise and fall of ocean and lake levels, and even the extinction of vast numbers of species. The last great mass extinction (on a global basis) appears to have occurred some 65 million years ago, possibly due to the impact of a large asteroid. The peak of the most recent period of glaciation generally is considered to have occurred about 18,000 years ago, when average global temperatures were about 5° Celsius (9° Fahrenheit) cooler than today.

Although such global changes are the inevitable results of major natural forces currently beyond human control, it is also apparent to scientists that humans have become a powerful agent for environmental change. For example, the chemistry of Earth's atmosphere has been altered significantly by both the agricultural and industrial revolutions. The erosion of the continents and sedimentation of rivers and shorelines have been influenced dramatically by agricultural and construction practices. The production and release of toxic chemicals have affected the health and natural distributions of biotic populations. The ever-expanding human need for water resources has affected the patterns of natural water exchange that take place in the hydrological cycle (the oceans, surface and ground water, clouds, etc.). One example is the enhanced evaporation rate from large human-engineered reservoirs compared to the smaller natural evaporation rate from wild, unregulated rivers. This increased evaporation rate from large-engineered reservoirs demonstrates how human activities can change natural processes significantly on a local or even regional scale. Such environmental changes may not always be beneficial and often may not have been anticipated at the start of the project or activity. As the world population grows and human civilization undergoes further technological development in the next century, the role of our planet's most influential animal species as an agent of environmental change undoubtedly will expand.

Over the past three decades, scientists have accumulated technical evidence that indicates that ongoing environmental changes are the result of complex interactions among a number of natural and human-related systems. For example, the changes in Earth's climate now are considered to involve not only wind patterns and atmospheric cloud populations but also the interactive effects of the biosphere and ocean currents, human influences on atmospheric chemistry, Earth's orbital parameters, the reflective properties of our planetary system (Earth's ALBEDO) and the distribution of water among the atmosphere, hydrosphere, and cryosphere (polar ice). The aggregate of these interactive linkages among our planet's major natural and human-made systems that appear to affect the environment has become known as *global change.*

The governments of many nations, including the United States, have begun to address the issues associated with global change. Over the last decade, preliminary results from global observation programs (many involving space-based systems) have stimulated a new set of concerns that the dramatic rise of industrial and agricultural activities during the 19th and 20th centuries may be adversely affecting the overall Earth system. Today the enlightened use of Earth and its resources has become an important contemporary political and scientific issue.

The global changes that may affect both human well-being and the quality of life on this planet include global climate warming, sea-level change, ozone depletion, deforestation, desertification, drought, and a reduction in biodiversity. Although complex phenomena in themselves, these individual global change concerns cannot be fully understood and addressed unless they are studied collectively in an integrated, multidisciplinary fashion. An effective and well-coordinated international research program, which includes use of advanced environmental observation satellite systems, will be required to significantly improve our scientific knowledge of natural and human-induced changes in the global environment and their regional impacts.

See also: MISSION TO PLANET EARTH; REMOTE SENSING.

Global Positioning System (GPS) The Global Positioning System or *Navstar Global Positioning System* (GPS) is a constellation of over 20 orbiting satellites that provides navigation data to military and civilian users all over the world. The system was developed for the Department of Defense and is operated by the U.S. Air Force. GPS satellites orbit Earth every 12 hours, emitting continuous navigation signals. With proper equipment, users can receive these signals and use them to calculate location, time, and velocity. The signals provided by GPS are so accurate, time can be calculated to within a millionth of a second, velocity within a fraction of a kilometer per hour, and location within a few meters or less. GPS receivers have been developed for use in aircraft, ships, and land vehicles as well as hand-held applications by individuals in the field.

The Global Positioning System has significantly enhanced functions such as mapping, aerial refueling and rendezvous, geodetic surveys, and search and rescue operations. Many military applications were put to the test during the U.S. involvement in Operations Desert Shield and Storm. Allied troops relied heavily on GPS data to navigate the featureless regions of the Saudi Arabian desert. Forward air controllers, pilots, tank drivers, and support personnel all used the system so successfully that U.S. defense officials cited GPS as a key to the Desert Storm victory.

The 985-kilogram (2,175 pounds-mass [lbm]) GPS Block II-A satellites are placed in a circular 20,350-kilometer (10,988 nautical mile) altitude orbit. The Delta II launch vehicle is used to place the GPS satellites in orbit from Cape Canaveral Air Force Station in Florida. GPS Block II-A satellites have a design lifetime of approximately 7.5 years.

globular cluster Compact cluster of up to 1 million, generally older, stars.
See also: GALACTIC CLUSTER.

Glonass Russian global positioning satellites used in a constellation to provide navigation support.
See also: GLOBAL POSITIONING SYSTEM.

Goddard, Robert H. Often referred to as the Father of American Rocketry, Dr. Robert H. Goddard (1882–1945) successfully launched the world's first liquid-fuel rocket on March 16, 1926. The rocket engine itself was just 1.2 meters (m) (4 feet [ft]) tall and 15.2 centimeters (6 inches) in diameter. It was supported in a metal frame structure that resembled a child's play gym. (See Figure 46.) Launched from a snow-covered field at his Aunt Effie Goddard's farm in Auburn,

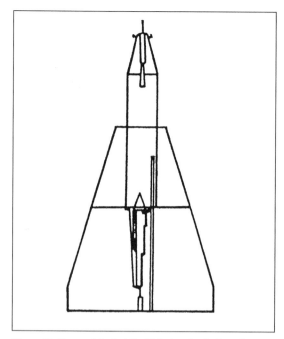

Figure 46. The world's first liquid-fuel rocket built and launched by Dr. Robert H. Goddard on March 16, 1926 *(Drawing courtesy of NASA)*

Massachusetts, this historic rocket rose 12 m (40 ft) and landed about 56 m (184 ft) away, in a brief but successful flight that lasted just 2.5 seconds. Despite its tiny size and essentially unnoticed inaugural flight, Goddard's rocket was the forerunner of all liquid-propellant rockets. His liquid-propellant rocket experiments in the 1930s in the desert of southern New Mexico provided the sound engineering basis for the rockets that ushered in the space age. During his lifetime, Goddard's pioneering work on liquid-propellant rockets was essentially ignored by the U.S. Government, but not by the German rocket team that developed the V-2 rocket during World War II. NASA's Goddard Space Flight Center is named in his honor.

go no-go The condition or state of operability of a component or aerospace system: "go" means functioning properly, while "no-go" means not functioning properly. For example, a test missile's guidance system at launch time is "go," but a malfunctioning fuel pump would be "no-go," leading to an aborted launch attempt.

Gorizont A series of geostationary Russian communications satellites.

governor A device that regulates the speed, output, or motion of a mechanism despite variations in the load, using the principle of negative feedback.

GOX Gaseous oxygen.

grain 1. In rocketry, the integral piece of molded or extruded solid propellant that comprises both fuel and oxidizer in a solid rocket motor and is shaped to produce, when burned, a specified performance versus time relation. *See also:* SOLID-PROPELLANT ROCKET. 2. In photography, a small particle of metallic silver remaining in a photographic emulsion after development and fixing. In the agglomerate, these grains form the dark area of a photographic image. Excessive graininess reduces the quality of a photographic image, especially when the image is enlarged or magnified. 3. In materials science, an individual crystal in a polycrystalline metal or alloy.

grain anomaly A nonhomogeneity, such as a void or a fuel-rich pocket, in a cured solid-propellant grain.
See also: SOLID-PROPELLANT ROCKET.

grain-conditioned temperature The uniform temperature environment of the solid-propellant grain just before ignition.
See also: SOLID-PROPELLANT ROCKET.

gram (symbol: g) The fundamental unit of mass in the centimeter-gram-second (CGS) unit system. One gram is equal to one-thousandth (1/1000) of a kilogram.

grant In general, an asset, such as money, bestowed or transferred for a specific purpose. Space scientists and astronomers often depend on grants from various agencies and organizations, such as NASA or the European Space Agency, to conduct their research programs.

granules The small bright features found in the photosphere of the Sun. Also called: *granulation.*
See also: SUN.

Grashof number (N_{GR}) A nondimensional number used in fluid mechanics to describe the characteristics of free convection in the vicinity of a hot body. It is defined as

$$N_{GR} = \frac{(\text{inertial force}) \times (\text{buoyant force})}{(\text{viscous force})^2}$$

$$N_{GR} = \frac{\rho^2 \, g \, l^3 \, \beta \, \Delta T}{\mu^2}$$

where ρ is (mass) density, g is gravitational acceleration, l is the characteristic length, β is the temperature coefficient of volume expansion, ΔT is temperature difference, and μ is the absolute viscosity. The Grashof number often is associated with the Reynolds number and the Prandtl number in the study of convection.

See also: PRANDTL NUMBER; REYNOLDS NUMBER.

gravitation The acceleration produced by the mutual attraction of two masses, directed along the line joining their centers of mass, and of magnitude inversely proportional to the square of the distance between the two centers of mass. In classical physics, the force of attraction ($\mathbf{F_g}$) between two masses (m and M), is given by NEWTON'S LAW OF GRAVITATION:

$$\mathbf{F_g} = [G \, m \, M] / r^2$$

where G is the gravitational constant (6.6726×10^{-11} N m^{2}kg^{-2}) and r is the distance between the two masses.

gravitational constant (symbol: G) The coefficient of proportionality in NEWTON'S LAW OF GRAVITATION.

$$G = 6.672 \times 10^{-11} \text{ newton - meter}^2 \text{ - kilogram}^{-2} \text{ (N m}^2 \text{ kg}^{-2})$$

gravitational potential 1. The potential associated with the force of gravitation arising from the attraction between mass points, for example, Earth's center and a particle in space. 2. At any point in a gravitational field, the work needed to remove an object from that point to infinity.

gravitational tide An atmospheric tide due to the gravitational attraction of the Sun or Moon. The semidiurnal lunar atmospheric tide is totally gravitational, while the semidiurnal solar atmospheric tide is partly gravitational.

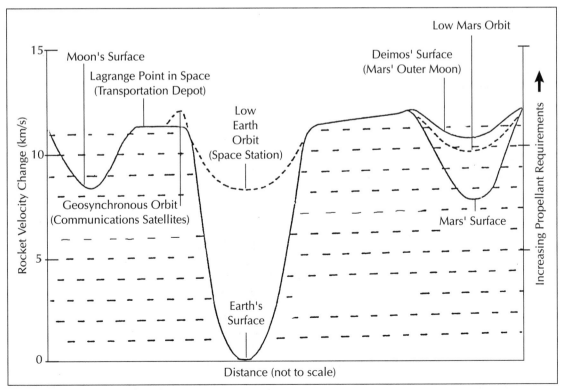

Figure 47. The gravity well of Earth   *(NASA)*

gravity In general, the attraction of a celestial object for any nearby mass. Specifically, the downward force imparted by Earth on a mass near Earth or on its surface. Since Earth is rotating, the force observed as "gravity" is actually the resultant of the force of gravitation and the centrifugal force arising from its rotation.

See also: GRAVITATION.

gravity anomaly A region on a celestial body where the local force of gravity is lower or higher than expected. If the celestial object is assumed to have a uniform density throughout, then we would expect the gravity on its surface to have the same value everywhere.

See also: MASCON.

gravity assist The change in a spacecraft's direction and velocity achieved by a carefully calculated flyby through a planet's gravitational field. The change in direction and velocity is achieved without the use of supplementary propulsive energy.

See also: ORBITS OF OBJECTS IN SPACE; VOYAGER.

gravity well An analogy in which the gravitational field of a planetary body is considered as a deep well or pit out of which a space vehicle has to climb to escape from this celestial object. For example, as shown in Figure 47, Earth is considered to sit in a deep gravity well; considerable energy is needed to lift material and human crews from that well and to put these cargoes into space. The rocket velocity change (ΔV) shown here is indicative of the minimum propellant needed to travel to low Earth orbit and to other destinations in the inner solar system, including the Moon and Mars. It should be noted that this figure is not a potential energy diagram, since the rocket velocity change depends on the actual path taken as well as the potential energy difference between locations. However, this diagram is a good indication of the relative propellant requirements for travel from one location to another. This illustration also does not take into account the travel times associated with minimum ΔV trajectories. One-way travel times range from less than an hour to low Earth orbit, to three days to lunar orbit, to months to a year or more for Mars.

gray (symbol: Gy) In radiation protection, the SI UNIT of absorbed dose of ionizing radiation. One gray (1 Gy) is equal to the absorption of 1 joule of energy per kilogram of matter. This unit is named

in honor of L. H. Gray (1905–1965), a British radiologist. The gray is related to the traditional radiation dose unit system as follows:

$$1 \text{ Gy} = 100 \text{ rad}$$

gray body A body that absorbs some constant fraction, between zero and one, of all electromagnetic radiation incident upon it. The fraction of electromagnetic radiation absorbed is called the *absorptivity* (symbol: α) and is independent of wavelength for a gray body. Many objects fit the gray body model, which represents a surface of absorptive characteristics intermediate between those of a white body and a blackbody. In radiation transport theory, a white body is a hypothetical body whose surface absorbs no electromagnetic radiation at any wavelength, i.e., it is a perfect reflector. Since the white body exhibits zero absorptivity at all wavelengths, it is an idealization that is exactly opposite to that of the blackbody. The gray body is also called *grey body*.

See also: BLACKBODY.

Greek alphabet

alpha A, α	beta B, β	gamma Γ, ν	delta Δ, δ
epsilon E, ϵ	zeta Z, ζ	eta H, η	theta Θ, θ
iota I, ι	kappa K, κ	lambda Λ, λ	mu M, μ
nu N, ν	xi Ξ, ξ	omicron O, o	pi Π, π
rho P, ρ	sigma Σ, σ	tau T, τ	upsilon Ψ, υ
phi Φ, ϕ	chi Ξ, ξ	psi Ψ, ψ	omega Ω, ω

greenhouse effect The general warming of the lower layers of a planet's atmosphere caused by the presence of "greenhouse gases," such as water vapor (H_2O), carbon dioxide (CO_2), and methane (CH_4). On Earth, the greenhouse effect might occur because our atmosphere is relatively transparent to visible light from the Sun (typically 0.3 to 0.7 micrometer wavelength) but is essentially opaque to the longer-wavelength (typically 10.6 micrometer) thermal infrared radiation emitted by the planet's surface. Because of the presence of greenhouse gases in our atmosphere—such as carbon dioxide, water vapor, methane, nitrous oxide (NO_2) and man-made chlorofluorocarbons (CFCs)—this outgoing thermal radiation from Earth's surface could be blocked from escaping to space, and the absorbed thermal energy causes a rise in the temperature of the lower atmosphere. Therefore, as the presence of greenhouse gases increases in the

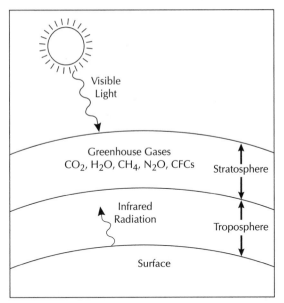

Figure 48. The greenhouse effect in Earth's atmosphere
(Drawing courtesy of the U.S. Environmental Protection Agency)

Earth's atmosphere, more outgoing thermal radiation is trapped, and a global warming trend occurs. (See Figure 48.)

Scientists around the world are concerned that human activities, such as increased burning of vast amounts of fossil fuels, are increasing the presence of greenhouse gases in our atmosphere and upsetting the overall planetary energy balance. These scientists are further concerned that we may be creating the conditions of a *runaway greenhouse,* as appears to have occurred in the past on the planet Venus. Such an effect is a planetary climatic extreme in which all of the surface water has evaporated from the surface of a life-bearing or potentially life-bearing planet. Planetary scientists believe that the current Venusian atmosphere allows sunlight to reach the planet's surface, but its thick clouds and rich carbon dioxide content prevent surface heat from being radiated back to space. This condition has led to the evaporation of all surface water on Venus and has produced the present infernolike surface temperatures of approximately 485° Celsius (900° Fahrenheit)—a temperature hot enough to melt lead.

green satellite An Earth-orbiting satellite that collects environmental data.

See also: EARTH OBSERVING SATELLITE; EARTH OBSERVATION SYSTEM (EOS).

Greenwich mean time (GMT) Mean solar time at the meridian of Greenwich, England used as a basis for standard time throughout the world. Normally expressed in four numerals, 0001 through 2400. Also called: *universal time, Z-time,* and *zulu time.*

gross liftoff weight (GLOW) The total weight of an aircraft, aerospace vehicle, rocket, as loaded; specifically, the total weight with full crew, full tanks, and payload.

Ground-based Electro-Optical Deep Space Surveillance (GEODSS) There are now more than 7,000 known objects in orbit around Earth. These objects range from active satellites to pieces of space debris, or *space junk,* such as expended upper-stage vehicles, fragments from exploded rockets, and even "missing" tools and cameras from astronaut extravehicular activities. The U.S. Space Command Space Surveillance Center, located within Cheyenne Mountain in Colorado, is responsible for keeping track of everything in orbit. The center continuously receives data about Earth-orbiting objects, including those objects considered to be in "deep space" (i.e., at an altitude of more than 4,800 kilometers [3,000 miles]).

The modern Ground-based Electro-Optical Deep Space Surveillance [GEODSS] system is the successor to the Baker-Nunn camera developed in the mid-1950s and performs this space-object tracking mission by bringing together telescopes, low-light-level television, and modern computers. Each operational GEODSS site has at least two main telescopes and one auxiliary telescope. Operational GEODSS sites are located at Socorro, New Mexico; Maui, Hawaii (on top of Mount Haleakala); Choe Jong-San, South Korea; and Diego Garcia, British Indian Ocean Territories.

The GEODSS telescopes move across the sky at the same rate as the stars appear to move. This keeps the distant stars in the same positions in the field of view. As the telescopes slowly move, the GEODSS cameras take very rapid electronic snapshots of the field of view. Computers then take these snapshot images and overlay them on each other. Star images, which essentially remain fixed, are erased electronically. Human-made space objects circling Earth, however, do not remain fixed, and their movements show up as tiny streaks that can be viewed on a console screen. Computers then measure these streaks and use the data to determine the orbital positions of objects. The GEODSS system can track objects as small as a basketball orbiting Earth at an altitude of more than 32,200 kilometers (20,000 miles).

See also: CHEYENNE MOUNTAIN AIR STATION; SPACE DEBRIS.

ground elapsed time (GET) The time since launch. For example, at two hours GET, the space shuttle crew will open the orbiter's cargo bay doors and prepare to deploy a payload on orbit.

ground entry point (GEP) The location or point where satellite sensor data and other information are received by a ground station.

ground environment 1. The environment that surrounds and affects a system or piece of aerospace equipment while it operates on the ground. 2. The system or part of a system, such as a guidance system, that functions on the ground; the aggregate of equipment, conditions, facilities, and personnel that go to make up a system, or part of a system, functioning on the ground.

ground-handling equipment Equipment on the ground used to move, lift, or transport an aerospace vehicle, a rocket, or component parts. Such equipment includes the GANTRY, the transporter, and the forklift.

ground receiving station A facility on the surface of Earth that records data transmitted by an Earth observation satellite.

ground speed The rate of motion of an aerospace vehicle, spacecraft, or aircraft along its groundtrack.

See also: GROUNDTRACK.

ground state The state of a nucleus, atom, or molecule at its lowest (stable) energy level. Compare with EXCITED STATE.

ground support equipment (GSE) Any nonflight (i.e., ground-based) equipment used for launch, checkout, or in-flight support of an aerospace vehicle, expendable rocket, spacecraft, or payload. More specifically, GSE consists of nonflight equipment, devices, and implements that are required to inspect, test, adjust, calibrate, appraise, gauge, measure, repair, overhaul, assemble, transport,

safeguard, record, store, or otherwise function in support of a rocket, space vehicle, or the like, either in the research and development phase or in the operational phase. In general, GSE is not considered to include land and buildings but may include equipment needed to support another item of GSE.

ground swath In remote sensing, the width of the terrain strip imaged by a scanner system.

groundtrack The path followed by a spacecraft over Earth's surface.

ground truth In remote sensing, measurements made on the ground to support, confirm, or help calibrate observations made from aerial or space platforms. Typical ground truth data include weather, soil conditions and types, vegetation types and conditions, and surface temperatures. Best results are obtained when these ground truth measurements are performed simultaneously with the airborne or spaceborne sensor measurements. Also referred to as *ground data* and *ground information*.

growth potential In aerospace engineering, the potential of a launch vehicle or spacecraft for future development, usually demonstrated by the adaptability of the basic design to evolving mission requirements and needs.

g-suit (or G-suit) A suit that exerts pressure on the abdomen and lower parts of the body to prevent or retard the collection of blood below the chest under conditions of positive acceleration.

See also: G.

g-tolerance A tolerance in a person or other animal, or in a piece of equipment, to an acceleration of a particular value.

See also: G.

guidance system A system that evaluates flight information; correlates it with target or destination data; determines the desired flight path of the missile, spacecraft, or aerospace vehicle; and communicates the necessary commands to the vehicle's flight control system.

guided missile (GM) An unmanned, self-propelled vehicle moving above the surface of Earth whose trajectory or course is capable of being controlled while in flight. (See Figure 49.) An air-to-air guided missile (AAGM) is an air-launched vehicle for use against aerial targets. An air-to-surface guided missile (ASGM) is an air-launched missile for use against surface targets. A surface-to-air guided missile (SAGM) is a surface-launched guided missile for use against targets in the air. Finally, a surface-to-surface guided missile (SSGM) is a surface-launched missile for use against surface targets.

See also: BALLISTIC MISSILE.

guided missile cruiser (U.S. Navy Designation: CGN) A warship designed to operate with strike and amphibious forces against air, surface, and subsurface threats. Normal armaments consist of 3-inch or 5-inch guns, an advanced area-defense anti-air-warfare missile system, and antisubmarine-warfare weapons.

guided missile destroyer (U.S. Navy Designation: DDG) This U.S. Navy destroyer type is equipped with Terrier/Tartar guided missiles, an improved naval gun battery, long-range sonar, and antisubmarine warfare weapons, including the antisubmarine rocket (ASROC).

guided missile equipment carrier A self-propelled, full-tracked, amphibious, air-transportable, unarmored carrier for various guided missile systems and their equipment.

guided missile frigate (U.S. Navy Designation: FFG) A modern U.S. Navy warship equipped with Tartar or SM-1 missile launchers. This vessel also can be equipped with a 5-inch gun battery or a 54-mm or 70-mm gun battery.

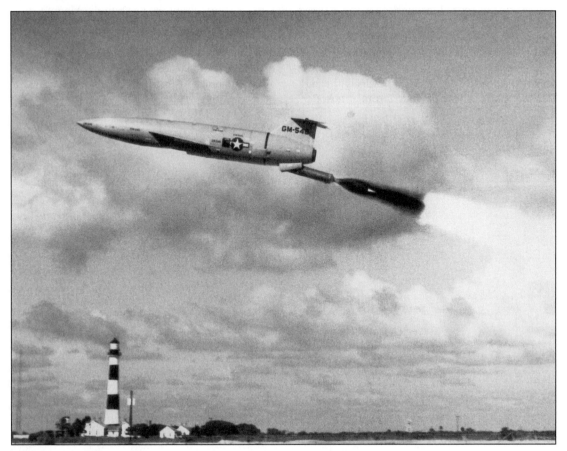

Figure 49. Early flight (July 18, 1951) of Matador surface-to-surface guided missile at Cape Canaveral Air Force Station. Historic Cape Canaveral Lighthouse can be seen in the lower portion of the photograph. *(U.S. Air Force)*

guided missile submarine (nuclear) (U.S. Navy Designation: SSGN) A nuclear-powered submarine designed to have an additional capability to launch guided missile attacks.

guide vane A control surface that may be moved into or against a rocket's jetstream; used to change the direction of the jet flow for thrust vector control.

gun-launch to space (GLTS) An advanced launch concept involving the use of a long and powerful electromagnetic launcher to hurl small satellites and payloads into orbit. One recent concept suggests the development of a hypervelocity coilgun launcher to place 100-kilogram (221 pound-mass [lbm]) payloads into Earth orbit at altitudes ranging from 200 to 500 kilometers (km) (125 to 310 miles [mi]). This coilgun launcher would accelerate the specially designed (and acceleration-hardened) payload package to an initial velocity of about 6 km per second through a long, evacuated tube. The payload package would consist of the payload itself (e.g., a satellite or bulk cargo), a solid-propellant orbital insertion rocket, a guidance system, and an aeroshell. The specially designed payload would penetrate easily through the atmosphere and be protected from atmospher-

ic heating by its aeroshell. Once out of the sensible atmosphere, the aeroshell would be discarded and the solid-propellant rocket would be fired to provide the final velocity increment necessary for orbital insertion and circularization. Payloads launched (or perhaps more correctly "shot") into orbit by such electromagnetic guns would experience peak accelerations ranging from hundreds to thousands of gs (with one g being the normal acceleration due to gravity at Earth's surface). This approach also has been suggested for use on the lunar surface, where the absence of an atmosphere and the Moon's reduced gravitational field (about one-sixth that experienced on Earth's surface) make this concept even more potentially attractive. Launch concepts involving this approach are sometimes referred to as the "Jules Verne Approach to Orbit" (in recognition of the giant gun used by the author Jules Verne to send his explorers on a voyage around the Moon in the famous story "From the Earth to the Moon").

gyro A device that utilizes the angular momentum of a spinning mass (rotor) to sense angular motion of its base about one or two axes orthogonal (mutually perpendicular) to the spin axis. Also called a *gyroscope*.

H-II launch vehicle An advanced expendable booster sponsored by the National Space Development Agency of Japan (NASDA). The H-II is a two-stage launch vehicle capable of delivering a 2,000-kilogram (kg) (4,400 pound-mass [lbm]) payload into geostationary orbit. The H-II is equipped with high-performance rocket engines using liquid hydrogen and liquid oxygen. The thrust of the first stage is supplemented by two large solid rocket boosters. The first stage uses a large liquid oxygen/liquid hydrogen rocket engine called the LE-7, which employs a staged-combustion cycle. The second stage engine uses a liquid oxygen/liquid hydrogen engine called the LE-5A, which employs a hydrogen bleed cycle. The first launch of the H-II vehicle from the Tanegashima Space Center, Japan, occurred on February 4, 1994; it successfully placed several experimental payloads into their planned orbits.

See also: LAUNCH VEHICLE; NATIONAL SPACE DEVELOPMENT AGENCY OF JAPAN (NASDA).

habitable payload A payload with a pressurized compartment suitable for supporting a crewperson in a shirtsleeve environment.

half-angle In rocketry, the angle between the nozzle center line and a line parallel to the inner surface of the nozzle exit cone; also called the *divergence angle.*

half-life 1. (radioactive) The time in which half the atoms of a particular radioactive isotope disintegrate to another nuclear form. Measured half-lives vary from millionths of a second to billions of years. The half-life ($T_{1/2}$) is given by the expression:

$$T_{1/2} = (\ln 2)/\lambda = 0.69315/\lambda$$

where λ is the decay constant for the particular radioactive isotope and ln 2 is the natural (Napierian) logarithm of the number 2 with a numerical value of approximately 0.69315. 2. (effective) The time required for a radionuclide contained in a biological system, such as a human being or an animal, to reduce its activity by half as a combined result of radioactive decay and biological elimination. 3. (biological) The time required for the elimination of one-half of the total amount of a toxic substance contained in a biological system by natural processes. 4. (environmental) The time required for a pollutant to lose half its effect on the environment. For example, the half-life of the insecticide DDT in the environment is about 15 years.

See also: LOGARITHM; NAPIERIAN BASE.

hangfire A faulty condition in the ignition system of a rocket engine.

hardened site A site constructed to provide protection against the effects of conventional and nuclear explosions. It also may be equipped to provide protection against a chemical or biological attack.

hard kill The destruction of a target in such a way as to produce unambiguous visible evidence of its neutralization. For example, the explosive fragmentation of a rocket, reentry vehicle, or satellite after a kinetic energy weapon strike would indicate (at a distance) that the target was destroyed.

hard landing A relatively high-velocity impact landing of a "lander" spacecraft or probe on the surface of a planet or moon that destroys all equipment, except perhaps a very rugged instrument package or payload container. This hard landing could be intentional, as occurred during the early U.S. Ranger missions to the lunar surface; or unintentional, as when a retrorocket system fails and the "lander" spacecraft strikes the planetary surface at an unplanned high speed.

hard line A line or duct that incorporates no flexible joints but is provided with deflection capability by the use of loops and elbows or thin-walled material to accommodate temperature-induced expansion or contraction.

hard missile base A launch complex that is protected against a nuclear explosion.

hardness 1. In BALLISTIC MISSILE DEFENSE (BMD), a property of a target measured by the power needed per unit area to destroy it by means of a DIRECTED-ENERGY WEAPON (DEW). A "hard" target is more difficult to kill than a "soft" target. 2. In aerospace engineering, the resistance of a metal to plastic deformation, scratching, abrasion, or cutting. Often measured on the basis of indentation hardness, as, for example, the BRINELL HARDNESS scale.

hard radiation Nuclear radiation of very great penetrating power; usually refers to energetic X rays and gamma rays.

hard targets Ground targets, such as missile silos or deeply buried command centers, that could survive a nuclear blast unless it were to hit within a few hundred meters.

hard vacuum A very high vacuum; the level of vacuum often associated with deep space. This term often is considered to mean a pressure exerted by any gas of less than [10^{-8} millimeters (mm) of mercury (Hg) (about 1.33×10^{-10} newtons per square meter [N/m^2])].

hardware 1. A generic term dealing with physical items, as distinguished from ideas or "paper designs"; includes aerospace equipment, tools, instruments, devices, components, parts, assemblies, and subassemblies. Satellites and rockets often are referred to as *space hardware*. The term also can be used in aerospace engineering to describe the stage of development, as in the passage of a device or component from the design stage into the hardware stage as a finished object. 2. In computer science and data automation, the physical equipment or devices that make up a computer or one of its peripheral components (e.g., a printer), as opposed to the *software*, which operates and controls the computer system.

HARM missile The AGM-88 High-Speed Antiradiation Missile (HARM) is an air-to-surface tactical missile designed to seek out and destroy enemy radar-equipped air defense systems. An antiradiation missile passively homes in on enemy electronic signal emitters, especially those associated with radar sites used to direct antiaircraft guns and surface-to-air missiles. The AGM-88 can detect, attack, and destroy a target with minimum aircrew input. Used extensively by the U.S. Air Force and Navy.

harmonic 1. An integral multiple or submultiple of a given frequency; a sinusoidal component of a periodic wave. 2. A signal or wave that has a frequency which is a whole-number (integral) multiple of a fundamental (sinusoidal) wave or signal.

harmonic analyzer A device that resolves a periodic curve into its harmonic constituents.

Harpoon missile The AGM-84D is an all-weather, over-the-horizon, antiship missile. The Harpoon's active radar guidance, warhead design, and low-level, sea-skimming cruise trajectory assure high survivability and effectiveness. This missile is capable of being launched from surface ships, submarines, or (without its booster component) from aircraft. Originally developed for the U.S. Navy to serve as its basic antiship missile for fleetwide use, the AGM-84D also has been adapted for use on the U.S. Air Force's B-52G bombers.

hatch A door in the pressure hull of a spacecraft, aerospace vehicle, or space station. The hatch is sealed tightly to prevent the cabin or pressurized module atmosphere from escaping to the vacuum of space outside the pressure hull.

hat section Extruded, machined, or formed metal stringers, or slender, lengthwise structural members, for stiffening spacecraft skin.

hazardous systems In aerospace operations, systems that use or handle hazardous substances or devices such as liquid propellants, solid propellants, rocket engine igniters, ordnance, lasers, and radiofrequency (RF) emitters.

head (or headrise) The increase in fluid pressure supplied by a pump; the difference between pressure at the pump inlet and pressure at pump discharge. Fluid pressure sometimes is expressed as an equivalent height of a fluid column, such as 960 millimeters mercury; or else as pascals (newtons per meter-squared [N/m^2] or pounds-force (lbf) per inch-squared [psi]).

head-up display A display of flight, navigation, attack, or other information superimposed on the pilot's forward field of view.

health physics The branch of science that is concerned with the recognition, evaluation, and control of health hazards from ionizing radiation.

heat Energy transferred by a thermal process. Heat (or *thermal energy*) can be measured in terms of the mechanical units of energy, such as the joule (J), or in terms of the amount of energy required to produce a definite thermal change in some substance, as, for example, the energy required to raise the temperature of a unit mass of water at some initial temperature (e.g., calorie or British thermal unit [BTU]).

$$1 \text{ joule} = 0.239 \text{ calorie}$$

See also: THERMODYNAMICS.

heat balance 1. The equilibrium that exists on the average between the radiation received by a planet and its atmosphere from the Sun and that emitted by the planet and its atmosphere. *See also:* GREENHOUSE EFFECT. 2. The equilibrium that is known to exist when all sources of heat (thermal energy) gain and loss for a given region or object are accounted for. In general, this balance includes conductive, convective, evaporative, and other terms as well as a radiation term.

heat capacity (usual symbol: C) In general, a measure of the increase in energy content of an object or system per degree of temperature rise. This thermodynamic property describes the ability of a substance to store the energy that has been delivered

to it as heat (i.e., thermal energy flow). The *specific heat capacity* (c) is related to the *total heat capacity* (C) as follows:

$$c = C/\rho$$

where c has the units (joules/kg- $^\circ$K), C has the units (joules/m^3-$^\circ$K) and ρ is the density of the substance (kg/m^3). The specific heat capacity (c), sometimes shortened to *specific heat,* has very special significance and meaning in classical thermodynamics. For example, the *specific heat at constant volume* (c_v) is defined as:

$$c_v = (\partial u / \partial T)_v$$

where u is internal energy (joules/kg) and T is temperature ($^\circ$Kelvin [K]). The expression $(\partial u / \partial T)_v$ means the partial derivative of internal energy (u) with respect to temperature (T) holding volume (v) constant. Similarly, the *specific heat at constant pressure* (c_p) is defined as:

$$c_p = (\partial h / \partial T)_p$$

where h is enthalpy (joules/kg) and T is temperature ($^\circ$K). The terms c_v and c_p are very important thermodynamic derivative functions.

Heat Capacity Mapping Mission (HCMM) NASA's Heat Capacity Mapping Mission, or HCMM, was launched on April 26, 1978 and operated successfully between April 1978 and September 1980 in a near-polar orbit at 620 kilometers (385 miles) altitude. This Earth-observing spacecraft was the first NASA research effort directed mainly toward observations of the thermal state of Earth's land surface by a satellite . The HCMM sensor measured reflected solar radiation and thermal emission from the surface with a spatial resolution of 600 meters (~1970 feet). The satellite was placed in an orbit that permitted it to survey thermal conditions during midday and at night. HCMM data have been used to produce temperature difference and apparent thermal inertia images for selected areas within much of North America, Europe, North Africa, and Australia. These data can be used by scientists for rock-type discrimination, soil-moisture detection, assessment of vegetation states, thermal current monitoring in water bodies, urban heat-island assessments, and other environmental studies of Earth.

heat engine A thermodynamic system that receives energy in the form of heat and that, in the performance of an energy transformation on a working fluid, does work. Heat engines function in cycles. An ideal heat engine works in accordance with the CARNOT CYCLE, while practical heat engines use thermodynamic cycles such as BRAYTON, RANKINE, and STIRLING. The steam engine, which helped create the Industrial Revolution, is a heat engine. Gas turbines and automobile engines are also heat engines.

heater blanket An electrical heater, usually in strip or sheet form, that is wrapped around all or a portion of a cryogenic component (e.g., a valve or actuator) to prevent the temperature within the component from falling below a stated operating minimum.

heat exchanger A device for transferring thermal energy (heat) from one fluid to another without intermixing the fluids. There is a great variety of heat exchanger designs. For example, in a *parallel flow heat exchanger,* both fluids flow in the same direction; while in a *counter-flow heat exchanger,* one fluid flows in the opposite direction of the other. In a *gas-liquid heat exchanger,* one of the fluids is in the gaseous state, while the other is in the liquid state.

heat flux (common symbol: q″) The amount of thermal energy (heat) that is transported across a surface of unit area per unit time; the heat flux (q'') often has the units (joules/meter-squared-second) [J/(m^2-sec)] or (British thermal units/foot-squared-second [BTU/(ft^2-sec)]).

heat of ablation A measure of the effective heat capacity of an ablating material; numerically defined as the heating (thermal energy transfer) rate into the substance divided by the mass loss rate resulting from ablation.
See also: ABLATION.

heat pipe A very-high-efficiency heat (thermal energy) transport device. The basic heat pipe is a closed system that contains a working fluid that transports thermal energy by means of phase change (i.e., through the use of the latent heat of vaporization). An external thermal energy (heat) source is applied to the outside of the evaporator section of the heat pipe. This heat addition causes the working fluid contained in a wick to undergo a phase change from liquid to vapor. The vapor leaves the wick, flows through the central region of

the heat pipe, and eventually arrives at the condenser region. At the condenser section of the heat pipe, the vapor also experiences phase change—this time, however, going from a gas to a liquid. The condensation process releases heat, which then is removed through the external portion of the evaporator section. The wick (which lines the interior surface of the entire heat pipe) uses capillary action to return the liquid to the evaporator section. Once there, the liquid can again evaporate, continuing the overall heat transport process.

heat pump A thermodynamic device that operates in the exact opposite manner from a heat engine. The heat pump uses work (mechanical energy input) to take thermal energy (heat) from a lower-temperature environment or source and then to discharge that heat into a higher-temperature environment. An ideal heat pump sometimes is referred to as a *reverse Carnot engine.*
See also: CARNOT CYCLE; HEAT ENGINE.

heat shield 1. In general, any device that protects something from unwanted thermal energy (heat). 2. In aerospace engineering, the special structure used to protect a reentry body or aerospace vehicle from aerodynamic heating on flight through a planet's atmosphere; or the protective structure used to block unwanted heat from entering into a spacecraft, its components, or sensing instruments.

heat sink In thermodynamics, a material, region, or environment in which thermal energy (heat) is stored or to which heat is rejected from a heat engine. The term also is used to describe a material capable of absorbing large quantities of heat, such as the special thermal protection materials used on reentry bodies and aerospace vehicles.

heat-sink chamber In rocketry, a combustion chamber in which the heat capacity of the chamber wall limits wall temperature. This approach is effective only for short-duration firings.

heat soak The increase in the temperature of rocket-engine components after firing has ceased. This increase results from heat transfer through contiguous parts of the engine when no active cooling is present.

heat soakback Thermal energy (heat) on the surface or skin flowing back into a reentry body or an aerospace vehicle structure, usually by means of conduction heat transfer. A good aerothermodynamic design will permit only a few percent of the total aerodynamic heating load to reach the interior of the vehicle.

heat transfer The transfer or exchange of thermal energy (heat) by conduction, convection, or radiation within an object and between an object and its surroundings. Thermal energy also is transferred when a working fluid experiences phase change, such as evaporation or condensation.

heat-transfer coefficient An analytically or empirically determined parameter that expresses the rate of heat transfer per unit area per unit temperature difference between two objects, substances, or regions.

heat treatment Heating and cooling a solid metal or alloy in such a way as to obtain desired conditions and properties. Normally, heating for the sole purpose of hot-working a piece of metal is excluded from this definition.

heavy hydrogen An expression for deuterium (D), the nonradioactive isotope of hydrogen with one proton and one neutron in its nucleus.

heavy-lift launch vehicle (HLLV) A proposed large-capacity space-lift vehicle capable of carrying tens of metric tons of cargo into LOW EARTH ORBIT (LEO) at substantially less cost than contemporary launch vehicles. Several designs, involving varying degrees of reusability, have been studied.

hecto- (symbol: h) A prefix in the SI UNIT system meaning multiplied by 10^2.

hectare A unit of area equal to 10,000 square meters; 1 hectare = 2.4711 acres.

height (symbol: h) Vertical distance; the height above some reference point or plane, as *height above sea level*. The vertical dimension of an object.

height of burst (HOB) The vertical distance from a target on Earth's surface to the point of burst of a nuclear or conventional weapon.

heliocentric Relative to the Sun as a center, as in *heliocentric orbit* or *heliocentric space*.

heliopause The boundary in deep space thought to be roughly circular or perhaps teardrop-shaped, marking the edge of the Sun's influence. It occurs perhaps 100 astronomical units (AU) from the Sun.

heliosphere The space within the boundary of the *heliopause,* containing the Sun and the solar system.

heliostat A mirrorlike device arranged to follow the Sun as it moves through the sky and to reflect the Sun's rays on a stationary collector or receiver.

Helmholtz function (symbol: A or a) A mathematically defined thermodynamic function of state, the decrease of which during a reversible isothermal process is equal to the work done by the system. The Helmholtz function (a) per unit mass is defined as:

$$a = u - Ts$$

where u is the specific internal energy (joules/kilogram), T is absolute temperature (degrees Kelvin), and s is the specific ENTROPY (joules/kilogram-degree Kelvin). Also called the *Helmholtz free energy.* *See also:* THERMODYNAMICS.

henry (symbol: H) The SI UNIT of inductance (L). Inductance relates the production of an electromotive force ($\mathcal{E}$) in a conductor when there is a change in the magnetic flux (Φ) in that conductor. The induced electromotive force ($\mathcal{E}$) is proportional to the time rate of change of the current (dI/dt), namely:

$$\mathcal{E} = -L\,(dI/dt)$$

where the inductance (L) serves as a proportionality constant and depends on the geometric design of the circuit.

One henry (H) is defined as the inductance occurring in a closed electric circuit in which an electromotive force (or emf) of 1 volt is produced when the current (I) in the circuit is varied uniformly at the rate of 1 ampere per second. This unit has been named in honor of the American physicist Joseph Henry (1797–1878).

Hermes An aerospace plane proposed for development by the European Space Agency (ESA). If developed, it would be launched into Earth orbit by the *Ariane 5* vehicle from the Kourou, French Guiana site.

hermetic seal A seal evidencing no detectable leakage or permeation of gas or moisture.

hertz (symbol: Hz) The SI UNIT of frequency. One hertz is equal to 1 cycle per second. Named in honor of the German physicist H. R. Hertz (1857–94).

high altitude By aerospace convention, an altitude above 10,000 meters (33,000 feet).

high-altitude burst The explosion of a nuclear weapon that takes place at a height in excess of 30,000 meters (100,000 feet).

high-Earth orbit (HEO) An orbit around Earth at an altitude greater than 5,600 kilometers (3,500 miles).

high-energy laser (HEL) A space-based laser capable of generating high-energy beams (i.e., 20 kilowatts or greater average power; 1 kilojoule or more per pulse) in the infrared, visible, or ultraviolet portion of the electromagnetic spectrum. When projected to a target this beam would accomplish damage ranging from degradation to destruction.

high explosive (HE) A chemical explosive that when used in its normal manner detonates rather than deflagrates or burns; that is, the rate of advance of the reaction zone into the unreacted material exceeds the speed of sound.

highlands Oldest exposed areas on the surface of the Moon; extensively cratered and chemically distinct from the *maria*.
See also: MOON.

high-power microwave (HPM) system A proposed space-based weapon system that would be capable of destroying not only targets in space but also airborne and ground targets. This type of weapon system typically would involve peak powers of 100 megawatts or more and a single pulse energy of 100 joules or more. Target damage would result from electronic upset or burnout.

hit-to-kill vehicle A kinetic (hypersonic velocity) vehicle that destroys its target by hitting it and thereby transferring a lethal amount of kinetic energy to it.

hohlraum In radiation heat transfer, a cavity whose walls are in radiative equilibrium with the radiant energy within the cavity. This idealized cavity can be approximated in practice by making a small hole or perforation in the walls of a hollow container of any opaque material. The radiant energy escaping through such a tiny hole will be a reasonable approximation to BLACKBODY radiation at the temperature of the interior of the container.

Hohmann transfer orbit The most efficient orbit transfer path between two coplanar circular orbits. It consists of two impulsive high-thrust "burns" (or firings) of a spacecraft's propulsion system. The first burn is designed to change the original circular orbit to an elliptical orbit whose perigee is tangent with the lower-altitude circular orbit and whose apogee is tangent with the higher-altitude circular orbit. After coasting for half of the elliptical transfer orbit (i.e., the *Hohmann transfer orbit*) and when tangent with the destination circular orbit, the second impulsive high-thrust burn is performed by the spacecraft's onboard propulsion system (sometimes called an *apogee kick motor*), circularizing the orbit at the desired new altitude. (See Figure 50.) This technique also can be used to lower the altitude of a satellite from one circular orbit to another circular orbit (of less altitude). In this case

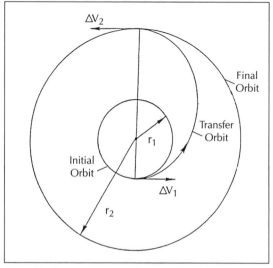

Figure 50. The Hohmann transfer for orbit raising from a lower altitude circular orbit to a higher altitude circular orbit   *(Author's collection)*

two impulsive retrofirings are required. The first retroburn (i.e., the thrust is opposite to the direction of travel) places the spacecraft on an elliptical transfer orbit; while the second retroburn occurs at perigee of the elliptical transfer orbit and circularizes the spacecraft's orbit at the desired lower altitude. Named after the German engineer Walter Hohmann, who first suggested this minimum energy orbital transfer technique in a publication in 1925.

See also: ORBITS OF OBJECTS IN SPACE.

hold In rocketry, to halt the sequence of events during a countdown until an impediment has been removed so that the countdown to launch can be resumed; for example, "T minus 25 and *holding* because of a sudden change in weather conditions."

holddown test The testing of some system or subsystem in a rocket, while the rocket is firing but restrained in a test stand.

homing 1. In general, the technique whereby a mobile station or system directs itself, or is directed, toward a source of primary or reflected energy, or to a specified point. 2. In BALLISTIC MISSILE DEFENSE (BMD), the ability of an interceptor to locate its target and to modify its trajectory to ensure that it approaches its target close enough to destroy it. Homing may be based on infrared, radar, or laser-radar (ladar) systems.

homing guidance A guidance system, by which a missile steers itself toward a target by means of a self-contained mechanism that is activated by some distinguishing characteristics of the target. The process is called: *active homing guidance,* if the target information is received in response to signals transmitted by the missile (e.g., reflected radar beams when the search radar is carried by the missile); *semiactive homing guidance,* if the missile's homing system follows a reflected signal from the target and the source of the reflected signal is other than the missile or the target (e.g., a missile following laser light reflected from the target when the laser beam [also called a target designator beam] is placed or "painted" on the target by the attacking aircraft platform); and *passive guidance,* if the missile follows a signal emitted by the target itself (e.g., an infrared signature associated with an exhaust plume).

Honest John An early surface-to-surface missile deployed by the U.S. Army. It has a range of about 50 kilometers (30 miles).

hook Aerospace industry jargon for a design feature to accommodate the addition or upgrade of computer software at some future time; as, for example, the new space platform has been *hooked* and *scarred* to accommodate a telerobotic laboratory capability.

horizon The line marking the apparent junction of Earth and sky.

Horizon Mission Methodology (HMM) A systematic NASA methodology for identifying and evaluating innovative aerospace technology concepts that offer revolutionary, breakthrough-type capabilities for advanced space missions and for assessing the potential mission impact of these advanced technologies. The methodology is based on the concept of the *horizon mission,* which is defined as a hypothetical space mission having performance requirements that cannot be met even by extrapolating known space technologies. Horizon missions include: an interstellar probe, the thousand-astronomical-unit (TAU) observatory, an Oort Cloud probe, and human-tended planetary stations in the Jupiter or Saturn systems.

horizonal takeoff and landing (HOTOL) A British aerospace industry proposed aircraftlike reusable vehicle that would take off and land on runways, similar to advanced performance supersonic jet aircraft. On its ascent to low-Earth orbit the HOTOL aerospace vehicle would first be accelerated by a sledlike undercarriage system for about 2 kilometers (1.2 miles) and then, drawing oxygen from the atmosphere, would use its onboard engines to climb up through the atmosphere and achieve the velocity necessary to reach orbit. As proposed, it would be capable of carrying payloads of up to about 7,000 kilograms (15,400 pounds-mass) into LOW EARTH ORBIT (LEO).

horsepower (symbol: hp) a traditional engineering unit of power defined as:

1 hp = 550 foot-pounds force/second = 746 watts

hot-core injector In rocketry, an injector that produces a central hot-gas combustion region surrounded by a "cold" fuel sheath.

hot fire Term applied to a test of a liquid-fuel rocket engine system in which the engine is started (ignited) and operated while performance of the system and its components is observed and measured; the period of operation need not be full operational duration.
See also: HOT TEST.

hot-gas valve Valve that controls the flow of hot gases, opening at low liquid-fuel engine power levels, but restricting the flow at mainstage conditions; it operates at temperatures in excess of 366° Kelvin (K) and as high as 811° K or higher.

hot streaking Stratification of burning gases in a combustion chamber into longitudinal zones of high-temperature gases that do not break up and mix with cooler gases. The term derives from the localized heat marks visible on the combustion chamber wall after firing has ended.

hot test A liquid-fuel propulsion system test conducted by actually firing the engines (usually for a short period of time) with the rocket vehicle secured to the launch pad by holddown bolts.

Hound Dog An early U.S. Air Force air-to-surface missile with a range of about 800 kilometers (500 miles). It was externally carried under the wing of long-range strategic bombers, such as the B-52.

hour (symbol: h) A unit of time equal to 3,600 seconds or 60 minutes.

"housekeeping" The collection of routine tasks that must be performed to keep an aerospace vehicle or spacecraft functioning properly. For example, the astronaut crew or ground support team performing frequent status checks and making minor adjustments on the life support and waste management systems of a human-occupied space vehicle; or the mission control team performing regular telemetry management checks and trajectory adjustments on an interplanetary spacecraft as it cruises toward its planetary target.

housing The physical structure that forms the containing envelope for an assembly.

Hubble constant (symbol: H_0) The "constant" that relates the recession velocity of a galaxy (as determined by the REDSHIFT) to its distance from Earth. This number, named in honor of American astronomer Edwin Hubble (1889–1953), helps establish an upper limit to the age and size of an expanding universe. Unfortunately, there is still much debate and controversy among astrophysicists and cosmologists as to what the accepted value of the Hubble constant really is (based on measurements of distant receding galaxies). Recently proposed values for H_0 fall between 50 and 90 kilometers per second per megaparsec (km s^{-1} Mpc^{-1}). The inverse of the Hubble constant ($1/H_0$, the *Hubble time*) has the dimension of time and is considered a measure of the age of the universe, especially if a constant expansion rate is assumed. If H_0 is given a value of 80 km s^{-1} Mpc^{-1}, this would suggest that the universe is between about 8 and 12 billion years old. However, if H_0 is given a value of 50 km s^{-1} Mpc^{-1}, then the universe has an estimated age of about 20 billion years. The smaller the value assigned to the Hubble constant, the older the estimated age of the universe (since the primordial "Big Bang").
See also: ASTROPHYSICS; "BIG BANG" THEORY; COSMOLOGY.

Hubble Space Telescope (HST) A cooperative program of the European Space Agency (ESA) and NASA to operate a long-lived space-based observatory for the benefit of the international astronomical community. The visible-light element of NASA's Great Observatories program, the orbiting facility is named for the American astronomer Edwin P. Hubble (1889–1953), who revolutionized our knowledge of the size, structure, and makeup of the universe through his pioneering observations in the first half of the 20th century. The Hubble Space Telescope (HST) is being used by astronomers and space scientists to observe the visible universe to distances never before obtained and to investigate a wide variety of interesting astronomical phenomena.

The HST is 13.1 meters (m) (43 feet [ft]) long and has a diameter of 4.27 m (14 ft). (See Figure 51.) This space-based observatory is designed to provide detailed observational coverage on the visible and ultraviolet portions of the electromagnetic (EM) spectrum. The HST power supply system consists of two large solar panels (unfurled on orbit), batteries, and power-conditioning equip-

Figure 51. NASA's Hubble Space Telescope (HST)—a long-lived space-based optical observatory capable of being serviced in low Earth orbit by the space shuttle   *(Artist rendering courtesy of NASA/MSFC)*

ment. The 11,000 kilogram (24,300 pounds-mass) free-flying astronomical observatory initially was placed into a 600-kilometer (375-mi) LOW EARTH ORBIT (LEO) during the STS-31 Space Shuttle *Discovery* mission on April 25, 1990.

The years since the launch of HST have been momentous. The initial discovery of a spherical aberration in the telescope optical system severely threatened its usefulness. A practical solution, however, was found when the STS-61 Space Shuttle *Endeavour* mission (December 1993) of on-orbit servicing of the telescope was a complete success. The effects of the spherical aberration were overcome and the HST was restored to full functionality. During this mission, the astronauts changed out the original Wide Field/Planetary Camera (WF/PC1) and replaced it with the WF/PC2. The relay mirrors in WF/PC2 are spherically aberrated to correct for the spherically aberrated primary mirror of the observatory. HST's pri-

mary mirror is two micrometers (2 microns) too flat at the edge, so corrective optics within WF/PC2 are too high by that same amount. A corrective optics package, called the *Corrective Optics Space Telescope Axial Replacement,* or *COSTAR,* displaced the High Speed Photometer during the STS-61 servicing mission to HST. COSTAR is designed to optically correct the effect of the primary mirror's aberration on the three remaining scientific instruments: the Faint Object Camera (FOC) [built by ESA], Faint Object Spectrograph (FOS), and the Goddard High Resolution Spectrograph (GHRS).

A second on-orbit HST servicing mission was accomplished in February 1997 during the STS-82 space shuttle *Discovery* mission.

Although HST operates around the clock, not all of its time is spent observing the universe. Each orbit lasts about 95 minutes, with time allocated for "housekeeping" functions and for observations. Housekeeping functions include turning the telescope to acquire a new target, or to avoid the Sun or the Moon, switching communications antennas and data transmission modes, receiving command loads and downloading data, calibrating, and similar activities. Responsibility for conducting and coordinating the science operations of the Hubble Space Telescope rests with the Space Telescope Science Institute (STScI).

Because of HST's location above Earth's atmosphere, its science instruments can produce high-resolution images of astronomical objects. Ground-based telescopes, influenced by atmospheric effects, seldom can provide resolution better than 1.0 arc-second, except perhaps momentarily under the very best observing conditions. The Hubble Space Telescope's resolution is about 10 times better, or 0.1 arc-second.

Here are just a few of the exciting discoveries provided so far by the Hubble Space Telescope: (1) it gave astronomers their first detailed view of the shapes of 300 ancient galaxies located in a cluster 5 billion light-years away; (2) it also gave astronomers their best look yet at the workings of a black hole "engine" in the core of the giant elliptical galaxy NGC4261, located 45 million light-years away in the constellation Virgo; (3) its detailed images of newly forming stars help confirm more than a century of scientific hypothesis and conjecture on how a solar system begins; and (4) HST gave astronomers their earliest look at a rapidly ballooning bubble of gas blasted off a star (Nova Cygni, which erupted February 19, 1992).

See also: STAR(S).

human factors engineering The branch of engineering involved in the design, development, testing, and construction of devices, equipment, and artificial living environments to the anthropometric, physiological, and/or psychological requirements of the human beings who will use them. In aeroscope, human factors engineering is involved in such diverse areas as the design of a functional microgravity toilet (for both male and female crewpersons), the creation of crew living and sleeping quarters that are both efficient (from a size perspective) and yet provide a suitable level of aesthetics and privacy, and the development of crew workstations that can accommodate a variety of mission needs and still provide immediate attention to hazardous or emergency situations (i.e., a warning light that "jumps out" immediately and

can be recognized easily amid 100 so other lights and indicators).

humidity The amount of water vapor in the air; the "wetness" of the atmosphere. The *relative humidity* represents the ratio of the amount of water vapor present in the air at a given temperature to the greatest amount of water vapor possible for that temperature. For example, a 10% relative humidity is very dry air, while a 90% relative humidity is very moist air.

hydraulic Operated, moved, or affected by liquid used to transmit energy.

hydrazine (symbol: N_2H_4) A toxic, colorless liquid that often is used as a rocket propellant because it reacts violently with many oxidizers. It is spontaneously ignitable with concentrated hydrogen peroxide (H_2O_2) and nitric acid. When decomposed by a suitable catalyst, hydrazine is also a good monopropellant and can be used in simple, small rocket engines, such as those for spacecraft attitude control.

hydrodynamics The branch of science that studies the motion of incompressible fluids and fluid-boundary interactions.

hydrogen (symbol: H) A colorless, odorless gas, the lightest and most abundant of all the elements in the universe. There are three isotopes: ordinary hydrogen [^1_1H], which is nonradioactive and contains a single proton in the nucleus; deuterium [^2_1D], which is also nonradioactive and contains a proton and a neutron in the nucleus; and tritium [^3_1T], which is radioactive (12.3 year half-life) and contains a proton and two neutrons in the nucleus. Ordinary hydrogen is sometimes referred to a *protium* and has a natural abundance of about 99.985%. Deuterium as found naturally in hydrogen has an abundance of about 0.015%.

Liquid hydrogen (LH_2) when burned with liquid oxygen (LOX) or liquid fluorine (LF) makes an excellent high-performance chemical rocket propellant. It is used, for example, as the propellant (along with liquid oxygen) for the three main engines on the space shuttle. However, to be useful as a propellant, it must be stored as a cryogenic liquid, at very low (cryogenic) temperatures (i.e., less than -267° Celsius or -423° Fahrenheit). This presents some handling and storage problems both at the launch complex and in design of the propellant storage tanks. Once liquid hydrogen evaporates, it becomes potentially explosive gaseous hydrogen, requiring additional safety precautions and venting procedures.

Liquid hydrogen, because of its low molecular weight of 2.016, also has been considered as the monopropellant of choice in nuclear thermal rocket systems, both demonstrated and proposed. These nuclear rocket systems would use the thermal energy released by a nuclear reactor to heat the liquid hydrogen propellant to extremely high (gaseous) exit temperatures.

Visionary planners also see hydrogen coming into much wider use in the terrestrial energy economy in the 21st century as a premier energy carrier and transportation sector source. Whether hydrogen is produced by electrolytic or thermochemical methods, whether the initial source of energy is a coal-fired or nuclear plant, a solar power tower or a field of photovoltaic cells, the resulting hydrogen "fuel" represents an energy carrier much more convenient and versatile than the coal, uranium, or even solar energy from which it derives. Procedures for producing, handling, and storing large quantities of hydrogen that have been developed in the aerospace industry as part of launch vehicle operations could pave the way for routine handling of large quantities of hydrogen in the terrestrial energy economy of the next century. More modestly scaled hydrogen economies also can play a role in the fully regenerative life-support systems of future lunar and Mars surface bases.

hydrogen bomb A nuclear weapon that derives its yield (energy) largely from thermonuclear (fusion) reactions.

See also: FUSION (NUCLEAR).

hydrogen embrittlement Decrease in a metal's tensile strength, notched tensile strength, fatigue strength, resistance-to-crack growth, and especially ductility as a result of absorption by the metal of newly formed gaseous hydrogen.

hydroponics The technique of growing plants without soil, in nutrient solutions. "Space greenhouses," an integral part of reliable controlled ecological life-support systems (CELSS) at future lunar and Mars surface bases, might use hydroponics.

hydrostatic equation In the vector equation of motion, the form assumed by the vertical component, when all Coriolis, Earth-curvature, frictional, and vertical-acceleration terms are considered negligible compared with those involving the vertical pressure force and the force of gravity. Therefore,

$$dP = - \rho \, g \, dZ$$

where dP is a differential (i.e., tiny) change in fluid pressure; ρ is the fluid density; g is the acceleration of gravity; and dZ is a differential change in geometric height. Since the geometric height (Z) is measured positively upward, the negative sign on the right side of the above equation indicates that pressure decreases with an increase in height. The error in applying the hydrostatic equation to the atmosphere (even though density, r, is not truly constant but rather decreases with height) for cyclonic-scale motions is less than 0.01 percent. Strong vertical accelerations in thunderstorms and mountain waves may be 1% of gravity or more in extreme situations.

In integral form, this equation is written as:

$$_1\!\int^2 dP/\rho g = - (Z_2 - Z_1)$$

Finally, for the case of an incompressible fluid (i.e., a fluid whose density [ρ] can be treated as constant) and assuming that the acceleration of gravity (g) is also constant over the change in geometric height, the hydrostatic equation becomes simply:

$$P_2 - P_1 = - \rho g \, (Z_2 - Z_1)$$

hydrostatic equilibrium 1. The state of a fluid whose surfaces of constant pressure and constant mass (or density) coincide and are horizontal throughout. Complete balance exists between the force of gravity and the pressure force in accordance with the HYDROSTATIC EQUATION. 2. Of a rotating body, a state in which the body maintains (or returns to) the figure generated by this rotation in spite of small disturbances.

hydrostatic pressure The pressure exerted by a column of fluid; fluid pressure due to the force of gravity.

See also: HYDROSTATIC EQUATION.

hydrostatic seal Seal that incorporates features which maintain an interfacial film thickness by means of pressure provided either by an external source or by the pressure differential across the seal.

hyperbaric Pertaining to breathing atmospheric pressures above sea level normal.

hyperbaric chamber A chamber used to induce an increase in ambient pressure as would occur in descending below sea level, in a water or air environment. It is the only type of chamber suitable for use in the treatment of decompression sickness.

hyperbola An open curve with two branches, all points of which have a constant difference in distance from two fixed points called *focuses* (or foci).

hyperbolic Of or pertaining to a HYPERBOLA.

hyperbolic velocity A velocity sufficient to allow escape from a planetary system or the solar system; for example, all interplanetary spacecraft missions follow hyperbolic orbits, both for Earth departure and then again upon arrival at the target planet. Comets, if not gravitationally captive to the Sun, can have hyperbolic velocities; their trajectories would be escape trajectories or hyperbolas.
See also: ORBITS OF OBJECTS IN SPACE.

hypergolic fuel (hypergol) A rocket fuel that spontaneously ignites when brought into contact with an oxidizing agent (oxidizer); for example, aniline ($C_6H_5NH_2$) mixed with red fuming nitric acid (85% HNO_3 and 15% N_2O_4) produces spontaneous combustion.

hypergolic ignition Ignition that involves no external energy source but results entirely from the spontaneous reaction of two materials when they are brought into contact; materials may be two liquids or a liquid impinging on a solid.

hyperoxia An aerospace medicine term describing a condition in which the total oxygen content of the body is increased above that normally existing at sea level.

hypersonic Of or pertaining to speeds equal to or in excess of five times the speed of sound (i.e., ≥ Mach 5).

hypersonic flow In aerodynamics, flow of a fluid over a body at speeds much greater than the speed of sound and in which the shock waves start at a finite distance from the surface of the body.

hypersonic glider An unpowered aerospace vehicle designed to fly and maneuver at hypersonic speeds upon reentering a planetary atmosphere.

hypervelocity Extremely high velocity. The term is applied by physicists to speeds approaching the speed of light; but in aerospace applications, the term generally implies speeds of the order of satellite or spacecraft speed and greater (i.e., 5 to 10 kilometers per second and greater).

hypervelocity gun (HVG) A gun that can accelerate projectiles to 5 kilometers per second or more; for example, an electromagnetic gun.
See also: GUN-LAUNCH TO SPACE.

hypobaric Pertaining to low atmospheric pressure, especially the low pressure of high altitudes.

hypobaric chamber A chamber used to induce a decrease in ambient pressure as would occur in ascending altitude. This type of chamber is used primarily for flight training purposes and for aerospace experiments. Also called an *altitude chamber*.

hypothesis A scientific theory proposed to explain a set of data or observations; can be used as basis for further investigation and testing.

hypoxia An aerospace medicine term describing an oxygen deficiency in the blood, cells, or tissues of the body in such degree as to cause psychological and physiological disturbances.

hypsithermal period The period about 4,000 to 8,000 years ago, when Earth apparently was several degrees warmer than it is now. More rainfall occurred in most of the subtropical desert regions and less in the central Midwest United States and Scandinavia. Also called the *altithermal period*. It can serve as a past climate analog for predicting the regional pattern of climate change that might occur should the mean Earth surface temperature increase due to an increase in atmospheric carbon dioxide concentration.
See also: GREENHOUSE EFFECT.

hysteresis 1. Any of several effects resembling a kind of internal friction, accompanied by the generation of thermal energy (heat) within the substance affected. *Magnetic hysteresis* occurs when a ferromagnetic is subjected to a varying magnetic intensity. *Electric hysteresis* occurs when a dielectric is subjected to a varying electric intensity. *Elastic hysteresis* is the internal friction in an elastic solid subjected to varying stress. 2. The delay of an indicator in registering a change in a parameter being measured.

HZE particles The most potentially damaging cosmic rays, with high atomic number (Z) and high kinetic energy (E). Typically, HZE particles are atomic nuclei with Z greater than 6 and E greater than 100 million electron volts (100 MeV). When these extremely energetic particles pass through a substance, they deposit a large amount of energy along their tracks. This deposited energy ionizes the atoms of the material and disrupts molecular bonds.

See also: COSMIC RAYS.

ice catastrophe A planetary climatic extreme in which all the liquid water on the surface of a life-bearing or potentially life-bearing planet has become frozen or completely glaciated.

See also: GLOBAL CHANGE.

ice point The equilibrium temperature of a mixture of water and ice at standard pressure. Formerly, the zero point of the Celsius relative temperature scale was based on this temperature point. For water at the ice point, this equilibrium temperature point is 273.15° Kelvin, 0° Celsius, 32.00° Fahrenheit, and 491.67° Rankine depending on the choice of temperature scale.

See also: ABSOLUTE TEMPERATURE SCALE.

ideal gas The pressure (p), volume (V), and temperature (T) behavior of many gases at low pressures and moderate temperatures is approximated quite well by the ideal (or *perfect*) gas equation of state, which is

$$p V = N R_U T$$

where N is the number of moles of gas and R_U is the universal gas constant.

$$R_U = 8314.5 \text{ joules/kg-mole-°K} = 1.986$$
$$\text{Btu/lb}_{mass}\text{-mole-°R}$$

This very useful relationship is based on the experimental work originally conducted by Boyle (Boyle's Law), Charles (Charles Law) and Gay-Lussac (the Gay-Lussac Law). In the ideal gas approximation, we assume that there are no forces exerted between the molecules of the gas and that these molecules occupy negligible space in the containing region. The ideal gas equation

above and its many equivalent forms has widespread application in thermodynamics, as, for example, in describing the performance of an IDEAL ROCKET.

ideal nozzle The nozzle of an ideal rocket, or a nozzle designed according to the ideal gas laws.

ideal rocket A theoretical rocket postulated for design and performance parameters that are then corrected (i.e., modified) in aerospace engineering practice. The ideal rocket model often assumes one or more of the following conditions: a homogeneous and invariant propellant; exhaust gases that behave in accordance with the ideal (perfect) gas laws; the absence of friction between the exhaust gases and the nozzle walls; the absence of heat transfer across the rocket engine and/or nozzle wall(s); an axially directed velocity of all exhaust gases; a uniform gas velocity across every section normal to the nozzle axis; and chemical equilibrium established in the combustion chamber and maintained in the nozzle.

See also: ROCKET.

idiot pin A locating pin that matches two parts in correct orientation so that mating components cannot be joined incorrectly.

ignitable Capable of burning or causing fire.

igniter A device used to begin combustion, such as a SQUIB used to ignite the fuel in a solid propellant rocket. The igniter typically contains a specially arranged charge of a ready-burning composition (such as blackpowder) and is used to amplify the initiation of a primer.

ignition The attainment of self-sustaining combustion of propellants in a rocket engine or motor.

ignition delay In solid rocket motors, the time period from the moment of arrival of the thermal energy (heat) from the igniter at the propellant grain surface until an exothermic gas-phase reaction is self-sustaining (i.e., the solid propellant is burning); in liquid rocket engines, the time from initial contact of fuel and oxidizer until a measurable pressure is generated.

ignition temperature The surface temperature of a solid-propellant grain at the moment combustion begins; this temperature depends on the extent of pyrolysis (high-temperature–induced chemical decomposition), on the thermal energy (heat) generation rate, and on the pressure, especially at low pressures and high heat flux levels.

illuminance (symbol: E) The amount of visible radiation incident on a given surface per unit time per unit area; the luminous flux (Φ) per unit area. Illuminance is often measured in *lux* (lumens per square-meter). Also called *illumination.*

illumination from space Suggested in the early 1970s by space visionaries (such as Dr. Krafft A. Ehricke) large, lightweight mirrors or reflecting surfaces could be placed in orbit around Earth to provide routine nighttime illumination of cities, to serve as emergency lighting sources during disaster relief operations, to enhance regional agriculture through the stimulation of photosynthesis, to accomplish the controlled melting of snowpacks, to help reduce ice fields that were blocking navigation, and to enhance terrestrial solar power installations. NASA investigations of solar-sail applications also have provided the technical characteristics for a large space mirror constructed out of aluminized mylar, possibly just 0.0025 millimeter (0.01 mil) thick. It is anticipated that such giant mirrors (if developed) eventually could have areal densities as low as 6 grams per square meter, which corresponds to 6 metric tons per square kilometer.

Such giant mirrors could be placed in appropriate orbits around the Moon to help illuminate mining and exploration operations during the long lunar night (approximately 14 Earth days' duration) or to help prevent excessive facilities and equipment "cold soak" during these extended periods of lunar darkness.

image A graphic representation of a physical object or scene formed by a mirror, lens, or electro-optical recording device. In remote sensing, the term "image" generally refers to a representation acquired by nonphotographic methods.
See also: REMOTE SENSING.

image compensation Movement intentionally imparted to a photographic film system or electro-optical imagery system at such a rate as to compensate for the forward motion of an air or space vehicle when observing objects on the ground. Without image compensation, the forward motion of the air or space vehicle would cause blurring and degradation of the image produced by the system.

image converter An electro-optical device capable of changing the spectral (i.e., wavelength) characteristics of a radiant image. The conversion of an infrared image to a visible image, an X-ray image to a visible image, and a gamma ray image to a visible image are all examples of image conversion performed by this type of device.

image degradation The reduction of the inherent optimum potential of individual sensor systems caused by error in sensor operations or, processing procedures or incorrect data handling. This term generally is not used to refer to a reduction in the quality of an image caused by unavoidable factors not associated with the sensor systems, such as atmospherics, snow, and the like.

image enhancement The manipulation of individual pixels in an image so that certain features might be observed and analyzed more easily by a human being. For example, we might brightly "color" all pixels in a thermal infrared image of an object (e.g., a power transformer or a radiator system) that are in excess of a certain temperature (radiant thermal energy) level to determine quickly the presence and location of "hot spots," representing malfunctioning parts within the object.

image processing A general term describing the contemporary technology used for acquiring, transferring, analyzing, displaying, and applying digital imagery data. Often this image processing can take place in real time or near real time. It is especially useful in defense applications that involve the use of mobile sensors for real-time target acquisition and guidance, the processing and display of large complex data sets, timely data transmission and compression techniques, and the three-dimensional presentation of battlefield information. The remote sensing of Earth and other planetary objects also has been greatly enhanced by advanced image processing techniques. These techniques (often conducted on today's personal computers) enable remote sensing analysts to compare, interpret, archive, and recall vast quantities of "signature" information emanating from objects on Earth or other planetary bodies. Modern image processing supports applications in such important areas as crop forecasting, rangeland and forest management, land use planning, mineral and petroleum exploration, mapmaking, water quality evaluation, and disaster assessment.

See also: REMOTE SENSING.

imagery Collectively, the representations of objects produced by image-forming devices such as electro-optical sensor systems or photographic systems. (See Figure 52.)

imagery correlation The mutual relationship between the different signatures on imagery from different types of sensors in terms of position and the physical characteristics signified.

imagery exploitation The cycle of processing and printing imagery to the positive or negative state, assembly into imagery packs, identification, interpretation, mensuration, information extraction, preparation of reports, and dissemination of information.

imagery intelligence Intelligence information derived from the exploitation of imagery collected by visual photography, infrared sensors, lasers, electro-optics, and radar sensors (e.g., synthetic aperture radar). Images of objects and target scenes may be reproduced optically or electronically on film, electronic display devices or other media. Also called *IMINT.*

imagery interpretation 1. The process of location, recognition, identification, and description of objects, activities, and terrain represented on imagery. 2. The extraction of information from photographs or other recorded images.

Figure 52. Reconnaissance satellite imagery. This photograph is the first intelligence target taken from the first successful CORONA mission. (CORONA was the first-generation U.S. photo-reconnaissance satellite). It shows a military airfield near Mys Schmidta on the Chukchi Sea in far northeastern Russia. *(Photograph courtesy of Central Intelligence Agency)*

imaging The process of identifying an object by obtaining a high-quality image (representation) or profile of it.

imaging instruments Optical imaging from scientific spacecraft is performed by two families of detectors: *vidicons* and the newer *charge coupled devices* (CCDs). Although the detector technology differs, in each case an image of the target celestial object is focused by a telescope onto the detector, where it is converted to digital data. Color imaging requires three exposures of the same target, through three different color filters selected from a filter wheel. Ground processing combines data from the three black-and-white images, reconstructing the original color by using three values for each picture element (pixel).

A vidicon is a vacuum tube resembling a small cathode ray tube (CRT). An electron beam is swept across a phosphor coating on the glass where the image is focused, and its electrical potential varies slightly in proportion to the levels of light it encounters. This varying potential becomes the basis of the video signal produced. Viking, Voyager, and many earlier spacecraft used vidicon-based imaging systems to send back spectacular images of Mars (Viking) and the outer planets: Jupiter, Saturn, Uranus, and Neptune (Voyager).

The newer charge coupled device (CCD) imaging system is typically a large-scale integrated circuit that has a two-dimensional array of hundreds of thousands of charge-isolated wells, each representing a pixel. Light falling on a well is absorbed by a photoconductive substrate (e.g., silicon) and releases a quantity of electrons proportional to the intensity of the incident light. The CCD then detects and stores an accumulated electrical charge, representing the light level on each well. These charges subsequently are read out for conversion to digital data. CCDs are much more sensitive to light over a wider portion of the electromagnetic spectrum than vidicon tubes; they are also less massive and require less energy to operate. In addition, they interface more easily with digital circuitry, simplifying (to some extent) onboard data processing and transmission back to Earth. The Galileo spacecraft's solid state imaging (SSI) instrument contains a CCD with an 800 x 800 pixel array. (See Figure 53.)

See also: GALILEO PROJECT; VIKING PROJECT; VOYAGER.

impact 1. A single, forceful collision of one mass in motion with a second mass that may be either in motion or at rest; for example, the *impact* of a meteoroid traveling at high velocity with the surface of the Moon. 2. Specifically in aerospace operations, the action or event of an object, such as a rocket or a space probe, striking the surface of a planet or natural satellite; the time of this event, as in from launch to *impact*. 3. To strike an object or surface, as in the kinetic energy weapon *impacted* its target at a velocity of 5 kilometers per second or the missile *impacted* 20 minutes after launch.

impact area 1. In general, an area having designated boundaries within the limits of which all ordnance is to make contact with the ground. 2. In aerospace operations, the area in which a rocket or missile strikes the surface of Earth or a space probe or spacecraft strikes the surface of a planet. With respect to missile range safety, an area surrounding an approved impact point. The extent and configuration of this area is based on the rocket vehicle or stage dispersion characteristics.

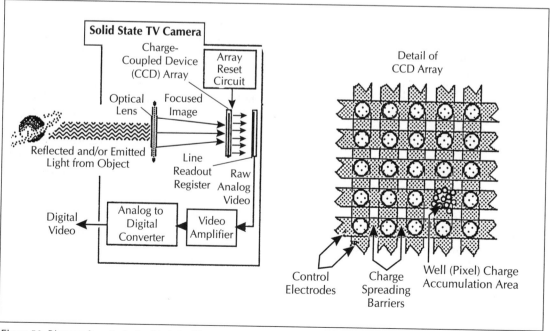

Figure 53. Diagram for a typical solid-state video imaging system with charge-coupled device (CCD) array *(Drawing courtesy of NASA/JPL)*

impact convoy An emergency response force, specifically to support aborted launch operations with technical direction and on-scene coordination being provided by missile range safety personnel.

impact crater A crater formed on the surface of a planetary body because of a high-velocity impact from a meteroid, asteroid, or comet. Impact craters are a common feature on most planetary bodies because cosmic projectiles (e.g., meteoroids, asteroids, and comets) have collided with planetary surfaces for billions of years. Some planetary objects, like the Moon, have no atmosphere and all of the encountered projectiles (called *impactors*) can approach the surface unimpeded. For other planetary objects with atmospheres (e.g., Earth, Venus, and Mars), only some of the encountered cosmic projectiles are able to penetrate the planet's atmosphere and impact the solid surface at velocities of ten or more kilometers per second with enough energy to generate shock waves in crustal rocks. These shock waves propagate to produce craters by the ejection of vapors, melted rocks, hot particles and fragments, and large blocks of fractured rock. Generally, impact craters have a circular outline, a raised rim, and a depth that is shallow relative to the diameter. The crater is surrounded by ejecta deposits that decrease in thickness outward from the crater rim.

Impact craters exhibit a wide range of degradation on different planetary bodies. On Earth, for example, craters are rapidly degraded and destroyed by weathering processes. In contrast, Venusian craters remain pristine because they are young, and very little weathering affects them. The heavily cratered lunar surface is essentially an "undisturbed" history of the cosmic bombardment that has occurred in the inner solar system since the Moon was formed.

See also: ASTEROID; COMET; METEOROIDS; MOON.

impact line With respect to missile range safety, an imaginary line on the outside of the DESTRUCT LINE and running parallel to it, which defines the outer limits of impact for fragments from a rocket or missile destroyed under command destruct procedures. Also called *impact limit line.*

See also: ABORT.

impact melt 1. Part of the spacecraft or target material that is melted by the impact of a hyperve-

locity projectile. 2. Rock melt produced on or within a planetary body by the hypervelocity impact of a meteoroid, asteroid, or comet. The term generally includes the small particles dispersed in various impact deposits and ejecta and larger pools and sheets of melt that coalesce in low areas within an impact crater. Impact melts are extremely uniform in their composition but highly variable in texture. They are composed predominantly of the target rocks but can contain a small amount of the impactor.

impact microphone A sensitive instrument that records the vibration of one object impacting another. This type of instrument is used on scientific spacecraft and space probes to record the impact of small meteoroids and cometary dust particles.

impactor 1. The meteoroid, asteroid, or comet that strikes a planetary surface at high velocity creating an impact crater. 2. The hypervelocity projectile fired by a kinetic energy weapon (KEW) system that strikes its target. 3. A piece of space debris that strikes an aerospace vehicle or spacecraft at hypervelocity.

impact pressure 1. Pressure of a moving fluid brought to rest that is in excess of the pressure the fluid has when it does not flow, that is, total pressure less static pressure. Impact pressure is equal to dynamic pressure in incompressible flow; but in compressible flow, impact pressure includes the pressure change owing to the compressibility effect. 2. A measured quantity obtained by placing an open-ended tube, known as an impact tube or PITOT TUBE, in a gas stream and noting the pressure in the tube on a suitable instrument, such as a manometer. Since pressure is exerted at a stagnation point, the impact pressure sometimes is referred to as the stagnation pressure.

impedance (symbol: Z) A quantity describing the total opposition to current flow [both resistance (R) and reactance (X)] in an alternating current (a.c.) circuit. For an a.c. circuit, the impedance can be expressed as:

$$Z^d = R^2 + X^2$$

where Z is the impedance, R is the resistance, and X is the reactance, all expressed in ohms (Ω).

impeller A device that imparts motion to a fluid; for example, in a centrifugal compressor, the impeller is a rotary disk that, faced on one or both sides with radial vanes, accelerates the incoming fluid outward into a diffuser.

impinging-stream injector In a liquid-propellant rocket engine, a device that injects the fuel and oxidizer into the combustion chamber in such a manner that the streams of fluid intersect one another.

implosion The rapid inward collapse of the walls of an evacuated system or device, as a result of the failure of the walls to sustain the ambient pressure. An implosion also can occur when a sudden sharp inward pressure force is exerted uniformly on the surface of an object or composite structure, causing it to crush and collapse inward. A submarine diving below the "crush depth" of its hull design will experience an implosion. The Galileo probe plunging into the depths of the Jovian atmosphere in December 1995 also experienced an implosion at the end of its brief but successful scientific mission. If the application of external pressure is sufficiently rapid and intense, even a solid metal object will experience some degree of "squeezing" and compression as its volume is decreased and its density increased during an implosion.

impulse (symbol: I) In general, a mechanical "jolt" delivered to an object that represents the total change in momentum the object experiences. Physically, the thrust force (F) integrated over the period of time (t_1 to t_2) it is applied. The impulse theorem is expressed mathematically as:

$$\text{Impulse (I)} = {}_1\!\int^2 F \, dt = \text{change of momentum of object,}$$

where F is the time-dependent thrust force applied from t_1 to t_2. If the thrust force is constant (or can be treated as approximately constant) during the period, then the impulse (I) becomes simply:

$$I = F \, \Delta t \text{ (the impulse approximation)}$$

where Δt is the total time increment. Impulse (I) has the units of newton-second (N-s) in the SI system. Also called the total impulse, I_{total}. Compare with but do not confuse with SPECIFIC IMPULSE (I_{sp}).

impulse intensity Mechanical impulse per unit area. The SI UNIT of impulse intensity is the pascal-second (Pa-s). A conventionally used unit of impulse intensity is the *tap*, which is 1 dyne-second per square centimeter.

$$1 \text{ tap} = 0.1 \text{ Pa-s}$$

impulse kill The destruction of a target by ablative shock using a directed energy weapon (DEW). The intensity of directed energy (e.g., a high-energy laser pulse) may be so great that the surface of the target violently and rapidly boils off, delivering a mechanical shock to the rest of the target and causing structural failure.

impulse stage Stage in a pump or turbine in which there is no change in static pressure across the rotor.

impulse tagging A possible technique for interactive target discrimination in ballistic missile defense. A high-powered laser strikes an object, ablating a small amount of surface material. The object recoils, and the speed of the recoil is inversely proportional to its mass. "Real" targets (e.g., warhead-equipped reentry vehicles) should be heavier than decoys and therefore recoil less. It is reasoned that an attacker would not spend the resources to deliver a mass-replicated decoy, since the same "booster expense" could be invested more wisely in sending another live warhead against the intended target, thereby increasing the probability of its destruction.
See also: BALLISTIC MISSILE DEFENSE.

incandescence Emission of light due to high temperature of the emitting material, as, for example, the very hot filament in an incandescent lamp. Any other emission of light is called *luminescence*.

inch (symbol: in) A unit of length found in the English (traditional engineering) system. An inch is defined as equal to 1/36 yard. By international agreement, 1 inch = 2.540 centimeters exactly.

inclination (symbol: i) One of the six Keplerian elements, it indicates the angle of the orbital plane to the central body's equator. The orbital plane always goes through the center of Earth but may be

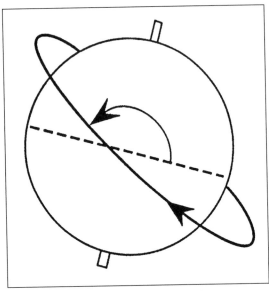

Figure 54. Inclination (i) is one of the six Keplerian elements used to describe the orbit of an object around its primary (central body). The inclination is the angle of the orbital plane with respect to the equatorial plane of the central body.   *(Diagram courtesy of NASA)*

tilted at any angle relative to the equator. Inclination (i) is the angle between the equatorial plane and the orbital plane measured counterclockwise at the ascending node. (See Figure 54.) A satellite traveling eastward in an orbit that exactly matches the equator has an inclination of 0°, whereas one whose orbit crosses the Earth's poles has an inclination of 90°. Because the angle is measured in a counterclockwise direction, it is quite possible for a satellite to have an inclination of more than 90 degrees. An inclination of 180 degrees would mean the satellite is orbiting the equator in a westward direction, that is, in the opposite direction of Earth's rotation. Some sun-synchronous satellites that maintain the same ground track throughout the year have inclinations of as much as 98 degrees. A satellite traveling generally "eastward" with an inclination between 0 degrees and 90 degrees is considered to be in a *prograde orbit*; a satellite traveling generally "westward" with an inclination greater than 90° is said to be in a RETRO-GRADE ORBIT.

See also: KEPLERIAN ELEMENTS; ORBITS OF OBJECTS IN SPACE.

incompressible fluid A fluid for which the density (ρ) is assumed constant.

increment An increase in the value of a variable. Compare DECREMENT.

independent system In aerospace engineering, a system not influenced by other systems. For example, an independent circuit would not require other circuits to be functioning properly in order to perform its task. This "independent" characteristic requires that the circuit to be powered from an independent power supply, be controlled from a single source, and (in terms of redundancy) be tolerant of all credible failure modes in the corresponding redundant circuit or system. To make a system truly independent, the aerospace engineer also must exclude interface items such as mounting brackets and connectors that can create a common failure.

indications and warning (I&W) Those intelligence activities intended to detect and report time-sensitive intelligence information on foreign developments that could involve a threat to the United States or allied military, political, or economic interests or to U.S. citizens abroad. It includes forewarning of enemy actions or intentions; the imminence of hostilities; insurgency; nuclear and nonuclear attack on the United States, its overseas forces, or allied nations; hostile reactions to U.S. reconnaissance activities (as, e.g., interfering with or destroying a satellite system); terrorist attacks; and other similar events.

induction heating The heating of an electrically conducting material using a varying electromagnetic field to induce eddy currents within the material. This may be an undesirable effect in electric power generation and distribution equipment but a desirable effect in materials processing (e.g., an induction heating furnace).

inert In aerospace operations, not containing an explosive or other hazardous material such that checkout operations can be conducted in a less restrictive manner and so that anomalies can occur in a safe configuration.

inert atmosphere A gaseous medium that because of its lack of chemical reaction is used to enclose tests or equipment. Helium (He) often is used to provide an inert atmosphere.

inert gas Any one of six "noble" gases: helium (He), neon (Ne), argon (Ar), krypton (Kr), xenon

(Xe), and radon (Rn), all of which are almost completely chemically inactive. All of these gases are found in Earth's atmosphere in small amounts.

inertia The resistance of a body to a change in its state of motion. Mass (m) is an inherent property of a body that helps us quantify inertia. *Newton's First Law of Motion* sometimes is called the "Law of Inertia"—namely: a body in motion will remain in motion unless acted upon by an external force and a body at rest will remain at rest unless acted upon by an external force.
See also: NEWTON'S LAWS OF MOTION.

inertial guidance system A guidance system designed to project a missile or rocket over a predetermined path, wherein the path of the vehicle is adjusted after launching by (inertial) devices wholly within the missile or rocket and independent of outside information. The inertial guidance system measures and converts accelerations experienced to distance traveled in a certain direction.
See also: GUIDANCE SYSTEM.

inertial orbit An orbit that conforms with Kepler's laws of celestial motion. Kepler's laws describe the behavior of natural celestial bodies and spacecraft that are not under any type of propulsive power.
See also: KEPLER'S LAWS; ORBITS OF OBJECTS IN SPACE.

inertial upper stage (IUS) An orbital transfer vehicle (OTV) used to boost payloads from LOW EARTH ORBIT (LEO) to higher-altitude destinations, such as GEOSYNCHRONOUS EARTH ORBIT (GEO). The inertial upper-stage (IUS) vehicle was developed by the U.S. Air Force for use with the space shuttle or with the Titan family of expendable launch vehicles (ELVs). The standard two-stage IUS measures approximately 2.9 meters (m) (9.5 feet [ft]) in diameter by about 4.9 m (16 ft) in height. It has an initial mass of approximately 14,500 kilograms (k) (32,000 pounds-mass (lbm)). A space shuttle–deployed IUS upper stage is capable of boosting payloads with a mass of up to 2,270 k (5,000 pounds-mass (lbm)) into geosynchronous Earth orbit. A Titan IV expendable launch vehicle–deployed IUS is capable of boosting a 2,360 k (5,250 lbm) payload to GEO.

IUS propulsion on the standard two-stage unit is provided by two solid rocket motors. The first-stage solid-propellant rocket motor contains about 9,700 k (21,400 lbm) of solid propellant and gener-

ates a thrust of about 185,000 newtons (41,600 pounds-force). The second-stage solid-propellant rocket motor contains about 2,720 k (17,600 lbm) of propellant and generates about 78,300 newtons (17,600 lbf) of thrust. The second stage has an extendable exit cone for increased system performance.
See also: UPPER STAGE.

inferior planet(s) Planets that have orbits that lie inside Earth's orbit around the Sun—namely, Mercury and Venus.

infinity (symbol: ∞) A quantity beyond measurable limits.

inflection Reversal of direction of curvature; the point on a curve where the tangent changes from rotation in one direction to rotation in the opposite direction. The point at which this reversal takes place is called the *inflection point.*

in-flight phase The flight of a missile or rocket from launch to detonation or impact; the flight of a spacecraft from launch to the time of planetary flyby, encounter and orbit, or impact.

in-flight start An engine ignition sequence after take-off and during flight. This term includes starts both within and above the sensible atmosphere.

infrahuman A live animal (other than a man or woman) that is used as a substitute for a human being in aerospace life-science experiments.

Infrared Astronomical Satellite (IRAS) The *Infrared Astronomical Satellite (IRAS)*, which was launched in January 1983, was the first extensive scientific effort to explore the universe in the infrared portion of the electromagnetic spectrum. *IRAS* was an international effort involving the United States, the United Kingdom, and the Netherlands. By the time *IRAS* ceased operations in November 1983, this successful space-based infrared telescope had completed the first all-sky survey in a wide range of IR wavelengths with a sensitivity 100 to 1,000 times greater than any previous telescope.

infrared (IR) astronomy The branch of astronomy dealing with infrared (IR) radiation from celestial objects. Most celestial objects emit some quantity of infrared radiation. However, when a star is not quite hot enough to shine in the visible portion of the electromagnetic spectrum, it emits the bulk of its energy in the infrared. IR astronomy, consequently, involves the study of relatively cool celestial objects, such as interstellar clouds of dust and gas (typically about 100° Kelvin [K]) and stars with surface temperatures below about 6,000° K.

Many interstellar dust and gas molecules emit characteristic infrared signatures that astronomers use to study chemical processes occurring in interstellar space. This same interstellar dust also prevents astronomers from viewing visible light coming from the center of our Milky Way Galaxy. However, IR radiation from the galactic nucleus is absorbed not as severely as radiation in the visible portion of the electromagnetic spectrum, and IR astronomy enables scientists to study the dense core of the Milky Way.

Infrared astronomy also allows astrophysicists to observe stars as they are being formed (called protostars) in giant clouds of dust and gas (called nebula), long before their thermonuclear furnaces have ignited and they have "turned on" their visible emission.

Unfortunately, water and carbon dioxide in Earth's atmosphere absorb most of the interesting IR radiation arriving from celestial objects. Earth-based astronomers can use only a few narrow IR spectral bands or windows in observing the universe; and even these IR windows are distorted by "sky noise" (undesirable IR radiation from atmospheric molecules). With the arrival of the space age, however, astronomers have placed sophisticated IR telescopes (such as the INFRARED ASTRONOMICAL SATELLITE) in space, above the limiting and disturbing effects of Earth's atmosphere, and have produced comprehensive catalogs and maps of significant infrared sources in the observable universe.

infrared (IR) imagery That imagery produced as a result of electro-optically sensing electromagnetic radiations emitted or reflected from a given object or target surface in the infrared portion of the electromagnetic spectrum (which extends from approximately 0.72 micrometers [near infrared] to about 1,000 micrometers [far infrared]). *Thermal imagery* is infrared imagery associated with the 8- to 14-micrometer thermal infrared region. Note: Infrared imagery *is not* the same as photographs produced using infrared film.

infrared (IR) photography Photography employing an optical system and direct image recording on "infrared film" that is sensitive to near-infrared wavelengths (about 1.0 micrometer). Note: Infrared photography *is not* the same as infrared imagery.

infrared (IR) radiation That portion of the electromagnetic (EM) spectrum lying between the optical (visible) and radio wavelengths. It is generally considered to span three decades of the EM spectrum, from 1 micrometer to 1,000 micrometers wavelength. The English-German astronomer Sir William Herschel (1738–1822) is credited with the discovery of infrared radiation.
See also: ELECTROMAGNETIC SPECTRUM.

infrared (IR) radiometer A telescope-based instrument that measures the intensity of thermal (infrared) energy radiated by targets. This type of instrument often is found as part of the instrument package on a scientific spacecraft. For example, by filling the IR radiometer's field of view completely with the disc of a target planet and measuring its total thermal energy output, the planet's thermal energy balance can be computed, revealing to space scientists the ratio of solar heating to the planet's internal heating.

infrared (IR) sensor A sensor (often placed on a military satellite) that detects the characteristic infrared (IR) radiation from a missile plume, a reentry vehicle, or a "cold body" target in space. Depending on the detector materials and instrument design (e.g., actively cooled versus passively cooled), IR sensors respond to different portions of the IR region of the electromagnetic spectrum and, therefore, support different applications in defense and space science.
See also: BALLISTIC MISSILE DEFENSE; INFRARED ASTRONOMY.

infrasonic frequency A frequency below the audiofrequency range; that is, below the audible limit of about 15 to 20 hertz. The word "infrasonic" may be used as a modifier to indicate a device or system intended to operate at an infrasonic frequency.

infrastructure A term generally applicable to all fixed and permanent installations or facilities for the support and control of aerospace systems.

inhibit device A electromechanical device that prevents a hazardous event from occurring. This device has direct control—that is, it is not simply a device monitoring a potentially hazardous situation, nor is it in indirect control of some device experiencing the hazardous circumstances. All inhibit devices are independent from each other and are verifiable. A temperature limit switch that shuts down a device or system before a potentially hazardous temperature condition is reached (i.e., at some safe preset temperature limit) is an example of an inhibit device.

inhibitor In general, anything that inhibits; specifically, a substance bonded, taped, or dip-dried onto a solid propellant to restrict the burning surface and to give direction to the burning process.

initial mass The mass of a rocket vehicle at launch.

initiation 1. In general, the process of starting combustion, explosion, or detonation of materials by such means as impact, friction, electrostatic discharge, shock, fragment impact, flame, or heat. 2. The action of a device used as the first element of an explosive train, which, upon receipt of the proper impulse, causes the detonation or burning of an explosive item. 3. With respect to nuclear weapons, the action that sets off a chain reaction in a fissile mass of nuclear material (such as uranium-235 or plutonium-239) that has reached the critical state; generally achieved by the emission of a "burst" or "spurt" of neutrons.

initiator The part of the solid rocket igniter that converts a mechanical, electrical, or chemical input stimulus to an energy output that ignites the energy release system. Also called an *initiation system*.

injection 1. The introduction of fuel and oxidizer in the combustion chamber of a liquid propellant rocket engine. 2. The time following launch when nongravitational forces (e.g., thrust, lift, and drag) become negligible in their effect on the trajectory of a rocket or aerospace vehicle. 3. The process of putting a spacecraft up to escape velocity or a satellite into orbit around Earth.

injection cooling The method of reducing heat transfer to a body by mass transfer cooling, which is accomplished by injecting a fluid into the local flow field through openings in the surface of the body.

injector A device that propels (injects) fuel and/or oxidizer into a combustion chamber of a liquid-propellant rocket engine. The injector atomizes and mixes the propellants so that they can be combusted more easily and completely. Numerous types of injectors have been designed, including splash plate injectors, shower head (nonimpinging) injectors, and spray-type injectors.

inlet An entrance or orifice for the admission of fluid. Frequently used in compounds, such as inlet air, inlet air temperature, inlet casing, inlet duct, inlet guide wave, inlet port, inlet valve.

inner planets The terrestrial planets: Mercury, Venus, Earth, and Mars. These planets all have orbits around the Sun that lie inside the main asteroid belt.

input 1. The path through which information is applied to a device. 2. Information or data entered into a computer system for processing. 3. The quantity to be measured, or otherwise operated upon, that is received by an instrument. Also called the *input signal*. 4. Information or energy entering into a system. Compare with OUTPUT.

insertion The process of putting an artificial satellite, aerospace vehicle, or spacecraft into orbit.

instrument 1. (verb) To provide a rocket, aerospace vehicle, spacecraft, or component with instrumentation. 2. (noun) A device that detects, measures, records, or otherwise provides data about certain quantities (e.g., propellant supply available), activities (e.g., vehicle velocity), or environmental conditions (e.g., space radiation environment or surface temperature on a planet).

instrumentation 1. The installation and use of electronic, gyroscopic, and other instruments for the purpose of detecting, measuring, recording, telemetering, processing, or analyzing different values or quantities as encountered in the flight of a rocket, aerospace vehicle, or spacecraft. 2. The collection of such instruments in a rocket, aerospace vehicle, or spacecraft, as, for example, the *instrumentation package* for a scientific spacecraft. 3. The specialized branch of aerospace engineering concerned with the design, composition, arrangement, and operation of such instruments.

intact abort An abort of an aerospace vehicle mission in which the crew, payload, and vehicle are returned to the landing site.

See also: ABORT; ABORT MODES (SPACE TRANSPORTATION SYSTEM).

integer A whole number, such as 1, 7, 11, 34; a number that is not a fraction.

integral tank A fuel or oxidizer tank built within the normal contours of an aircraft or rocket vehicle and using the skin of the vehicle as a wall of the tank.

integrated circuit (IC) Electronic circuits, including transistors, resistors, capacitors, and their interconnections, fabricated on a single small piece of semiconductor material (chip). Categories of integrated circuits such as LSI (large-scale integration) and VLSI (very large-scale integration) refer to the level of integration, which denotes the number of transistors on a chip.

integrated simulation An aerospace training session that includes the aerospace vehicle crew, flight operations support personnel, and payload operations support personnel in combined operations simulating a portion of the flight.

integration 1. In aerospace, a combination of activities and processes leading to the assembly of payload and launch vehicle components, subsystems and system elements into a desired final configuration, and then the verification of compatibility among the assembled elements. 2. In computer technology, the process of combining software and hardware elements, networks, personnel, and procedures into an overall well-functioning system.

intelligence The product resulting from the processing of information concerning foreign nations, hostile or potentially hostile elements, or areas of actual or potential operations. The term also is applied to the activity that results in the product and to organizations engaged in such activity. The steps by which information is converted into intelligence and made available to users is called the *intelligence cycle*. There are five major steps in this cycle: (1) planning and direction, (2) collec-

tion, (3) processing, (4) production, and (5) dissemination.

intensive property A thermodynamic property that is independent of mass. Temperature (T), pressure (p), specific volume (v), and density (ρ) are examples of intensive properties. The internal energy (u), enthalpy (h), or entropy (s) of a thermodynamic system can be either an extensive property (if it represents the total value of the property) or an intensive property (if it represents the value per unit mass). For example, the total internal energy (U) of a system is expressed in joules and is an extensive thermodynamic property, while the specific internal energy (u) of a system is expressed in joules per kilogram (J/kg) and is an intensive property. Intensive thermodynamic properties are used in many thermodynamic analyses. However, mass (m) and total volume (V) are extensive thermodynamic properties, since these properties vary directly with the mass (or "extent") of the system.

See also: THERMODYNAMICS.

interactive discrimination Techniques for target discrimination that involve perturbing a target and observing its reactions to the perturbation. Examples include neutral particle beams producing neutrons or electrons in the target, impulse tagging with a laser (to cause the object to recoil), and laser thermal tagging (heating an object and observing the temperature rise).

See also: BALLISTIC MISSILE DEFENSE.

interception The act of destroying a moving target.

intercontinental ballistic missile (ICBM) A ballistic missile with a range capability in excess of 5,500 kilometers (3,000 nautical miles).

interdigitate To align two or more sets of fins or projections on a rocket so that each fin or projection of one set lies in a plane between the planes established by fins or projections of the other set or sets.

interface 1. In general, a common boundary, whether material or nonmaterial, between two parts of a system. 2. In engineering, a mechanical, electrical, or operational common boundary between two elements of an aerospace system, subsystem, or component. 3. In aerospace operations, the point or area where a relationship exists between two or more parts, systems, programs, persons, or procedures wherein physical and functional compatibility is required. 4. In fluid mechanics, a surface separating two fluids across which there is a dissimilarity of some fluid property, such as density or velocity, or some derivative of these properties. The equations of motion do not apply at the interface but are replaced by the boundary conditions.

interface verification Testing of space flight hardware interfaces by an acceptable method that confirms that those interfaces are compatible with the affected systems of an aerospace launch vehicle, missile, or spacecraft.

interference 1. Extraneous signals, noises, and the like that hinder proper reception of the desired signal in electronic, optical, or audio equipment. 2. In physics, the mutual effect of the meeting of two or more traveling waves or vibrations of any kind. Sometimes called *wave interference.*

interference fit The retention of a component in a mounting solely by virtue of the friction between the interfaces; the degree of friction (and therefore retention force) is governed by the relative dimensions of the mating parts. Also called *press fit.*

interferometer An instrument used to produce and measure interference fringes from two or more coherent wave trains from the same source. Interferometers are used to measure wavelengths, to measure the angular width of sources, to determine the angular position of sources (as in satellite tracking), and for many other scientific purposes. Radio (wavelength) interferometers represent one of the basic instruments of radio astronomy.

intergalactic Between or among the galaxies. Although no place in the universe is truly "empty," the space between clusters of galaxies comes very close. These intergalactic regions are thought to contain less than one atom in every 10 cubic meters (350 cubic feet).

intermediate-range ballistic missile (IRBM) A ballistic missile with a range capability from about 1,000 to 5,500 kilometers (550 to 3,000 nautical miles).

internal energy (symbol: u) A thermodynamic property interpretable through statistical mechanics as a measure of the microscopic energy modes (i.e., molecular activity) of a system. This property appears in a first law of thermodynamics energy balance for a closed system as:

$$du = dq - dw$$

where du is the increment of specific internal energy, dq is the increment of thermal energy (heat) added to system, and dw is the increment of work done by the system per unit mass.

See also: THERMODYNAMICS.

International System of Units (SI) The metric system of units based on the meter (m), kilogram (kg), second (s), ampere (A), Kelvin degree (°K), mole (mol), and candela (cd). Other derived and supplementary SI units include: hertz (Hz), henry (H), joule (J), newton (N), watt (W), becquerel (Bq), gray (Gy), sievert (Sv), volt (V), ohm (Ω),pascal (Pa), coulomb (C), lumen (lm), lux (lx), radian (rad), steradian (sr), siemens (S), weber (Wb) and farad (F). Also called *Système International d'Unités,* or *SI units.*

International Telecommunications Satellite (INTELSAT) The international organization involved in the development of a family of highly successful commercial communications satellites of the same name.

See also: COMMUNICATIONS SATELLITE.

International Ultraviolet Explorer (IUE) A highly successful scientific spacecraft launched in January 1978. Operated jointly by NASA and the European Space Agency (ESA), the *IUE* has helped astronomers from around the world obtain access

FUNDAMENTAL SI UNITS	
Name (and Symbol)	**Physical Quantity Represented**
meter (m)	length
kilogram (kg)	mass
second (s)	time
ampere (A)	electric current
candela (cd)	luminous intensity
kelvin (K)	thermodynamic temperature
mole (mol)	amount of substance

DERIVED AND SUPPLEMENTARY SI UNITS	
Name (and Symbol)	Physical Quantity Represented
becquerel (Bq)	radioactivity
coulomb (C)	electric charge
farad (F)	electric capacitance
gray (Gy)	absorbed dose of ionizing radiation
henry (H)	inductance
hertz (Hz)	frequency
joule (J)	energy
lumen (lm)	luminous flux
lux (lx)	illuminance
newton (N)	force
ohm (Ω)	electric resistance
pascal (Pa)	pressure
radian (rad)	plane angle
siemens (S)	electric conductance
sievert (Sv)	ionizing radiation dose equivalent
steradian (sr)	solid angle
tesla (T)	magnetic flux density
volt (V)	electric potential difference
watt (W)	power
weber (Wb)	magnetic flux

to the ultraviolet (UV) radiation of celestial objects in unique ways not available by other means. The spacecraft contains a 0.45-meter (1.48-foot) aperture telescope solely for spectroscopy in the wavelength range from 115 to 325 nanometers (nm) [1150 to 3250 angstroms (Å)]. *IUE* data helps support fundamental studies of comets and their evaporation rate when they approach the Sun and of the mechanisms driving the stellar winds that make many stars lose a significant fraction of their mass (before they die slowly as white dwarfs or suddenly in supernova explosions). This long-lived international spacecraft also has assisted astrophysicists in their search to understand the ways by which BLACK HOLES possibly power the turbulent and violent nuclei of active galaxies.

Internet An enormous global computer network that links many government agencies, research laboratories, universities, private companies, and individuals. This worldwide computer network has its origins in the "ARPA-net"—a small experimental computer network established by the Advanced Research Project Agency (ARPA) of the U.S. Department of Defense in the 1970s to permit rapid communication among universities, laboratories, and military project offices.

interplanetary Between the planets; within the solar system.

interplanetary dust (IPD) Tiny particles of matter (typically less than 100 micrometers in diameter) that exist in space within the confines of our solar system. By convention, the term applies to all solid bodies ranging in size from submicrometer diameter to tens of centimeters in diameter, with corresponding masses ranging from 10^{-17} gram to approximately 10 kilograms. Near Earth the IPD flux is taken as approximately 10^{-13} to 10^{-12} gram per square meter per second [g/m^2-s)]. Space scientists have made rough estimates that Earth collects about 10,000 metric tons of IPD per year. They also estimate that the entire IPD "cloud" in the solar system has a total mass of between 10^{+16} and 10^{+17} kilograms.

interstage section A section of a missile or rocket that lies between stages.

interstellar Between or among the stars.

interstellar communication and contact Several methods of achieving contact with (postulated) intelligent extraterrestrial life-forms have been suggested. These methods include: (1) interstellar travel by means of starships, leading to physical contact between different civilizations; (2) indirect contact through the use of robot (i.e., uncrewed) interstellar probes; (3) serendipitous contact, such as finding a derelict alien starship or probe drifting in the main asteroid belt; (4) interstellar communication involving the transmission and reception of electromagnetic signals; and (5) very "exotic" techniques involving information transfer through the modulation of gravitons, neutrinos, or streams of tachyons; the use of some form of telepathy; and perhaps even matter transport by means of distortions in the space-time continuum that help "beat" the speed-of-light barrier that now underlies our understanding of the physical universe.

See also: SEARCH FOR EXTRATERRESTRIAL INTELLIGENCE (SETI).

interstellar medium (ISM) The gas and dust particles that are found between the stars in our galaxy, the Milky Way. Up until about three decades ago, the interstellar medium was considered to be an uninteresting void. Today, through advances in astronomy (especially infrared and radioastronomy), we now know that the interstellar medium contains a rich and interesting variety of atoms and molecules as well as a population of fine-grained dust particles. Over 100 interstellar molecules have been discovered to date, including many organic molecules considered essential in the development of life. Interstellar dust (which "reddens" the visible light from the stars behind it because of its preferential scattering of shorter-wavelength photons) is considered to consist of very fine silicate particles, typically 0.1 micrometers in diameter. These interstellar "sands" sometimes may have an irregularly shaped coating of water ice, ammonia ice, or solidified carbon dioxide.

interstellar probe A highly automated interstellar spacecraft sent from our solar system to explore other star systems. Most likely this type of probe would make use of very smart machine systems capable of operating autonomously for decades or centuries. Once the robot probe arrives at a new star system, it would begin a detailed exploration procedure. The target star system is scanned for possible life-bearing planets, and if any are detected, they become the object of more intense scientific investigations. Data collected by the "mother" interstellar probe and any miniprobes (deployed to explore individual objects of interest within the new star system) are transmitted back to Earth. There, after light-years of travel, the signals are intercepted and analyzed by scientists, and interesting discoveries and information are used to enrich our understanding of the universe.

Robot interstellar probes also might be designed to carry specially engineered microorganisms, spores, and bacteria. If a probe encounters ecologically suitable planets on which life has not yet evolved, then it could "seed" such barren but potentially fertile worlds with primitive life-forms or at least life precursors. In that way, human beings (through their robot probes) would not only be exploring neighboring star systems but would be participating in the spreading of life itself through some portion of the Milky Way Galaxy.

interstellar travel In general, matter transport between star systems in a galaxy; specifically, trav-

el beyond our own solar system. The "matter" transported may be: (1) a robot interstellar probe on an exploration mission; (2) an automated spacecraft that carries a summary of the cultural and technical heritage of a civilization (e.g., the plaques on the *Pioneer 10* and *11* spacecraft and the "recorded message" on the *Voyager 1* and *2* spacecraft); (3) a "crewed" starship on a long-term round-trip voyage of scientific exploration; or even (4) a giant "interstellar ark" that is designed to transport a portion of the human race on a one-way mission beyond the solar system in search of new, suitable planetary systems to explore and inhabit.

intravehicular activity (IVA) Crew activities performed inside an orbiting aerospace vehicle or space station; for example, an astronaut going from the habitation module to a research module on the space station using appropriate tunnels and passageways would be performing intravehicular activity. This term can be a bit confusing, however, since it is dependent on where the activity is performed and is independent of the local atmospheric pressure. With respect to the space shuttle orbiter, therefore, IVA means crew activities performed inside the orbiter vehicle, within a payload module (such as the Spacelab) carried in the cargo bay, or within the cargo bay itself (a space-suit–required environment) when the cargo bay doors are closed. An emergency response team, wearing space suits and traveling *on the inside* of a space station module to repair a pressure hull leak, also would be engaged in IVA. Compare with EXTRAVEHICULAR ACTIVITY.

intrinsically safe In aerospace operations, incapable of producing sufficient energy to ignite an explosive atmosphere.

inverse-square law A relation between physical quantities of the form: x proportional to $1/y^2$, where y is usually a distance; and x terms are of two kinds, forces and fluxes. NEWTON'S LAW OF GRAVITATION is an example of the inverse-square law. This relationship is:

$$F = [Gm_1 m_2]/r^2$$

where F is the gravitational force between two objects having masses, m_1 and m_2, respectively, G is the gravitational constant, and r is the distance between these two masses. Note that the force of gravitational attraction decreases as the inverse of the distance squared (i.e., as $1/r^2$).

inverter A device for changing direct current (d.c.) into alternating current (a.c.)

inviscid fluid A hypothesized "perfect" fluid that has zero coefficient of viscosity. Physically this means that shear stresses are absent despite the occurrence of shearing deformations in the fluid. The inviscid fluid also glides past solid boundaries without sticking. No real fluids are inviscid. In fact, since real fluids are viscous, they stick to solid boundaries during flow processes creating thin boundary layers where shear forces are significant. However, the inviscid (perfect) fluid approximation provides a useful model that approximates the behavior of real fluids in many flow situations.

in vitro Literally, "in glass." A life sciences term describing biological tests using cells from an organism but occuring outside that living organism in a laboratory apparatus, such as a glass test tube.

in vivo Literally, "in a living organism (body)." A life sciences term describing biological experiments that take place within (or using) a living organism, such as a test animal or human volunteer. Astronauts often participate in an interesting variety of in vivo life science experiments while on extended flights in microgravity.

ion An atom or molecule that has lost or (more rarely) gained one or more electrons. By this *ionization process,* it becomes electrically charged.

ion engine An electrostatic rocket engine in which a propellant (e.g., cesium, mercury, argon, or xenon) is ionized and the propellant ions are accelerated by an imposed electric field to very high exhaust velocity.
See also: ELECTRIC PROPULSION.

ionization The process of producing ions by the removal of electrons from, or the addition of electrons to, atoms or molecules. High temperatures, electrical discharges, or nuclear radiations can cause ionization.

ionizing radiation Any type of nuclear radiation that displaces electrons from atoms or molecules,

thereby producing ions within the irradiated material. Examples include: alpha (α) radiation, beta (β) radiation, gamma (γ) radiation, protons, neutrons, and X rays.

ionospheric storm Disturbances of Earth's ionosphere (caused by solar flare activity), resulting in anomalous variations in its characteristics and effects on radio wave propagation. In general, ionospheric storms can persist for several days and cover large portions of the globe. Two types of storms of particular interest are: the polar-cap absorption (PCA) event and the geomagnetically induced storm. As the name implies, the polar-cap absorption (PCA) event occurs at high latitudes and is associated with the arrival of very energetic solar flare protons. Radio communications blackouts usually occur as a result of a PCA event. The geomagnetically induced ionospheric storm occurs along with periods of special auroral activity. Unlike PCA events, the geomagnetic storms are more intense at night. Finally, the sudden ionospheric disturbance (SID) appears within a few minutes of the occurrence of strong solar flares and causes a fade-out of long-distance radio communications on the sunlit part of Earth.

ion pair A closely associated positive ion and negative ion (usually an electron) having charges of the same magnitude and formed from a neutral atom or molecule by nuclear radiation.

irradiance (symbol: E) The total radiant flux (electromagnetic radiation of all wavelengths) received on a unit area of a given surface; usually measured in watts per meter-squared (W/m^2). Compare ILLUMINANCE.

irradiated food Food that has been treated with specified doses of nuclear radiation (usually gamma rays) to kill insects, bacteria, and mold, and to preserve the food without need for refrigeration or freezing. Some of the food consumed by astronauts during space flight has been irradiated food. (Note: Irradiated food does *not* become radioactive; it is merely better preserved using this modern processing technique.)

irreversible process In thermodynamics, a process that cannot return both the system and the surroundings to their original conditions. Four common causes of irreversibility in a thermodynamic process are: friction, heat transfer through a finite temperature difference, the mixing of two different substances, and unrestrained expansion of a fluid. The exhausting of combustion gases through a rocket engine's nozzle is an irreversible process.

isentropic Of equal or constant entropy.
See also: ENTROPY; THERMODYNAMICS.

isentropic process In thermodynamics, a reversible, adiabatic process is an isentropic (constant entropy) process.
See also: THERMODYNAMICS.

isobaric Of equal or constant pressure.

isochoric Of equal or constant volume; usually applied to a thermodynamic process during which the volume of the system remains unchanged.

isomer 1. In nuclear physics, one of two or more nuclides with the same numbers of neutrons and protons in their nuclei but with different energies; a nuclide in an excited state and a similar nuclide in the ground state are isomers. 2. In chemistry, one of two or more molecules having the same atomic composition and molecular weight but differing in geometric configuration.

isomeric transition A radioactive transition from one nuclear isomer (in an excited energy state) to another of lower energy. This transition often is accompanied by the emission of a gamma ray or by internal conversion (IC) followed by the emission of X rays and/or Auger electrons.

isothermal process In thermodynamics, any process or change of state of a system that takes place at constant temperature.
See also: THERMODYNAMICS.

isothermal solidification In materials processing, the cooling and subsequent solidification of a melt that occurs under uniform temperature conditions throughout the phase-changing melt.

isotope One of two or more atoms with the same *atomic number* (Z) (i.e., the same chemical element) but with different atomic weights. An equivalent statement is that the nuclei of isotopes have the same number of protons but different numbers of neutrons. Therefore, carbon-12 ($^{12}_6C$), carbon-13 ($^{13}_6C$), and carbon-14 ($^{14}_6C$) are all isotopes of the element carbon. The subscripts denote their common atomic number (i.e., $Z = 6$), while the superscripts denote their differing *atomic mass numbers* (i.e., $A = 12$, 13, and 14 respectively), or approximate atomic weights. Isotopes usually have very nearly the same chemical properties but different physical and nuclear properties. For example, the isotope carbon-14 is radioactive, while the isotopes carbon-12 and carbon-13 are both stable (nonradioactive).

isotope power system A device that uses the thermal energy deposited by the absorption of alpha or beta particles from a radioisotope (radioactive material) as the heat source to produce electric power by direct energy conversion or dynamic conversion (thermodynamic cycle) processes. (Note: Radioisotopes that emit gamma rays are not normally considered suitable for this application because of the shielding requirements.) A variety of radioisotope thermoelectric generators (RTGs), powered by the alpha-emitting radioisotope plutonium-238 ($^{238}_{94}Pu$), has been used very successfully to provide continuous, long-term electric power to spacecraft such as *Pioneer 10* and *11*, *Voyager 1* and *2*, *Ulysses*, *Galileo*, and the *Viking* Mars Landers.
See also: GALILEO PROJECT; PIONEER 10, 11; SPACE NUCLEAR POWER; ULYSSES MISSION; VIKING PROJECT; VOYAGER.

isotropic Having uniform properties in all directions.

isotropic radiator An energy source that radiates (emits) particles or photons uniformly in all directions.

jacket 1. A covering or casing of some kind. 2. Specifically, a shell around the combustion chamber of a liquid-fuel rocket, through which the propellant is circulated in regenerative cooling. 3. A coating of one material over another to prevent oxidation, micrometeoroid penetration, and so on.

jamming Intentional transmission or reradiation of radio or radar frequency signals in such a way as to interfere with reception of desired signals by the intended receiver.

jansky (symbol: Jy) A unit used to describe the strength of an incoming electromagnetic wave signal. The jansky frequently is used in radio and infrared astronomy. It is named after the American radio engineer Karl G. Jansky (1905–1950), who discovered extraterrestrial radiowave sources in the 1930s, a discovery generally regarded as the birth of radio astronomy.

$$1 \text{ jansky (Jy)} = 10^{-26} \text{ watts per meter-squared per hertz } [\text{W}/(\text{m}^2\text{-Hz})]$$

See also: RADIO ASTRONOMY.

Japanese Earth Resources Satellite (JERS) The Japanese Earth Resources Satellite (JERS-1) was launched successfully by an H-1 rocket vehicle from the Tanegashima Space Center in Japan and placed into a Sun-synchronous, 568-kilometer (353-mile) altitude orbit on February 11, 1992. This spacecraft observes Earth with a high-performance synthetic aperture radar (SAR) (1.275 gigahertz frequency [L-band] microwave) system and a companion optical sensor (OPS) that covers seven spectral bands from the visible to near-infrared portion of the electromagnetic spectrum. Global JERS-1 data are being used for national land surveys, agriculture and forestry assessment, environmental protection, disaster prevention, and coastal monitoring. Also called *Fuyo-1*.

See also: REMOTE SENSING.

jet 1. A strong, well-defined stream of fluid either issuing from an orifice or moving in a contracted duct, such as the jet of combustion gases coming out of a reaction engine or the jet in the test section in a wind tunnel. 2. A tube or nozzle through which fluid passes or emerges in a "jet," such as the jet in a liquid propellant rocket motor's injector. 3. A jet engine 4. A jet aircraft

jet propulsion Reaction propulsion in which the propulsion unit obtains oxygen from the air, as distinguished from rocket propulsion, in which the unit carries its own oxidizer (i.e., oxygen-producing material). In connection with aircraft propulsion, the term refers to a turbine jet unit (usually burning hydrocarbon fuel) that discharges hot gas through a tail pipe and a nozzle, producing a thrust that propels the aircraft.

See also: ROCKET PROPULSION.

Jet Propulsion Laboratory (JPL) NASA's Jet Propulsion Laboratory (JPL) is located near Pasadena, California, approximately 32 kilometers (20 miles) northeast of Los Angeles. JPL is a government-owned facility operated by the California Institute of Technology under a NASA contract. In addition to the Pasadena site, JPL operates the worldwide Deep Space Network (DSN), including a DSN station, at Goldstone, California.

This laboratory is engaged in activities associated with deep-space automated scientific missions, such as subsystem engineering, instrument development, and data reduction and analysis required by deep space flight. The Galileo spacecraft's exploration of the Jovian system is a current JPL mission.

See also: NATIONAL AERONAUTICS AND SPACE ADMINISTRATION (NASA).

jetstream A *jet* issuing from an orifice into a much more slowly moving medium, such as the stream of combustion products ejected from a reaction engine. This term also is used in meteorology, but appears as two words, namely *jet stream*.

See also: JET STREAM.

jet stream A strong band of wind or winds in the upper troposphere or in the stratosphere, moving in the general direction from west to east and often reaching velocities of hundreds of kilometers an hour.

See also: JETSTREAM.

jettison To discard. For example, when the propellant in the booster stage of a multistage rocket vehicle is used up, the now-useless booster stage is *jettisoned*—that is, it is separated from the upper stage(s) of the launch vehicle and allowed to fall back to Earth, usually impacting in a remote ocean area.

jet vane A vane, either fixed or movable, used in a JETSTREAM, especially in the jetstream of a rocket, for the purposes of stability or control under conditions where external aerodynamic controls are ineffective.

jitter 1. Instability of the signal or trace of a cathode ray tube. 2. Small rapid variations in a signal or waveform due to accidental or deliberate disturbances in the key components of a sensing system, such as unwanted mechanical motions or unexpected and electrical transients.

Johnson Space Center (JSC) NASA's Lyndon B. Johnson Space Center (JSC) is located about 32 kilometers (20 miles) southeast of downtown Houston, Texas. This center was established in September 1961 as NASA's primary center for: (1) the design, development, and testing of spacecraft and associated systems for human space flight; (2) the selection and training of astronauts; (3) the planning and supervision of crewed space missions; and (4) extensive participation in the medical, engineering, and scientific experiments aboard human crew space flights. The Mission Control Center (MCC) at JSC is the central facility from which all U.S. crewed space flights are monitored.

joule (symbol: J) The unit of energy or work in the INTERNATIONAL SYSTEM OF UNITS (SI). It is defined as the work done (or its energy equivalent) when the point of application of a force of one newton moves a distance of one meter in the direction of the force.

1 joule (J) = 1 newton-meter (N-m) =
1 watt-second (W-s) = 10^7 erg =
0.2388 calories

This unit is named in honor of the British physicist James Prescott Joule (1818–1889).

Joule heating The generation of heat (thermal energy) as a result of the passage of an electric current through a conductor material. The heat (Q) produced by a constant-value electric current (I) flowing through a resistance (R) for a fixed time (t) is given by the expression:

$$Q_{Joule} = [I^2R] \, t$$

where Q_{Joule} is the amount of Joule heating (joules), I is the current (amperes), R is the resistance (ohms), and t is the time (seconds). The above-stated principle is sometimes also called *Joule's law* or *Joule's law of heating*.

Joule-Thomson effect The change (decrease) in temperature that takes place when a gas expands through a throttling device, such as a nozzle or a porous plug, into a lower-pressure region. In the Joule-Thomson effect, the rate of change of temperature (T) with pressure (p) is called the Joule-Thomson coefficient (symbol: μ) expressed as

$$\mu = (\partial T/\partial p)_h$$

where h denotes constant ENTHALPY. Also called the *Joule-Kelvin effect*.

Jovian Of or relating to the planet Jupiter.

Jovian planet One of the major, or giant, planets that is characterized by a great total mass, low average density, and an abundance of the lighter elements (especially hydrogen and helium). The

Jovian planets are Jupiter, Saturn, Uranus, and Neptune.

See also: JUPITER; NEPTUNE; SATURN; URANUS.

JP-4 A liquid, hydrocarbon fuel for jet and rocket engines, the chief ingredient of which is kerosene.

Juno The Juno I and Juno II were early NASA expendable launch vehicles adapted from existing U.S. Army missiles. These rocket vehicles were named after the ancient Roman goddess, Juno, queen of the gods, and wife of Jupiter, king of the Gods. The Juno I, a four-stage configuration of the Jupiter C vehicle, orbited the first U.S. satellite, *Explorer 1*, on January 31, 1958. The Juno V was the early designation of the launch vehicle that eventually became the Saturn I rocket.

Table 1.
PHYSICAL AND DYNAMIC PROPERTIES OF JUPITER

Diameter (equatorial)	142,982 km
Mass	1.9×10^{27} kg
Density (mean)	1.32 g/cm^3
Surface gravity (equatorial)	23.1 m/s^2
Escape velocity	59.5 km/s
Albedo (visual geometric)	0.52
Atmosphere	Hydrogen (~89%), helium (~11%), also ammonia, methane, and water.
Natural satellites	16
Rings	3 (1 main, 2 minor)
Period of rotation (a "Jovian day")	0.413 day
Average distance from Sun	7.78×10^8 km (5.20 AU) [43.25 light-min]
Eccentricity	0.048
Period of revolution around Sun (a "Jovian year")	11.86 years
Mean orbital velocity	13.1 km/s
Magnetosphere	Yes (intense)
Radiation belts	Yes (intense)
Mean atmospheric temperature (at cloud tops)	~129 K
Solar flux at planet (at top of atmosphere)	50.6 W/m^2 (at 5.2 AU)

Source: NASA.

See also: EXPLORER I; LAUNCH VEHICLE.

Jupiter The largest planet in our solar system with more than twice the mass of all the other planets and their moons combined and a diameter of approximately 143,000 kilometers (km). It is the fifth planet from the Sun and is separated from the four terrestrial planets by the main asteroid belt. The giant planet, named after Jupiter, king of the gods in Roman mythology (Zeus in Greek mythology), rotates at a dizzying pace—about once every 9 hours and 55 minutes. It takes Jupiter almost 12 Earth-years to complete a journey around the Sun. Its mean distance from the Sun is about 5.2 astronomical units (AU), or 7.78×10^8 km. Table 1 provides a summary of the physical and dynamic characteristics of this giant planet.

The planet is distinguished by bands of colored clouds that change their appearance over time. One distinctive feature, the Great Red Spot, is a huge oval-shaped atmospheric storm that has persisted for at least three centuries. (See Figure 55.) In July 1994, 20 large fragments from the Comet Shoemaker-Levy crashed into the clouds of Jupiter, producing gigantic "Earth-size" disturbances in the Jovian cloud system. Scientists estimated that

Figure 55. The dynamic atmosphere of the planet Jupiter, as imaged by the Voyager spacecraft (1979)—including the Great Red Spot, which appears in the lower central portion of the image *(Photo courtesy of NASA—B&W Photo # 79-H-301)*

Table 2.
PROPERTIES OF THE MOONS OF JUPITER

Moon	Diameter (km)	Semimajor Axis of Orbit (km)	Period of Rotation (days)
Sinope	30 (approx)	23,700,000	758 (retrograde)
Pasiphae	40 (approx)	23,500,000	735 (retrograde)
Carme	30 (approx)	22,600,000	692 (retrograde)
Ananke	20 (approx)	21,200,000	631 (retrograde)
Elara	80 (approx)	11,740,000	260.1
Lysithea	20 (approx)	11,710,000	260
Himalia	180 (approx)	11,470,000	251
Leda	10 (approx)	11,110,000	240
Callisto[a]	4,820	1,880,000	16.70
Ganymede[a]	5,270	1,070,000	7.16
Europe[a]	3,130	670,900	3.55
Io[a]	3,640	422,000	1.77
Thebe (1979J2)	80 (approx)	222,000	0.675
Amalthea	270 (approx)	181,300	0.498
Adrastea (1979J1)	40 (approx)	129,000	0.298
Metis (1979J3)	40 (approx)	127,900	0.295

[a]Galilean satellite.
Source: NASA.

the largest cometary fragments (about 3 to 5 km in diameter) produced a blast in the Jovian atmosphere equivalent perhaps to as much as 6 million megatons per fragment.

Jupiter's atmosphere, explored in situ by the Galileo atmospheric probe (on December 7, 1995) is composed primarily of hydrogen and helium in approximately "stellar composition" abundances —that is, about 89% hydrogen (H) and 11% helium (He). In fact, Jupiter is sometimes called a near star. If it had been only about 100 times larger, nuclear burning could have started in its core, and Jupiter would have become a star to rival the Sun itself. Its

interesting complement of natural satellites even resembles a miniature solar system.

Jupiter has 16 known natural satellites and one artificial satellite, the Galileo spacecraft, which orbited the Jovian system in late 1995 on a multi-year mission of detailed scientific investigation. The four largest of Jupiter's moons are often called the Galilean satellites. They are: Io, Europa, Ganymede, and Callisto. These moons were discovered in 1610 by the Italian astronomer Galileo Galilei. Very little actually was known about the Jovian moons until the *Pioneer 10* and *11* and *Voyager 1* and *2* spacecraft encountered Jupiter

Table 3.
PHYSICAL DATA FOR THE GALILEAN MOONS

Galilean Moon	Diameter (km)	Mass (kg)	Density (g/cm^3)	Albedo
Callisto	4,820	1.07×10^{23}	1.8	0.17
Ganymede	5,270	1.49×10^{23}	1.9	0.43
Europa	3,130	0.487×10^{23}	3.0	0.64
Io	3,640	0.891×10^{23}	3.5	0.63

Source: NASA.

between 1973 and 1979. These flybys provided a great deal of valuable information and initial imagery, including the discovery of three new moons (Metis, Adrastea, and Thebe), active volcanism on Io, and a possible liquid-water ocean beneath the smooth icy surface of Europa. The highly elliptical orbit of the Galileo spacecraft is now providing the opportunity for several close-up inspections of Jupiter's major moons and will greatly supplement the current knowledge base for the Jovian system. Tables 2 and 3 provide selected physical and dynamic data for moons of Jupiter.

See also: GALILEO PROJECT; PIONEER 10, 11; VOYAGER.

Jupiter C A modified version of the Redstone ballistic missile developed by the U.S. Army and a direct descendant of the V-2 rocket developed in Germany during World War II. The Juno I, a four-stage configuration of the Jupiter C rocket, orbited the first American satellite (*Explorer I*) on January 31, 1958.

See also: EXPLORER I; JUNO.

Kapustin Yar A minor Russian launch complex that is located on the banks of the Volga River near Volgograd at approximately 48.4 degrees north latitude and 45.8 degrees east longitude. This complex originally was built to support the early Soviet ballistic missile test program; its first missile launch occurred in 1947. Since the launch of *Kosmos I* in 1962, the Kapustin Yar site has conducted relatively few (less than 100) space launches in comparison to the other two Russian launch complexes: Tyuratam (now in the Kazakstan Republic) and the Plesetsk Cosmodrome (south of Archangel in the northwest corner of Russia), which is sometimes called the world's busiest spaceport. However, Kapustin Yar has been used for small and intermediate-size payloads, including those launched for or in cooperation with other nations. For example, on April 19, 1975, with 50 scientists and technicians from India in attendance, the Indian satellite *Aryabhata* was sent into orbit from this complex.

keep-out zone A volume of space around a space asset (e.g., a military surveillance satellite) that is declared to be forbidden (i.e., "off-limits") to parties who are not owners/operators of the asset. Enforcement of such a zone is intended to protect space assets against attack, especially by space mines. Keep-out zones can be negotiated or unilaterally declared. The right to defend such a zone by force and the legality of unilaterally declared zones under the terms of the current Outer Space Treaty remain to be determined in space law.

kelvin (symbol: K) The International System (SI) unit of thermodynamic temperature. One kelvin is defined as the fraction 1/273.16 of the thermodynamic temperature of the triple point of water. The absolute zero of temperature has a temperature of 0° K. This unit is named after the British physicist Lord Kelvin (1824–1907).

See also: ABSOLUTE TEMPERATURE SCALE; INTERNATIONAL SYSTEM OF UNITS.

Kennedy Space Center (KSC) NASA's John F. Kennedy Space Center (KSC) is located on the east coast of Florida 241 kilometers (km) (150 miles [mi]) south of Jacksonville and approximately 80 km (50 mi) east of Orlando. KSC is immediately north and west of Cape Canaveral Air Force Station. The center is about 55 km (34 mi) long and varies in width from 8 km (5 mi) to 16 km (10 mi). The total land and water occupied by the installation is 56,817 hectares (140,393 acres). Of this total area, 34,007 hectares (84,031 acres) are NASA-owned. The remainder is owned by the State of Florida. This large area, with adjoining bodies of water, provides the buffer space necessary to protect the nearby civilian communities during space vehicle launches. Agreements have been made with the U.S. Department of the Interior supporting the use of the nonoperational (buffer) area as a wildlife refuge and national seashore.

KSC was established in the early 1960s to serve as the launch site for the Apollo-Saturn V lunar landing missions. After the Apollo program ended in 1972, Launch Complex 39 was used to support both the Skylab program (early nonpermanent U.S. space station) and the Apollo-Soyuz test project (an international rendezvous and docking demonstration involving spacecraft from the United States and Russia [former Soviet Union]).

The Kennedy Space Center now serves as the primary center within NASA for the test, checkout,

Figure 56. The space shuttle orbiter *Columbia,* being towed in front of the gigantic (160-meter tall) Vehicle Assembly Building (VAB) at the Kennedy Space Center   *(Photo courtesy of NASA)*

Keplerian Elements

a semi-major axis, gives the size of the orbit

e eccentricity, gives the shape of the orbit

i inclination angle, gives the angle of the orbit plane to the central body's equator

Ω right ascension of the ascending node, which gives the rotation of the orbit plane from reference axis

ω argument of perigee gives the rotation of the orbit in its plane

θ true anomaly gives the location of the satellite on the orbit

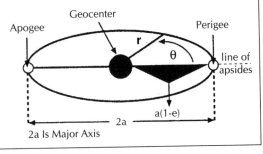

Figure 57. The six Keplerian or classical orbital elements that uniquely define the position of a satellite   *(Illustration courtesy of NASA)*

and launch of space vehicles. KSC responsibility includes the launching of crewed (space shuttle) vehicles at Launch Complex (LC) 39 and NASA uncrewed, expendable launch vehicles (such as a Delta II rocket) at both nearby Cape Canaveral Air Force Station and at Vandenberg Air Force Base in California.

The assembly, checkout, and launch of the space shuttle vehicles and their payloads takes place at the center. Weather conditions permitting, the orbiter vehicle lands at the Kennedy Space Center (after an orbital mission) and undergoes "turn-around," or processing between flights. The Vehicle Assembly Building (VAB) and the two shuttle launch pads at LC 39 may be the best-known structures at KSC, but other facilities also play critical roles in prelaunch processing of payloads and elements of the space shuttle system. Some buildings, such as the 160-meter (525-foot) tall VAB, were originally designed for the Apollo Project in the 1960s and then altered to accommodate the space shuttle. Other facilities, such as the Orbiter Processing Facility (OPF) high bays, were

designed and built exclusively for the space shuttle program. (See Figure 56.)

See also: NATIONAL AERONAUTICS AND SPACE ADMINISTRATION (NASA); SPACE TRANSPORTATION SYSTEM (STS).

Keplerian elements The Keplerian elements, or *orbital elements,* are the six parameters that uniquely specify the position and path of a satellite (natural or human-made) in its orbit as a function of time. These elements and their characteristics are described in Figure 57.

See also: ORBITS OF OBJECTS IN SPACE.

Kepler's laws Three empirical laws describing the motion of the planets in their orbits around the Sun, first formulated by the German astronomer Johannes Kepler (1571–1630), on the basis of the detailed observations of the Danish astronomer Tycho Brahe (1546–1601). These laws are:(1) the orbits of the planets are ellipses, with the Sun at a common focus; (2) as a planet moves in its orbit, the line joining the planet and the Sun sweeps over

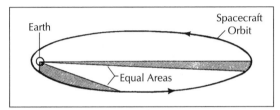

Figure 58. Kepler's second law of satellite and planet motion, the law of equal areas *(Illustration courtesy of NASA)*

equal areas in equal intervals of time (sometimes called the *law of equal areas*); and (3) the square of the orbital period (P) of any planet is proportional to the cube of its mean distance (a) from the Sun (i.e., the semimajor axis "a" for the elliptical orbit). An empirical statement of Kepler's third law is that for any planet, P^2/a^3 = a constant (with a value of approximately 2.98 x 10^{-19} [2.98 x 10^{-19} seconds squared per cubic meter (s^2/m^3)]. About a century after Kepler's initial formulation of these laws of planetary motion, NEWTON'S LAW OF GRAVITATION and LAWS OF MOTION provided the mathematical basis for a more complete physical understanding the motion of planets and satellites. (See Figure 58.)

kerosene A liquid hydrocarbon fuel used in certain rocket and jet engines. Also spelled **kerosine.**

keV A unit of energy, corresponding to 1,000 electron volts; keV means kiloelectron volts.
See also: ELECTRON VOLT; INTERNATIONAL SYSTEM OF UNITS

kill assessment The detection and assimilation of information indicating the destruction of an object under attack. Kill assessment is one of the many functions to be performed by a battle management system.

kill probability A measure of the probability of destroying a target.

kilo- (symbol: k) An SI UNIT system prefix meaning that a basic space/time/mass unit is multiplied by (1,000); as, for example, a *kilogram (kg)* or a *kilometer (km)*. Note, however, that in computer technology and digital data processing, kilo designated with a capital "K" refers to a precise value of 1,024 (which corresponds in binary notation to 2^{10}). Therefore, a kilobyte (abbreviated KB or K-byte) is actually 1,024 bytes; similarly, a kilobit (Kb or K-bit) stands for 1,024 bits.

kilobit (Kb or K-bit) One thousand twenty-four (1,024) bits.
See also: BIT; KILO-.

kilobyte (KB or K-byte) One thousand twenty-four (1,024) bytes.
See also: BYTE; KILO-.

kilogram (symbol: kg) The fundamental unit of mass in the International System (SI).

> 1 kilogram (kg) = 1,000 grams =
> 2.205 pounds-mass (lbm) (approximately)

See also: INTERNATIONAL SYSTEM OF UNITS.

kilohertz (kHz) One thousand hertz; the hertz is the SI unit of frequency.

> 1 kHz = 1,000 cycles per second

See also: INTERNATIONAL SYSTEM OF UNITS.

kilometer (km) An SI UNIT of distance corresponding to 1,000 meters or approximately 0.6214 statute miles (0.54 nautical miles).

> 1 kilometer (km) = 1,000 meters =
> 3280.8 feet = 0.62137 statute miles

kiloparsec (kpc) A distance of 1,000 parsecs or approximately 3,261.6 light-years.

kiloton (symbol: kT) A unit of energy defined as 10^{12} calories (4.2 x 10^{12} joules). This unit is used to describe the energy released in a nuclear detonation. It is approximately the amount of energy that would be released by the explosion of 1,000 metric tons (1 kiloton) of TNT (trinitrotoluene).

kinematics The branch of science that deals with describing the motion of solid objects or fluids without reference to the forces producing the motion.

kinematic viscosity (symbol: υ) A coefficient defined as the ratio of the dynamic viscosity of a fluid (μ) to its density (ρ). The units of kinematic viscosity are meters-squared per second (m^2/s) or feet-squared per second (ft^2/s). The kinematic viscosity is used to modify *perfect (ideal) fluid* equations of motion to include phenomena characteristic of a real (viscous) fluid.

kinetic energy (symbol: KE or E_{KE}) The energy that a body possesses as a result of its motion, defined as one-half the product of its mass (m) and the square of its speed (v), that is: $E_{KE} = 1/2$ m v^2.

kinetic energy interceptor An interceptor that uses a nonexplosive projectile moving at very high speed (e.g., several kilometers per second) to destroy a target on impact. The projectile may include homing sensors and onboard rockets to improve its accuracy, or it may follow a preset trajectory (as with a projectile launched from a high-velocity gas or electromagnetic gun).

kinetic energy weapon (KEW) A weapon that uses kinetic energy, or the energy of motion, to destroy or "kill" an object. Kinetic energy weapon projectiles strike their targets at very high velocities (typically more than 5 kilometers per second) and achieve a great deal of impact damage, which destroys the target. Typical KEW projectiles include spherical or shaped plastic pellets (fired by high-velocity gas guns) or tiny metal rods, pellets, or shaped shells (fired by electromagnetic railgun systems.) Even tiny grains of sand, explosively dispersed into a cloud directly in the path of a high-velocity reentry vehicle, can achieve a "kinetic energy" kill, as the hostile reentry vehicle (and its warhead) is quite literally "sand-blasted" out of existence.
See also: BALLISTIC MISSILE DEFENSE.

kinetic kill vehicle (KKV) In space defense, a rocket that homes in on its target and then kills it either by striking it directly or by showering it with fragments of material from a specially designed exploding device.

kinetic theory A physical theory, initially developed in the 19th century, that describes the "macroscopic" physical properties of matter (e.g., pressure and temperature) in terms of the "microscopic" behavior (i.e., motions and interactions) of the constituent atoms and molecules. For example, the simple kinetic theory of a gas explains pressure in terms of a statistical treatment of the continuous impacts of gas molecules (or atoms) on the walls of the container—that is, the pressure is described as being proportional to the average translational kinetic energy of the system of particles per unit volume.

Kirchhoff's law (of radiation) The physical law of radiation heat transport states that at a given temperature, the ratio of the emisivity (ε) to the absorptivity (α) for a given wavelength is the same for all bodies and is equal to the emissivity of an ideal BLACKBODY at that temperature and wavelength.

Kirkwood gaps Gaps or "holes" in the main asteroid belt between Mars and Jupiter where essentially no asteroids are located. These gaps initially were explained in 1857 by Daniel Kirkwood, an American astronomer (1814–1895), as being the result of complex orbital resonances with Jupiter. Specifically, the gaps correspond to the absence of asteroids with orbital periods that are simple fractions (e.g., 1/2, 2/5, 1/3, 1/4, etc.) of Jupiter's orbital period. Consider, for example, an asteroid that orbits the Sun in exactly half the time it takes Jupiter to orbit the Sun. (This example corresponds to a 2:1 orbital resonance.) The minor planet in this particular orbital resonance would then experience a regular, periodic pull (i.e., gravitational tug) from Jupiter at the same point in every other orbit. The cumulative effect of these recurring gravitational pulls is to deflect the asteroid into a chaotic (elongated) orbit that could then cross the orbit of Earth or Mars.
See also: ASTEROID.

klystron A high-powered electron tube that converts direct current (d.c.) electric energy into radiofrequency waves (microwaves) by alternately speeding up and slowing down the electrons (i.e., by electron beam velocity oscillation).

knot (symbol: kn) A unit of speed originating in the late 16th century sailing industry, which represents a speed equal to 1 nautical mile per hour.

> 1 knot (kn) = 1 nautical mile/hr =
> 1.1508 statute miles/hr = 1.852 kilo-
> meters/hr

Knudsen number (symbol: Kn) A nondimensional number used to describe the flow of a low-pressure (low-density) gas. It is defined as the ratio λ/l, where l is the mean free path (cm) of the gas molecule and λ is some characteristic dimension (cm) of the flow system, such as the pipe diameter. If the Knudsen number (Kn) is much greater than unity (i.e., Kn>>1), then the flow is called *molecular flow* (or Knudsen flow) and the gas behaves like a collection of independent particles. If the Knudsen number is much less than unity (i.e., Kn<<1), then viscous or continuous flow is involved.

Kuiper belt A hypothetical, disk-shaped reservoir of objects ranging in size from tiny particles to Plutonian-size planetary bodies (or even larger) that lies beyond the orbit of Neptune. Since 1992 almost 20 objects have been discovered in the Kuiper belt with diameters of 100 to 300 kilometers, leading to estimates that perhaps 20,000 to 40,000 such objects might exist in this distant, outer region of the solar system. A HUBBLE SPACE TELE-SCOPE study in 1995 discovered about 30 objects (approximately 6 to 10 kilometers in size) that also may be part of this postulated belt.

laddering down A proposed technique for over-coming a terminal phase ballistic missile defense (BMD) system. Successive salvos of salvage-fuzed reentry vehicles (RVs) attack. The detonations of one salvo disable local BMD capabilities so that fol-lowing salvos are able to approach the target more closely before being intercepted in turn. Eventually, by repeating the process, the target is reached and destroyed.

See also: BALLISTIC MISSILE DEFENSE.

lag 1. The delay between change of conditions and the indication of the change on an instrument. 2. Delay in human reaction. 3. The amount one cyclic motion is behind another, expressed in units of time (e.g., seconds) or in degrees. The opposite of *lead,* which is the amount one cyclic motion is ahead another.

Lagrangian libration points The five points in outer space where a small object can have a stable orbit in spite of the gravitational attractions exert-ed by two much more massive celestial objects when they orbit about a common center of mass. The existence of such points was first postulated by the French mathematician Joseph Louis Lagrange (1736–1818). The Trojan group of asteroids, which occupy such Lagrangian points 60 degrees ahead of and 60 degrees behind the planet Jupiter in its orbit around the Sun, are one example.

In cislunar space—that is, the region of space associated with the Earth-Moon system—the five Lagrangian points arise from a balancing of the gravitational attractions of Earth and the Moon with the centrifugal force that an observer would feel in the rotating Earth-Moon coordinate system. The main feature of these points or regions in cis-

lunar space (see Figure 59) is that an object placed there will keep a fixed relation with respect to Earth and the Moon as the entire system revolves around the Sun.

The Lagrangian points called L_1, L_2, and L_3 in the figure, are saddle-shaped "gravity-wells," with the interesting property that if you move an object at right angles (i.e., perpendicularly) to a line con-necting Earth and the Moon (called the Earth-Moon axis), this object will slide backward toward the axis; however, if you displace the object along this axis, it will move away from the Lagrangian point indefinitely. Because of this, these three Lagrangian points are called *points of unstable equi-librium.*

In contrast, the Lagrangian points L_4 and L_5 present bowl-shaped "gravity-valleys." If an object at L_4 or L_5 is moved slightly in any direction, it

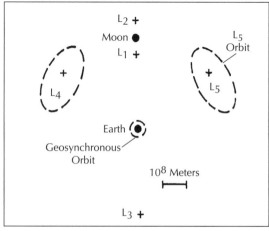

Figure 59. Five Lagrangian libration points in the Earth-Moon system   *(Drawn by author)*

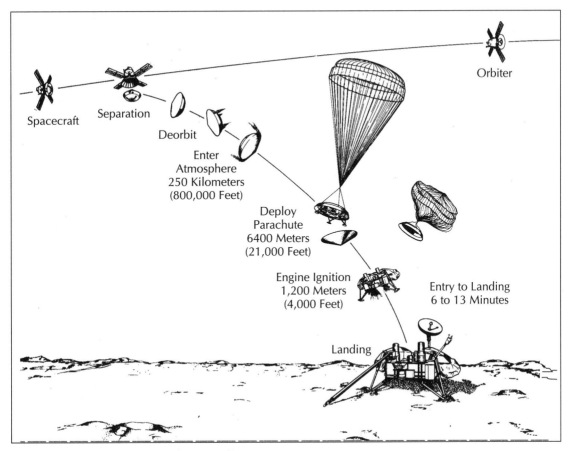

Figure 60. The Viking lander spacecraft entry profile *(Drawing courtesy of NASA)*

returns to the Lagrangian point. These two points therefore are called *points of stable equilibrium.* Lagrangian points L_4 and L_5 are located on the Moon's orbit about Earth, at equal distance from both the Moon and Earth. They have been proposed as the sites for large human settlements in cislunar space.

lambert (symbol: L) A unit of luminance defined as equal to 1 LUMEN of (light) flux emitted per square centimeter of a perfectly diffuse surface. This unit is named in honor of the German mathematician Johann H. Lambert (1728–1777).

laminar boundary layer In fluid flow, the layer next to a fixed boundary layer. The fluid velocity is zero at the boundary but the molecular viscous stress is large because the velocity gradient normal to the wall is large. The equations describing the flow in the laminar boundary layer are the Navier-Stokes equations containing only inertia and molecular viscous terms.

laminar flow In fluid flow, a smooth flow in which there is no crossflow of fluid particles occurring between adjacent stream lines. The flow velocity profile for laminar flow in circular pipes is parabolic in shape with a maximum flow in the center of the pipe and a minimum flow at the pipe walls. Compare TURBULENT FLOW.

lander (spacecraft) A spacecraft designed to reach the surface of a planet and capable of surviving long enough to telemeter back data to Earth. The U.S. *Viking 1* and *2* landers on Mars and Surveyor landers on the Moon are examples of highly successful lander missions. (See Figure 60.) The Russian Venera landers were able to briefly survive the extremely harsh surface environment of Venus and carried out chemical composition analyses of Venusian rocks and relayed images of the surface.

landing gear The apparatus comprising those components of an aircraft, spacecraft, or aerospace vehicle that support and provide mobility for the craft on land, water, or other planetary surface. The landing gear consists of wheels, floats, skis, or other devices, together with all associated struts, bracing, shock absorbers, and the like.

LANDSAT A family of NASA-developed Earth-observing satellites that have demonstrated numerous applications of multispectral imagery. The first spacecraft in this series, *LANDSAT-1* (originally called the *Earth Resources Technology Satellite,* or *ERTS-1*) was launched successfully in July 1972 and quite literally changed the way we looked at our home planet. It was the first civilian (scientific) spacecraft to provide relatively high-resolution images of Earth's land surfaces simultaneously in several important bands of the electromagnetic spectrum (primarily visible to near infrared). Scientists from around the world were given access to these multispectral images and quickly applied them to a wide variety of important areas, including: agriculture, water resource evaluation, forestry, urban planning, and pollution monitoring, to name just a few.

LANDSAT-2 (launched in January 1975) and *LANDSAT-3* (launched in March 1978) were similar to *LANDSAT-1.* Then, in July 1982, the "second generation" of remote sensing spacecraft entered service with the successful launching of *LANDSAT-4,* which had both an improved multispectral scanner (MSS) and a new thematic mapper (TM) instrument. *LANDSAT-5,* carrying a similar complement of advanced instruments, was launched successfully in March 1984. Unfortunately, an improved *LANDSAT-6* failed to achieve orbit in October 1993.

A more advanced *LANDSAT-7* spacecraft is currently scheduled for launch by an expendable Delta II rocket in 1998. The Earth-observing instrument on *LANDSAT-7,* called the enhanced thematic mapper plus (ETH+), replicates the capabilities of the highly successful thematic mapper (TM) instruments on *LANDSAT-4* and *LANDSAT-5* and is similar to the improved ETH instrument that was onboard the lost *LANDSAT-6* spacecraft. The ETH+ instrument on *LANDSAT-7* also includes new features that make it a more versatile and effi-

Summary of *LANDSAT-7* Capabilities		

ETH+ Sensor Characteristics

Band Number	Spectral Range (μm)	Ground Resolution
1	.45–.515	30
2	.525–.605	30
3	.63–.690	30
4	.75–.90	30
5	1.55–1.75	30
6	10.40–12.5	60
7	2.09–2.35	30
Pan	.52–.90	15

- Swath width: 185 km
- Repeat coverage interval: 16 days (233 orbits)
- Altitude: 705 km
- Quantization: Best 8 of 9 bits
- On-board data storage: ~375 Gb (solid state)
- Inclination: Sun-synchronous, 98.2°
- Equatorial crossing: Descending node, 10:00 A.M. ±15 min.
- Launch vehicle: Delta II
- Launch date: December 1998

Source: NASA

cient instrument for global change studies, land cover monitoring and assessment, and large-area mapping than its design predecessors. Some of the major new ETH+ instrument features on *LANDSAT-7* include: a panchromatic band with 15-meter spatial resolution; onboard, full-aperture, 5% absolute radiometric calibration; and a thermal infrared (IR) channel with 60-meter spatial resolution. (See table.)

The areas where LANDSAT multispectral imagery data have been applied successfully include: agriculture, cartography, water management, flood and hurricane damage assessment, environmental monitoring and protection, rangeland management, urban planning, and geology.

See also: REMOTE SENSING.

lapse rate The decrease of atmospheric temperature with increasing altitude. The *dry adiabatic lapse rate* for air not saturated with water vapor is about 1° Celsius per 100-meter rise in altitude, while the *wet adiabatic lapse rate* is approximately 0.6° Celsius per 100-meter rise in altitude.

large space structures The building of very large and complicated structures in space will be one of the hallmarks of space activities in the 21st century. The capability to supervise deployment and construction operations on orbit is a crucial factor in the effective use of space. Space planners and visionaries already have identified three major categories of large space structures: (1) very large surfaces (i.e., 100s square meters to perhaps a few square kilometers in area) to provide power (solar energy collection), to reject thermal energy (from a multimegawatt power-level space nuclear reactor), or to reflect sunlight (illumination of Earth's surface from space); (2) very large antennas (50-meter to 100-meter diameter and more) to receive and transmit energy over the radio-frequency portion of the electromagnetic spectrum; and (3) large space platforms (perhaps 200 meters or more in dimension) that provide the docking, assembly, checkout, and resupply facilities to service spacecraft and orbital transfer vehicles or that accommodate the highly automated "factory" facilities for space-based manufacturing operations. In the beginning, these large space structures will be deployed on-orbit—that is, erected or inflated from some stowed launch configuration. However, there is a limit to the size of such deployable and erectable systems. Larger, more sophisticated space structures (i.e., those with dimensions exceeding 25 meters or so) will require assembly on orbit—most likely by teams of space workers supported by fleets of robotic spacecraft that can intelligently assist in their fabrication, assembly, and maintenance. (See Figure 61.)

Figure 61. A large satellite power system under construction in Earth orbit (sometime in the early 21st century). A fleet of robotic orbital transfer vehicles can also be seen approaching the "construction site." *(Artist rendering courtesy of NASA)*

laser A device capable of producing an intense beam of coherent light. The term is an acronym derived from the expression *light amplification by the stimulated emission of radiation*. In a laser, the beam of light is amplified when photons (quanta of light) strike excited atoms or molecules. These atoms or molecules are thereby stimulated to emit new photons (in a cascade or chain reaction) that have the same wavelength and are moving in phase and in the same direction as the original photon. Modern lasers come in a wide variety of wavelengths and power levels. Very-high-energy lasers, for example, can destroy a target by heating, melting, or vaporizing the object. Other types of lasers (operating at much lower power levels) are used in such diverse areas as medicine, communications, environmental monitoring, and geophysics research (i.e., to study movement of Earth's crust).

See also: BALLISTIC MISSILE DEFENSE.

laser designator A device that emits a low-power beam of laser light that is used to mark a specific place or object. A weapon system equipped with a special tracking sensor that detects this reflected laser light can then home in on the designated target with great accuracy.

Laser Geodynamics Satellite (LAGEOS) A series of passive, spherical satellites launched by NASA and the Italian Space Agency (Agenzia Spaziale Italiana [ASI]) and dedicated exclusively to satellite laser ranging (SLR) technologies and demonstrations. These SLR activities include measurements of global tectonic plate motion, regional crustal deformation near plate boundaries, Earth's gravity field, and the orientation of its polar axis and its spin rate. The *LAGEOS-1* satellite was launched in 1976 and the *LAGEOS-2* in 1992. Each satellite was placed into a nearly circular, 5,800-kilometer (km) (3,600-mile [mi]) orbit but with a different inclination (110 degrees for *LAGEOS-1* and 52 degrees for *LAGEOS-2*). The small, spherical satellites are just 60 centimeters (cm) (24-inches) [in] in diameter but have a mass of 405 kilograms (900 pounds-mass). This compact, dense design makes their orbits as stable as possible, thereby accommodating satellite laser ranging measurements of submillimeter precision. An identically designed *LAGEOS-3* spacecraft is planned for the late 1990s. It will be placed in a 5,800-km (3,600-mi) circular orbit with an inclination of 70 degrees, supplementing the existing spacecraft.

The *LAGEOS* satellite looks like a dimpled golf ball with its surface covered by 426 nearly equally spaced retroreflectors. Each retroreflector has a flat, circular front face with a prism-shaped back. These retroreflectors are three-dimensional prisms that reflect laser light directly back to its source. A timing signal starts when the laser beam leaves the ground station and continues until the pulse, reflected from one of the spacecraft's retroreflectors, returns to the ground station. Since the speed of light is constant, the distance between the ground station and the satellite can be determined precisely. This process is called *satellite laser ranging* (SLR). Scientists use this technique to accurately measure movements of Earth's surface—centimeters per year in certain locations. For example, *LAGEOS-1* data have shown that the island of Maui (in Hawaii) is moving toward Japan at a rate of approximately 7 cm (2.8 in) per year and away from South America at 8 cm (3.1 in) per year.

laser guided weapon A weapon that utilizes a seeker to detect laser energy reflected from a laser-marked/designated target and through signal processing provides guidance commands to a control system that guides the weapon to the point from which the laser energy is being reflected.

laser illuminator A device for enhancing the illumination in a zone of action by irradiating with a laser beam.

laser propulsion system A proposed form of advanced propulsion in which a high-energy laser beam is used to heat a propellant (working fluid) to extremely high temperatures and then the heated propellant is expanded through a nozzle to produce thrust. If the high-energy laser is located away from the space vehicle, as, for example, on Earth or the Moon or at a different orbital position in space, the laser energy used to heat the propellant would be beamed into the space vehicle's thrust chamber. This concept offers the advantage that the space vehicle being propelled need not carry a heavy onboard power supply. A fleet of laser-propelled orbital transfer vehicles operating between low-Earth orbit and lunar orbit has been suggested as part of a lunar base transportation system. This propulsion concept also has been suggested for deep space probes on one-way missions to the edges of the solar system and beyond. In this case, the laser energy ("light energy") might first be gathered by a large optical collector and then converted into electric energy, which would be used to operate some type of advanced electric propulsion system.

See also: BEAMED ENERGY PROPULSION.

laser radar An active remote sensing technique analogous to radar but that uses laser light rather than radio- or microwave radiation to illuminate a target. Also called *ladar* or *lidar*.

See also: LIDAR.

laser rangefinder A device that uses laser energy for determining the distance from the device to a place or object. A short pulse of laser light usually is placed on the target and the time required for the reflected laser signal to return to the device is used to determine the range.

laser seeker A device based on a direction-sensitive receiver that detects the energy reflected from a laser-designated target and defines the direction of the target relative to the receiver.

See also: LASER GUIDED WEAPON.

laser tracker 1. A device that locks on to the reflected energy from a laser-marked/designated target and defines the direction of the target relative to itself. 2. The process of using a laser to illuminate a target so that specialized sensors can detect the reflected laser light and track the target.

latch A device that fastens one object or part to another but is subject to ready release on demand so the objects or parts can be separated. For example, a sounding rocket can be held on its launcher by a latch or several latches and then quickly released after ignition and proper thrust development.

latent heat The amount of thermal energy (heat) added to or removed from a substance to produce an isothermal (constant temperature) change in phase. There are three basic types of latent heat. The *latent heat of fusion* is the amount of thermal energy added or removed from a unit mass of substance to cause an isothermal change in phase between liquid and solid (e.g., freezing water or melting an ice cube). The *latent heat of vaporization* is the amount of thermal energy added to or removed from a unit mass of substance to cause an isothermal change of phase between liquid and gas

(e.g., evaporating water or condensing steam). The latent heat of vaporization is sometimes called the *latent heat of condensation,* when the change in phase is from gas to liquid. Finally, the *latent heat of sublimation* is the amount of thermal energy added to or removed from a unit mass of substance to cause an isothermal change in phase from solid to vapor (e.g., a block of "dry ice" disappearing in a cloud of carbon dioxide vapor). In the thermodynamic literature, the latent heat is often treated as the ENTHALPY of: vaporization, condensation, melting, solidification (fusion), sublimation, as appropriate. Note: The term "latent heat" is used to describe only the amount of thermal energy (heat) added to or removed from a substance that causes a change in phase but no change in temperature; term "sensible heat" is used to describe energy transfer as heat that produces a temperature change. This somewhat confusing nomenclature has its roots in the historic evolution of the science of thermodynamics.

lateral 1. Of or pertaining to the side; directed or moving toward the side. 2. Of or pertaining to the lateral axis; directed, moving, or located along, or parallel to, the lateral axis.

Latin space designations The language of the Roman Empire (from over two millennia ago) is used today by space scientists to identify places and features found on other worlds. This is done by international agreement to avoid confusion or contemporary language favoritism in the naming of newly discovered features on the planets and their moons. As in biology and botany, Latin is treated as a "neutral" language in space science. Two of the more common Latin terms that are encountered in space science and planetary geology are: *mare maria* (pl:) meaning "sea" e.g., *Mare Tranquillitatis*—the Sea of Tranquility—site of the first human landing (*Apollo 11* mission) on the Moon; and *mons monte* (pl:) meaning "mountain" e.g., *Olympus Mons*—the largest volcano on Mars). As an interesting historical footnote, when Galileo first explored the Moon with his newly invented telescope (circa 1610), he thought the dark (lava-flow) regions he saw where bodies of water and mistakenly called them *maria* (or seas).

latitude The angle between a perpendicular at a location and the equatorial plane of Earth. Latitude

Figure 62. An assembled space shuttle vehicle slowly works its way to Launch Complex 39-A at the NASA Kennedy Space Center *(Photo courtesy of NASA)*

is measured in degrees north or south of the equator with the equator being defined as 0 degrees, the North Pole as 90 degrees north and the South Pole as 90 degrees south latitude, respectively.

launch 1. (noun) a. The action taken in launching a rocket or aerospace vehicle from a planetary surface. b. The transition from static repose to dynamic flight of a missile or rocket. c. The action of sending forth a rocket, probe, or other object from a moving vehicle such as an aircraft, aerospace vehicle, or spacecraft. 2. (verb) a. To send off a rocket or missile under its own propulsive power. b. To send off a missile, rocket, or aircraft by means of a catapult, as in the case of the German V-1 cruise missile (World War II era), or by means of inertial force, as in the release of a bomb from a flying aircraft. c. To give a payload or space probe an added boost for flight into space just before separation from its launch vehicle.

launch aircraft The aircraft used to air launch a missile, rocket, human-crewed experimental aircraft, air-launched space booster or remotely piloted vehicle (RPV). Launch aircraft, such as the NASA/Air Force B-52s used during the X-15 hypersonic flight program, often are called "motherships."

See also: PEGASUS; X-15.

launch azimuth The initial compass heading of a powered vehicle at launch. The term often is applied to space launch vehicles.

launch complex In general, the site, facilities, and equipment used to launch a rocket, missile, or aerospace vehicle. (See Figure 62.)

See also: LAUNCH SITE.

launch configuration The assembled combination of strap-on booster rockets, primary launch vehicle, spacecraft/payload, and upper stages (if appropriate) that must be lifted off the ground at launch.

launch crew The group of engineers, technicians, managers, and safety personnel that prepare and launch a rocket, missile, or aerospace vehicle.

launch danger area A land area drawn as a circle about the launch point with tangents to the circle extending to the ocean, parallel to the intended flight azimuth of the missile, rocket, or aerospace vehicle. This area is based on calculated explosive velocities, explosive yield (i.e., trinitrotoluene [TNT] equivalents), toxic propellant dispersion, fragment dispersion, and the ability of an erratic vehicle to maneuver off the launch pad before range safety destruction action can be taken.

launch danger zone A sea area and air space measured from the launch point and extending downrange along the intended flight azimuth of a rocket, missile, or aerospace vehicle. The size of this danger zone is based on the potential hazard to ships and aircraft.

launcher 1. In general, a structure, machine, or device, including the catapult, by means of which airplane, rockets, or missiles, are hurled, directed, or launched. 2. Specifically, a structure or device, often incorporating a tube, a group of tubes, or a set of tracks, from which self-propelled missiles or rockets are sent forth and by means of which the missiles or rocket usually are aimed or given initial guidance—distinguished in this specific sense from a catapult.

launching angle The angle between a horizontal plane and the longitudinal axis of a rocket, missile, or aerospace vehicle being launched.

launching rail A rail that gives initial support and guidance to a missile or rocket launched in a non-vertical position.

launchpad In general, the load-bearing base of platform from which a rocket, missile, or aerospace vehicle is launched. Often simply called "the pad."

launch ring The metal ring used at some launch pads on which a missile or rocket stands before launch.

launch site A defined area from which a aerospace or rocket vehicle is launched, either operationally or for test purposes. Major launch sites in the United States include the Eastern Space and Missile Center (ESMC) at Cape Canaveral Air Force Station/Kennedy Space Center on the central east coast of Florida, the Western Space and Missile Center (WSMC) at Vandenberg Air Force Base on the west central coast of California, and NASA's Wallops Island facility on the east coast of Virginia. Major Russian launch sites include Plesetsk, Kapustin Yar, and Tyuratam (also called the Baikonur Cosmodrome), which is located in Kazakhstan. The European Space Agency (ESA) has a major launch site in Kourou, French Guiana, on the northeast coast of South America.

launch stand A facility or station at which a rocket vehicle is launched, normally incorporating a launch pad with launcher.

launch time The time at which an aircraft, missile, rocket, or aerospace vehicle is scheduled for flight.

launch under attack (LUA) Execution by National Command Authorities (e.g., the president) of Single Integrated Operational Plan (SIOP) forces subsequent to tactical warning of strategic nuclear

CHARACTERISTICS OF SOME OF THE WORLD'S LAUNCH VEHICLES

Country	Launch Vehicle	Stages	First Launch	Performance
China	Long March 2(CZ-2C)	2 hypergolic, optional solid upper stage	1975	3,175 kg to LEO
	Long March 2E	2 hypergolic, 4 hypergolic strap-on rockets	1992	8,800 kg to LEO
	Long March 3	2 hypergolic, 1 cryogenic	1984	5,000 kg to LEO
	Long March 3A	2 hypergolic, 1 cryogenic	1994	8,500 kg to LEO
	Long March 4	3 hypergolic	1988	4,000 kg to LEO
Europe (ESA/France)	Ariane 40	2 hypergolic, 1 cryogenic	1990	4,625 kg to LEO
	Ariane 42P	2 hypergolic, 1 cryogenic, 2 strap-on solid rockets	1990	6,025 kg to LEO
	Ariane 42L	2 hypergolic, 1 cryogenic, 2 hypergolic, strap-on rockets	1993	3,550 kg to GTO
	Ariane 5	2 large solid boosters, cryogenic core, hypergolic upper stage	1996	18,000 kg to LEO, 6,800 kg to GTO
India	Polar Space Launch Vehicle (PSLV)	2 solid stages, 2 hypergolic, 6 strap-on solid rockets	1993	3,000 kg to LEO
Israel	Shavit	3 solid rocket stages	1988	160 kg to LEO
Japan	M-3SII	3 solid rocket stages, 2 strap-on solid rockets	1985	770 kg to LEO
	H-2	2 cryogenic, 2 strap-on solid rockets	1994	10,000 kg to LEO, 4,000 kg to GTO
Russia	Soyuz	2 cryogenic, 4 cryogenic strap-on rockets	1963	6,900 kg to LEO
	Rokot 3	hypergolic	1994	1,850 kg to LEO
	Tsyklon	3 hypergolic	1977	3,625 kg to LEO
	Proton (D-1)	3 hypergolic	1968	20,950 kg to LEO
	Energia	cryogenic core, 4 cryogenic strap-on rockets, optional cryogenic upper stages	1987	105,200 kg to LEO
United States	Atlas I	1 1/2 cryogenic lower stage, 1 cryogenic upper stage	1990	5,580 kg to LEO, 2,250 GTO
	Atlas II	1 1/2 cryogenic lower stage, 1 cryogenic upper stage,	1991	6,530 kg to LEO, 2,800 kg to GTO
	Atlas IIAS	1 1/2 cryogenic lower stage, 1 cryogenic upper stage, 4 strap-on solid rockets	1993	8,640 kg to LEO, 4,000 kg to GTO
	Delta II	1 cryogenic, 1 hypergolic, 1 solid stage, 9 strap-on solid	1990	5,050 kg to LEO, 1,820 kg to GTO
	Lockheed Martin Launch Vehicle (LMLV 1)	2 solid stages	1995	815 kg to LEO
	Pegasus (aircraft-launched)	3 solid stages	1990	290 kg to LEO
	Space Shuttle	2 large solid rocket boosters, cryogenic core	1981	25,000 kg to LEO
	Taurus	4 solid stages	1994	1,300 to LEO
	Titan 4	2 hypergolic stages, 2 large strap-on solid rockets, variety of upper stages	1989	18,100 to LEO

LEO = low Earth orbit.
GTO = geostationary transfer orbit.

Scout	Delta	Delta 2	Atlas 1	Atlas 2	Titan 3	Titan 4	Shuttle
475 lbs.	7,800 lbs.	11,100 lbs.	12,300 lbs.	14,400 lbs.	33,000 lbs.	40,000 lbs.	55,000 lbs.

Pounds to Low Earth Orbit

Figure 63. Performance comparison for some contemporary U.S. launch vehicles *(Drawing courtesy of NASA)*

attack against the United States and prior to first impact of an enemy's nuclear warheads.

launch vehicle An expendable or reusable rocket vehicle that propels and guides a payload, such as a spacecraft, into orbit around Earth or into a trajectory to another celestial body or deep space. Also called *booster* or *space lift vehicle*. Launch vehicles come in many sizes and capabilities. An expendable launch vehicle (ELV), such as the Delta, is used only once; a reusable launch system, such as the space shuttle, is refurbished and reflown. The table identifies some of the major launch vehicles now used in the world or planned for use in the upcoming years. Figure 63 compares several contemporary U.S. launch vehicles on the basis of payload delivery to low Earth orbit (LEO). Expendable launch vehicle capabilities range from about 215 kilograms (kg) (475 pounds-mass (lbm) for the Scout to 18,150 kg (40,000 lbm) for the Titan-4; the reusable space shuttle can lift about 25,000 kg (55,000 lbm) into LEO.

See also: ATLAS; DELTA; SCOUT; SPACE TRANSPORTATION SYSTEM; TITAN.

launch window An interval of time during which a launch may be made to satisfy some mission objec-

tive. Usually a short period of time each day for a certain number of days. An interplanetary launch window generally is constrained within a number of weeks each year by the location of Earth in its orbit around the Sun, in order to permit the launch vehicle to use Earth's orbital motion for its trajectory as well as to time the spacecraft to arrive at its destination when the target planet is in the correct position. A launch that involves a rendezvous in Earth orbit with another spacecraft or platform must be timed precisely to account for the orbital motion of the "target" space object, creating launch windows of just a few minutes each day. Similarly, an interplanetary launch window is further constrained to just a few hours each appropriate day in order to take full advantage of Earth's rotational motion.

layered defense An approach to ballistic missile defense (BMD) consisting of several relatively independent layers of missile defense technologies/systems designed to operate against different portions of the trajectory of an enemy's ballistic missile. For example, there could be a boost-phase (first layer) defense with any remaining targets being passed on to succeeding layers (i.e., midcourse, terminal) of the defense system.

See also: BALLISTIC MISSILE DEFENSE.

leakage The percentage of warheads that get through a defensive system intact and operational.
See also: BALLISTIC MISSILE DEFENSE.

leakage rate The quantity of fluid escaping past a seal in a given length of time.

"leak-before-burst" condition Condition requiring that cracks penetrating a pressure vessel wall do so without reaching the (critical) size for unstable propagation (i.e., the size that leads to brittle fracture).

length (symbol: L, l or *l*) The dimension of an aircraft, rocket, or aerospace vehicle from nose to tail; the measurement of this dimension.

lens A curve piece of glass, quartz, plastic, or other transparent material that has been ground, polished, and shaped accurately to focus light from a distant object so as to form an image of that object.

lethal radius The maximum distance from an exploding nuclear or nonnuclear warhead within which a target would be destroyed.

leverage In ballistic missile defense (BMD), the advantage gained by boost-phase intercept, when a single booster kill may eliminate many reentry vehicles (RVs) and decoys before they can be deployed. This could provide a favorable cost-exchange ratio for the defense and would reduce the stress on later layers of the defense system.
See also: BALLISTIC MISSILE DEFENSE.

lever link Mechanical linkage between the actuator and the valving element of a rotary valve that consists of a lever or crank on the rotary member and a link with clevis connections from the lever to the actuator shaft.
See also: CLEVIS.

Lewis number (symbol: Le) In fluid mechanics, a dimensionless number (or parameter) describing the ratio of mass diffusivity to thermal diffusivity

$$Le = \frac{\text{mass diffusivity}}{\text{thermal diffusivity}} = \frac{D \rho c_p}{k}$$

where D is mass diffusivity, ρ is mass density, c_p is specific heat at constant pressure, and k is thermal conductivity.

libration A real or apparent oscillatory motion, particularly the apparent oscillation of the Moon. Because of libration, more than half (about 59%) of the Moon's surface actually can be seen over time by an observer on Earth despite the fact that it is in synchronous motion around our planet (i.e., keeping the same side always facing Earth).

libration points The unique positions of gravitational balance measured from a celestial body and its satellite at which points smaller objects can orbit in stable equilibrium with the other two bodies.
See also: LAGRANGIAN LIBRATION POINTS.

lidar An active remote-sensing technique analogous to radar but that uses laser light rather than radio- or microwave radiation to illuminate a target. The laser light is reflected off a target and then detected. Using time-of-flight techniques to analyze the returned beam, information on both the distance to and velocity of the target can be obtained. The term is an acronym for *light detec*tion *and ranging. Sometimes referred to as *ladar* (*laser detection and ranging).

life cycle In general, all the phases through which an item, component, or system passes from the time it is conceived and initially developed until the time it is either consumed in use (e.g., expended during a mission) or disposed of as being excess to known requirements (e.g., a flight spare that is not needed because of the success of the original system). A NASA space mission, such as an interplanetary probe to Mars, often is considered as having the following "life cycle": Pre-Phase A (Conceptual Study), Phase A (Preliminary Analysis), Phase B (Definition), Phase C/D (Design and Development), and the Operations Phase. During the Pre-Phase A process the proposed space mission is studied and evaluated for merit, and if accepted, "the idea" moves forward through a feasibility screening process and becomes a *project*. During Phase A of the mission life cycle, the new project develops a preliminary design and project plan that specifies what is going to be built, when the launch will be needed, the trajectory the spacecraft is to take, and what operations will be carried out during the cruise phase and encounter phase of the mission when the spacecraft reaches its target planet. During Phase B the preliminary plan of the project becomes more rigorously defined, schedules are determined, and specifications are pre-

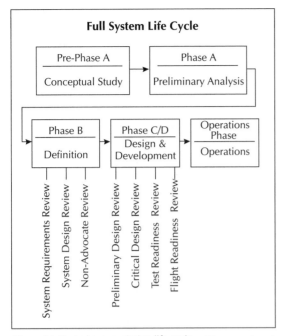

Full System Life Cycle

Pre-Phase A

Conceptual Study

Phase A

Preliminary Analysis

Phase B

Definition

Phase C/D

Design & Development

Operations Phase

Operations

System Requirements Review

System Design Review

Non-Advocate Review

Preliminary Design Review

Critical Design Review

Test Readiness Review

Flight Readiness Review

Figure 64. Typical space mission life cycle   *(Diagram courtesy of NASA/JPL)*

pared to initiate system design and development process. During Phase C/D, the space flight system is designed, developed, integrated, tested, launched and/or deployed, and verified. Finally, during the Operations Phase, the spacecraft travels to the target planet and obtains the scientific data for which the mission was conceived and designed. Many factors enter into this space mission life cycle, including technical considerations, budget, design changes, and competition for both fiscal and physical resources (e.g., tracking support and launch vehicle capacity). (See Figure 64.)

life cycle cost (LCC) The entire cost of a program, project, or system from inception to ultimate disposition. Estimating life cycle cost is important to understanding long-term impacts of decision making early in the life of an aerospace program.

life support system (LSS) In general, the system (or collection of various subsystems) that will maintain life throughout the flight environment. Depending on the aerospace mission, the flight environment could include travel in space, activities on the surface of another would (e.g., the lunar surface), and ascent and descent through Earth's

atmosphere. The life support system provides a human crew with their daily needs of clean air, potable water, food, and reliable waste removal, thereby insuring healthy and productive lives while the crew is in space.

Life support system technologies deal with three major considerations: (1) water reclamation, (2) air revitalization, and (3) waste management. Water reclamation is responsible for providing the potable water needs of a space inhabitant. Air revitalization maintain a habitable atmosphere of the proper gas composition, temperature, humidity, and pressure. This area of life support system technology also addresses the control of airborne contaminants. Finally, waste management is responsible for the efficient handling, treatment, and disposal of human by-products, both liquid and solid

For long-duration space missions, a regenerative life support system (RLS) will be designed to help recover and recycle some (or all) of the daily human crew needs for air and water. However, a regenerative life support system is much more complex than the "once-through" or "open-loop" life support systems previously designed and used on short duration space missions. In the regenerative life support system, for example, the water reclamation and air revitalization elements must be concerned with safely and reliably recovering water and oxygen from the secondary raw materials of human waste products. Also, any treatment of the solid waste component must minimize the generation of final residue waste material. In contrast, of missions relatively short duration (including Earth-orbiting space station mission that can be resupplied at frequent intervals) employ an "open-loop" life support system approach in which the air, water, and food needed by each crew member are stored aboard the spacecraft or space vehicle at launch (or else frequently resupplied) and the waste products then are stored for return to Earth or else simply jettisoned into space (e.g., a "dirty" water dump while on orbit).

For future long-duration missions away from Earth, such as a human expedition to Mars, continuous resupply from Earth of life support system consumables is not practical. Similarly, with a population of 100 or more persons, a permanently occupied surface base on the Moon or Mars cannot use the "open-loop" approach to life support, since the logistic and cost would be overwhelming. Instead, a partially closed or completely regenerative life support system (sometimes called a *controlled ecological life support system,* or *CELSS*) must be developed and used. Finally, giant space habitats, with populations of perhaps 10,000 or more human beings, will use life support systems based on the full-scale recycling and treatment of air, water, and waste products.

lift 1. That component (commonly used symbol, L) of the total aerodynamic force acting upon a body perpendicular to the undisturbed airflow relative to the body. *See also:* AERODYNAMIC FORCES. 2. To lift off, or to take off in a vertical ascent. Said of a rocket or an aerostat.

lift coefficient (symbol: C_L) A coefficient representing the *lift* of a given airfoil or other aerodynamic body. The lift coefficient is obtained by dividing the lift by the free-stream dynamic pressure and by the representative areas under consideration.
See also: AERODYNAMIC FORCES; LIFT.

lift-drag (L/D) ratio The ratio of lift to drag obtained by dividing the lift component of the aerodynamic forces by the drag component of the aerodynamic forces; or by dividing the lift coefficient (C_L) by the drag coefficient (C_D).
See also: AERODYNAMIC FORCES.

lifting brake A spacecraft aerodynamically shaped to provide some lift and much drag to change its path as it passes through a planetary atmosphere.
See also: AEROASSIST.

liftoff The action of a rocket or aerospace vehicle as it separates from its launch pad in a vertical ascent. Compare TAKEOFF. Note: *Liftoff* is applicable only to vertical ascent; *takeoff* is applicable to ascent at any angle. A liftoff is an action performed by a rocket, missile, or aerospace vehicle (e.g., the space shuttle); a launch is action performed upon a rocket, missile, or aerospace vehicle or upon a satellite or spacecraft carried by the rocket or aerospace vehicle.

light Electromagnetic radiation, ranging from about 0.4 to 0.7 micrometers (microns) in wavelength, to which the human eye is sensitive. Light helps us form our visual awareness of the universe and its contents.

light flash A momentary flash of light seen by astronauts in space, even with their eyes closed. Scientists believe that there are probably at least three causes for these light flashes. First, energetic cosmic rays passing through the eye's "detector" (the retina) ionize a few atoms or molecules, resulting in a signal in the optic nerve. Second, extremely energetic HZE particles can produce Cerenkov radiation in the eyeball. (Cerenkov radiation is the bluish light emitted by a particle traveling very near the speed of light when it enters a medium in which the velocity of light is less than the particle's speed.) Finally, alpha particles from nuclear collisions caused by very energetic Van Allen belt protons can produce ionization in the retina, again triggering a signal in the optic nerve. Astronauts have reported seeing these flashes in a variety of sizes and shapes.
See also: COSMIC RAYS; HZE PARTICLES.

light-minute (lm) A unit of length equal to the distance traveled by a beam of light (or any electromagnetic wave) in the vacuum of outer space in one minute. Since the speed of light (c) is 299,792.5 kilometers per second (km/s) in free space, a light-minute corresponds to a distance of approximately 18 million kilometers.

lightning protection Aerospace launch complexes and the launch vehicle themselves must be protected from lightning strikes. At any given instant, more than 2,000 thunderstorms are taking place throughout the world. All of these combine to produce about 100 lightning flashes per second.

On November 14, 1969 an out-of-the-blue lightning bolt struck and temporarily disabled the electrical systems on the *Apollo 12* spacecraft onboard a Saturn V launch vehicle about 1.6 kilometers (1 mile) above NASA's Kennedy Space Center (KSC) on the way to the Moon. On March 26, 1987 a NASA Atlas/Centaur vehicle and its payload were lost when the vehicle was hit by lightning while climbing up through the atmosphere after launch from Cape Canaveral Air Force Station (CCAFS). The lightning strike caused the rocket's computer to upset and issue an extreme yaw command that led to the vehicle's breakup in flight.

Lightning tends to strike the highest points in any given area, and aerospace safety engineers take special care to protect tall structures at a launch complex from these high-voltage bolts. The U.S. Lightning Protection Code for structures requires a pathway, or conductor, that will lead a lightning bolt safely to the ground. Additional protection is provided by circuit breakers, fuses, and electrical surge arrestors.

KSC operates extensive lightning protection and detection systems in order to keep workers, the space shuttle vehicle, launchpads, and processing facilities safe from harm. While the NASA lightning protection system is exclusively on KSC property, the lightning detection system incorporates equipment and personnel both at the Kennedy Space Center and CCAFS, which is located just east of the NASA complex. The Launch Pad Lightning Warning System (LPLWS) and the Lightning Surveillance System (LSS) provide the data necessary for evaluating weather conditions that can lead to the issuance of lightning warnings for the entire KSC/CCAFS launch complex. When the treat of lightning is present (typically within 8 kilometers [5 miles] of critical facilities), a lightning policy is put into effect. This lightning policy restricts certain outdoor activities and hazardous operations, such as the start of launch vehicle fueling.

Facilities such as the service tower structures at Launch Complex 39A and 39B, the Vehicle Assembly Building (VAB), and the Orbiter Processing Facility (OPF), have extensive lightning shielding devices incorporated in their construction. A 24-meter(m)-high (80-foot [ft]) fiberglass mast on top of the Fixed Service Structure at both Launch Complex 39-A and 39-B is perhaps the most visible means of protecting the launch structure itself, the shuttle vehicle (while on the launch pad), and any enclosed launch operations equipment. This mast supports a 2.54-centimeter (1-inch) diameter stainless steel cable that runs over its top. This steel cable stretches about 300 m (1,000 ft) in two directions to where each end is anchored and grounded. Its appearance is similar to that of a suspension bridge tower and its supporting cables. A 1.3-m-high (4-ft) lightning rod on top of this mast is connected to the cable. The lightning rod's purpose is to prevent lightning current from passing directly through the space shuttle vehicle and the launch pad structures. Any lighting strikes in this area would be conducted by this cable, called a *catenary wire* because of its shape, to the grounded anchor points.

Other grounding systems in the Launch Complex 39 area include a network of buried, interconnected metal rods that run under the launch pads and surrounding support structures. All structures in the launch complex area are grounded, including the 160-m-tall (525-ft) VAB. For example, the VAB has a system of eleven 7.6-m (25-ft) high lightning conductor towers on its roof. When lightning hits the system, the wires conduct the charge to the towers, which then directs the current down the sides of the VAB and into the structure's foundation pilings, which are driven into bedrock.

Finally, overhead gridwires protect hypergolic fuel storage areas at the pads. The giant liquid-oxygen and liquid-hydrogen storage tanks at each pad are constructed of metal, however, and therefore do not need overhead lightning protection, since these metallic structures provide their own grounding pathways.

Do these lighting protection systems work? Since their installation, the lightning masts at Launch Pads 39A and 39B have been struck at least five times with a space shuttle vehicle on the pad, with no damage to any equipment.

LightSat A small, lightweight satellite that can be built quickly and economically. An common LightSat project fiscal goal is to build and launch the tiny, single-mission spacecraft for under $1 million total cost. LightSats appear to have promising role in telecommunications, especially in use with the rapidly growing, mobile, pocket-size, two-way satellite communicators that work anywhere in the world.

light-second (ls) A unit of length equal to the distance traveled by a beam of light (or any electromagnetic wave) in the vacuum of outer space in one second. Since the speed of light (c) in free space is 299,792.5 kilometers per second (km/s), a light-second corresponds to a distance of approximately 300,000 kilometers.

light time The amount of time it takes light or radio signals to travel a certain distance at light speed (i.e., c = 299,792.5 kilometers/second).

light water Ordinary water (H_2O), as distinguished from heavy water (D_2O), where D is deuterium.

light-year (ly) The distance that light travel at 3 x 10^8 meters per second in one year (3.15 x 10^7 seconds). One light-year is equal to a distance of

9.46 x 10^{12} kilometers, or about 63,000 times the distance from Earth to the Sun.

limb The outer edge of a celestial body, such as Earth or the Sun.

limit load The maximum anticipated load or combination of loads a part, component, or structure is expected to experience at any time during its intended operation and expected operational environment. Also called *design load.*

limit switch A mechanical device that can be used to determine the physical position of equipment. For example, an extension on a valve shaft mechanically trips a limit switch as it moves from open to shut or shut to open. The limit switch gives "ON/OFF" output that corresponds to valve position. Normally, limit switches are used to provide full open or full shut indications. Many limit switches are the push-button variety. When the valve extension comes in contact with the limit switch, the switch depresses to complete, or turn on, the electrical circuit. As the valve extension moves away from the limit switch, spring pressure opens the switch, turning off the circuit.

line (or duct) Enclosed passageway (usually circular in cross section with relatively thin walls) that conveys fluid under pressure.

linear 1. Of or pertaining to a line. 2. Having a relation such that a change in one quantity is accompanied by an exactly proportional change in a related quantity, such as input and output of electronic equipment.

linear acceleration The time rate of change of linear velocity, namely: $a = dv/dt$.

linear accelerator A long straight tube (or series of tubes) in which charged particles, such as electrons or protons, gain in energy by the action of oscillating electromagnetic fields.
See also: ACCELERATOR.

linear energy transfer (LET) The energy lost (ΔE) per unit path length (Δx) by ionizing radiation as it passes through matter. Often it is used as a measure of the relative ability of different types of ionizing radiation to produce a potentially harmful effect on living matter; that is, the higher the LET

value, the greater the potential for biological effect. LET = ΔE/Δx = energy deposited/unit path length; often expressed in units of: keV/micrometer.

linear variable differential transformer (LVDT) A device that provides an accurate position indication throughout the range of valve travel, from "OPEN" or "CLOSED" and all positions in between.

line of apsides The line connecting the two points of an orbit that are nearest and farthest from the center of attraction, as the *perigee* and *apogee* of a satellite in orbit around Earth or the *perihelion* and *aphelion* of a planet around the Sun; the major axis of any elliptical orbit and extending indefinitely in both directions.
See also: ORBITS OF OBJECTS IN SPACE.

line of flight The line in air or space along which an aircraft, rocket, aerospace vehicle, or spacecraft travels. This line can be either the intended (i.e., planned) line of movement or the actual line of movement of the vehicle or craft.

line of force A line indicating the direction that a force acts.

line of nodes The straight line created by the intersection of a satellite's orbital plane and a reference plane (usually the equatorial plane) of the planet or object being orbited.

line of sight (LOS) 1. The straight line between a sensor or the eye of an observer and the object or point being observed. Sometimes called the *optical path*. 2. A direct line of propagation that does not go below the horizon.

liner 1. With respect to solid-propellant rocket motors, the thin layer of material used to bond the solid propellant to the motor case; this material also can provide thermal insulation. 2. With respect to a rocket nozzle, the thin layer of ablative material placed on the nozzle wall (especially in the throat area) to help reduce heat transfer from the hot exhaust gases to the nozzle wall structure.

line spectra The discontinous lines produced when bound electrons go from a higher energy level to a lower energy level in an excited atom, spontaneously emitting electromagnetic radiation.

This radiation is essentially emitted at a single frequency, which is determined by the transition or "jump" in energy. Each different "jump" in energy level, therefore, has its own characteristic frequency. The overall collection radiation emitted by the excited atom is called the line spectra. Since these line spectra are characteristic of the atom, they can be used for identification purposes.

link In telecommunications, a general term used to indicate the existence of communications pathways and/or facilities between two points. In referring to communications between a ground station and a spacecraft or satellite, the term "uplink" describes communications from the ground site to the spacecraft, while the term "downlink" describes communications from the spacecraft to the ground site.

lip seal Pressure-actuated seal that prevents leakage in dynamic and static applications by employing a scraping or wiping action on the mating surface.

liquefaction of gases The process of converting gases into liquids, such as separating and extracting liquid oxygen (LOX) and liquid nitrogen (LN) from air. Involves cooling the gases to low temperatures and then applying one of several thermodynamic processes, such as the Joule-Thomson effect.
See also: JOULE-THOMSON EFFECT.

liquid A phase of matter between a solid and a gas. A substance in a state in which the individual particles move freely with relation to each other and take the shape of the container but do not expand to fill the container. Compare with FLUID.

liquid fuel A rocket fuel that is liquid under the conditions in which it is stored and used in a rocket engine.
See also: LIQUID PROPELLANT.

liquid hydrogen (LH$_2$) A liquid propellant used as the fuel with liquid oxygen serving as the oxidizer in high-performance cryogenic rocket engines. Hydrogen remains a liquid only at very low (cryogenic) temperatures, typically about 20° Kelvin (-253° Celsius or -423° Fahrenheit) or less. This cryogenic temperature requirement creates significant propellant storage and handling problems. However, the performance advantage experienced with the use of liquid hydrogen/liquid oxygen in high-energy space boosters often offsets these cryogenic handling problems.
See also: LIQUID PROPELLANT.

liquid length The distance along a chamber wall over which film coolant remains in a liquid state.

liquid oxygen (LOX or LO$_2$) A cryogenic liquid propellant requiring storage at temperatures below 90 Kelvin (i.e., -183° Celsius or -298° Fahrenheit). Often used as the oxidizer with RP-1 (a kerosene-type) fuel in many expendable boosters or with liquid hydrogen (LH$_2$) fuel in high-performance cryogenic-propellant rocket engines.
See also: LIQUID PROPELLANT.

liquid propellant Any liquid combustible fed to the combustion chamber of a rocket engine. The petroleum used as a rocket fuel is a type of highly refined kerosene, called RP-1 (for *refined petroleum-1*). Usually it is burned with liquid oxygen (LOX) in rocket engines to provide thrust.

Cryogenic propellants are very cold liquid propellants. The most commonly used are LOX, which serves as an oxidizer, and liquid hydrogen (LH$_2$), which serves as the fuel. Cooling and compressing gaseous hydrogen and oxygen into liquids vastly increases their density, making it possible to store them (as cryogenic liquids) in smaller tanks. Unfortunately, the tendency of cryogenic propellants to return to their gaseous form unless kept supercool makes them difficult to store for long periods of time. Therefore, cryogenic propellants are less satisfactory for use in strategic nuclear missiles or tactical military rockets, which must be kept launch-ready for months to years at a time. However, cryogenic propellants are favored for use in space boosters, because of the relatively high thrust achieved per unit mass of chemical propellant consumed. For example, the space shuttle's main engines burn LH$_2$ and LOX.

Hypergolic propellants are liquid fuels and oxidizers that ignite on contact with each other and need no ignition source. This easy start and restart capability makes these liquid propellants attractive for both crewed and uncrewed spacecraft maneuvering systems. Another positive feature of hypergolic propellants is the fact that, unlike cryogenic propellants, these liquids do not have to be stored at extremely low temperatures. One favored hypergolic combination is monomethyl hydrazine

(MMH) as the fuel and nitrogen tetroxide (N_2O_4) as the oxidizer. However, both of these fluids are highly toxic and must be handled under the most stringent safety conditions. Hypergolic propellants are used in the core liquid propellant stages of the Titan family of launch vehicles.

Some of the desirable properties of a liquid rocket propellant are: high specific gravity (to minimize tank space); low freezing point (to permit cold-weather operation); stability (to minimize chemical deterioration during storage); favorable thermophysical properties (e.g., a high boiling point and high thermal conductivity—especially valuable in support of regenerative cooling of the combustion chamber and nozzle throat); and low vapor pressure (to support more efficient propellant pumping operations). Some of the physical hazards encountered in the use of liquid propellants include: toxicity, corrosion, ignitability (when exposed to air or heat), and explosive potential (when the propellant deteriorates, is shocked, or excessively heated).

See also: ROCKET.

liquid rocket engine A rocket engine that uses liquid propellants for the fuel and oxidizer.
See also: LIQUID PROPELLANT; ROCKET.

liter (symbol: l or L) A unit of volume in the metric (SI) system. Defined as the volume of 1 kilogram of pure water at standard (atmospheric) pressure and a temperature of 4° Celsius. Also spelled *litre*. 1 liter = 0.2642 gallons = 1.000028 cubic decimeters (dm^3).
See also: INTERNATIONAL SYSTEM OF UNITS.

lithium hydroxide (LiOH) A white crystalline compound used for removing carbon dioxide from a closed atmosphere, such as found on a crewed spacecraft, aerospace vehicle, or space station. Spacesuit life support systems also use lithium hydroxide canisters to purge the suit's closed atmosphere of the carbon dioxide exhaled by the astronaut occupant.

little Green men (LGM) A popular expression (originating in science fiction literature) for extraterrestrial beings, presumably intelligent.

live testing The testing of a rocket, missile, or aerospace vehicle by actually launching it. Compare STATIC TESTING.

load factor In aerospace engineering, a factor that accounts for unavoidable deviations of the actual load from the nominal value. Examples of load factors include: wind load factor, shock load factor, dynamic load factor, and seismic load factor.

lobe An element of a beam of focused electromagnetic (e.g., radio frequency, or RF) energy. Lobes define surfaces of equal power density at varying distances and directions from the radiating antenna. Their configuration is governed by two factors: (1) the geometrical properties of the antenna reflector and feed system; and (2) the mutual interference between the direct and reflected rays for an antenna situated above a reflecting surface. In addition to the major lobes of an antenna system, there exist side lobes (or minor lobes) that result from the unavoidable finite size of the reflector. The exist at appreciable angles from the axis of the beam, and, while objectionable, they normally contain much less energy than in the major lobe.

Local Group A small cluster of about 20 galaxies, of which the Milky Way (our galaxy) and the Andromeda Galaxy are dominant members.
See also: CLUSTER OF GALAXIES; GALAXY.

local time Time adjusted for location around Earth or other planets in time zones.

local vertical The direction in which the force of gravity acts at a particular point on the surface of Earth (or other planet).

Lockheed Martin Launch Vehicle (LMLV) A planned new family of small- to medium-payload-capacity commercial boosters that combine already proven rocket technologies. The LMLV-1 is a two-stage solid-propellant rocket capable of placing about 815 kilograms (kg) (1,800 pounds-mass (lbm) [lb_{mass}]) into LOW-EARTH ORBIT (LEO). The first stage of the LMLV-1 uses a large solid rocket motor (called the Thiokol Castor 120 motor), which is based on the first stage of the air force MX/Peacekeeper intercontinental ballistic missile (ICBM). The planned LMLV-2 will have a third, solid-propellant stage, while the LMLV-3 will used a third solid-propellant stage plus from two to six solid-propellant strap-on rocket motors. The LMLV-2 will place about 1,810 kg (4,000 lbm) into LEO, while the LMLV-3 will be capable of putting about 3,600 kg (8,000 lbm) into LEO.
See also: LAUNCH VEHICLE.

lock on Signifies that a tracking or target-seeking system is continuously and automatically tracking a target in one or more coordinates (e.g., range, bearing, elevation).

lockwire 1. (noun) Flexible slender rod or thread of material (usually metal) that is passed through matching holes in two (rotating) parts so as to fasten together securely. 2. (verb) To fasten securely in place by means of a wire.

logarithm The power (p) to which a fixed number (b), called the base (usually 10 or e [2.71828 . . .]), must be raised to produce the number (n) to which the logarithm corresponds. Any number (n) can be written in the form: $n = b^p$. The term "p" is then the logarithm to the base "b" of the number "n"; that is, $p = \log_b n$. *Common logarithms* have 10 as the base and usually are written: log or $\log_{10}$. *Natural logarithms* (also called Napierian logarithms) have e as the base and often are denoted: ln or $\log_e$. The irrational number e is defined as the limit as x tends to infinity (∞) of the expression $[1 + 1/x]^x$ An antilogarithm (or inverse logarithm) is the value of the number corresponding to a given logarithm. Using the previous nomenclature, if "p" is the logarithm, then "n" is the antilogarithm.

logarithmic scale A scale in which the line segments that are of equal length are those representing multiples of 10.

logistics carriers Carriers that deliver payloads to a permanent space station (or other platform/depot in orbit) and do not require a pressurized environment.

logistic modules Modules that deliver payloads to a permanent space station (or other platform/depot in orbit) and require a pressurized environment.

Long Duration Exposure Facility (LDEF) NASA's Long Duration Exposure Facility, a free-lying spacecraft the size of a bus, studied the space environment during its 69-month mission in Earth orbit from April 1984 to January 1990. Launched by a space shuttle in April 1984, this giant, essentially passive spacecraft was designed to intentionally expose a selected set of materials to the harsh environment of outer space. LDEF was then retrieved by another space shuttle mission (in January 1990)

and returned to Earth so the exposed samples could be studied in detail by scientists and engineers. The LDEF experiments gathered information on space radiation, atomic oxygen, meteoroids, spacecraft contamination, and space debris. For example, LDEF was the first satellite to detect *beta meteoroids*—minute particles accelerated by solar radiation. An LDEF meteoroid experiment recorded the direction and precise time of more than 15,000 impacts, providing important clues to the natural meteoroid and human-generated space debris environment currently existing in low-Earth orbit. Understanding how materials and equipment behave after long periods of exposure to the space environment is very important in the successful development and operation of permanent space stations, the establishment of lunar bases, and sending human expeditions to Mars and beyond.

longeron The main longitudinal member of a fuselage or nacelle (a streamlined enclosure).

longitude 1. Great circles that pass through both the north and south poles. Also called *meridians*. 2. Angular distance along a primary great circle, from the adopted reference point; the angle between a reference plane through the polar axis (often called the *prime meridian*) and a second plane through that axis. On Earth, longitude is measured eastward and westward through the prime meridian through 180 degrees.

longitudinal axis The fore-and-aft line through the center of gravity of a craft.

longitudinal slot With respect to solid rocket motors, a slot inside a propellant grain parallel to the axis of the grain.

Long March (LM) launch vehicle A series of launch vehicles developed by China. The Long March-2 (LM-2), or Cang Zheng-2C (CZ-2C), has two hypergolic stages and an optional solid rocket upper stage. It can place approximately 3,175 kilograms (kg) (7,000 pounds-mass [lbm]) into LOW EARTH ORBIT (LEO). This booster was first launched in 1975. The Long March-3 (LM-3) vehicle has two hypergolic stages (essentially the Long March-2 vehicle) and a cryogenic third stage. The Long March-3 vehicle was first launched in 1984 and is capable of a placing 5,000 kg (11,000 lbm) payload

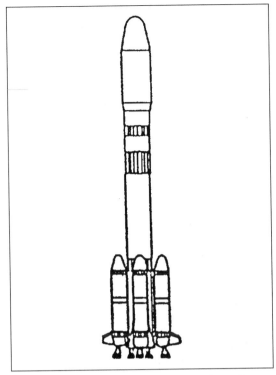

Figure 65. China's Long March-2E, or Cang Zheng-2E, launch vehicle.   *(Drawing courtesy of U.S. Congress [Office of Technology Assessment])*

into LEO. The Long March-3A (LM-3A) vehicle has two hypergolic stages and a cryogenic upper stage. It was first launched in 1994 and can place 8,500 kg (18,700 lbm) into LEO. The Long March-4 (LM-4) vehicle was first launched in 1988. It consists of three hypergolic stages and can place a 4,000 kg (8,800 lbm) payload into LEO. Finally, the Long March-2E vehicle (LM-2E or CZ-2E) has two hypergolic stages and four hypergolic strap-on rockets. It can place 8,800 kg (19,400 lbm) into LEO and was first launched in 1992. (See Figure 65.)

See also: LAUNCH VEHICLE.

look angles   The elevation and azimuth at which a particular satellite is predicted to be found at a specified time. Look angles are used for satellite tracking and data acquisition to minimize the amount of searching needed to acquire the satellite in the telescopic field of view or the antenna beam.

Loschmidt number (symbol: N_L)   The number of atoms or molecules per unit volume of an IDEAL GAS at standard pressure and temperature. The

Loschmidt number is equal to 2.687×10^{25} particles per cubic meter. Also called the *Loschmidt constant.*

See also: AVOGADRO'S NUMBER.

low Earth orbit (LEO)   An orbit, usually close to a circle, just beyond Earth's appreciable atmosphere at a height (typically 300 to 400 kilometers (185 to 250 miles) or more) sufficient to prevent the orbit from decaying rapidly because of normal conditions of atmospheric drag.

low explosive (LE)   An explosive that, when used in its normal manner, deflagrates or burns rather than detonates; that is, the rate of advance of the reaction zone into the unreacted material is less than the velocity of sound in the material. Low explosives include most rocket propellants and certain primer mixtures. Compare HIGH EXPLOSIVE.

low-gain antenna (LGA)   A spacecraft's low-gain antenna (LGA) provides wide-angle coverage at the expense of gain. Coverage is nearly omnidirectional, except for areas that may be shadowed by the spacecraft body. For interplanetary space missions, especially in the inner solar system, low-gain antennas often are designed to be usable for relatively low data rates, as long as the spacecraft is within relatively close "interplanetary range" (typically a few astronomical units) and the Earth-to-spacecraft transmitter is powerful enough. For example, a LGA can be used on a mission to Venus, but a spacecraft exploring Saturn or Uranus must use a high-gain antenna (HGA) because the distances involved. An LGA sometimes is mounted on top of a HGA's subreflector.

low-temperature deep space   The universe has a background temperature of about 3° Kelvin (K). If we look away from the Sun and Earth, this very cold background predominates and can be used by a spacecraft as a low-temperature reservoir or heat sink. The cosmic background behaves like a 3° K BLACKBODY radiator with a predominant wavelength at 1 millimeter (although the cosmic radiation background has components at other wavelenghts). The cosmic background temperature of deep space is both constant in time and uniform in all direction (i.e., isotropic) and can be used to calibrate radiofrequency (RF) receivers.

LOX   Liquid oxygen at a temperature of 90° Kelvin (-183° Celsius) or lower. A common propellant (the oxidizer) for liquid rocket engines. Encountered in a variety of aerospace uses, such as *LOX tank, LOX valve, or loxing* (e.g., to fill a rocket vehicle's propellant tank with liquid oxygen).

lox-hydrogen engine A rocket engine that uses liquid hydrogen as the fuel and liquid oxygen (LOX) as the oxidizer, such as the space shuttle main engines (SSMEs).

lubrication (in space) Under the very low pressures encountered in outer space (typically 10^{-11}–10^{-18} millimeters of mercury [mm Hg]), conventional oils and the oil components of greases evaporate very rapidly. Even soft metals, such as copper, lead, tin, and cadmium used in bearing materials here on Earth, evaporate at significant rates in space. Vaporization of substances within space vehicles has the added disadvantage that the vapors can condense on other surfaces, such as optical and electrical equipment, thereby impairing the operation of the equipment or even causing its complete failure. If these vapors diffuse into a crew habitat (perhaps through airlock operations during an extravehicular operation), they may prove annoying to the astronaut inhabitants or possibly toxic.

Another consequence of the extremely low pressures in space is that bare metal surfaces can weld together when placed in contact. The more similar the metals are, the more readily they can *cold weld.* Metal surfaces do not cold weld under usual conditions on Earth because of the presence of protective oxide coatings or adsorbed gases on their surfaces. Under the low pressures in space, however, some oxide coatings decompose and adsorbed gases are desorbed, exposing the bare metal surfaces. When metal surfaces rub together in space, therefore, there is a great likelihood that they will cold weld, thus greatly increasing the frictional force between them and possibly leading to malfunction of the equipment.

Temperature is another environmental factor that reaches extreme proportions during space missions. At once extreme, unheated structures, such as antennas and sensor booms, can reach very low temperatures when viewing (i.e., radiating to) the temperature of deep space, which is near absolute zero (about 3° Kelvin). At the other extreme, high temperatures can occur within components inside a spacecraft, especially if proper thermal management techniques have not been incorporated in the design. So lubricants must be

selected to work not only under extremely low pressure conditions but also over a wide temperature range.

Considering the environmental demands imposed by space flight, aerospace engineers use two main techniques of lubrication in space vehicles: thick-film lubrication and thin-film lubrication. (See Figure 66.)

Thick-film lubrication is also known as *hydrodynamic* or *hydrostatic lubrication,* depending on whether the fluid pressure is maintained by the lubricated mechanism itself or by external means, respectively. It occurs when bearing (or contacting) surfaces are held sufficiently far apart by the lubricant that irregularities or asperities in the bearing surfaces do not come in contact with each other. In thick-film lubrication the lubricant must remain sufficiently viscous during operation so that the bearing surfaces do not come in contact with each other.

Thin-film lubrication occurs whenever the film of lubricant between surfaces is squeezed out until the two surfaces come into physical contact with each other. Because of surface irregularities or asperities, the actual points of contact have a total area much less than the apparent area of contact.

Spacecraft and satellites are lubricated with dry films, liquids, metallic coatings, special greases, or combinations of these lubricants. Liquid lubrication systems generally are used for mission life requirements of over a year. The primary function of a liquid lubricant in space applications is to separate surfaces in relative motion so that the surfaces do not sustain major damage and to keep the coefficient of friction between the surfaces relatively low.

See also: SPACE TRIBOLOGY.

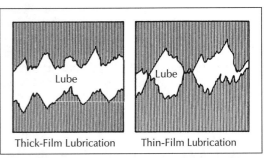

Figure 66. Thick-film and thin-film lubrication. Surface irregularities or asperities do not come into contact with each other during normal operation of a thick-film lubricant. *(Drawing courtesy of NASA)*

lumen (symbol: lm) The SI UNIT of luminous flux. It is defined as the luminous flux emitted by a uniform point source with an intensity of one candela in a solid angle of one steradian.

See also: CANDELA.

luminance (symbol: L) In photometry, a measure of the intrinsic luminous intensity emitted by a source in a given direction; the illuminance produced by light from the source upon a given surface area with an orientation to the line of sight at any distance from the source, divided by the solid angle subtended by the source at the receiving surface. It is assumed that the medium between the source and receiver is perfectly transparent; therefore, luminance is independent of extinction between source and receiver. The source may or may not be self-luminous. Luminance is a measure of light only; the comparable term for electromagnetic radiation in general is *radiance.* Luminance is expressed in units of candela per square meter (Cd/m^2).

luminous intensity Luminous energy per unit time per unit solid angle; the intensity (i.e., flux per unit solid angle) of visible radiation weighted to take into account to variable response of the human eye as a function of the wavelength of light; usually expressed in candelas. Sometimes called *luminous flux density.*

lumped mass Concept in engineering analysis wherein a mass is treated as if it were concentrated at a point.

Luna A series of Russian spacecraft sent to the Moon in the 1960s and 1970s. For example, *Luna 9,* a 1,581-kilogram (kg) (3,485 (pounds-mass [lbm]) spacecraft, was launched on January 31, 1966 and successfully soft-landed on the Ocean of Storms on February 3, 1966. This spacecraft transmitted several medium-resolution photographs of the lunar surface before its batteries failed four days after landing. The lander spacecraft also returned data on radiation levels at the landing site. *Luna 12* was an orbiter spacecraft that was launched on October 22, 1966 successfully orbited the Moon and returned television pictures of the surface. *Luna 16,* launched on September 12, 1970, was the first successful automated (robotic) sample-return mission to the lunar surface. (Of course, the U.S. *Apollo 11* and *12* lunar landing missions in July 1969 and

November 1969 respectively, already had returned lunar samples collected by astronauts who walked on the Moon's surface.) After landing on the Sea of Fertility, this robot spacecraft deployed a drill that bore 35 centimeters (about 1 foot) into the surface. The lunar soil sample, which had a mass of about 0.1 kg (0.22 lbm), was transferred automatically to a return vehicle, which left the lunar surface and landed in the former Soviet Union on September 24, 1970, *Luna 17* introduced the first robot roving vehicle, called Lunokhod I, on the lunar surface. The spacecraft successfully touched down on the Sea of Rains and deployed the sophisticated Lunokhod I rover. This eight-wheel vehicle was radio-controlled from Earth. The rover covered 10.5 kilometers (6.5 miles) during a surface exploration mission that lasted 10.5 months. The rover's cameras transmitted more than 20,000 images of the Moon's surface and instruments of the vehicle analyzed properties of the lunar soil at many hundreds of locations. *Luna 20* (launched February 14, 1972) and *Luna 24* (launched August 9, 1976) were also successful robot soil sample return missions. *Luna 21,* launched in January 1973, successfully deployed another robot rover, Lunokhod 2, in the Le Monnier crater in the Sea of Tranquility. This 840-kg (1,852 lbm) rover vehicle traveled about 37 kilometers (23 miles) during its four-month-long surface exploration mission. Numerous photographs were taken and surface experiments conducted by this robot rover under radio-control by Russian scientists and technicians on Earth.

See also: MOON.

lunar Of or pertaining to the Moon.

lunar base A permanently inhabited complex on the surface of the Moon. In the first permanent lunar base camp, a team of from 10, up to perhaps 100, lunar workers will set about the task of fully investigating the Moon. (The word "permanent" here means that the facility will always be occupied by human beings, but individuals probably will serve tours of from one to three years before returning to Earth.) These lunar base inhabitants will take advantage of the Moon as a science-in-space platform and perform the fundamental engineering studies needed to confirm and define the specific roles the Moon will play in the full development of space in the 21st century. For example, the discovery of frozen volatiles (including water) in the perpetually frozen recesses of the Moon's polar

lunar gravity **223**

Figure 67. An early lunar surface base—this one intended to supply lunar materials to support space-based manufacturing operations. The four large horizontal cylinders contain the base habitat, maintenance facility, soil-packaging plant, and loading facility. An electromagnetic mass driver (partially illustrated) launches 4-kilogram mass packages of lunar material to a point in space where they are collected and taken to an orbiting processing plant. *(Artist rendering courtesy of NASA)*

regions could change lunar base logistics strategies and accelerate development of a large lunar settlement of up to 10,000 or more inhabitants. Many lunar base applications have been proposed. Some of these concepts include: (1) a lunar scientific laboratory complex; (2) a lunar industrial complex to support space-based manufacturing; (3) an astrophysical observatory for solar system and deep space surveillance; (4) a fueling station for orbital transfer vehicles that travel through cislunar-space; and (5) a training site and assembly point for the first human expedition to Mars. (See Figure 67.)

lunar crater A depression, usually circular, on the surface of the Moon. It frequently occurs with a raised rim called a *ringwall.* Lunar craters range in size up to 250 kilometers (155 miles) in diameter. The largest lunar craters are sometimes called "walled plains." The smaller crater—say, 15 to 30 kilometers (9.3 to 18.6 miles) across—often are called "craterlets"; while the very smallest, just a

few hundred meters across, are called "beads." Many lunar craters have been named after famous people, usually astronomers.

See also: IMPACT CRATER; MOON.

lunar day The period of time associated with one complete orbit of the Moon about Earth. It is equal to 27.322 "Earth" days. The lunar day is also equal in length to the sidereal month.

lunar eclipse The phenomenon observed when the Moon enters the shadow of Earth. A lunar eclipse is called *penumbral,* if the Moon enters only the penumbra of Earth; *partial,* if the Moon enters the umbra without being totally immersed; and *total,* if the Moon is entirely immersed in the umbra.

lunar gravity The force imparted by the Moon to a mass that is at rest relative to the lunar surface. It is approximately one-sixth the acceleration experienced by a mass at rest on the surface (sea level) of Earth. On the Moon's surface, the acceleration due to gravity is about 1.62 meters per second per second (m/s^2) [5.32 feet per second per second (ft/s^2)].

lunar highlands The light-colored, heavily cratered mountainous part of the lunar landscape.
See also: MOON.

lunar module (LM) The lander spacecraft used to bring the Apollo astronauts to the surface of the Moon. The lunar module (LM) lifted off from Earth enclosed in a compartment of the *Saturn V* launch vehicle, below the command-service module (CSM) that housed the astronauts. Once the craft was on its way to the Moon, the CSM pulled the LM from its storage area. In lunar orbit, the two Apollo astronauts who were to explore the lunar surface climbed into the LM, undocked, and "flew" the lander spacecraft to the Moon's surface. The descent stage of the LM contained a main, centrally located retrorocket engine that accomplished the "soft-landing." Upon completion of the surface expedition, the crew lifted off from the lunar surface using the top segment of the LM, which was powered by another, smaller rocket. The "four-legged" bottom portion of the LM remained on the

Figure 68. *Apollo 11* astronaut Edwin "Buzz" Aldrin, Jr., descends the ladder of the lunar module and becomes the second human being to walk on the Moon (July 20, 1969). *(Photograph courtesy of NASA—B&W Photo #69-H-1264)*

Moon. After reaching lunar orbit with the now-smaller LM spacecraft, the crew rendezvoused with and transferred back into the Apollo CSM. The ascent stage of the LM was then jettisoned and placed in a decaying orbit that sent it crashing into the lunar surface to avoid possible interference with the Apollo CSM or a future mission. (See Figure 68.)

During the aborted *Apollo 13* mission, the LM served as a lifeboat for all three Apollo astronauts, providing them the emergency life support that helped get them safely home after the CSM suffered a catastrophic explosion on the way to the Moon.

The LM is also referred to as the *lunar excursion module,* or simply "LEM."
See also: APOLLO PROJECT.

lunar orbit Orbit of a spacecraft around the Moon.

Lunar Orbiter Five Lunar Orbiter missions were launched by NASA in 1966 through 1967 with the purpose of mapping the Moon's surface prior to the landings by the Apollo astronauts (which occurred from 1969 to 1972). All five missions were highly successful; 99% of the lunar surface was photographed with a 60-meter (197-feet) spatial resolution or better. The first three Lunar Orbiter missions were dedicated to imaging 20 potential Apollo landing sites, which had been preselected based on observations from Earth. The fourth and fifth missions were committed to broader scientific objectives and were flown in high-altitude polar orbits around the Moon. *Lunar Orbiter 4* photographed the entire nearside and 95% of the farside, and *Lunar Orbiter 5* completed the farside coverage and acquired medium- (20-meter) and high- (2-meter) resolution images of 36 preselected areas. These probes were sent into orbit around the Moon to gather information and then purposely crashed at the end of each mission to prevent possible interference with future projects.
See also: APOLLO PROJECT; MOON.

lunar probe A probe for exploring and reporting conditions on or about the Moon.

Lunar Prospector A NASA spacecraft designed for a low-polar-orbit investigation of the Moon, including mapping of surface composition and possible deposits of polar ice, measurements of magnetic and gravity fields, and study of lunar

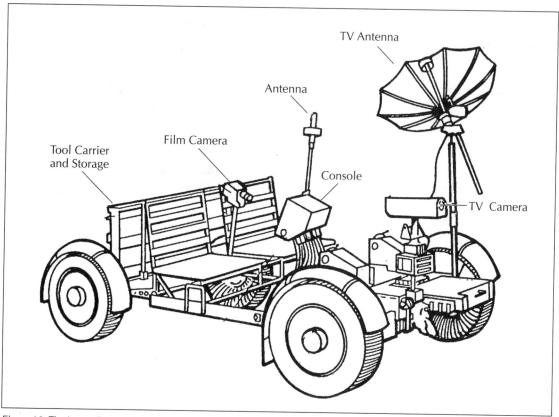

Figure 69. The Lunar Rover Vehicle used by the Apollo astronauts to explore the Moon's surface far from their landing site
(Drawing courtesy of NASA)

outgassing events. The *Lunar Prospector* was launched successfully from Cape Canaveral Air Force Station, Florida by a Lockheed Athena II vehicle on January 6, 1998 at approximately 9:28 PM local (EST) time. The spacecraft swung into orbit around the Moon early on January 11 and prepared to start its science mission. Data from this one- to three-year duration mission will permit construction of a detailed map of the surface composition of the Moon and improve our understanding of its origin, evolution, current state, and resources. The 126-kilogram (278 pound-mass) spacecraft carries the following scientific equipment: a gamma ray spectrometer (GRS), a neutron spectrometer (NS), a magnetometer (MAG), an electron reflectometer (ER), an alpha particle spectrometer (APS), and a Doppler gravity experiment (DGE).

See also: MOON.

lunar rover(s) Crewed or automated (robot) vehicles used to help explore the Moon's surface. The Lunar Rover Vehicle (LRV), shown in Figure 69, also was called a space buggy and the "Moon car." It was used by American astronauts during the *Apollo 15, 16,* and *17* expeditions to the Moon. This vehicle was designed to climb over steep slopes, go over rocks, and move easily over sandlike lunar surfaces. It was able to carry more than twice its own mass (about 210 kilograms [463 pounds-mass]) in passengers, scientific instruments, and lunar material samples. This electric-powered (battery) vehicle could travel about 16 kilometers (10 miles) per hour on level ground. The vehicle's power came from two 36-volt silver zinc batteries that drove independent 1/4-horsepower electric motors in each wheel. Apollo astronauts used their space buggies to explore well beyond their initial lunar-landing sites. With these vehicles, they were able to gather Moon rocks and travel much farther and quicker across the lunar surface than if they had to explore on foot. For example, during the *Apollo 17* expedition, the lunar rover traveled 19 kilometers (12 miles) on just one of its three excursions.

Automated or robot rovers also can be used to explore the lunar surface. For example, during the Russian *Luna 17* mission to the Moon in 1970, the "mother" spacecraft soft-landed on the lunar surface in the Sea of Rains and deployed the Lunokhod 1, robot rover vehicle. Controlled from Earth by radio signals, this eight-wheeled lunar rover vehicle traveled for months across the lunar surface, transmitting more than 20,000 television images of the surface and performing more than 500 lunar soil tests at various locations. The Russian *Luna 21* mission to the Moon in January 1973 successfully deployed another robot rover, called Lunokhod 2.

See also: APOLLO PROJECT; LUNA; MOON.

lunar satellite A human-made object that is placed in orbit (one or more revolutions) around the Moon. For example, the American Lunar Orbiter spacecraft was a lunar satellite.

See also: LUNAR ORBITER.

Lunokhod A Russian eight-wheeled robot vehicle, controlled by radio signals from Earth and used to conduct surface exploration of the lunar surface.

See also: LUNA; LUNAR ROVER(S).

lux (symbol: lx) The SI unit of illuminance. It is defined as 1 lumen per square meter.

See also: INTERNATIONAL SYSTEM OF UNITS; LUMEN.

Mace An improved version of the air force's Matador missile (MGM-1C), differing primarily in its improved guidance system, longer-range, low-level attack capability, and higher-yield warhead. The Mace was designated as the MGM-13. This early "winged missile" was guided by a self-contained radar guidance system (MGM-13A) or by an inertial guidance system (MG-13B).

Mach cone 1. The cone-shaped shock wave that theoretically emanates from an infinitesimally small particle moving at supersonic speed through a fluid medium. It is the locus of Mach lines. 2. The cone-shaped shock wave generated by a sharp-pointed object, such as the nose of a high-speed jet aircraft.

Mach number (symbol: M) A number expressing the ratio of the speed of a body or of a point on a body with respect to the surrounding air or other fluid, or the speed of a flow, to the speed of sound in the medium. It is named after the Austrian scientist Ernst Mach (1838–1916).

If the Mach number is less than one (i.e., M < 1), the flow is called *subsonic,* and local disturbances can propagate ahead of the flow. If the Mach number is equal to unity (i.e., M = 1), the flow is called *sonic.* If the Mach number is greater than one (i.e., M > 1), the flow is called *supersonic,* and disturbances cannot propagate ahead of the flow, with the general result that oblique shock waves form (i.e., shock waves inclined in the direction of flow). The formation and characteristics of such oblique shock waves involve complicated compressible flow phenomena. Sometimes the oblique shock wave is attached to the surface of the body, but this usually occurs only when the supersonic stream encounters a sharp, narrow-angled object. Most times, however, the oblique shock wave takes the form of a rounded, detached shock that appears in front of a more blunt-shaped object moving at supersonic speeds through a compressible fluid medium.

Magellanic Clouds The two dwarf galaxies that are closest to our Milky Way Galaxy. The Large Magellanic Cloud (LMC) is about 150,000 light-years away and the Small Magellanic Cloud (SMC) is approximately 170,000 light-years away. Both are visible to observers in the Southern Hemisphere and resemble luminous clouds several times the size of the full Moon. Their presence was first recorded in 1519 by the Portuguese explorer Ferdinand Magellan, after whom they are named.

Magellan Mission A NASA solar system exploration mission to the planet Venus. On May 4, 1989 the 3,550 kilogram (7,825 pound-mass) *Magellan* spacecraft was delivered to Earth orbit by the space shuttle *Atlantis* during the STS 30 mission and then sent on an interplanetary trajectory to the cloud-shrouded planet by a solid-fueled inertial upper stage (IUS) rocket system. *Magellan* was the first interplanetary spacecraft to be launched by the space shuttle. On August 10, 1990 the *Magellan* (named for the famous 16th-century Portuguese explorer Ferdinand Magellan) was inserted into orbit around Venus and began initial operations of its very successful radar mapping mission.

Magellan used a sophisticated imaging radar system to make the most detailed map of Venus ever captured during its four years in orbit around Earth's "sister planet" from 1990 to 1994. After concluding its radar mapping mission, *Magellan* made global maps of the Venusian gravity field. During this phase of the mission, the spacecraft did not use its radar mapper but instead transmitted a constant radio signal back to Earth. When it passed over an area on Venus with higher than normal gravity, the spacecraft would speed up slightly in its orbit. This movement then would cause the frequency of *Magellan*'s radio signal to change very slightly due to the DOPPLER EFFECT. Because of the ability of the radio receivers in the NASA Deep Space Network to measure radio frequencies extremely accurately, scientists were able to construct a very detailed gravity map of Venus. In fact, during this phase of its mission, the spacecraft provided high-resolution gravity data for about 95% of the planet's surface. Flight controllers also tested a new maneuvering technique called *aerobraking,* a technique that uses a planet's atmosphere to slow or steer a spacecraft.

The craters revealed by *Magellan*'s detailed radar images suggested to planetary scientists that the Venusian surface is relatively young—perhaps "recently" resurfaced or modified about 500 million years ago by widespread volcanic eruptions. The planet's current harsh environment has persisted at least since then. No surface features were detected that suggest the presence of oceans or lakes at any time in the planet's past. Furthermore, scientists found no evidence of plate tectonics, that is, the movements of huge crustal masses.

Magellan's mission ended with a dramatic plunge through the dense atmosphere to the planet's surface. This was the first time an operating planetary spacecraft has ever been crashed intentionally. Contact was lost with the spacecraft on October 12, 1994 at 10:02 Universal Time (3:02 AM Pacific Daylight Time). The purpose of this last maneuver was to gather data on the Venusian atmosphere before the spacecraft ceased functioning during its fiery descent. Although much of the *Magellan* is believed to have been vaporized by atmospheric heating during this final plunge, some sections may have survived and hit the planet's surface intact.

See also: VENUS.

magma Molten rock material beneath the surface of a planet or moon. It may be ejected to the surface by volcanic activity.

magnet A substance with the property of attracting certain other substances. Some metals, such as cobalt, iron, and nickel, can be magnetized to attract other magnetic metals. A magnet has a MAGNETIC FIELD, which is a region around it where there are forces exerted on other magnetic materials. Earth has a magnetic field, as do several other planets. An electric current, flowing through a conductor, also creates a magnetic field.

magnetic field A region of space with a detectable magnetic force at every location within the region. Often it is represented as an array of imaginary lines of force that exist in relation to a magnetic pole.

magnetic field strength (symbol: H) The strength of the magnetic force on a unit magnetic pole in a region of space affected by other magnets or electric currents. The magnetic field strength is a vector quantity that is measured in amperes per meter.

magnetic flux (symbol: Φ_M) A measure of the total size of a magnetic field. The flux through any area in the medium surrounding a magnet is equal to the integral of the magnetic flux density (B) over the area (A). That is,

$$\Phi_M = \int B \cdot d\,A$$

The weber (Wb) is the SI UNIT of magnetic flux.

magnetic flux density (symbol: B) The magnetic flux that passes through a unit area of a MAGNETIC FIELD in a direction at right angles to the magnetic force. It is a vector quantity. The SI UNIT of magnetic flux density is the tesla (T), which is equal to one weber of magnetic flux per square meter.

magnetic storm A sudden, worldwide disturbance of Earth's magnetic field, believed caused by solar disturbances, such as a solar flare. The onset of a magnetic storm may occur in an hour, while the gradual return to normal conditions may take several days.

magnetohydrodynamics (MHD) converter A device that directly converts the kinetic energy of a hot working fluid into electrical energy. This direct energy conversion (DEC) process is achieved by flowing a high-temperature, electrically conducting gas or gas-liquid metal combination through a stationary magnetic field. MHD conversion systems can either be closed-cycle or open-cycle systems. In a closed-cycle MHD system, the working fluid is continuously recirculated; in an open-cycle MHD system, the working fluid passes just once through the converter region and is then discharged.

magnetometer An instrument for measuring the strength and sometimes the direction of a magnetic field. Magnetometers often are used to detect and measure the interplanetary and solar magnetic fields in the vicinity of a scientific spacecraft. These direct-sensing instruments typically detect the strength of magnetic fields in three dimensions (i.e., in the x-, y-, and z-planes). As a magnetometer sweeps an arc through a magnetic field when the spacecraft rotates, an electrical signal is produced proportional to the magnitude and structure of the field.

magnetomotive force (symbol: F_M) The magnetomotive force (mmf) can be considered as the physical parallel of the electromotive force (emf) in a magnetic circuit. It is defined mathematically as the closed path (circular) integral of the magnetic field strength (H), namely

$$F_M = \oint H\, dx$$

The magnetomotive force is measured in ampere-turns. Also called *magnetic potential*.

magnetoplasmadynamic (MPD) thruster An advanced electric propulsion device capable of operating with a wide range of propellants in both pulsed and steady-state modes. MPD thrusters are well suited for orbit transfer and spacecraft

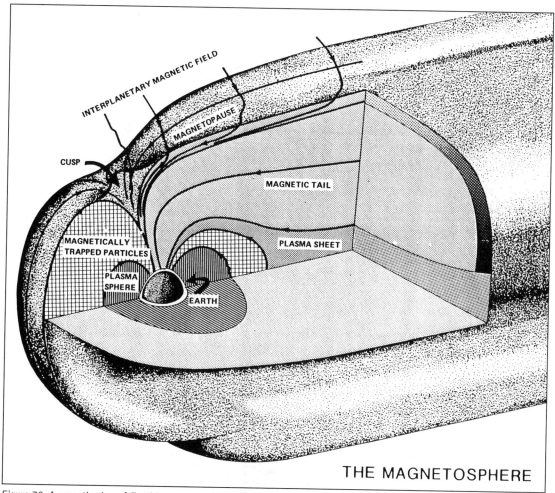

THE MAGNETOSPHERE

Figure 70. A synoptic view of Earth's magnetosphere   *(Drawing courtesy of NASA)*

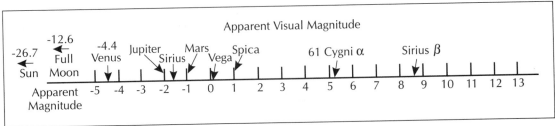

Figure 71. The apparent visual magnitude of several celestial objects   *(Chart courtesy of NASA)*

maneuvering applications. In an MPD thruster device, the current flowing from the cathode to the anode sets up a ring-shaped magnetic field. This magnetic field then pushes against the plasma in the arc. As propellant, such as argon, flows through the arc plasma, it is ionized and forced away by the magnetic field. A thrusting force therefore is created by the interaction of an electrical current and a magnetic field.

See also: ELECTRIC PROPULSION.

magnetosphere The region around a planet in which charged atomic particles are influenced by the planet's own MAGNETIC FIELD rather than by the magnetic field of the Sun, as projected by the solar wind. Because Earth has its own magnetic field, the interaction of Earth's magnetic field and the solar wind results in this very dynamic and complicated region surrounding Earth. As shown in Figure 70, studies by spacecraft and probes have now mapped much of the region of magnetic field structures and streams of trapped particles around Earth. The *solar wind,* a plasma of electrically charged particles (mostly protons and electrons) that flows at speeds of 1 million kilometers per hour or more from the Sun, shapes Earth's magnetosphere into a teardrop, with a long magnetic tail (called the *magnetotail*) stretching out opposite the Sun.

Earth and other planets of the solar system exist in the *heliosphere*—the region of space dominated by the magnetic influence of the Sun. Interplanetary space is not empty but filled with the solar wind. The geomagnetic field of Earth presents an obstacle to the solar wind, behaving much like a rock in a swiftly flowing stream of water. A shock wave, called the BOW SHOCK, forms on the sunward side of Earth and deflects the flow of the solar wind. The bow shock slows down, heats, and compresses the solar wind, which then flows around the geomagnetic field, creating Earth's magnetos-

phere. The steady pressure of the solar wind compresses the otherwise spherical field lines of Earth's magnetic field on the sunward side at about 15 Earth radii, or some 100,000 kilometers, a distance still inside the Moon's orbit around Earth. On the night side of Earth away from the Sun, the solar wind pulls the geomagnetic field lines out to form a long magnetic tail (i.e., the *magnetotail*). The magnetotail is believed to extend for hundreds of Earth radii, although it is not known precisely how far it actually extends into space away from Earth.

The outermost boundary of Earth's magnetosphere is called the *magnetopause*. Some solar wind particles do pass through the magnetopause and become trapped in the inner magnetosphere. Some of those trapped particles then travel down through the *polar cusps* at the North and South poles and into the uppermost portions of the Earth's atmosphere. These trapped solar wind particles then have enough energy to trigger the *aurora,* which are also called the *Northern* (aurora borealis) and *Southern Lights* (aurora australis) because they occur in circles around the North and South poles. These spectacular aurora are just one dramatic manifestation of the many connections among the Sun, the solar wind, and Earth's magnetosphere and atmosphere.

magnitude A number, now measured on a logarithmic scale, used to indicate the relative brightness of a celestial body. The smaller the magnitude number, the greater the brightness. When ancient astronomers studied the heavens, they observed objects of varying brightness and color and decided to group them according to their relative brightness. The 20 brightest stars of the night sky were called *stars of the first magnitude.* Other stars were called 2nd, 3rd, 4th, 5th, and 6th magnitude stars according to their relative brightness. The 6th magnitude stars are the faintest stars visible to the unaided (i.e., "naked") human eye under the most favorable observing conditions. By convention the star Vega (Alpha Lyra) was defined as having a magnitude of zero. Even brighter objects, such as the star Sirius or the planets Mars and Jupiter thus acquired *negative magnitude* values. In 1856 the British astronomer N. R. Pogson, proposed a more precise logarithmic magnitude in which a difference of five magnitudes represented a relative brightness ratio of 100 to 1. Consequently, with Pogson's proposed scale, two stars differing by five magnitudes would differ in brightness by a factor of 100. Today the Pogson magnitude scale is used almost universally in astronomy. (See Figure 71.)

See also: STAR(S).

main-belt asteroid An asteroid located in the main asteroid belt, which occurs between Mars and Jupiter. This term sometimes is limited to asteroids found in the most populous portion of the main asteroid belt, namely those asteroids about 2.2 to 3.3 astronomical units (AUs) from the Sun.

See also: ASTEROID.

main stage 1. In a multistage rocket vehicle, the stage that develops the greatest amount of thrust, with or without booster engines. 2. In a single-stage rocket vehicle powered by one or more engines, the period when "full thrust" (i.e., at or above 90% of the rated thrust) is attained. 3. A sustainer engine that is considered as a stage after booster engines have fallen away, as in the main stage of the Atlas launch vehicle.

See also: ROCKET.

maintenance The actions taken to maintain an item in a specified condition, including systematic inspection, detection of flaws, and servicing to prevent failure. Also the actions taken to restore an item to a specified operational condition, including fault identification, item replacement, repair, and verification of serviceability.

main valve The valve, usually located just upstream of the thrust chamber injector, that controls the propellant to the injector in a liquid rocket engine.

See also: ROCKET.

make safe One or more actions necessary to prevent or interrupt complete function of the system.

Among the necessary actions are: (1) install safety devices such as pins or locks; (2) disconnect hoses, linkages, or batteries; (3) bleed (i.e., drain) fluids from accumulators and reservoirs; (4) remove explosive devices such as initiators, fuzes, and detonators; and (5) intervene by welding components in place or fixing their movement with lockwires. Often used to describe the "disarming" or "disabling" of a weapon or rocket system.

malfunction Improper functioning of a component or subsystem that causes improper operation of a system.

mandrel The tool that forms the geometry of the central cavity in the casting of a solid-propellant grain.

maneuvering booster A booster that can change course in a preprogrammed manner. A maneuvering booster might be used in an effort to avoid attack during the boost phase by space-based interceptors.

See also: BALLISTIC MISSILE DEFENSE.

maneuvering reentry vehicle (MaRV) A reentry vehicle that can maneuver in the late-midcourse or terminal phase of its flight, either to enhance its accuracy or to avoid antiballistic missiles. Maneuvers within the atmosphere usually can be accomplished by aerodynamic means, while maneuvers in space could be accomplished by small rockets.

See also: BALLISTIC MISSILE DEFENSE.

maneuver pad Data or information on spacecraft attitude, thrust values, event times, and the like that is transmitted in advance of a maneuver.

manifold A fluid-flow enclosure that distributes the flow in a desired manner from an inlet or inlets to an outlet or outlets.

manipulators Mechanical devices used for handling objects; frequently involving remote operations (i.e., teleoperation) and/or hazardous substances or environmental conditions. That portion of a robot system which is capable of grasping or handling. A manipulator often has a versatile end effector (i.e., the special tool or "grasping element" installed at the end of the manipulator) that can respond to a variety of different handling requirements. For example, the U.S. space shuttle has a very useful manipulator called the *remote manipulator system* (*RMS*).

man-machine interface The boundary where human and machine characteristics and capabilities are joined in order to obtain optimum operating conditions and maximum efficiency of the combined *man-machine system*. A joystick and a control panel are examples of man-machine interfaces. Also called *human-machine interface*.

manned An aerospace vehicle or system that is occupied by one or more persons, male or female. The terms "crewed," "human," or "personed" are preferred today in the aerospace literature. For example, a "manned mission to Mars" should be called a "human mission to Mars."

manned vehicle An older aerospace term describing a rocket or spacecraft that carried one or more human beings, male or female. Used to distinguish that craft from a robot (i.e., pilotless) aircraft, a ballistic missile, or an automated (and uncrewed) satellite or planetary probe. The expression "crewed vehicle" or "personed vehicle" is now preferred.

manometer An instrument for measuring the pressure of fluids (either gases or liquids) both above and below atmospheric pressure.

man-rated A launch vehicle, spacecraft, aerospace system, or component considered safe and reliable enough to be used by human crew members. The term "human-rated" is now preferred.

man-tended capability A space facility or orbiting platform designed to operate without a permanent human crew on board. However, astronauts will visit this type of orbiting facility periodically to conduct servicing operations and maintenance. The HUBBLE SPACE TELESCOPE (HST) is an example. The term "crew-tended" or "human-tended" is now preferred.

Mariner spacecraft A series of NASA planetary exploration spacecraft that performed reconnaissance flyby and orbital missions to Mercury, Mars, and Venus in the 1960s and 1970s. *Mariner 2* encountered Venus at a distance of about 41,000 kilometers (km) (25,480 miles [mi]) on December

14, 1962. It provided important scientific data about conditions in interplanetary space (e.g., solar wind, interplanetary magnetic field, cosmic rays, etc.) and on the planet Venus. *Mariner 4* flew by Mars on July 14, 1965 and returned images of the planet's surface. The closest encounter distance for its mission was 9,846 km (6,118 mi) from the Martian surface. The *Mariner 5* spacecraft passed within 4,000 km (2,486 mi) of Venus on October 19, 1967. Its instruments successfully measured both interplanetary and Venusian magnetic fields, charged particles, plasmas, as well as certain properties of the Venusian atmosphere. *Mariner 6* passed within 3,431 km (2,132 mi) of the Martian surface on July 31, 1969. The spacecraft's instruments took images of the planet's surface and measured ultraviolet and infrared emissions of the Martian atmosphere. The *Mariner 7* spacecraft was identical to the *Mariner 6* spacecraft. *Mariner 7* passed within 3,430 km (2,131 mi) of Mars on August 5, 1969 and acquired images of the planet's surface. Emissions of the Martian atmosphere also were measured. *Mariner 9* arrived at and orbited Mars on November 14, 1971. This spacecraft gathered data on the atmospheric composition, density, pressure, and temperature of the Martian atmosphere as well as performing studies of the Martian surface. After depleting its supply of attitude control gas, the spacecraft was turned off on October 27, 1972. *Mariner 10* was the seventh successful launch in the Mariner series. (*Mariner 1* and *Mariner 8* experienced launch failures, while *Mariner 3* ceased transmissions nine hours after launch and entered solar orbit.) The *Mariner 10* spacecraft was the first to use the gravitational pull of one planet (Venus) to reach another planet (Mercury). It passed Venus on February 5, 1974 at a distance of 4,200 km (2,610 mi). The spacecraft then crossed the orbit of Mercury at a distance of 704 km (437 mi) from the surface on March 29, 1974. A second encounter with Mercury occurred on September 21, 1974 at an altitude of about 47,000 km (29,210 mi). A third and final Mercury encounter occurred on March 16, 1975, when the spacecraft passed the planet at an altitude of 327 km (203 mi). Many images of the planet's surface were acquired during these flybys, and magnetic field measurements were performed. When the supply of attitude control gas became depleted on March 24, 1975, this highly successful mission was terminated.

See also: MARS; MERCURY; VENUS.

marmon clamp A ring-shaped clamp, consisting of three equal-length segments held together by explosive bolts, used to couple the main subsections of a rocket vehicle.

Mars The fourth planet in the solar system with an equatorial diameter of 6,794 kilometers. Throughout human history Mars, the Red Planet, has been at the center of astronomical thought. The ancient Babylonians, for example, followed the motions of this wandering red light across the night sky and named it after Nergal, their god of war. In time the Romans, also honoring their own god of war, gave the planet its present name. The presence of an atmosphere, polar caps, and changing patterns of light and dark on the surface caused many pre–space age astronomers and scientists to consider Mars an "Earthlike planet"—the possible abode of extraterrestrial life. In fact, when actor Orson Welles broadcast a radio drama in 1938 based on H. G. Wells's science-fiction classic *War of the Worlds,* enough people believed the report of invading Martians to create a near panic in some areas.

Over the past three decades, however, sophisticated robot spacecraft—flybys, orbiters, and landers—have shattered these romantic myths of a race of ancient Martians struggling to bring water to the more productive regions of a dying world. Spacecraft-derived data have shown instead that the Red Planet is actually a "halfway" world. Part of the Martian surface is ancient, like the surfaces of the Moon and Mercury, while part is more evolved and Earthlike. Contemporary information about Mars is presented in Table 1.

In August and September 1975, two Viking spacecraft were launched on a mission to help answer the question: Is there life on Mars? Each Viking spacecraft consisted of an orbiter and lander. While scientists did not expect these spacecraft to discover Martian cities bustling with intelligent life, the exobiology experiments on the lander were designed to find evidence of primitive life-forms, past or present. Unfortunately, the results sent back by the two robot landers were teasingly inconclusive.

The Viking Project was the first mission to successfully soft-land a robot spacecraft on another planet (excluding the Earth's Moon.) All four Viking spacecraft (two orbiters and two landers) exceeded by considerable margins their design goal lifetime of 90 days. The spacecraft were launched in 1975 and began to operate around or on the Red Planet in 1976. When the *Viking 1* lander touched down on the Plain of Chryse on July 20, 1976, it found a bleak landscape. (See Figure 72.) Several weeks later its twin, the *Viking 2* lander, set down on the Plain of Utopia and discovered a more gentle, rolling landscape. One by one these robot explorers finished their highly successful visits to Mars. The *Viking Orbiter 2* spacecraft ceased operation in July 1978; the Lander 2 fell silent in April 1980; *Viking Orbiter 1* managed at least partial operation until August 1980; the *Viking Lander 1* made its final transmission on November 11, 1982. NASA officially ended the Viking mission to Mars on May 21, 1983.

As a result of these interplanetary missions, we now know that Martian weather changes very little. For example, the highest atmosphere tempera-

Table 1.
PHYSICAL AND DYNAMIC DATA
FOR MARS

Diameter (equatorial)	6,794 km
Mass	6.42×10^{23} kg
Density (mean)	3.9 g/cm^3
Surface gravity	3.73 m/sec^2
Escape velocity	5.0 km/sec
Albedo	0.15
Atmosphere (main components by volume)	
Carbon dioxide (CO_2)	95.32%
Nitrogen (N_2)	2.7%
Argon (Ar)	1.6%
Oxygen (O_2)	0.13%
Carbon monoxide (CO)	0.07%
Water vapor (H_2O)	0.03%[a]
Natural satellites	2 (Phobos and Deimos)
Period of rotation (a Martian day)	1.026 days
Average distance from Sun	2.28×10^8 km (1.523 AU)
Eccentricity	0.093
Period of revolution around Sun (a Martian year)	687 days
Mean orbital velocity	24.1 km/sec
Solar flux at planet (at top of atmosphere)	590 W/m^2 (at 1.52 AU)

[a]variable
Source: Based on NASA data.

Figure 72. A panoramic view of the surface of Mars at the *Viking 1* lander site   *(Photograph courtesy of NASA/JPL)*

ture recorded by either Viking lander was minus 21° Celsius (mid-summer at the *Viking 1* site) while the lowest recorded temperature was minus 124° Celsius (at the more northerly *Viking 2* site during winter).

The atmosphere of Mars was found to be primarily carbon dioxide (CO_2). Nitrogen, argon, and oxygen are present in small percentages, along with trace amounts of neon, xenon, and krypton. The Martian atmosphere contains only a wisp of water (about 1/1000th as much as found in Earth's atmosphere). But even this tiny amount can condense out and form clouds that ride high in the Martian atmosphere or form patches of morning fog in valleys. There is also evidence that Mars had a much denser atmosphere in the past—one capable of permitting liquid water to flow on the plan-

et's surface. Physical features resembling riverbeds, canyons and gorges, shorelines, and even islands hint that large rivers and maybe even small seas once existed on the Red Planet.

Mars has two small, irregularly shaped moons called Phobos ("fear") and Deimos ("terror"). These natural satellites were discovered in 1877 by the American astronomer Asaph Hall (1829–1907). They both have ancient, cratered surfaces with some indication of REGOLITHS to depths of possibly 5 meters or more. The physical properties of these two moons are presented in Table 2. It is hypothesized that these moons actually may be asteroids "captured" by Mars.

Scientists believe that at least 12 unusual meteorites found on Earth actually are pieces of Mars that were blasted off the Red Planet by ancient

Table 2.
PHYSICAL AND DYNAMIC PROPERTIES OF THE MARTIAN MOONS,
PHOBOS AND DEIMOS

Property	Phobos	Deimos
Characteristic dimensions (both are irregularly shaped)		
Longest dimension	27 km	15 km
Intermediate dimension	21 km	12 km
Shortest dimension	19 km	11 km
Mass	9.8×10^{15} kg	2.0×10^{15} kg
Density	2.0 g/cm³	1.9 g/cm³
Albedo	0.05	0.06
Surface gravity	1 cm/sec²	0.5 cm/sec²
Rotation	Synchronous	Synchronous
Semimajor axis of orbit	9,378 km	23,459 km
Eccentricity	0.018	0.0008
Sidereal period (approx.)	7 hr, 39 min	30 hr, 18 min

Source: Based on NASA data.

meteoroid impact collisions. One particular Martian meteorite, called ALH84001, has stimulated a great deal of interest in the possibility of life on Mars. In the summer of 1996, a NASA research team at the Johnson Space Center (JSC) announced that they had found evidence in ALH84001 that "strongly suggests primitive life may have existed on Mars more than 3.6 billion years ago." The NASA team found the first organic molecules thought to be of Martian origin; several mineral features characteristic of biological activity; and possibly microfossils (i.e., very tiny fossils) of primitive, bacterialike organisms inside this ancient Martian rock that fell to Earth as a meteorite.

Stimulated by the exciting possibility of life on Mars, two NASA missions, Mars Global Surveyor and Mars Pathfinder were launched successfully in late 1996 to start a new decade of expanded U.S. and international exploration of Mars. These robot explorers will be followed by many others as the Red Planet again becomes the center of intense scientific investigation by space scientists from around Earth.

See also: MARS BASE; MARS GLOBAL SURVEYOR; MARS PATHFINDER; MARS SURFACE ROVER(S); MARTIAN METEORITES.

Mars base For automated Mars missions, the spacecraft and robotic surface rovers generally will be small and self-contained. For human expedi-

tions to the surface of the Red Planet, however, two major requirements must be satisfied: life support (habitation) and surface transportation (mobility). Habitats, power supplies, and life support systems will tend to be more complex in a permanent Martian surface base that must sustain human beings for years at a time. Surface mobility systems will also grow in complexity and sophistication as early Martian explorers and settlers travel tens to hundreds of kilometers from their base camp. (See Figure 73.) At a relatively early time in any Martian surface base program, the use of Martian resources to support the base must be tested vigorously and then quickly integrated in the development of an eventually self-sustaining surface infrastructure.

In one possible scenario, the initial Martian habitats will resemble standardized lunar base (or space station) pressurized modules and will be transported from cislunar space to Mars in prefabricated condition by interplanetary nuclear-electric propulsion (NEP) cargo ships. These modules will be configured and connected as needed on the surface of Mars and then covered with a meter or so thickness of Martian soil for protection against the lethal effects of solar flare radiation or continuous exposure to cosmic rays on the planet's surface. (Unlike Earth's atmosphere, the very thin Martian atmosphere does not shield very well against ionizing radiations from space.)

See also: MARS.

Mars Global Surveyor (MGS) mission The Mars Global Surveyor (MGS) mission is designed as a rapid, low-cost recovery of the Mars Observer mission objectives. (Contact with the Mars Observer spacecraft was lost on August 21, 1993, just three days before orbit insertion around Mars.) The science objectives of this mission include: high-resolution imaging of the planet's surface, studies of the Martian topography and gravity field, the role of water and dust on the surface and in the atmosphere of Mars, the weather and climate of Mars, the composition of the surface and atmosphere, and the existence and evolution of the Martian magnetic field.

The 1,031-kilogram (2,733 pound-mass) spacecraft was launched successfully from Cape Canaveral Air Force Station by an expendable Delta II rocket on November 07, 1996 and placed on a 10-month-long interplanetary trajectory to Mars. The spacecraft entered orbit around Mars on September 11, 1997. On September 17 the NASA flight team started performing a series of orbit changes to lower the spacecraft's perigee (lowest point of its orbit) into the fringes of the Martian atmosphere. On every pass through the atmosphere, the spacecraft slowed down a slight amount because of atmospheric resistance, and consequently the apogee (or high point of its orbit around Mars) began to drop. The original plan was to use the "aerobraking" scheme to lower the high point of the orbit from about 54,000 kilometers (km) (33,560 miles [mi]) down to about 400 km (250 mi) repeatedly flying through the Martian atmosphere for about four months. However, on October 11, 1997 this aerobraking maneuver was suspended temporarily because pressure from the Martian atmosphere caused one of the spacecraft's two solar panels to bend backward a slight amount. The solar panel in question had been slightly damaged shortly after launch in November 1996, and the NASA flight team did not want to risk overstressing it.

Then, following several weeks of intense analysis, the NASA flight team decided on November 7 to resume aerobraking—provided that it now occurred at a more gentle pace (i.e., less atmospheric pressure each pass) than proposed by the original mission plan. Under the new mission plan, aerobraking will occur with the low point of the spacecraft at an average altitude of 120 km (74.6 mi), rather than the original low-point altitude of 110 km (68.4 mi). This slightly higher low-point altitude results in a decrease of about 66% in terms of atmospheric resistance pressure experienced by the spacecraft. Aerobraking is now scheduled to be completed in March 1999. At that time, the spacecraft will be in the proper orbit (i.e., a nearly circular polar orbit with an average altitude of about 378 km [235 mi]) for the Mars Global Surveyor Orbiter Camera (MOP) to conduct the high-resolution imaging program for which it was designed. High-resolution images of the planet's surface then will be collected for about one Martian year (approximately two Earth years).

Figure 73. An artist rendering of a 21st-century Mars base near Pavonis Mons, a large shield volcano on the Martian equator that overlooks the ancient water-eroded canyon in which the base is located. The base infrastructure depicted here includes a habitation module, a power module, central base work facilities, a greenhouse, a launch and landing complex, and even a Martian airplane (ultra-light construction). In the foreground, human explorers have taken their surface rover vehicle to an interesting spot, where one of the Mars explorers has just made the discovery of the 21st century—a large fossil of an ancient Martian creature! *(Artwork courtesy of NASA/JSC—Artist: Pat Rawlings)*

Despite this setback in schedule, the scientific instruments have performed flawlessly since the spacecraft arrived at Mars and are now providing new information about the Martian atmosphere, surface features, temperatures and mineralogy.

See also: MARS; MARS OBSERVER.

Marshall Space Flight Center (MSFC) A major NASA complex in Huntsville, Alabama. It was the center where Dr. Wernher von Braun (1912–77) and his team of German rocket scientists developed a series of highly successful rockets, including the giant Saturn V vehicle that sent human expeditions to the lunar surface.

See also: NATIONAL AERONAUTICS AND SPACE ADMINISTRATION.

Mars Observer mission NASA's *Mars Observer,* the first of the Observer series of planetary missions, was designed to study the geoscience of Mars. The primary science objectives for the mission were to: (1) determine the global elemental and mineralogical character of the surface; (2) define globally the topography and gravitational field of the planet; (3) establish the nature of the Martian magnetic field; (4) determine the temporal and spatial distribution, abundance, sources, and sinks of volatiles (substances that readily evaporate) and dust over a seasonal cycle; and (5) explore the structure and circulation of the Martian atmosphere. The 1,018-kilogram (2,245 pound-mass) spacecraft was launched successfully on September 25, 1992. Unfortunately, for unknown reasons, contact with the *Mars Observer* was lost on August 21, 1993, just three days before scheduled orbit insertion around Mars. Contact with the spacecraft was not reestablished, and it is not known whether this spacecraft was able to follow its automatic programming and go into Mars orbit or if it flew by Mars and is now in a heliocentric orbit. Although none of the primary objectives of the mission was achieved, cruise mode (i.e., interplanetary) data were collected up to loss of contact.

See also: MARS; MARS GLOBAL SURVEYOR MISSION.

Mars Pathfinder mission NASA's *Mars Pathfinder* was launched successfully on December 4, 1996 by a Delta II expendable vehicle. This mission, formerly called the Mars Environmental Survey (or MESUR) Pathfinder, had the primary objective of demonstrating the feasibility of low-cost landing on and exploration of the Martian surface. This objective was met successfully by tests of communications between the rover and lander, the lander and Earth, and tests of imaging devices and sensors. The scientific objectives of this mission included atmospheric entry science and long-range and close-up surface imaging, with the general objective being to characterize the Martian environment for further exploration.

The Mars Pathfinder mission consisted of a stationary "lander" and a "surface rover." The lander had a mass of 264 kilograms (kg) (582 pound-mass (lbm)) and the small surface rover, named the Sojourner, had a mass of 10.5 kg (23.2 lbm). The spacecraft entered the Martian atmosphere directly from its approach trajectory at a velocity of about 7,300 meters per second (m/s) [23,950 feet per second (ft/s)] without going into orbit around the planet. The cruise stage was jettisoned 30 minutes before atmospheric entry. The lander spacecraft recorded atmospheric measurements as it descended. In about 160 seconds, the entry vehicle's heat shield slowed the craft to a velocity of approximately 400 m/s (1,312 ft/s). A parachute was then deployed, slowing the lander to about 65 m/s (213 ft/s). The heat shield was released 20 seconds after parachute deployment, and the bridle (a 20-meter-long (65.6-foot-long) Kevlar tether) deployed below the spacecraft. Next, the lander separated from the backshell and slid down to the bottom of bridle, a process taking about 25 seconds. At an altitude of approximately 1.5 km (0.93 miles) above the surface of Mars, the spacecraft's radar altimeter acquired the ground. Then, about 8 seconds before landing, four airbags quickly inflated (in about 0.3 second), forming a 5.2-meter-diameter (17.1-foot) protective "ball" around the lander. Four seconds later the three solid rockets (which were mounted in the backshell) fired to slow the descent. Two seconds later the bridle was cut, releasing the airbag-encased lander from the backshell. The lander then dropped to the ground in about 2 seconds and impacted at 16:57 Universal Time on July 4, 1997 at an overall velocity of about 18 m/s (59 ft/s). The airbag-encased lander bounced about 15 meters (49 feet) into the atmosphere and continued to bounce at least another 15 times and to roll before coming to rest approximately 150 seconds after impact. When it finally stopped bouncing and rolling, the airbag-encased lander was about 1 km (0.62 mile) from the initial impact site. After landing, the airbags deflated and the Mars Pathfinder lander opened its three metallic triangular solar panels (petals).

The landing site is at 19.33 N, 33.55 W in the Ares Vallis region of Mars—a large outwash plain near Chryse Planitia (the Plains of Gold) where the *Viking 1* lander had successfully touched down on July 20, 1976. Planetary geologists speculate that this region is one of the largest outflow channels on Mars, the result of a huge, ancient flood that had occurred over a short period of time and flowed into the Martian northern lowlands.

The lander, renamed by NASA as the Carl Sagan Memorial Station, first transmitted engineering and science data collected during atmospheric entry and landing. Then its imaging system (which was on a pop-up mast) obtained views of the rover and the immediate surroundings. These images were transmitted back to Earth to assist the flight team in planning the rover's operations on the surface of Mars. After some maneuvers to clear an airbag out of the way, ramps were deployed and the mini-rover (Sojourner), which had been stowed against one of the petals, rolled onto the Martian surface. Following rover deployment, the bulk of the lander's remaining tasks were to support the rover by imaging rover operations and relaying data from the rover back to Earth. Solar cells on the lander's three petals, in combination with rechargeable batteries, powered the lander, which also was equipped with a meteorology station. (see Figure 74.)

The rover, named Sojourner (but previously called Rocky IV), was a six-wheeled vehicle that was controlled ("teleoperated—operated over great distances by remote control) by the Earth-based flight team at the Jet Propulsion Laboratory (JPL) in Pasadena, California, who used images obtained by both the rover and the lander systems. These teleoperations required that the rover be capable of some semiautonomous operation, since a time delay of the signals averaged between 10 and 15 minutes, depending on the relative position of Earth and Mars over the course of the mission. For example, the rover had a hazard avoidance system, and surface movement was performed very slowly.

The small rover was 280 millimeters (mm) high (about 11 inches [in]), 630 mm (24.8 in) long, and 480 mm (18.9 in) wide with a ground clearance of 130 mm (5.1 in). While stowed in the lander, the rover had a height of just 180 mm (about 7.1 in). However, after deployment on the Martian surface, the rover extended to its full height and rolled down a deployment ramp. The rover was powered by solar cells (0.2 square meter (2.16 square foot area), which provided energy for several hours of surface operations per "sol" (a "sol" is one Martian day, which is about 24.6 Earth-hours). Backup power for the rover was provided by nonrechargeable batteries. (See Figure 75.)

The rover was equipped with a black-and-white imaging system that was used to image the lander and take images of the surrounding Martian terrain and of the rover wheel tracks to help scientists estimate soil properties. An alpha proton X-ray spectrometer (APXS) onboard the rover was used to assess the composition of Martian rocks and soil.

The primary objectives of the rover mission were scheduled to occur in the first seven sols and took

Figure 74. A magnificent 360-degree panorama of the Ares Vallis landing site taken by the Mars Pathfinder lander's imaging system on July 6, 1997 (also referred to as Sol 3 of the mission). All three of the landers petals, the perimeter of the deflated airbags, the deployed minirover (Sojourner), the lander's forward and backward ramps, and prominent Martian surface features are all visible. The Imager for Mars Pathfinder (IMP) was developed by the University of Arizona Lunar and Planetary Laboratory under contract with NASA/JPL. *(NASA/JPL)*

Figure 75. The Mars Pathfinder rover, Sojourner, during tests on Earth just prior to its mission to the Red Planet *(Image courtesy of NASA)*

place within about 10 meters (32.8 feet) of the lander spacecraft. The extended mission for the rover included longer trips away from the lander that lasted over 80 sols. In fact, the last successful data transmission cycle from the Mars Pathfinder lander occurred on September 27, 1997 (Sol 83 of the mission)—almost three times the lander's design lifetime of 30 days.

The Mars Pathfinder mission is regarded as an outstanding success. Some of the preliminary scientific highlights of this mission include: (1) Martian dust contains magnetic, composite particles with a mean size of 1 micrometer (1 μμ); (2) the soil chemistry of the Ares Vallis region appears to be similar to that observed at the *Viking 1* and 2 landing sites; (3) dust is confirmed as the dominant absorber of solar radiation in the Martian atmosphere; (4) rock chemistry at the landing site (possibly basaltic andesite composition) may be different from the chemistry of the Martian meteorites found on Earth; (5) the rock size distribution is consistent with a flood-related deposit; and (6) the weather observed at the landing site was similar to the weather observed by the *Viking 1* lander. Perhaps the most intriguing result is that the Mars Pathfinder mission has provided evidence that strongly suggests that Mars was once warm, moist, and more Earthlike than its current forbidding surface environment suggests. This provides strong encouragement that future Mars missions could discover direct evidence that life did once exist on the Red Planet.

The Mars Pathfinder mission also achieved important aerospace engineering milestones, including the successful demonstration of a new

way to deliver a spacecraft to the surface of Mars (by way of direct atmospheric entry and airbag cushion) and successful teleoperation of a semiautonomous robot rover on Mars via a lander spacecraft. These technical accomplishments provide the heritage for more ambitious robot missions to the surface of Mars in the early part of the 21st century.

See also: MARS; MARS SURFACE ROVER(S); MARTIAN METEORITES; VIKING PROJECT.

Mars Sample Return Mission (MSRM) The purpose of a Mars Sample Return Mission is, as the name implies, to use a combination of robot spacecraft and lander systems to collect soil and rock samples from Mars and then return them to Earth for detailed laboratory analysis. A wide variety of options for this type of mission are being explored. For example, one or several small robot rover vehicles could be carried and deployed by the lander vehicle. These rovers (under the control of operators on Earth) would travel away from the original landing site and collect a wider range of rock and soil samples for return to Earth. Another option is to design a nonstationary, or mobile, lander that could travel (again guided by controllers on Earth) to various surface locations and collect interesting specimens. After the soil collection mission was completed, the upper portion of the lander vehicle would lift off from the Martian surface and rendezvous in orbit with a special "carrier" spacecraft. This automated rendezvous/return "carrier" spacecraft would remove the soil sample canisters from the ascent portion of the lander vehicle and then depart Mars orbit on a trajectory that would bring the samples back to Earth. After an interplanetary journey of about one year, this automated "carrier" spacecraft with its precious cargo of Martian soil and rocks would achieve orbit around Earth.

To avoid any potential problems of extraterrestrial contamination of Earth's biosphere by alien microorganisms that might possibly be contained in the Martian soil or rocks, the sample canisters might first be analyzed in a special, human-tended orbiting quarantine facility. An alternate return mission scenario would be to bypass an Earth-orbiting quarantine process altogether and use a direct reentry vehicle operation to bring the encapsulated Martian soil samples to Earth.

Whatever sample return mission profile ultimately is selected, contemporary analysis of Martian meteorites (that have fallen to Earth) has stimulated a great scientific interest in obtaining well-documented and well-controlled "virgin" samples of Martian soil and rocks. Carefully analyzed in laboratories on Earth, these samples will provide a wealth of important and unique information about the Red Planet. These samples might even provide further clarification of the most intriguing question of all: Is there (or, at least, has there been) life on Mars? A successful Mars Sample Return Mission is also considered a significant and necessary step toward eventual human expeditions to Mars in the 21st century.

See also: EXTRATERRESTRIAL CONTAMINATION; MARS; MARS PATHFINDER MISSION; MARS SURFACE ROVER(S); MARTIAN METEORITES.

Mars surface rover(s) Automated rovers and mobility systems can be used to satisfy a number of exploration needs on the surface of Mars. For example, they can acquire specific samples of surface materials for automated evaluation in onboard laboratories, they can deploy instruments on or beneath the Martian surface, or they can perform extensive site investigations. The mobility of surface rovers also can be used to extend the range of landers. For example, a small, solar-powered rover called Sojourner was sent to Mars in December 1996 as part of NASA's Mars Pathfinder mission. This robot minirover, under the control its human operators on Earth, successfully deployed from the lander spacecraft on July 5, 1997 and wandered across the Martian surface for many days, collecting scientific data that were then relayed back to Earth by the lander spacecraft.

Following upon the success of the 1997 Mars Pathfinder mission, NASA plans to send another lander/rover combination spacecraft to the surface of Mars in the years 2001–2002. This mission is being called NASA's 2001 Mars Surveyor Lander/Rover mission. The 2001 robot rover will be similar to the Sojourner but will be larger and have the capability to travel much farther (i.e., 10–20 kilometers (6.2–12.4 miles) versus about 100 meters (328 feet)) and to last much longer (about one year) than the Sojourner (which had just a 7-day expected lifetime but actually operated for several months). The 2001 rover will carry an integrated science payload, called Athena. The instruments on the Athena payload will work together, giving complementary scientific data that can be used to understand the geology of Mars. The main job of the Athena payload will be to investigate the geo-

logical record of the ancient terrain of Mars and to collect samples at sites on the planet's surface where evidence of life might be preserved.

NASA's long-range goals currently include a plan to retrieve samples of the Martian surface for return to Earth for detailed study and analysis. Consequently, the Athena payload includes a coring drill and sample container to acquire and store interesting samples of Martian surface materials. It is now envisioned that a spacecraft sent to Mars in 2005 will gather these samples from the 2001 rover and possibly from a similar 2003 rover and then return them to Earth in about the year 2008.

Even more ambitious future surface rover missions to Mars could involve the operation of large, advanced-design mobile robot explorers in teams of two or four. Mission data would be transmitted back to Earth via a Mars-orbiting "mothership." Two pair of surface rovers might travel up to 5 kilometers each Martian day and assist one another as needed.

Planetary surface rovers can be designed to meet a full range of mission requirements. They can vary in mass from 10 to approximately 2,000 kilograms [22 to 4410 pounds-mass (lbm)]. Large, autonomous full-capacity rovers typically would have a total mass of between 400 and 500 kilograms [880 and 1100 lbm], including a scientific payload capability of between 80 and 100 kilograms [176 and 221 lbm]. For operation in hostile planetary environments (including operations in darkness), these rovers could be powered by radioisotope thermoelectric generator (RTG) systems. They would be capable of autonomously traveling approximately 400 meters (1310 feet) per Martian day and would have a total range of several hundred kilometers. Full-capacity, automated rovers would have a mission design lifetime of at least one Martian year.

See also: LUNAR ROVER(S); MARS PATHFINDER MISSION.

Mars Surveyor '98 (MARS98)

1. Orbiter (MARS98S) NASA's *Mars Surveyor '98* orbiter is the companion spacecraft to the *Mars Surveyor '98* lander spacecraft. The two spacecraft will be launched separately but comprise a single mission to study the Martian weather, climate, and water and carbon dioxide (CO_2) budget. These observations will help scientists further understand the reservoirs, behavior, and atmospheric role of volatiles (substances that readily evaporate) on Mars and to search for evidence of long-term and episodic climate changes. The orbiter has as its primary science objectives: (1) monitoring the daily weather and atmospheric conditions; (2) recording changes on the Martian surface due to wind and other atmospheric effects; (3) determining temperature profiles of the atmosphere; and (4) monitoring the water vapor and dust content of the Martian atmosphere. The orbiter will use two instruments to conduct these investigations. The Mars Surveyor '98 Orbiter Color Imager, or MARCI, will acquire daily atmospheric weather images and high-resolution surfaces images. The Pressure Modulator Infrared Radiometer, or PMIRR, will allow measurement of the atmospheric temperature, water vapor abundance, and dust concentration. The orbiter spacecraft also will serve as a data relay satellite to the *Mars Surveyor '98* lander and other future U.S. and international missions to the surface of Mars.

The orbiter will use aerobraking in the Martian atmosphere to achieve a polar orbit around the planet. The orbit will be a Sun-synchronous, nearly circular polar orbit with an altitude of about 380 kilometers (236 miles). The nominal mission is planned for one Martian year (approximately 1.9 Earth-years) duration. A launch date in December 1998 currently is planned.

This spacecraft is also called *Mars '98* or *Mars '98* orbiter.

2. Lander (MARS98L) The *Mars Surveyor '98* lander is the companion spacecraft to the *Mars Surveyor '98* orbiter. As mentioned above, these two spacecraft will be launched separately but comprise a single NASA mission to study Mars. The lander has as its primary science objectives: (1) recording local meteorological conditions near the Martian South Pole; (2) analyzing samples of the polar deposits for volatiles, particularly water and carbon dioxide; (3) digging trenches in the Martian soil and then imaging the interior of these trenches; and (4) imaging the immediate landing site and the surrounding region. These goals will be accomplished using a number of scientific instruments, including a Mars Volatiles and Climate Surveyor (MVACS) instrument package. The MVACS instrument package is comprised of a robotic arm and attached camera, mast-mounted surface stereo imager and meteorology package, and a gas analyzer. In addition, a Descent Imager will capture regional views during atmospheric descent. Image collection with this instrument will start from the

moment of parachute deployment (at about 8 kilometers (5 miles) altitude) and continue until the spacecraft lands on the surface of Mars.

The lander consists of a base with three landing legs and an exposed upper deck to hold the instruments. Two solar power arrays extend from the upper deck parallel to the ground on opposite sides. The imaging and meteorology masts extend upward from the deck. A two-meter- (about 6.6-foot-) long robotic arm is attached to one side of the deck, and a small parabolic dish antenna is on the opposite side. A thermally regulated payload electronics enclosure houses the temperature sensitive components.

The lander is scheduled for launch in January, 1999. After an 11-month cruise through interplanetary space, the lander spacecraft will make a direct entry into the Martian atmosphere in December 1999. After using an active descent propulsion system and deploying a parachute at about 8 kilometers (5 miles) altitude, the spacecraft will making a soft landing on the surface of Mars at about 71 degrees south latitude, 210 degrees west longitude. This landing spot represents the most northerly extent of the South Pole–layered deposits. These layered deposits appear to be made of alternating layers of clean and dust-laden ice. This region may, therefore, represent an important volatile reservoir as well as contain a long-term record of the Martian climate. The lander will touch down during the late "spring season" in the Martian Southern Hemisphere and immediately begin its primary mission, which is scheduled to last until the end of February 2000. The lander's secondary mission will continue until May 31, 2000. If all goes well, there are even plans for a later spring mission from about July 1 to September 30, 2001.

This spacecraft is also called *Mars '98* and *Mars '98* lander.

See also: MARS; MARS GLOBAL SURVEYOR MISSION; MARS PATHFINDER MISSION.

Martian Of or relating to the planet Mars.

Martian meteorites Scientists now believe that at least 12 unusual meteorites are pieces of Mars that were blasted off the Red Planet by meteoroid impact collisions. These interesting meteorites were previously called *SNC meteorites,* after the first three type samples discovered (namely: Shergotty, Nakhla, and Chassigny) but are now generally referred to as *Martian meteorites.* The

MARTIAN METEORITES

Name	Classification	Mass (kg)	Find/Fall	Year
Shergotty	S-basalt (pyx-plag)	4.00	fall	1865
Zagami	S-basalt	18.00	fall	1962
EETA 79001	S-basalt	7.90	find-A	1980
QUE94201	S-basalt	0.012	find-A	1995
ALHA77005	S-lherzolite (ol-pyx)	0.48	find-A	1978
LEW88516	S-lherzolite	0.013	find-A	1991
Y793605	S-lherzolite	0.018	find-A	1995
Nakhla	N-clinopyroxenite	40.00	fall	1911
Lafayette	N-clinopyroxenite	0.80	find	1931
Gov. Valadares	N-clinopyroxenite	0.16	find	1958
Chassigny	C-dunite (olivine)	4.00	fall	1815
ALH84001	orthopyroxenite	1.90	find-A	1993

Classification: S=shergottite, N=nakhlite, C=chassignite. ALH84001 is none of these.

find-A designates Antarctic meteorites (all recent finds). *Year* is recovery date for non-Antarctic meteorites and date of Martian classification for Antarctic meteorites.

Source: NASA.

Chassigny meteorite was discovered in Chassigny, France on October 3, 1815. It establishes the name of the *chassignite* type subgroup of the SNC meteorites. Similarly, the *Shergotty meteorite* fell on Shergotty, India on August 25, 1865 and provides the name of the *shergottite* type subgroup of SNC meteorites. Finally, the *Nakhla meteorite* was found in Nakhla, Egypt on June 28, 1911 and establishes the name for the *nakhlite* type subgroup of SNC meteorites.

All 12 known SNC meteorites are igneous rocks crystallized from molten lava in the crust of the parent planetary body. The Martian meteorites discovered so far on Earth represent five different types of igneous rocks, ranging from simple plagioclase-pyroxene basalts to almost monomineralic cumulates of pyroxene or olivine. These Martian meteorites are summarized in the table.

The only natural process capable of launching Martian rocks to Earth is meteoroid impact. To be ejected from Mars, a rock must reach a velocity of 5 kilometers (3.1 miles [mi]) per second or more. (The escape velocity for Mars is 5 km/sec [3.1 mi/sec].) During a large meteoroid impact on the surface of Mars, the kinetic energy of the incoming cosmic "projectile" causes shock deformation, heating, melting, and vaporization as well as crater excavation and ejection of target material. The impact and shock environment of such a collision provide sci-

entists with an explanation as to why the Martian meteorites are all igneous rocks. Martian sedimentary rocks and soil would not be consolidated sufficiently to survive the impact as intact rocks and then wander through space for millions of years and eventually land on Earth as meteorites.

One particular Martian meteorite, called ALH84001, has stimulated a great deal of interest in the possibility of life on Mars. In the summer of 1996, a NASA research team at the Johnson Space Center (JSC) announced that they had found evidence in ALH84001 that "strongly suggests primitive life may have existed on Mars more than 3.6 billion years ago." The NASA research team found the first organic molecules thought to be of Martian origin; several mineral features characteristic of biological activity; and possibly microscopic fossils of primitive, bacterialike organisms inside of an ancient Martian rock that fell to Earth as a meteorite. While the NASA research team did not claim that they had conclusively proved life existed on Mars some 3.6 billion years ago, they did believe that "they have found quite reasonable evidence of past life on Mars."

Martian meteorite ALH84001 is a 1.9-kilogram (4.2 pound-mass (lbm)), potato-sized igneous rock that has been age-dated to about 4.5 billion years, the period when the planet Mars formed. This rock is believed to have originated underneath the

Martian surface and to have been extensively fractured by impacts as meteorites bombarded the planet during the early history of the solar system. Between 3.6 and 4.0 billion years ago, Mars is believed to have been a warmer and wetter world. "Martian" water is thought to have penetrated fractures in the subsurface rock, possibly forming an underground water system. Since the water was saturated with carbon dioxide from the Martian atmosphere, carbonate materials were deposited in the fractures. The NASA research team estimates that this rock from Mars entered Earth's atmosphere about 13,000 years ago and fell in Antarctica as a meteorite. ALH84001 was discovered in 1984 in the Allan Hills ice field of Antarctica by an annual expedition of the National Science Foundation's Antarctic Meteorite Program. It was preserved for study at the NASA JSC Meteorite Processing Laboratory, but its possible Martian origin was not fully recognized until 1993. It is the oldest of the Martian meteorites yet discovered.

See also: MARS; METEORITE; METEOROID.

mascon A term meaning "mass concentration." An area of mass concentration or high density within a celestial body, usually near the surface. In 1968 data from five U.S. lunar orbiter spacecraft indicated that regions of high density, or "mascons," existed under circular maria (i.e., the extensive dark areas) on the Moon. The Moon's gravitational attraction is somewhat higher over such mass concentrations, and their presence perturbs (causes variations in) the orbits of spacecraft around the Moon.

See also: MOON.

mass (symbol: m) The amount of material present in an object. This fundamental unit describes "how much" material makes up an object. The SI UNIT for mass is the kilogram (kg), while it is the pound-mass (lbm) in the traditional or engineering unit system. The term "mass" and "weight" are very often confused in the traditional or engineering unit system, because they have similar names: the pound-mass (lbm) and the pound-force (lbf). However, these terms are *not* the same, since "weight" is a derived unit that describes the action of the local force of gravity on the "mass" of an object. An object of 1 kilogram mass on Earth will also have a 1 kilogram mass on the surface of Mars. However, the "weight" of this 1-kilogram-mass object will be different on the surface of each planet, since the acceleration of gravity is different on each planet (i.e., about 9.8 meters per second per second on Earth's surface versus 3.7 meters per second per second on Mars).

mass driver An electromagnetic device (currently under study and development) that can accelerate payloads (nonliving and nonfragile) to a very high terminal velocity. Small, magnetically levitated vehicles, sometimes called "buckets," would be used to carry the payloads. These buckets would then contain superconducting coils and be accelerated by pulsed magnetic fields along a linear trace or guideway. When these buckets reach an appropriate terminal velocity (e.g., several kilometers per second), they release their payloads and are then decelerated for reuse. Mass drivers have been suggested as a way "shooting" lunar ores into orbit around the Moon for collection and subsequent use by space-based manufacturing facilities.

See also: GUN-LAUNCH TO SPACE.

mass-energy equation (mass-energy equivalence) The statement developed by Albert Einstein (1879–1955), German-born American physicist, that "the mass of a body is a measure of its energy content," as an extension of his 1905 *Special Theory of Relativity*. The statement subsequently was verified experimentally by measurements of mass and energy in nuclear reactions. This equation is written as: $E = m c^2$, and illustrates that when the energy of a body changes by an amount, E, the mass, m, of the body will change by an amount equal to E/c^2. (Note: The factor c^2, the square of the speed of light in a vacuum, may be regarded as the conversion factor relating units of mass and energy.) This famous equation predicted the possibility of releasing enormous amounts of energy in the nuclear chain reaction (e.g., as found in a nuclear explosion) by the conversion of some of the mass in the atomic nucleus into energy. This equation is sometimes called the *Einstein equation*.

See also: RELATIVITY.

mass flow rate (symbol: ṁ) The mass of fluid flowing through or past a reference point per unit time. Typical units are kilograms per second (kg/s) and pounds-mass per second (lbm/s).

mass fraction The fraction of a rocket's (or of a rocket stage's) mass that is taken up by propellant. The remaining mass is structure and payload.

mass number (symbol: A) The number of nucleons (i.e., the number of protons and neutrons) in an atomic nucleus. It is the nearest whole number to an atom's atomic weight. For example, the mass number of the isotope uranium-235 is 235.

mass ratio In rocketry, the ratio of the mass of the propellant charge of a rocket to the total mass of the rocket when fully charged with propellant.

mass spectrometer An instrument used to measure the relative atomic masses and relative abundances of isotopes. A sample (usually gaseous) is ionized, and the resultant stream of charged particles is accelerated into a high vacuum region where electric and magnetic fields deflect the particles and focus them on a detector. A *mass spectrum* (i.e., a series of lines related to mass/charge values) then is created. This characteristic pattern of lines helps scientists identify different molecules.

mass transfer cooling Heat transfer or thermal control accomplished primarily by the use of an amount of mass to cool a surface or region. There are three general categories of mass transfer cooling: (1) *transpiration cooling,* (2) *film cooling,* or (3) *ablation cooling.* Aerospace designers have long recognized mass transfer to the boundary layer as an effective technique for significantly altering the adverse aerodynamic heating phenomena associated with a body in hypersonic flight through a planetary atmosphere. Similarly, rocket engineers often use some form of mass transfer cooling to prevent the overheating or destruction of thermally sensitive rocket nozzle components.

Matador An early medium-range, surface-to-surface winged missile developed by the U.S. Air Force in the 1950s.

mate To fit together two major components of an aerospace system.

materials processing in space (MPS) *Materials processing* is the science by which ordinary and comparatively inexpensive raw materials are made into useful crystals, chemicals, metals, ceramics, and countless other manufactured products. Modern materials processing on Earth has taken us into the space age and opened up the microgravity environment of Earth orbit. The benefits of extended periods of "weightlessness" promise to open up new and unique opportunities for the science of materials processing. In the microgravity environment of an orbiting spacecraft, scientists can use materials processing procedures that are all but impossible on Earth.

In orbit, materials processing can be accomplished without the effects of gravity, which on Earth causes materials of different densities and temperatures to separate and deform under the influences of their own masses. However, when scientists refer to an orbiting object as being "weightless," they do not literally mean there is an absence of gravity. Rather, they are referring to the microgravity conditions, or the absence of relative motion between objects in a free-falling environment, as experienced in an Earth-orbiting spacecraft. These useful "free-fall" conditions can be obtained only briefly on Earth using drop towers or "zero-gravity" aircraft. Extended periods of microgravity can be achieved only on an orbiting spacecraft, such as the space shuttle orbiter, a space station, or a crew-tended free-flying platform.

Materials science experiments conducted on Skylab, the Apollo-Soyuz Test Project (ASTP), the space shuttle, and the Russian Mir space station already have demonstrated that new knowledge can be gained through the effective use of the microgravity environment found in orbit. Metals, for example, can be solidified without the disturbing effects of gravity-driven convection. Convection is the spontaneous mixing or stirring in a liquid or gas as (fluid) currents flow between temperature gradients. Convective phenomena are unpredictable and chaotic, and often lead to undesirable structural and compositional differences in a material after it has solidified. Both crystal growth and solidification processes are enhanced if convective disturbances are suppressed. An extended microgravity environment gives material scientists the opportunity to reduce or completely eliminate such undesirable convective phenomena.

On Earth, gravity causes heavier components of a mixture to settle to the bottom (a process called *sedimentation*) while less dense materials rise to the top (a process called *buoyancy*). As a result, sedimentation or buoyancy effects complicate terrestrial manufacturing processes involving different-density alloys or composite materials. There are hundreds of potentially interesting metallic combinations that, like oil and water, just do not mix properly on Earth. As long as these metallic mixtures remain essentially separated through sedimentation or buoyancy effects, they are not particularly useful. But when combined in microgravity, the lighter-density components of such mixtures or alloys will remain suspended indefinitely and therefore permit the formation of essentially uniform solid composites or alloys whose constituents have large density differences. When uniformly mixed and properly solidified, many of these new composite materials take on unusual properties, such as very high strengths, excellent semiconductor behavior, or perhaps outstanding performance as a superconductor.

Hydrostatic pressure places a strain on materials during solidification processes on Earth. Certain crystals are sufficiently dense and delicate that they are subject to strain under the influence of their own weight during growth. Such strain-induced deformations in crystals degrade their overall performance. In microgravity, heat-treated, melted, and resolidified crystals and alloys can be developed free of such deformations.

Containerless processing in microgravity eliminates the problems of container contamination and wall effects. Often these are the greatest source of impurities and imperfections when a molten material is formed on Earth. But in space a material can be melted, manipulated, and shaped free of contact with a container wall or crucible, by acoustic, electromagnetic, or electrostatic fields. In microgravity, the surface tension of the molten material helps hold it together, while on Earth this cohesive force is overpowered by gravity.

Over the next few decades, space-based materials processing research will emphasize both scientific and commercial goals. Potential space-manufactured products include special crystals, metals, ceramics, glasses, and biological materials. Processes will include containerless processing and fluid and chemical transport. As research in these areas progresses, specialized new materials and manufactured products could become available in the 21st century for use in space as well as on Earth.

See also: DROP TOWER; MICROGRAVITY; ZERO-GRAVITY AIRCRAFT.

mating The act of fitting together two major components of a system, such as the mating of a launch vehicle and a spacecraft. Also, the physical joining of two orbiting spacecraft either through a docking or a berthing process.

matter The substance of which a physical object is composed. All materials in the universe have the same inner nature, that is, they are composed of atoms, arranged in different (and often complex) ways; the specific atoms and the specific arrangements identify the various materials.

matter-antimatter propulsion Spacecraft propulsion by use of matter-antimatter annihilation reactions.

Maverick (AGM-65) A tactical, air-to-surface guided missile designed for close air support, interdiction, and defense suppression missions. It provides standoff capability and high probability of strike against a wide range of tactical targets, including armor, air defenses, ships, transportation equipment, and fuel storage facilities. Maverick A and B models have an electro-optical television guidance system; the Maverick D and G models have an imaging infrared guidance system. The U.S. Air Force accepted the first AGM-65A Maverick missile in August 1972. AGM-65 missiles were used successfully by F-16 and A-10 aircraft in 1991 to attack armored targets in the Persian Gulf during Operation Desert Storm.

max-Q An aerospace term describing the condition of maximum dynamic pressure—the point in the flight of a launch vehicle when it experiences the most severe aerodynamic forces, as it rises up through Earth's atmosphere toward outer space.

"mayday" A distress call.

mean free path (symbol: λ) The average distance traveled by a particle, atom, or molecule between collisions or interactions.

mean motion The averaged speed of a satellite in a noncircular orbit (i.e., in an orbit with an eccentricity greater than zero). Satellites in circular orbits travel at a constant speed. Satellites in noncircular orbits move faster when closer to Earth (or other planet they are traveling around) and slower when farther away. It is common aerospace industry practice to compute the mean motion (i.e., average the speed), which usually is measured in revolutions per day. For an Earth-orbiting spacecraft, this number may be greater than 0.0 and less than 20.0.

mean solar day The duration of one rotation of Earth on its axis, with respect to the uniform motion of the mean Sun. The length of the mean solar day is 24 hours of *mean solar time* or 24 hours 3 minutes 56.555 seconds of *mean sidereal time*. A mean solar day beginning at midnight is called a *civil day;* one beginning at noon is called an *astronomical day.*

mean solar time Time based on Earth's rate of rotation, which originally was assumed to be constant.
   See also: MEAN SOLAR DAY.

mean time between failures (MTBF) The average time between the failure of elements in a system composed of many elements.

mean time to repair (MTTR) In a multielement system, the average time required to repair the system in the event of a failure.

medium-range ballistic missile (MRBM) A ballistic missile with a range capability from about 1,100 kilometers (km) (680 miles [mi]) to 2,780 km (1,725 mi).

mega- (symbol: M) A prefix in the SI UNIT system meaning multiplied by 1 million (10^6), as, for example, megahertz (MHz), meaning 1 million hertz.

megabit (Mb) Approximately 1 million bits; actually, 2^{20} or 1,048,576 bits.

megabyte (MB) Approximately 1 million bytes; actually, 2^{20} or 1,048,576 bytes; often used as a unit of processor storage capacity and real or virtual memory in a computer system.

megaflops (MFLOPS) One million floating-point operations per second. A floating-point operation is a computer processing operation in which numbers are expressed in *floating-point format;* for example, a 3,300 is represented as 3.3E+3; 0.0033 becomes 3.3E-3. (Note E+3 represents 10^3, while E-3 means 10^{-3}.) Floating-point methods are used to quickly calculate a large range of numbers.

megahertz (MHz) One million hertz; 1 million cycles per second.

megaparsec (Mpc) One million parsecs; a distance of approximately 3,260,000 light-years.
   See also: LIGHT-YEAR; PARSEC.

megaton (MT) A measure of the explosive yield of a nuclear weapon that is equivalent to the explosion of 1 million tons of trinitrotoluene (TNT), a chemical high explosive. By definition, 1 MT = 10^{15} calories or 4.2 x 10^{15} joules. (Here, a ton represents 1,000 kilograms or approximately 2,000 pounds-mass of TNT.)

megawatt (MW) One million watts.
   See also: WATT.

melting In thermodynamics, the transition of a material from the solid phase to the liquid phase, generally as a result of heating.

melting ablator An ablative cooling material characterized by melting of the thermal protection material at the aerodynamically heated surface.

Mercurian Of or pertaining to the planet Mercury.

Mercury The innermost planet in the solar system, orbiting the Sun at approximately 0.4 astronomical unit (AU). This planet, named for the messenger

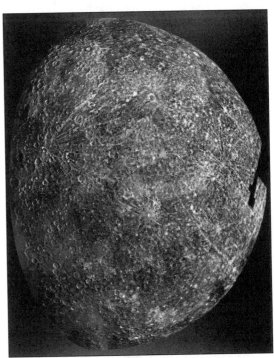

Figure 76. The mosaic of several hundred images from the *Mariner 10* provides an enhanced view of Mercury's southern hemisphere. *(Photograph courtesy of NASA/JPL)*

god of Roman mythology, is a scorched, primordial world that is only 40% larger in diameter than Earth's Moon.

NASA's *Mariner 10* spacecraft provided the first close-up views of Mercury. (See Figure 76.) This spacecraft was launched from Cape Canaveral in November 1973. After traveling almost five months (including a flyby of Venus), this spacecraft passed within 805 kilometers (km) (483 miles [mi]) of Mercury on March 29, 1974. *Mariner 10* then looped around the Sun and made another rendezvous with Mercury on September 21, 1974. This encounter process was repeated a third time on March 16, 1975, before the control gas used to orient the spacecraft was exhausted. This triple flyby of the planet Mercury by *Mariner 10* is sometimes referred to as Mercury I, II, and III in the technical literature.

The images of Mercury transmitted back to Earth by *Mariner 10* revealed an ancient, heavily cratered world that closely resembled Earth's Moon. Unlike the Moon, however, huge cliffs (called *lobate scarps*) crisscross Mercury. These great cliffs apparently were formed when Mercury's interior cooled and shrank, compressing the planet's crust. The cliffs are as high as 2 km (1.2 mi) and as long as 1,500 km (900 mi).

To the surprise of scientists, instruments on board *Mariner 10* discovered that Mercury has a weak magnetic field. It also has a wisp of an atmosphere—a trillionth of the density of Earth's atmosphere and made up mainly of traces of helium, hydrogen, sodium, and potassium.

Temperatures on the sunlit side of Mercury reach approximately 700° Kelvin (427° Celsius)—a temperature that exceeds the melting point of lead; on the dark side, temperatures plunge to a frigid 100° Kelvin (minus 173° Celsius). Quite literally, Mercury is a world seared with intolerable heat in the daytime and frozen at night.

In the late 1960s, scientists on Earth bounced radar signals off the surface of Mercury. Analysis of the scattered radar signals indicated that the planet actually rotated slowly on its axis with a period of about 59 days. Consequently, the "days" and "nights" on this planet are quite long by terrestrial standards, 1 Mercurian day equals 59 Earth-days. It takes the planet approximately 88 days to orbit around the Sun.

As shown in Figure 101, Mercury's surface features include large regions of gently rolling hills and numerous impact craters like those found on the Moon. Many of these craters are surrounded by

PHYSICAL AND DYNAMIC PROPERTIES OF THE PLANET MERCURY

Radius (mean equatorial)	2,439 km
Mass	3.30×10^{23} kg
Mean density	5.44 g/cm^3
Acceleration of gravity (at the surface)	3.70 m/sec^2
Escape velocity	4.25 km/sec
Normal albedo (averaged over visible spectrum)	0.125
Surface temperature extremes	-173° C to +427° C
Atmosphere	negligible
Number of natural satellites	none
Flux of solar radiation	
Aphelion	6,290 W/m^2
Perihelion	14,490 W/m^2
Semimajor axis	5.79×10^7 km (0.387 AU)
Perihelion distance	4.60×10^7 km (0.308 AU)
Aphelion distance	6.98×10^7 km (0.467 AU)
Eccentricity	0.20563
Orbital inclination	7.004 degrees
Mean orbital velocity	47.87 km/sec
Sidereal day (a Mercurean "day")	58.646 Earth days
Sidereal year (a Mercurean "year")	87.969 Earth days

Source: NASA

blankets of ejecta (material thrown out at the time of a meteoroid impact) and secondary craters that were created when chunks of ejected material fell back down to the planet's surface. Because Mercury has a higher gravitational attraction than the Moon, these secondary craters are not spread as widely from each primary crater as occurs on the Moon. One major surface feature discovered by *Mariner 10* is a large impact basin called Caloris, which is about 1,300 km (780 mi) in diameter. Scientists now believe that Mercury has a large iron-rich core—the source of its weak, but detectable, magnetic field. The table presents some contemporary physical- and dynamic-property data about the Sun's closest planetary companion.

Because Mercury lies deep in the Sun's gravity well, detailed exploration with sophisticated orbiters and landers will require the development of advanced planetary spacecraft that take advantage of intricate "gravity-assist" maneuvers involving both the Earth and Venus.

See also: MARINER SPACECRAFT.

Mercury Project America's pioneering project to put a human being into orbit. The series of six suborbital and orbital flights was designed to demonstrate that human beings could withstand the high acceleration of a rocket launching, a prolonged period of weightlessness, and then a period of high deceleration during reentry.

The Mercury Project became an official program of NASA on October 7, 1958. Seven astronauts were chosen in April 1959, after a nationwide call for jet pilot volunteers. The one-person Mercury spacecraft was designed and built with a maximum orbiting mass of about 1,452 kilograms (3,200 pounds-mass [lbm]). Shaped somewhat like a bell, this small spacecraft was about 189 centimeters (74.5 inches) wide across the bottom and about 2.7 meters (9 feet) tall. The astronaut escape tower added another 5.2 meters (17 feet) for an overall length of approximately 8 meters (26 feet) at launch.

Two boosters were chosen: the U.S. Army Redstone with its 346,944 newtons (78,000 pounds-force [lbf]) thrust for the suborbital flights and the U.S. Air Force Atlas with its 1,601,280 newtons (360,000 lbf) thrust for the orbital missions.

On May 5, 1961 Astronaut Alan B. Shepard, Jr., was launched from Complex 5 at Cape Canaveral Air Force Station (CCAFS) by a Redstone booster on the first U.S. crewed space flight. His brief suborbital mission lasted just 15 minutes, and his *Freedom 7* Mercury capsule traveled 186.7 kilometers (116 miles) high into space. On July 21, 1961 another Redstone booster hurled Astronaut Virgil I. "Gus" Grissom through the second and last suborbital flight in the *Liberty Bell 7* Mercury capsule.

Following these two successful suborbital missions, NASA then advanced the project to the Mercury-Atlas series of orbital missions. Another space milestone was reached on February 20, 1962 when Astronaut John H. Glenn, Jr., became the first American in orbit, circling the Earth three times in the *Friendship 7* spacecraft.

On May 24, 1962 Astronaut M. Scott Carpenter completed another three-orbit flight in the *Aurora 7* spacecraft. Astronaut Walter M. Schirra, Jr. doubled the flight time in space and orbited six times, landing the *Sigma 7* Mercury capsule in a Pacific Ocean recovery area. All previous Mercury Project landings had been in the Atlantic Ocean. Finally, on May 15–16, 1963 Astronaut L. Gordon Cooper, Jr. completed a 22-orbit mission in the *Faith 7* spacecraft, triumphantly concluding the program and paving the way for the Gemini Project and ultimately the Apollo Project, which took American astronauts to the lunar surface. The table summarizes the Mercury Project missions.

See also: APOLLO PROJECT; MERCURY PROJECT.

MERCURY PROJECT MISSIONS (1961–1963)				
Mission	Date(s)/Recovery Ship, Ocean	Astronaut	Mission Duration	Remarks
Mercury Redstone 3 (*Freedom 7*)	May 5, 1961 *Lake Champlain*, Atlantic	Navy Comdr. Alan B. Shepard, Jr.	0:15:22	suborbital
Mercury Redstone 4 (*Liberty Bell 7*)	July 21, 1961 *Randolph*, Atlantic	USAF Maj. Virgil I. Grissom	0:15:37	suborbital
Mercury Atlas 6 (*Friendship 7*)	Feb. 20, 1962 *Noa*, Atlantic	Marine Lt. Col. John H. Glenn	4:55:23	3 orbits
Mercury Atlas 7 (*Aurora 7*)	May 24, 1962 *Pierce*, Atlantic	Navy Lt. Comdr. Scott Carpenter	4:56:05	3 orbits
Mercury Atlas 8 (*Sigma 7*)	Oct. 3, 1962 *Kearsarge*, Pacific	Navy Comdr. Walter M. Schirra, Jr.	9:13:11	6 orbits
Mercury Atlas 9 (*Faith 7*)	May 15-16, 1963 *Kearsarge*, Pacific	USAF Maj. L. Gordon Cooper	34:19:49	22 orbits

Note: Names in parentheses in column 1 are those given to Mercury spacecraft.
Source: NASA.

meridians Great circles that pass through both the North and South poles; also called *lines of longitude*.

mesosphere The region of Earth's atmosphere above the stratosphere that is characterized by temperature decreasing with height. The top of this layer, called the *mesopause,* occurs between 80 and 85 kilometers (48–50 miles) altitude. The mesopause is the coldest region of the entire atmosphere and has a temperature of approximately 180° Kelvin (-93° Celsius).
See also: ATMOSPHERE.

meteor The luminous phenomena that occurs when a meteoroid enters Earth's atmosphere. Sometimes called a *shooting star*.
See also: METEOROIDS.

meteorite Metallic or stony material that has passed through the atmosphere and reached Earth's surface. Meteorites are of extraterrestrial origin. Known sources of meteorites include asteroids and comets; some even originated on the Moon or on Mars. Presumably meteorites from the Moon and Mars were ejected by impact cratering events. The term "meteorite" also is applied to meteoroids that land on planetary bodies other than Earth.
See also: MARTIAN METEORITES; METEOROIDS.

meteoroids An all encompassing term that refers to solid objects found in space, ranging in diameter from micrometers to kilometers and in mass from less than 10^{-12} gram to more than 10^{+16} grams. If these pieces of extraterrestrial material are less than 1 gram, they often are called *micrometeoroids.* When objects of more than approximately 10^{-6} gram reach Earth's atmosphere, they are heated to incandescence (i.e., they glow with heat) and produce the visible effect popularly called a *meteor*. If some of the original meteoroid survives its glowing plunge into Earth's atmosphere, the remaining unvaporized chunk of space matter is then called a *meteorite.*

Scientists currently think that meteoroids originate primarily from asteroids and comets that have perihelia (portions of their orbits nearest the Sun) near or inside Earth's orbit around the Sun. The parent celestial objects are assumed to have been broken down into a collection of smaller bodies by numerous collisions. Recently formed meteoroids tend to remain concentrated along the orbital path

TIME BETWEEN METEOROID COLLISIONS FOR A SPACE SHUTTLE ORBITER IN LOW EARTH ORBIT (300-KM ALTITUDE)

Minimum Meteoroid Mass (g)	Estimated Time Between Collisions (yr)
10	350,000
1	25,000
0.1	1,800
0.01	130

Source: Based on NASA data.

of their parent body. These "stream meteoroids" produce the well-known meteor showers that can be seen at certain dates from Earth.

Meteoroids generally are classified by composition as stony meteorites (chondrites), irons, and stony-irons. Of the meteorites that fall on Earth, stony meteorites make up about 93%, irons about 5.5%, and stony-irons about 1.5%. Space scientists estimate that about 10^{+7} kilograms (or 10,000 metric tons) of "cosmic rocks" now fall on our planet annually.

Some of the meteorites found on Earth are thought to have their origins on the Moon or on Mars. It is now believed that these lunar or Martian meteorites were ejected by ancient impact-cratering events. If an asteroid or comet of sufficient mass and velocity hits the surface of the Moon, a small fraction of the material ejected by the impact collision could depart from the Moon's surface with velocities greater than its escape velocity (2.4 kilometers per second [km/sec]). A fraction of that ejected material eventually would reach Earth's surface, with Moon-to-Earth transit times ranging from under 1 million years to upward of 100 million years. Similarly, a very energetic asteroid or comet impact collision on Mars (which has an escape velocity of 5.0 km/sec) could be the source of the interesting "Martian" meteorites found recently in Antarctica.

Micrometeoroids and small meteoroids large enough to damage an Earth-orbiting spacecraft are considered "somewhat rare" by space scientists. For example, the table presents a contemporary estimate for the time between collisions between an object the size of a space shuttle orbiter in

LOW-EARTH ORBIT and a meteoroid of mass greater than a given meteoroid mass.

On a much larger "collision scale," meteoroid impacts now are considered by planetary scientists to have played a basic role in the evolution of planetary surfaces in the early history of the solar system. Although still dramatically evident in the cratered surfaces found on other planets and moons, here on Earth this stage of surface evolution has essentially been lost due to later crustal recycling and weathering processes.

See also: ASTEROID; COMET; MARTIAN METEORITES.

meteorological rocket A rocket designed for routine upper-air observation (as opposed to scientific research), especially in that portion of Earth's atmosphere inaccessible to weather balloons, namely above 30,500 meters (100,000 feet) altitude.

meteorological satellite An Earth-observing spacecraft that senses some or most of the atmospheric phenomena (e.g., wind and clouds) related to weather conditions on a local, regional, or hemispheric scale.

See also: WEATHER SATELLITE.

meteorology The branch of science dealing with phenomena of the atmosphere. This includes not only the physics, chemistry, and dynamics of the atmosphere but also many of the direct effects of the atmosphere upon Earth's surface, the oceans, and life in general. Meteorology is concerned with actual weather conditions, while *climatology* deals with average weather conditions and long-term weather patterns.

See also: WEATHER SATELLITE.

Meteosat spacecraft A geostationary weather satellite operated by the European Space Agency (ESA). The main payload of the Meteosat spacecraft is a multispectral radiometer that provides visible and infrared radiances of Earth in three spectral bands: 0.5 to 0.9 micrometers for the visible part of the spectrum; 5.7 to 7.1 micrometers for the infrared water-vapor absorption band, and 10.5 to 12.5 micrometers for thermal infrared radiation. The Meteosat images have a spatial resolution at the satellite subpoint of approximately 5 kilometers for the thermal infrared and water-vapor absorption band images and 2.5 kilometers for the visible images.

See also: WEATHER SATELLITE.

meter (symbol: m) The fundamental SI UNIT of length. 1 meter = 3.281 feet. Also spelled *metre* (British spelling).

metric system The international system (SI) of weights and measures based on the *meter* as the fundamental unit of length, the *kilogram* as the fundamental unit of mass, and the *second* as the fundamental unit of time. Also called the *mks system*.

See also: SI UNITS.

metrology The science of dimensional measurement; sometimes includes the science of weighing.

MeV An abbreviation for 1 million electron volts, a common energy unit encountered in the study of nuclear reactions. $1 \text{ MeV} = 10^6 \text{ eV}$.

micro- (symbol: μ) A prefix in the SI UNIT system meaning divided by 1 million; for example, a micrometer (mm) is 10^{-6} meter. The term also is used as a prefix to indicate something is very small, as in *micrometeoroid* or *micromachine*.

microbar (symbol: μb) A unit of pressure in the centimeter-gram-second (cgs) system equal to 1 dyne per square centimeter. $1 \text{ μb} = 1 \text{ dyne/cm}^2$.

See also: BAR.

microenvironment An environment created and maintained within a very small space, such as a pressurized space capsule, a space suit, a space station, or a planetary surface base, and sufficient to support life in a reasonably normal manner.

microelectronic upsets Some minor, as well as major, spacecraft anomalies have resulted from the passage of galactic ionizing radiation through radiation-sensitive microelectronic circuits. Single-event upsets (SEUs) are basically "bit flips" in microelectronic circuits that can cause damage to stored data, a failure of the central processing unit (CPU), damage to software, or even unplanned mission events, including a total loss of the mission. The passage of very energetic, heavy ion galactic cosmic rays (GCRs) through microelectronic circuit materials and the associated nuclear reactions and ionization produces these microelectronic upsets.

microgravity Because the inertial trajectory of a spacecraft (e.g., the space shuttle orbiter) compensates for the force of Earth's gravity, an orbiting spacecraft and all its contents approach a state of free-fall. In this state of free-fall, all objects inside the spacecraft appear "weightless."

It is important to understand how this condition of weightlessness, or the apparent lack of gravity, develops. NEWTON'S LAW OF GRAVITATION states that any two objects have a gravitational attraction for each other that is proportional to their masses and inversely proportional to the square of the distance between their centers of mass. It is also interesting to recognize that a spacecraft orbiting Earth at an altitude of 400 kilometers is only 6% farther away from the center of Earth than it would be if it were on Earth's surface. Using Newton's law, we find that the gravitational attraction at this particular altitude is only 12% less than the attraction of gravity at the surface of Earth. In other words, an Earth-orbiting spacecraft and all its contents are very much under the influence of Earth's gravity! The phenomenon of weightlessness occurs because the orbiting spacecraft and its contents are in a continual state of free-fall.

Figure 77 describes the different orbital paths a falling object may take when "dropped" from a point above Earth's sensible atmosphere. With no tangential-velocity component, an object would fall straight down (trajectory 1) in this simplified demonstration. As the object receives an increasing tangential-velocity component, it still "falls" toward Earth under the influence of terrestrial gravitational attraction, but the tangential-velocity component now gives the object a trajectory that is

a segment of an ellipse. As shown in trajectories 2 and 3 in the figure, as the object receives a larger tangential velocity, the point where it finally hits Earth moves farther and farther away from the release point. If we keep increasing this velocity component, the object eventually "misses Earth" completely (trajectory 4). As the tangential velocity is increased further, the object's trajectory takes the form of a circle (trajectory 5) and then a larger ellipse, with the release point representing the point of closest approach to Earth (or "perigee"). Finally, when the initial tangential-velocity component is about 41% greater than that needed to achieve a circular orbit, the object follows a parabolic, or escape, trajectory and will never return (trajectory 6).

Einstein's principle of equivalence states that the physical behavior inside a system in free-fall is identical to that inside a system far removed from other matter that could exert a gravitational influence. Therefore, the term "zero gravity" (also called "zero g") or "weightlessness" often is used to describe a free-falling system in orbit.

Sometimes people ask what is the difference between mass and weight. Why do we say, for example, "weightlessness" and not "masslessness"? *Mass* is the physical substance of an object—it has the same value everywhere. *Weight*, on the other hand, is the product of an object's mass and the local acceleration of gravity (in accordance with Newton's second law of motion, F = ma). For example, you would weigh about one-sixth as much on the Moon as on Earth, but your mass remains the same in both places.

A "zero-gravity" environment is really an ideal situation that can never be totally achieved in an orbiting spacecraft. The venting of gases from the space vehicle, the minute drag exerted by a very thin terrestrial atmosphere at orbital altitudes, and even crew motions create nearly imperceptible forces on people and objects alike. These tiny forces are collectively called "microgravity." In a microgravity environment, astronauts and their equipment are almost, but not entirely, weightless.

Microgravity represents an intriguing experience for space travelers. However, life in microgravity is not necessarily easier than life on Earth. For example, the caloric (food-intake) requirements for people living in microgravity are the same as those on Earth. Living in microgravity also calls for special design technology. A beverage in an open container, for instance, will cling to the

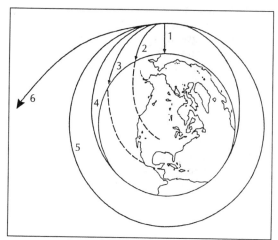

Figure 77. Various optical paths of a falling body around Earth *(Drawing courtesy of NASA)*

inner or outer walls and, if shaken, will leave the container as free-floating droplets or fluid globs. Such free-floating droplets are not merely an inconvenience. They can annoy crew members, and they represent a definite hazard to equipment, especially sensitive electronic devices and computers.

Therefore, water usually is served in microgravity through a specially designed dispenser unit that can be turned on or off by squeezing and releasing a trigger. Other beverages, such as orange juice, typically are served in sealed containers through which a plastic straw can be inserted. When the beverage is not being sipped, the straw is simply clamped shut.

Microgravity living also calls for special considerations in handling solid foods. Crumbly foods are provided only in bit-size pieces to avoid having crumbs floating around the space cabin. Gravies, sauces, and dressings have a viscosity (stickiness) that generally prevents them from simply lifting off food trays and floating away. Typical space food trays are equipped with magnets, clamps, and double-adhesive tape to hold metal, plastic, and other utensils. Astronauts are provided with forks and spoons. However, they must learn to eat without sudden starts and stops if they expect the solid food to stay on their eating utensils.

Personal hygiene is also a bit challenging in microgravity. For example, space shuttle astronauts must take sponge baths rather than showers or regular baths. Because water adheres to the skin in microgravity, perspiration also can be annoying, especially during strenuous activities. Waste elimination in microgravity represents another challenging design problem. Special toilet facilities are needed that help keep an astronaut in place (i.e., prevent drifting). The waste products themselves are flushed away by a flow of air and a mechanical "chopper-type" device.

Sleeping in microgravity is another interesting experience. For example, shuttle astronauts can sleep either horizontally or vertically while in orbit. Their fireproof sleeping bags attach to rigid padded boards for support. But the astronauts themselves quite literally sleep "floating in air."

Working in microgravity requires the use of special tools (e.g., torqueless wrenches), handholds, and foot restraints. These devices are needed to balance or neutralize reaction forces. If these devices were not available, an astronaut might find him-/herself helplessly rotating around a "work piece."

Exposure to microgravity also causes a variety of physiological (bodily) changes. For example, space travelers appear to have "smaller eyes," because their faces have become puffy. They also get rosy cheeks and distended veins in their foreheads and necks. They may even be a little bit taller than they are on Earth, because their body masses no longer "weigh down" their spines. Leg muscles shrink, and anthropometric (measurable postural) changes also occur. Astronauts tend to move in a slight crouch, with head and arms forward.

Some space travelers suffer from a temporary condition resembling motion sickness. This condition is called space sickness or *space adaptation syndrome.* In addition, sinuses become congested, leading to a condition similar to a cold.

Many of these microgravity-induced physiological effects appear to be caused by fluid shifts from the lower to the upper portions of the body. So much fluid goes to the head that the brain may be fooled into thinking that the body has too much water. This can result in an increased production of urine.

Extended stays in microgravity tend to shrink the heart, decrease production of red blood cells, and increase production of white blood cells. A process called resorption occurs. This is the leaching of vital minerals and other chemicals (e.g., calcium, phosphorous, potassium, and nitrogen) from the bones and muscles into the body fluids that are then expelled as urine. Such mineral and chemical losses can have adverse physiological and psychological effects. In addition, prolonged exposure to a microgravity environment might cause bone loss and a reduced rate of bone-tissue formation.

While a relatively brief stay (say from 7 to 70 days) in microgravity may prove a nondetrimental experience for most space travelers, long-duration (i.e., one to several years) missions, such as a human expedition to Mars, could require the use of artificial gravity (created through the slow rotation of the living modules of the spacecraft) to avoid any serious health effects that might arise from such prolonged exposure to a microgravity environment. While cruising to Mars, this artificial gravity environment also would help condition the astronauts for activities on the Martian surface, where they will once again experience the "tug" of a planet's gravity.

Besides providing an interesting new dimension for human experience, the microgravity environment of an orbiting space system offers the ability to create new and improved materials that cannot be made on Earth. Although microgravity can be simulated from here on Earth using drop towers, special airplane trajectories, and sounding rocket flights, these techniques are only short-duration simulations (lasting only seconds to minutes) that are frequently "contaminated" by vibrations and other undesirable effects. However, the long-term microgravity environment found in orbit provides an entirely new dimension for materials science research, life science research, and even manufacturing of specialized products.

See also: DROP TOWER; MATERIALS PROCESSING IN SPACE; ZERO-GRAVITY AIRCRAFT.

micrometeoroids Tiny particles of meteoritic dust in space ranging in size from about 1 to 200 or more micrometers (microns) in diameter.

micrometer 1. An SI UNIT of length equal to one-millionth (10^{-6}) of a meter; also called a *micron*. $1 \mu m = 10^{-6}$ m. 2. An instrument or gauge for making very precise linear measurements (e.g., thicknesses and small diameters) in which the displacements measured correspond to the travel of a screw of accurately known pitch.

micron (symbol: μm) An SI UNIT of length equal to one-millionth (10^{-6}) of a meter. Also called a *micrometer.*

microsecond (symbol: μs) A unit of time equal to one-millionth (10^{-6}) of a second.

microspacecraft Proposed "softball"-size, miniature spacecraft based on micromachine, microsensor, and microelectronics technologies. Launched in swarms (of up to 100 or more) these 5-kilogram mass, laser-beam–interlinked miniature spacecraft would form a constellation of highly autonomous probes in deep space. Asteroid flybys, comet landers, and deep-space astrophysics sensor networks are candidate missions for such tiny spacecraft.

microwave A comparatively short-wavelength electromagnetic (EM) wave in the radio-frequency portion of the EM spectrum. The term "micro-wave" usually is applied to those EM wavelengths that are measured in centimeters, approximately 30 centimeters to 1 millimeter (with corresponding frequencies of 1 gigahertz [GHz] to 300 gigahertz [GHz]).

See also: ELECTROMAGNETIC SPECTRUM.

Mie scattering Any scattering produced by spherical particles without special regard to the comparative size of radiation wavelength and particle diameter.

mil 1. As a unit of length, a mil is 1/1000 (10^{-3}) of an inch. 2. As a unit of angular measurement, a mil is 1/6400 of a circle or 1/1000 (10^{-3}) of a radian. (A radian is approximately equal to 57.296 degrees.)

mile (symbol: mi) 1. (statute or land mile) A unit of distance in the English unit system equal to 1,760 yards or 5,280 feet. 1 statute mile = 1,609.344 meters. Note: In this book, "mile (mi)" indicates statue mile, unless otherwise specified. 2. (nautical mile) The nautical mile is defined as the length of 1 minute of latitude. By international agreement, 1 nautical mile = 1,852 meters (i.e., 1 minute of arc at 45 degrees latitude). Note: When a unit of distance is expressed in nautical miles in this book, it is specifically identified as "nautical miles (n.mi.)"

milestone An important event or decision point in a program or plan. The term originates from the use of stone markers set up on roadsides to indicate the distance in miles to a given point. Milestone charts are used extensively in aerospace programs and planning activities.

military satellite (MILSAT) A satellite used for military or defense purposes such as missile surveillance, navigation, and intelligence gathering.

Milky Way Galaxy Our home galaxy. The immense band of stars stretching across the night sky represents our "inside view" of the Milky Way. Classified as a spiral galaxy, the Milky Way is characterized by the following general features: a spherical central bulge at the galactic nucleus; a thin disk of stars, dust, and gas formed in a beautiful, extensive pattern of spiral arms; and a halo defined by an essentially spherical distribution of globular clusters. This disk is between 2,000 and 3,000 light-years thick and is some 100,000 light-years in diameter. It contains primarily younger, very luminous, metal-rich stars (called Population I stars) as well as gas and dust. Most of the stars found in the halo are older, metal-poor stars (called Population II stars), while the galactic nucleus appears to contain a mixed population of older and

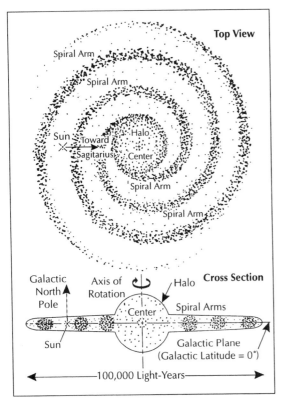

Figure 78. Top view and cross section of the Milky Way galaxy, a gigantic rotating disk of stars, gas, and dust about 100,000 light-years in diameter and about 3,000 light-years thick, with a bulge or halo around the center of mass
(Drawing courtesy of NASA)

younger stars. Some astrophysicists now speculate that a massive black hole, containing millions of "devoured" solar masses, may lie at the center of many galaxies, including our own. Current estimates suggest that our galaxy contains between 200 and 600 billion solar masses. (A solar mass is a unit used for comparing stellar masses, with one solar mass being equal to the mass of our Sun.) Our solar system is located about 30,000 light-years from the center of the galaxy. (See Figure 78.)

See also: BLACK HOLE(S); GALAXY; STARS.

milli- (symbol: m) The SI UNIT system prefix meaning multiplied by 1/1000 (10^{-3}). For example, a *millivolt* (mV) is 0.001 volt; a *millimeter* (mm) is 0.001 meter; and a *millisecond* (msec) is 0.001 second.

millibar (symbol: mbar or mb) A unit of pressure equal to 0.001 bar (i.e., 10^{-3} bar) or 1,000 dynes per square centimeter. The millibar is used as a unit of

measure of atmospheric pressure, with a *standard atmosphere* being equal to about 1,013 millibars or 29.92 inches (760 mm) of mercury. 1 mbar = 100 newtons/m^2 = 1,000 dynes/cm^2.

See also: BAR, DYNE.

millimeter (symbol: mm) One-thousandth (1/1000; 10^{-3}) of a meter. 1 mm = 0.001 m = 0.1 cm = 0.03937 in.

millisecond (symbol: msec or ms) One-thousandth (1/1000, 10^{-3}) of a second. 1 msec = 0.001 sec = 1,000 µsec.

Milstar Satellite Communications System Milstar is a joint U.S. armed services military communications satellite system that provides secure, jam-resistant worldwide communications to meet essential wartime requirements for high-priority military users. The multisatellite constellation links command authorities with a wide variety of resources, including ships, submarines, aircraft, and ground stations. Milstar is the most advanced military communications satellite developed to date and represents the future of U.S. military communications capability. The operational Milstar satellite constellation will be composed of four satellites positioned around Earth in geosynchronous orbits plus a polar adjunct system. Each satellite has a mass of approximately 4,550 kilograms (10,000 pound-mass) and a design life of about 10 years. The first Milstar satellite was launched on February 7, 1994 by a Titan IV expendable launch vehicle. The second satellite was launched on November 6, 1995. Beginning with the third launch in 1998, these satellites will have greatly increased capacity. A total of six launches are planned.

mini- An abbreviation for "miniature."

miniature homing vehicle (MHV) An air-launched, direct-ascent (i.e., "pop-up") kinetic-energy kill, antisatellite (ASAT) weapon.

minor planet An asteroid.
See also: ASTEROID.

minute 1. A unit of time equal to the 60th part of an hour; that is, 60 minutes = 1 hour. 2. A unit of angular measurement such that 60 minutes (60′) equal 1 degree (1°) of arc.

Minuteman (LGM-30) A three-stage solid-propellant ballistic missile that is guided to its target by an all-inertial guidance and control system. These strategic missiles are equipped with nuclear warheads and designed for deployment in hardened and dispersed underground silos. The LGM-30 Minuteman intercontinental ballistic missile (ICBM) is an element of the U.S. strategic deterrent force. The "L" in LGM stands for silo-configuration; "G" means surface attack; and "M" means guided missile.

The Minuteman weapon system was conceived in the late 1950s and deployed in the mid-1960s. Minuteman was a revolutionary concept and an extraordinary technical achievement. Both the missile and basing components incorporated significant advances beyond the relatively slow-reacting, liquid-fueled, remotely controlled ICBMs of the previous generation of missiles (such as the Atlas and the Titan). From the beginning, Minuteman missiles have provided a quick-reacting, inertially guided, highly survivable component of America's nuclear Triad. Minuteman's maintenance concept capitalizes on high reliability and a "remove-and-replace" approach to achieve a near 100% alert rate.

Through state-of-the-art improvements, the Minuteman system has evolved over three decades to meet new challenges and assume new missions. Modernization programs have resulted in new versions of the missile, expanded targeting options, and significantly improved accuracy. For example, when the Minuteman I became operational in October 1962, it had a single-target capability. The Minuteman II became operational in October 1965.

Figure 79. The Mir space station complex   *(Drawing courtesy of NASA)*

While looking similar to the Minuteman I, the Minuteman II had greater range and targeting capability. Finally, the Minuteman III became operational in June 1970. This missile, with its improved third stage and the postboost vehicle, can deliver multiple independently targetable reentry vehicles and their penetration aids onto multiple targets. Over 500 Minuteman III's are currently deployed at bases in the United States.

Mir The third-generation Russian space station and the first permanent space station, that is, the first space station designed for continuous occupancy and expansion through the addition of new modules while on orbit. The Mir complex is at an orbital inclination of 51.6 degrees and an orbital altitude of 300 to 400 kilometers. Except for two brief periods (July 1986 to February 1987 and April to September 1989), Russian cosmonauts and their guest cosmonauts or astronauts from other countries have lived aboard the Mir continuously.

The Mir core module was launched in February 1986 and provides basic services, crew living quarters, life support, power, and scientific research capabilities. Soyuz-TM crewed transports and automated Progress-M supply ships dock at two axial docking ports, fore and aft. Up to 1990, the Russians added three expansion modules to the Mir core module: Kvant, Kvant 2, and Krystall. The Kvant berthed at the core module's aft axial port in 1987. This module carries telescopes and equipment for attitude control and life support. Although the Kvant module blocked the core module's aft port, it had its own aft port, which then took over as the station's aft port. The Kvant 2 module berthed at a radial port in 1989. This module carried an airlock for extravehicular activity (EVA), two solar arrays, and science and life support equipment. The Krystall module berthed opposite the Kvant 2 module in 1990. It carried two stowable solar arrays, science and technology equipment, and a docking and a special androgynous (having "male" and "female" characteristics in one apparatus) docking mechanism designed to receive large spacecraft (e.g., the American space shuttle) that are equipped with the same kind of docking unit. (See Figure 79.)

As part of Russian-American space cooperation in support of the International Space Station project, the American space shuttle has rendezvoused (*Discovery*, 1995) and docked (*Atlantis*, starting in 1995) with the Mir. Equipment and crew have been exchanged while docked in orbit, and American astronauts have flown on Mir with the Russian cosmonaut crew for extended periods of time. Since 1995 three more modules (carrying U.S. equipment) have been added to the Mir. These modules are: Spektr (carrying solar arrays and scientific equipment), Priroda (carrying Earth observation and microgravity research equipment), and a docking module (berthed at Krystall's androgynous docking port) to make shuttle orbiter dockings with Mir easier.

See also: SPACE STATION.

mirror matter A popular name for antimatter, which is the "mirror image" of ordinary matter. For example, an antielectron (also called a positron) has a positive charge, while an ordinary electron has a negative charge.

See also: ANTIMATTER.

mirror system In the context of BALLISTIC MISSILE DEFENSE (BMD), a BMD system that one side builds in response to its adversary that contains similar elements and has similar functions and missions.

misfire 1. Failure to fire or explode properly. 2. Failure of a primer or the propelling charge of a round or projectile to function wholly or in part.

missile Any object thrown, dropped, fired, launched, or otherwise projected with the purpose of striking a target. Short for *ballistic missile* or *guided missile*. "Missile" should *not* be used loosely as a synonym for rocket or launch vehicle.

missile assembly-checkout facility A building, van, or other type of structure located near the operational missile launching location and designed for final assembly and checkout of the missile system.

missile intercept zone That geographical division of the destruction area where surface-to-air missiles have primary responsibility for the destruction of incoming airborne objects.

missile release line The line at which an attacking aircraft could launch an air-to-surface missile against a specific target.

missile silo A hardened protective container, buried in the ground, in which land-based long-range ballistic missiles are placed for launching.

missilry The art and science of designing, developing, building, launching, directing, and sometimes guiding a rocket-propelled missile; any phase or aspect or aspect of this art or science. Also called *missilery*.

mission 1. In aerospace operations, the performance of a set of investigations or operations in space to achieve program goals. For example, the *Voyager 2* "Grand Tour" *mission* to the outer planets. 2. In military operations, a duty assigned to an individual or unit; a task. Also, the dispatching of one or more aircraft to accomplish one particular task. For example, a search-and-destroy *mission*.

mission control center (MCC) In general, the operational headquarters of a space mission. Specifically, the NASA facility responsible for providing total support for all phases of a crewed space flight (e.g., space shuttle flight)—prelaunch, ascent, on-orbit activities, reentry, and landing. It provides systems monitoring and contingency support, maintains communications with the crew and onboard systems, performs flight data collection, and coordinates flight operations. NASA's MCC is located at the Johnson Space Center in Houston, Texas.

mission specialist The space shuttle crew member (and career astronaut) responsible for coordinating payload/Space Transportation System (STS) interaction and, during the payload operation phase of a shuttle flight, directing the allocation of STS and crew resources to accomplish the combined payload objectives.

Mission to Planet Earth (MTPE) From its origins, the planet Earth has experienced change. Change is a natural process. However, there are now strong scientific indications that natural change is being accelerated by certain human activities. For example, we have altered Earth by reconfiguring the landscape, by changing the composition of the atmosphere, and by stressing the biosphere in numerous ways. In our quest for an improved quality of life, we also have become a force for change on the planet.

As a result of certain human activities, Earth may face the possibility of rapid environmental change, including climate warming, sea level rise, deforestation, desertification, ozone depletion, acid rain, and an irreversible reduction in biodiversity (since extinction is forever). Such adverse environmental changes would have an impact on all nations. However, scientists today do not fully understand either the short-term effects of human activities on the overall process of global change or their possible long-term implications. In fact, many important questions in this field remain unanswered. For example, while many scientists concur that global warming is a likely consequence of a continued carbon dioxide (CO_2) increase in the atmosphere, the magnitude and timing of this global warming episode are quite uncertain, especially at the regional level. Therefore, additional information on the rate, causes (natural as well as human-induced), and potential effects of global change is essential.

The National Aeronautics and Space Administration (NASA) is working with the national and international scientific communities to establish a sound scientific basis for addressing these critical issues through research efforts coordinated under the U.S. Global Change Research Program (USGCRP), the International Geosphere-Biosphere Program (IGBP), and the World Climate Research Program (WCRP). Mission to Planet Earth (MTPE) is NASA's contribution to the U.S. Global Change Research Program. It is using space- and ground-based measurement systems to provide the scientific basis for understanding global change. The space-based components of MTPE will provide a constellation of satellites to monitor Earth from space. A major component of Mission to Planet Earth is the *Earth Observation System* (EOS). The EOS will provide sustained space-based observations that will allow researchers to monitor climate variables over time to determine trends. However, space-based monitoring alone is not sufficient. A comprehensive data and information system, a community of scientists performing research with the data acquired, and extensive ground-based and aerial data collection efforts are also important components of the EOS program. The EOS constellation of satellites will start acquiring global data at the end of this century and extend these collection efforts well into the 21st century.

Developing an understanding of how Earth functions in response to interactions among land, oceans, and atmosphere has presented a critical challenge that must be met if we are to predict the impacts of human activities on local, regional, and global climate change. The Earth system science concept promotes the study of Earth as an integrated system of atmosphere, ocean, and land, while bridging the traditional disciplines of physics, chemistry, and biology. The field of Earth science has matured from the point of understanding processes in ocean, land, and atmosphere components treated separately to studying their connections on a global scale. Also called NASA's Earth Science Enterprise (ESE) program.

See also: EARTH OBSERVATION SYSTEM (EOS); GLOBAL CHANGE; GREENHOUSE EFFECT.

mixture ratio In liquid-propellant rockets, the mass flow rate of oxidizer to the combustion chamber divided by the mass flow rate of fuel to the combustion chamber.

MKS system The INTERNATIONAL SYSTEM OF UNITS based on the *meter* (length), the *kilogram* (mass), and the *second* (time) as fundamental units of measure.

See also: SI UNITS.

mobile launch platform (MLP) The structure on which the elements of the space shuttle are stacked in the Vehicle Assembly Building (VAB) and then moved to the launch pad (Complex 39) at the NASA Kennedy Space Center in Florida.

See also: SPACE TRANSPORTATION SYSTEM.

mobility aids Handrails and footrails that help crew members move about an orbiting spacecraft or space station.

mock test An operational test of a complete launch vehicle or rocket system performed without actually firing the rocket engine(s).

mock-up A full-size replica or dummy of something, such as a spacecraft, often made of some substitute material, such as wood, and sometimes incorporating actual functioning pieces of equipment, such as engines or power supplies. Mock-ups are used to study construction procedures, to examine equipment interfaces, or to train personnel.

modeling A scientific investigative technique that uses a mathematical or physical representation of a system or theory. This representation, or "model," accounts for all, or at least some, of the known properties of the system or the characteristics of the theory. Models are used frequently to test the effects of changes of system components on the overall performance of the system or the effects of variation of critical parameters on the behavior of the theory.

modulation The process of modifying a radio frequency (RF) signal by shifting its phase, frequency, or amplitude to carry information. The respective processes are called *phase modulation* (PM), *frequency modulation* (FM), and *amplitude modulation* (AM).

module 1. A self-contained unit of a launch vehicle or spacecraft that serves as a building block for the overall structure. It is common in aerospace practice to refer to the module by its primary function, for example, the Apollo spacecraft "command module" that was used in the Apollo Project to the Moon. 2. A pressurized, crewed laboratory suitable for conducting science, applications, and technology activities; for example, the spacelab module in the Space Transportation System. 3. A one-package assembly of functionally related parts, usually a "plug-in" unit arranged to function as a system or subsystem; a "black box."

mole (symbol: mol) The SI UNIT of the amount of substance. It is defined as the amount of substance that contains as many *elementary units* as there are atoms in 0.012, kilograms of carbon-12, a quantity known as *Avogadro's number* (N_A). (The Avogadro Number, N_A, has a value of about 6.022×10^{23} molecules/mole.) These elementary units may be atoms, molecules, ions, or radicals, and are specified. For example, often it is convenient to express the amount of an "ideal" gas in a given volume in terms of the number of moles (n). As previously stated, a mole of any substance is that mass of the substance that contains a specific number of atoms or molecules. Therefore, the number of moles of a substance can be related to its mass (m) (in grams) by the equation:

$$n = m/M_W$$

where M_W is the *molecular weight* of the substance (expressed as grams per mole or g/mol.) For the case of oxygen (O_2) which has a molecular weight (M_W) of 32 g/mol, the mass of *1 mole* of oxygen is 32.0 grams; *a 1/2 mole* of oxygen would have a mass of 16.0 grams, and so on.

molecular flow The flow of gas through a duct under conditions such that the mean free path is greater than the largest dimension of a transverse section of the duct.

molecule A group of atoms held together by chemical forces. The atoms in the molecule may be identical, as in hydrogen (H_2), or different, as in water (H_2O) and carbon dioxide (CO_2). A molecule is the smallest unit of matter that can exist by itself and retain all its chemical properties.

Molniya launch vehicle A Russian launch vehicle that is descended from the first Russian intercontinental ballistic missile (ICBM). This vehicle, first used in 1961, consists of three cryogenic stages and four cryogenic strap-on motors. It can place a 1,590-kilogram (3,500 pound-mass [lbm]) payload into a highly elliptical (*Molniya*) orbit. This vehicle was used to launch communication satellites (of the same name, i.e., "Molniya" satellites), as well as many of the Russian interplanetary missions in the 1960s.

Molniya orbit A highly elliptical 12-hour orbit that places the apogee (about 40,000 kilometers [km] (24,855 miles [mi])) of a spacecraft over the Northern Hemisphere and the perigee (about 500 km [311 mi]) of the spacecraft over the Southern Hemisphere. Developed and used by the Russians for their communications satellites (called *Molniya satellites*). A satellite in a Molniya orbit spends the bulk of its time (i.e., apogee) above the horizon in view of the high northern latitudes and very little of its time (i.e., perigee) over southern latitudes.

Molniya satellite One of a family of Russian communications spacecraft that operate in highly elliptical orbits, called *Molniya orbits,* so that the spacecraft spends most of its time above the horizon in the Northern Hemisphere.

moment (symbol: M) A tendency to cause rotation about a point or axis, as of a control surface about its hinge or of an airplane about its center of gravity; the measure of this tendency, equal to the product of the force and the perpendicular distance between the point or axis of rotation and the line of action of the force.

moment of inertia (symbol: I) For a massive body made up of many particles or "point masses" (m_i), the moment of inertia (I) about an axis is defined as the sum (Σ) of all the products formed by multi-

plying each point mass or particle (m_i) by the square of its distance (r_i)^2 from the line or axis of rotation; that is: $I = \Sigma_i \, m_i \, (r_i)^2$. The moment of inertia can be considered as the analog in rotational dynamics of mass in linear dynamics.

momentum (linear) The linear momentum (p) of a particle of mass (m) is given by the equation: $p = m \cdot v$, where v is the particle's velocity. Newton's Second Law of Motion states that the time rate of change of momentum of a particle is equal to the resultant force (F) on the particle, namely: $F = dp/dt$.

monopropellant A liquid rocket propellant consisting of a single chemical substance (such as hydrazine) that decomposes exothermally and produces a heated exhaust jet without the use of a second chemical substance. Often used in attitude control systems on spacecraft and aerospace vehicles.

Moon The Moon (the term is capitalized when used in this sense) is Earth's only natural satellite and closest celestial neighbor. (See Figure 81.) While life on Earth is made possible by the Sun, it is also regulated by the periodic motions of the Moon. For example, the months of our year are measured by the regular motions of the Moon around Earth, and the tides rise and fall because of the gravitational tug-of-war between Earth and the Moon. Throughout history, the Moon has had a significant influence on human culture, art, and literature. Even in the space age, it has proved to be a major technical stimulus. It was just far enough away to represent a real technical challenge to reach it; yet it was close enough to allow us to be successful on the first concentrated effort. Starting in 1959 with the U.S. *Pioneer 4* and the Russian *Luna 1* lunar flyby missions, a variety of American and Russian missions have been sent to and around the Moon. The most exciting of these missions, the Apollo expeditions to the Moon from 1968 to 1972, are summarized on page 24. In 1994 the Clementine spacecraft, which was developed and flown by the Ballistic Missile Defense Organization of the U.S. Department of Defense as a demonstration of certain advanced space technologies, spent 70 days in lunar orbit mapping the Moon's surface. Figure 82 is a detailed composite view of the lunar surface, centered on the Moon's South Pole. This mosaic image was constructed from 1,500

Clementine images. The area shown in the figure contains part of the South Pole–Aitken impact basin, the deepest known crater in the solar system and one that is essentially in permanent darkness. Scientists previously had hypothesized that because of the depth of this crater and its permanent shadow, it was large enough and cold enough to trap (as ice) any water brought to the Moon by cometary impact. In December 1996 scientists announced an exciting discovery. A detailed analysis of the Clementine data from this area had revealed a signature of water ice. Water on the Moon (as trapped surface ice) is an extremely valuable resource that would present many exciting possibilities for future lunar base development.

From evidence gathered by the early uncrewed lunar missions (such as Ranger, Surveyor, and the lunar orbiter spacecraft), and by the Apollo missions, lunar scientists have learned a great deal more about the Moon and have been able to construct a geologic history dating back to its infancy. Table 1 provides selected physical and dynamic properties of the Moon.

Because the Moon does not have any oceans or other free-flowing water and lacks a sensible atmosphere, appreciable erosion, or "weathering," has not occurred there. In fact, the Moon is actually a "museum world." The primitive materials that lay on its surface for billions of years are still in an excellent state of preservation. Scientists believe

Figure 80. Astronaut Irwin with the Lunar Rover during the Apollo 15 mission, which launched July 26, 1971. *(courtesy of NASA)*

Figure 81. An excellent view of a near full moon, as photographed by the *Apollo 16* crew (June 1972). Most of the lunar area in this picture is on the far side of the Moon and not visible from Earth. *(Photograph courtesy of NASA—B&W Photo # 72-H-848)*

that the Moon was formed over 4 billion years ago and then differentiated quite early, perhaps only 100 million years later. Tectonic activity ceased eons ago on the Moon. The lunar crust and mantle are quite thick, extending inward to more than 800 kilometers (480 miles). However, the deep interior of the Moon is still unknown. It may contain a small iron core at its center, and there is some evidence that the lunar interior may be hot and even partially molten. Moonquakes have been measured within the lithosphere and interior, most being the result of gravitational stresses.

Chemically, Earth and the Moon are quite similar, although compared to Earth, the Moon is depleted in more easily vaporized materials. The lunar surface consists of highlands composed of alumina-rich rocks that formed from a globe-encircling molten sea and maria made up of volcanic melts that surfaced about 3.5 billion years ago. However, despite all we have learned in the past three decades about our nearest celestial neighbor, lunar exploration really has only just started. Several puzzling mysteries still remain, including the origin of the Moon itself.

Table 1.
PHYSICAL AND ASTROPHYSICAL PROPERTIES OF THE MOON

Diameter (equatorial)	3,476 km
Mass	$7.350 \ 10^{22}$ kg
Mass (Earth's mass = 1.0)	0.0123
Average density	3.34 g/cm³
Mean distance from Earth (center-to-center)	384,400 km
Surface gravity (equatorial)	1.62 m/sec²
Escape velocity	2.38 km/sec
Orbital eccentricity (mean)	0.0549
Inclination of orbital plane (to ecliptic)	5° 09'
Sidereal month (rotation period)	27.322 days
Albedo (mean)	0.07
Mean visual magnitude (at full)	- 12.7
Surface area	37.9×10^{6} km²
Volume	2.20×10^{10} km³
Atmospheric density (at night on surface)	2×10^{5} molecules/cm³
Surface temperature	102 K–384 K

Source: NASA.

Figure 82. A remarkable view of the lunar south pole, constructed from 1,500 Clementine spacecraft images (taken in 1994). This area contains part of the South Pole–Aitken impact basin, the deepest known crater in the solar system. Some of its permanently shadowed regions are now believed to contain "Moon ice," that is, surface deposits of frozen water brought to the Moon by ancient cometary impacts.
(Digital photo courtesy of NASA and Dept. of Defense)

Recently, a new lunar origin theory has been suggested: a cataclysmic birth of the Moon. Scientists supporting this theory suggest that near the end of Earth's accretion from the primordial solar nebula materials (i.e., after its core was formed, but while Earth was still in a molten state), a Mars-size celestial object (called an "impactor") hit Earth at an oblique angle. This ancient explosive collision sent vaporized-impactor and molten-Earth material into Earth orbit, and the Moon then formed from these materials.

As previously mentioned, the surface of the Moon has two major regions with distinctive geologic features and evolutionary histories. First is the relatively smooth, dark areas that Galileo originally called "maria" (because he thought they were seas or oceans). Second is the densely cratered, rugged highlands (uplands), which Galileo called "terrae." The highlands occupy about 83% of the Moon's surface and generally have a higher elevation (as much as 5 kilometers above the Moon's mean radius.) In other places the maria lie about 5 kilometers below the mean radius and are concentrated on the "near side" of the Moon (i.e., on the side of the Moon always facing Earth).

The main external geologic process modifying the surface of the Moon is meteoroid impact. Craters range in size from very tiny pits only micrometers in diameter to gigantic basins hundreds of kilometers across.

The surface of the Moon is strongly brecciated, or fragmented. This mantle of weakly coherent debris is called regolith. It consists of shocked fragments of rocks, minerals, and special pieces of glass formed by meteoroid impact. Regolith thickness is quite variable and depends on the age of the bedrock beneath and on the proximity of craters and their ejecta blankets. Generally, the maria are covered by 3 to 16 meters of regolith, while the older highlands have developed a "lunar soil" at least 10 meters thick. Table 2 provides a summary of the major chemical elements currently known to be on the lunar surface.

See also: LUNAR BASE; LUNAR PROSPECTOR.

moon A small natural body that orbits a larger one; a natural satellite.

multi- More than one; for example, *multimedia.*

multiple-degree-of-freedom system A mechanical system (e.g., a robot arm) for which two or more

Table 2.
MAJOR CHEMICAL ELEMENTS FOUND ON THE LUNAR SURFACE

	Highland Rocks		Mare Basalts	
	Anorthositic Gabbro	Gabbroic Anorthosite	Olivine Basalt (A12)	Green Glass (A15)
SiO_2 [silicon oxide (silica, quartz)]	44.5	44.5	45.0	45.6
TiO_2 [titanium oxide (rutile)]	0.39	0.35	2.90	0.29
Al_2O_3 [aluminum oxide (corundum)]	26.0	31.0	8.59	7.64
FeO [iron oxide]	5.77	3.46	21.0	19.7
MnO [manganese oxide]	—	—	0.28	0.21
MgO [magnesium oxide]	8.05	3.38	11.6	16.6
CaO [calcium oxide]	14.9	17.3	9.42	8.72
Na_2O [sodium oxide]	0.25	0.12	0.23	0.12
K_2O [potassium oxide]	—	—	0.064	0.02
P_2O_5 [phosphorous oxide (phosphate)]	—	—	0.07	—
Cr_2O_3 [chromium oxide]	0.06	0.04	0.55	0.41
Total	99.9	100.2	99.77	99.4

Source: NASA.

coordinates are required to define completely the position of the system at any instant.

multiple independently-targetable reentry vehicle (MIRV) A package of two or more reentry vehicles that can be carried by a single ballistic missile and guided to separate targets. MIRVed ballistic missiles use a warhead-dispensing mechanism called a postboost vehicle to target and release the reentry vehicles.

multiple scattering Any scattering process in which radiation being observed or detected is scattered more than once before reaching the sensor system.

multipropellant A rocket propellant consisting of two or more substances fed separately to the combustion chamber.

multispectral sensing A method of using many different bands of the electromagnetic spectrum (e.g., the visible, near-infrared, and thermal infrared bands) to sense a target. When several bands are used to sense a target, deceptive measures become much less effective.

multistage compressor An axial-flow compressor with two or more stages of rotor and stator blades; a radial-flow compressor with two or more impeller wheels.

multistage launch A launch that uses several stages to boost the payload into orbit. After the first-stage rocket booster has consumed its propellant, it is jettisoned and the second-stage rocket is fired. When the second-stage rocket engine's propellant is depleted, the second-stage rocket also is discarded, and so on. In the early aerospace literature also called a *step-rocket launch.*

multistage rocket A vehicle having two or more rocket units, each firing after the one in back of it has exhausted its propellant. Normally, each unit, or stage, is jettisoned after completing its firing. Also called a *multiple-stage rocket* or, infrequently, a *step rocket.*

mutual assured destruction (MAD) The strategic situation that existed during the cold war in which either superpower (i.e., either the United States or the former Soviet Union) could inflict massive nuclear destruction on the other, no matter which side struck first.

mutual assured survival (MAS) The hypothetical cold war strategic situation wherein each superpower (i.e., the United States and the former Soviet Union) would know that it could survive a nuclear attack launched by the other with only minimal casualties, because of the high effectiveness of its defensive systems. The desire to achieve a mutual-assured-survival situation stimulated the U.S. Strategic Defense Initiative (SDI) Program and its high-technology approach to ballistic missile defense (BMD) in the 1980s.

See also: BALLISTIC MISSILE DEFENSE.

nadir 1. The direction from a spacecraft directly down toward the center of the planet. Opposite of the *zenith*. 2. That point on the celestial sphere directly beneath the observer and directly opposite the zenith.

nano- (symbol: n) A prefix in the SI UNIT system meaning multiplied by 10^{-9}.

nanometer (nm) A billionth of a meter (i.e., 10^{-9} meter)

nanosecond (ns) A billionth of a second (i.e., 10^{-9} second).

nanotechnology A general term that describes the manufacture and application of microminiature machines, electronic devices, and chemical and biological sensors all of which have characteristic dimensions on the order of a micron (10^{-6} meter) or less.

Napierian base The logarithmic base, *e*.
See also: LOGARITHM.

National Aeronautics and Space Administration (NASA) The civilian space agency of the United States, created in 1958 by an act of Congress (i.e., the National Aeronautics and Space Act of 1958). NASA belongs to the executive branch of the federal government. Its overall mission is to plan, direct, and conduct civilian (including scientific) aeronautical and space activities for peaceful purposes. This mission is implemented by NASA Headquarters in Washington, D.C. and by ten major centers throughout the United States. In addition to NASA Headquarters, some of the major NASA facilities and installations include: Ames Research Center (Moffett Field, California), Dryden Flight Research Center (Edwards Air Force Base, California), Goddard Space Flight Center (Greenbelt, Maryland), Jet Propulsion Laboratory (Pasadena, California), Johnson Space Center (Houston, Texas), Kennedy Space Center (Cape Canaveral, Florida), Langley Research Center (Hampton, Virginia), Lewis Research Center (Cleveland, Ohio), Marshall Space Flight Center (Huntsville, Alabama), Stennis Space Center (Mississippi), and the Wallops Flight Facility (Wallops Island, Virginia).

NASA Headquarters in Washington, D.C. exercises management over the space flight centers, research centers, and other installations that make up NASA. Responsibilities include general determination of programs and projects, establishment of policies and procedures, and evaluation and review of all phases of the NASA aerospace program.

The Ames Research Center (ARC), at Moffett Field, California specializes in research aimed toward creating new knowledge and new technology. Contemporary activities include such diverse topics as: information systems technologies, air traffic control and human factors, understanding the effects of gravity on living things, and the overall search for life in the universe.

The Dryden Flight Research Center (DFRC) is NASA's major installation for aeronautical flight research. It is located at Edwards Air Force Base, California, on the western edge of the Mojave Desert, about 130 kilometers (80 miles) north of metropolitan Los Angeles. In addition to aeronautical research, this center also supports the space shuttle program as a primary and backup landing site and as a facility to test and validate design concepts and systems used in the development and operation of the orbiter aerospace vehicles.

The Goddard Space Flight Center (GSFC) was created on January 15, 1959 and named in commemoration of Dr. Robert H. Goddard (1882–1945), the American pioneer in rocket research. The mission of this center is to expand knowledge of Earth and its environment, the solar system, and the universe through observations from space. GSFC is the lead center in NASA's Mission to Planet Earth program.

The Jet Propulsion Laboratory (JPL) in Pasadena, California, is managed for NASA by the California Institute of Technology. JPL is the lead NASA center for robotic exploration of the solar system. In fact, JPL spacecraft have now visited all the known planets except Pluto (and a Pluto mission is currently under study). In addition, JPL manages the worldwide Deep Space Network (DSN), which communicates with spacecraft and conducts scientific investigations from its complexes in California's Mojave Desert near Goldstone; near Madrid, Spain; and near Canberra, Australia.

The Johnson Space Center (JSC) near Houston, Texas was established in September 1961 as NASA's primary center for: the design, development, and testing of spacecraft and associated systems for human flight; the selection and training of astronauts; planning and conducting human space flight missions; and participation in the medical, engineering, and scientific experiments carried aboard crewed space flights.

The Kennedy Space Center (KSC) at Cape Canaveral, Florida is currently responsible for ground turnaround and support operations, prelaunch checkout, and launch of the space shuttle and its payloads. Launch Complex 39 at KSC was also the departure point for the Apollo Project's manned expeditions to the Moon. This center also has responsibility for the NASA facilities and ground operations at Vandenberg Air Force Base, California and the designated contingency shuttle landing sites around the world.

The Langley Research Center (LaRC) at Hampton, Virginia develops airframe and synergistic spaceframe systems technologies. This center also is involved with the scientific understanding of Earth's atmosphere in support of NASA's Mission to Planet Earth program. The Lewis Research Center (LeRC) in Cleveland, Ohio defines and develops advanced technology for high-priority national needs. Contemporary work at this center is directed toward new propulsion, power, and communications technologies for application to aeronautics and space.

The Marshall Space Flight Center (MSFC) in Huntsville, Alabama develops and maintains space transportation and propulsion systems and conducts microgravity research. The Stennis Space Center (SSC) in Hancock County, Mississippi is NASA's primary center for testing large rocket propulsion systems for the space shuttle and future generations of space launch vehicles. Finally, NASA's Wallops Flight Facility (WFF) on Wallops Island, Virginia includes the following mission areas: sounding rockets, scientific balloons, observational science, and scientific aircraft. The Wallops Test Range includes a launch range (for sounding rockets and small expendable launch vehicles), an aeronautical research airport, and associated tracking, data acquisition, and control instrumentation systems. This range supports NASA, Department of Defense, other government agencies, and commercial missions.

National Aerospace Plane (NASP) A Department of Defense (DoD) and NASA research program to develop and demonstrate the technologies of hypersonic flight in a revolutionary piloted research vehicle called the X-30. *Hypersonic flight* usually is defined as flight through Earth's atmosphere at speeds of at least Mach 5—that is, five times the speed of sound. The speed of sound (Mach number = 1) in dry air is 331.4 meters per second (741.4 miles per hour) at a temperature of 0° Celsius (273° Kelvin) (32° Fahrenheit). As envisioned, the X-30 aerospace plane would be capable of flying between North America and Asia in less than two hours (hence its nickname, "Orient Express"); or it could serve as a launch vehicle capable of flying from a conventional 3,050-meter (10,000-foot) runway, accelerating to Mach 25 in the upper portions of Earth's atmosphere, achieving Earth orbit, and then returning to Earth, landing on a conventional airport runway.

National Oceanic and Atmospheric Administration (NOAA) In 1970 the National Oceanic and Atmospheric Administration (NOAA) was established within the U.S. Department of Commerce to ensure the safety of the general public from atmospheric phenomena and to provide the public with an understanding of Earth's environment and resources. NOAA includes: the National Ocean Service, the National Marine Fisheries Service, the NOAA Corps (which operates ships and flies aircraft), and the Office of Oceanic and Atmospheric Research. NOAA has two main components; the National Weather Service (NWS) and the National Environmental Satellite, Data, and Information Service (NESDIS).

See also: WEATHER SATELLITE.

National Reconnaissance Office (NRO) The National Reconnaissance Office (NRO) is the national program to meet the needs of the U.S. government through spaceborne reconnaissance. The NRO is an agency of the Department of Defense (DoD) and receives its budget through that portion of the National Foreign Intelligence Program (NFIP) known as the National Reconnaissance

Program (NRP), which is approved both by the secretary of defense and the director of Central Intelligence (DCI). The existence of the NRO was declassified by the deputy secretary of defense, as recommended by the DCI, on September 18, 1992.

The mission of the NRO is to ensure that the United States has the technology and spaceborne assets needed to acquire intelligence worldwide. This mission is accomplished through research, development, acquisition, and operation of the nation's intelligence satellites. The NRO's assets collect intelligence to support such functions as intelligence and warning, monitoring of arms control agreements, military operations and exercises, and monitoring of natural disasters and environmental issues.

The director of the NRO is appointed by the president and confirmed by the Congress as the

Figure 83. An example of early *Corona* imagery. The Yurya ICBM complex in the Soviet Union photographed on June 28, 1962 during Mission 9038. This image shows construction of an SS-7 launch site. *(Courtesy of National Reconnaissance Office)*

assistant secretary of the air force for space. The secretary of defense has the responsibility, which is exercised in concert with the DCI, for the management and operation of the NRO. The DCI establishes the collection priorities and requirements for the collection of satellite data. The NRO is staffed by personnel from the Central Intelligence Agency (CIA), the military services, and civilian DoD personnel.

The *Corona* program was the first satellite photo reconnaissance program developed by the United States. Corona was a product of the cold war. Soviet nuclear weapons coupled with the long-range bomber and missile delivery systems created the possibility of a devastating surprise attack—a "nuclear Pearl Harbor"—and President Dwight D. Eisenhower demanded better intelligence. But the Iron Curtain and the sheer size of the Soviet landmass made traditional intelligence collection methods marginally useful, at best. The U-2 reconnaissance aircraft served admirably for four years collecting data over the Soviet Union, but its effectiveness was known to be limited by advancements in Soviet air defenses. That, coupled with the urgency for a national space program stimulated by *Sputnik* (the first satellite launched by the former Soviet Union on October 4, 1957), gave birth to the Corona satellite program.

The air force, under a program with the innocuous designation Weapon System 117L, Advanced Reconnaissance System, had been developing a family of satellites since 1956 in connection with development of the ballistic missile, which would serve as the satellite launch vehicle. But priority for the satellite program had been low, and funding was limited.

Following *Sputnik,* all that changed. The most promising near-term project was split out from Weapon System-117L in early 1958 and named Corona. The program was provided increased priority and funding and designated for streamlined management under a joint air force/CIA team. That team was told to take a space booster, a spacecraft, a reentry vehicle, a camera, photographic film, and a control network, all untested, and to make them work together as a system quickly. However, strong leadership, coupled with unwavering White House support, would be needed (and provided) to take this pioneering reconnaissance satellite program through many early setbacks. And there were numerous setbacks! All but one of the first 13 Corona launches (numbered

0–12) resulted in failure of one type or another. But each failure was investigated, identified, and corrected as the team moved closer to an operational photo reconnaissance capability.

Then, on August 10, 1960, *Corona XIII* was launched with diagnostic equipment rather than an actual camera payload. A day later the film capsule reentered and was recovered in the Pacific Ocean. On August 18 *Corona XIV,* with a camera/film payload, was launched in a perfect mission ending with a successful midair capsule recovery. The film retrieved *Corona XIV* was processed quickly and exploited by the intelligence community. This film capsule provided more coverage than all previous U-2 flights over the Soviet Union combined. The United States now had the space-based "eyes" so necessary to protect its people and keep the peace throughout the cold war. The 145th and final Corona launch took place on May 15, 1972.

From a technical perspective, Corona was the first space program to recover an object from orbit and the first to deliver photo reconnaissance information from a satellite. It would go on to be the first program to use multiple reentry vehicles, pass the 100 mission mark, and produce stereoscopic space imagery. Its most remarkable technological advance, however, was the improvement in its ground resolution from an initial 25- to 40-foot (about 7.6 to 12.2-meter) capability to an ultimate 6-foot (1.82-meter) resolution. (See Figure 83.)

National Space Development Agency of Japan (NASDA) Japan's space development activities are implemented primarily by the National Space Development Agency (NASDA) and the Institute of Space and Astronautical Science (ISAS), in cooperation with other related organizations and in accordance with the space development program established by the Space Activities Commission, an advisory committee to the prime minister. NASDA was established on October 1, 1969.

NASDA's activities are limited to the peaceful uses of space. The agency is engaged primarily in research and development involving satellites and launch vehicles for practical uses, launch and tracking operations for Japanese satellites, and the development of remote sensing technologies and applications-oriented experiments (e.g., materials processing in space).

The Engineering Test Satellites (ETS) play a crucial role for NASDA in creating the basic technology that will be used in operational Japanese satellites. For example, the *Engineering Test Satellite V* (ETS-V), which is also called *Kiku-5,* was placed in orbit by an H-I expendable launch vehicle in August 1987. Its smooth injection into orbit and subsequent performance confirmed the in-flight capabilities of NASDA's 550-kilogram (kg) class three-axis stabilized geostationary satellite bus system and its apogee engine for geostationary orbit injection (first Japanese domestically developed version), giving both systems the go-ahead for actual use. *ETS-V* also conducted important mobile satellite communications experiments. The *ETS-VI* (also called *Kiku-6*) was launched in August 1994 by NASDA's H-II launch vehicle (second flight). Although a malfunction of the apogee engine prevented it from completing its mission, it helped establish the use of high-performance, long-life, and large-scale satellites with high-precision orbit maintenance, ion engines and nickel-hydrogen batteries. *Engineering Test Satellite VII* (ETS-VII) was successfully launched by an H-II rocket vehicle on November 28, 1997. *ETS VII* is actually composed of a chaser satellite (called *Hikoboshi*) and a target satellite (called *Orihime*) and is conducting rendezvous and docking (RVD) experiments, as well as space robotics technology (RBT) experiments.

NASDA's H-IIA rocket is designed to meet the demand of various missions in the 21st century with lower cost and a high degree of reliability, using the technology of the current H-II launch vehicle. The H-IIA in its standard configuration is capable of launching a 2-ton class payload into geosynchronous Earth orbit (GEO), which is the same capability for the H-II vehicle. The H-IIA can also launch a 3-ton class payload into GEO with the configuration augmented by a large liquid rocket booster. The vehicle for 3-ton class GEO payloads will be launched from the Tanegasima Space Center early in the first decade of the 21st century. The first stage of the H-IIA vehicle consists of the first-stage core vehicle equipped with the LE-7A liquid hydrogen/liquid oxygen engine and two solid rocket boosters (SRB-A). The LE-7A engine is an improved LE-7 engine (developed for the first stage of the H-II launch vehicle) with 110 tons of thrust (in vacuum). The SRB-As are also newly developed for the H-IIA vehicle with a composite material motor case and polybutadiene composite solid propellant. Each SRB-A booster provides 230 tons of thrust (in vacuum) at liftoff. The liquid rocket booster (LRB) consists of the first stage core structure and two LE-7A engines. It is used for launching 3-ton class (or heavier) payloads into geostationary orbit. The second stage of the H-IIA launch vehicle is equipped with the LE-5B liquid hydrogen/liquid oxygen engine. The LE-5B engine is an improved LE-5A engine, developed for the H-II second stage, and provides 14 tons of thrust (in vacuum). The guidance and control of the second stage is performed by the thrust vector control of the LE-5B engine nozzle with an electrical actuation system and the hydrazine gas-jet reaction control systems.

The main NASDA facilities include the Tsukuba Space Center (Ibaraki), Kakuda Propulsion Center, and Tanegashima Space Center. The Tanegashima Space Center is located on the southeastern portion of Tanegashima Island, Kagoshima. This center includes the Takesake Range for small rockets, the Osaki Range for the H-I launch vehicle, and the Yoshinobu Launch Complex for the H-II expendable vehicle.

JAPANESE LAUNCH VEHICLE PERFORMANCE CHARACTERISTICS

Launch Vehicle	Length (m)	Diameter (m)	Launch Performance Capability to Geostationary Orbit (Payload Mass, kg)
N-I	33	2.4	130
N-II	35	2.4	350
H-I	40	2.4	550
H-II	49	4.0	2,200

Source: Data courtesy of NASDA.

NASDA's Lunar-A mission is scheduled for launch in 1999. This 545 kg spacecraft will orbit the Moon and fire three spear-shaped penetrators about 1.3-meters beneath the lunar surface to make seismology and heat-flow measurements.

Following Luna-A, the next major Japanese lunar project is SELENE (SELenological and ENgineering Explorer) named after the Moon goddess in Greek mythology. SELENE is a joint project between NASDA and the Institute of Space and Astronomical Science (ISAS). This project is currently scheduled for launch in 2003. It consists of placing a satellite in polar orbit around the Moon (at about 100 km altitude) and a relay satellite in an elliptical orbit (100 km by 2,400 km altitude) around the Moon. The major objectives of this project are to obtain scientific data necessary to clarify the origin and evolution of the Moon and to develop technologies that support future lunar exploration efforts (such as advanced soft-landing technology).

These turn-of-the-century lunar missions are considered precursors of more ambitious Japanese lunar activities, including a possible lunar astronomical observatory sometime between the years 2010 and 2020 and involvement in an international lunar base.

NATO III A constellation of military communications satellites launched from Cape Canaveral, Air Force Station, Florida between April 1976 and November 1984. These satellites, designated A, B, C, and D, have provided communications for North Atlantic Treaty Organization (NATO) officials in Belgium, Canada, Denmark, the United Kingdom (England), Germany, as well as Greece, Iceland, and Italy. The United States, Netherlands, Norway, Portugal and Turkey also have used the satellite communications system. NATO III simultaneously accommodated hundreds of NATO users and provided voice and facsimile services. The 2.13-meter (7-foot) diameter, 2.74-meter- (9-foot-) high cylinder-shaped, spinning spacecraft are located in geostationary orbit. Each satellite has three "horn" antennas mounted on a platform that spins in the opposite direction of the body of the spacecraft, enabling the antennas to point at the same place on Earth constantly.

nautical mile (nm) A unit of distance used mainly in navigation. Defined as the distance spanned by one minute of arc of any great circle on Earth. Also called the *sea mile*.

1 nautical mile = 1.852 kilometers = 1.15 statute (land) miles

Navstar The Navstar Global Positioning System is a constellation of advanced radio navigation satellites developed for the U.S. Department of Defense and operated by the U.S. Air Force. In addition to serving defense navigation needs this system, also supports many civilian applications.

See also: GLOBAL POSITIONING SYSTEM (GPS).

Near Earth Asteroid Rendezvous (NEAR) mission NASA's Near Earth Asteroid Rendezvous (NEAR) mission was launched on February 17, 1996 by an expendable Delta II vehicle. It is the first of NASA's Discovery missions, a series of small-scale spacecraft designed to proceed from development to flight in under three years for a cost of less than $150 million. The spacecraft is equipped with an X ray/gamma ray spectrometer, a near-infrared imaging spectograph, a multispectral camera fitted with a charge-coupled device (CCD) imaging detector, a laser altimeter, and a magnetometer. The ultimate goal of this mission is to rendezvous with and achieve orbit around near-Earth asteroid, 433 Eros, in January 1999. The NEAR spacecraft then will study the asteroid for about one year. Eros is an S-class asteroid about 14 x 14 x 40 kilometers (8.7 x 6.2 x 6.2 miles) in size. Studies will be made of the asteroid's size, shape, mass, magnetic field, composition, and surface and internal structure.

See also: ASTEROID.

near infrared That portion of the electromagnetic spectrum involving the shorter wavelengths in the infrared region; generally considered to extend from just beyond the visible red portion of the spectrum (about 0.7 micrometer wavelength) out to about 3.0 micrometers wavelength.

See also: ELECTROMAGNETIC SPECTRUM; INFRARED (IR) RADIATION.

nearside The side of the Moon that always faces Earth.

See also: MOON.

nebula (plural: nebulae) A cloud of interstellar gas or dust. It can be seen either as a dark hole or a band against a brighter background (called a *dark nebula*) or as a luminous patch of light (called a *bright nebula*).

needle valve Valve with a long tapered rod for gradual opening or closing of the valve throat when the rod is moved.

Nemesis A postulated dark stellar companion to the Sun whose close passage every 26 million years is thought to be responsible for the cycle of mass extinctions that seem also to have occurred on Earth at 26-million-year intervals. This "death star" companion has been named for the Greek goddess of retributive justice or vengeance. If it really does exist, it might be a white dwarf, a rogue star that was captured by the Sun, or possibly a tiny but gravitationally influential neutron star. The passage of such a death star through the Oort Cloud (a postulated swarm of comets surrounding the solar system) could lead to a massive shower of comets into the solar system. One or several of these "perturbed" comets impacting on Earth then would trigger massive extinctions and catastrophic environmental changes within a very short period of time.

neper (symbol: N or Np) A natural logarithmic unit (x) used to express the ratio of two power levels, P_1(input) and P_2(output), such that x (nepers) = $1/2 \ln (P_1/P_2)$. The unit is named after John Napier (1550–1617), the Scottish mathematician who developed natural logarithms (symbol: ln). This unit is often encountered in telecommunications engineering. 1 neper = 8.686 decibels.

See also: BEL.

Neptune The outermost of the Jovian planets and the first planet to be discovered using theoretical predictions. Neptune's discovery was made by J. G. Galle (1812–1910) at the Berlin Observatory in 1846. This discovery was based on independent orbital perturbation (disturbance) analyses by the French astronomer Jean Joseph Urbain Le Verrier (1811–77) and the British scientist J. Adams (1819–1892). It is considered to be one of the triumphs of 19th-century theoretical astronomy.

Because of its great distance from Earth, little was known about this majestic blue giant planet until the *Voyager 2* spacecraft swept through the Neptunian system on August 25, 1989. Neptune's characteristic blue color comes from the selective absorption of red light by the methane (CH_4) found in its atmosphere—an atmosphere consisting primarily of hydrogen (over 89%) and helium

Table 1.
PHYSICAL AND DYNAMIC
PROPERTIES OF NEPTUNE

Diameter (equatorial)	49,528 km
Mass	1.02×10^{26} kg
Density (mean)	1.64 g/cm^3
Surface gravity	11 m/sec^2 (approx.)
Escape velocity	23 km/sec (approx.)
Albedo (visual geometric)	0.4 (approx.)
Atmosphere	Hydrogen(>89%), helium (~11%), methane (ppm)
Temperature (blackbody)	45 Kelvin
Natural satellites	8
Rings	4 [Galle, LeVerrier, 1989N4R, Adams (arcs)]
Period of rotation (a Neptunian day)	0.6715 day (16 hr 7 min)
Average distance from Sun	4.5×10^9 km (30.06 AU)
Eccentricity	0.0097
Period of revolution around Sun (a Neptunian year)	165 yr
Mean orbital velocity	5.4 km/sec
Magnetic field	Yes (strong, complex; tilted 50° to planet's axis of rotation)
Radiation belts	Yes (complex structure)
Solar flux at planet (at top of atmosphere)	1.5 W/m^2 (at 30 AU)

Source: NASA.

(about 11%) with minor amounts of methane, ammonia ice, and water ice. At the time of the *Voyager 2* encounter, Neptune's most prominent "surface" feature was called the Great Dark Spot (GDS), which was somewhat analogous in relative size and scale to Jupiter's Red Spot. However, unlike Jupiter's Red Spot, which has been observed for at least 300 years, Neptune's GDS, which was located in the Southern Hemisphere in 1989, had disappeared by June of 1994, when the Hubble Space Telescope looked for it. Then, a few months later, a nearly identical spot appeared in

Table 2.
PHYSICAL DATA FOR NEPTUNE'S MOONS

Name	Distance from Planet's Center (km)	Period (day)	Diameter (km)
Naiad (1989N6)	48,000	0.30	50 (approx.)
Thalassa (1989N5)	50,000	0.31	80 (approx.)
Despina (1989N3)[a]	52,500	0.33	150 (approx.)
Galatea (1989N4)[a]	62,000	0.43	160 (approx.)
Larissa (1989N2)	73,600	0.55	200 (irreg shape)
Proteus (1989N1)	117,600	1.12	400 (irreg shape)
Triton	354,000	5.88 (retrograde)	2,706
Nereid	5,513,000	360.1	340

[a] Ring shepherd satellite

Source: NASA.

Neptune's northern hemisphere. Neptune is an extraordinarily dynamic planet that continues to surprise space scientists. The *Voyager 2* encounter also revealed the existence of six additional satellites and an interesting ring system. Table 1 provides contemporary physical and dynamic data for Neptune; Table 2 describes Neptune's eight known satellites.

Triton, Neptune's largest moon, is one of the most interesting and coldest objects (about 35° Kelvin surface temperature) yet discovered in the solar system. Because of its inclined retrograde orbit, density (2.0 grams per centimeter cubed), rock and ice composition, and frost-covered (frozen nitrogen) surface, space scientists consider Triton to be a "first cousin" to the planet Pluto. Triton shows remarkable geologic history; *Voyager 2* images have revealed active geyserlike eruptions spewing invisible nitrogen gas and dark dust several kilometers into space.

See also: PLUTO; URANUS; VOYAGER.

Neptunian Of or pertaining to the planet Neptune.

NERVA *Nuclear Engine for Rocket Vehicle Application.* The acronym applied to a series of nuclear reactors developed as part of the overall U.S. nuclear rocket development program (i.e., the ROVER Program) from 1959 to 1973.

See also: NUCLEAR ROCKET; SPACE NUCLEAR PROPULSION.

neutral Without an electrical charge; neither positive nor negative.

neutral atmosphere That portion of a planetary atmosphere consisting of neutral (uncharged) atoms or molecules, as opposed to electrically charged ions.

neutral buoyancy simulator Orbiting objects in space, being "weightless," behave a little like neutral buoyancy objects in water here on Earth. Astronauts have trained for certain on-orbit tasks by working with and moving space hardware while underwater in a large tank or submersion facility. These activities help simulate the actual mission activities to be performed during weightlessness.

neutral burning With respect to a solid-propellant rocket, a condition of propellant burning such that the burning surface or area remains constant, thereby producing a constant pressure and thrust.

neutral density filter A filter that attenuates, or reduces, all regions of the electromagnetic spectrum equally; it is not spectrally (e.g., color) selective.

neutron (symbol: n) An uncharged elementary particle with a mass slightly greater than that of the proton. It is found in the nucleus of every atom heavier than hydrogen. A free neutron is unstable, with a half-life of about 12 minutes, and decays into an electron, a proton, and a neutrino. Neutrons sustain the fission chain reaction in a nuclear reactor.

neutron stars Remnants of supernovae explosions. These stars, typically about 10 kilometers in diameter, consist of extremely high-density matter that is composed entirely of neutrons (i.e., all the atomic electrons and protons have been squeezed together by the force of gravity exerted by the collapsing matter in the supernova explosion to form neutrons). Neutron stars send out rapidly varying radio signals.

See also: PULSAR; STAR(S).

new moon The Moon at conjunction, when little or none of it is visible to an observer on Earth because the illuminated side is away from him or her.

See also: MOON.

newton (symbol: N) The unit of force in the INTERNATIONAL SYSTEM OF UNITS. It is defined as the force that provides a 1-kilogram mass with an acceleration of 1 meter per second per second.

$$1 \, N = 1 \, kg\text{-}m/s^2$$

Newtonian mechanics The system of mechanics based on Newton's laws of motion in which mass and energy are considered as separate, conservative mechanical properties, in contrast to their treatment in relativistic mechanics, in which mass and energy are treated as equivalent (from the Einstein mass-energy equivalency formula: $E = m \, c^2$).

See also: NEWTON'S LAWS OF MOTION.

Newtonian telescope A reflecting telescope in which a small plane mirror reflects the convergence beam from the objective (primary mirror) to an eyepiece at the side of the telescope. After the second reflection the rays travel approximately perpendicular to the longitudinal axis of the telescope. This type of telescope, the first reflecting telescope to be constructed was developed by Sir Isaac Newton (1642–1727) around 1670.

Newton's law of gravitation Every particle of matter in the universe attracts every other particle with a force (F), acting along the line joining the two particles, proportional to the product of the masses (m_1 and m_2) of the particles and inversely proportional to the square of the distance (r) between the particles, or

$$F = [G \, m_1 \, m_2]/r^2$$

where F is the force of gravity (newtons), m_1, m_2 are the masses of the (attracting) particles (kg); r is

the distance between the particles (m); and G is the universal gravitational constant.

$$G = 6.6732 \, (\pm 0.003) \times 10^{-11} \, N\cdot m^2/kg^2$$
(in SI units)

Newton's laws of motion A set of three fundamental postulates that form the basis of the mechanics of rigid bodies. These laws were formulated in about 1685 by the brilliant English scientist and mathematician Sir Isaac Newton (1642–1727), as he was studying the motion of the planets around the Sun. Newton described this work in the book *Mathematical Principles of Natural Philosophy*, which is often referred to simply as Newton's *Principia*.

Newton's first law is concerned with the principle of inertia and states that if a body in motion is not acted upon by an external force, its momentum remains constant. This law also can be called the *law of conservation of momentum*.

The second law states that the rate of change of momentum of a body is proportional to the force acting upon the body and is in the direction of the applied force. A familiar statement of this law is the equation: F = m a, where F is the vector sum of applied forces, m is the mass, and a is the vector acceleration of the body.

Newton's third law is the principle of action and reaction. It states that for every force acting upon a body, there is a corresponding force of the same magnitude exerted by the body in the opposite direction.

nickel-cadmium (nicad) batteries Long-lived, rechargeable batteries frequently used in spacecraft applications as a secondary source of power. For example, in a typical Earth-orbiting spacecraft, solar cell arrays capture sunlight and provide electric power to operate the spacecraft's electrical systems and also to charge the nickel-cadmium batteries. Then, when the spacecraft is shadowed by Earth and is not illuminated by the Sun, spacecraft electric power is provided by the nickel-cadmium batteries. This cycle continues many times during the lifetime of the spacecraft. While the nicad batteries have a low energy density (typically 15 to 30 watt-hours per kilogram), they have a good deep-discharge tolerance and long cycle life, making their use nearly standard in contemporary spacecraft operations.

Nike Hercules A U.S. Army air defense surface-to-air guided missile system that provides nuclear or conventional, medium- to high-altitude air defense coverage against manned bombers and air-breathing missiles. The system is designed to operate in either a mobile or fixed-site configuration and has a capability of performing surface-to-surface missions. Also designated as the MIM-14.

The army developed two other surface-to-air missiles in the Nike missile family: the Nike Ajax and the Nike Zeus.

Nimbus satellites A series of second-generation weather satellites created by NASA and the National Oceanographic and Atmospheric Administration (NOAA) as a follow-up to the Tiros satellites, which were the first polar orbiting meteorological satellites. The Nimbus satellites were more complex than the Tiros satellites. For example, they carried advanced television (TV) cloud-mapping cameras and an infrared radiometer that permitted the collection of cloud images at night for the first time. From 1964 to 1978 seven Nimbus spacecraft were placed in polar orbit from Vandenberg Air Force Base, California, creating a 24-hour-per-day capability to observe weather conditions on the planet.
See also: WEATHER SATELLITE.

node 1. In orbital mechanics, one of the two points of intersection of the orbit of a planet, planetoid, or comet with the ecliptic, or of the orbit of a satellite with the plane of the orbit of its primary. By convention, that point at which the body crosses to the north side of the reference plane is called the *ascending node;* the other node is called the *descending node.* The line connecting these two nodes is called the *line of nodes.* 2. In physics, a point, line, or surface in a standing wave where some characteristic of the wave field has essentially zero amplitude. By comparison, a position of maximum amplitude in a standing wave is referred to as an *antinode.* 3. In communications, a network junction or connection point (e.g., a terminal).

no-fire limit Maximum current, power, voltage, or capacitance that can be applied to the firing circuit of an electroexplosive device without firing the device.

"no-go" In aerospace operations, an expression indicating an operation or activity is not ready to proceed; the opposite of "go." During a launch countdown, the launch director will poll all key individuals responsible for various aspects of the launch operations. If everything is proper in a particular area or activity, an individual will respond "go"; if, however, a problem has suddenly developed, the individual responsible for overseeing that particular aspect of the launch activities will respond "no-go." For example, the weather officer might say "no-go" because a thunderstorm has moved too close to the launch site.

"nominal" In the context of aerospace operations and activities, a word meaning "within prescribed or acceptable limits." For example, the Mars mission is now on a "nominal" interplanetary trajectory; or the pressure in the combustion chamber is "nominal."

noncavitating valve Flow-control valve that meters the flow of liquid propellant without cavitation occurring in its operating range.

noncoherent communication Communications mode wherein a spacecraft generates its downlink frequency independent of any uplink frequency.
See also: TELECOMMUNICATIONS.

noncondensable gas A gas whose temperature is above its critical temperature, so that it cannot be liquefied by an increase of pressure alone.

noncooperative launch A launch that is made separate, and not coordinated with, a crewed launch already in orbit.

nondestructive testing Testing to detect internal and concealed defects in materials and components using techniques that do not damage or destroy the items being tested. X rays, gamma rays, and neutron irradiation, as well as ultrasonics, frequently are used to accomplish nondestructive testing.

nondimensional parameter Any parameter of a problem or equation that has the dimensions of a pure number, usually rendered deliberately. A pure number (e.g., the ratio of two speeds) does not involve any physical dimensions. Also called *nondimensional number.*

nonequilibrium In thermodynamics, a state within a gas mixture in which reactions have not reached equilibrium. If left in this condition, the composition of the gas mixture would change in time.

nonequilibrium composition In rocketry, the exhaust gas chemical composition resulting from incomplete chemical reaction of the products of combustion.

nonflight unit An aerospace unit that is not intended for flight usage. Also called *test article* or a *hangar queen*.

nonimpinging injector An injector used in liquid rocket engines that employs parallel streams of propellant usually emerging normal to the face of the injector. In this type injector, propellant mixing usually is obtained by turbulence and diffusion. The World War II era German V-2 rocket used a nonimpinging injector.
   See also: INJECTOR.

nonionizing electromagnetic radiation Radiation that does not change the structure of atoms but does heat tissue and may cause harmful biological effects. Microwaves, radio waves, and low-frequency electromagnetic fields from high-voltage transmission lines are considered to be nonionizing radiation.

normal 1. Equivalent to usual, regular, rational, or standard conditions. 2. Perpendicular. A line is *normal* to another line or a plane when it is perpendicular to it. A line is *normal* to a curve or curved surface when it is perpendicular to the tangent line or plane at the point of tangency.

normal distribution In statistics, the fundamental frequency distribution defined by a mathematical formula involving the arithmetic mean (μ) and the standard deviation (σ). When the normal distribution is plotted as a function of the variable (x), the plot has a characteristic bell shape. Also called *Gaussian distribution*.

normal emittance Emittance in a direction perpendicular to the surface or in a small solid angle whose axial ray is perpendicular to the surface.

normally closed valve Powered valve that returns to a closed position on shutoff or on failure of the actuating energy or signal.

normally open valve Powered valve that returns to an open position on shutoff or on failure of the actuating energy or signal.

"normal" propellants In rocketry, bipropellants (two propellants mixed together) that derive thermal energy primarily from oxidizer-fuel reactions.

normal shock wave In supersonic flow, a shock wave perpendicular (or substantially so) to the direction of flow. Sometimes shortened to *normal shock*.

North American Aerospace Defense Command (NORAD) The North American Aerospace Defense Command (NORAD) is the binational United States–Canadian command charged with safeguarding the sovereign airspace of the United States and Canada. The mission objectives of NORAD are threefold: (1) to assist each nation to safeguard the sovereignty of its airspace; (2) to contribute to the deterrence of an attack on North America by providing a capability for aerospace surveillance, threat evaluation and attack warning, and defense against attack by air or space; and (3) should deterrence fail, to ensure an appropriate defense against attack by providing for the effective use of the forces of the two countries available for defense.

   NORAD has specific responsibilities for providing warning of an intercontinental ballistic missile (ICBM) attack or a submarine-launched ballistic missile (SLBM) attack against North America. This responsibility includes an assessment of the nature of such an attack. To carry out this responsibility, NORAD receives information from a worldwide network of ground-based missile warning systems and from space-based surveillance systems that detect the thermal (infrared) energy from ballistic missile plumes and provide the first indication that potentially threatening missiles have been launched.

   The U.S. Space Command provides NORAD with both surveillance of space activities of strategic or tactical interest and warning of space events that may threaten North America. Space surveillance includes responsibility for detecting, tracking, identifying, cataloging, and maintaining the status of human-made objects in space.

   In addition to its responsibility for providing surveillance and control of the airspace of Canada and the United States, NORAD also is tasked to provide warning of bomber and/or air-launched cruise missile (ALCM) or sea-launched cruise missile (SLCM) attack on North America and to defend against that attack.

NORAD's Air Defense Operations Center is located at Cheyenne Mountain Air Force Base, Colorado.

See also: BALLISTIC MISSILE DEFENSE; CHEYENNE MOUNTAIN AIR STATION.

nose cone The cone-shaped leading edge of a rocket vehicle. Designed to protect and contain a warhead or payloads, such as satellites, instruments, animals, or auxiliary equipment. The outer surface and structure of a nose cone is built to withstand the high temperatures associated with the aerodynamic heating and vibrations (buffeting) that results from flight through the atmosphere.

See also: REENTRY VEHICLE; ROCKET.

nova (plural: novae) A star that exhibits a sudden and exceptional brightness, usually of a temporary nature, and then returns to its former luminosity. A *supernova* is a much brighter explosion of a giant star during which a large fraction of its mass is blown outward into space. The term derives from the Latin word *nova,* which means "new."

See also: STAR(S).

nozzle In a rocket engine, the carefully shaped aft portion of the thrust chamber that controls the expansion of the exhaust gas so that the thermal energy of combustion is converted effectively into kinetic energy of the combustion product gases, thereby propelling the rocket vehicle. The nozzle is a major component of a rocket engine, having a significant influence on the overall engine performance and representing a large fraction of the engine structure. The design of the nozzle consists of solving simultaneously two different problems: defining the shape of the wall that forms the expansion surface and delineating the nozzle structure and hydraulic system.

In general, the nozzle shape is selected to maximize performance within the constraints placed on the rocket system. The nozzle structure of a large rocket must provide strength and rigidity to a system in which mass is at a high premium and the loads are not readily predictable. The maximum loads on the nozzle structure often occur during the start transients (i.e., initial rapid rise in pressure and fluid flow rates) before full flow is established.

(a) Bell   (b) Conical

(c) Annular Bell   (d) Expansion-Deflection (E-D)

(e) Plug (Truncated Aerospike)

Figure 84. Basic types of nozzles used in liquid rocket engines   *(Drawing courtesy of NASA)*

The nozzles used on liquid rocket engines now are inherently very efficient components, since they are the product of many years of engineering development. (See Figure 84.) With increasing area ratio (i.e., exit area to throat area), the nozzle becomes a proportionally larger part of the rocket engine. Because there is relatively little to be gained in trying to increase the efficiencies of conventional bell and conical nozzles, recent aerospace engineering activities in nozzle development have focused on obtaining the same nozzle efficiency from a shorter package through the use of short bell nozzles and annular nozzles, such as expansion-deflection (E-D) and plug (aerospike) nozzles.

An *aerospike nozzle* is an annular nozzle that allows the combustion gas to expand from one surface—a centerbody spike—to ambient pressure. A *bell nozzle* is a nozzle with a circular opening for a throat and an axisymmetric contoured wall downstream of the throat that gives the nozzle a characteristic bell shape. The *expansion-deflection,* or *E-D, nozzle* is a nozzle that has an annular throat that discharges exhaust gas with a radial outward component. A *plug nozzle* is an annular nozzle that discharges exhaust gas with a radial inward component—a truncated aerospike.

The nozzle configuration best suited to a particular application depends on a variety of factors, including the altitude regime in which the nozzle will be used, the diversity of stages in which the same nozzle will be employed, and limitations imposed by available development time and funding. The propellant combination, chamber pressure, mixture ratio, and thrust level for a rocket engine generally are determined on the basis of factors other than the nozzle configuration. These parameters will have only a minor effect on the selection of a nozzle configuration but will have a significant effect on the selection of nozzle cooling method.

Figure 85 presents a typical bell nozzle configuration and associated nozzle nomenclature. The throat of the nozzle is the region of transition from subsonic to supersonic flow. For typical rocket nozzles, local mass flux and, consequently, the rate of heat transfer to the wall are highest in this area of the nozzle. The shape of the nozzle wall in the vicinity of the throat dictates the distribution of exhaust-gas flow across the nozzle at the throat. The nozzle wall geometry immediately upstream of the throat determines the distribution of gas properties at the throat. The expansion geometry extends from the throat to the nozzle exit. The function of this part of the nozzle is to accelerate the exhaust gases to a high velocity in a short distance, while providing near-ideal performance. Both engine length and propellant specific impulse strongly influence the payload capability of a rocket vehicle. Therefore, aerospace engineers give considerable attention to the design of the nozzle expansion geometry in order to obtain the maximum performance from a nozzle length consistent with optimum vehicle payload.

The *area ratio* of a nozzle is defined as the ratio of the geometric flow area of the nozzle exit to the geometric flow area of the nozzle throat. This important nozzle parameter is also called the *expansion area ratio*. An *ideal nozzle* is a nozzle that provides theoretically perfect performance for the given area ratio when analyzed on the basis of one-dimensional point-source flow. The *aerodynamic throat area* of a nozzle is the effective flow area of the throat, which is less than the geometric flow area because the flow is not uniform. A *nozzle extension* is a nozzle structure that has been added to the main nozzle in order to increase the expansion area ratio or to provide a change in nozzle construction. Finally, *overexpansion* is a condition that occurs when a nozzle expands the exhaust gas to an ambient pressure that is higher than that for which the nozzle was originally designed.

See also: ROCKET.

nozzle extension Nozzle structure that is added to the main nozzle in order to increase the expansion

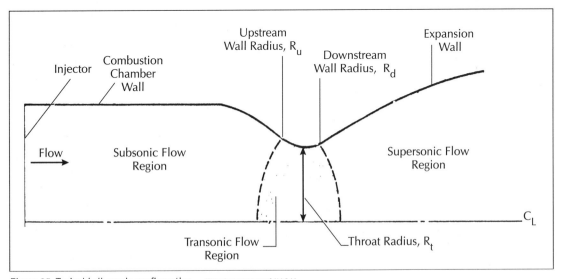

Figure 85. Typical bell nozzle configuration *(Drawing courtesy of NASA)*

area ratio or to provide a change in nozzle construction.

See also: NOZZLE.

nuclear airburst The explosion of a nuclear weapon in the air, at a height greater than the maximum radius of the fireball.

nuclear cross section (symbol: σ) A measure of the probability that some particular nuclear reaction will take place. It is mathematically defined by the expression:

$$dI = I \, n \, \sigma \, dx$$

where I is the intensity of the incident particle beam; n is the number of target nuclei per cubic centimeter of target; σ is the cross section for the particular nuclear reaction (expressed in square centimeters); and x is the target thickness (in centimeters). In physics, the nuclear cross section (σ) is often expressed in *barns*, where 1 barn = 10^{-28} centimeters squared.

nuclear defense The methods, plans, and procedures involved in establishing and exercising defensive measures against the effects of an attack by nuclear weapons or radiological warfare agents. It encompasses both the training for and the implementation of these methods, plans, and procedures.

nuclear delivery vehicle That portion of the weapon system that provides the means of delivery of a nuclear weapon to the target.

nuclear detonation detection and warning system A system employed to provide surveillance coverage of critical friendly target areas and indicate location, height of burst, yield, and ground zero (actual or projected) of nuclear detonations.

nuclear-electric propulsion (NEP) system A propulsion system in which a nuclear reactor is used to produce the electricity needed to operate the electric propulsion engine(s). Unlike the solar-electric propulsion (SEP) system, the nuclear electric propulsion (NEP) system can operate anywhere in the solar system and even beyond, since the NEP system's performance is independent of its position relative to the Sun. Furthermore, it can provide shorter trip times and greater payload

capacity than any of the advanced chemical propulsion technologies that might be used in the next two decades or so for detailed exploration of the outer planets, especially Saturn, Uranus, Neptune, Pluto, and their respective moons. Closer to Earth, a NEP orbital transfer vehicle (OTV) can serve effectively in cislunar space, gently transporting large cargoes and structures from LOW EARTH ORBIT to geosynchronous orbit or to a logistics depot in lunar orbit that supports the needs of an expanding lunar settlement. Finally, advanced nuclear electric propulsion systems can become the main space-based transport vehicles for both human explorers and their equipment as permanent surface bases are established on Mars in the 21st century.

See also: ELECTRIC PROPULSION; SPACE NUCLEAR POWER; SPACE NUCLEAR PROPULSION.

nuclear energy Energy released as a result of interactions involving atomic nuclei; that is, reactions in which there is a rearrangement of the constituents (i.e., protons and neutrons) of the nucleus. Any nuclear process in which the total mass of the products is less than the mass before interaction is accompanied by the release of energy. The amount of energy release is related to the decrease in (nuclear) mass by the famous Einstein mass-energy equivalence formula:

$$E = m \, c^2$$

where E is the energy release, m is the *decrease* in mass, and c is the speed of light. The disappearance of 1 atomic mass unit (i.e., the mass of a proton or a neutron) results in the release of about 931 million electron volts (MeV) of energy.

See also: FISSION (NUCLEAR); FUSION (NUCLEAR).

nuclear exoatmospheric burst The explosion of a nuclear weapon above Earth's sensible atmosphere (e.g., about 120 kilometers (75 miles) altitude), where atmospheric interaction is minimal.

nuclear explosive An explosive based on the fission or fusion of atomic nuclei.

See also: FISSION (NUCLEAR); FUSION (NUCLEAR).

nuclear fission The splitting of a heavy atomic nucleus into two smaller masses accompanied by the release of neutrons, gamma rays, and about 200 million electron volts (MeV) of energy.

See also: FISSION (NUCLEAR).

nuclear fusion The nuclear reaction (process) whereby several smaller nuclei combine to form a more massive nucleus, accompanied by the release of a large amount of energy (which represents the difference in nuclear masses between the sum of the smaller particles and the resultant combined, or "fused," nucleus). Nuclear fusion is the source of energy in stars, including the Sun. For example, the nuclear fusion processes now taking place within the Sun convert approximately 5 million metric tons of mass into energy every second.

See also: FUSION (NUCLEAR).

nuclear radiation Particles (e.g., alpha particles, beta particles, and neutrons) and very energetic electromagnetic radiation (i.e., gamma ray photons) emitted from atomic nuclei during various nuclear reaction processes, including radioactive decay, fission, and fusion. Nuclear radiations are ionizing radiations.

nuclear reaction A reaction involving a change in an atomic nucleus, such as neutron capture, radioactive decay, fission, or fusion. A nuclear reaction is distinct from and far more energetic than a chemical reaction, which is limited to changes in the electron structure surrounding the nucleus.

See also: FISSION (NUCLEAR); FUSION (NUCLEAR).

nuclear reactor A device in which a fission chain reaction can be initiated, maintained, and controlled. Its essential component is the core, which contains the fissile fuel. Depending on the type of reactor, its purpose and design, the reactor also can contain a moderator, a reflector, shielding, coolant, and control mechanisms.

See also: FISSION (NUCLEAR); SPACE NUCLEAR POWER; SPACE NUCLEAR PROPULSION.

nuclear rocket In general, a rocket vehicle that derives its propulsive thrust from nuclear energy sources, primarily fission. There are two general classes of nuclear rockets: the *nuclear-thermal rocket* and the *nuclear-electric propulsion* (NEP) *system*. The nuclear thermal rocket uses a nuclear reactor to heat the propellant (generally hydrogen) to extremely high temperatures before it is expelled through a rocket nozzle. The nuclear electric propulsion system uses the nuclear reactor to produce electric power, which in turn is used to operate an electric propulsion system. (See Figure 86.)

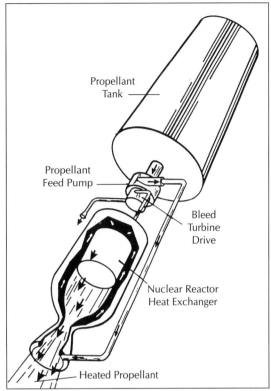

Figure 86. Basic components of a nuclear thermal rocket. The propellant tank carries liquid hydrogen (at cryogenic temperatures). This single propellant is heated to extremely high temperatures as it passes through the nuclear reactor, and then very hot gaseous hydrogen is expelled out the rocket's nozzle to produce thrust. *(Drawing courtesy of NASA and U.S. Department of Energy)*

See also: NUCLEAR-ELECTRIC PROPULSION (NEP) SYSTEM; SPACE NUCLEAR PROPULSION.

Nuclear Rocket Development Station (NRDS) Major test facilities for the U.S. nuclear rocket program (from 1959 to 1973) were located at the Nuclear Rocket Development Station (NRDS) at the Nevada Test Site (NTS) in southern Nevada. Both nuclear reactors and complete nuclear rocket engine assemblies were tested (in place) at the NRDS, which had three major test areas: Test cells A and C and Engine Test Stand Number One (ETS-1). The reactor test facilities were designed to test a reactor in an upward-firing position, while the engine test facility tested nuclear rocket engines in a downward-firing mode. During a nuclear rocket test at the NRDS, the surrounding desert basin (called Jackass Flats after some of the indigenous wildlife) literally became an inferno as the very hot hydrogen gas spontaneously ignited upon contact with the air and burned (with atmospheric oxygen) to form water.

See also: NUCLEAR ROCKET: SPACE NUCLEAR PROPULSION.

nuclear surface burst An explosion of a nuclear weapon at the surface of land or water or above the surface, at a height less than the maximum radius of the fireball.

nuclear weapon A device in which the explosion results from the energy released by reactions involving atomic nuclei, either fission or fusion, or both. The basic fission weapon can either be a gun-assembly type weapon or an implosion-type weapon, while a thermonuclear weapon involves the use of the energy of a fission weapon to ignite the desired thermonuclear reactions.

nuclear yields The energy released in the detonation of a nuclear weapon, measured in terms of the kilotons or megatons of TNT (trinitrotoluene) required to produce the same energy release. Yields are categorized as: *very low,* less than 1 kiloton; *low,* 1–10 kilotons; *medium,* over 10–50 kilotons; *high,* 50–500 kilotons; and *very high,* over 500 kilotons.

nucleate boiling Formation and breaking away of bubbles from active bubble formation sites (i.e., nucleation sites) on a submerged heated surface; the rising bubbles stir the liquid so that thermal energy (heat) transfer from the surface to the liquid is much greater than that due to normal convection heat transfer.

nucleon The common name for a major constituent particle of the atomic nucleus. It is applied to protons and neutrons. The number of nucleons in a nucleus represents the atomic mass number (A) of that nucleus. For example, the isotope uranium-235 has 235 nucleons in its nucleus (92 protons and 143 neutrons). This isotope also is said to have an atomic mass number of 235 (i.e., A = 235).

nucleosynthesis The production of heavier chemical elements from the fusion or joining of lighter chemical elements (e.g., hydrogen or helium nuclei) in thermonuclear reactions in stellar interiors.

See also: FUSION (NUCLEAR); STAR(S).

nucleus 1. In physics, the central portion of an atom, consisting of protons and neutrons bound together by a strong nuclear force. It is positively charged and contains most of the mass of the atom. The total number of protons plus neutrons is the mass number (A). Also called the *atomic nucleus.* 2. In biology, a clearly delineated central body or region within a living cell that contains the genetic material DNA and serves as the control center for the cell. The *cellular nucleus is* surrounded by the cytoplasm. 3. In astronomy, the small (perhaps 1 kilometer or so in diameter), permanent, central body of a comet. Also called a *cometary nucleus.*

nuclide A general term applicable to all forms of the elements. The term is used erroneously as a synonym for "isotope," which properly has a more limited definition. Whereas isotopes are the various forms of a single element (therefore they are a family of nuclides) and all have the same atomic number (i.e., the same number of protons), nuclides comprise all the isotopic forms of all the elements. Nuclides are distinguished by their atomic number (Z), mass number (A), and nuclear energy state.

In accordance with the recommendations of the International Unions of Pure and Applied Chemistry, the following designations, as shown in Figure 87, are used for nuclides:

The *mass number* (A) of a nuclide is placed as a superscript to the left of the symbol for the chemical element of the nuclide, rather than to its right, as was formerly done; for example, ^{14}N rather than N^{14} for nitrogen-14.

The *atomic number* (Z) is placed as a left subscript; for example $^{14}_{6}C$ for carbon-14 or $^{235}_{92}U$ for uranium-235.

The state of ionization is shown as a right superscript; for example, Ca++ (a calcium atom that has a double positive charge).

Figure 87. Nuclide designation   *(Courtesy of U.S. Department of Energy)*

The number of neutrons in the nucleus is shown as a right subscript; for example, $^{40}_{20}Ca_{20}$ for the isotope calcium-40, which contains 20 protons (its atomic number—indicated by the left subscript) and 20 neutrons (indicated by the right subscript).

Excited states are shown as part of the left superscript or, sometimes, the right superscript; for example, ^{110m}Ag or $^{110}Ag^m$ is used to indicate an excited state of a silver-110 nucleus; while He* indicates an excited state of a helium atom.

Nusselt number (symbol: Nu) 1. In heat transfer, a nondimensional number used to describe the heat transfer between a solid boundary and a moving fluid.

$$Nu \equiv (total\ heat\ transfer)/(conductive\ heat\ transfer) \equiv h\,l/k$$

where h is the heat transfer coefficient; l is the characteristic length; and k is the thermal conductivity of the fluid. 2. A nondimensional number used to characterize mass transfer problems.

$$Nu \equiv (mass\ diffusivity)/(molecular\ diffusivity) \equiv k_c\,l\,/D_m$$

where k_c is the mass transfer coefficient; l is the characteristic length; and D_m is the molecular diffusivity. These dimensionless parameters are named in honor of the German engineer Wilhelm Nusselt (1882–1957), who derived them in 1905.

oblate spheroid A sphere flattened such that its polar diameter is smaller than its equatorial diameter.

oblique shock wave A shock wave inclined at an oblique angle to the direction of flow in a supersonic flow field. Compare with NORMAL SHOCK WAVE.

obscurant A substance, such as chaff or smoke, used to conceal an object from observation by a radio-frequency (i.e., radar) or optical sensor. Chaff helps conceal an object from radar detection by creating numerous false images and returns, while smoke simply helps hide an object from direct observation by an optical sensor.

observed In astronomy and navigation, pertaining to a value that has been measured, in contrast to one that has been computed.

occult, occulting The disappearance of one celestial object behind another. For example, a solar eclipse is an *occulting* of the Sun by the Moon; that is, the Moon comes between Earth and the Sun, temporarily blocking the Sun's light and darkening regions of Earth.

ocean remote sensing Covering about 70 % of Earth's surface, the oceans are central to the continued existence of life on our planet. The oceans are where life first appeared on Earth. Today the largest creatures on the planet (whales) and the smallest creatures (bacteria and viruses) live in the global oceans. Important processes between the atmosphere and the oceans are linked. Oceans store energy. The wind roughens the ocean surface, and the ocean surface, in turn, extracts more energy from the wind and puts it into wave motion, currents, and mixing. When ocean currents change, they cause changes in global weather patterns and can cause droughts, floods, and storms.

However, our knowledge of the global oceans is still limited. Ships, coastlines, and islands provide places from which we can observe, sample, and study small portions of the oceans. But from Earth's surface, we can look at only a very small part of the global ocean. Satellites orbiting Earth can survey an entire ocean in less than an hour. Sensors on these satellites can "look" at clouds to study the weather or at the sea surface to measure its temperature, wave heights, and the direction of the waves. Some satellite sensors use microwave (radar) wavelengths to look through the "clouds" at the sea surface. One other important characteristic that we can see from space is the color of the ocean. Changes in color of ocean water over time or across a distance on the surface provide additional valuable information.

When we look at the ocean from space, we see many shades of blue. Using instruments that are more sensitive than the human eye, we can measure the subtle array of colors displayed by the global ocean. To skilled remote-sensing analysts and oceanographers, different ocean colors can reveal the presence and concentration of phytoplankton, sediments, and dissolved organic chemicals. Phytoplankton are small, single-celled ocean plants, smaller than the size of a pinhead. These tiny plants contain the chemical chlorophyll. Plants use chlorophyll to convert sunlight into food using a process called *photosynthesis*. Because different types of phytoplankton have different concentrations of chlorophyll, they appear as different colors

IMPORTANT DATA PROVIDED BY OCEAN REMOTE SENSING FROM SPACE

Sensor	Data	Science question	Application
Ocean-color sensor	Ocean color	Phytoplankton concentration; ocean currents; ocean surface temperature; pollution and sedimentation	Fishing productivity; ship routing; monitoring coastal pollution
Scatterometer	Wind speed; wind direction	Wave structure; currents; wind patterns	Ocean waves; ship routing; currents; ship, platform safety
Altimeter	Altitude of ocean surface; wave height; wind speed	El Niño onset and structure	Wave and current forecasting.
Microwave imager	Surface wind speed; ice edge; precipitation	Thickness, extent of ice cover; internal stress of ice; ice growth and ablation rates	Navigation information; ship routing; wave and surf forecasting
Microwave radiometer	Sea-surface temperature	Ocean-air interactions	Weather forecasting

Source: US. Congress, Office of Technology Assessment, 1994.

to sensitive satellite instruments. Therefore, looking at the color of an area of the ocean allows scientists to estimate the amount and general type of phytoplankton in that area, such information tells them about the health and chemistry of that portion of the ocean. Comparing images taken at different periods reveals any changes and trends in the health of the ocean that are occurring over time.

Why are phytoplankton so important? Besides acting as the first link in a typical oceanic food chain, phytoplankton are a critical part of ocean chemistry. Carbon dioxide in the atmosphere is in balance with carbon dioxide (CO_2) in the ocean. During photosynthesis, phytoplankton remove carbon dioxide from sea water and release oxygen as a by-product. This allows the oceans to absorb additional carbon dioxide from the atmosphere. If fewer phytoplankton existed, atmospheric carbon dioxide would increase.

Phytoplankton also affect carbon dioxide levels when they die. Phytoplankton, like plants on land, are composed of substances that contain carbon. Dead phytoplankton can sink to the ocean floor. The carbon in the phytoplankton is soon covered by other material sinking to the ocean bottom. In this way, the oceans serve as a reservoir (i.e., a place to dispose of global carbon), which otherwise would accumulate in the atmosphere as carbon dioxide.

Observation of the ocean from space with a variety of special instruments provides oceanographers and environmental scientists with very important data. The table summarizes some of the data that these satellite sensors can provide.

See also: MISSION TO PLANET EARTH; REMOTE SENSING.

oersted (symbol: Oe) The unit of magnetic field strength in the centimeter-gram-second (c.g.s.) system of units.

$$1 \text{ oersted} = 79.58 \text{ amperes/meter}$$

This unit is named in honor of Hans Christian Oersted (1777–1851), a Danish physicist who was first to demonstrate the relationship between electricity and magnetism.

O/F ratio With respect to liquid-propellant rocket engines, the mass flow rate of oxidizer (O) to the mass flow rate of fuel (F) at the time of combustion.

offgassing The emanation of volatile matter of any kind from materials.

off-line In aerospace operations, an activity conducted independent of the main launch vehicle or space vehicle activities. For example, an activity conducted independent of any element of the

Space Transportation System (i.e., the space shuttle). *Off-line integration* involves assembly of payload elements or multiple payloads in a way that does not involve any STS element (e.g., the orbiter vehicle).

ogive The tapered or curved front of a missile.

ohm (symbol: Ω) The unit of electrical resistance in the INTERNATIONAL SYSTEM OF UNITS. It is defined as the resistance (R) between two points on a conductor produced by a current flow (I) of one ampere when there is a constant voltage difference (potential) (V) of one volt between these points. From Ohm's law, the resistance in a conductor is related to the voltage and the current by the equation: R = V/I, so that, 1 ohm (W) of resistance = 1 volt per ampere. The unit and physical law are named in honor of the German physicist George Simon Ohm (1787–1854).

ohmmeter A direct-reading instrument for measuring electrical resistance. A simple ohmmeter consists of a power supply (battery), a meter movement calibrated in ohms, and a variable resistor.

Ohm's law Statement that the current (I) in a linear constant current electric circuit is inversely proportional to the resistance (R) of the circuit and directly proportional to the voltage difference (V) (i.e., the electromotive force) in the circuit. Expressed as an equation, V = I · R. First postulated by the German physicist George S. Ohm (1787–1854).
See also: OHM.

omni- A prefix meaning "all," as in *omnidirectional.*

one-g The downward acceleration of gravity at Earth's surface; at sea level, "one-g" corresponds to an acceleration of 9.8 meters per second per second (m/s^2), or about 32.1 per second per second (ft/s^2).
See also: G.

one-way communications Communications mode consisting only of downlink received from a spacecraft.

one-way light time (OWLT) Elapsed time (in units of light-seconds or light-minutes) for a radio signal to travel (one way) between Earth and a spacecraft or solar system body.

on-line 1. Operating, as distinct from dormant. 2. In aerospace operations, an activity that directly involves the launch vehicle or aerospace vehicle, especially as it is being prepared for flight; for example, *on-line integration* involves the mating payloads with the space shuttle orbiter, an expendable launch vehicle, or an upper stage vehicle. 3. In computer operations, a peripheral device, such as a printer, that is connected and ready to operate. 4. The application of databases that are accessible on or from computer resources; data or communications that are transmitted or made available through the use of computer resources and networks.

Oort Cloud A large number, or "cloud," of comets theorized to orbit the Sun at a distance of between 50,000 and 80,000 astronomical units (AU) (i.e., out to the limits of the Sun's gravitational attraction). First proposed in 1950 by the Dutch astronomer Jan Hendrik Oort (1900–92).

open loop A control system operating without feedback or perhaps with only partial feedback. An electrical or mechanical system in which the response of the output to an input is preset; there is no feedback of the output for comparison and corrective adjustment.

open orbit An orbit that does not return to its starting point; an escape orbit.
See also: ORBITS OF OBJECTS IN SPACE.

open system In thermodynamics, a system as defined by a control volume in space across whose boundaries energy and mass can flow. Compare with CLOSED SYSTEM.

open universe The open or unbounded universe model in cosmology assumes that there is not enough matter in the universe to halt completely (by gravitational attraction) the currently observed expansion of the galaxies. Therefore, the galaxies will continue to move away from each other and the expansion of the universe (which started with the "Big Bang") will continue forever.
See also: "BIG BANG" THEORY.

operating life The maximum operating time (or number of cycles) that an item can accrue before replacement or refurbishment without risk of degradation of performance beyond acceptable limits.

operating pressure Nominal pressure to which the fluid-system components are subjected under steady-state conditions in service operations.

operational deflections Deflections imposed on a structure during engine operation or flight (e.g., by thrust vector gimballing, thermal differential, flight accelerations, and mechanical vibration).

operational missile A missile that has been accepted by the armed services for tactical and/or strategic application.

operational pressure transients Rises in operating pressure (due to rapid startup or shutdown, or water hammer) with sufficient duration to be felt as loads on the system or structure.

operations planning Performing those tasks that must be done to ensure that the launch vehicle systems and ground-based flight control operations support flight objectives. Consumables analyses and the preparation of flight rules are a part of operations planning.

operator 1. In aero space engineering, a device that causes an actuator to function. 2. In mathematics, a symbol that specifies a certain operation should be carried out; for example, the operator $\sqrt{}$ in the expression $\sqrt{}$ a indicates that the square root of a should be taken.

opposition In astronomy, the alignment of a superior planet (e.g., Mars, Jupiter, etc.) with the Sun so that they appear to an observer on Earth to be in opposite parts of the sky; that is, the planetary object has a celestial longitude differing from that of the Sun by 180 degrees. More simply put, these bodies lie in a straight line with Earth in the middle. Compare with CONJUNCTION.

optimum height of burst For nuclear weapons, the optimum height of burst for a particular target (or area) is that at which it is estimated a weapon of a specific energy yield will produce a certain desired effect over the maximum possible area.

optoelectronic device A device that combines optical (light) and electronic technologies, such as a fiber optics communications system.

orbit 1. In physics, the region occupied by an electron as it moves around the nucleus of an atom. 2. In astronomy and space science, the path followed by a satellite around an astronomical body, such as Earth or the Moon. When a body is moving around a primary body, such as Earth, under the influence of gravitational force alone, the path it takes is called its orbit. If a spacecraft is traveling along a closed path with respect to the primary body, its orbit will be a circle or an ellipse. Perfectly circular orbits are not achieved in practice. However, the ellipse approaches a circle when the eccentricity becomes small (i.e., approaches zero). The planets, for example, have the Sun as their primary body and follow nearly circular orbits. When a satellite makes a full trip around its primary body, it is said to complete a *revolution,* and the time required is called its *period* or the *period of revolution.*
See also: ORBITS OF OBJECTS IN SPACE.

orbital Taking place in orbit, as *orbital refueling;* or pertaining to an orbit, as *orbital plane.*

orbital elements A set of six parameters used to specify a Keplerian orbit and the position of a satellite in such an orbit at a particular time. These six parameters are: semimajor axis (a), which gives the size of the orbit; eccentricity (e), which gives the shape of the orbit; inclination angle (i), which gives the angle of the orbit plane with respect to the central (primary) body's equator; right ascension of the ascending node (Ω), which gives the rotation of the orbit plane from the reference axis; argument of perigee (Ω) which is the angle from the line of the ascending node to perigee point, measured along the orbit in the direction of the satellite's motion; and true anomaly (θ), which gives the location of the satellite on the orbit.
See also: KEPLERIAN ELEMENTS.

orbital injection The process of providing a space vehicle with sufficient velocity to establish an orbit.

orbital maneuvering system (OMS) Two orbital maneuvering engines, located in external pods on each side of the aft fuselage of the space shuttle orbiter structure, which provide thrust for orbit insertion, orbit change, orbit transfer, rendezvous and docking, and deorbit. Each pod contains a high-pressure helium storage bottle, the tank, pressurization regulators and controls, a fuel tank, an oxidizer tank, and a pressure-fed regeneratively cooled rocket engine. Each OMS engine develops a vacuum thrust of 27 kilonewtons (6,000 pounds-force (lbf)) and uses a hypergolic propellant combination of nitrogen tetroxide and monomethyl hydrazine. These propellants are burned at a nominal oxidizer-to-fuel mixture ratio of 1.65 and a chamber pressure of 860 kilonewtons per square meter (kN/m^2) [125 pounds-force per square inch (psi)]. The system can provide a velocity change of 305 meters per second (1,000 feet per second) when the orbiter carries a payload of 29,500 kilograms (65,000 pounds-mass [lbm]).

See also: SPACE TRANSPORTATION SYSTEM (STS).

orbital period The interval between successive passages of a satellite or spacecraft through the same point in its orbit. Often called *period*.

See also: ORBITS OF OBJECTS IN SPACE.

orbital plane The imaginary plane that contains the orbit of a satellite and passes through the center of the primary (i.e., celestial body being orbited). The angle of inclination (θ) is defined as the angle between Earth's equatorial plane and the orbital plane of the satellite.

See also: ORBITS OF OBJECTS IN SPACE.

orbital replacement unit (ORU) The lowest level of component or subsystem hardware or software that can be replaced in orbit.

orbital transfer vehicle (OTV) A propulsion system used to transfer a payload from one orbital location to another—as, for example, from LOW EARTH ORBIT (LEO) to geostationary Earth orbit (GEO). Orbital-transfer vehicles can be expendable or reusable; many involve chemical, nuclear, or electric propulsion systems. An expendable orbital transfer vehicle frequently is referred to as an upper-stage unit, while a reusable OTV is sometimes called a space tug. OTVs can be designed to move people and cargo between different destinations in cislunar space.

See also: UPPER STAGE.

orbital velocity The average velocity at which a satellite, spacecraft, or other orbiting body travels around its primary.

orbit determination The process of describing the past, present, or predicted (i.e., future) position of a satellite or other orbiting body in terms of its orbital parameters.

orbiter 1. Class of space exploration missions, involving the insertion of a space vehicle into orbit around another celestial body, as, for example, the Mars Global Surveyor mission; the spacecraft inserted into orbit around another celestial body. *See also:* ORBITER SPACECRAFT. 2. The reusable, aerospace vehicle used by the astronauts during space shuttle missions, as in the space shuttle orbiter vehicle.

See also: SPACE TRANSPORTATION SYSTEM (STS).

orbiter spacecraft A spacecraft especially designed to travel to a distant planet and then to orbit around that planet and conduct a program of scientific investigation. Unlike a flyby spacecraft, an orbiter spacecraft must have substantial propulsive capability to decelerate at just the right moment and thereby achieve orbit insertion around the target planet. This type of spacecraft, also must be designed to accommodate the fact that while it is orbiting the target planet, numerous solar occultations will occur (i.e., the spacecraft will be in the planet's shadow), cutting off the production of electric power by the solar panels and subjecting the vehicle to extreme thermal variations. Frequent Earth occultations also will occur, cutting off uplink and downlink communications with the mission control team on Earth. Orbiter spacecraft, such as the Mars Global Surveyor, represent the next phase of solar system exploration, following up the initial reconnaissance (flyby) missions with detailed study of the planets.

See also: MARS GLOBAL SURVEYOR.

orbit inclination The angle between an orbital plane and Earth's equatorial plane.

See also: ORBITS OF OBJECTS IN SPACE.

Orbiting Astronomical Observatory (OAO) A series of large astronomical observatories developed by NASA in the late 1960s to significantly broaden our understanding of the universe. The first successful large observatory placed in Earth orbit was the *Orbiting Astronomical Observatory 2 (OAO-2)*, nicknamed *Stargazer*, which was launched on December 7, 1968. In its first 30 days of operation, *OAO-2* collected more than 20 times the celestial ultraviolet (UV) data than had been acquired in the previous 15 years of sounding rocket launches. *Stargazer* also observed Nova Serpentis for 60 days after its outburst in 1970. These observations confirmed that mass loss by the nova was consistent with theory. NASA's Orbiting Astronomical Observatory 3 (OAO-3), named *Copernicus* in honor of the famous Polish astronomer, was launched successfully on August 21, 1972. This satellite provided much new data on stellar temperatures, chemical compositions, and other properties. It also gathered data on the BLACK HOLE candidate Cygnus X-1, so named because it was the first X-ray source discovered in the constellation Cygnus.

Orbiting Geophysical Observatory (OGO). A series of six NASA scientific spacecraft placed in Earth-orbit between 1961 and 1965. At the beginning of the U.S. civilian space program, data from the Orbiting Geophysical Observatory (OGO) spacecraft made significant contributions to an initial understanding of the near-Earth space environment and Sun-Earth interrelationships. For example, they provided the first evidence of a region of low-energy electrons enveloping the high-energy VAN ALLEN RADIATION BELT region.

orbiting laser power station A large orbiting system that collects incoming solar radiation and concentrates it to operate a direct solar-pumped laser. The orbiting facility then directs the beam from this solar-pumped laser to a suitable collection facility (e.g., on the lunar surface), where photovoltaic converters tuned to the laser wavelength produce electric power with an efficiency of perhaps 50%. Figure 88 shows one scheme for the proposed orbiting laser power station. A nearly parabolic solar collector, with a radius of about 300 meters, captures sunlight and directs it, in a line focus, onto a 10-meter-long laser, with an average concentration of several thousand solar constants. (A solar constant is the total amount of the Sun's radiant energy that crosses normal to a unit area at the top of Earth's atmosphere. At one astronomical unit from the Sun a solar constant is about 1371 ± 5 watts per meter squared [(W/m^2].) An organic iodide gas lasant flows through the laser, circulated by a turbine-compressor combination. (A lasant is a chemical substance that supports stimulated light emission in a laser.) The hot lasant then is cooled and purified at the radiator. New lasant is added from the supply tanks to make up for the small amount of lasant lost in each pass through

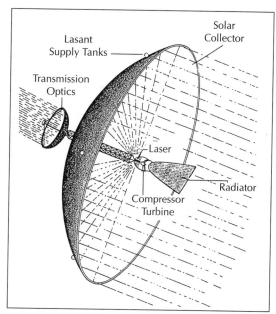

Figure 88. Proposed 1 megawatt-class solar-pumped iodine laser orbiting power station *(Drawing courtesy of NASA)*

the laser. Power from the laser then is spread and focused by a combination of transmission mirrors to provide a one-meter-diameter spot at distances up to 10,000 kilometers (6,200 miles) away or more.

Orbiting Quarantine Facility (OQF) A proposed Earth-orbiting laboratory in which soil and rock samples from other worlds—for example, Martian soil and rock specimens—could first be tested and examined for potentially harmful alien microorganisms, before the specimens are allowed to enter Earth's biosphere. A space-based quarantine facility provides several distinct advantages: (1) it eliminates the possibility of a sample-return spacecraft's crashing and accidentally releasing its potentially deadly cargo of alien microorganisms; (2) it guarantees that any alien organisms which might escape from the orbiting laboratory's confinement facilities cannot immediately enter Earth's biosphere; and (3) it ensures that all quarantine workers remain in total isolation during protocol testing of the alien soil and rock samples. Three hypothetical results of such protocol testing are: (1) no replicating alien organisms are discovered; (2) replicating alien organisms are discovered, but they are also found not to be a threat to terrestrial life-forms; or (3) hazardous replicating alien life-forms are discovered. If potentially harmful replicating alien organisms were discovered during these protocol tests, then orbiting quarantine facility workers would: render the sample harmless (e.g., through heat- and chemical-sterilization procedures); retain it under very carefully controlled conditions in the orbiting complex and perform more detailed studies on the alien life-forms; or properly dispose of the sample before the alien life-forms could enter Earth's biosphere and infect terrestrial life-forms.

See also: EXTRATERRESTRIAL CONTAMINATION.

Orbiting Solar Observatory (OSO) A series of eight NASA Earth-orbiting scientific satellites that were used to study the Sun from space, with emphasis on its electromagnetic radiation emissions in the range from ultraviolet to gamma rays. These scientific observatories were launched between 1962 and 1975. They acquired an enormous quantity of important solar data during an 11-year solar cycle, when solar activity went from low to high and then back to low again.

See also: SUN.

orbits of objects in space We must know about the science and mechanics of orbits to launch, control, and track spacecraft and to predict the motion of objects in space. An *orbit* is the path in space along which an object moves around a primary body. Common examples of orbits include Earth's path around its celestial primary (the Sun) and the Moon's path around Earth (its primary body). A single orbit is a complete path around a primary as viewed from space. It differs from a revolution. A

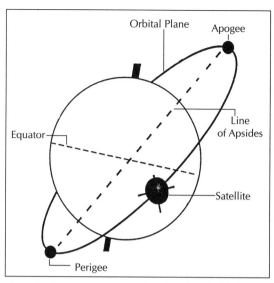

Figure 90. The terms *apogee* and *perigee* described in terms of a satellite's orbit around Earth   *(Drawing courtesy of NASA)*

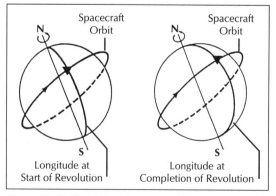

Figure 89. An illustration of a spacecraft's west-to-east orbit around the Earth and how the Earth's west-to-east rotation moves longitude ahead. As shown here, the period of one revolution can be longer than the orbital period.   *(Courtesy of NASA)*

single *revolution* is accomplished whenever an orbiting object passes over the primary's longitude or latitude from which it started. For example, the space shuttle *Columbia* completed a revolution whenever it passed over approximately 80 degrees west longitude on Earth. However, while *Columbia* was orbiting from west to east around the globe, Earth itself was also rotating from west to east. Consequently, *Columbia*'s period of time for one revolution actually was longer than its orbital period. (See Figure 89.) If, on the other hand, *Columbia* were orbiting from east to west (not a practical flight path from a propulsion-economy standpoint), then because of Earth's west-to-east spin, its period of revolution would be shorter than its orbital period. An east-to-west orbit is called a *retrograde orbit* around Earth; a west-to-east orbit is called a *posigrade orbit*. If *Columbia* were traveling in a north-south orbit, or *polar orbit*, it would complete a period of revolution whenever it passed over the latitude from which it started. Its orbital period would be about the same as the revolution period, but not identical, because Earth actually wobbles slightly north and south.

Other terms are used to describe orbital motion. The *apoapsis* is the farthest distance in an orbit from the primary; the *periapsis,* the shortest. For orbits around planet Earth, the comparable terms are *apogee* and *perigee*. The *line of apsides* is the line connecting the two points of an orbit that are nearest and farthest from the center of attraction, as the perigee and apogee of a satellite in orbit around the Earth. (See Figure 90.)

For objects orbiting the Sun, *aphelion* describes the point on an orbit farthest from the Sun; *perihelion*, the point nearest to the Sun.

Another term we frequently encounter is the *orbital plane.* An Earth satellite's orbital plane can be visualized by thinking of its orbit as the outer edge of a giant, flat plate that cuts Earth in half. This imaginary plate is called the orbital plane.

Inclination is another orbital parameter. This term refers to the number of degrees the orbit is inclined away from the equator. The inclination also indicates how far north and south a spacecraft will travel in its orbit around Earth. If, for example, a spacecraft has an inclination of 56 degrees, it will travel around Earth as far north as 56 degrees north latitude and as far south as 56 degrees south latitude. Because of Earth's rotation, it will not, however, pass over the same areas of Earth on each orbit. A spacecraft in a polar orbit has an inclination of about 90 degrees. As such, this spacecraft orbits Earth traveling alternately in north and south directions. A polar-orbiting satellite eventually passes over the entire Earth because Earth is rotating from west to east beneath it. The LANDSAT spacecraft is an example of a spacecraft whose cameras and multispectral sensors observe the entire Earth from a nearly polar orbit, providing valuable information about the terrestrial environment and resource base.

A satellite in an equatorial orbit around Earth has zero inclination. The Intelsat communications satellites are examples of satellites in equatorial orbits. By their placement into near-circular equatorial orbits at just the right distance above Earth, these spacecraft can be made essentially to "stand still" over a point on Earth's equator. Such satellites are called *geostationary.* They are in *synchronous orbits,* meaning they take as long to complete an orbit around Earth as it takes for Earth to complete one rotation about its axis (i.e., approximately 24 hours). A satellite at the same "synchronous" altitude but in an inclined orbit also may be called synchronous. While this particular spacecraft would not move much east and west, it would move north and south over Earth to the latitudes indicated by its inclination. The terrestrial ground track of such a spacecraft resembles an elongated figure eight, with the crossover point on the equator.

All orbits are elliptical, in accordance with Kepler's first law of planetary motion (described shortly). However, a spacecraft generally is considered to be in a circular orbit if it is in an orbit that is nearly circular. A spacecraft is taken to be in an elliptical orbit when its apogee and perigee differ substantially.

Two sets of scientific laws govern the motions of both celestial objects and human-made spacecraft. One is Newton's law of gravitation; the other, Kepler's laws of planetary motion.

The brilliant English scientist and mathematician Sir Isaac Newton (1642–1727) observed the following physical principles:

1. All bodies attract each other with what we call gravitational attraction. This applies to the largest celestial objects and to the smallest particles of matter.
2. The strength of one object's gravitational pull upon another is a function of its mass—that is, the amount of matter present.
3. The closer two bodies are to each other, the greater their mutual attraction.

These observations can be stated mathematically as:

$$F = \frac{G\, m_1\, m_2}{r^2}$$

where F is the gravitational force acting along the line joining the two bodies (N); m_1, m_2 are the masses (in kilograms) of body one and body two, respectively; r is the distance between the two bodies (m); and G is the universal gravitational constant (6.6732×10^{-11} newton-meter^2/kilogram^2)

Specifically, Newton's law of gravitation states that two bodies attract each other in proportion to the product of their masses and inversely as the square of the distance between them. This physical principle is very important in launching spacecraft and guiding them to their operational locations in space and frequently is used by astronomers to estimate the masses of celestial objects. For example, Newton's law of gravitation tells us that for a spacecraft to stay in orbit, its velocity (and therefore its kinetic energy) must balance the gravitational attraction of the primary object being orbited. Consequently, a satellite needs more velocity in low than in high orbit. For example, a spacecraft with an orbital altitude of 250 kilometers (km) (150 miles [mi]) will have an orbital speed of about 28,000 (km) (17,500 mi) per hour.

Our Moon, on the other hand, which is about 442,170 km (238,857 mi) from Earth, has an orbital velocity of approximately 3,660 km (2,287 mi) per hour. Of course, to boost a payload from the surface of Earth to a high-altitude (versus low-attitude) orbit requires the expenditure of more energy, since we are in effect lifting the object farther out of Earth's "gravity well."

Any spacecraft launched into orbit moves in accordance with the same laws of motion that govern the motions of the planets around our Sun and the motion of the Moon around Earth. The three laws that describe these planetary motions, first formulated by the German astronomer Johannes Kepler (1571–1630), may be stated as follows:

1. Each planet revolves around the Sun in an orbit that is an ellipse, with the Sun as it focus, or primary body.
2. The radius vector—such as the line from the center of the Sun to the center of a planet, from the center of Earth to the center of the Moon, or from the center of Earth to the center (of gravity) of an orbiting spacecraft—sweeps out equal areas in equal periods of time.
3. The square of a planet's orbital period is equal to the cube of its mean distance from the Sun. We can generalize this last statement and extend it to spacecraft in orbit about Earth by saying that a spacecraft's orbital period increases with its mean distance from the planet.

In formulating his first law of planetary motion, Kepler recognized that purely circular orbits did not really exist—rather, only elliptical ones were found in nature, being determined by gravitational pertubations (disturbances) and other factors. Gravitational attractions, according to Newton's law of gravitation, extend to infinity, although these forces weaken with distance and eventually become impossible to detect. However, spacecraft orbiting Earth, while influenced primarily by the gravitational attraction of Earth (and anomalies in Earth's gravitational field), also are influenced also by the Moon and the Sun and possibly other celestial objects, such as the planet Jupiter.

Kepler's third law of planetary motion states that the greater a body's mean orbital altitude, the longer it will take for it to go around its primary. Let's take this principle and apply it to a rendezvous maneuver between a space shuttle orbiter and a satellite in LOW EARTH ORBIT (LEO). To catch up with and retrieve an uncrewed spacecraft in the same orbit, the space shuttle first must be decelerated. This action causes the orbiter vehicle to descend to a lower orbit. In this lower orbit, the shuttle's velocity would increase. When properly positioned in the vicinity of the target satellite, the orbiter then would be accelerated, raising its orbit and matching orbital velocities for the rendezvous maneuver with the target spacecraft.

Another very interesting and useful orbital phenomenon is the Earth satellite that appears to "stand still" in space with respect to a point on Earth's equator. Such satellites were first envisioned by the English scientist and writer Arthur C. Clarke (1917–), in a 1945 essay in *Wireless World*. Clarke described a system in which satellites carrying telephone and television would circle Earth at an orbital altitude of approximately 35,580 km (22,240 mi) above the equator. Such spacecraft move around Earth at the same rate that the Earth rotates on its own axis. Therefore, they neither rise nor set in the sky like the planets and the Moon but rather always appear to be at the same longitude, synchronized with Earth's motion. At the equator, Earth rotates about 1,600 km (1,000 mi) per hour. Satellites placed in this type of orbit are called *geostationary* or *geosynchronous* spacecraft.

It is interesting to note here that the spectacular Voyager missions to Jupiter, Saturn, and beyond used a "gravity-assist" technique to help speed them up and shorten their travel time. How can a spacecraft can be speeded up while traveling past a planet? A spacecraft increases in speed as it approaches a planet (due to gravitational attraction), but the gravity of the planet also should slow it down as it begins to move away again. So where does this increase in speed really come from?

There are three basic possibilities for a spacecraft trajectory when it encounters a planet. (See Figure 91.) The first possible trajectory involves a direct hit or hard landing. This is an *impact trajectory*. (See trajectory a.) The second type of trajectory is an *orbital-capture trajectory*. The spacecraft is simply "captured" by the gravitational field of the planet and enters orbit around it. (See trajectories b and c.) Depending on its precise speed and altitude (and other parameters), the spacecraft can enter this captured orbit from either the leading or trailing edge of the planet. In the third type of trajectory, a *flyby trajectory*, the spacecraft remains far enough away from the planet to avoid capture but passes close enough to be strongly affected by its gravity. In this case, the speed of the spacecraft will be increased if it approaches from the trailing side of the planet

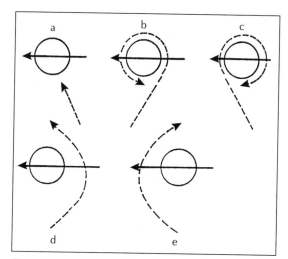

Figure 91. Possible trajectories of a spacecraft encountering a planet   *(Drawing by NASA—modified by author)*

of the Sun and with asymptotic velocity (V_a). The heliocentric arrival velocity (V_1) is then computed by vector addition:

$$V_1 = V_j + V_a$$

The spacecraft departs Jupiter in a new direction, determined by the amount of bending that is caused by the effects of the gravitational attraction of Jupiter's mass on the mass of the spacecraft. The asymptotic departure speed (V_d) on the hyperbola is equal to the arrival speed. Thus, the length of V_a equals the length of V_d. For the heliocentric departure velocity, $V_2 = V_j + V_d$. This vector sum is also depicted in Figure 92.

During the relatively short period of time that the spacecraft is near Jupiter, the orbital velocity of

(see trajectory d) and diminished if it approaches from the leading side (see trajectory e). In addition to changes in speed, the direction of the spacecraft's motion also changes.

Thus the increase in speed of the spacecraft actually comes from a decrease in speed of the planet itself. In effect, the spacecraft is being "pulled" by the planet. Of course, this has been a greatly simplified discussion of complex encounter phenomena. A full account of spacecraft trajectories must consider the speed and actual trajectory of the spacecraft and planet, how close the spacecraft will come to the planet, and the size (mass) and speed of the planet in order to make even a simple calculation.

Perhaps an even better understanding of gravity assist can be obtained if we use vectors in a more mathematical explanation. The way in which speed is added to the flyby spacecraft during close encounters with the planet Jupiter is shown in Figure 92. During the time that spacecraft, such as *Voyager 1* and *2*, were near Jupiter, the heliocentric (Sun-centered) path they followed in their motion with respect to Jupiter closely approximated a hyperbola.

The heliocentric velocity of the spacecraft is the vector sum of the orbital velocity of Jupiter (V_j) and the velocity of the spacecraft with respect to Jupiter (i.e., tangent to its trajectory—the hyperbola). The spacecraft moves toward Jupiter along an asymptote, approaching from the approximate direction

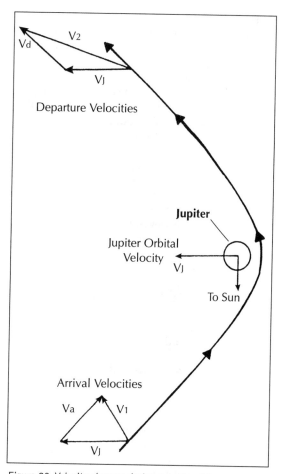

Figure 92. Velocity changes during a Jupiter flyby   *(Drawing courtesy of NASA)*

Jupiter (V_j) changes very little, and we assume that V_j is equal to a constant.

The vector sums in Figure 116 illustrate that the deflection, or bending, of the spacecraft's trajectory caused by Jupiter's gravity results in an increase in the speed of the spacecraft along its hyperbolic path, as measured relative to the Sun. This increase in velocity reduces the total flight time necessary to reach Saturn and points beyond. This "indirect" type of deep-space mission to the outer planets saves two or three years of flight time when compared to "direct-trajectory" missions, which do not take advantage of gravity assist.

Of course, while the spacecraft gains speed during its Jovian encounter, Jupiter loses some of its speed. However, because of the extreme difference in their masses, the change in Jupiter's velocity is negligible.

orbit trim maneuvers Small changes in a spacecraft's orbit around a planet for the purpose of adjusting an instrument's field-of-view footprint, improving sensitivity of a gravity field survey, or preventing too much orbital decay. To make a change increasing the altitude of periapsis ("perigee" for an Earth-orbiting satellite), an orbit trim maneuver (OTM) would be designed to increase the spacecraft's velocity when it is at apoapsis (or "apogee" for an Earth-orbiting satellite). To decrease the apoapsis altitude, an OTM would be performed at periapsis, reducing the spacecraft's velocity. Slight changes in the orbital plane's orientation also can be made with orbit trim maneuvers. However, the magnitude of such changes is necessarily small due to the limited amount of "maneuver" propellant typically carried by a spacecraft.

order of magnitude A value expressed to the nearest power of ten; for example, a cluster containing 925 stars would be said to have approximately 1,000 stars in an "order-of-magnitude" estimate.

ordnance train A network of small explosive charges.

O-ring Sealing ring with a circular cross section, which may be either hollow or solid; generally made of elastomer or plastic but also can be metal.

orthogonal At right angles; pertaining to or composed of right angles.

oscillation 1. Fluctuation or vibration on each side of a mean value or position 2. The variation, usually with time, of the magnitude of a quantity with respect to a specific reference when the magnitude is alternately greater and smaller than the reference.

oscillatory combustion Unstable combustion in a rocket engine or motor, characterized by pressure oscillations.

oscilloscope 1. An instrument for producing a visual representation of the variation (oscillation) of a parameter, such as current or voltage. 2. Specifically, a cathode ray oscilloscope.

ounce (symbol: oz) 1. A unit of mass in the U.S. Standard System equal to 1/16th of a pound. 1 ounce (oz) = 0.02833 kilogram. 2. A unit of (fluid) volume in the U.S. Standard System equal to 1/16th of a pint. 1 fluid ounce (oz) = 0.0296 liters.

outer planets The planets in the solar system with orbits greater than the orbit of Mars. These are Jupiter, Saturn, Uranus, Neptune, and Pluto. Of these outer planets, all except Pluto also are called the *giant planets*.

outer space A general term referring to any region beyond Earth's atmospheric envelope. By informal international agreement, outer space usually is considered to begin at between 100 and 200 kilometers (km) (60 to 120 miles [mi]) altitude. Within the U.S. aerospace program, persons who have traveled beyond about 80 km altitude (50 mi) often are recognized as space travelers or astronauts.

outgassing Release of gas from a material when it is exposed to an ambient pressure lower than the vapor pressure of the gas. Generally refers to the gradual release of gas from enclosed surfaces when an enclosure is vacuum pumped or to the gradual release of gas from a spacecraft's surfaces and components when they are first exposed to the vacuum conditions of outer space following launch. Outgassing presents a problem to spacecraft designers because the released vapor might recondense on optical surfaces (instruments) or other special spacecraft surfaces where these unwanted material depositions can then degrade performance of the component or sensor. Aerospace engineers try to avoid such outgassing problems by carefully selecting the materials used in the spacecraft. In addition, certain (outgassing-prone) components also can be placed through a lengthy thermal vacuum ("bake-out") treatment to remove unwanted substances prior to final installation and launch.

output 1. The yield or product of an activity furnished by a person, a machine, or a system. 2. Power or energy delivered by an engine, generator, or the like. 3. The electrical signal coming out of a transducer; usually a function of the applied stimulus. Compare with INPUT.

overexpanding nozzle A nozzle in which the working fluid is expanded to a lower pressure than the external pressure; that is, an overexpanding nozzle has an exit area larger than the optimum exit area for the particular external pressure environment. For example, a nozzle designed to operate in space (where the ambient or external pressure is essentially zero) would overexpand the rocket's exhaust gases, if that particular rocket engine-nozzle configuration were used in Earth's atmosphere, where the ambient pressure is greater than the vacuum conditions found in space.

See also: NOZZLE.

overpressure The pressure resulting from the blast wave of an explosion. It is referred to as "positive" when it exceeds atmospheric pressure and "negative" during the passage of the wave when resulting pressures are less than atmospheric pressure.

override Generally means one function prevails over or preempts another function. The prevailing function is regarded as having more importance with respect to the aerospace mission. This is especially true for safety-related functions, which generally should "override" all other activities or functions.

oxidizer Material whose main function is to supply oxygen or other oxidizing materials for deflagration (burning) of a solid propellant or combustion of a liquid fuel.

pad The platform from which a rocket vehicle is launched.

See also: LAUNCHPAD.

pad deluge Water sprayed upon certain launch pads during the launch of a rocket so as to reduce the temperatures of critical parts of the pad or the rocket.

pair production The gamma ray interaction process in which a high-energy [> 1.02 million electron volts (MeV)] photon is annihilated in the vicinity of the nucleus of an absorbing atom with the simultaneous formation of a negative and positive electron (positron) pair.

pallet An unpressurized platform designed for installation in the space shuttle orbiter's cargo bay for mounting instruments and equipment that require direct space exposure.

See also: SPACELAB; SPACE TRANSPORTATION SYSTEM.

pallet train More than one pallet rigidly connected to form a single unit in the space shuttle orbiterís cargo bay. Used for mounting instruments and equipment that require direct space exposure.

See also: SPACELAB; SPACE TRANSPORTATION SYSTEM.

parabolic Pertaining to, or shaped like, a *parabola*. A parabola is a conic section with an eccentricity (*e*) equal to unity (i.e., *e* = 1). If a parabola is symmetrical about the x-axis and has its vertex at the origin, then it is defined by the equation: $y^2 = 4ax$, where a is the distance from the vertex to the focus and 4a is the length of the latus rectum.

See also: CONIC.

parabolic antenna A radio reflector used for radar, microwave, and space communications. In receivers, the parabolic reflecting surface concentrates parallel beams on to a single focus point, where the active element of the antenna is located. In transmitters, the parabolic reflecting surface converts the source signal into a parallel beam that then is projected outward.

parabolic orbit An orbit shaped like a parabola; the orbit representing the least eccentricity for escape from an attracting body.

See also: ORBITS OF OBJECTS IN SPACE.

parabolic reflector A reflecting surface having a cross section along the axis in the shape of a parabola. Incoming parallel rays striking the reflector are brought to a focus point, or if the source of the rays is located at the focus, the rays are reflected as a parallel beam. Also called *parabolic effect*.

See also: CONIC; PARABOLIC.

parachute recovery system With respect to the U.S. Space Transportation System (STS), a component of the space shuttle solid rocket booster (SRB). This system (pilot, drogue, and main parachutes) is designed to permit the recovery of the spent (used) solid rocket boosters (SRBs) by gently returning them to an ocean impact area where they can be recovered for refurbishing and subsequent reuse.

See also: SPACE TRANSPORTATION SYSTEM.

parallax In general, the difference in the apparent position of an object when viewed from two different points. Specifically, the angular displacement in the apparent position of a celestial body when observed from two widely separated points (e.g.,

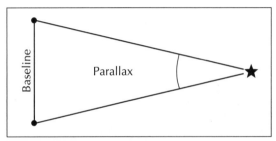

Figure 93. The concept of parallax. (Note: dimensions shown are not to scale, since angle involved in parallax measurement is very small—typically, arc seconds.) *(Drawing courtesy of NASA—modified by author)*

when Earth is at the extremities of its orbit around the Sun). This difference is very small and expressed as an angle, usually in arc seconds (where 1 arc second = 1/3,600 of a degree). (See Figure 93.)
See also: ASTROMETRY; PARSEC.

parking orbit An orbit of a spacecraft around a celestial body, used for assembly and/or transfer of components (e.g., the rendezvous and docking of a lander spacecraft with its mothership) or to wait for conditions favorable for departure from that orbit.

parsec (symbol: pc) A unit of distance frequently encountered in astronomical studies. The parsec is defined as a parallax shift of one second of arc. The term itself is a shortened from of "parallax second." The parsec is the extraterrestrial distance at which the main radius of Earth's orbit (one astronomical unit [AU] by definition) subtends an angle of one arc-second. It is therefore also the distance at which a star would exhibit an annual parallax of one arc-second.

$$1 \text{ parsec} = 3.2616 \text{ light-years (or } 206,265 \text{ AU)}$$

The kiloparsec (kpc) represents a distance of 1,000 parsecs (or 3,261.6 light-years); and the megaparsec (Mpc), a distance of 1 million parsecs (or about 3.262 million light-years).
See also: PARALLAX.

part One of the constituents into which a thing may be divided. Applicable to a major assembly, subassembly, or smallest individual piece of a given thing.

partial pressure In general, the pressure exerted by a designated component or components of a gaseous mixture; as, for example, the partial pressure of carbon dioxide (CO_2) in the atmosphere. In the atmosphere, the partial pressure of CO_2 is defined as the pressure the CO_2 would exert if all other gases were removed. The sum of the partial pressure of all the atmospheric gases then equals the atmospheric pressure. The partial pressure of CO_2 in the atmosphere is determined by the atmospheric CO_2 concentration and the atmospheric temperature.
See also: DALTON LAW.

particle A minute constituent of matter, generally one with a measurable mass. An elementary atomic particle such as a proton, neutron, electron (beta particle), or alpha particle.

particle accelerator A device that accelerates charged nuclear and subnuclear particles by means of changing electromagnetic fields. Accelerators impart energies of millions of electron volts (MeV) and higher to particles, such as protons or electrons. Accelerators used in nuclear physics research have achieved energy levels of over 10^{12} electron volts. Accelerators useful in a BALLISTIC MISSILE DEFENSE (BMD) role, such as neutral particle beam (NPB) accelerators and free electron laser (FEL) devices, need only achieve particle energies of between 10^8 and 10^9 electron volts but generally require much higher beam currents.

particle beam A focused, collimated stream of nuclear or subnuclear particles (e.g., protons, electrons, or alpha particles) that have been accelerated to high velocities (often a considerable portion of the speed of light).

pascal (symbol: Pa) The SI UNIT of pressure. It is defined as the pressure that results from a force of one newton (N) acting uniformly over an area of 1 square meter.

$$1 \text{ pascal [Pa]} = 1 \text{ N/m}^2$$

This unit is named after the French scientist Blaise Pascal (1623–1662).

pass 1. A single circuit of Earth (or a planet) by a spacecraft or satellite. Passes start at the time the satellite crosses the equator from the Southern Hemisphere into the Northern Hemisphere (the ascending node). 2. The period of time a satellite or spacecraft is within telemetry range of a ground station.

passive Containing no power sources to augment output power or signal, such as a *passive electrical network* or a *passive reflector.* Applied to a device that draws all its power from the input signal. A dormant device or system, that is, one that is not active.

passive defense Measures taken to reduce the probability and to minimize the effects of damage caused by hostile action without the intention of taking the initiative (e.g., short of launching a preemptive first strike). Compare with ACTIVE DEFENSE.

passive discrimination Discrimination of decoys from real targets by observing infrared, optical, or other emissions from the object. In ballistic missile defense (BMD), for example, passive infrared observations of threat objects may be made in an attempt to discriminate between reentry vehicles and simple decoys. Infrared sensors in the defensive system would depend on the characteristic emissions of the hostile objects (real and decoy) to determine their actual nature. The more sophisticated the decoy objects become, the less valuable becomes passive discrimination in an actual defensive system. However, if an enemy is forced to expend considerable resources in making a decoy "look" real, then (relatively inexpensive) passive discrimination techniques can provide some overall resource expenditure advantage to the defense.
See also: BALLISTIC MISSILE DEFENSE.

passive homing The guidance (homing) of an aircraft, missile, aerospace vehicle, or spacecraft wherein the craft directs itself toward the target by means of electromagnetic waves or signals emitted by the target itself. For example, a heat-seeking missile would aim toward an enemy aircraft by "homing" in on the thermal signature of the engine exhaust. Compare with ACTIVE HOMING GUIDANCE.
See also: GUIDANCE SYSTEM.

passive homing guidance A system of homing guidance wherein the receiver in the missile uses radiation from the target. Compare with ACTIVE HOMING GUIDANCE.
See also: GUIDANCE SYSTEM.

passive satellite A satellite that does not transmit a signal. This type of "silent" human-made space object could be a dormant (but still functional) replacement satellite, a retired or decommissioned satellite, a satellite that has failed prematurely (and is now a piece of "space junk"), or possibly even a silent, stalking space mine.

passive sensor A sensor that detect radiation naturally emitted by (e.g., infrared) or reflected (e.g., sunlight) from a target.

passive target A "target" orbital payload or satellite that is stabilized along its three axes and is detected, acquired, and tracked by means of electromagnetic energy reflected from the target's surface (or skin).

path 1. Of a satellite or spacecraft, the projection of the orbital plane on Earth's surface. Since Earth is turning under the satellite, the path of a single orbital pass will not be a closed curve. The terms "path" and "track" are used interchangeably. On a cylindrical map projection, a satellite's path is a sine-shaped curve. 2. Of an aircraft or aerospace vehicle, the flight path. 3. Of a meteor, the projection of the trajectory on the celestial sphere as seen by an observer.
See also: GROUNDTRACK; ORBITS OF OBJECTS IN SPACE.

Patriot The U.S. Army's Patriot missile system provides high- and medium-altitude defense against aircraft and tactical ballistic missiles. The combat element of the Patriot missile system is the fire unit, which consists of a radar set, an engagement control station (ECS), equipment powerplant (EPP), an antenna mast group (AMG), and eight remotely located launchers. The single phased-array radar provides the following tactical functions: airspace surveillance, target detection and tracking, and missile guidance. The ECS provides the human interface for command and control operations. Each firing battery launcher currently contains four ready-to-fire missiles, sealed in canisters, that serve a dual purpose as shipping containers and launch tubes. The Patriot's fast reaction capability, high firepower, ability to track up to 50 targets simultaneously with a maximum range of 68.5 kilometers (42.6 miles), and the ability to operate in a severe electronic-countermeasures (ECM) environment are features not available in previous air defense systems. The Patriot Advance Capability-3 (PAC-3) upgrade program will incorporate 16 advanced hit-to-kill missiles into two of the eight launchers per firing battery, thereby increasing the system's firepower and ballistic missile defense capabilities. The primary mission of the PAC-3 missile is to kill both maneuvering and non-maneuvering tactical ballistic missiles. The PAC-3 missile also will have a capability to counter cruise missiles and aircraft.

payload 1. Originally, the revenue-producing portion of an aircraft's load, such as passengers, cargo, and mail. By extension, the term "payload" has become applied to that which a rocket, aerospace vehicle, or spacecraft carries over and above what is necessary for the operation of the vehicle during flight. 2. With respect to the Space Transportation System (or space shuttle), the total complement of specific instruments, space equipment, support hardware and consumables carried in the orbiter vehicle (especially in the cargo bay) to accomplish a discrete activity in space but not included as part of the basic orbiter payload support (e.g., the remote manipulator system, or RMS). 3. With respect to the space station, an aggregate of instruments and software for the performance of specific scientific or applications investigations, or for commercial activities. Payloads may be located inside the pressurized modules of the space station, attached to the space station structure, or attached to a platform, or they may be free-flyers. 4. With respect to a military missile, the payload generally consists of a warhead, its protective container, and activating devices.

Payload Assist Module (PAM) A family of upper-stage vehicles, developed by the McDonnell Douglas Astronautics Company, for use with the Space Transportation System (STS) or expendable launch vehicles, such as the Delta. The PAM takes a payload from LOW EARTH ORBIT (LEO) and delivers it to a final operational location, such as geosynchronous orbit (GEO). There are three main versions of the PAM system: PAM-D, PAM-DII, and PAM-A. The PAM-D is compatible with either the space shuttle or the Delta expendable launch vehicle. In the space shuttle (or STS) configuration, it has a maximum payload capacity of 1,260 kilograms (kg) [2,780 pounds-mass (lbm)]. The first PAM-D space shuttle mission was accomplished in November 1982. The PAM-DII is compatible with many expendable launch vehicles as well as the space shuttle. In the STS application the PAM-DII

Figure 94. Family of versatile PAM upper stages *(Drawing courtesy of McDonnell Douglas Astronautics Company)*

has a 1,900-kg (4,200-lbm) payload capacity. The first space shuttle mission with the PAM-DII upper stage was completed in November 1985. Finally, the PAM-A vehicle has a maximum payload capacity of 1,950 kg (4,300 lbm) and can be mounted horizontally in the shuttle's cargo bay to accommodate larger-diameter and longer-length spacecraft. (See Figure 94.)

See also: DELTA; SPACE TRANSPORTATION SYSTEM; UPPER STAGE.

payload bay The 4.57-meter- (150-foot-) diameter by 18.3-meter- (60-foot-) long enclosed volume within the space shuttle Orbiter vehicle designed to carry payloads, upper-stage vehicles with attached payloads, payload support equipment, and associated mounting hardware. Also called the *cargo bay.*

See also: SPACE TRANSPORTATION SYSTEM.

payload buildup The process by which the instrumentation (e.g., sensors, detectors, etc.) and equipment, including the necessary mechanical and electronic subassemblies, are combined into a complete operational package capable of achieving the objectives of a space particular mission.

payload canister Environmentally controlled transporter for use at the space shuttle launch site (Complex 39 A/B, Kennedy Space Center). It is the same size and configuration as the orbiter vehicle's cargo bay.
See also: SPACE TRANSPORTATION SYSTEM.

payload carrier With respect to the Space Transportation System (STS), one of the major classes of standard payload carriers certified for use with the space shuttle to support payload operations. Payload carriers are identified as: habitable modules (e.g., spacelab) and attached but uninhabitable modules and equipment (e.g., pallets, free-flying systems, satellites, and propulsive upper stages).
See also: SPACE TRANSPORTATION SYSTEM.

payload changeout room An environmentally controlled room on a movable support structure (including a manipulator system) at the space shuttle launch pad (Complex 39 A/B at the Kennedy Space Center). It used for inserting payloads vertically into the Orbiter vehicle's cargo bay at the launch pad and supports payload transfer between the transport canister and the cargo bay.
See also: SPACE TRANSPORTATION SYSTEM.

pico- A prefix in the SI unit system meaning multiplied by 10^{-12}; for example, a *picosecond* is 10^{12} second.
See also: INTERNATIONAL SYSTEM OF UNITS

payload discipline training The process of acquiring the knowledge and skills related to the operation of a particular space shuttle payload. This training is flight dependent and includes (for scientific payloads) basic experiment science, experiment design and operation, and experiment objectives. It is accomplished external to the basic Space Transportation System (STS) training program.
See also: SPACE TRANSPORTATION SYSTEM.

payload integration The compatible installation of a complete payload package into the spacecraft and space launch vehicle.

payload operations control center (POCC) Central area at a NASA center from which space shuttle payload operations are monitored and controlled. For example, attached payloads use the POCC at the Johnson Space Center (Houston, Texas). Often the payload sponsor/user will have direct command of a payload from this control center.
See also: SPACE TRANSPORTATION SYSTEM.

payload retrieval mission A space shuttle mission in which an orbiting payload is captured, secured in the cargo bay, and then returned to Earth.
See also: SPACE TRANSPORTATION SYSTEM.

payload servicing mission A space shuttle mission in which an orbiting payload is given inspection, maintenance, modification, and/or repair. This type of mission generally involves rendezvous and capture operations as well as extravehicular activity (EVA), during which shuttle astronauts perform repair and servicing activities while outside of orbiter vehicle's pressure cabin. Sometimes called *payload repair mission.*
See also: HUBBLE SPACE TELESCOPE; SPACE TRANSPORTATION SYSTEM.

payload specialist The noncareer astronaut who flies as a space shuttle passenger and is responsible for achieving the payload/experiment objectives. He/she is the onboard scientific expert in charge of payload/experiment operations. The payload specialist has a detailed knowledge of the payload instruments and their subsystems, operations, requirements, objectives and supporting equipment. As such, he/she is either the principal investigator (PI) conducting experiments while in orbit or the direct representative of the principal investigator. Of course, the payload specialist also must be knowledgeable about certain basic orbiter systems, such as food and hygiene accommodations, life support systems, hatches, tunnels, and caution and warning systems.

payload station Location on the orbiter vehicle aft flight deck from which payload-specific operations are performed, usually by the payload specialist or mission specialist. Also the locations in the orbiter's flight decks and cargo bay at which payloads are mounted.
See also: SPACE TRANSPORTATION SYSTEM.

payload support equipment (PSE) The flight equipment needed to support a (space shuttle) payload, such as caution and warning indicators, data recording devices, controllers, instrumentation, and the like.

See also: SPACE TRANSPORTATION SYSTEM.

payload system The combination of a spacecraft, instrument module, and other mission-unique equipment, such as a solar array and antenna system, that can be used together to meet a specified mission objective.

Peacekeeper (LGM-118A) The Peacekeeper (also called LGM-118A) is America's newest intercontinental ballistic missile (ICBM). Its deployment filled a key goal of the strategic modernization program and increased the strength and credibility of the ground-based leg of the U.S. strategic (nuclear) triad. The Peacekeeper is capable of delivering ten independently targeted warheads with greater accuracy than any other ballistic missile. It is a three-stage rocket ICBM system consisting of three major sections: the boost system, the post-boost vehicle system, and the reentry system.

The boost system consists of three rocket stages that launch the missile into space. These rocket stages are mounted atop one another and fire successively. Each of the first three stages exhausts its solid-propellant materials through a single movable nozzle that guides the missile along its flight path. The post-boost vehicle is made up of a maneuvering rocket and a guidance and control system. The reentry vehicle system consists of the deployment module, containing up to 10 cone-shaped reentry vehicles and a protective shroud.

The air force achieved initial operational capability of 10 deployed Peacekeeper missiles at F.E. Warren Air Force Base, Wyoming in December 1986. Full operational capability was achieved in December 1988 with the establishment of a squadron of 50 missiles. However, with the end of the cold war, the United States has begun to revise its strategic nuclear policy and has agreed to eliminate the multiple reentry vehicle Peacekeeper ICBMs by the year 2003 as part of the Strategic Arms Reduction Treaty II.

peak overpressure The maximum value of overpressure at a given location that generally is experienced at the instant the shock (or blast) wave from an explosion reaches that location.

Peclet number (symbol: N_{Pe} or Pe) 1. A nondimensional number arising in problems of heat transfer in fluids. It is defined as the ratio of heat convection to heat conduction.

$$N_{Pe} = (\text{heat convection})/(\text{heat conduction}) = (\rho \, c_p \, v \, l) / k$$

where ρ is the mass density of the fluid, c_p is the specific heat at constant pressure, v is the fluid velocity, l is the characteristic length, and k is the heat (thermal) conductivity of the fluid. 2. A nondimensional number arising in mass transfer problems. It is defined as the ratio of the bulk mass transfer to diffusive mass transfer.

$$N_{Pe} = (\text{bulk mass transfer})/(\text{diffusive mass transfer}) = (l \, v) / D$$

where l is the characteristic length, v is the fluid velocity, and D is the mass diffusivity.

Pegasus (space launch vehicle) The Pegasus air-launched space booster is produced by Orbital Sciences Corporation and Hercules Aerospace Company to provide small satellite users with a cost-effective, flexible, and reliable method for placing payloads into LOW EARTH ORBIT (LEO). Launching a Pegasus rocket from an airplane flying at an altitude of approximately 12 kilometers (40,000 feet)—the same altitude most commercial jet airliners fly—reduces the amount of thrust needed to overcome Earth's gravity by 10 to 15%. (See Figure 95.)

See also: LAUNCH VEHICLE.

Peltier effect The production or absorption of thermal energy (heat) that occurs at the junction of two dissimilar metals or semiconductors when an electric current flows through the junction. If thermal energy is generated by the flow of current in one direction, it will be absorbed when the current flow is reversed. This phenomenon, discovered by the French physicist J. C. A. Peltier (1785—1845), can be used in direct conversion cooling applications (e.g., infrared sensor arrays), especially for small volumes or regions where regular refrigeration and cooling techniques are impractical.

See also: DIRECT CONVERSION.

penetration aid In general, techniques and/or devices employed by offensive aerospace weapon

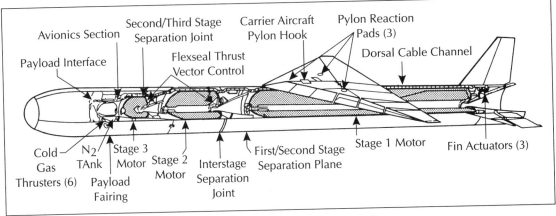

Avionics Section
Second/Third Stage Separation Joint
Carrier Aircraft Pylon Hook
Pylon Reaction Pads (3)
Dorsal Cable Channel
Payload Interface
Flexseal Thrust Vector Control
Cold Gas Thrusters (6)
N2 TAnk
Stage 3 Motor
Payload Fairing
Stage 2 Motor
Interstage Separation Joint
First/Second Stage Separation Plane
Stage 1 Motor
Fin Actuators (3)

Figure 95. Cutaway view of the Pegasus space launch vehicle *(Drawing courtesy of NASA)*

systems to increase the probability of penetration of enemy defenses. With respect to ballistic missiles, a device, or group of devices that accompanies a reentry vehicle (RV) during its flight to misdirect defenses and thereby allow the RV to reach its target and detonate its warhead.

See also: BALLISTIC MISSILE DEFENSE.

penetrator Space scientists have concluded that experiments performed from a network of penetrators can provide essential facts needed to begin understanding the evolution, history, and nature of a planetary body, such as Mars. The scientific measurements performed by penetrators might include seismic, meteorologic, and local site characterization studies involving heat flow, soil moisture content, and geochemistry. A typical penetrator system consists of four major subassemblies: (1) the launch tube, (2) the deployment motor, (3) the decelerator (usually a two-stage device), and (4) the penetrator itself. The launch tube attaches to the host spacecraft and houses the penetrator, deployment motor, and two-stage decelerator. The deployment motor is based on well-proven solid rocket motor technology and provides the required deorbit velocity. If the planetary body has an atmosphere, the two-stage decelerator includes a furlable umbrella heat shield for the first stage of hypersonic deceleration. The penetrator itself is a steel device, shaped like a rocket, with a blunt ogive (curved) nose and conical-flared body. The aftbody (or afterbody) of the penetrator remains at the planet's surface, with the forebody penetrating the subsurface material. Communications with scientists on Earth from the surface/subsurface penetrator sites is accom-

plished by means of an orbiting mothership, which interrogates each penetrator at regular intervals. (See Figure 96.)

A network of penetrators can be used to study planets with solid surfaces (e.g., Mercury, Venus, Mars, and Pluto) as well as many of the interesting moons in the solar system (e.g., Titan, Io, Callisto, Ganymede, Triton, and Charon). The Jovian moon, Europa, is an especially interesting target because of the possibility of a liquid water ocean underneath its smooth, icy surface. A network of penetrators also can be deployed on Earth's own Moon to conduct a variety of scientific experiments, including in-situ evaluation and assessment of surface deposits of frozen volatiles now suspected to occur in certain permanently shadowed polar regions.

NASA's Deep Space 2 project consists of two small cylindrical probes (each has a mass of less than 2 kilograms) that will penetrate the surface of Mars near the South Pole layered terrain and send back data on the subsurface properties. Also called the Mars Microprobe Project, the mission has the following scientific objectives: to test for presence of ice below the surface, to determine the thermal properties and temperature gradient of the subsurface material and to measure the atmospheric pressure and temperature in the vicinity of the impact points. This mission also will serve as a technology test for many of the components of the probes and as a demonstration of passive atmospheric entry and survivable hard impact.

The Deep Space 2 mission will be carried to Mars as part of the Mars Surveyor '98 lander mission (early 1999 launch date). About 18 seconds after the Mars Surveyor '98 Lander separates from its cruise stage, the two probes also will separate from this cruise stage and free-fall through the atmosphere to the Martian surface, impacting at about 160 to 200 meters per second. On impact, the aeroshells protecting the probes will shatter; and the forebody of the probes will separate and penetrate a distance of 0.3 to 2 meters below the surface (depending on the composition of the subsurface material).

A few minutes after impact, a small drill will be deployed out the side of the forebody. This drill will bring approximately 0.1 gram of subsurface material sample into the forebody, where it will be examined for the presence of ice. The sample will then be heated in 10° Celsius increments and measurements performed concerning the amount of water vapor released at each stage.

The aftbody of the probes, which are connected by a flexible cable to the forebody, will remain on the surface. A Sun detector on the aftbody will be used to verify that it did indeed remain on the Martian surface after the high-velocity impact landing. The aftbody is a short cylinder that contains the primary batteries, pressure sensors, and

communications equipment, including an antenna. Data are stored on board and then transmitted to the Mars Global Surveyor spacecraft, which will serve as the mothership for the microprobes and relay their data back to Earth. Atmospheric pressure and subsurface temperature measurements should be made every hour for the planned two-day duration mission. However, these measurements could continue for an additional 20 days, should the primary batteries last that long.

See also: MARS; MARS GLOBAL SURVEYOR MISSION; MARS SURVEYOR '98; MOON.

perfect fluid In simplifying assumptions made as part of preliminary engineering analyses, a fluid chiefly characterized by a lack of viscosity and, usually, by incompressibility. Also called an *ideal fluid* or an *inviscid fluid*.

perfect gas A gas that obeys the following equation of state: pv = RT, where p is pressure, v is specific volume, T is absolute temperature, and R is the gas constant.

See also: IDEAL GAS.

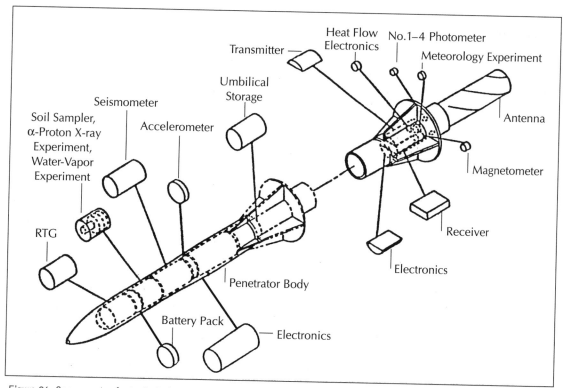

Figure 96. Components of a typical planetary penetrator *(Drawing courtesy of NASA)*

perforation With respect to a solid-propellant rocket, the central cavity or hole down the center of a propellant grain. This perforation can take different shapes, ranging from a right circular cylinder to a complex star pattern. The geometry and dimensions of the perforation affect the solid-propellant burn rate and, consequently, the thrust delivered by the rocket as a function of time.
See also: ROCKET.

peri- A prefix meaning near, as in *perigee.*

periapsis The point in an orbit closest to the body being orbited.
See also: ORBITS OF OBJECTS IN SPACE.

periastron That point of the orbit of one member of a binary star system at which the stars are nearest to each other. The opposite of *apastron.*
See also: BINARY STARS.

pericynthian That point in the trajectory of a vehicle that is closest to the Moon.

perifocus An orbiting body's nearest approach to the surface of the central body. Also called *periapsis.*
See also: ORBITS OF OBJECTS IN SPACE.

perigee In general, the point at which a satellite's orbit is the closest to the primary (central body); the minimum altitude attained by an Earth-orbiting object.
See also: ORBITS OF OBJECTS IN SPACE.

perigee propulsion A programmed-thrust technique for escape from a planet by an orbiting space vehicle. The technique involves the intermittent application of thrust at perigee (when the object's orbital velocity is high) and coasting periods.

perihelion The place in a solar orbit that is nearest the Sun, when the Sun is the center of attraction. Compare with APHELION.

perilune In an orbit around the Moon, the point in the orbit nearest the lunar surface.

period (common symbol: T) 1. In general, the time required for one full cycle of a regularly repeated series of events. 2. The time taken by a satellite to travel once around its orbit. Also called the *orbital period.* 3. The time between two successive swings of a pendulum or between two successive crests in a wave, such as a radio wave. 4. The time required for one oscillation; consequently, the reciprocal of frequency. 5. In nuclear engineering, the time required for the power level of a reactor to change by the factor e (2.718, the base of natural logarithms). Also called the *reactor period.*

permanently crewed capability (PCC) The capability to operate a space station (or a planetary surface base) with a human crew on board, 24 hours a day, 365 days a year. Sometimes called *permanently manned capability* (PMC).

permeability 1. In general, the ability to permit penetration or passage. In this sense, the term is applied particularly to substances that permit the penetration or passage of fluids. 2. (magnetic, μ) For a magnetic material, the (magnetic) permeability (μ) is defined as the ratio of the magnetic induction (B) to the magnetic field intensity (H) in the same region, namely $\mu = B/H$. The permeability of free space (μ_0) (a constant) has the value $4\pi \times 10^{-7}$ weber per ampere per meter [wb/(A·m)]. If $\mu < m_0$, the substance is called a *diamagnetic* substance (e.g., copper, bismuth, hydrogen). If $\mu > \mu_0$, the substance is *paramagnetic* (e.g., platinum). Finally, if $\mu \gg \mu_0$, the substance is *ferromagnetic* (e.g., cobalt, nickel, iron).

Pershing (MGM-31A) A U.S. Army mobile surface-to-surface inertially guided missile of a two-stage solid-propellant type. It possesses a nuclear warhead capability and is designed to support ground forces by attacking long-range ground targets.

persistence In environmental science, the length of time a compound, once introduced into the environment, stays there. For example, a compound may persist for less than a second or indefinitely.

perturbation 1. Any departure introduced into an assumed steady-state system, or a small departure from the nominal path, such as a specified trajectory. 2. In astronomy, a disturbance in the regular motion of a celestial body, resulting from a force that is additional to that which causes the regular motion, specifically a gravitational force. For example, the orbit of an asteroid or comet is strongly *perturbed* when the small celestial object passes near a major planetary body such as Jupiter.

phase 1. The fractional part of a periodic quantity through which the particular value of an independent variable has advanced as measured from an arbitrary reference. 2. The physical state of a substance, such as solid, liquid, or gas. 3. The extent that the disk of the Moon or a planet, as seen from Earth, is illuminated by the Sun.

phase change The physical process that occurs when a substance changes between the three basic phases (or states) of matter: solid, liquid, and vapor. *Sublimation* is a change of phase directly from the solid phase to the vapor phase. *Vaporization* is a change of phase from the liquid phase to the vapor (gaseous) phase. *Condensation* is the change of phase from the vapor phase to the liquid phase (or from the vapor phase directly to the solid phase). *Fusion* is the change of phase from the liquid phase to the solid phase, while *melting* is a change of phase from the solid phase to the liquid phase. Phase change is a thermodynamic process involving the addition or removal of heat (thermal energy) from the substance. The temperature at which these processes occur is dependent on the pressure.

phased deployment With respect to ballistic missile defense (BMD), the deployment of successively more effective systems, as they are developed.
See also: BALLISTIC MISSILE DEFENSE.

phase modulation (PM) A type of modulation in which the relative phase of the carrier wave is modified or varied in accordance to the amplitude of the signal. Specifically, a form of angle modulation in which the angle of a sine-wave carrier is caused to depart from the carrier angle by an amount proportional to the instantaneous value of the modulating wave.
See also: AMPLITUDE MODULATION; FREQUENCY MODULATION.

Phobos The larger of the two small moons of Mars. Phobos has a mean diameter of 22 kilometers, a period of rotation of 0.3188 days, and a mean distance from the planet of 9,380 kilometers.
See also: MARS.

Phoenix (AIM-54A) A long-range air-to-air missile with electronic guidance/homing developed by the U.S. Navy. Usually carried in clusters of up to six missiles on an aircraft such as the Tomcat,

this missile is an airborne weapons control system with multiple-target—handling capabilities. It is used to kill multiple air targets with conventional warheads. Near-simultaneous launch is possible against up to six targets in all weather and heavy jamming environments. This missile is powered by a solid-propellant rocket motor. It is 3.9 meters (13 feet) long, 38.1 centimeters (15 inches) wide, and has a wing span of 0.9 meters (3 feet). It has a range in excess of 184 kilometers (115 miles). Its conventional warhead has a mass of 60.75 kilograms (135 pounds-mass), while the entire missile has a total mass of 460.8 kilograms (1,024 pounds-mass).

photoelectric effect The emission of an electron from a surface as the surface absorbs a photon of electromagnetic radiation. Electrons so emitted are called *photoelectrons.* The effectiveness of the process depends on the surface metal involved and the wavelength of the radiant energy to which it is exposed. For example, cesium will emit photoelectrons when exposed to visible radiation. The energy of the photoelectron produced is equal to the energy of the incident photon (hν) minus the amount of work (Φ) needed to raise the electron to sufficient energy level to free it from the surface. This relationship is expressed in Einstein's photoelectric effect equation:

$$E_{photoelectron} = h\nu - \Phi$$

where h is the Planck constant, ν is the frequency of the incident photon, and Φ is the work function of the solid (metal) surface. In 1905 Albert Einstein (1879–1955) published an important physics paper that described the photoelectric effect.

photon According to quantum theory, the elementary bundle or packet of electromagnetic radiation, such as a photon of light. Photons have no mass and travel at the speed of light. The energy (*E*) of the photon is equal to the product of the frequency (ν) of the electromagnetic radiation and Planck's constant (*h*):

$$E = h\nu$$

where *h* is equal to 6.626×10^{-34} joule-sec; and ν is the frequency (hertz).

photon engine A conceptual reaction engine in which thrust would be obtained by emitting photons, such as light rays. Although the thrust from such an engine would be very small, it would be applied continuously in the vacuum of outer space (if a suitable power source became available) and eventually might achieve significant speeds—perhaps even supporting interstellar flight.

See also: LASER PROPULSION SYSTEM.

photosphere The intensely bright, visible portion (surface) of the Sun.

See also: SUN.

photovoltaic material A substance (semiconductor material) that converts sunlight directly into electricity, using the photovoltaic effect. This effect involves the production of a voltage difference across a p–n junction, resulting from the absorption of a photon of energy. The p–n junction is the region at which two dissimilar types of semiconductor materials (i.e., materials of opposite polarity) meet. The voltage difference in the semiconductor material is caused by the internal drift of holes and electrons.

Crystalline silicon (Si) and gallium arsenide (GaAs) are the photovoltaic materials often used in spacecraft power system applications. The typical silicon *solar cell* delivers about 11.5% solar energy-to-electric energy conversion efficiency, while the newer but more expensive gallium arsenide cell promises to provide about 18% or more conversion efficiency. Solar panels and solar arrays are constructed in a variety of configurations from large numbers of individual solar cells that are made of these photovoltaic materials. The series-parallel pattern of electrical connections between the cells determines the total output voltage of the solar panel or array.

On orbit, prolonged exposure to sunlight causes the performance of these photovoltaic materials to degrade, typically by 1 or 2% per year. Exposure to radiation (both the permanently trapped radiation belts surrounding Earth and transitory solar flare radiations) can cause even more rapid degradation in the performance of photovoltaic materials. Solar cells constructed from gallium arsenide are more radiation resistant that silicon solar cells.

See also: SOLAR CELL.

piggyback experiment An experiment that rides along with the primary experiment on a space-available basis without interfering with the mission of the primary experiment.

pilot 1. In general, the person who handles the controls of an aircraft, aerospace vehicle, or spacecraft from within the craft and, in so doing, guides or controls it in three-dimensional flight. 2. An electromechanical system designed to exercise control functions in an aircraft, aerospace vehicle, or spacecraft; for example, the *automatic pilot.* 3. (verb) To operate, control, or guide an aircraft, aerospace vehicle, or spacecraft from within the vehicle so as to move in three-dimensional flight through the air or space. 4. With respect to the U.S. Space Transportation System (STS), the second in command of a space shuttle flight. He or she assists the commander as required in conducting all phases of the orbiter vehicle flight. The pilot has such authority and responsibilities as are delegated him/her by the commander. The pilot normally operates the remote manipulator system (RMS) at the Orbiter's payload handling station, using the RMS to deploy, release, or capture payloads. The pilot also is generally the second crewperson (behind the mission specialist) for extravehicular activity (EVA).

See also: SPACE TRANSPORTATION SYSTEM.

pilot chute A small parachute to pull a drogue or main parachute from stowage.

pilot valve A low-capacity valve that amplifies a low-power control signal to operate a larger valve.

Pioneer spacecraft NASA's solar-orbiting Pioneer spacecraft have contributed enormous amounts of data concerning the solar wind, solar magnetic field, cosmic radiation, micrometeoroids, and other phenomena of interplanetary space. *Pioneer 4,* launched March 3, 1959, was the first U.S. spacecraft to go into orbit around the Sun. It provided excellent radiation data. *Pioneer 5,* launched March 11, 1960, confirmed the existence of interplanetary magnetic fields and helped explain how solar flares trigger magnetic storms and the northern and southern lights (auroras) on Earth. *Pioneers 6* through *9* were launched between December 1965 and November 1968. These spacecraft provided large quantities of valuable data concerning the solar wind, magnetic and electrical fields, and cosmic rays in interplanetary space. Data from these spacecraft helped space scientists draw a new picture of the

Sun as the dominant phenomenon of interplanetary space.

See also: PIONEER 10, 11; PIONEER VENUS.

Pioneer 10, 11 The *Pioneer 10* and *11* spacecraft, as their names imply, are true deep-space explorers—the first human-made objects to navigate the main asteroid belt, the first spacecraft to encounter Jupiter and its fierce radiation belts, the first to encounter Saturn, and the first spacecraft to leave the solar system. These spacecraft also investigated magnetic fields, cosmic rays, the solar wind, and the interplanetary dust concentrations as they flew through interplanetary space.

At Jupiter and Saturn, scientists used the spacecraft to investigate the giant planets and their interesting complement of moons in four main ways: (1) by measuring particles, fields, and radiation; (2) by spin-scan imaging the planets and some of their moons; (3) by accurately observing the paths of the spacecraft and measuring the gravitational forces of the planets and their major satellites acting on them; and (4) by observing changes in the frequency of the S-band radio signal before and

Figure 97. The *Pioneer 10* (and *11*) spacecraft with its complement of scientific instruments. Power is provided by a long-lived radioisotope-thermoelectric generator (RTG). *(Drawing courtesy of NASA)*

after occultation (the temporary "disappearance" of the spacecraft caused by their passage behind these celestial bodies) to study the structures of their ionospheres and atmospheres. (See Figure 97.)

The *Pioneer 10* spacecraft was launched from Cape Canaveral Air Force Station, Florida by an Atlas-Centaur rocket on March 2, 1972. It became the first spacecraft to cross the main asteroid belt and the first to make close-range observations of the Jovian system. Sweeping past Jupiter on December 3, 1973 (its closest approach to the giant planet), it discovered no solid surface under the thick layer of clouds enveloping the giant planet— an indication that Jupiter is a liquid hydrogen planet. *Pioneer 10* also explored the giant Jovian magnetosphere, made close-up pictures of the intriguing Red Spot, and observed at relatively close range the Galilean satellites Io, Europa, Ganymede, and Callisto. When *Pioneer 10* flew past Jupiter, it acquired sufficient kinetic energy to carry it completely out of the solar system.

Departing Jupiter, *Pioneer 10* continued to map the heliosphere (the Sun's giant magnetic bubble, or field, drawn out from it by the action of the solar wind). Then, on June 13, 1983, *Pioneer 10* crossed the orbit of Neptune, which at the time was (and until 1999 will be) the planet farthest out from the Sun, due to the eccentricity in Pluto's orbit, which now takes it inside that of Neptune. This historic date marked the first passage of a human-made object beyond the known planetary boundary of the solar system. Beyond this solar system boundary, *Pioneer 10* continues to measure the extent of the heliosphere as it flies through interstellar space. Along with its sister ship, *Pioneer 11*, this spacecraft is still helping scientists investigate the deep space environment.

The *Pioneer 11* spacecraft was launched on April 5, 1973 and swept by Jupiter at an encounter distance of only 43,000 kilometers (26,720 miles) on December 2, 1974. It provided additional detailed data and pictures of Jupiter and its moons, including the first views of Jupiter's polar regions. Then, on September 1, 1979, *Pioneer 11* flew by Saturn, demonstrating a safe flight path through the rings for the more sophisticated Voyager spacecraft to follow. *Pioneer 11* (officially renamed *Pioneer Saturn*) provided the first close-up observations of Saturn, its rings, satellites, magnetic field, radiation belts, and atmosphere. It found no solid surface on Saturn but discovered at least one additional satellite and ring. After rushing past Saturn, *Pioneer 11*

also headed out of the solar system toward the distant stars.

Finally, both Pioneer spacecraft carry a special message (the "Pioneer plaque") for any intelligent alien civilization that might find them wandering through the interstellar void millions of years from now. This message is drawing map, engraved on an anodized aluminum plaque. The plaque depicts the location of Earth and the solar system, a man and a woman, and other points of science and astrophysics that should be decipherable by a technically intelligent civilization.

See also: JUPITER; SATURN.

Pioneer Venus mission The Pioneer Venus mission consisted of two separate spacecraft launched by the United States to the planet Venus in 1978. The *Pioneer Venus* orbiter spacecraft (also called *Pioneer 12*) was a 553-kilogram (1220 pounds-mass [lbm]) spacecraft that contained a 45-kilogram (100 lbm) payload of scientific instruments. It was launched on May 20, 1978 and placed into a highly eccentric orbit around Venus on December 4, 1978. For 14 years (1978–1992) the Orbiter spacecraft gathered a wealth of scientific data about the atmosphere and ionosphere of Venus and their interactions with the solar wind as well as details about the planet's surface. Then in October 1992, this spacecraft made an intended, final entry into the Venusian atmosphere, gathering data up to its final fiery plunge and dramatically ending the operations portion of the Pioneer Venus mission.

The Pioneer Venus Multiprobe spacecraft (also called *Pioneer 13*) consisted of a basic bus spacecraft, a large probe, and three identical small probes. The Multiprobe spacecraft was launched on August 8, 1978, and separated about three weeks before entry into the Venusian atmosphere. The four (now-separated) probes and their (spacecraft) bus successfully entered the Venusian atmosphere at widely dispersed locations on December 9, 1978 and returned important scientific data as they plunged toward the planet's surface. Although the probes were not designed to survive landing, one hardy probe did and transmitted data for about an hour after impact.

The *Pioneer Venus* orbiter and multiprobe spacecraft provided a wealth of scientific data about Venus, its surface, atmosphere, and interaction with the solar wind. For example, the orbiter spacecraft made an extensive radar map, covering about 90% of the Venusian surface. Using its radar to look

Figure 98. Pitch, yaw, and roll *(Drawing courtesy of NASA)*

through the dense Venusian clouds, this spacecraft revealed that the planet's surface was mostly gentle, rolling plains with two prominent plateaus: Ishtar Terra and Aphrodite Terra. This highly successful, two-spacecraft mission also provided important groundwork for NASA's subsequent Magellan mission to Venus.

See also: MAGELLAN MISSION; VENUS.

pitch 1. In acoustics, the "highness" or "lowness" of a sound. Pitch depends mainly on the frequency of the sound stimulus but also on the pressure and waveform of the stimulus. 2. In aerospace technology, the rotation (angular motion) of an aircraft, aerospace vehicle, or spacecraft about its lateral axis. (See Figure 98.) 3. In engineering, the distance between corresponding points on adjacent teeth of a gear or an adjacent blades on a turbine wheel, as measured along a prescribed arc, called the *pitch-line*.

pitch angle The angle between an aircraft's or missile's longitudinal axis and Earth's horizontal plane. Also called *inclination angle*.

pitchover The programmed turn from the vertical that a rocket or launch vehicle (under power) takes as it describes an arc and points in a direction other than vertical.

pitot tube An open-ended tube that, when immersed in a moving fluid with its mouth pointed upstream, can be used to measure the stagnation pressure of the fluid for subsonic flow or the stagnation pressure behind the tube's normal shock wave for supersonic flow.

pitting Creation of surface voids by mechanical erosion, chemical corrosion, or cavitation.

pixel Contraction for *picture element*; the smallest unit of information on a screen or in an image; the more pixels, the higher the potential resolution of the video screen or image.

Planck's constant (symbol: h) A fundamental constant in modern physics that is equal to the ratio of the energy (E) of a quantum of energy to the frequency (ν) of this quantum (or photon); that is,

$$h = E/\nu = 6.626 \times 10^{-34} \text{ joule-second.}$$

This unit is named in honor of the German physicist Max Planck (1858–1947), who first developed quantum theory.

Planck's radiation law The fundamental physical law that describes the distribution of energy radiated by a BLACKBODY. Introducing the concept of the *quantum* (or photon) as a small unit of energy transfer, the German physicist Max Planck (1858–1947) first proposed this law in 1900. It is an expression for the variation of monochromatic radiant flux per unit area of source as a function of wavelength (λ) of blackbody radiation at a given thermodynamic temperature (T). Mathematically, Planck's law can be expressed as:

$$dw = [2\pi hc^2] / \{\lambda^5 [e^{hc/\lambda kT} - 1]\}d\lambda$$

where *dw* is the radiant flux from a blackbody in the wavelength interval $d\lambda$, centered around wavelength λ, per unit area of blackbody surface at thermodynamic temperature T. In this equation, c is the velocity of light, h is a constant (later named the *Planck constant*), and k is BOLTZMANN'S CONSTANT.

planet A nonluminous celestial body that orbits around the Sun or some other star. There are nine such large objects, or "major planets," in the solar system, and numerous "minor planets," or asteroids. The distinction between a planet and a satellite may not always be clear-cut, except for the fact that a satellite orbits around a planet. For example, our Moon is nearly the size of the planet Mercury and is very large in comparison to its parent planet, Earth. In some cases, Earth and the Moon can be treated almost as a "double-planet system"; the same is true for icy Pluto and its large satellite, or moon, Charon.

The largest planet is Jupiter, which has more mass than all the other planets combined. Mercury is the planet nearest the Sun, while (on the average) Pluto is the farthest away. At perihelion (the point in an orbit at which a celestial body is nearest the Sun), Pluto actually is closer to the Sun than Neptune. Saturn is the least dense planet in the solar system. If we could find some giant cosmic swimming pool, Saturn would float, since it is less dense than water. Seven of the nine planets have satellites, or moons, some of which are larger than the planet Mercury.

See also: ASTEROID; EARTH; JUPITER; MARS; MERCURY; NEPTUNE; PLUTO; SATURN; URANUS; VENUS.

planetary albedo The fraction of incident solar radiation that is reflected by a planet (and its atmosphere) and returned to space. For example, Earth has a planetary albedo of approximately 0.3 —that is, it reflects about 30% of the incident solar radiation back to space, mostly by backscatter from clouds in the atmosphere.

planetary orbital operations Planetary spacecraft can engage in two general categories of orbital operations: exploration of the planetary system and mapping of the planet. Exploring a planetary system includes making observations of the target planet and its system of satellites and rings. A mapping mission generally is concerned with acquiring large amounts of data about the planet's surface features. An orbit of low inclination at the target planet usually is well suited to a planetary system exploration mission, since it provides repeated exposure to satellites (moons) orbiting with the equatorial plane as well as adequate coverage of the planet and its magnetosphere. However, an orbit of high inclination is much better suited for a mapping mission, because the target planet will fully rotate below the spacecraft's orbit, thereby providing eventual exposure to every portion of the planet's surface. During either type of mission, the orbiting spacecraft is involved in an extended encounter period with the target planet and requires continuous (or nearly continuous) support from the flight team members at mission control on Earth. Galileo is an example of a planetary system

exploration mission, while Magellan is an example of a planetary mapping mission.

See also: GALILEO PROJECT; MAGELLAN MISSION.

planetary orbit insertion The same type of highly precise navigation and course correction procedures used in flyby missions are applied during the cruise phase for a planetary orbiter mission. This process then places the spacecraft at precisely the correct location at the correct time to enter into an orbit about the target planet. However, orbit insertion requires not only the precise position and timing of a flyby mission but also a controlled deceleration. As the spacecraft's trajectory is bent by the planet's gravity, the command sequence aboard the spacecraft fires its retroengine(s) at the proper moment and for the proper duration. Once this retroburn (or retrofiring) has been completed successfully, the spacecraft is captured into orbit by its target planet. If the retroburn fails (or is improperly sequenced), the spacecraft will continue to fly past the planet. It is quite common for this retroburn to occur on the far side of a planet as viewed from Earth—requiring this portion of the orbit insertion sequence to occur essentially automatically (based on onboard commands) and without any interaction with the flight controllers on Earth.

planetesimals Small celestial objects in the solar system, such as asteroids, comets, and moons.

planet fall The landing of a spacecraft or space vehicle on a planet.

planetoid An asteroid, or minor planet.
See also: ASTEROID.

plasma An electrically neutral gaseous mixture of positive and negative ions. Sometimes called the "fourth state of matter," since a plasma behaves quite differently from solids, liquids, or gases.

plasma engine A reaction (rocket) engine using electromagnetically accelerated plasma as propellant.
See also: ELECTRIC PROPULSION.

plasma instruments Plasma detectors on a scientific spacecraft measure the density, composition, temperature, velocity, and three-dimensional distribution of plasmas that exist in interplanetary space and within planetary magnetospheres. Plasma detectors are typically sensitive to solar and planetary plasmas, and they can observe the solar wind and its interactions with a planetary system.

See also: MAGNETOSPHERE; SOLAR WIND.

plasma rocket A rocket engine in which the ejection of plasma generates thrust; a rocket using a plasma engine.

See also: ELECTRIC PROPULSION.

plasticity The tendency of a loaded body to assume a (deformed) state other than its original state, when the load is removed.

platform 1. An uncrewed (unmanned) orbital element of the space station program that provides standard support services to payloads not attached to the space station. *See also:* SPACE STATION. 2. With respect to ballistic missile defense, a satellite in space that is used as a carrier for weapons, sensors, or both. *See also:* BALLISTIC MISSILE DEFENSE.

platform decoy A relatively inexpensive object intended to fool an adversary's sensors into deciding that the object is really a much more valuable platform in space.

See also: BALLISTIC MISSILE DEFENSE.

plug nozzle An annular nozzle that discharges exhaust gas with a radial inward component; a truncated aerospike.

See also: NOZZLE.

plume 1. In aerospace, the hot, bright exhaust gases from a rocket. 2. In environmental studies, a visible or measurable discharge of a contaminant from a given point of origin; can be visible or thermal in water, or visible in the air (e.g., a plume of smoke).

Pluto Pluto, the smallest planet in the solar system, has remained a mystery since its discovery by astronomer Clyde Tombaugh in 1930. Pluto is the only planet not yet viewed close-up by spacecraft, and given its great distance from the Sun and tiny size, study of the planet continues to challenge and extend the skills of planetary astronomers. In fact, most of what scientists know about Pluto has been learned since the late 1970s. Such basic char-

acteristics as the planet's radius and mass were virtually unknown before the discovery of Pluto's moon Charon in 1978. Since then observations and speculations about the Pluto-Charon system—it is now considered a "double planet" system—have progressed steadily to a point where many of the key questions remaining about the system must await the close-up observation of a flyby space mission, such as NASA's planned Pluto Express mission.

Table 1. DYNAMIC PROPERTIES AND PHYSICAL DATA FOR PLUTO	
Diameter	2,274 km
Mass	1.25×10^{22} kg
Mean Density	2.05 g/cm³
Albedo (visual)	0.3
Surface Temperature (average)	~ 50 K
Surface gravity	0.4 - 0.6 m/s²
Escape velocity	1.1 km/s
Atmosphere (a transient phenomenon)	Nitrogen (N_2) and methane (CH_4)
Period of rotation	6.387 days
Inclination of axis (of rotation)	122.46°
Orbital period (around Sun)	248 years (90,591 days)
Orbit inclination	17.15°
Eccentricity of orbit	0.2482
Mean orbital velocity	4.75 km/s
Distance from Sun	
Aphelion	7.38×10^9 km (49.2 AU) (409.2 light-min)
Perihelion	4.43×10^9 km (29.5 AU) (245.3 light-min)
Mean Distance	5.91×10^9 km (39.5 AU) (328.5 light-min)
Solar flux (at 30 AU ~perihelion)	1.5 W/m²
Number of known natural satellites	1

(Note: Some of these data are speculative.)
Source: NASA.

Table 2.
DYNAMIC PROPERTIES AND PHYSICAL DATA FOR CHARON

Diameter	1,270 km
Mass	1.7×10^{21} kg
Mean density	1.8 g/cm^3
Surface gravity	0.2 m/s^2
Escape velocity	0.58 m/s
Albedo (visual)	0.375
Mean distance from Pluto	19,640 km
Sidereal period (gravitationally synchronized orbit)	6.387 days
Orbital inclination	96.56°
Orbital eccentricity	0

Note: Some of these data are speculative.
Source: NASA.

For example, there is a strong variation in brightness, or albedo, as Pluto rotates, but planetary scientists do not know if what they are observing is a system of varying terrains, areas of different composition, or both. Scientists know there is a dynamic, largely nitrogen and methane atmosphere around Pluto that waxes (grows) and wanes (diminishes) with the planet's elliptical orbit around the Sun, but they still need to understand how the Plutonian atmosphere arises, persists, is again deposited on the surface, and how some of it escapes into space.

Telescopic studies (both Earth-based telescopes and NASA's Earth-orbiting HUBBLE SPACE TELESCOPE) indicate that Pluto and Charon are very different bodies. Pluto is more rock, while Charon appears more icy. How and when the two bodies in this interesting double-planet system could have evolved so differently is another key question that awaits data from a close-up observation. Data about Pluto and Charon, as gathered using ground-based and Earth-orbiting observatories, have helped improve our fundamental understanding of these planetary bodies. The most recent of these data are presented in Table 1 for Pluto and Table 2 for Charon.

Because of Pluto's highly eccentric orbit, its distance from the Sun varies from about 4.4 to 7.4 billion kilometers, or some 29.5 to 49.2 astronomical units (AU). For most of its orbit, Pluto is the outermost of the planets. However, since 1979 it actually has been orbiting closer to the Sun than Neptune. This condition will remain until 1999, when Pluto again becomes the outermost planet in the solar system. Upon its discovery in 1930, Clyde Tombaugh (keeping with astronomical tradition) named the planet Pluto—after the god of the underworld in Roman mythology. Incidentally, this discovery was not a real astronomical surprise, since astronomers at the turn of the century had predicted Pluto's existence from perturbations (disturbances) observed in the orbits of both Uranus and Neptune.

However, the discovery of Charon by James W. Christy of the U.S. Naval Observatory in 1978, triggered a revolution in our understanding of Pluto. Charon was the boatman in Greek and Roman mythology who ferried the dead across the River Styx to the underworld, ruled by Pluto ("Hades" in Greek myth). This large moon has a diameter of about 1,270 kilometers, compared tiny Pluto's diameter of 2,274 kilometers. These similar sizes encourage many planetary scientists to regard the pair as the only true double-planet system in our solar system. Charon circles Pluto at a distance of 19,640 kilometers. Its orbit is gravitationally synchronized with Pluto's rotation period (approximately 6.4 days) so that both the planet and its moon keep the same hemisphere facing each other at all times.

Planetary scientists currently believe that Pluto possesses a very thin atmosphere that contains nitrogen (N_2) and methane (CH_4). Pluto's atmosphere is unique in the solar system in that it undergoes a formation-and-decay cycle each orbit around the Sun. The atmosphere begins to form several decades before perihelion (the planet's closet approach to the Sun) and then slowly collapses and freezes out decades later, as the planet's orbit takes it farther and farther away from the Sun to the frigid outer extremes of the solar system. In September 1989 Pluto experienced perihelion. Several decades from now its thin atmosphere will freeze out and collapse, leaving a fresh layer of nitrogen and methane snow on the planet's surface.

See also: PLUTO EXPRESS MISSION.

Pluto Express mission Originally designated the Pluto Fast Flyby (PFF), the Pluto Express mission is planned to be a two-spacecraft mission designed to make studies of the planet, Pluto, and its moon, Charon. Its major science objectives are to: (1) characterize the global geology and geomorphology of

Pluto and Charon; (2) map the composition of Pluto's surface; and (3) determine the composition and structure of Pluto's atmosphere. This mission is intended to reach Pluto as quickly as possible—before the tenuous Plutonian atmosphere can refreeze onto the surface as the planet recedes from perihelion (its closest approach to the Sun). Launched sometime between 2001 and 2003, the two spacecraft will arrive about one year apart, after traveling some 12 years through interplanetary space. The interplanetary transit time will depend greatly on the final mass of the spacecraft, now nominally 85.00 kilograms (187.4 pounds-mass [lbm]). Studies of this interesting "double-planet" system will begin some 12 to 18 months prior to closest approach.

The overall structure of the Pluto Express spacecraft is an aluminum hexagonal bus with no deployable structures. Power will be provided by radioisotope thermoelectric generators (RTGs) similar in design to those used on earlier missions (such as Galileo and Cassini). Communications with Earth will be accomplished by means of a fixed, 1.47-meter- (4.82-foot-) diameter high-gain antenna, employing an X-band uplink receiver and downlink transponder. Pointing control will be maintained by a wide-field star tracker and a set of three solid-state rate sensors.

Planned science experiments include a visible-light imaging system, an infrared mapping spectrometer, an ultraviolet spectrometer, and a radio occultation experiment. The Pluto Express spacecraft will be launched by an expendable launch vehicle, such as the Delta II rocket. Current mission plans call for the use of three gravity assists from Venus and one from Jupiter in order to obtain sufficient velocity to arrive within the required travel time to Pluto of about 12 years. Because the Pluto-Charon double-planet system has a rotation period of 6.4 days, the two spacecraft will arrive at an odd multiple of 3.2 days apart so that both sides of each planetary body can be imaged. To accomplish the mission goal of 1-kilometer (0.62 mile) resolution mapping, the closest approach distance will be about 15,000 kilometers (about 9,300 miles).

See also: PLUTO; SPACE NUCLEAR POWER.

Plutonian Of or relating to the planet Pluto.

pneumatic Operated, moved, or effected by a pressurized gas (typically air) that is used to transmit energy.

pod An enclosure, housing, or detachable container of some kind; for example, an *instrument pod* or an *engine pod.*

pogo A term developed within the aerospace industry to describe the longitudinal (vertical) dynamic oscillations (vibrations) generated by the interaction of the launch vehicle's structural dynamics with the propellant and engine combustion process. The name appears to have originated from the similarity of this bumping phenomenon to the up-and-down bumping motion of a pogo stick.

pogo suppressor A device within a liquid rocket engine that absorbs any vibration of the vehicle's structure during the engine combustion process.
See also: POGO.

point of impact The point at which a projectile, bomb, or reentry vehicle inpacts or is expected to impact.

point of no return 1. The point along the launch track of an aerospace vehicle or space vehicle from which it can no longer return to its launch base. 2. For a human surface expedition on Mars, the point at which the team can no longer return to its surface base with the remaining supplies (e.g., air, food, water, or fuel). 3. For an aircraft, a point along its flight track beyond which its endurance will not permit return to its own or some other associated base with its remaining fuel supply.

poise (symbol: P) Unit of dynamic viscosity in the centimeter-gram-second (cgs) unit system. It is defined as the tangential force per unit area (e.g., dynes/cm^2) required to maintain a unit difference in velocity (e.g., 1 cm/sec) between two parallel plates in a liquid that are separated by a unit distance (e.g., 1 centimeter).

1 poise = (1 dyne-second)/(centimeter)^2 = 0.1 (newton-second)/(meter)^2

The unit is named after the French scientist Jean Louis Poiseuille (1799–1869). The centipoise, or 0.01 poise, is encountered often. For example, the dynamic viscosity of water at 20° Celsius is approximately 1 centipoise.

polar coordinates A coordinate system in which a point (P) that is defined as P(x, y) in two-dimensional Cartesian coordinates is now represented as P(r, θ), where x = r cosθ and y = r sinθ. Physically, in the polar coordinate system: r is the radial distance in the x-y plane from the origin (O) to point P and θ is the angle formed between the x-axis and the radial vector (i.e., the line of length r from the origin O to point P).

In three dimensions, the Cartesian coordinate system point P(x,y,z) becomes P(r,θ,z) in *cylindrical polar coordinates*—where the point P (r,θ,z) is now regarded as lying on the surface of a cylinder. The terms r and θ are as previously defined, while z represents the height above (or below) the x-y plane.

See also: CARTESIAN COORDINATES; CYLINDRICAL COORDINATES.

Polaris (UGM-27) An underwater/surface-launched, surface-to-surface, solid-propellant ballistic missile with inertial guidance and nuclear warhead. The Polaris (version UGM-27C) has a range of 4,600 kilometers (2,500 nautical miles).

polar orbit An orbit around a planet that passes over or near its poles; an orbit with an inclination of about 90 degrees.

See also: ORBITS OF OBJECTS IN SPACE.

polar orbiting platform (POP) An uncrewed (unmanned) spacecraft in polar or near-polar inclination that is operated from ground stations but dependent on the space station program to provide services for its complement of payloads.

See also: SPACE STATION.

Polar-orbiting Operational Environmental Satellite (POES) The National Oceanic and Atmospheric Administration's (NOAA's) Polar-orbiting Operational Environmental Satellites follow orbits that pass close to the North and South Pole as Earth rotates beneath them. Orbiting at an altitude of about 840 kilometers (520 miles), these satellites provide continuous global coverage of the state of Earth's atmosphere, including such essential information as atmospheric temperature, humidity, cloud cover, ozone concentration, and Earth's energy (radiation) budget. They also provide important surface data, such as sea-ice and sea-surface temperature and snow and ice coverings.

See also: MISSION TO PLANET EARTH; WEATHER SATELLITE.

Polar Space Launch Vehicle (PSLV) A launch vehicle developed by the Indian Space Research Organization (ISRO). It consists of two solid stages, two hypergolic stages, and six strap-on solid rocket motors. This vehicle can place up to 3,000 kilograms into LOW EARTH ORBIT (LEO). It was first launched in 1993.

See also: LAUNCH VEHICLE.

popping Sudden, short-duration surges of pressure in a combustion chamber.

pop-up The use of the rapidly reacting, ground-launched elements of a ballistic missile defense system. These "pop-up" elements may be sensors (e.g., for midcourse tracking and discrimination) or weapons (e.g., kinetic energy kill vehicles).

See also: BALLISTIC MISSILE DEFENSE.

port 1. An opening; a place to access an aerospace system through which energy, data, or fluids may be supplied to or withdrawn from the system. For example, an *observation port,* a *refueling port,* or a *communications port.* 2. The left-hand side of an aerospace vehicle as a person looks from the rear of the craft to the nose.

posigrade rocket An auxiliary rocket that fires in the direction in which the vehicle is pointed, used, for example, in separating two stages of a vehicle. A posigrade course correction adds to the spacecraft's speed, in contrast to a *retrograde* correction, which slows it down.

See also: ORBITS OF OBJECTS IN SPACE.

position 1. A point in space. 2. A point defined by stated or implied coordinates, particularly one on the surface of Earth. 3. A crew member's station or status onboard a space vehicle or space station; for example, the *mission specialist position* on the space shuttle.

positron (symbol: β⁺) An elementary particle with the mass of an electron, but charged positively. It is the "antielectron." A positron is emitted in some types of radioactive decay and also is formed in pair production by the interaction of high-energy gamma rays with matter.

See also: ANTIMATTER.

post-boost phase The phase of a missile trajectory, after the booster's stages have finished firing, in

which the various reentry vehicles (RVs) are independently placed on ballistic trajectories toward their targets. In addition, penetration aids can be dispensed from the post-boost vehicle during this phase, which typically lasts between 3 to 5 minutes.
See also: BALLISTIC MISSILE DEFENSE.

post-boost vehicle (PBV) The portion of a ballistic missile payload that carries the multiple warheads and has maneuvering capability to place each warhead on its final trajectory to a target. Also referred to as a *bus.*
See also: BALLISTIC MISSILE DEFENSE.

potential energy (PE) Energy possessed by an object by virtue of its position in a gravity field. In general, the potential energy (PE) of an object can be expressed as:

$$PE = m \cdot g \cdot z$$

where m is the mass of the object, g is the acceleration due to gravity, and z is the height of the object above some reference position or datum.

pound (symbol: lb) 1. pound (mass) [lbm]: The unit of mass in the foot-pound-second (or U.S. customary) unit system. 1 lbm = 0.45359237 kilogram. 2. pound (force) [lbf]: The unit of force in the foot-pound-second (or U.S. customary) unit system equal to the force required to give a 1 pound mass at sea level on Earth an acceleration of 32.175 feet/second^2. 1 lbf = 4.448 newtons.

power (symbol: P) 1. In physics and engineering, the rate with respect to time at which work is done or energy is transformed or transferred to another location. In the SI UNIT system, power typically is measured in multiples of the watt, which is defined as one joule (of energy) per second. 2. In mathematics, the number of times a quantity is multiplied by itself; for example, b^3 means that b has been raised to the *third power,* or simply b^3 = b·b·b.

power plant In the context of aerospace engineering, the complete installation of an engine (or engines) with supporting subsystems (e.g., cooling subsystem, ignition subsystem) that generates the motive power for a self-propelled vehicle or craft, such as an aircraft, rocket, or aerospace vehicle.

Prandtl number (symbol: Pr) An important nondimensional parameter used in many heat-

transfer and mass problems involving fluid flow. Named in honor of German scientist Ludwig Prandtl (1875–1953).

In heat transfer problems, the Prandtl number expresses the ratio of momentum diffusivity to thermal diffusivity:

$$Pr = (momentum\ diffusivity)/(thermal\ diffusivity) = (c_p\ \mu)/k$$

where c_p is the specific heat at constant pressure, μ is the absolute viscosity, and k is the thermal conductivity.

In mass transfer problems, the Prandtl number expresses the ratio of momentum diffusivity to mass diffusivity:

$$Pr = (momentum\ diffusivity)/(mass\ diffusivity) = \mu/(\rho\ D)$$

where μ is the absolute viscosity, ρ is the density, and D is the mass diffusivity.

preburners Some liquid-hydrogen–fueled rocket engines, such as the space shuttle main engines (SSMEs), have fuel and oxidizer preburners that provide hydrogen-rich hot gases at approximately 1030° Kelvin (760° Celsius) (1400° Fahrenheit). These gases then are used to drive the fuel and oxidizer high-pressure turbopumps.

precession The gradual periodic change in the direction of the axis of rotation of a spinning body due to the application of an external force (torque).

precombustion chamber In a liquid-propellant rocket engine, a chamber in which the propellants are ignited and from which the burning mixture expands torchlike to ignite the mixture in the main combustion chamber.

preemptive attack An attack initiated on the basis of incontrovertible evidence that an enemy attack is imminent.

preferential defense The defensive tactic of protecting some targets strongly, while leaving others defended less strongly or not at all. This concentration of (usually limited) defensive assets on a subset of sites is done in order to assure the survival of some of them. This preferential allocation of defense resources is to be hidden from the offense and often forces an attacker to waste offensive resources.

preferential offense The concentration of offensive assets on a subset of potential targets, thereby increasing the probability of their destruction.

preflight In aerospace operations, something that occurs before launch vehicle liftoff.

prelaunch survivability The probability that a warhead delivery system and/or its launch vehicle will survive an enemy attack under an established condition of warning.

preset guidance A technique of missile control wherein a predetermined flight path is set into the control mechanism and cannot be adjusted after launching.
See also: GUIDANCE SYSTEM.

pressurant Gas that provides ullage pressure in a propellant tank.

pressure (symbol: p) A thermodynamic property that two systems have in common when they are in mechanical equilibrium. Pressure can be defined as the normal component of force per unit area exerted by a fluid on a boundary. According to the *Pascal Principle,* the pressure at any point in a fluid at rest is the same in all directions. (Blaise Pascal [1623–62] was the French scientist who discovered this hydrostatic principle in the 1650s.) The fundamental principle of hydrostatics is:

$$dp/dz = -\rho g$$

where dp is the change in pressure corresponding to a change in height or depth (dz), ρ is the fluid density, and g is the acceleration due to gravity. Assuming that the density (ρ) of the fluid is constant, we can compute the hydrostatic pressure of a liquid from the following relationship:

$$p(z) = \rho\, g\, z$$

where p is the pressure and z is the height or depth with respect to some reference or datum, such as sea level.

In aerostatics, density varies (decreases) with height in the atmosphere, and, therefore, pressure cannot be evaluated as a function of height until the density is specified in some manner. The ideal gas law often can be used to describe the thermodynamic properties of a gas, such as air. Using this relationship

$$p = \rho\, R\, T$$

where p is the pressure of the gas, ρ is the density, T is the absolute temperature, and R is the specific gas constant.

The pascal (named in honor of Blaise Pascal) is the SI UNIT of pressure. It is defined as:

$$1 \text{ pascal} = 1 \text{ newton}/(\text{meter})^2$$

pressure-actuated seal A seal designed such that the pressure of the fluid being sealed activates or increases the sealing action.

pressure altimeter An altimeter that uses the change of atmospheric pressure with height to measure altitude. The *aneroid altimeter* is commonly used as pressure altimeter in aerospace applications, because of its rugged composition. Also called *barometric altimeter.*

pressure fed In rocketry, a propulsion system in which tank ullage pressure expels the propellants from the tanks into the combustion chamber of the engine.

pressure-laden sequence In rocketry, a method to accomplish fail-safe liquid-propellant engine starts by sequencing the operation of rocket engine control valves; the sequencing is achieved by vent mechanisms on the control system or propellant feed system, or both, that are triggered by pressure changes.

pressure recovery The conversion of velocity head to pressure head in a fluid system. In fluid dynamics, the term "head" (with various qualifications) generally refers to a difference in fluid energy as might be brought about by a change in pressure, a change in velocity, or a change in height.

pressure regulator A pressure control valve that varies the volumetric flow rate through itself in response to a downstream pressure signal so as to maintain the downstream pressure nearly constant.

pressure suit In general, a garment designed to provide pressure upon the body so that the respiratory and circulatory functions may continue normally, or nearly so, under low-pressure conditions, such as occur at high altitudes or in space without benefit of a pressurized module or crew compartment. 1. (partial) A skintight suit that does not completely enclose the body but that is capable of exerting pressure on the major portion of the body in order to counteract an increased intrapulmonary oxygen pressure. 2. (full) A suit that completely encloses the body and in which a gas pressure, sufficiently above ambient pressure for maintenance of respiratory and circulatory functions, may be sustained.

pressurization For a launch vehicle prior to liftoff, the sequence of operations that increases the propellant tank ullage pressure to the desired level just before the main sequence of propellant flow and engine firing.

pressurization system The set of fluid system components that provides and maintains a controlled gas pressure in the ULLAGE space of the launch vehicle propellant tanks.

pressurized habitable environment Any module or enclosure in space in which an astronaut may perform activities in a "shirt-sleeve" environment.

prestage A step in the action of igniting a large liquid-propellant rocket taken prior to the ignition of the full flow. It involves igniting a partial flow of propellants into the thrust chamber.

primary body The celestial body about which a satellite, moon, or other object orbits or from which it is escaping or toward which it is falling. For example, the primary body of Earth is the Sun; the primary body of the Moon is Earth.

primitive atmosphere The atmosphere of a planet or other celestial object as it existed in the early stages of its formation. For example, the primitive atmosphere of Earth some 3 billion years ago was thought to consist of water vapor, carbon dioxide, methane, and ammonia.

principal investigator (PI) The research scientist who is responsible for a space experiment and reporting the results.

probe 1. Any device inserted in an environment for the purpose of obtaining information about the environment. 2. An instrumented spacecraft or vehicle moving through the upper atmosphere or outer space or landing on another celestial body in order to obtain information about the specific environment, as, for example, a *deep-space probe*, a *lunar probe*, a *Jovian atmosphere probe*. 3. A slender device (e.g., a pitot tube) projected into a moving fluid for measurement purposes. 4. A ground-based set of sensors that could be launched rapidly into space on warning of attack and then function as tracking and acquisition sensors to support weapon allocation and firing by BALLISTIC MISSILE DEFENSE (BMD) weapons against enemy intercontinental ballistic missiles (ICBMs) and reentry vehicles (RVs). 5. An extended structure on one spacecraft that is inserted into a compatible receptacle (called a *drogue*) on another spacecraft, creating a linkage (docking) of the two spacecraft.

Prognoz A series of scientific Russian spacecraft placed in highly elliptical Earth orbits for the purpose of investigating the Sun, the effects of the solar wind on Earth's magnetosphere, and solar flares. The first spacecraft in this series, *Prognoz 1*, was launched from Tyuratam on April 14, 1972. This 845-kilogram pound-mass spacecraft was placed in a highly elliptical Earth orbit that had a perigee of 950 kilometers and an apogee of 200,000 kilometers, an inclination of 65 degrees, and a period of 4.04 days.

prograde orbit An orbit having an inclination of between 0 and 90 degrees.
See also: ORBITS OF OBJECTS IN SPACE.

program In an aerospace context, a major activity that involves the human resources, material, funding, and scheduling necessary to achieve desired space exploration or space technology goals. For example, the *space shuttle program*, the *space station program*, and the *Hubble Space Telescope program*.

Progress An uncrewed supply spacecraft, configured to perform automated rendezvous and docking with orbiting Russian space stations, such as the Salyut and the Mir. After the Russian cosmonauts have unloaded the *Progress* cargo ship, it separates from the space station, deorbits, and then burn up in the upper regions of Earth's atmosphere.

progressive burning The condition in which the burning area of a solid-propellant rocket grain increases with time, thereby increasing pressure and thrust as the burning progresses.

progressivity ratio Ratio of final burning surface area to initial burning surface area of a solid-propellant rocket grain.

project A planned undertaking of something to be accomplished, produced, or constructed, having a finite beginning and a finite ending; for example, the *Mercury Project* or the *Apollo-Soyuz Test Project.*

projectile An object propelled by an applied exterior force and continuing in motion by virtue of its own inertia, such as a bullet, shell, or missile.

proof test Pressure test to prove the structural integrity of a component or assembly without exceeding allowable stresses or producing any permanent deformation.

propellant In general, a material, such as a fuel, an oxidizer, an additive, a catalyst, or any compound or mixture of these, carried in a rocket vehicle that releases energy during combustion and thus provides thrust to the vehicle. Propellants commonly are in either liquid or solid form. Modern launch vehicles use three types of liquid propellants: petroleum-based, cryogenic, and hypergolic.

The petroleum used as a rocket fuel is a type of kerosene similar to the compound burned in heaters and lanterns. However, the rocket petroleum is highly refined and is called RP-1 (Refined Petroleum). It usually is burned with liquid oxygen (LOX) to produce thrust. However, the RP-1/LOX propellant combination delivers considerably less *specific impulse* (I_{sp}) than that delivered by cryogenic propellant combinations.

The specific impulse is an important parameter in describing the performance of a rocket engine and the propellant combination being used. It is defined as:

$$I_{sp} = (\text{thrust force})/(\text{mass flow rate of propellant})$$

In the SI UNIT system, specific impulse has the units of: newtons/(kilogram/second), which then reduces to meter/second. In the U.S. standard (or engineering) unit system, this important propellant performance parameter has the units of: pounds-force [lbf] per pounds-mass [lbm] per second (lbf/[lbm/s]), which often is simplified to just "sec-

ond(s)," since 1 lbf = 1 lbm at sea level on Earth. This is a somewhat confusing situation, but as long as the basic definition is used consistently within a system of units, the specific impulse (expressed as lbf/(lbm/s), "seconds", or m/s) will describe the relative performance capabilities of different types of rocket propellant combinations.

The most important cryogenic propellants are liquid oxygen (LOX), which serves as the oxidizer, and liquid hydrogen (LH_2), which serves as the fuel. The word "cryogenic" is a derivative of the Greek word "kruos" (κρυος) meaning "very cold." Oxygen remains in a liquid state at temperatures of -183° Celsius (C) (-298° Fahrenheit [F]) and below. Hydrogen remains in a liquid state at temperatures of -253° C (-423° F) and below.

In gaseous form, oxygen and hydrogen have such low densities that extremely large tanks would be required to store them onboard a rocket or launch vehicle. But cooling and compressing these propellants into liquids greatly increases their densities, making it possible to store large quantities in much smaller volume tanks. However, the tendency of liquid cryogenic propellants to return to gaseous form unless kept very cold makes them difficult to store over long periods of time. Therefore, cryogenic propellant generally are not considered suitable, for military rockets, which must be kept launch-ready for months at a time.

But the high-performance capability of the LH_2/LOX combination makes this low-temperature storage problem acceptable when the launch vehicle reaction time and propellant storability issues are not too critical. The LOX/LH_2 combination of cryogenic propellants has been used for a variety of U.S. rockets including: the RL-10 engines on the Centaur upper stage, the J-2 engines used on the Saturn V rocket vehicle's second and third stages, and the space shuttle's main engines (SSMEs).

Using the simplified U.S. customary unit of specific impulse for comparison purposes, the Centaur RL-10 engine has a specific impulse of 444 seconds, the J-2 engines of the Saturn V upper stages had specific impulse ratings of 425 seconds, and the space shuttle main engines have a specific impulse rating of 455 seconds. In contrast, the giant cluster of F-1 engines in the Saturn V vehicle first stage burned LOX and kerosene and had a specific impulse rating of just 260 seconds. This same propellant combination was used by the booster stages of the Atlas/Centaur rocket combination and yielded a specific impulse rating of 258 seconds in the Atlas' booster engine and a 220 seconds rating in its sustainer engine.

Hypergolic propellants are fuels and oxidizers that ignite on contact with each other and, therefore, need no ignition source. This easy start/restart capability makes them attractive for both crewed and uncrewed spacecraft maneuvering systems. Another advantage of hypergolic propellants is the fact that they do not have the extremely low storage temperature requirements needed for cryogenic propellants.

Typically, monomethyl hydrazine (MMH) is used as the hypergolic fuel and nitrogen tetroxide (N_2O_4) as the oxidizer. Hydrazine is a clear, nitrogen/hydrogen compound with a "fishy" smell; it is similar to ammonia. Nitrogen tetroxide is a reddish fluid that has a pungent, sweetish smell. Both of these fluids are highly toxic and must be handled under the most stringent safety precautions.

Hypergolic propellants are used in the core liquid propellant stages of the Titan family of launch vehicles and on the second stage of the Delta launch vehicle. The space shuttle orbiter uses hypergolic propellants (or "hypergols") in its orbital maneuvering system (OMS), which is used for orbital insertion, major orbital maneuvers, and deorbit operations. The orbiter's reaction control system (RCS) also uses hypergols to accomplish attitude control.

The solid-propellant rocket motor is the oldest and simplest of all forms of rocketry, dating back to the ancient Chinese. In its simplest form, the solid-propellant rocket is just a casing (usually steel) that is filled with a mixture of chemicals (fuel and oxidizer) in solid form that burn at a rapid rate after ignition, expelling hot gases from the nozzle to produce thrust. Solid-propellant rocket motors do not require turbopumps or complex propellant feed systems. A simple squib device at the top of the motor directs a high-temperature flame along the surface of the propellant grain, igniting it instantaneously.

Generally, solid propellants are stable and storable. Unlike a liquid-propellant rocket engine, however, a solid-propellant motor cannot be shut down. Once ignited, it will burn until all the propellant is exhausted.

Solid-propellant rockets have a variety of uses in space operations. Small solids often power the final stage of a launch vehicle or are attached to payload elements to boost satellites and spacecraft to higher orbits.

Medium-size solid-propellant rocket motors are used in special upper-stage systems that are designed specifically to boost a payload from LOW EARTH ORBIT (LEO) to geosynchronous Earth orbit (GEO) or to place a spacecraft on an interplanetary trajectory. The Payload Assist Module (PAM) and the Inertial Upper Stage (IUS) are examples of upper-stage systems.

The Scout launch vehicle is a four-stage rocket used to place small satellites into orbit. All four stages are solid-propellant rockets.

Finally, liquid-propellant launch vehicles such as the Titan, Delta, and space shuttle use solid-propellant rockets to provided added thrust at liftoff. The space shuttle, for example, uses the largest solid rocket motors ever built and flown. Each reusable solid rocket booster (SRB) contains 453,600 kilograms (1.1 million-pounds-mass) of propellant, in the form of a hard, rubbery substance with a consistency like that of a pencil eraser. A solid-propellant rocket motor always contains its own oxygen supply. The oxidizer in the shuttle's solid-rocket booster is ammonium perchlorate, which forms 69.93% of the mixture. The fuel is a form of powdered aluminum (16%), with an iron oxidizer powder (0.07%) as a catalyst. The binder that holds the mixture together is polybutadiene acrylic acid acrylonitrile (12.04%). In addition, the mixture contains an epoxy-curing agent (1.96%). The binder and epoxy also burn as fuel, adding thrust. The specific impulse of the shuttle's solid rocket booster is 242 seconds at sea level.

propellant mass fraction (symbol: ζ) In rocketry, the ratio of the propellant mass (m_p) to the total initial mass (m_o) of the vehicle before operation, including propellant load, payload, and structure.

$$\zeta = m_p/m_o$$

propulsion system The launch vehicle or space vehicle system that includes the rocket engines, propellant tanks, fluid lines, and all associated equipment necessary to provide the propulsive force as specified for the vehicle. For example, typical launch vehicles, expendable or reusable, depend on chemical propulsion systems (i.e., solid-propellant and/or liquid-propellant rockets) to take a payload from the surface of Earth into orbit (generally LOW EARTH ORBIT). Upper-stage chemical rockets also serve as the propulsion system used to take certain payloads from low Earth orbit to geosynchronous Earth orbit or to place a spacecraft on an interplanetary trajectory. However, nuclear propulsion systems (thermal or electric) also might be used to take a payload/spacecraft from Earth orbit to Mars, to the outer reaches of the solar system and even beyond. Solar-electric propulsion systems can be used to take nonpriority payloads from Earth orbit to various locations in the inner solar system. Finally, very exotic propulsion systems, based on nuclear fusion reactions or even matter-antimatter annihilation reactions, have been suggested (stretching our current knowledge of physics and engineering) as the propulsive systems necessary for interstellar travel.

See also: ELECTRIC PROPULSION; LAUNCH VEHICLE; ROCKET; SPACE NUCLEAR PROPULSION; UPPER STAGE.

propulsive efficiency (symbol: η_p) The efficiency with which energy available for propulsion is converted into thrust by a rocket engine. It is defined as:

$$\eta_p = \text{(vehicle energy)}/[\text{vehicle energy} + \text{residual kinetic energy in exhaust jet}]$$
$$\eta_p = [2\,V_{abs}/V_{jet}]/[1 + (V_{abs}/V_{jet})^2]$$

where V_{abs} is the absolute vehicle velocity (m/s) and V_{jet} is the effective (jet) exhaust velocity with respect to the vehicle (m/s). The propulsive efficiency describes how much of the kinetic energy of the rocket's exhaust jet is actually useful in propelling the vehicle. It reaches a maximum when the forward vehicle velocity is exactly equal to the exhaust velocity, that is, when $V_{abs}=V_{jet}$.

protogalaxy A galaxy at the early stages of its evolution.

proton (symbol: p) A stable elementary nuclear particle with a single positive charge and a rest mass of about 1.672×10^{-27} kilograms, which is about 1,836 times the mass of an electron. A single proton makes up the nucleus of an ordinary (or light hydrogen atom. Protons are also constituents of all other nuclei. The atomic number (Z) of an atom is equal to the number of protons in its nucleus.

Proton A Russian liquid-propellant expendable launch vehicle. The four-stage configuration of this vehicle often is used for interplanetary missions. It consists of three hypergolic stages and one cryogenic stage and is capable of placing 4,790 kilograms (kg) into geostationary transfer orbit (GTO), that is, an elliptical orbit with an apogee of 35,400 kilometers and a perigee of 725 kilometers. The Proton D-1 vehicle consists of three hypergolic stages and can place up to 20,950 kg into LOW EARTH ORBIT. The three-stage Proton vehicle configuration was used to place Salyut and Mir space station modules into orbit.

See also: LAUNCH VEHICLE.

proton storm The burst or flux of protons sent into space by a solar flare.

See also: SUN.

protoplanet Any of a star's planets as such planets emerge during the process of accretion (accumulation), in which planetesimals collide and coalesce into large objects.

protostar A star in the making. Specifically, the stage in a young star's evolution after it has separated from a gas cloud but prior to its collapsing sufficiently to support thermonuclear reactions.

protosun The Sun as it emerged in the formation of the solar system.

prototype 1. Of any mechanical device, a production model suitable for complete evaluation of mechanical and electrical form, design, and performance. 2. The first of a series of similar devices. 3. A physical standard to which replicas are compared. 4. A spacecraft or component that has passed or is undergoing tests, qualifying the design for fabrication of complete flight units or components thereof. 5. A model suitable for evaluation of design, performance, and production potential.

proving stand A test stand for reaction engines, especially rocket engines.

pulsar A stellar radio source that emits radio waves in a pulsating rhythm; believed to be a rotating neutron star.

pulse The variation of a quantity whose value is normally constant; this variation is characterized by a rise and a decay, and has a finite duration. This definition is so broad that it covers almost any transient phenomenon, such as the short burst of electromagnetic energy associated with a radar pulse. The only features common to all pulses are rise, finite duration, and decay (fall). The rise, duration, and decay must be of a quantity that is constant (not necessarily zero) for some time before the pulse and must have the same constant value for some time afterward.

pulse code modulation (PCM) The transmission of information by controlling the amplitude, position, or duration of a series of pulses. An analog signal (e.g., an image, music, a voice, etc.) is broken up into a digital signal (i.e., binary code) and then transmitted in this series of pulses via telephone line or radio waves.

pulsejet A jet engine containing neither compressor or turbine in which combustion takes place intermittently, producing thrust by a series of "miniexplosions," or combustion pulses. This type of engine is equipped with valves or shutters in the front that open and shut to take in air for the periodic combustion pulses. The World War II German V-1 "buzz-bomb" contained a pulsejet engine.

pump A machine for transferring mechanical energy from an external source to the fluid flowing through it. The increased energy is used to lift the fluid, to increase its pressure, or to increase its rate of flow.

pump-fed Term used to describe a propulsion system that incorporates a pump that delivers propellant to the combustion chamber at a pressure greater than the tank ullage pressure.

purge To rid a line or tank of residual fluid; especially of fuel or oxide in the tanks or lines of a rocket after a test firing or simulated test firing.

pyrogen A small rocket motor used to ignite a larger rocket motor.

pyrolysis Chemical decomposition of a substance due to the application of intense heat (thermal energy).

pyrometer An instrument for the remote (noncontact) measurement of temperatures. This term is generally applied to instruments that measure temperatures above 600° Celsius (1112° Fahrenheit).

pyrophoric fuel A fuel that ignites spontaneously in air. Compare this term with HYPERGOLIC FUEL (HYPERGOL).

pyrotechnic As an adjective, term used to describe a mixture of chemicals that, when ignited, is capable of reacting exothermically to produce light, heat, smoke, sound, or gas and also may be used to introduce a delay into an explosive train because of its known burning time. The term includes propellants and explosives; for example, *pyrotechnic device* and *pyrotechnic delay.*

pyrotechnics As a noun, igniters (other than pyrogens) in which solid explosives or energetic propellantlike chemical formulations are used as the heat-producing materials.

pyrotechnic subsystems Space system designers use electrically initiated pyrotechnic devices to open certain valves, ignite solid rocket motors, explode bolts to separate or jettison hardware, and to deploy spacecraft appendages. Pyrotechnic subsystems receive their electrical power from a bank of capacitors that are charged from the spacecraft's main power bus a few minutes prior to the planned detonation (activation) of a particular pyrotechnic device.

quad A unit in the U.S. Standard System used to express very large amounts of energy. One quad is defined as a quadrillion (i.e., 10^{15}) British thermal units (BTUs). As a point of reference, the total annual energy consumption of the United States is less than 100 quads.

$$1 \text{ quad} = 1 \times 10^{15} \text{ BTU} = 1.055 \times 10^{18}$$
$$\text{joules} = 2.93 \times 10^{11} \text{ kilowatt-hours}$$

quantity/distance (Q/D) Aerospace safety term for criteria that specify safe distances for the location of buildings that process or store rocket propellants or propellant ingredients (liquid or solid).

quantum (plural: quanta) 1. In general, a discrete small unit; in any given physical process, it is considered the minimum permissible unit of energy. 2. In modern physics, the discrete bundle of energy possessed by a photon (e.g., a light wave or a gamma ray). The energy of the photon (E) is related to its frequency (ν) by the equation:

$$E = h \cdot \nu$$

where E is the photon energy (joules), ν is the frequency (hertz), and h is Planck's constant (6.626×10^{-34} joule-seconds).

quantum theory The theory, first stated in 1900 by German physicist Max Planck (1858–1947), that all electromagnetic radiation is emitted and absorbed in "quanta," or discrete energy packets, rather than continuously. Each quantum of energy has a magnitude, hν, where h is the Planck constant (a quantity having the dimensions of energy x time, namely h = 6.626×10^{-34} joule-seconds) and ν is the

frequency. Planck's classic equation is, therefore, $E = h\nu$.

In his theory, Planck further postulated that a system (e.g., a BLACKBODY radiator) could change its energy only in discrete packets or an integral number of quanta (i.e., by hν, 2hν, 3hν, . . . nhν). Albert Einstein (1879–1955) used this quantum of energy concept in 1905 to explain the photoelectric effect, by assuming that light was radiated in quanta or photons. In 1913 the Danish physicist Niels Bohr (1885–1962), developed his theory of atomic spectra, by assuming that an atom (in this case, the hydrogen atom) can exist only in certain energy states and that photons (light) are emitted or absorbed when the atom changes from one energy state to another. Bohr proposed that the angular momentum of an orbiting electron can assume only an integral value (i.e., nh/2π, where n = 0, 1, 2, 3 . . . and h is the Planck constant).

In quantum theory, therefore, physical quantities are "quantized"—that is, certain restrictions are imposed on these physical quantities limiting them to a set of discrete values. Quantum changes in energy are small and, subsequently, observable only on the atomic scale. Classical mechanics (as developed from Newton's laws) can adequately describe the behavior of large-scale (nonrelativistic) systems. The original quantum theory applied the "quantum of energy" concept to problems in classical mechanics. More precise developments and refinements, involving the formulation of a new system of mechanics, resulted in the creation of *quantum mechanics* in the 1920s. Finally, the extension of quantum mechanics to include Einstein's special theory of relativity resulted in the formulation of relativistic quantum mechanics.

quasars Mysterious objects that appear almost like stars but are far more distant than any individual star we can now observe. These unusual objects were first discovered in the 1960s with radio telescopes, and they were called "quasi-stellar radio sources"—or quasars, for short. Quasars emit tremendous quantities of energy from very small volumes. Some of the most distant quasars yet observed are so far away that they are receding at more than 90% of the speed of light.

As bright, concentrated radiation sources, quasars are thought to be the nuclei of active galaxies. The optical brightness of some quasars has been observed to change by a factor of two in about a week, with detectable changes occurring in just one day. Therefore, astrophysicists now speculate that such quasars cannot be much larger than about one light-day across (a distance about twice the dimension of our solar system), because a light source cannot change brightness significantly in less time than it takes for light itself to travel. The problem facing scientists today is to explain how quasars can generate more energy than is possessed by an entire galaxy and generate this energy in so small a region of space. Also called *quasi-stellar objects* (QSOs).

See also: ACTIVE GALAXIES.

quiet Sun A term used by solar physicists to describe the minimum portion of the sunspot cycle for the Sun.

See also: SUN.

rad The traditional unit in radiation protection and nuclear technology for absorbed dose of ionizing radiation. A dose of 1 rad means the absorption of 100 ergs of ionizing radiation energy per gram of absorbing material (or 0.01 joule per kilogram in SI UNITS). The term is an acronym derived from *rad*iation *a*bsorbed *d*ose.

See also: ABSORBED DOSE.

radar An active form of remote sensing generally used to detect objects in the atmosphere and space by transmitting electromagnetic waves (e.g., radio or microwaves) and sensing the waves reflected by the object. The reflected waves (called "returns" or "echos") provide information on the distance to the object (or target) and the velocity of the object (or target). The reflected waves also can provide information about the shape of the object (or target). The term is an acronym for *ra*dio *d*etection *a*nd *r*anging.

Satellite-borne radar systems (called *synthetic aperture radar* or *SAR systems*) can be used to study the features of a planet's surface when conditions (e.g., clouds or night time) obscure the surface from observation in the visible portion of the electromagnetic spectrum.

See also: RADAR ASTRONOMY; RADAR IMAGING; RADARSAT; REMOTE SENSING.

radar altimeter An active instrument, carried onboard an aircraft, aerospace vehicle, or spacecraft, used for measuring the distance (or altitude) of the vehicle or craft above the surface of a planet. An accurate determination of altitude is obtained by carefully timing the travel of a radar pulse down to the surface and back.

radar astronomy The use of radar by astronomers to study objects in our solar system, such as the Moon, the planets, asteroids, and even planetary ring systems. For example, a powerful radar telescope, such as the Arecibo Observatory, can hurl a radar signal through the "opaque" Venusian clouds (some 80 kilometers thick) and then analyze the faint return signal to obtain detailed information for the preparation of high-resolution surface maps. Radar astronomers can precisely measure distances to celestial objects, estimate rotation rates, and also develop unique maps of surface features, even when the actual physical surface is obscured from view by thick layers of clouds.

See also: ARECIBO OBSERVATORY; MAGELLAN MISSION.

radar imaging An active remote sensing technique in which a radar antenna first emits a pulse of microwaves that illuminates an area on the ground (called a *footprint*). Any of the microwave pulse that is reflected by the surface back in the direction of the imaging system is then received and recorded by the radar antenna. An image of the ground thus is made as the radar antenna alternately transmits and receives pulses at particular microwave wavelengths and polarizations. Generally, a radar imaging system operates in the wavelength range of one centimeter to one meter, which corresponds to a frequency range of about 300 megahertz (MHz) to 30 gigahertz (GHz). The emitted pulses can be polarized in a single vertical or horizontal plane. About 1,500 high-power pulses per second are transmitted toward the target or surface area to be imaged, with each pulse having a pulse width (i.e., pulse duration) of between 10 to 50 microseconds (μs). The pulse typically involves

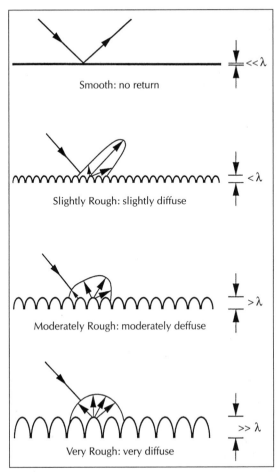

Figure 99. The effect of surface roughness on radar signal backscatter. Surfaces whose roughness is much less than the radar wavelength (λ), scatter in the specular direction. Rougher surfaces scatter more radar signal energy in all directions, including the direction back to the receiving antenna. *(NASA)*

As the radar imaging system moves along its flight path, the surface area illuminated by the radar also moves along the surface in a swath, building the image as a result of the radar platform's motion. The length of the radar antenna determines the resolution in the azimuth (i.e., along-track) direction of the image. The longer the antenna, the finer the spatial resolution in this dimension. The term "synthetic aperture radar" (SAR) refers to a technique used to synthesize a very long antenna by electronically combining the reflected signals received by the radar as it moves along its flight track.

As the radar imaging system moves, a pulse is transmitted at each position and the return signals (or echoes) are recorded. Because the radar system is moving relative to the ground, the returned signals (or echoes) are Doppler-shifted. This Doppler shift is negative as the radar system approaches a target and positive as it moves away from a target. When these Doppler-shifted frequencies are compared to a reference frequency, many of the returned signals can be focused on a single point, effectively increasing the length of the antenna that is imaging the particular point. This focusing operation, often referred to as *SAR processing,* is done rapidly through the use of high-speed digital computers and requires a very precise knowledge of the relative motion between the radar platform and the objects (surface) being imaged.

The synthetic aperture radar is now a well-developed technology that can be used to generate high-resolution radar images. The SAR imaging system is a unique remote sensing tool. Since it provides its own source of illumination, it can image at any time of the day or night, independent of the level of sunlight available. Because its radio-frequency wavelengths are much longer than those of visible light or infrared radiation, the SAR imaging system can penetrate through clouds and dusty conditions, imaging surfaces that are obscured to observation by optical instruments.

Radar images are composed of many picture elements, or pixels. Each dot or picture element in a radar image represents the radar backscatter from that area of the surface. Typically, dark areas in a radar image represent low amounts of backscatter (i.e., very little radar energy being returned from the surface), while bright areas indicate a large amount of backscatter (i.e., a great deal of radar energy being returned from the surface).

a small band of frequencies, centered on the operating frequency selected for the radar. The bandwidths used in imaging radar systems generally range from 10 to 200 MHz.

At the surface of Earth (or other planetary body, such as cloud-enshrouded Venus), the energy of this radar pulse is scattered in all directions, with some reflected back toward the antenna. The roughness of the surface affects radar backscatter. Surfaces whose roughness is much less than the radar wavelength scatter in the specular direction. Rougher surfaces scatter more energy in all directions, including the direction back to the receiving antenna. (See Figure 99.)

A variety of conditions determine the amount of radar signal backscatter from a particular target area. These conditions include: the geometric dimensions and surface roughness of the scattering objects in the target area, the moisture content of the target area, the angle of observation, and the wavelength of the radar system. As a general rule, the greater the amount of backscatter from an area (i.e., the brighter it appears in an image), the rougher the surface being imaged. Therefore, flat surfaces that reflect little or no radar (microwave) energy back toward the SAR imaging system usually appear dark or black in the radar image. In general, vegetation is moderately rough (with respect to most radar imaging system wavelengths) and consequently appears as gray or light gray in a radar image. Natural and human-made surfaces that are inclined toward the imaging radar system will experience a higher level of backscatter (i.e., appear brighter in the radar image) than similar surfaces that slope away from the radar system. Some areas in a target scene (e.g., the back slope of mountains) are shadowed and do not receive any radar illumination. These shadowed areas also will appear dark or black in the image. Urban areas provide interesting radar image results. When city streets are lined up in such a manner that the incoming radar pulses can bounce off the streets and then bounce off nearby buildings (a "double-bounce") directly back toward the radar system, the streets appear very bright (i.e., white) in a radar image. However, open roads and highways are generally physically flat surfaces that reflect very little radar signal, so often they appear dark in a radar image. Buildings that do not line up with an incoming radar pulse so as to reflect the pulse straight back to the imaging system actually appear light gray in a radar image, because buildings behave like very rough (diffuse) surfaces.

The amount of signal backscattered also depends on the electrical properties of the target and its water content. For example, a wetter object will appear bright, while a drier version of the same object will appear dark. A smooth body of water is the exception to this general rule. Since a smooth body of water behaves like a flat surface, it backscatters very little signal and will appear dark in a radar image.

Spacecraft-carried radar imaging systems have been used to explore and map the cloud-enshrouded surface of Venus. Earth-orbiting radar systems, such as NASA's Spaceborne Imaging Radar-C/X-band Synthetic Aperture Radar (SIR-C/X-SAR), which is carried into space in the space shuttle's cargo bay, support a variety of contemporary Earth resource observation and monitoring programs.

See also: MAGELLAN MISSION; PIONEER VENUS MISSION; RADARSAT; REMOTE SENSING.

Radarsat *Radarsat,* Canada's first remote sensing satellite, was placed in an 800-kilometer polar orbit by a U.S. Delta II expendable launch vehicle on November 4, 1995 from Vandenberg Air Force Base in California. The principal instrument onboard this spacecraft is an advanced synthetic aperture radar (SAR), which produces high-resolution surface images of Earth despite clouds and darkness. The *Radarsat's* SAR is an active sensor that transmits and receives a microwave signal (variations of C-band) that is sensitive to the moisture content of vegetation and soil and supports crop assessments in Canada and around the world. SAR imagery can provide important geological information for mineral and petroleum exploration. The instrument also delineates ice cover and its extent (e.g., first-year ice versus heavier multiyear ice), thereby permitting the identification of navigable Arctic sea routes. *Radarsat* was developed under the management of the Canadian Space Agency (CSA) in cooperation with the U.S. National Aeronautics and Space Administration (NASA), the National Oceanic and Atmospheric Administration (NOAA), the provincial governments of Canada, and the private sector. The U.S. supplied the launch vehicle for the 2,700-kilogram satellite in exchange for 15% of its viewing time. Canada has 51% of the observation time. The rest of the observation time is being marketed by Radarsat International. The spacecraft has a five-year life expectancy and probably will be followed by at least one more satellite.

See also: RADAR IMAGING; REMOTE SENSING.

radial-burning In rocketry, a solid-propellant grain that burns in the radial direction, either outwardly (e.g., an internal-burning grain) or inwardly (e.g., an internal-external burning tube or rod and tube grain).

See also: ROCKET.

radian A unit of angle. One radian is the angle subtended at the center of a circle by an arc equal in length to a radius of the circle.

$$1 \text{ radian} = 360°/(2\pi) = 57.2958°$$

radiance (symbol: L_e or L) For a point source of radiant energy, radiance is defined as the radiant intensity (I_e) in a specified direction per unit projected area; namely, $L_e = [\mathrm{d}\,I_e/\mathrm{d}\,A] \cdot \cos\theta$, where A is the area and θ is the angle between the surface and the specified direction. Radiance is expressed in watts per steradian per square meter (W sr^{-1} m^{-2}).

radiant flux (symbol: Φ_e or Φ) The total power (i.e., energy per unit time) emitted or received by a body in the form of electromagnetic radiation. Generally expressed in watts (W).

radiant heat transfer The transfer of thermal energy (heat) by electromagnetic radiation that arises due to the temperature of a body. Most energy transfer of this type is in the infrared portion of the electromagnetic spectrum. However, if the emitting object has a high enough temperature, it also will radiate in the visible spectrum and beyond (e.g., the Sun). The term "thermal radiation" often is used to distinguish this form of electromagnetic radiation from other forms, such as radio waves, light, X rays, and gamma rays. Unlike convection and conduction, radiant heat transfer takes place in and through a vacuum.

radiant intensity (symbol: I_e or I) The radiant flux (Φ_e) emitted by a point source per unit solid angle; measured in watts per steradian (W sr^{-1}).

radiation The propagation of energy by electromagnetic waves (photons) or streams of energetic nuclear particles. The energy so propagated. *Nuclear radiation* generally is emitted from atomic nuclei (as a result of various nuclear reactions) in the form of alpha particles, beta particles, neutrons, protons, and/or gamma rays.

radiation cooling In rocketry, the process of cooling a combustion chamber or nozzle in which thermal energy losses by radiation heat transfer from the outer combustion chamber or nozzle wall (to the surroundings) balances the heat gained (on the inner wall) from the hot combustion gases. As a result of radiation cooling, the combustion chamber or nozzle operates in a state of thermal equilibrium. To accommodate such heat transfer processes, radiatively cooled rocket engine components often are made of refractory metals or graphite.

radiation hardness The ability of electronic components and systems to function in high-intensity nuclear (ionizing) radiation environments. Spacecraft passing through or operating in a planet's trapped radiation belts would experience high-intensity nuclear radiation environments. Similarly, spacecraft exposed to solar flare conditions also can experience high-intensity radiation environments, depending on their distance from the Sun and the relative strength of the solar flare event. Techniques for increasing the radiation hardness of electronic components and systems include use of semiconductors that are less susceptible to ionizing radiation upset, shielding, reduction in size of the equipment/components, and redundancy.

radiation laws The collection of empirical and theoretical laws that describe radiative transport phenomena. The four fundamental laws that together provide a fundamental description of the behavior of blackbody radiation are: (1) *Kirchoff's law of radiation*—which is essentially a thermodynamic relationship between emission and absorption at any given wavelength and a given temperature; (2) *Planck's radiation law*—which describes the variation of intensity of a blackbody radiator at a given temperatures as a function of wavelength; (3) the *Stefan-Boltzmann law*—which relates the time rate of radiant energy emission from a blackbody to the fourth power of its absolute temperature; and (4) *Wien's displacement law*—which relates the wavelength of maximum intensity emitted by a blackbody to its absolute temperature.

See also: BLACKBODY; KIRCHOFF'S LAW (OF RADIATION); PLANCK'S RADIATION LAW; STEFAN-BOLTZMANN LAW; WIEN'S DISPLACEMENT LAW.

radiation sickness An illness resulting from excessive exposure to ionizing radiation. The earliest symptoms are blood cell changes, nausea, vomiting, and diarrhea, which may be followed by loss of hair, hemorrhage, inflammation of the mouth and throat, and general loss of energy. For radiation dose equivalent values of about 450 to 500 rem (4.5 to 5 sievert), this condition will prove fatal to 50% of the individuals so exposed. For radiation dose equivalent values of 1,000 rem or more (10 sievert or more), this illness is eventually fatal to all individuals so exposed. Sometimes called *acute radiation syndrome.*

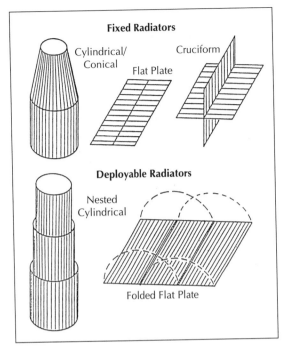

Fixed Radiators

Cylindrical/
Conical   Cruciform
        Flat Plate

Deployable Radiators

Nested
Cylindrical

Folded Flat Plate

Figure 100. Some radiator configurations. *(Drawing courtesy of U.S. Department of Energy)*

radiator 1. Any source of radiant energy. 2. In aerospace engineering, a device that rejects waste heat from a spacecraft or satellite to outer space by radiant heat transfer processes. Radiator design depends on both operating temperature and the amount of thermal energy to be rejected. The amount of waste heat that can be radiated to space by a given surface area is determined by the Stefan-Boltzmann law and is proportional to the fourth power of the radiating surface temperature. The surface area and mass of the thermal radiator are very sensitive to the heat rejection temperature. Higher heat rejection temperatures correspond to smaller radiator areas and, therefore, lower radiator masses. For radioisotope thermoelectric generator (RTG) power systems, for example, radiator temperatures are typically about 575° Kelvin (K).

Radiators can be fixed or deployable. Flat plate and cruciform configurations often are used. The radiator can be solid, all-metal construction, or else contain embedded coolant tubes and passageways to assist in the transport of thermal energy to all portions of the radiator surface. However, radiators with embedded coolant tubes and channels must be sufficiently thick ("armored") to protect against meteoroid impact damage and the subse-

quent loss of coolant. Heat pipe radiator configurations also have been considered. (See Figure 100.)

See also: STEFAN-BOLTZMANN LAW; SPACE NUCLEAR POWER.

radioactivity The spontaneous decay or disintegration of an unstable atomic nucleus, usually accompanied by the emission of ionizing radiation, such as alpha particles, beta particles, and gamma rays. The radioactivity, often shortened to just "activity," of natural and human-made (artificial) radioisotopes decreases exponentially with time, governed by the fundamental relationship:

$$N = N_0 e^{-\lambda t}$$

where N is the number of radionuclides (of a particular radioisotope) at time (t), N_0 is the number of radionuclides of that particular radioisotope at the start of the count (i.e., at t = 0), λ is the decay constant of the radioisotope, and t is time.

The decay constant (λ) is related to the half-life ($T_{1/2}$) of the radioisotope by the equation:

$$\lambda = (\ln 2)/T_{1/2} = 0.69315/T_{1/2}$$

The half-lives for different radioisotopes vary widely in value, from as short as about 10^{-8} seconds to as long as 10^{10} years and more. The longer the half-life of the radioisotope, the more slowly it undergoes radioactive decay. For example, the natural radioisotope uranium-238 has a half-life of 4.5 x 10^9 years and therefore is only slightly radioactive (emitting an alpha particle when it undergoes decay).

Radioisotopes that do not normally occur in nature but are made in nuclear reactors or accelerators are called *artificial radioactivity* or *human-made radioactivity*. Plutonium-239, with a half-life of 24,400 years, is an example of artificial radioactivity.

radio astronomy Branch of astronomy that collects and evaluates radio signals from extraterrestrial sources. Radio astronomy is a relatively young branch of astronomy. It was started in the 1930s, when Karl Jansky (1905–1950), an American radio engineer, detected the first extraterrestrial radio signals. Until Jansky's discovery, astronomers had used only the visible portion of the electromagnetic spectrum to view the universe. The detailed observation of cosmic radio sources is difficult, however, because these sources shed so little energy on Earth. But starting in the mid-1940s with the pioneering work of the British astronomer Sir

Alfred Charles Bernard Lovell (1913–), at the United Kingdom's Nuffield Radio Astronomy Laboratories at Jodrell Bank, the radio telescope has been used to discover some extraterrestrial radio sources so unusual that their very existence had not even been imagined or predicted by scientists.

One of the strangest of these cosmic radio sources is the pulsar—a collapsed giant star that emits pulsating radio signals as it spins. When the first pulsar was detected in 1967, it created quite a stir in the scientific community. Because of the regularity of its signal, scientists thought they had just detected the first interstellar signals from an intelligent alien civilization.

Another interesting celestial object is the quasar, or quasi-stellar radio source. Discovered in 1964, quasars now are considered to be entire galaxies in which a very small part (perhaps only a few light-days across) releases enormous amounts of energy—equivalent to the total annihilation of millions of stars. Quasars are the most distant known objects in the universe; some of them are receding from us at over 90% of the speed of light.

See also: ARECIBO OBSERVATORY; PULSAR; QUASAR.

radio frequency (RF) In general, a frequency at which electromagnetic radiation is useful for communication purposes; specifically, a frequency above 10,000 hertz and below 3×10^{11} hertz. One hertz is defined as 1 cycle per second.

See also: ELECTROMAGNETIC SPECTRUM.

radio galaxy A galaxy (often exhibiting a dumbbell-shaped structure) that produces very strong signals at radio wavelengths. Cygnus A, one of the closest bright radio galaxies, is about 650 million light-years away.

See also: RADIO ASTRONOMY.

radioisotope A radioactive isotope. An unstable isotope of an element that spontaneously decays or disintegrates, emitting nuclear radiation (e.g., an alpha particle, beta particle, or gamma ray). More than 1,300 natural and artificial radioisotopes have been identified.

radioisotope thermoelectric generator (RTG) A space power system in which thermal energy (heat) deposited by the absorption of alpha particles from a radioisotope source (generally plutonium-238) is converted directly into electricity.

Radioisotope thermoelectric generators, or RTGs, have been used in space missions where long life, high reliability, operation independent of the distance or orientation to the Sun, and operation in severe environments (e.g., lunar night, Martian dust storms) are critical. The first RTG used by the United States in space was the SNAP 3B design for the U.S. Navy's *Transit 4A* and *4B* satellites, which were launched successfully into orbit around Earth in June and November 1961, respectively. SNAP is an acronym that stands for *S*ystems for *A*uxiliary *N*uclear *P*ower.

SNAP-27 units provided electric power to instruments left on the lunar surface by the Apollo astronauts. SNAP-19 units provided electric power to the two highly successful Viking lander spacecraft that touched down on Mars in 1976. The *Pioneer 10/11* spacecraft that visited Jupiter and Saturn (*Pioneer 11* only) also were powered by SNAP-19 units. The *Voyager 1/2* spacecraft that explored the outer regions of our solar system, including flybys of Jupiter, Saturn, Uranus (*Voyager 2* only) and Neptune (*Voyager 2* only) were powered by an RTG unit called the Multihundred Watt (MHW) Generator. Finally, an RTG unit called the General Purpose Heat Source (GPHS) is providing electric power to more recent spacecraft, such as Galileo and Ulysses.

The radioisotope thermoelectric generators currently designed for space missions (i.e., the GPHS) contain several kilograms of an isotopic mixture of plutonium (primarily the isotope plutonium-238) in the form of an oxide, pressed into a ceramic pellet. The pellets are arranged in a converter housing and function as a heat source to generate the electricity provided by the RTG. The radioactive decay of plutonium-238, which has a half-life of 87.7 years, produces heat, some of which is converted into electricity by an array of thermocouples made of silicon-germanium junctions. Waste heat then is radiated into space from an array of metal fins.

Plutonium, like all radioactive substances and many nonradioactive materials, can be a health hazard under certain circumstances, especially if inadvertently released into the terrestrial environment. Consequently, RTGs fueled by plutonium are designed under rigorous safety standards with the specific goal that these devices be capable of surviving all credible launch accident environments without releasing their plutonium content.

Prior to launch, a nuclear-powered spacecraft undergoes a thorough safety analysis and review by various agencies of the government, including the Department of Energy. The results of that safety analysis and review also are evaluated by an independent panel of experts. Both these safety reviews are then sent to the White House; where the staff makes a final evaluation concerning the overall risk presented by the mission. Finally, presidential approval is required before a spacecraft carrying an RTG can be launched by the United States.

See also: SPACE NUCLEAR POWER; THERMOELECTRIC CONVERSION.

radiometer An instrument for detecting and measuring radiant energy, especially infrared radiation.

See also: REMOTE SENSING.

radionuclide A radioactive isotope characterized according to its atomic mass (A) and atomic number (Z). Radionuclides experience spontaneous decay in accordance with their characteristic half-life and can be either naturally occurring or human-made.

radio telescope A large, metallic device, generally parabolic (dish-shaped), that collects radio wave signals from extraterrestrial objects (e.g., active galaxies and pulsars) or from distant spacecraft and focuses these radio signals onto a sensitive radio-frequency (RF) receiver.

See also: ARECIBO OBSERVATORY; RADIO ASTRONOMY.

radio waves Electromagnetic waves of wavelength between about 1 millimeter (0.001 meter) and several thousand kilometers; and correspond-

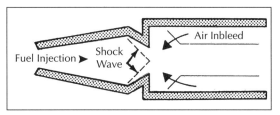

Figure 101. Shock wave-induced ignition in an air-breathing hypersonic ramjet engine. The fuel and air are heated to combustion temperatures as they pass through the shock wave. *(Drawing courtesy of NASA)*

ing frequencies between 300 gigahertz and a few kilohertz. The higher frequencies are used for spacecraft communications.

See also: ELECTROMAGNETIC SPECTRUM.

rail gun A device that uses the electromagnetic force experienced by a moving current in a transverse magnetic field to accelerate very small objects to very high velocities.

See also: GUN-LAUNCH TO SPACE.

ramjet A reaction (jet-propulsion) engine containing neither compressor nor turbine that depends for its operation on the air compression accomplished by the forward motion of the vehicle. The ramjet has a specially shaped tube or duct open at both ends into which fuel is fed at a controlled rate. The air needed for combustion is shoved, or "rammed," into the duct and compressed by the forward motion of the vehicle/engine assembly. This rammed air passes through a diffuser and is

Mission	Launch Date	Objective	Result(s)
Ranger 1	08/23/61	Lunar mission prototype	Launch failure
Ranger 2	11/18/61	Lunar mission prototype	Launch failure
Ranger 3	01/26/62	Lunar (impact) probe	Spacecraft failed; missed Moon
Ranger 4	04/23/62	Lunar (impact) probe	Spacecraft failed; impact farside
Ranger 5	10/18/62	Lunar (impact) probe	Spacecraft failed; missed Moon
Ranger 6	01/30/64	Lunar (impact) probe	Successful impact; cameras failed
Ranger 7	07/28/64	Lunar (impact) probe	Successful impact; numerous images
Ranger 8	02/17/65	Lunar (impact) probe	Successful impact; numerous images
Ranger 9	03/21/65	Lunar (impact) probe	Successful impact; numerous images

RANGER MISSION SUMMARY (1961–1965)

Source: NASA data.

mixed with fuel and burned. The combustion products then are expanded in a nozzle. A ramjet cannot operate under static conditions. The duct geometry depends on whether the ramjet operates at subsonic or supersonic speeds. (See Figure 101.)

range 1. The distance between any given point and an object or target. 2. Extent or distance limiting the operation or action of something, such as the *range* of a surface-to-air missile. 3. An area in and over which rockets, missiles, or aerospace vehicles are fired for testing.

Ranger Project The Ranger spacecraft were the first U.S. robot spacecraft sent toward the Moon in the early 1960s to pave the way for the Apollo Project's human landings at the end of that decade. The Rangers were a series of fully attitude-controlled spacecraft designed to photograph the lunar surface at close range before impacting. *Ranger 1* was launched on August 23, 1961 and set the stage for the rest of the Ranger missions, by testing spacecraft navigational performance. *Ranger 2* through *9* were launched from November 1961 through March 1965. (See Table) All of the early Ranger missions (*Ranger 1* through *6*)suffered setbacks of one type or another. Finally, *Ranger 7, 8,* and *9* succeeded with flights that returned many thousands of images (before impact) and greatly advanced scientific knowledge about the lunar surface.

See also: APOLLO PROJECT; MOON; SURVEYOR.

Figure 102. In this version of the basic Rankine cycle, a regenerator is used to increase overall efficiency. The regenerator captures some of the waste heat from the working fluid as it exits the turbine (5) (as a spent vapor) and then uses this "captured waste heat" to preheat the working fluid (2) (now a liquid) before it enters the boiler (3). *(Drawing courtesy of NASA)*

Rankine cycle A fundamental thermodynamic heat engine cycle in which a working fluid is converted from a liquid to a vapor by the addition of heat (in a boiler), and the hot vapor then is used to spin a turbine, thereby providing a work output. This work output often is used to rotate a generator and produce electric power. After passing through the turbine, the vapor is cooled in a condenser (rejecting heat to the surroundings). While being cooled, the working fluid changes phase (from vapor to liquid) and then passes through a pump to start the cycle again. (See Figure 102.)

See also: BRAYTON CYCLE; CARNOT CYCLE; HEAT ENGINE; THERMODYNAMICS.

Rankine temperature scale (symbol: R) An absolute temperature scale with the degree-interval of the Fahrenheit (F) temperature scale and the zero point at absolute zero. Consequently, 0° R is equivalent to -459.67° F; the normal boiling point of water is 671.67° R or 212° F.

See also: ABSOLUTE TEMPERATURE SCALE.

rate gyro A single-degree-of-freedom gyro having primarily elastic restraint of its spin axis about the output axis. In this type of gyro, an output signal is produced by gimbal angular displacement (relative to the base) that is proportional to the angular rate of the base about the input axis.

See also: GYRO.

rate integrating gyro A single-degree-of-freedom gyro having primarily viscous restraint of its spin axis about the output axis. In this type of gyro, an output signal is produced by gimbal angular displacement (relative to the base) that is proportional to the integral of the angular rate of the base about the input axis.

See also: GYRO.

raw data Data that have not been reduced or processed.

Rayleigh number (symbol: N_{Ra}) The dimensionless ratio between the product of buoyancy forces and heat advection and the product of viscous forces and heat conduction in a fluid. It can be expressed as:

$$N_{Ra} = \frac{\text{gravity}}{\text{thermal diffusivity}}$$
$$= \frac{c_p \, \rho^2 \, g \, l^3 \, \beta \, \Delta T}{\mu \, k}$$

where c_p is the specific heat at constant pressure, ρ is the density, g is the acceleration due to gravity, l is the characteristic length, β is the volume expansion coefficient with temperature, ΔT is the temperature difference, μ is the absolute viscosity, and k is the thermal conductivity of the fluid. Named after the British physicist Lord Rayleigh (1842–1919). The Rayleigh number equals the product of the Grashof and Prandtl numbers. It is a critical parameter in the theory of thermal instability.

See also: GRASHOF NUMBER; PRANDTL NUMBER.

Rayleigh scattering Selective scattering process caused by spherical particles (e.g., gas molecules) whose characteristic dimensions are about one-tenth (or less) of the wavelength (λ) of the radiation being scattered. Rayleigh scattering is inversely proportional to the fourth power of the wavelength—that is, this scattering process goes as λ^{-4}. For the scattering of visible light, this means that blue light ($\lambda = 0.4\ \mu m$) is scattered much more severely by Earth's atmosphere than longer-wavelength red light ($\lambda = 0.7\ \mu m$). For a clear daytime atmosphere, this selective scattering causes the sky to appear blue to an observer who is not along the direction of illumination. However, at sunrise and sunset, sunlight must pass through a much thicker column of the atmosphere and the preferential scattering blue light is so complete that essentially only red, orange, and yellow light reaches an observer on Earth. Named after the British physicist Lord Rayleigh (1842–1919).

Another selective scattering process is called *Mie scattering.* It involves scattering of radiation by particles whose characteristic size is between one-tenth (0.1) and 10 times the wavelength of the incident radiation. Smoke, fumes, and haze in Earth's atmosphere result in this type of scattering, which is inversely proportional to the wavelength of the radiation (i.e., the process goes as λ^{-1}).

Nonselective scattering is caused by particles (such as found in clouds and fog) with characteristic dimensions of more than about 10 times the wavelength of the radiation being scattered. These larger particles scatter all wavelengths of light equally well, so that clouds and fog appear white, even though they contain particles of water, which is actually colorless.

See also: MIE SCATTERING.

reaction 1. In chemistry, a chemical change that occurs when two or more substances are mixed, usually in solution; chemical activity between substances. 2. In physics, the equal in magnitude but opposite in direction force that occurs in response to the action of some other force in accordance with Newton's Third Law of Motion (i.e., the action-reaction principle).

See also: NEWTON'S LAWS OF MOTION.

reaction-control jets Small propulsion units on a spacecraft or aerospace vehicle that are used to rotate the craft or to accelerate it in a specific direction.

reaction control system (RCS) The collection of thrusters on the space shuttle orbiter vehicle that provides attitude control and three-axis translation during orbit insertion, on-orbit operations, and reentry.

See also: SPACE TRANSPORTATION SYSTEM.

reaction decoy In ballistic missile defense (BMD), a decoy deployed only upon warning or suspicion of imminent attack.

See also: BALLISTIC MISSILE DEFENSE.

reaction engine An engine that develops thrust by its physical reaction to the ejection of a substance (including possibly photons and nuclear radiations) from it; commonly, the reaction engine ejects a stream of hot gases created by combusting a propellant within the engine.

A reaction engine operates in accordance with Newton's Third Law of Motion (i.e., the action-reaction principle). Both rocket engines and jet engines are reaction engines. Sometimes called a *reaction motor.*

See also: NEWTON'S LAWS OF MOTION; ROCKET.

reaction time In human factors engineering, the interval between an input signal (physiological) or a stimulus (psychophysiological) and a person's response to it. Normally it takes a human being at least three-tenths of a second (0.3 sec) to begin to respond to a crisis or emergency situation (e.g., applying the brakes of an automobile). Training and special alarms and signals can reduce this reaction time a bit, while inexperience, panic, or fear can significantly lengthen it.

reaction turbine A type of turbine that has rotary blades shaped so that they form a ring of nozzles.

The turbine then is rotated by the reaction of the fluid ejected from between the blades.

See also: TURBINE.

readout 1. (verb) The action of a spacecraft's transmitter sending data that either are being instantaneously acquired or else extracted from storage (often by playing back a magnetic tape upon which the data have been recorded previously). 2. (noun) The data transmitted by the action described in sense 1. 3. (verb) In computer operations, to extract information from storage.

readout station A recording (or receiving) station at which the data-carrying radio-frequency signals transmitted by a spacecraft or space probe are acquired and initially processed.

real-time Time in which reporting on or recording events is simultaneous with the events; essentially, "as it happens."

real-time data Data presented in usable form at essentially the same time the event occurs.

reconnaissance satellite An Earth-orbiting military satellite intended to perform reconnaissance missions against enemy nations and potential adversaries. In the 1960s the United States developed and flew its first generation of photoreconnaissance satellites, called the CORONA, ARGON, and LANYARD systems.

In 1958 during the cold war, President Dwight D, Eisenhower approved a program that would answer questions about Soviet missile capability

Figure 103. A recently declassified U.S. reconnaissance satellite image of a major Soviet strategic bomber base near Dolon, Kazakhstan. This image (taken on August 20, 1966) demonstrates the ability of the early satellite imagery systems to distinguish between heavy bombers and transport aircraft seen on the airfield's main parking apron. The photograph is a 30X enlargement of the original image.   *(Photograph courtesy of the National Reconnaissance Office [NRO])*

and replace risky U-2 reconnaissance flights over Soviet territory. The Central Intelligence Agency (CIA) and the U.S. Air Force would jointly develop satellites to photograph denied areas from space. The program had both a secret mission and a secret name—CORONA.

The CIA and the air force developed this first-generation space program with great speed and tight secrecy. In August 1960, after numerous unsuccessful attempts, a CORONA satellite was launched successfully and its film capsule was recovered from space. During the next 12 years, CORONA satellites ushered in a new era of technical intelligence and a new era of space "firsts" that also contributed to advancements in other areas of the national space program. For example, the CORONA program provided valuable experience on how to recover objects from orbit—experience that was later used to recover astronauts from orbit during NASA's Mercury, Gemini, and Apollo projects. CORONA also provided a fast and relatively inexpensive way to map Earth from space.

But the most important contribution of the CORONA system to national security came from the intelligence it provided. During the cold war, CORONA looked through the Iron Curtain and helped lay the groundwork for important disarmament agreements. For example, with reconnaissance satellites, the United States could verify reductions in missiles without on-site inspections. Satellite imagery gave U.S. leaders the confidence to enter into negotiations and to sign important arms control agreements with the Soviet Union. Successor programs continued to monitor intercontinental ballistic missile (ICBM) sites and verify strategic arms agreements and the Nuclear Nonproliferation Treaty.

The CORONA program operated from August 1960 to May 1972 and collected both intelligence and mapping imagery. ARGON was a mapping system that used the organizational framework of CORONA and achieved 7 of 12 successful missions from May 1962 to August 1964. Finally, LANYARD was an attempt to gain higher-resolution imagery. It flew one successful mission in 1963.

Early imagery collections were driven, for the most part, by the pressures of the cold war and the needs of the United States to confirm suspected developments in Soviet strategic arms capabilities. (See Figure 103.) Worldwide photographic coverage also was used to produce maps and charts for the Department of Defense and other U.S. government mapping programs.

A presidential executive order (dated February 24, 1995) has declassified more than 800,000 images collected by these early photoreconnaissance systems from 1960 to 1972. The historic, declassified imagery (some with a resolution of 1.82 meters [6 feet]) is being made available to assist environmental scientists improve their understanding of global environmental processes and to develop a baseline in the 1960s for assessing important environmental changes.

See also: NATIONAL RECONNAISSANCE OFFICE (NRO).

recovery The procedure or action that occurs when the whole of a satellite, spacecraft, scientific instrument package, or component of a rocket vehicle is recovered after a launch or mission; the result of this procedure.

rectifier A device for converting alternating current (a.c.) into direct current (d.c.); usually accomplished by permitting current flow in one direction only.

recurring training The process by which an astronaut maintains and updates the knowledge and skills required for flight certification. This training is flight independent.

recycle In aerospace launch operations, to stop the count and to return to an earlier point in the countdown; as, for example, in "we have *recycled* and are now at T minus two hours and counting."

Redeye (FIM-43) A U.S. Army, lightweight, person-portable, shoulder-fired air defense artillery weapon for low-altitude air defense of forward combat area troops.

red fuming nitric acid (RFNA) Concentrated nitric acid (HNO_3) in which nitrogen dioxide (NO_2) has been dissolved. This toxic and corrosive mixture typically contains between 5 and 20% nitrogen dioxide. It is used as an oxidizer in liquid-propellant rockets.

redline 1. (noun) Term denoting a critical value for a parameter or a condition that, if exceeded, threatens the integrity of a system, the performance of a vehicle, or the success of a mission. 2. (verb) To establish a critical value as described in sense 1.

redshift The apparent increase in the wavelength of a light source caused by the receding motion of the source. The Doppler-effect shift of the visible spectra of distant galaxies toward red light (i.e., longer wavelength) indicates that these galaxies are receding. The greater redshift observed in more distant galaxies has been interpreted that the universe is expanding. Compare with BLUESHIFT.

Redstone An early, liquid-propellant, medium-range surface-to-surface missile used by the U.S. Army. The Redstone served as the first stage of the Jupiter-C vehicle that launched the first American satellite, *Explorer-1*, in January 1958. It also served as the launch vehicle for Astronaut Alan Shepard's suborbital flight on May 5, 1961 in the Mercury *Freedom 7* capsule—the first American human space mission.
See also: EXPLORER-1; MERCURY PROJECT.

Reech number A nondimensional number expressing the ratio of gravity force to inertial force, that is

$$\text{Reech number} = \frac{\text{gravity force}}{\text{inertia force}} = \frac{lg}{V^2}$$

where l is the characteristic length, g is the acceleration of gravity, and V is the velocity. The Reech number is the reciprocal of the Froude number.
See also: FROUDE NUMBER.

reentry The return of objects, originally launched from Earth, back into the sensible (measurable) atmosphere; the action involved in this event. The major types of reentry are: ballistic, gliding, and skip. To perform a safe controlled reentry, a spacecraft or aerospace vehicle must be capable of achieving a controlled dissipation of its kinetic and potential energies. The kinetic and potential energy values are determined by the returning object's velocity and altitude at the atmospheric reentry interface. Successful reentry, culminating in a safe landing on the surface of Earth (land or water), requires a very carefully designed and maintained flight trajectory.

Random or uncontrolled reentry, as might occur with a derelict satellite or piece of space debris, normally results in excessive aerodynamic heating and the burnup of the object in the upper atmosphere. On certain occasions, however, natural or human-made objects have undergone uncontrolled

reentry and actually survived the fiery plunge through the atmosphere, impacting on Earth. Also called *entry* in the aerospace literature.

reentry body That part of a rocket or space vehicle that reenters Earth's atmosphere after flight above the sensible (measurable) atmosphere.

reentry corridor The narrow region or pathway, established primarily by velocity and altitude, along which a spacecraft or aerospace vehicle must travel in order to return safely to Earth's surface. The design of the vehicle and the operational circumstances (e.g., normal end-of-mission return to Earth, emergency reentry, etc.) also contribute to the dimensions of the reentry corridor.

reentry nose cone A nose cone designed especially for reentry; usually consisting of one or more chambers protected by a specially designed outer surface that serves as both an aerodynamic surface and a heat shield.

reentry phase That portion of the trajectory of a ballistic missile or aerospace vehicle where there is a significant interaction of the vehicle and Earth's sensible (measurable) atmosphere, following flight in outer space.
See also: BALLISTIC MISSILE DEFENSE.

reentry trajectory The trajectory or pathway followed by an aerospace vehicle, spacecraft, or other object during reentry. If the object is unguided after passing the reentry interface at the top of the sensible (measurable) atmosphere, its trajectory will be essentially ballistic. With controlled aerodynamic maneuvering and guidance during reentry, however, the object would follow a glide or skip trajectory as it descends to the surface of Earth.

reentry vehicle (RV) 1. In general, that part of a space vehicle designed to reenter Earth's atmosphere in the terminal portion of its trajectory. 2. In the context of ballistic missile defense (BMD), that part of a ballistic missile (or post-boost vehicle) that carries the nuclear warhead to its target. The reentry vehicle is designed to enter Earth's atmosphere in the terminal portion of its trajectory and proceed to its target. The reentry vehicle is designed to survive rapid heating during high-velocity flight through the atmosphere and to protect its warhead until the nuclear weapon can detonate at the target.

See also: BALLISTIC MISSILE DEFENSE.

reentry window The area at the limits of Earth's sensible (measurable) atmosphere through which an aerospace vehicle or spacecraft in a given trajectory should pass to accomplish a successful reentry.

reflectance (symbol: ρ) In radiation heat transfer, the reflectance (ρ) of a body is defined as the ratio of the incident radiant energy reflected by the body to the total radiant energy falling on the body. The reflecting surface of the body may be *specular* (mirrorlike) or *diffuse*. For the special case of an ideal BLACKBODY, all the radiant energy incident upon this blackbody is absorbed and none is reflected, regardless of wavelength or direction. Therefore, the reflectance for a blackbody has a value of zero, that is, $\rho_{blackbody} = 0$. All other "real-world" solid objects have a reflectance of greater than (or perhaps approximately equal to) zero. Also called *reflectivity*. Compare with ABSORPTANCE and TRANSMITTANCE.

reflecting telescope A telescope that collects and focuses light from distant objects by means of a mirror (called the *primary mirror*). The first reflecting telescope was introduced by Sir Isaac Newton (1642–1727) in 1670, and his design is sometimes referred to as a *Newtonian reflector*.

See also: TELESCOPE.

refracting telescope A telescope that collects and focuses light from distant objects by means of a lens (called the *objective lens*) or system of lenses. Also called a *refractor*.

See also: TELESCOPE.

refraction The deflection or bending of electromagnetic waves when these waves pass from one type of transparent medium into another. For example, visible light, passing through a prism at a suitable angle, is dispersed into a continuum of colors. This happens because of refraction. When visible light waves cross an interface between two transparent media of different densities (e.g., from air into glass) at an angle other than 90 degrees, the light waves are bent (or refracted). Different wavelengths of visible light are bent different amounts; this causes them to be dispersed into a continuum of colors.

The *index of refraction* is defined as the ratio of the speed of light in a vacuum to the speed of light in the transparent substance of the observed medium. Each type of transparent substance lowers the speed of light slightly and by a different amount; low-density air has a different index of refraction from high-density air and from water, glass, carbon dioxide (gas), and so on.

regenerative cooling A common approach to cooling large liquid-propellant rocket engines and nozzles, especially those that must operate for an appreciable period of time. In this cooling technique, one of the liquid propellants (e.g., liquid oxygen) is first sent through special cooling passages in the thrust chamber and nozzle walls before being injected into the combustion chamber.

regenerative life support system A controlled ecological life support system in which biological and physiochemical subsystems produce plants for food and process solid, liquid, and gaseous wastes for reuse in the system.

regenerator A device used in a thermodynamic process for capturing and returning to the process thermal energy (heat) that otherwise would be lost. The use of a regenerator helps increase the thermodynamic efficiency of a heat engine cycle like the RANKINE CYCLE.

regolith The lunar regolith is the unconsolidated mass of surface debris that overlies the Moon's bedrock. This blanket of pulverized lunar "dust and soil" was created by eons of meteoric and cometary impacts. The "fines" are the fraction of the lunar regolith containing particles that are less than one millimeter in diameter.

See also: MOON.

regressive burning With respect to a solid-propellant rocket, the condition in which the thrust, pressure, or burning surface decreases with time or with the amount of web burned.

See also: WEB.

regulator Flow-control device that adjusts the pressure and controls the flow of fluid (propellant) to meet the demands of a liquid-propellant rocket engine.

reheating In thermodynamics, the addition of thermal energy (heat) to a working fluid in a heat engine after a partial expansion in a multistage turbine. Reheating is used to increase the thermodynamic efficiency of a cycle like the RANKINE CYCLE.

relative state In aerospace operations, the position and motion of one spacecraft relative to another.

relative temperature scale A temperature scale of common convenience, usually defined with respect to such easily reproduced reference points as the normal boiling point of water (100° Celsius [C]) or the ice point of water (0° C). The Celsius (formerly Centigrade) scale and the Fahrenheit scale are relative temperature scales. Note: In many aerospace engineering calculations, absolute temperatures (i.e., temperature expressed in Kelvin or Rankine units) are required.

See also: ABSOLUTE TEMPERATURE SCALE.

relativistic In general, pertaining to an object (including nuclear particles) moving at speeds that are an appreciable fraction of the speed of light (c).

relativity The theory of space and time developed by Albert Einstein (1879–1955), which has become one of the foundations of modern physics. Einstein's theory of relativity often is discussed in two general categories: the *special theory of relativity,* which he first proposed in 1905, and the *general theory of relativity,* which he presented in 1915.

The special theory of relativity is concerned with the laws of physics as seen by observers moving relative to one another at constant velocity—that is, by observers in nonaccelerating or inertial reference frames. Special relativity has been well demonstrated and verified by many types of experiments and observations.

Einstein proposed two fundamental postulates in formulating special relativity: (1) *First Postulate of Special Relativity:* The speed of light (c) has the same value for all (inertial-reference-frame) observers, regardless and independent of the motion of the light source or the observers. (2) *Second Postulate of Special Relativity:* All physical laws are the same for all observers moving at constant velocity with respect to each other.

From the theory of special relativity, scientists now conclude that only a "zero-rest-mass" particle, such as a photon, can travel at the speed of light. Another major consequence of special relativity is the equivalence of mass and energy, which is expressed in Einstein's famous formula:

$$E = \Delta m\, c^2$$

where E is the energy equivalent of an amount of matter (Δm) that is annihilated or converted completely into pure energy and c is the speed of light.

In 1915 Einstein introduced his general theory of relativity. He used this development to describe the space-time relationships developed in special relativity for cases where there was a strong gravitational influence—such as white dwarf stars, neutron stars, and black holes. One of Einstein's conclusions was that gravitation is not really a force between two masses (as Newtonian mechanics indicates) but rather arises as a consequence of the curvature of space and time. In a four-dimensional universe (x, y, z, and time), space-time becomes curved in the presence of matter.

The fundamental postulate of general relativity is also called *Einstein's principle of equivalence:* The physical behavior inside a system in free-fall is indistinguishable from the physical behavior inside a system far removed from any gravitating matter (i.e., the complete absence of a gravitational field).

Several experiments have been performed to confirm the general theory of relativity. These experiments included observation of the bending of electromagnetic radiation (starlight and radio-wave transmissions from the Viking Project on Mars) by the Sun's immense gravitational field and recognizing the subtle perturbations (disturbances) in the orbit (at perihelion) of the planet Mercury as caused by the curvature of space-time in the vicinity of the Sun. While some scientists do not think that these experiments have demonstrated the validity of general relativity conclusively, data from more powerful space-based observatories in the upcoming years should provide additional experimental evidence.

reliability The probability of specified performance of a piece of equipment or system under stated conditions for a given period of time.

relief valve Pressure-relieving device that opens automatically when a predetermined pressure is reached.

rem In radiation protection and nuclear technology, the traditional unit for dose equivalent (symbol: H). The dose equivalent in rem is the product of the absorbed dose (symbol: D) in rad and the quality factor (QF) as well as any other modifying factors considered necessary to characterize and evaluate the biological effects of ionizing radiation doses received by human beings or other living creatures. The term is an acronym derived from the expression: *roentgen equivalent man*. The rem is related to the *sievert*, the SI UNIT of dose equivalent, as follows: 100 rem = 1 sievert.

See also: DOSE EQUIVALENT.

remaining body That part of an expendable rocket vehicle that remains after the separation of a fallaway section or companion body. In a multistage rocket, the remaining body diminishes in size as each section or part is cast away and successively becomes a different body.

remote control Control of an operation from a distance, especially by means of telemetry and electronics; a controlling switch, level, or other device used in this type of control, as in *remote-control arming switch*.

See also: TELEOPERATION.

remotely piloted vehicle (RPV) An aircraft or aerospace vehicle whose pilot does not fly on board but rather controls it at a distance (i.e., remotely) using a telecommunications link from a crewed aircraft, aerospace vehicle, or ground station. RPVs often are used on extremely hazardous missions or on long-duration missions involving extended loitering and surveillance activities. Also called an *unmanned* (or *uncrewed*) *aerial vehicle (UAV)*.

remote manipulator system (RMS) The Canadian-built, 15.2-meter- (50-foot-) long articulating arm that is remotely controlled from the aft flight deck of the space shuttle orbiter. The elbow and waist movements of the RMS permit payloads to be grappled for deployment out of the cargo bay or to be retrieved and secured in the cargo bay for on-orbit servicing or return to Earth. Because the RMS can be operated from the shirt-sleeve environment of the orbiter cabin, an extravehicular activity (EVA) often is not required to perform certain orbital operations.

See also: SPACE TRANSPORTATION SYSTEM.

remote sensing The sensing of an object, event, or phenomenon without having the sensor in direct contact with the object being studied. Information transfer from the object to the sensor is accomplished through the use of the electromagnetic spectrum. Remote sensing can be used to study Earth in detail from space or to study other objects in the solar system, generally using flyby and orbiter spacecraft. Modern remote sensing technology uses many different portions of the electromagnetic spectrum, not just the visible portion we see with our eyes. As a result, often very different and very interesting "images" are created by these new remote sensing systems.

For example, Figure 104 is a radar image showing the volcanic island of Reunion, about 700 kilometers (434 miles) east of Madagascar in the southwest Indian Ocean. The southern half of the island is dominated by the active volcano Piton de la Fournaise. This is one of the world's most active volcanoes, with more than 100 eruptions in the last 300 years. The most recent activity occurred in the vicinity of Dolomieu Crater, shown in the lower center of the image within a horseshoe-shaped collapse zone. The radar illumination is from the left side of the image and dramatically emphasizes the precipitous cliffs at the edges of the central canyons of the island. These canyons are remnants from the collapse of formerly active parts of the volcanoes that built the island. This image was acquired by the Spaceborne Imaging Radar-C/X-Band Synthetic Aperture Radar (SIR-C/X-SAR) flown aboard the space shuttle *Endeavour* on October 5, 1994. The SIR-C/X-SAR is part of the Mission to Planet Earth (MTPE) program of the National Aeronautics and Space Administration (NASA). The radars illuminate Earth with microwaves, allowing detailed observations at any time regardless of weather or sunlight conditions. SIR-C/X-SAR, a joint mission of the German (DARA), Italian (ASI), and American (NASA) space agencies, uses three microwave wavelengths: L-band (24 centimeters [cm]), C-band (6 cm), and X-band (3 cm). The international scientific community is using these multifrequency radar imagery data to better understand the global environment and how it is changing.

Earth receives and is heated by energy in the form of electromagnetic radiation from the Sun. Some of this incoming solar radiation is reflected by the atmosphere, while most penetrates the atmosphere and subsequently is reradiated by atmospheric gas molecules, clouds, and the surface of Earth itself (including, e.g., oceans, mountains, plains, forests, ice sheets, and urbanized areas). All remote sensing systems (including those used to observe Earth from space) can be divided into two general classes: *passive sensors* and *active sensors*. Passive sensors observe reflected solar radiation (or emissions characteristic of and produced by the target itself), while active sensors (like a radar system) provide their own illumination on the target. Both passive and active remote sensing systems can be used to obtain images of the target or scene or else simply to collect and measure the total amount of energy (within a certain portion of the spectrum) in the field of view.

Passive sensors collect reflected or emitted radiation. Types of passive sensors include: *imaging radiometers* and *atmospheric sounders.* Imaging radiometers sense the visible, near-infrared, thermal-infrared, or ultraviolet wavelength regions and provide an image of the object or scene being viewed. Atmospheric sounders collect the radiant energy emitted by atmospheric constituents, such as water vapor or carbon dioxide, at infrared and microwave wavelengths. These remotely sensed data are then used to infer temperature and humidity throughout the atmosphere.

Active sensors provide their own illumination (radiation) on the target and then collect the radiation reflected back by the object. Active remote sensing systems including:*imaging radar, scatterometers, radar altimeters,* and *lidar altimeters.* An imaging radar emits pulses of microwave radiation from a radar transmitter and collects the scattered radiation to generate an image. (Look again at Figure 104 for an example of a detailed radar image collected from space.) Scatterometers emit microwave radiation and sense the amount of energy scattered back from the surface over a wide field of view. These type of instruments are used to measure surface wind speeds and direction and to determine cloud content. Radar altimeters emit a narrow pulse of microwave energy toward the surface and accurately time the return pulse reflected from the surface, thereby providing a precise measurement of the distance (altitude) above the surface. Similarly, lidar altimeters emit a narrow pulse of laser light (visible or infrared) toward the surface and time the return pulse reflected from the surface.

Today, remote sensing of Earth from space provides scientific, military, governmental, industrial, and individual users with the capacity to gather data to perform a variety of important tasks. These tasks include: (1) simultaneously observing key

Figure 104. A radar image (C and X band) of the volcanic island of Réunion, which lies about 700 kilometers east of Madagascar in the southwest Indian Ocean. This image was acquired by NASA's Spaceborne Imaging Radar-C/X Band-Synthetic Aperture Radar (SIR-C/X-SAR) system flown onboard the space shuttle *Endeavour* on October 5, 1994 *(Courtesy of NASA/JPL)*

elements of an interactive Earth system; (2) monitoring clouds, atmospheric temperature, rainfall, wind speed, and direction; (3) monitoring ocean surface temperature and ocean currents; (4) tracking anthropogenic and natural changes to the environment and climate; (5) viewing remote or difficult-to-access terrain; (6) providing synoptic views of large portions of Earth's surface without being hindered by political boundaries or natural barriers; (7) allowing repetitive coverage of the same area over comparable viewing conditions to support change detection and long-term environmental monitoring; (8) identifying unique surface features (especially with the assistance of multispectral imagery); and (9) performing terrain analysis and measuring moisture levels in soil and plants.

Space-based remote sensing is a key technology in our intelligent stewardship of planet Earth, its resources, and interwoven biosphere in the 21st century. Monitoring of the weather and climate supports accurate weather forecasting and identifies trends in the global climate. Monitoring of the land surface assists in global change research, the management of known natural resources, the exploration for new resources (e.g., oil, gas, and minerals), detailed mapping, urban planning, agriculture, forest management, water resource assessment, and national security. Monitoring of the oceans helps determine such properties as ocean productivity, the extent of ice cover, sea-surface winds and waves, ocean currents and circulation, and ocean-surface temperatures. These type of ocean data have particular value to scientists as well as to the fishing and shipping industries.

The concept of a civilian Earth resources satellite was developed in the U.S. Department of the Interior in the mid-1960s. NASA then embarked on an initiative to develop and launch the first Earth monitoring satellite to meet the needs of resource managers and Earth scientists. The U.S. Geological Survey (USGS) entered into a partnership with NASA in the early 1970s to assume responsibility for the archive management of Landsat data products. On July 23, 1972, NASA successfully launched the first in a series of satellites designed to provide repetitive global coverage of Earth's landmasses. This remote sensing spacecraft initially was called the *Earth Resources Technology Satellite-A* (*ERTS-A*). It used a Nimbus-spacecraft type platform that was modified to carry remote sensing systems and data relay equipment. When operational orbit was achieved, the satellite was designated *ERTS-1*. Later its name was changed again to *Landsat-1*. This satellite continued to function beyond its design life of one year and finally ceased operation on January 6, 1978—more than five years after its launch date.

The second in this series of Earth resources satellites (called initially *ERTS-B*) was launched successfully on January 22, 1975. Three additional Landsats (called *Landsats 3, 4,* and *5* respectively) were launched in 1978, 1982, and 1984. Each successive satellite system had improved sensor and communications capabilities. *Landsat 6*, developed by Earth Observation Satellite (EOSAT) Company under a U.S. Department of Commerce contract, was launched by a Titan 2 expendable vehicle from Vandenberg Air Force Base, California on October 5, 1993. The advanced remote sensing spacecraft separated from the Titan booster but failed to achieve orbit. A review board has attributed the failure to a ruptured hydrazine manifold that rendered the satellite's reaction engine assemblies useless because the hydrazine fuel could not reach the engines. As a consequence, there was a failure to maintain attitude control during the apogee kick motor (AKM) burn. This failure caused the spacecraft to tumble during the AKM burn and not accumulate sufficient energy to attain a proper orbit.

Landsats 1 through *3* operated in a near-polar orbit at an altitude of 920 kilometers (570 miles) with an 18-day repeat coverage cycle. These remote sensing satellites carried two passive sensors: a return beam vidicon (RBV) and a multispectral scanner (MSS). The RBV sensor was essentially a television camera that did not achieve the popularity of the MSS sensor. The MSS sensors were line scanning devices, observing Earth perpendicular to the orbital track. The cross-track scanning was accomplished by an oscillating mirror; six lines were scanned simultaneously in each of four spectral bands for each mirror sweep. The forward motion of the satellite provided the along-track scan line progression. *Landsats 1* to *5* all carried an MSS sensor that responded to Earth-reflected sunlight in four spectral bands, from the visible green to the near-infrared wavelengths. The resolution of the MSS sensor was approximately 80 meters (m) (262 feet [ft]) in the four spectral bands covered. *Landsat 3* carried an MSS sensor with an additional band (called band 8) that responded to thermal infrared radiation.

Landsats 4 and *5* carry both the multispectral scanner (MSS) and a thematic mapper (TM). These more recent Landsat spacecraft orbit Earth at an altitude of 705 kilometers (438 miles) and provide a 16-day, 233-orbit coverage cycle. The MSS sensors onboard *Landsats 4* and *5* are identical to the MSS sensors carried on *Landsats 1* and *2*. In late 1992 routine collection of MSS data was terminated. The thematic mapper (TM) sensor also primarily detects reflected radiation from Earth in the visible and infrared (IR) wavelengths, but the TM sensor provides more radiometric information than the older MSS sensor. The wavelength range for the *Landsat 4* and *5* thematic mapper is from the visible (blue), through the mid-infrared, and into the thermal infrared portion of the electromagnetic spectrum. Sixteen detectors for the visible and mid-infrared wavelength bands in the TM sensor provide 16 scan lines on each active scan. Four detectors for the thermal infrared band provide four scan lines on each active scan. The TM sensor has a spatial resolution of 30 m (98 ft) for the visible, near-infrared, and mid-infrared wavelengths and a spatial resolution of 120 m (393 ft) for the thermal infrared band.

Since 1972 the Landsat remote sensing satellites (and similar Earth-resource monitoring spacecraft launched by other nations) have provided multispectral imagery with repetitive, synoptic, global coverage. The characteristics of Landsat's MSS and TM sensors were selected to maximize their capabilities for detecting and monitoring different types of Earth resources. For example, band 1 of the *Landsat 4* and *5* MSS sensor (called band 4 on

Landsats 1 to *3*) can be used to detect green (sunlight) reflectance from healthy vegetation; while band 2 of the MSS sensor (called band 5 on *Landsats 1* to *3*) is designed to detect chlorophyll absorption in vegetation. Similarly, MSS bands 3 and 4 (called bands 6 and 7 on *Landsats 1* to *3*) are ideal for recording near-infrared reflectance peaks in healthy green vegetation and for detecting water-land interfaces.

Remote sensing analysts can combine MSS sensor bands 4, 2, and 1 (called bands 7, 5, and 4 on *Landsats 1* to *3*) to create interesting and very useful false-color composite images. In this case, band 4 controls the red, band 2 the amount of green, and band 1 the amount of blue in the composite image. This particular combination of bands makes vegetation appear as shades of red, with brighter reds indicating more vigorously growing vegetation. Soils with no or sparse vegetation will range in color from white (indicating sand) to greens or browns, depending on moisture and organic matter content. Bodies of water will appear blue. Deep, clear water will be dark blue to black in color, while sediment-laden or shallow waters will appear lighter in color. Urban areas will appear blue-gray in color, while clouds and snow will appear as bright white. Remote sensing analysts usually can distinguish between clouds and snow by the shadows associated with clouds.

This brief discussion highlights just one example of the power of modern remote sensing and of multispectral imagery analysis and interpretation. Landsat's more sophisticated thematic mapper (TM) data and the higher spatial and spectral resolution data now becoming available from the new satellite systems of the international remote sensing community provide even greater details concerning conditions on the Earth's surface. Such multispectral and hyperspectral (many wavelengths collected simultaneously) images of Earth will be used by 21st century scientists to effectively study critical planetary processes.

The Landsat program has provided over two decades of calibrated remote sensing data to a

LANDSAT PROGRAM-SYSTEM SUMMARY

System	Launch (End of service)	I(s)	Resolution (meters)	Communications	Alt. Km	R Days	D Mbps
Landsat 1	7/23/72 (1/6/78)	RBV MSS	80 80	Direct downlink with recorders	917	18	15
Landsat 2	1/22/75 (2/25/82)	RBV MSS	80 80	Direct downlink with recorders	917	18	15
Landsat 3	3/5/78 (3/31/83)	RBV MSS	30 80	Direct downlink with recorders	917	18	15
*Landsat 4**	7/16/82	MSS TM	80 30	Direct downlink TDRSS	705	16	85
Landsat 5	3/1/84	MSS TM	80 30	Direct downlink TDRSS**	705	16	85
Landsat 6	10/5/93 (10/5/93)	ETM	15 (pan) 30 (ms)	Direct downlink with recorders	705	16	85
Landsat 7	12/98 (est.)	ETM+	15 (pan) 30 (ms)	Direct downlink with recorders (solid state)	705	16	150

I(s) = Instrument(s)
R = Revisit interval
D = Data rate
*TM data transmission failed in August 1993.
**Current data transmission by direct downlink only. No recording capability.

Note: *Landsat 6* failed to achieve orbit (October 1993).
Source: NASA.

broad user community, including the agricultural community, global change researchers, state and local governments, commercial users, and the military. The *Landsat 6* satellite, which failed to reach orbit in 1993, was intended to replace the existing *Landsat 4* and *5* satellites. *Landsat 4* and *5,* which were launched in 1982 and 1984 respectively and have operated well beyond their three-year design lifetimes, represent the only source of a global, calibrated, high-resolution measurement of Earth's surface that can be compared to previous data records. Dating back to 1972, the 25-year record of data acquired by Landsat spacecraft constitutes the longest continuous record of Earth's continental surfaces.

In 1992 the U.S. Congress authorized the procurement, launch, and operation of a new satellite, called *Landsat 7.* This spacecraft (scheduled for launch in December 1998) will help preserve the existing Landsat data record and continue this important capability into the 21st century. *Landsat 7* will have a unique and essential role in the realm of Earth-observing satellites in orbit at the end of this decade. No other remote sensing system will match Landsat's combination of synoptic coverage, high spatial resolution, spectral range, and radiometric calibration.

The Earth-observing instrument on *Landsat 7,* called the Enhanced Thematic Mapper Plus (ETM+), replicates the capabilities of the highly successful thematic mapper (TM) instruments flown on *Landsats 4* and *5* and is similar to the Enhanced Thematic Mapper (ETM) instrument that was lost on *Landsat 6.* However, the ETM+ instrument also includes new features that make it a more versatile and efficient instrument for global change studies, land-cover monitoring and assessment, and large area mapping than its technical predecessors. The primary new features associated with the ETM+ instrument are: a panchromatic band with a 15-m (49-ft) spatial resolution; onboard, full-aperture, 5% radiometric calibration; and a thermal infrared channel with a 60-m (196-ft) spatial resolution. (See the table.)

The Landsat Program, as defined by the U.S. Congress in 1992 and amended by the Presidential Decision Directive/NSTC-3 in May 1994, is now managed cooperatively by NASA, the National Oceanic and Atmospheric Administration (NOAA), and the U.S. Geological Survey (USGS). Responsibility for construction of the spacecraft lies with NASA (within the Mission to Planet Earth

office). Once in orbit, *Landsat 7* will be operated by NOAA. Data processing, archiving, and distribution will be performed by the USGS with direction from NOAA.

Remote sensing of Earth from outer space is one of the major contributions of modern space technology toward improving our overall quality of life. Future remote sensing systems will provide even more detailed information to assist us in the careful, enlightened stewardship of our home planet in the next century.

See also: EARTH OBSERVING SATELLITE; EARTH OBSERVATION SYSTEM (EOS); ELECTROMAGNETIC SPECTRUM; GLOBAL CHANGE; MISSION TO PLANET EARTH.

rendezvous The close approach of two or more spacecraft in the same orbit, so that docking can take place. These objects meet at a preplanned location and time with essentially zero relative velocity. A rendezvous would be involved, for example, in the construction, servicing, or resupply of a space station, or when the space shuttle orbiter performs on-orbit repair/servicing of a satellite. The term is also applied to a space mission, such as the *Near Earth Asteroid Rendezvous (NEAR) mission,* in which a scientific spacecraft is maneuvered so as to fly alongside a target body, such as a comet or asteroid, at zero relative velocity.

See also: NEAR EARTH ASTEROID RENDEZVOUS (NEAR) MISSION.

repressurization Sequence of operations during a rocket vehicle or spacecraft flight that uses an onboard pressurant supply to restore the ullage pressure to the desired level after an engine burn period.

resilience The property of a material that enables it to return to its original shape and size after deformation. For example, the resilience of a sealing material is the property that makes it possible for a seal to maintain sealing pressure despite wear, misalignment, or out-of-round conditions.

resistance (symbol: R) 1. Electrical resistance (R) is defined as the ratio of the voltage (or potential difference) (V) across a conductor to the current (I) flowing through it. In accordance with Ohm's law, $R = V/I$. The SI UNIT of resistance is the ohm (Ω), where 1 ohm = 1 volt per ampere. 2. Mechanical resistance is the opposition by frictional effects to forces tending to produce motion. 3. Biological resistance is the ability of plants and animals to withstand poor environmental conditions and/or attacks by chemicals or disease. This ability may be inborn or developed.

resolution 1. In general, a measurement of the smallest detail that can be distinguished by a sensor system under specific conditions. 2. The degree to which fine details in an image or photograph can be seen as separated or resolved. Spatial resolution often is expressed in terms of the most closely spaced line-pairs per unit distance that can be distinguished. For example, when the resolution is said to be 10 line-pairs per millimeter, this means that a standard pattern of black-and-white lines whose line plus space width is 0.1 millimeter is barely resolved by an optical system, finer patterns are not resolved, and coarser patterns are more clearly resolved.

responsive threat Offensive forces that have been modified to defeat a defensive system. For example, a ballistic missile threat that has been upgraded in quality or quantity or with added protective countermeasures in response to a projected ballistic missile defense (BMD) capability.
See also: BALLISTIC MISSILE DEFENSE.

restart In aerospace operations, the act of firing a spacecraft's or space vehicle's "restartable" rocket engine after a previous thrust period (powered flight) and a coast phase in a parking or transfer orbit.

rest mass (symbol: m_0) The mass that an object has when it is at (absolute) rest. From Einstein's special relativity theory, the mass of an object increases when it is in motion according to the formula:

$$m = m_0/\sqrt{(1 - [V^2 / c^2])}$$

where m is its mass in motion, m_0 is its mass at rest, v is the speed of the object, and c is the speed of light. This is especially significant at speeds approaching a considerable fraction of the speed of light. Newtonian physics, in contrast, makes no distinction between rest mass (m_0) and motion mass (m). This is acceptable in classical physics, as long as the object under consideration is traveling at speeds well below the speed of light–that is, when v<<c.

restricted propellant A solid propellant that has only a portion of its surface exposed for burning; the other propellant surfaces are covered by an inhibitor.

restricted surface The surface of a solid-propellant grain that is prevented from burning through the use of inhibitors.

retrieval With respect to the space shuttle, the process of using the remote manipulator system (RMS) and/or other handling aids to return a captured payload to a stowed or berthed position. No payload is considered retrieved until it is fully stowed for safe return or berthed for repair and maintenance.
See also: REMOTE MANIPULATOR SYSTEM; SPACE TRANSPORTATION SYSTEM.

retrofire To ignite a retrorocket.

retrofit The modification of or addition to a spacecraft, aerospace vehicle, or expendable launch vehicle after it has become operational.

retrograde In a reverse or backward direction.

retrograde motion Motion in an orbit opposite to the usual orbital direction of celestial bodies within a given system. Specifically, of a satellite, motion in a direction opposite to the direction of rotation of the primary.

retrograde orbit An orbit having an inclination of more than 90 degrees. In a retrograde orbit, the spacecraft or satellite has a motion that is opposite in direction to the rotation of the primary body (such as Earth). Compare with PROGRADE ORBIT.
See also: ORBITS OF OBJECTS IN SPACE.

retroreflection Reflection in which the reflected rays return along paths parallel to those of their corresponding incident rays.

retroreflector A mirrorlike instrument, usually a corner reflector design, that returns light or other electromagnetic radiation (e.g., an infrared laser beam) in the direction from which it comes.
See also: LASER GEODYNAMICS SATELLITE (LAGEOS).

retrorocket A small rocket engine on a satellite, spacecraft, or aerospace vehicle used to produce a retarding thrust or force that opposes the object's forward motion. This action reduces the system's velocity.

retrothrust Thrust used for a braking maneuver; a reverse thrust.

reusable launch vehicle (RLV) A launch vehicle that incorporates simple, fully reusable designs for airline-type operations using advanced technology and innovative operational techniques. NASA in partnership with the U.S. Air Force and private industry has created the Reusable Launch Vehicle (RLV) Technology Program. The main objective of this program is to develop and demonstrate new technologies for the next generation of fully reusable space transportation systems that can radically reduce the cost of access to space. An all-rocket-powered, single-stage-to-orbit (SSTO) reusable launch vehicle (RLV) is the goal of this technology program, which centers on two demonstrator designs: the X-33 and the X-34.
　　See also: X-33; X-34.

reverse thrust Thrust applied to a moving object in a direction to oppose the object's motion; used to decelerate a spacecraft or aerospace vehicle.

reversible process In thermodynamics, a process that goes in either the forward or the reverse direction without violating the SECOND LAW OF THERMODYNAMICS; a constant entropy process. For example, the entropy of a control mass experiencing a reversible, adiabatic process will not change. Such a constant entropy process is also called an *isentropic process*. However, the "reversible process" is just an idealization used in engineering analyses to help approximate the behavior of certain real-world systems. Some of the more commonly encountered reversible process idealizations are: frictionless motion, current flow without resistant, and "frictionless" pulleys. In contrast, irreversible processes, such as molecular diffusion, a spontaneous chemical reaction, or motion with friction, all produce entropy.
　　See also: ENTROPY; THERMODYNAMICS.

revetment In aerospace operations and safety, a wall of concrete, earth, or sandbags installed for the protection of launch crew personnel and equipment against the blast and flying shrapnel from an exploding rocket during a launch abort near the pad.

revolution 1. Orbital motion of a celestial body or spacecraft about a center of gravitational attraction, such as the Sun or a planet, as distinct from rotation around an internal axis. For example, Earth *revolves* around the Sun annually and *rotates* daily about its axis. 2. One complete cycle of the movement of a spacecraft or a celestial object around its primary.
　　See also: ORBITS OF OBJECTS IN SPACE.

Reynolds number (symbol: Re) A nondimensional number used in establishing and predicting changes in fluid flow regimes (i.e., laminar flow, transition flow, and turbulent flow). It is defined as the ratio of inertia force (momentum force) to viscous force in fluid flow. That is,

$$Re = \frac{\text{inertia force}}{\text{viscous force}} = \frac{\rho \, l \, V}{\mu}$$

where ρ is the mass density, l is the characteristic length, V is the fluid velocity, and μ is the absolute viscosity. At low Reynolds number the viscous force dominates the fluid flow and the motion is laminar. At high Reynolds number the inertia force dominates and leads to turbulent flow.

Richardson number (symbol: Ri) A nondimensional number that is defined as the ratio of buoyant force to turbulent force. That is,

$$\frac{\text{Richardson number}}{\text{(Ri)}} = \frac{\text{buoyant force}}{\text{turbulent force}} = \frac{g \, l \, \Delta\rho}{2 \, q}$$

where g is the acceleration of gravity, l is the characteristic length, $\Delta\rho$ is the density difference, q is the dynamic pressure [namely, $q = (\rho \, V^2) / 2$ and V is the velocity of the fluid.]. The Richardson number describes the stability of flow in terms of the velocity gradient at a fixed surface. Low values of the Richardson number indicate the fluid is homogeneous.

ring seal Piston-ring type of seal that assumes its sealing position under the pressure of the fluid to be sealed.

robotics Robotics is basically the science and technology of designing, building, and programming robots. Robotic devices, or robots as they are usually called, are primarily "smart machines" with manipulators that can be programmed to do a variety of manual or human labor tasks automatically. A robot, therefore, is simply a machine that does mechanical, routine tasks on human command. The expression "robot" is attributed to Czech writer Karel Capek, who wrote the play *R.U.R.* (*Rossum's Universal Robots.*) This play first appeared in English in 1923 and is a satire on the mechanization of civilization. The word "robot" is derived from *robata*, a Czech word meaning "compulsory labor" or "servitude."

A typical robot consists of one or more manipulators (arms), end effectors (hands), a controller, a power supply, and possibly an array of sensors to provide information about the environment in which the robot must operate. Because most modern robots are used in industrial applications, their classification is based on these industrial functions. Terrestrial robots frequently are divided into the following classes: nonservo (or pick-and-place), servo, programmable, computerized, sensory, and assembly robots.

The *nonservo robot* is the simplest type. It picks up an object and places it at another location. The robot's freedom of movement usually is limited to two or three directions.

The *servo robot* represents several categories of industrial robots. This type of robot has servomechanisms for the manipulator and end effector to enable it to change direction in midair (or mid stroke) without having to strip or trigger a mechanical limit switch. Five to seven directions of motion are common, depending on the number of joints in the manipulator.

The *programmable robot* is essentially a servo robot that is driven by a programmable controller. This controller memorizes (stores) a sequence of movements and then repeats these movements and actions continuously. Often this type of robot is programmed by "walking" the manipulator and end effector through the desired movement.

The *computerized robot* is simply a servo robot run by computer. This kind of robot is programmed by instructions fed into the controller electronically. These "smart robots" may even have the ability to improve upon their basic work instructions.

The *sensory robot* is a computerized robot with one or more artificial senses to observe and record its environment and to feed information back to the controller. The artificial senses most frequently employed are sight (robot or computer vision) and touch.

Finally, the *assembly robot* is a computerized robot, generally with sensors, that is designed for assembly-line and manufacturing tasks, both on Earth and eventually in space.

In industry, robots are designed mainly for manipulation purposes. The actions that can be produced by the end effector or hand include: (1) motion (from point to point, along a desired trajectory or along a contoured surface); (2) a change in orientation; and (3) rotation.

Nonservo robots are capable of point-to-point motions. For each desired motion, the manipulator moves at full speed until the limits of its travel are reached. As a result, nonservo robots often are called "limit sequence," "bang-bang," or "pick-and-place" robots. When nonservo robots reach the end of a particular motion, a mechanical stop or limit switch is tripped, stopping the particular movement.

Servo robots are also capable of point-to-point motions; but their manipulators move with controlled variable velocities and trajectories. Servo robot motions are controlled without the use of stop or limit switches.

Four different types of manipulator arms have been developed to accomplish robot motions. These are the rectangular, cylindrical, spherical, and anthropomorphic (articulated or jointed arm). Each of these manipulator arm designs features two or more degrees of freedom (DOF), a term that refers to the direction a robot's manipulator arm is able to move. For example, simple straight line or linear movement represents one DOF. If the manipulator arm is to follow a two-dimensional curved path, it needs two degrees of freedom: up and down and right and left. Of course, more complicated motions will require many degrees of freedom. To locate an end effector at any point and to orient this effector in a particular work volume requires six DOF. If the manipulator arm needs to avoid obstacles or other equipment, even more degrees of freedom will be required. For each DOF, one linear or rotary joint is needed. Robot designers sometimes combine two or more of these four basic manipulator arm configurations to increase the versatility of a particular robot's manipulator.

Actuators are used to move a robot's manipulator joints. Three basic types of actuators currently are used in contemporary robots: pneumatic,

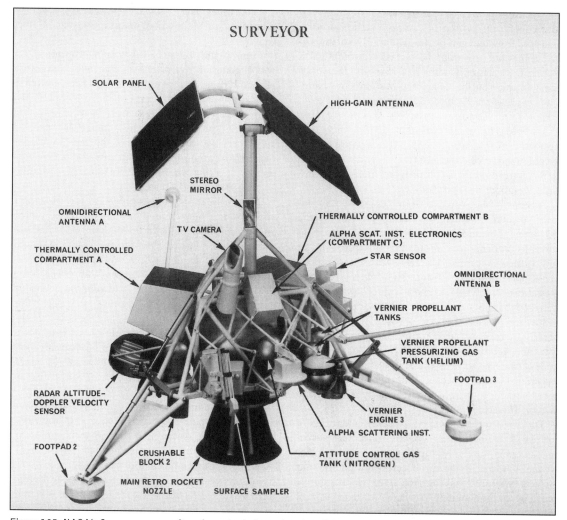

Figure 105. NASA's Surveyor spacecraft performed robotic exploration of the lunar surface from 1966 to 1968 in preparation for the landings by the Apollo astronauts (1969–1972). *(Photo courtesy of NASA)*

hydraulic, and electrical. Pneumatic actuators employ a pressurized gas to move the manipulator joint. When the gas is propelled by a pump through a tube to a particular joint, it triggers or actuates movement. Pneumatic actuators are inexpensive and simple, but their movement is not precise. Therefore, this kind of actuator usually is found in nonservo or pick-and-place robots. Hydraulic actuators are quite common and capable of producing a large amount of power. The main disadvantages of hydraulic actuators are their accompanying apparatus (pumps and storage tanks) and problems with fluid leaks. Electrical actuators provide smoother movements, can be

controlled very accurately, and are very reliable. However, these actuators cannot deliver as much power as hydraulic actuators of comparable mass. Nevertheless, for modest power actuator functions, electrical actuators often are preferred.

Many industrial robots are fixed in place or move along rails and guideways. Some terrestrial robots are built into wheeled carts, while others use their end effectors to grasp handholds and pull themselves along. Advanced robots use articulated manipulators as legs to achieve a walking motion.

A robot's end effector (hand or gripping device) generally is attached to the end of the manipulator arm. Typical functions of this end effector include grasping, pushing and pulling, twisting, using tools, performing insertions, and various types of assembly activities. End effectors can be mechanical, vacuum or magnetically operated, can use a snare device or have some other unusual design feature. The final design of the end effector is determined by the shapes of the objects that the robot must grasp. Usually most end effectors are some type of gripping or clamping device.

Robots can be controlled in a wide variety of ways, from simple limit switches tripped by the manipulator arm to sophisticated computerized remote sensing systems that provide machine vision, touch, and hearing. In the case of computer-controlled robots, the motions of the manipulator and end effector are programmed; that is, the robot "memorizes" what it is supposed to do. Sensor devices on the manipulator help to establish the proximity of the end effector to the object to be manipulated and feed information back to the computer controller concerning any modifications needed in the manipulator's trajectory.

Another interesting type of robot system, the *field robot,* has become practical recently. A field robot is a robot that operates in unpredictable, unstructured environments, typically outdoors (on Earth) and often operates autonomously or by teleoperation over a large workspace (typically a square kilometer or more). For example, in surveying a potentially dangerous site, a human operator will stay at a safe distance away in a protected work environment and control (by cable or radio frequency link) the field robot, which then actually operates in the hazardous environment. These terrestrial field robots can be considered as "technological first cousins" to the teleoperated robot planetary rovers that will roam the Moon, Mars, and other planetary bodies in the next century.

Robotic systems have played and will continue to play a major role in our exploration and development of the solar system. Early American space robots included: NASA's Surveyor spacecraft, which soft-landed on the lunar surface starting in 1966 operating soil scoops and preparing the way for the Apollo astronauts (see Figure 105); and NASA's Viking Lander spacecraft, which explored and examined the Martian surface for signs of microbial lifeforms starting in 1976. The Soviet Lunakhod remotely controlled robot moon rovers roamed across the lunar surface in the early 1970s, conducting numerous experiments and soil property investigations.

The space shuttle orbiter's remote manipulator system (RMS) was first flown in 1981. This versatile "robot arm" was designed to handle spacecraft deployment and retrieval operations, as well as to permit the assembly of large structures (e.g., a permanent space station). It is installed in the space shuttle orbiter's port (left) side cargo bay door hinges and is operated by a "shirt-sleeved" astronaut from inside the crew cabin. The RMS was designed and built by the National Research Council of Canada. It is a highly sophisticated robotic device that is similar to a human arm. The 15-meter-long (49-feet-long) RMS features a shoulder, wrist, and hand—although its "hand" does not look like a human hand. The skeleton of this mechanical arm is made of lightweight graphite composite materials. Covering the skeleton are skin layers consisting of thermal blankets. The muscles driving the joints are electric actuators (motors). Built-in sensors act like nerves and sense joint positions and rotation rates.

The RMS includes two closed-circuit television cameras, one at the wrist and one at the elbow. These cameras allow an astronaut, who is operating the RMS from the orbiter's aft flight deck, to see critical points along the arm and the target toward which the arm is moving.

Expanding on its previous space robot experience, NASA is now pursuing "intelligent teleoperation" technology as an interim step toward developing the technology needed for truly autonomous space robots. The goals of NASA's current space telerobotics program are to develop, integrate, and demonstrate the science and technology of remote telerobotics, leading to increases in operational capability, safety, cost effectiveness, and probability of success of NASA missions. Space telerobotics technology requirements can be characterized by the need for manual and automated control, non-repetitive tasks, time delay between operator and manipulator, flexible manipulators with complex dynamics, novel locomotion, operations in the space environment, and the ability to recover from unplanned events. There are three specific areas of focus: on-orbit servicing, science payload maintenance, and exploration robotics.

The on-orbit servicing telerobotics program is concerned with the development of space robotics for the eventual application to on-orbit satellite servicing by both free-flying and platform attached servicing robots. Relevant technologies include virtual reality telepresence, advanced display technologies, proximity sensing for perception technologies, and robotic flaw detection. Potential mission applications include: repair of free-flying small satellites, ground-based control of robotic servicers, and servicing of external space platform payloads (including payloads externally mounted on the international space station).

The science payload maintenance telerobotics program is intended to mature technologies for robotics that will be used inside pressurized living space to maintain and service payloads. Once developed, this telerobotic capability will off-load the requirements of intensive astronaut maintenance of these payloads and permit the operation of the payloads during periods when the astronauts may not be present. Relevant technologies include lightweight manipulators, redundant robotic safety systems, and self-deploying systems. One particular mission application involves intravehicular activity (IVA) robots for the space station.

The exploration robotics program involves the development of robot systems for the surface exploration of the Moon and Mars, including robotic reconnaissance and surveying systems as precursors to eventual human missions. During such surface exploration missions, these robots will explore potential landing sites and areas of scientific interest, deploy scientific instruments, gather samples for in-situ analysis or possible return to Earth, acquire and transmit video imagery, and provide the images needed to generate "virtual environments" of the lunar and Martian surface. The robotic systems for these operations will need high levels of local autonomy, including the ability to perform local navigation, identify areas of potential scientific interest, regulate on-board resources, and schedule activities—all with limited ground command intervention.

The *science rover/remote geologist robot* represents a 20-kilogram (44-pound-mass) class future microrover that can autonomously traverse many kilometers on the surface of Mars and perform scientist-directed experiments and then return relevant data back to Earth.

An *aerobot* is an autonomous robotic aerovehicle (e.g., a free-flying balloon or a specially designed "aeroplane") that is capable of flying in the atmospheres of Venus, Mars, Titan, or the outer planets. For Martian or Venusian aerobots, the robotic system would be capable of one or more of the following activities: autonomous state determination;

periodic altitude variations; altitude control and the ability to follow a designated flight path within a planetary atmosphere using prevailing planetary winds; and landing at a designated surface location.

Future exploration of interplanetary small bodies, such as comets and asteroids, requires telerobotic technology developments in a variety of areas. Landing and surface operations in the very-low-gravity environment of small interplanetary bodies (where the acceleration due to gravity is typically 10^{-4} to 10^{-2} meter per second-squared) is an extremely challenging problem. The robotic comet or asteroid explorer must have mechanisms and autonomous control algorithms to perform landing, anchoring, surface/subsurface sampling and sample manipulation for a complement of scientific instruments. A robotic lander might use, for example, crushable material on the underside of a base plate design to absorb almost all of the landing kinetic energy. An anchoring, or attachment system, then would be used to secure the lander and compensate for the reaction forces and moments generated by the sample acquisition mechanisms.

Recent advances in microtechnology and mobile robotics have made it possible to consider the creation and use of extremely small automated or remote-controlled vehicles, called *nanorovers*, in planetary surface exploration missions. A *nanorover* is a robotic vehicle with a mass of between 10 and 50 grams. One or several of these tiny robots could be used to survey areas around a lander and to look for a particular substance, such as water ice or microfossils. The nanorover would then communicate its scientific findings back to Earth via the lander spacecraft (possibly in conjunction with an orbiting "mothership").

Eventually, space robots will achieve higher levels of artificial intelligence, autonomy, and dexterity, so that servicing and exploration operations would become less and less dependent on a human operator being present in the control loop. These robots would be capable of interpreting very high-level command structures and executing commands without human intervention. Erroneous command structures, incomplete task operations, and the resolution of differences between the robot's built-in "world model" and the real-world environment it is encountering would be handled autonomously. This is especially important as more sophisticated robots are sent deeper into the outer solar system and telecommunications time delays of minutes become hours. This higher level of autonomy is also very important in the development and operation of permanent lunar or Martian surface bases, where smart machines become our permanent partners in the development of the space frontier.

These increasingly more sophisticated space robots will have working lifetimes of decades with little or no maintenance. Some space planners envision robots capable of repairing themselves or other robots—again with little or no direct human supervision. The brilliant Hungarian-American mathematician John von Neumann (1903–1957) was the first person to seriously explore the problem of *self-replicating systems (SRSS)*—that is, robots smart and dexterous enough to make copies of themselves. From von Neumann's work and the more recent work of other investigators, five broad classes of SRS behavior have been suggested:

1. *Production.* The generation of useful output from useful input. In the production process, the unit machine remains unchanged. Production is a simple behavior demonstrated by all working machines, including SRS devices.
2. *Replication.* The complete manufacture of a physical copy of the original machine unit by the machine unit itself.
3. *Growth.* An increase in the mass of the original machine unit by its own actions while still retaining the integrity of its original design. For example, the machine might add an additional set of storage compartments in which to keep a larger supply of parts or constituent materials.
4. *Evolution.* An increase in the complexity of the unit machine's function or structure. This is accomplished by additions or deletions to existing subsystems, or by changing the characteristics of these subsystems.
5. *Repair.* Any operation performed by a unit machine on itself that helps reconstruct, reconfigure, or replace existing subsystems but does not change the SRS unit population, the original unit mass, or its functional complexity.

In theory, such replicating systems can be designed to exhibit any or all of these machine behaviors. When such machines are actually built (perhaps in the mid- to late 21st century), a particular SRS unit most likely will emphasize just one or several kinds of machine behavior, even if it were capable of exhibiting all of them. For example, a particular SRS unit might be the fully autonomous, general-purpose, self-replicating lunar factory that first makes a sufficient number of copies of itself and then sets about harvesting lunar resources and converting these resources into products needed to support a permanently inhabited (by humans) lunar settlement.

Once we have developed the sophisticated robotic devices needed for the detailed investigation of the outer regions of this solar system, the next step becomes quite obvious. Sometime in the 21st century, humankind will build and launch its first fully automated robot explorer to a nearby star system. This interstellar explorer will be capable of searching for extrasolar planets around other suns, targeting any suitable planets for detailed investigation, and then initiating the search for extraterrestrial life. Light-years away, terrestrial scientists will wait for faint distant radio signals by which the robot starship describes any new worlds it has encountered, perhaps shedding light on the greatest cosmic mystery of all: Does life exist elsewhere in the universe?

See also: ARTIFICIAL INTELLIGENCE; LUNOKHOD; MARS PATHFINDER; MARS SAMPLE RETURN MISSION; MARS SURFACE ROVER(S); TELEOPERATION; TELEPRESENCE; THOUSAND ASTRONOMICAL UNIT (TAU) MISSION; VIKING PROJECT.

robust The ability of a system (e.g., a ballistic missile defense system) to endure and perform its mission in the face of nondestructive countermeasures (i.e., a reactive adversary) or a direct attack.

rocket In general, a completely self-contained projectile, pyrotechnic device, or flying vehicle propelled by a reaction (rocket) engine. Since it carries all of its propellant, a rocket vehicle can function in the vacuum of outer space and represents the key to space travel. Rockets obey Newton's Third Law of Motion, which states, "For every action there is an equal and opposite reaction." Rockets can be classified by the energy source used by the reaction engine to accelerate the ejected matter that creates the vehicle's thrust, as, for example: chemical rocket, nuclear rocket, and electric rocket. Chemical rockets, in turn, often are divided into two general subclasses: solid-propellant rockets and liquid-propellant rockets.

A *solid-propellant chemical rocket* is the simplest type of rocket. It can trace its technical heritage all the way back to the gunpowder-fueled "fire-arrow" rockets of ancient China (circa A.D. 1045). Those in use today generally consist of a solid propellant (i.e., fuel and oxidizer compound) with the following associated hardware: case, nozzle, insulation, igniter, and stabilizers. (See Figure 106.)

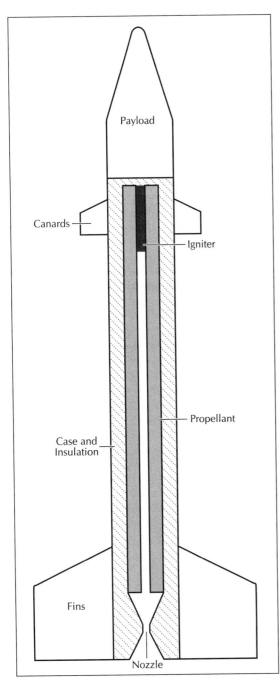

Figure 106. The basic components of a solid-propellant rocket   *(NASA—modified by author)*

Solid propellants, commonly referred to as the "grain," are basically a chemical mixture or compound containing a fuel and oxidizer that burn (combust) to produce very hot gases at high pressure. The important feature here is that these propellants are self-contained and can burn *without* the introduction of outside oxygen sources (such as air from Earth's atmosphere). Consequently, the solid-propellant rocket, and its technical sibling, the liquid-propellant rocket (which is discussed shortly), can operate in outer space. In fact, a rocket vehicle performs the best in space, as was originally postulated in 1919 by the brilliant American rocket scientist Dr. Robert H. Goddard (1882–1945). Goddard is often called the father of American rocketry.

Solid propellants often are divided into three basic classes: monopropellants, double-base, and composites. Monopropellants are energetic compounds such as nitroglycerin or nitrocellulose. Both of these compounds contain fuel (carbon and hydrogen) and oxidizer (oxygen). Monopropellants are rarely used in modern rockets. Double-base propellants are mixtures of monopropellants, such as nitroglycerin and nitrocellulose. The nitrocellulose adds physical strength to the grain, while the nitroglycerin is a high-performance, fast-burning propellant. Usually double-base propellants are mixed together with additives that improve the burning characteristics of the grain. The mixture becomes a puttylike material that is loaded into the rocket case.

Composite solid propellants are formed from mixtures of two or more unlike compounds that by themselves do not make good propellants. Usually one compound serves as the fuel and the other as the oxidizer. For example, the propellants used in the solid rocket boosters (SRBs) of the space shuttle fall into this category. The propellant type used in this case is known as PBAN, which means polybutadiene acrylic acid acrylonitrile terpolymer. This somewhat exotic-sounding chemical compound is used as a binder for ammonium perchlorate (oxidizer), powdered aluminum (fuel), and iron oxide (an additive). The cured propellant looks and feels like a hard rubber eraser.

The thrust produced by the propellants is determined by the combustive nature of the chemicals used and by the shape of their exposed burning surfaces. A solid propellant will burn at any point that is exposed to heat or hot gases of the right temperature. Grains usually are designed to be either end-burning or internal-burning. (See Figure 107.)

End-burning grains burn the slowest of any grain design. The propellant is ignited close to the nozzle, and the burning proceeds the length of the propellant load. The area of the burning surface is always at a minimum. While the thrust produced by end-burning is lower than for other grain designs, the thrust is sustained over longer periods.

Much more massive thrusts are produced by internal-burning. In this design, the grain is perforated by one or more hollow cores that extend the length of the case. With an internal-burning grain, the burning surface of the exposed cores is much larger than the surface exposed in an end-burning grain. The entire surfaces of the cores are ignited at the same time, and burning proceeds from the inside out. To increase the surface available for burning, a core may be shaped into a cruciform or star design.

By varying the geometry of the core design, the thrust produced by a large internal-burning grain also can be customized as a function of time to accommodate specific mission needs. For example, the massive solid rocket boosters (SRBs) used by the space shuttle feature a single core that has an 11-point star design in the forward section. At 65 seconds into the launch, the star points are burned away and thrust temporarily diminishes. This coincides with the passage of the space shuttle vehicle through the sound barrier. Buffeting occurs during this passage and the reduced SRB thrust helps alleviate strain on the vehicle.

The rocket case is the pressure and load-carrying structure that encloses the solid propellant. Cases are usually cylindrical, but some are spherical in shape. The case is an inert part of the rocket, and its mass is an important factor in determining how much payload the rocket can carry and how far it can travel. Efficient, high-performance rockets require that the casing be constructed of the lightest materials possible. Alloys of steel and titanium often are used for solid rocket casings. Upper-stage vehicles may use thin metal shells that are wound with fiberglass for extra strength.

Unless protected by insulation, the solid rocket motor case will lose strength rapidly and burst or burn through. Therefore, to protect the casing, insulation is bonded to the inside wall of the case before the propellant is loaded. The thickness of this insulation is determined by its thermal properties and how long the casing will be exposed to the high-pressure, very hot combustion gases. A fre-

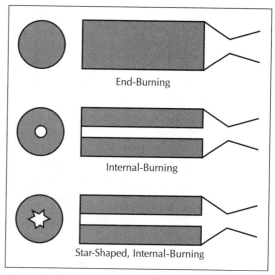

Figure 107. Typical solid-rocket motor grain designs
(*NASA—modified by author*)

quently used insulation for solid rockets is an asbestos-filled rubber compound that is thermally bonded to the casing wall.

During the combustion process, the resulting high temperature and high-pressure gases exit the rocket through a narrow opening, called the nozzle, that is located at the lower end of the motor. The most efficient nozzles are convergent-divergent designs. During operation, the exhaust gas velocity in the convergent portion of the nozzle is subsonic. The gas velocity increases to sonic speed at the throat and then to supersonic speeds, as it flows through and exits the divergent portion of the nozzle. The narrowest part of the nozzle is the throat. Escaping gases flow through this constricted region with relatively high velocity and temperature. Excessive heat transfer to the nozzle wall at the throat is a great problem. Often thermal protection for the throat consists of a liner that either withstands these high temperatures (for a brief period of operation) or else ablates (i.e., intentionally erodes carrying heat away). Large solid rocket motors, such as the space shuttle's solid rocket booster, generally rely on ablative materials to protect the nozzle's throat. Smaller solid rocket motors, such as might be used in an air-to-air combat missile or in a short-range surface-to-surface military missile, often use high-temperature–resistant materials to protect the nozzle. These temperature-resistant materials (possibly augmented by a thin layer of heat-resistant liner) can protect the nozzle's throat sufficiently, since the rocket's burn period is quite short (typically a few seconds).

To ignite the propellants of a solid rocket, the grain surface must be saturated with hot gases. The igniter is usually a rocket motor itself, but much smaller in size. The igniter can be placed inside the upper end of the hollow core, at the lower end of the core, or even completely outside the solid rocket motor. In the latter case, the exhaust of the igniter is directed into the nozzle of the larger solid rocket motor. An electrical circuit with a hot-wire resistor or an exploding bridgewire starts the igniter. The initial part of the ignition sequence begins with fast-burning pellets that, in turn, fire up the main igniter propellants.

Active directional control of solid-propellant rockets in flight generally is accomplished by one of two basic approaches. First, fins and possibly canards (small fins on the front end of the casing) can be mounted on the rocket's exterior. During flight in the atmosphere, these structures tilt to steer the rocket in much the same way that a rudder operates on a boat. Canards have an opposite effect on the directional changes of the rocket from the effect produced by the (tail) fins. Second, directional control also may be accomplished by using a gimbaled nozzle. Slight changes in the direction of the exhaust gases are accomplished by moving the nozzle from side to side. Large solid rocket motors, such as the space shuttle's solid rocket boosters, use the gimbaled-nozzle approach to help steer the vehicle.

When compared to liquid-propellant rocket systems, solid-propellant rockets offer the advantage of simplicity and reliability. With the exception of stability controls, solid-propellant rockets have no moving parts. When loaded with propellant and erected on a launch pad (or placed in an underground strategic missile silo or inside a launch tube in a ballistic missile submarine), solid rockets stand ready for firing at a moment's notice. In contrast, liquid-propellant rocket systems require extensive prelaunch preparations.

Solid rockets generally have an additional advantage in that a greater portion of their total mass can consist of propellants. Liquid-propellant rocket systems require fluid feed lines, pumps, and tanks, all adding additional (inert) mass to the vehicle. In fact, aerospace engineers often describe the performance of a rocket vehicle in terms of the *propellant mass fraction*. The propellant mass frac-

tion is defined as the rocket vehicle's propellant mass divided by its total mass (i.e., propellant, payload, structure, and supporting systems mass). A well-designed, "ideal" rocket vehicle should have a propellant mass fraction of between 91 and 93% (i.e., 0.91 to 0.93). This means that 91 to 93% of the rocket's total mass is propellant. Large liquid-propellant rocket vehicles generally achieve a mass fraction about 90% or less.

The principal disadvantage of solid-propellant rockets involves the burning characteristics of the propellants themselves. Solid propellants are generally less energetic (i.e., deliver less thrust per unit mass consumed) than the best liquid propellants. Also, once ignited, solid-propellant motors burn rapidly and are extremely difficult to throttle or extinguish. In contrast, liquid-propellant rocket engines can be started and stopped at will.

Today, solid-propellant rockets are used for strategic nuclear missiles (e.g., Minuteman), for tactical military missiles (e.g., Sidewinder), for small expendable launch vehicles (e.g., Scout), and as strap-on solid boosters for a variety of liquid-propellant launch vehicles, including the reusable space shuttle and the expendable Titan-IV. Solid-rocket motors also are used in small sounding rockets and in many types of upper-stage vehicles, such as the *Inertial Upper Stage* (*IUS*).

The liquid-propellant rocket engine was invented in 1926 by Dr. Goddard. So important were his contributions to the field of rocketry that it is even appropriate to state: "Every liquid propellant rocket is a Goddard rocket."

Figure 108 describes the major components of a typical liquid-propellant chemical rocket. Here, the propellants (liquid hydrogen for the fuel and liquid oxygen for the oxidizer) are pumped to the combustion chamber, where they begin to react. The liquid fuel often is passed through the tubular walls of the combustion chamber and nozzle to

Figure 108. Basic hardware associated with a bipropellant (here, LH_2 and LO_2) liquid rocket *(NASA)*

help cool them and prevent high-temperature degradation of their surfaces.

Liquid-propellant rockets have three principal components in their propulsion system: propellant tanks, the rocket engine's combustion chamber and nozzle assembly, and turbopumps. The propellant tanks are load-bearing structures that contain the liquid propellants. There is a separate tank for the fuel and for the oxidizer. The combustion chamber is the region into which the liquid propellants are pumped, vaporized, and reacted (combusted), creating the hot exhaust gases, which then expand through the nozzle generating thrust. The turbopumps are fluid-flow machinery that deliver the propellants from the tanks to the combustion chamber at high pressure and sufficient flow rate. (In some liquid-propellant rockets, the turbopumps are eliminated by using an "overpressure" in the propellant tanks to force the propellants into the combustion chamber.) A simplified liquid-propellant rocket engine is illustrated in Figure 109.

Propellant tanks serve to store one or two propellants until needed in the combustion chamber. Depending on the type of liquid propellants used, the tank may be nothing more than a low-pressure envelope, or it may be a pressure vessel capable of containing propellants under high pressure. In the case of cryogenic (extremely low temperature) propellants, the tank has to be an extremely well-insulated structure to prevent the very cold liquids from boiling away.

As with all rocket vehicle components, the mass of the propellant tanks is an important design factor. Aerospace engineers fully recognize that the lighter they can make the propellant tanks, the more payload that can be carried by the rocket or the greater its range. Many liquid-propellant tanks are made out of very thin metal or are thin metal sheaths wrapped with high-strength fibers and cements. These tanks are stabilized by the internal pressure of their contents, much the same way the wall of a balloon gains strength from the gas inside (at least up to a certain level of internal pressure). However, very large propellant tanks and tanks that contain cryogenic propellants require additional strengthening or layers. Structural rings and ribs are used to strengthen tank walls, giving the tanks the appearance of an aircraft frame. With cryogenic propellants, extensive insulation is needed to keep the propellants in their liquefied form. Unfortunately, even with the best available insula-

Figure 109. A simplified liquid-propellant rocket engine that employs regenerative cooling of the combustion chamber and nozzle walls *(NASA)*

tion, cryogenic propellants are difficult to store for long period of time and eventually will boil off (i.e., vaporize). For this reason, cryogenic propellants are not used in liquid-propellant military rockets, which must be stored for months at a time in a launch-ready condition.

Turbopumps provide the required flow of propellants from the low-pressure propellant tanks to the high-pressure combustion chamber. Power to operate the turbopumps is produced by combusting a fraction of the propellants in a preburner. Expanding gases from the burning propellants drive one or more turbines, which, in turn, drive the turbopumps. After passing through the turbines, these exhaust gases are either directed out of the rocket through a nozzle or are injected, along with liquid oxygen, into the combustion chamber for more complete burning.

The combustion chamber of a liquid-propellant rocket is a bottle-shaped container with openings

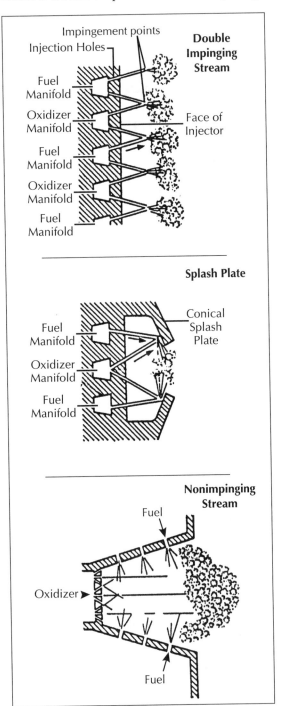

Figure 110. Some typical injector designs for liquid-propellant rocket engines *(NASA)*

at opposite ends. The openings at the top inject propellants into the chamber. Each opening consists of a small nozzle that injects either fuel or oxidizer. The main purpose of the injectors is to mix the propellants to ensure smooth and complete combustion and to avoid detonations. Combustion chamber injectors come in many designs, and one liquid-propellant engine may have hundreds of injectors. (See Figure 110.)

After the propellants have entered the combustion chamber, they must be ignited. Hypergolic propellant combinations ignite on contact, but other propellants need a starter device, such as a spark plug. Once combustion has started, the thermal energy released continues the process.

The opening at the opposite (lower) end of the combustion chamber is the throat or narrowest part of the nozzle. Combustion of the propellants builds up gas pressure inside the chamber, which then exhausts through this nozzle. By the time the gas leaves the exit cone (widest part of the nozzle), it achieves supersonic velocity and imparts forward thrust to the rocket vehicle.

Because of the high temperatures produced by propellant combustion, the chamber and nozzle must be cooled. For example, the combustion chambers of the space shuttle's main engines (i.e., the SSMEs) reach 3,590° Kelvin (3,317° Celsius) (6,000 ° Fahrenheit) during firing. All surfaces of the combustion chamber and nozzle need to be protected from the eroding effects of the high-temperature, high-pressure gases.

Two general approaches can be taken to cool the combustion chamber and nozzle. One approach is identical to the cooling approach taken with many solid-propellant rocket nozzles. The surface of the nozzle is covered with an ablative material that sacrificially erodes when exposed to the high-temperature gas stream. This intentional material erosion process keeps the surface underneath cool, since the ablated material carries away a large amount of thermal energy. However, this cooling approach adds extra mass to a liquid-propellant engine, which in turn reduces payload and range capability of the rocket vehicle. Therefore, ablative cooling is used only when the liquid-propellant engine is small or when a simplified engine design is more important than high performance. In considering such technical choices, an aerospace engineer is making "design tradeoffs."

The second method of cooling is called *regenerative cooling.* A complex plumbing arrangement inside the combustion chamber and nozzle walls circulates the fuel (in the case of the space shuttle's main engines, very cold (cryogenic) liquid hydrogen fuel) before it is sent through the preburner and into the combustion chamber. This circulating fuel then absorbs some of the thermal energy entering the combustion chamber and nozzle walls, providing a level of cooling. Although more complicated than ablative cooling, regenerative cooling reduces the mass of large rocket engines and improves flight performance.

Propellants for liquid rockets generally fall into two categories: monopropellants and bipropellants. Monopropellants consist of a fuel and an oxidizing agent stored in one container. They can be two premixed chemicals, such as alcohol and hydrogen peroxide, or a homogeneous chemical, such as nitromethane. Another chemical, hydrazine, becomes a monopropellant when first brought into contact with a catalyst. The catalyst initiates a reaction that produces heat and gases from the chemical decomposition of the hydrazine.

Bipropellants have the fuel and oxidizer separate from each other until they are mixed in the combustion chamber. Commonly used bipropellant combinations include: liquid oxygen (LO_2) and kerosene, liquid oxygen (LO_2) and liquid hydrogen (LH_2), and monomethylhydrazine (MMH) and nitrogen tetroxide (N_2O_4). The last bipropellant combination, MMH and N_2O_4, is hypergolic—meaning these two propellants ignite spontaneously when brought into contact with each other. Hypergolic propellants are especially useful for attitude control rockets where frequent firings and high reliability are required.

Aerospace engineers must consider many factors in selecting bipropellant combinations for a particular rocket system. For example, LH_2 and N_2O_4 would make a good combination based on propellant performance, but their widely divergent storage temperatures (cryogenic and room temperature, respectively) would require the use of large quantities of thermal insulation between the two tanks, adding considerable mass to the rocket vehicle. Another important factor is the toxicity of the chemicals used. MMH and N_2O_4 are both highly toxic. Rocket vehicles that use this propellant combination require special propellant handing and prelaunch preparation.

See also: ELECTRIC PROPULSION; LAUNCH VEHICLE; PROPELLANT; ROCKETRY; SPACE NUCLEAR PROPULSION.

rocket engine 1. In general, a reaction engine that contains within itself (or carries along with itself) all the substances (i.e., matter and energy sources) necessary for its operation. A rocket engine does not require the intake of any outside substance and is therefore capable of operating in outer space. The rocket engine converts energy from some suitable source and uses this energy to eject stored matter at high velocity. The ejected matter is called the rocket engine's *propellant*. Rocket engines often are classified according to the type of energy sources used to manipulate the ejected matter, as, for example: chemical rocket engines, nuclear rocket engines, and electric rocket engines. Very commonly, however, the term "rocket engine" is used to refer to chemical propulsion system engines as a class. Chemical propulsion system engines are further classified by the type of propellant liquid-propellant rocket engine or solid-propellant rocket engine. 2. Specifically, that portion of a rocket's chemical propulsion system in which combustible materials (propellants) are supplied to a chamber and burned under specified conditions. The thermal energy released in the chemical combustion reactions is converted into the kinetic energy of hot combustion gases that are ejected through a nozzle, creating the thrust (reaction force) that then propels the vehicle to which the rocket engine is attached. In common aerospace practice, the term "rocket engine" usually is applied to a device (machine) that burns liquid propellants and therefore requires a rather complex system of propellant tanks, ducts, pumps, flow control devices, and so on. The term "rocket motor" is customarily applied to a device (machine) that burns solid propellants and therefore is relatively simple, normally requiring just the solid-propellant grain within a case, an igniter, and a nozzle.

See also: ELECTRIC PROPULSION; ROCKET; SPACE NUCLEAR PROPULSION.

rocket propellant 1. In general, the matter ejected by a rocket (reaction) engine. 2. Any agent used for consumption or combustion in a rocket engine and from which the rocket derives its thrust, such as a chemical fuel, oxidizer, catalyst, or any compound or mixture of these. Chemical rocket propellants can be either liquid or solid propellants. For example, liquid hydrogen (fuel) and liquid oxygen (oxidizer) often are used as the cryogenic liquid propellants in modern, high-performance launch vehicles. Nuclear thermal rockets use a monopropellant, such as liquid hydrogen, which is heated to extremely high temperatures by a nuclear reactor; electric rockets use readily ionizable elements such as cesium, mercury, argon, or xenon as the propellant, which is accelerated and ejected at extremely high velocities by electromagnetic processes.

See also: ELECTRIC PROPULSION; PROPELLANT; ROCKET; SPACE NUCLEAR PROPULSION.

rocket propulsion Reaction propulsion by means of a rocket engine. Note: Rocket propulsion differs from "jet propulsion" in that a rocket propulsion system is completely self-contained (i.e., it carries all the substances necessary for its operation, such as chemical fuel and oxidizer), while a jet propulsion system needs external materials to achieve reactive propulsion (e.g., air from the atmosphere to support the chemical combustion processes). Rocket propulsion works both within and outside Earth's atmosphere; jet propulsion works only up to certain altitudes within Earth's atmosphere.

See also: JET PROPULSION; ROCKET; X-15.

rocket ramjet A ramjet engine that has a rocket mounted within the ramjet duct. This rocket is used to bring the ramjet up to the necessary operating speed.

See also: RAMJET.

rocketry The art or science of making rockets; the branch of science that deals with rockets, including theory, research, development, experimentation, and application.

According to certain historical records, the Chinese were the first to use gunpowder rockets, which they called "fire arrows," in military applications. In the battle of K'ai-Fung-Foo (A.D. 1232) these rocket fire-arrows helped the Chinese repel Mongol invaders. About A.D. 1300, the rocket migrated to Europe, where over the next few centuries (especially during the Renaissance) it ended up in most arsenals as a primitive bombardment weapon. However, artillery improvements eventually made the cannon more effective in battle, and military rockets remained in the background.

Rocketry legend suggests that around A.D. 1500, a Chinese official named Wan-Hu (also spelled Wan-Hoo) conceived of the idea of flying through the air in a rocket-propelled chair-kite assembly. Serving as his own test pilot, he vanished in a bright flash during the initial flight of this rocket-propelled device.

The rocket also found military application in the Middle East and in India. For example, in the late 1700s, Rajah Hyder Ali, Prince of Mysore, India, used iron-case stick rockets to defeat a British military unit. Profiting from their adverse rocket experience in India, the British, led by Sir William Congrieve, improved the design of these Indian rockets and developed a series of more efficient bombardment rockets, which ranged in mass from about 8 to 136 kilograms (18 to 300 pounds-mass [lbm]). Perhaps the most famous application of Congrieve's rockets was the British bombardment of the American Fort McHenry in the War of 1812. This rocket attack is now immortalized in the "rockets' red glare" phrase of "The Star-Spangled Banner."

An American named William Hale attempted to improve the inherently low accuracy of 19th-century military rockets through a technique called spin stabilization. U.S. Army units used bombardment rockets during the Mexican-American War (e.g., the siege of Veracruz in March 1847) and during the U.S. Civil War. However, improvements in artillery technology again outpaced developments in military rocketry; by the beginning of the 20th century, rockets remained more a matter of polite speculation rather than a widely accepted technology.

The Russian schoolteacher Konstantin Tsiolkovsky (1857–1935) wrote a series of articles about the theory of rocketry and space flight at the turn of the century. Among other things, his visionary works suggested the necessity for liquid-propellant rockets—the very devices that American physicist Dr. Robert H. Goddard would soon develop. (Because of the geopolitical circumstances in tsarist Russia, Goddard and many other scientists outside of Russia were unaware of Tsiolkovsky's work.) Today Tsiolkovsky is regarded as the Father of Russian Rocketry and one of the founders of modern rocketry. His tombstone bears the prophetic inscription: "Mankind will not remain tied to the Earth forever!"

Similarly, the brilliant physicist Dr. Robert H. Goddard (1882–1945) is regarded as the Father of American Rocketry and the developer of the practical modern rocket. He started working with rockets by testing solid-fuel models. In 1917 when the United States entered World War I, Goddard worked to perfect rockets as weapons. One of his designs became the technical forerunner of the *bazooka*—a tube-launched, antitank rocket. Goddard's device (about 45.7 centimeters [cm] long and 2.54 cm in diameter) (about 18 inches long and 1 inch in diameter) was tested in 1918, but the war ended before it could be used against enemy tanks.

In 1919 Goddard published the important technical paper, "Method of Reaching Extreme Altitudes," in which he concluded that the rocket actually would work better in the vacuum of outer space than in Earth's atmosphere. At the time, Goddard's "radical" (but correct) suggestion cut sharply against the popular (but wrong) belief that a rocket needed air to "push against." He also suggested that a multistage rocket could reach very high altitude and even attain sufficient velocity to "escape from Earth." Unfortunately, the press scoffed at his ideas and the general public failed to appreciate the great scientific merit of this paper. Despite this adverse publicity, Goddard continued to experiment with rockets, but now he intentionally avoided publicity. On March 16, 1926 he launched the world's first liquid-fueled rocket from a snow-covered field at his Aunt Effie Goddard's farm in Auburn, Massachusetts. This simple gasoline-and-liquid-oxygen–fueled device flew only 46 meters (about 152 feet)—by strange coincidence, nearly the same distance that the Wright Brothers covered during their first powered flight in 1903. Regardless of its initial "range," Goddard's liquid-propellant rocket successfully flew, and the world would never be quite the same. The technical progeny of this simple rocket have taken human beings into Earth orbit and to the surface of the Moon. They also have sent sophisticated space probes throughout the solar system and beyond.

After this initial success, Goddard flew other rockets in rural Massachusetts, at least until they started crashing into neighbors' pastures. After the local fire marshal declared that his rockets were a fire hazard, and Goddard terminated his New England test program. The famous aviator Charles Lindbergh came to Goddard's rescue and helped him receive a grant from the Guggenheim Foundation. With this grant, Goddard moved to sparsely populated Roswell, New Mexico, where he could experiment without disturbing anyone. At his Roswell test complex, Goddard developed the first gyro-controlled rocket guidance system. He also flew rockets faster than the speed of sound and at altitudes up to 2,300 meters (7,500 feet). Yet, despite his numerous technical accomplishments in rocketry, the U.S. Government never really

developed an interest in his work. In fact, only during World War II did he receive any government funding; and that was for him to design small rockets to help aircraft take off from Navy carriers. By the time he died in 1945, Goddard held over 200 patents in rocketry. It is essentially impossible to design, construct, or launch a modern liquid-propellant rocket without using some idea or device that originated from Goddard's pioneering work in rocketry.

While Goddard worked essentially unnoticed in the United States, a parallel group of "rocketeers" thrived in Germany, centered originally around the German Rocket Society. In 1923 Dr. Hermann Oberth published a highly prophetic book entitled *The Rocket Into Interplanetary Space*. In this important work, he proved that flight beyond the atmosphere was possible. One of the many readers inspired by this book was a brilliant young teenager named Werhner von Braun. Oberth published another book in 1929 entitled *The Road to Space Travel*. In this work, he proposed liquid-propellant rockets, multistage rockets, space navigation, and guided reentry systems. From 1939 to 1945 Oberth, along with other German rocket scientists (including von Braun), worked in the military rocket program. Under the leadership of von Braun this program produced a number of experimental designs, the most famous of which was the large, liquid-fueled A-4 rocket. The Germany military gave this rocket its more sinister and well-recognized name, V-2, for vengeance weapon number two. It was the largest rocket vehicle at the time, being about 14 meters (46 feet) long and 1.7 meters (5.5 feet) in diameter and developing some 249,000 newtons (56,000 pounds-force [lbf]) of thrust.

At the end of World War II, the majority of the German rocket development team from the Peenemunde rocket test site, led by von Braun, surrendered to the Americans. This team of German rocket scientists and captured V-2 rocket components were sent to White Sands Missile Range (WSMR), New Mexico to initiate an American military rocket program. The first reassembled V-2 rocket was launched by a combined American-German team on April 16, 1946. A V-2, assembled and launched on this range, was America's first rocket to carry a heavy payload to high altitude. (See Figure 111.) Another V-2 rocket set the first high-altitude and velocity record for a single-stage missile, and still another V-2 rocket was the first large missile to be controlled in flight.

Figure 111. Close-up view of a reassembled German V-2 rocket during refueling operations at the White Sands Missile Range (circa 1946) *(Photo courtesy of U.S. Army—White Sands Missile Range)*

Stimulated by the cold war, the American and German scientists at White Sands worked to develop a variety of missile and rocket systems including the Corporal, Redstone, Nike, Aerobee, and, Atlas.

The need for more room to fire rockets of longer range became evident in the late 1940s. In 1949 the Joint Long Range Proving Ground was established at a remote, deserted location on Florida's eastern coast known as Cape Canaveral. On July 24, 1950 a two-stage Bumper rocket became the first rocket vehicle to be launched from this now world-recognized location. The Bumper consisted of a V-2 first stage and a WAC-Corporal rocket second stage.

The Missile Race and the Space (Moon) Race of the cold war era triggered tremendous developments in rocketry during the second half of the 20th century. On October 4, 1957 the Russians launched *Sputnik 1,* the first artificial satellite to orbit Earth. The United States quickly responded on January 31, 1958 with the launching of *Explorer 1,* the first American satellite. The U.S. Army Ballistic Missile Agency (including von Braun's team of German rocket scientists then located at the Redstone Arsenal in Huntsville, Alabama) modified a Redstone-derived booster into a four-stage launch vehicle configuration, called the Juno I. (This Juno I launch vehicle was the satellite-launching version of the Army's Jupiter C rocket.) The Jet Propulsion Laboratory (JPL) was responsible for the fourth stage, which included America's first satellite.

Another descendent of the V-2 rocket, the mighty Saturn V launch vehicle, carried U.S. astronauts to the surface of the Moon between 1969 and 1972. The first flight of the space shuttle on April 12, 1981 opened up the era of aerospace vehicles and the reusable space transportation systems. NASA's current X-33 and X-34 programs will provide many major advances in "reusable" rocketry at the turn of the century.

With the end of the cold war in 1989, missile and space confrontation races have been replaced by cooperative programs that are truly international in their perspective. For example, in preparation for the construction and operation of the international space station, both American and Russian rockets now carry people and equipment to the *Mir* space station, where long-term cooperative flights are being performed.

As we enter the next millennium, the dream machines advocated by such visionaries as Tsiolkovsky, Oberth, Goddard and von Braun at the beginning of the 20th century have now become the well-recognized vehicles that will help fulfill our destiny among the stars.

See also: CAPE CANAVERAL AIR FORCE STATION; GODDARD; LAUNCH VEHICLE; ROCKET; SPACE TRANSPORTATION SYSTEM; WHITE SANDS MISSILE RANGE; X-33; X-34.

rocketsonde A rocket-borne instrument package for the measurement and transmission of upper-air meteorological data (up to about 76 kilometers [47 miles] altitude), especially that portion of the atmosphere inaccessible to radiosonde techniques. A meteorological rocket.

rocket thrust The thrust of a rocket engine, usually expressed in newtons (N) or pounds-force. One pound-force is equal to 4.448 newtons.

rocket vehicle A vehicle propelled by a rocket engine.
See also: ROCKET.

rockoon A high-altitude sounding system consisting of a small solid-propellant rocket carried aloft by a large plastic balloon. The rocket is fired near the maximum altitude of the balloon flight. It is relatively mobile sounding system and has been used extensively from ships.

roentgen A unit of exposure to ionizing radiation, especially X rays or gamma rays. The roentgen is defined as the quantity of X rays or gamma rays required to produce a charge of 2.58×10^{-4} coulomb in a kilogram of dry air under standard conditions. The unit is named after Wilhelm Roentgen (1845–1923), the German scientist who discovered X rays in 1895.

Roentgen Satellite (ROSAT) An Earth-orbiting X-ray observatory successfully launched by an expendable Delta II rocket on June 1, 1990 and placed into a 580-kilometer altitude, 53-degree inclination orbit. This mission represents a cooperative effort by the United States (NASA), the United Kingdom, and Germany. Germany constructed the spacecraft and main X-ray telescope; the United Kingdom contributed a wide field camera (WFC); and NASA provided the high-resolution imager (HRI), the launch vehicle, and launch services. Germany also performed the mission operations, including data collection and initial processing. During its first six months in orbit, ROSAT was dedicated to an all-sky survey and detected some 60,000 X-ray and extreme ultraviolet (EUV) sources. The spacecraft's primary mission (all-sky X-ray source survey) was completed by February 1992.
See also: X-RAY ASTRONOMY.

roll The rotational or oscillatory movement of an aircraft, aerospace vehicle, or missile about its longitudinal (lengthwise) axis.
See also: PITCH; YAW.

rollout That portion of the landing of an aircraft or aerospace vehicle following touchdown.

Rosetta Mission A planned European Space Agency (ESA) mission to rendezvous with Comet Wirtanen and perform remote sensing investigations as well as to carry and land two probes, called Roland and Champollion, on the surface of the comet's nucleus. The projected launch date for the *Rosetta* spacecraft is January 2003. The spacecraft also will perform flybys of two asteroids, 3840 Mimistrobell and 2530 Shipka, on its way to rendezvous with the comet. In August 2011, about 3,150 days after launch, the spacecraft will lower its velocity relative to that of Comet Wirtanen to a value low enough to enable it to go into elliptical polar orbit around the comet's nucleus. Mission controllers will use images the spacecraft has taken of the comet to refine the approach trajectory. Using images of the comet's nucleus, a landing site also will be selected for the two surface probes, Roland and Champollion. These surface science packages will be released in August 2012 and land with a relative velocity of less than five meters per second (5 m/s). The surface probes are expected to function for about 84 hours and the Rosetta spacecraft will relay their data back to Earth. The spacecraft then will remain with the comet and make observations through perihelion that will occur on October 21, 2013.

Rosetta will carry a full complement of scientific instruments, including a versatile remote imaging system, a gas and ion mass spectrometer, a cometary mass analyzer, a scanning electron microprobe, a dust production rate and velocity analyzer, and a solar wind flux monitor. The probe surface science packages will include an accelerometer, a variety of spectrometers, a gas chromatograph/mass spectrometer, and an in-situ imaging system.

See also: ASTEROID; COMET; EUROPEAN SPACE AGENCY.

rotary seal Mechanical seal that rotates with the shaft and is used with a stationary mating ring.

rotate To turn about an internal axis. Said especially of celestial bodies; for example, Earth rotates or spins on its axis once every 24 hours (approximately).

rotating service structure (RSS) An environmentally controlled facility at the launch pad that is used for inserting payloads vertically into the space shuttle orbiter's cargo bay.

See also: SPACE TRANSPORTATION SYSTEM.

rotation 1. The turning of an object (especially a celestial body) about an axis within the body, as the daily rotation of Earth. 2. One turn (i.e., a rotation) of a body about an internal axis. For example, Earth has a sidereal rotation period of 23.9345 hours.

See also: ORBITS OF OBJECTS IN SPACE.

round off To adjust or delete less significant digits from a number and possibly apply some rule of correction to the part retained.

rover A crewed or robotic vehicle used to explore a planetary surface.

See also: LUNAR ROVER(S); MARS SURFACE ROVER(S).

Rover Program The name given to the overall U.S. nuclear rocket development program conducted from 1959 to 1973. At the time, it was envisioned that nuclear (thermal) rockets, placed in Earth orbit by the giant Saturn V launch vehicle, would propel a human expedition to Mars (sometime in the 1980s) and safely return the astronauts back to Earth.

See also: NUCLEAR ROCKET; SPACE NUCLEAR PROPULSION.

RP-1 Rocket propellant number one (RP-1)—a common hydrocarbon-based, liquid-propellant rocket fuel that is essentially a refined kerosene mixture. It is relatively inexpensive and generally burned with liquid oxygen (LOX).

See also: PROPELLANT; ROCKET.

rubber-base propellant A solid-propellant mixture in which the oxygen supply is obtained from a perchlorate and the fuel is provided by a synthetic rubber compound.

See also: PROPELLANT; ROCKET.

rumble In rocketry, a form of combustion instability, especially in a liquid-propellant rocket engine, characterized by a low-pitched, low-frequency rumbling noise.

safe/arm (S/A) system Mechanism in a solid-propellant rocket motor igniter that, when in the "SAFE" condition, physically prevents the initiating charge from propagating to the energy release system, which would then ignite the main propellant charge. It is an aerospace safety device intended to prevent an accidental or premature ignition of a solid rocket motor.

Safeguard An early, midcourse, and terminal-phase ballistic missile defense system deployed by the United States in North Dakota in 1975. It was dismantled in 1976 because of its limited cost effectiveness.

See also: BALLISTIC MISSILE DEFENSE.

safety analysis The determination of potential sources of danger and recommended resolutions in a timely manner. A safety analysis addresses those conditions found in either the hardware/software systems, the human-machine interface, or the human/environment relationship (or combinations thereof) that could cause the injury or death of aerospace personnel, damage or loss of the aerospace system, injury or loss of life to the public, or harm to the environment.

safety critical 1. (noun) Aerospace facility, support, test, and flight systems containing: (1) pressurized vessels, lines, and components; (2) propellants, including cryogenic propellants; (3) hydraulics and pneumatics; (4) high voltages; (5) ionizing and nonionizing radiation sources; (6) ordnance and explosive devices or devices used for ordnance and explosive checkout; (7) flammable, toxic, cryogenic, or reactive elements or compounds; (8) high temperatures; (9) electrical equipment that oper-ates in the area where flammable fluids or solids are located; (10) equipment used for handling aerospace program hardware; and (11) equipment used by personnel for walking or as work platforms. 2. (adjective) Describes something (e.g., a function, a piece of equipment, a set of data) that may affect the safety of aerospace ground and flight personnel, the aerospace system or vehicle, payloads, the general public, or the environment.

safety device A device that prevents unintentional functioning.

safing 1. An action taken to retreat from an armed condition. 2. Actions taken to eliminate or control hazards.

SAINT An early U.S. satellite inspector system designed to demonstrate the feasibility of intercepting, inspecting, and reporting on the characteristics of satellites in orbit.

Salyut A series of Earth-orbiting space stations launched by the former Soviet Union (now Russian Federation) in the 1970s and early 1980s to support a variety of civilian and military missions. The name Salyut means "salute." *Salyut 1* to *5* often are regarded as first-generation crewed spacecraft in this series, while *Salyut 6* and *7* are considered to be an evolved, second-generation design. One major design difference is the fact that the first generation had just one docking port, while the second generation had two docking ports.

Salyut 1 was launched into Earth orbit on April 19, 1971. It functioned in a civilian research capacity as an observation platform, gathering data in the fields of astronomy, Earth resources monitoring, and meteorology. On June 29, the three cosmonauts, who had just spent 24 days aboard the space station, died during reentry operations. Cosmonauts Georgi Dobrovolsky, Vladislav Volkov, and Victor Patseyev suffocated when a vent valve on their *Soyuz 11* spacecraft opened and air rushed out of the capsule as they separated from the space station. Recovery crews found the cosmonauts dead after the capsule touched down. The *Salyut 1* station decayed from orbit on October 11, 1971.

Salyut 2, considered the first "military-mission" Salyut, was launched on April 3, 1973. However, before a cosmonaut crew could be sent to this station, it suffered a catastrophic explosion on April 14. This explosion tore away the space station's solar panels, telecommunications equipment, and docking apparatus. The derelict space station then tumbled out of orbit and on about May 28 burned up in Earth's atmosphere. *Salyut 3*, the first operational military Salyut, was launched into a low (219-kilometer by 270 kilometer) orbit in late June 1974. Apparently the cosmonaut crews performed military photoreconnaissance operations, although little information has been released about this spacecraft or the other military space station, *Salyut 5*.

Salyut 4, launched on December 26, 1974, was similar to *Salyut 1*. Its crews performed civilian missions including astronomical, Earth resources and biomedical observations, and materials processing experiments.

Salyut 5, the last station in this series dedicated primarily to military activities, was launched on June 22, 1976. In addition to military mission equipment, this station also had materials processing equipment.

Salyut 6 was launched on September 29, 1977. Its design represented an evolution of the earlier generation of civilian *Salyut* spacecraft. This station functioned successfully from 1977 to 1981, more than twice its design lifetime of 18 months. The addition of a second docking port gave this second-generation space station much greater flexibility. The use of the Progress supply ship also improved orbital operations. Civilian research activities included microgravity materials processing, Earth resource photography, and astronomical observations. The last cosmonaut crew left the *Salyut 6* on April 25, 1977 and the station reentered the atmosphere and was destroyed in July 1982.

Salyut 7 was launched on April 19, 1982 and, like the *Salyut 6* crew visit program, enjoyed a pattern of progressively longer flights by the resident cosmonaut crew. However, in early 1985, when it was not occupied by a crew, this station suffered several major technical problems. In June 1985 a cosmonaut crew (*Soyuz T-13* mission) was sent to repair and reoccupy the derelict space station. Repairs enabled it to perform one additional long-duration flight. However, the final *Salyut 7* crew suddenly departed in their spacecraft on November 11, 1985, terminating the mission early because of a serious illness involving one cosmonaut.

Building on the experience of the Salyut space stations, the Russian launched their third-generation space station, called Mir, on February 19, 1986. In March a crew from the Mir space station flew to the *Salyut 7*, visited for about six weeks, and then returned to the Mir. After this "space station" to "space station" visit, the *Salyut 7* was placed in a parking orbit for possible reuse. However, the uncrewed space station experienced a more rapid orbital decay than anticipated, was permanently abandoned, and reentered Earth's atmosphere in February 1991.

See also: MIR; SPACE STATION.

satellite A smaller (secondary) body in orbit around a larger (primary) body. Earth is a *natural satellite* of the Sun, and the Moon is a natural satellite of Earth. Human-made spacecraft placed in orbit around Earth are called *artificial satellites*, or more commonly just *satellites*.

satellite laser ranging (SLR) In satellite laser ranging (SLR), ground-based stations transmit short, intense laser pulses to a retroreflector-equipped satellite, such as the Laser Geodynamics Satellite (LAGEOS). The roundtrip time of flight of the laser pulse is measured precisely and corrected for atmospheric delay to obtain a geometric range. Transmitting pulses of light to these retroflector-equipped spacecraft with a global network of laser ranging stations (both fixed and mobile) allows scientists to determine both the precise orbit of a satellite and the position of the individual ground stations. By monitoring the carefully measured position of these ground stations over time (e.g., several months to years), researchers can deduce the motion of the ground site locations due to plate tectonics or other geodynamic processes, such as subsidence. In fact, a global network of more than

30 SLR stations already has provided a basic framework for determining plate motion, confirming the anticipated motion for most plates.

The theory of plate tectonics tries to explain how the continents arrived at their current positions and to predict where the continents will be in the future. Scientists theorize that up to about 200 million years ago, one giant continent existed where the Atlantic Ocean is today. It is called *Pangaea,* meaning "all lands." Then, about 180 million years ago, Pangaea started to break up into several continents. The plates carrying the continents drifted away from each other, and a low layer of rock formed between the plates. At present, the plates comprise the solid outer 100 kilometers (60 miles) of Earth. These plates move slowly, typically not faster than about 15 centimeters (cm) (6 inches [in.]) a year. For example, North America and Europe are moving apart at a rate of about 3 cm (1.2 in) per year. Although the accumulated motion of the plates is slow when averaged over time, the effects of their short-term drastic movements (such as during earthquakes) can be catastrophic. Plates may bump into one another, spread apart, or move horizontally past one another, in the process causing earthquakes, building mountains, or triggering volcanoes.

Scientists have used satellite laser ranging techniques for the past two decades to study the motions of Earth. These geodynamic studies include measurements of: global tectonic plate motions, regional crustal deformation near plate boundaries, Earth's gravity field, and the orientation of its polar axis and its spin rate. In the future, scientists will also "invert" the traditional SLR system by placing the laser ranging hardware onboard a satellite and then pulsing selected retroreflecting objects on Earth's surface from space. This "inverted" SLR technology, sometimes called a *laser altimeter system* (*LAS*), can be used to measure ice sheet topography and temporal changes, cloud heights, planetary boundary heights, aerosol vertical structure, and land and water topography. A laser altimeter system also can be used to perform similar laser ranging measurements on other planets, such as Mars.

See also: LASER GEODYNAMICS SATELLITE (LAGEOS).

Satellite Power System (SPS) A very large structure constructed in Earth orbit that takes advantage of the nearly continuous availability of sunlight to provide useful energy to a terrestrial power grid. The original SPS concept, called the "Solar Power Satellite," was first presented in 1968. The basic concept behind the SPS is quite simple. Each SPS unit is placed in geosynchronous orbit above Earth's equator, where it experiences sunlight over 99% of the time. The large orbiting space structure then gathers the incoming sunlight for use on Earth in one of three general ways: microwave transmission, laser transmission, or mirror transmission.

In the fundamental microwave transmission SPS concept, solar radiation collected by the orbiting SPS and converted into radio-frequency (RF) or microwave energy. This RF or microwave energy would then beamed precisely to a receiving antenna on Earth, where it is converted into electricity.

In the laser transmission SPS concept, solar radiation is converted into infrared laser radiation, which is then beamed down to special receiving facilities on Earth for the production of electricity.

Finally, in the mirror transmission SPS concept, very large (kilometer dimensions) orbiting mirrors would be used to reflect raw (unconverted) sunlight directly to terrestrial energy conversion facilities 24 hours a day.

In the microwave transmission SPS concept (described above), incoming sunlight is converted into electrical power on the giant space platform by either photovoltaic (solar cell) or heat engine (thermodynamic cycle-turbogenerator) techniques. This electric power then is converted at high efficiency into microwave energy. The microwave energy, in turn, is focused into a beam and aimed precisely at special ground stations. Ground station receiving antennas (also called *rectennas*) reconvert the microwave energy into electricity for distribution in a terrestrial power grid. One variation of the basic concept locates the receiving antennas on islands or human-made ocean platforms in remote equatorial areas. The SPS-provided electricity would be used to make hydrogen (by electrolysis from seawater), which then would be transported as a cryogenic liquid by special tankers to energy markets around the globe.

Because of its potential to satisfy long-term national and global energy needs, the Satellite Power System concept has been studied extensively. Some recent studies have suggested that the SPS units be constructed using extraterrestrial materials from the Moon and Earth-approaching asteroids, with manufacturing and construction activities being accomplished by space workers who would

SPS REFERENCE SYSTEM CHARACTERISTICS

System Characteristics
General capability (utility interface)
300 GW - total
5 GW - single unit

Number of units: 60
Design life: 30 years
Deployment rate: 2 units/year

Satellite
Overall dimensions: 10 x 5 x 0.5 km
Structural material: graphite composite

Satellite mass: 35-50 x 10^6 kg
Geostationary orbit: 35,800 km

Energy Conversion System
Photovoltaic solar cells: silicon or gallium aluminum arsenide

Power Transmission and Reception
D.C.-R.F. conversion: klystron
Transmission antenna diameter: 1 km
Frequency: 2.45 GHz
Rectenna dimensions (at 35° latitude)
   Active area: 10 x 13km
   Including exclusion area: 12 x 15.8 km

Rectenna construction time: ≈2 years
Rectenna peak power density: 23 mW/cm^2
Power density at rectenna edge: 1 m/W/cm^2
Power density at exclusion edge: 0.1 mW/cm^2
Active, retrodirective array control system with pilot beam reference

Space Transportation System
Earth-to-LEO - Cargo: vertical takeoff, winged two-stage (425 metric ton payload)
                 Personnel: modified Shuttle
LEO-to-GEO - Cargo: electric orbital transfer vehicle
                 Personnel: two-stage liquid oxygen/liquid hydrogen

Space Construction
Construction staging base - LEO: 480 km
Final construction - GEO: 35,800 km
Satellite construction time: 6 months

Construction crew: 600
System maintenance crew: 240

Source: NASA/Department of Energy.

reside in large permanent space settlements in cis-lunar space. Other SPS studies examined the development and construction of SPS units using only terrestrial materials, which were placed in LOW EARTH ORBIT (LEO) by a fleet of special heavy-lift launch vehicles (HLLVs). In this scenario, construction work could be accomplished in LEO, perhaps near a permanent space station or at the site of a special space construction base. Assembled SPS sections then would be ferried to GEOSYNCHRONOUS EARTH ORBIT (GEO) by a fleet of orbital transfer vehicles (OTVs). At GEO, a crew of space workers complete final assembly and prepare the SPS unit for operation.

It is too early to validate the SPS concept or to dismiss it. What can be stated at this time, however, is that the controlled beaming to Earth of solar energy (either as raw concentrated sunlight or as converted microwaves or laser radiation) appears to represent a major promise of space technology in the next century. This particular avenue of space technology development could be a powerful stimulus toward the creation of humanity's extraterrestrial civilization. However, the SPS concept also involves potential impacts on the terrestrial environment. Some such impacts are comparable in type and magnitude to those arising from other large-scale terrestrial energy technologies, while other impacts are unique to the SPS concept. Some SPS-unique environmental and health impacts are: potential adverse effects on Earth's upper atmosphere from launch vehicle effluents and from energy beaming (i.e., microwave heating of the ionosphere); potential hazards to terrestrial life-forms from nonionizing radiation (microwave or infrared wavelength laser), electromagnetic interference with other spacecraft, terrestrial communications, and astronomy; and potential hazards to space workers, especially exposure to ionizing radiation doses well beyond currently accepted industrial criteria. These issues will have to be resolved if the SPS concept is to emerge as a major pathway in humanity's creative use of the resources of outer space.

In 1980 the U.S. Department of Energy and NASA defined an SPS reference system to serve as the basis for conducting initial environmental, societal, and comparative assessments; alternative concept trade-off studies; and supporting critical technology investigations. This SPS reference system is, of course, not an optimum or necessarily the preferred system design. It does, however, represent one potentially plausible approach for achieving SPS concept goals.

The table summarizes the reference SPS system configuration and its main technical characteristics. The proposed configuration would provide 5 gigawatts (GW) of electric power at the terrestrial grid interface. In the reference scenario, 60 such SPS units would be placed in geostationary orbit and thus provide some 300 gigawatts of electric power for use on Earth. It has been optimistically estimated that only about six months would be required to construct each SPS unit.

satellite reconnaissance The use of specially designed Earth-orbiting spacecraft to collect intelligence data. Photoreconnaissance satellites are an example.

See also: NATIONAL RECONNAISSANCE OFFICE; RECONNAISSANCE SATELLITE.

satelloid A vehicle or object that revolves around Earth but at such an altitude as to require periodic sustaining thrust to balance the aerodynamic drag caused by the upper reaches of the atmosphere.

saturated liquid In thermodynamics, a substance that exists as a liquid at the saturation temperature and pressure of a mixture of vapor and liquid.

saturated vapor In thermodynamics, a substance that exists as a vapor at the saturation temperature and pressure of a mixture of vapor and liquid.

saturation A term in thermodynamics that defines a condition in which a mixture of vapor and liquid

can exist together at a given temperature and pressure. The vapor dome on a traditional pressure (p)–specific volume (v) plot for a simple compressible substance is bounded by the saturated liquid line on the left and the saturated vapor line on the right. The point where two lines meet at the peak of this dome-shaped region is called the *critical point.* It represents the highest pressure and temperature at which distinct liquid and vapor (gas) phases of a substance can coexist.

Saturn Family of expendable launch vehicles developed by NASA (Dr. Wernher von Braun's team at the Marshall Space Flight Center in Huntsville) to support the Apollo Project. The Saturn 1B was used initially to launch Apollo lunar spacecraft into Earth orbit to help the astronauts train for the manned flights to the Moon. The first launch of a Saturn 1B vehicle with an unmanned Apollo spacecraft took place in February 1966. A Saturn 1B vehicle launched the first crewed Apollo flight, *Apollo 7,* on October 11, 1968. After completion of the Apollo Project, the Saturn 1B was used to launch the three crews (three astronauts each crew) for the *Skylab* space station in 1973. Then, in 1975, a Saturn 1B launched the American astronaut crew for the *Apollo/Soyuz Test Project,* a joint American-Russian docking mission. With an Apollo spacecraft on top, the Saturn 1B vehicle was approximately 69 meters (233 feet) tall. This expendable launch vehicle developed 7.1 million newtons (1.6 million pounds-force) of thrust at liftoff.

The Saturn V rocket, America's most powerful staged rocket, successfully carried out the ambitious task of sending astronauts to the Moon during the Apollo Project. The first launch of the Saturn V vehicle, the unmanned *Apollo 4* mission, occurred on November 9, 1967. The first crewed flight of the Saturn V vehicle, the *Apollo 8* mission, was launched in December 1968. This historic mission was the first human flight to the Moon. The three astronauts aboard *Apollo 8* circled the Moon (but did not land) and then returned safely to Earth. On July 16, 1969 a Saturn V vehicle sent the *Apollo 11* spacecraft and its crew on the first lunar landing mission. The last crewed mission of the Saturn V vehicle occurred on December 7, 1972 when the *Apollo 17* mission lifted off on the final human expedition to the Moon this century. The Saturn V vehicle flew it last mission on May 14, 1973, when it lifted the unmanned Skylab space

Saturn V
363 feet
(111 meters)

Saturn IB
223 feet
(69 meters)

Figure 112. A side-by-side comparison of the Saturn V and Saturn 1B expendable launch vehicles *(Drawing courtesy of NASA)*

All three stages of the Saturn V vehicle used liquid oxygen (LO_2) as the oxidizer. The fuel for the first stage was kerosene, while the fuel for the upper two stages was liquid hydrogen (LH_2). The Saturn V vehicle, with the Apollo spacecraft and its small emergency escape rocket on top, stood 111 meters (363 feet) tall and developed 34.5 million newtons (7.75 million pounds-force) of thrust at liftoff. (See Figure 112.)

See also: APOLLO PROJECT; LAUNCH VEHICLE.

Saturn Saturn is the sixth planet from the Sun and to many the most beautiful celestial object in the solar system. To the naked eye the planet is yellowish in color. This planet is named after the elder god and powerful Titan of Roman mythology (Cronus in Greek mythology), who ruled supreme until he was dethroned by his son Jupiter (Zeus to the ancient Greeks).

Composed mainly of hydrogen and helium, Saturn (with an average density of just 0.7 grams per cubic centimeter) is so light that it would float on water, if there were some cosmic ocean large enough to hold it. The planet takes about 29.5 Earth years to complete a single orbit around the Sun. But a Saturnian day is only approximately 10 hours, 30 minutes long.

The first telescope observations of the planet were made in 1610 by Galileo Galilei (1564–1642). The existence of its magnificent ring system was not known until the Dutch astronomer Christian Huygens (1629–1695), using a better-resolution telescope, properly identified the ring system in 1655. Galileo had seen the rings but mistook them for large moons on either side of the planet. Huygens is also credited with the discovery of Saturn's largest moon, Titan, in 1655.

Astronomers had very little information about Saturn, its rings, and its constellation of moons, until the *Pioneer 11* spacecraft (September 1, 1979), *Voyager 1* spacecraft (November 2, 1980), and *Voyager 2* spacecraft (August 26, 1981) encountered the planet. These spacecraft encounters revolutionized our understanding of Saturn and have provided the bulk of the current information about this interesting giant planet, its beautiful ring system, and its large complement of moons (18 discovered and identified at present). The planet now is being observed, on occasion, by the Hubble Space Telescope and will be visited again for a detailed scientific mission by the Cassini spacecraft (and its Huygens probe for Titan) in July 2004. (See Figure 113.)

station into Earth orbit. Skylab later was occupied by three different astronaut crews for a total period of 171 days.

Table 1.
PHYSICAL AND DYNAMIC PROPERTIES OF THE PLANET SATURN

Diameter (equatorial)	120,540 km
Mass	5.68 x 10^{26} kg
Density	0.69 g/cm^3
Surface gravity (equatorial)	9.0 m/s^2 (approx)
Escape velocity	35.5 km/s (approx)
Albedo (visual geometric)	0.5
Atmosphere	Hydrogen (89%), helium (11%), small amounts of methane (CH_4), ammonia (NH_3), and ethane (C_2H_6); water-ice aerosols.
Natural satellites	18
Rings (thousands)	Complex system
Period of rotation (a Saturnian day)	0.44 days (approx)
Average distance from the Sun	14.27 x 10^8 km (9.539 AU) [79.33 light-min]
Eccentricity	0.056
Period of revolution around the Sun(a Saturnian year)	29.46 years
Mean orbital velocity	9.6 km/s
Solar flux at planet (at top of clouds)	15.1 watts/m^2 (at 9.54 AU)
Magnetosphere	Yes (strong)
Temperature (blackbody)	77 K

Source: NASA.

Figure 113. The Cassini spacecraft during the Saturn orbit insertion burn, just after the main engine has begun firing. This firing is to reduce the spacecraft velocity with respect to Saturn, so it can be captured by the planet's gravity. *(Artist's rendering courtesy of NASA/JPL)*

Saturn is a giant planet, second in size only to Jupiter. Like Jupiter, it has a stellar-type composition, rapid rotation, strong magnetic field, and intrinsic internal heat source. Saturn has a diameter of approximately 120,540 kilometers at it equator, but 10% less at the poles because of its rapid rotation. Saturn has a mass of approximately 5.68 x 10^{26} kilograms, the lowest of any planet in the solar system; this fact indicates that much of Saturn is in a gaseous state. Table 1 lists contemporary data for the planet.

Although the other giant planets—Jupiter, Uranus and Neptune—all have rings, Saturn has

an unrivaled, complex yet delicate ring system of billions of icy particles whirling around the planet in an orderly fashion. The main ring areas stretch from about 7,000 kilometers (km) above Saturn's atmosphere out to the F Ring—a total span of about 74,000 km. Within this vast region, the icy particles generally are organized into ringlets, each typically less than 100 km wide. Beyond the F Ring lies the G and E rings, with the latter extending some 180,000 to 480,000 km from the planet's center. The complex ring system contains a variety of interesting physical features, including: kinky rings, clump rings, resonances, spokes, shepherding moons (moons that keep the icy particles in an organized structure), and probably additional as-yet undiscovered moonlets.

Scientists think that the Saturnian rings resulted from one of three basic processes: a small moon venturing too close to the planet and ultimately getting torn apart by large gravitationally induced tidal forces; some of the planet's primordial material failing to coalesce into a moon; or collisions among several larger objects that orbited the planet.

Saturn is now known to have 18 satellites. (See Tables 2 and 3.) These moons form a diverse and remarkable constellation of celestial objects. The largest satellite, Titan, is in a class by itself because of its size and dense atmosphere. The six other major satellites (Iapetus, Rhea, Dione, Tethys, Enceladus, and Mimas) are somewhat similar; all are of intermediate size (some 400 to 1,500 km in diameter) and consist mainly of water ice. Saturn also has many smaller moons, ranging in size from the irregularly shaped Hyperion (about 350 by 200 km across) to tiny Pan (about 20 km in diameter). Hyperion orbits Saturn in a random, chaotic tum-

Table 2.
PHYSICAL AND DYNAMIC PROPERTIES OF THE MOONS OF SATURN

Moon	Diameter (km)	Semimajor Axis of Orbit (km)	Period of Rotation (days)
Phoebe	220 (approx.)	12,952,000	550.5 (retrograde)
Iapetus	1,440	3,561,300	79.33
Hyperion	350 x 200	1,481,000	21.28
Titan	5,150	1,221,850	15.95
Rhea	1,530	527,040	4.52
Helene	40 (approx.)	377,400	2.74
Dione	1,120	377,400	2.74
Calypso	30 (approx.)	294,660	1.89
Tethys	1,050	294,660	1.89
Telesto	25 (approx.)	294,660	1.89
Enceladus	500	238,020	1.37
Mimas	390	185,520	0.942
Janus	220 x 160	151,470	0.695
Epimetheus	140 x 100	151,420	0.694
Pandora	110 x 70	141,700	0.629
Prometheus	140 x 80	139,350	0.613
Atlas	40(approx.)	137,640	0.602
Pan	20 (approx.)	133,580	0.575

Source: NASA.

bling motion, an orbital condition perhaps indicative of an ancient, shattering collision. Phoebe, the outermost moon of Saturn, orbits in a retrograde direction (opposite the direction of the other moons) in a plane much closer to the ecliptic than Saturn's equatorial plane.

Titan is the largest and perhaps most interesting of Saturn's satellites. It is the second largest moon in the solar system and the only one known to have a dense atmosphere. The atmospheric chemistry now taking place on Titan may be similar to those processes that occurred in Earth's atmosphere several billion years ago.

Larger in size than the planet Mercury, Titan's density appears to be about twice that of water ice. Scientists believe, therefore, that it may be composed of nearly equal amounts of rock and ice. Titan's surface is hidden from spacecraft cameras

Table 3.
PHYSICAL DATA FOR THE LARGER MOONS OF SATURN

Moon	Diameter (km)	Mass (kg)	Density (g/cm³)	Albedo (visual geometric)
Iapetus	1,440	1.6×10^{21}	1.0	0.05-0.5
Titan	5,150	1.35×10^{23}	1.9	0.2
Rhea	1,530	2.3×10^{21}	1.2	0.7
Dione	1,120	1.05×10^{21}	1.4	0.7
Tethys	1,050	6.2×10^{20}	1.0	0.9
Enceladus	500	7.3×10^{19}	1.1	~1.0
Mimas	390	3.8×10^{19}	1.2	0.5

Source: NASA.

by a dense, optically thick photochemical haze whose main layer is about 300 km above its surface. The Titanian atmosphere is mostly nitrogen. Carbon-nitrogen compounds may exist on Titan because of the great abundance of both nitrogen and hydrocarbons.

What does the surface of Titan look like? Scientists currently speculate that there must be large quantities of methane on the surface, enough perhaps to form methane rivers or even a methane sea. The temperature on the surface is about 91° Kelvin (-182° Celsius), which is close enough to the temperature at which methane can exist as a liquid or solid under the atmosphere pressure near the surface. Some researchers have further speculated that Titan is like Earth (but colder), with methane playing the role that water plays on Earth. This analogy, if correct, leads to visions of methane-filled seas near Titan's equator and frozen methane ice caps in its polar regions. Titan's surface also might experience a constant rain of organic compounds from the upper atmosphere, perhaps creating up to a 100-meter-thick layer of tarlike materials. It is hoped that the Cassini spacecraft and the Huygens probe that will be released into the Titanian atmosphere in November 2004 will help answer this question.

See also: CASSINI MISSION; PIONEER 10, 11; VOYAGER.

Saturnian Of or relating to the planet Saturn.

scalar Any physical quantity whose field can be described by a single numerical value at each point in space. A scalar quantity is distinguished from a vector quantity by the fact that a scalar quantity possesses only magnitude, while a vector quantity possesses both magnitude and direction.

scar Aerospace jargon for design features to accommodate the addition or upgrade of hardware at some future time.

scattering 1. (particle) A process that changes a particle's trajectory. Scattering is caused by particle collisions with atoms, nuclei, and other particles or by interactions with fields of magnetic force. If the scattered particle's internal energy (as contrasted with its kinetic energy) is unchanged by the collision, *elastic scattering* prevails; if there is a change in the internal energy, the process is called *inelastic scattering*. 2. (photon) Scattering also may be viewed as the process by which small particles sus-

pended in a medium of a different refractive index diffuse a portion of the incident radiation in all directions. In scattering, no energy transformation results, only a change in the spatial distribution of the radiation. Along with absorption, scattering is a major cause of the attenuation of radiation by the atmosphere. Scattering varies as a function of the ratio of the particle diameter to the wavelength of the radiation. When this ratio is less than about one-tenth, *Rayleigh scattering* occurs in which the scattering process varies inversely as the fourth power of the wavelength. At larger values of the ratio of particle diameter to wavelength, the scattering varies in a complex fashion described by *Mie scattering* theory; at a ratio of the order of 10, the laws of geometric optics begin to apply.

See also: MIE SCATTERING; RAYLEIGH SCATTERING.

schlieren (German: *streaks, striae***)** 1. Regions of different density in a fluid, especially as shown by special apparatus. 2. Pertaining to a method or apparatus for visualizing or photographing regions of varying density in a fluid field.

See also: SCHLIEREN PHOTOGRAPHY.

schlieren photography A method of photography for flow patterns that takes advantage of the fact that light passing through a density gradient in a gas is refracted as if it were passing through a prism. Schlieren photography allows the visualization of density changes, and therefore shock waves, in fluid flow. Schlieren techniques have been used for decades in laboratory wind tunnels to visualize supersonic flow around special scale-model aircraft, missiles, and aerospace vehicles.

See also: WIND TUNNEL.

Schmidt number (Sc) A nondimensional transport number expressed by the relationship:

$$Sc = \eta/\rho D$$

where η is the viscosity coefficient of the fluid, ρ is the density of the fluid, and D is the diffusion coefficient.

science payload The complement of scientific instruments on a spacecraft, including both remote-sensing and direct-sensing devices that together cover large portions of the electromagnetic spectrum, large ranges in particle energies, or a detailed set of environmental measurements.

scientific airlock An opening in a crewed space-craft or space station from which experiment and research equipment can be extended outside (into space) while the interior of the vehicle retains its atmospheric integrity (i.e., remains pressurized).

scientific notation A method of expressing powers of 10 that greatly simplifies writing large numbers. In scientific notation, a number expressed in a positive power of 10 means the decimal point moves to the right (e.g., $3 \times 10^6 = 3,000,000$); a number expressed in a negative power of 10 means that the decimal moves to the left (e.g., $3 \times 10^{-6} = 0.000003$).

Scout A four-stage, all solid-propellant expendable launch vehicle developed and used by NASA to place small payloads into Earth orbit and to place probes on suborbital trajectories. The first Scout (Solid Controlled Orbital Utility Test) vehicle was launched on July 1, 1960, from the Mark 1 Launcher at the NASA Goddard Space Flight Center's Wallops Flight Facility, Wallops Island, Virginia. The Scout's first-stage motor was based on an earlier version of the navy's Polaris missile motor; the second-stage solid propellant motor was derived from the army's Sergeant surface-to-surface missile; and the third- and fourth-stage motors were adapted by NASA from the navy's Vanguard missile.

The standard Scout vehicle is a slender, all solid-propellant, four-stage booster system, approximately 23 meters (75 feet) in length with a launch mass of 21,500 kilograms (47,400 pounds-mass). This expendable vehicle is capable of placing a 186-kilogram (400 pounds-mass) payload into a 560-kilometer (350-mile) orbit around Earth.

See also: LAUNCH VEHICLE; ROCKET.

screaming A form of combustion instability, especially in a liquid-propellant rocket engine, of relatively high frequency and characterized by a high-pitched noise.

screeching A form of combustion instability, especially in an afterburner, of relatively high frequency and characterized by a harsh, shrill noise.

scrub To cancel or postpone a rocket firing, either before or during the countdown.

sealant Liquid/solid mixture installed at joints and junctions of components to prevent leakage of fluid (especially gas) from the joint or junction.

sealed cabin The crew-occupied space of an aircraft, aerospace vehicle, or spacecraft characterized by walls that do not allow any gaseous exchange between the cabin (inner) atmosphere and its surroundings and containing its own mechanisms for maintenance of the cabin atmosphere.

sea-level engine A rocket engine designed to operate at sea level; that is, the exhaust gases achieve complete expansion at sea-level ambient pressure.

See also: ROCKET; ROCKET ENGINE.

seal extrusion Permanent displacement (under the action of fluid pressure) of part of a seal into a gap provided for such displacement.

sealing rings Mechanical devices designed to fit together tightly when two spacecraft or a spacecraft and a space station are docked so that their cabin atmospheres will not leak out during crew and equipment transfers.

search for extraterrestrial intelligence (SETI) The major aim of SETI programs is to listen for evidence of radio-frequency (microwave) signals generated by intelligent extraterrestrial civilizations. This search is an attempt to answer an important philosophical question: Are we alone in the universe? The classic paper by Giuseppe Cocconi and Philip Morrison entitled "Searching for Interstellar Communications" (*Nature*, 1959) often is regarded as the start of modern SETI. With the arrival of the space age, the entire subject of extraterrestrial intelligence (ETI) has left the realm of science fiction and now is regarded as a scientifically respectable (although currently speculative) field of endeavor.

The current understanding of stellar formation leads scientists to think that planets are normal and frequent companions of most stars. As interstellar clouds of dust and gas condense to form stars, they appear to leave behind clumps of material that form into planets. The Milky Way Galaxy contains at least 100 billion to 200 billion stars.

Current theories on the origin and chemical evolution of life indicate that it probably is not unique to Earth but may be common and widespread throughout the galaxy. Further, some scientists believe that life on alien worlds could have developed intelligence, curiosity, and the technology necessary to build the devices needed to transmit and receive electromagnetic signals across the interstellar void. For example, an intelligent alien civilization might, like humans, radiate electromagnetic energy into space. This can happen unintentionally (as a result of planetary-level radio-frequency communications) or intentionally (through the beaming of structured radio signals out into the galaxy in the hope some other intelligent species can intercept and interpret these signals against the natural electromagnetic radiation background of space).

SETI observations may be performed using radio telescopes on Earth, in space, or even (some day) on the far side of the Moon. Each location has distinct advantages and disadvantages.

Until now only very narrow portions of the electromagnetic spectrum have been examined for "artifact signals" (i.e., those generated by intelligent alien civilizations). Human-made radio and television signals—the kind radio astronomers reject as clutter and interference—actually are similar to the signals SETI researchers are hunting for.

The sky is full of radio waves. In addition to the electromagnetic signals we generate as part of our technical civilization (e.g., radio, TV, radar, etc.), the sky also contains natural radio-wave emissions from such celestial objects as the Sun, the planet Jupiter, radio galaxies, pulsars, and quasars. Even interstellar space is characterized by a constant, detectable radio-noise spectrum.

And just what would a radio-frequency signal from an intelligent extraterrestrial civilization look like? Figure 114 presents a spectrogram that shows a simulated "artifact signal" from outside the solar system. This particular signal was sent by *Pioneer 10* from beyond the orbit of Neptune and was received by a Deep Space Network (DSN) radio telescope at Goldstone, California using a 65,000-channel spectrum analyzer. The three signal components are quite visible above the always-present background radio noise. The center spike appearing in the figure has a transmitted signal power of approximately 1 watt—about half the power of a miniature Christmas tree light. SETI scientists are looking for a radio-frequency signal that might appear this clearly, or for one that may actually be quite difficult to distinguish from the background radio noise. To search through this myriad of radio-frequency signals, SETI scientists have devel-

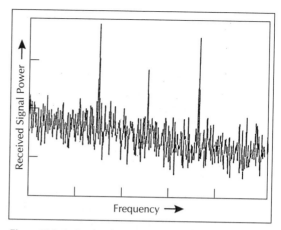

Figure 114. A simulated signal from an extraterrestrial civilization (using the *Pioneer 10* spacecraft transmitting a signal from beyond the orbit of Neptune) *(Courtesy of NASA)*

oped state-of-the-art spectrum analyzers that can sample millions of frequency channels simultaneously and identify candidate "artifact signals" automatically for further observation and analysis.

If an alien signal is ever detected and decoded, the people of Earth would face another challenging question: Do we answer? For now, SETI scientists are content to listen passively for "artifact signals" that might arrive across the interstellar void.

See also: ARECIBO OBSERVATORY; RADIOASTRONOMY.

Seasat A NASA Earth observation spacecraft designed to demonstrate techniques for global monitoring of oceanographic phenomena and features, to provide oceangraphic data, and to determine key features of an operational ocean-dynamics system. *Seasat-A* was launched on June 26, 1978 by an expendable Atlas-Agena launch vehicle from Vandenberg Air Force Base, California. It was placed into a near-circular (~800 kilometer (~500 miles) altitude) polar orbit. The major difference between *Seasat-A* and previous Earth observation satellites was the use of active and passive microwave sensors to achieve an all-weather capability. After 106 days of returning data, contact with *Seasat-A* was lost when a short circuit drained all power from its batteries.

See also: OCEAN REMOTE SENSING; REMOTE SENSING.

Sea Sparrow (RIM-7M) The U.S. Navy's Sea Sparrow missile, designated RIM-7, is a radar-guided, air-to-air missile with a high-explosive (HE) warhead. It has a cylindrical body with four wings (canards) at midbody and four tail fins. A solid-propellant rocket motor powers this versatile all-weather, all-altitude operational weapon system that can attack high-performance aircraft and missiles from any direction. The navy also uses the Sea Sparrow aboard ships as a surface-to-air antimissile defense system.

See also: SPARROW.

second 1. The SI UNIT of time (symbol: s), now defined as the duration of 9,192,631,770 periods of radiation corresponding to the transition between two hyperfine levels of the ground state of the cesium-133 atom. Previously, this unit of time had been based on astronomical observations. 2. A unit of angle (symbol: ″) equal to 1/3600 of a degree or 1/60 of a minute of angle.

secondary radiation Electromagnetic (photons) or particulate ionizing radiation resulting from the absorption of other (primary) ionizing radiation in matter. For example, the ionizing occurring within a spacecraft, when high-energy cosmic rays impact the wall of a spacecraft and remove electrons or nuclei from the matter in the wall. These removed electrons or nuclei are called secondary radiations.

Second Law of Thermodynamics An inequality asserting that it is impossible to transfer thermal energy (heat) from a colder to a warmer system without the occurrence of other simultaneous changes in the two systems or in the environment.

It follows from this important physical principle that during an adiabatic process, ENTROPY cannot decrease. For reversible adiabatic processes, entropy remains constant; while for irreversible adiabatic processes, it increases.

An equivalent formulation of the law is that it is impossible to convert the heat of a system into work without the occurrence of other simultaneous changes in the system or its environment. This version of the Second Law, which requires a heat engine to have a cold sink as well as a hot source, is particularly useful in engineering applications.

Another important statement of the Second Law is that the change in entropy (ΔS) for an isolated system is greater than or equal to zero. Mathematically,

$$(\Delta S)_{isolated} \geq 0$$

See also: FIRST LAW OF THERMODYNAMICS; THERMODYNAMICS.

section One of the cross-section parts that a rocket vehicle is divided into, each adjoining another at one or both of its ends. Usually described by a designating word, as in *nose section, aft section, center section, tail section, thrust section, propellant tank section.*

Seebeck effect The establishment of an electric potential difference that tends to produce a flow of current in a circuit of two dissimilar metals, the junctions of which are at different temperatures. It is the physical phenomenon involved in the operation of a thermocouple and is named for the German scientist Thomas Seebeck (1770–1831), who first observed it in 1822.

See also: THERMOCOUPLE; THERMOELECTRIC CONVERSION.

Selenian Of or relating to Earth's Moon. Once a permanent lunar base is established, a resident of the Moon.

See also: MOON.

selenocentric 1. Relating to the center of Earth's Moon; referring to the Moon as a center. 2. Orbiting about the Moon as a central body.

selenodesy That branch of science (applied mathematics) that determines, by observation and measurement, the exact positions of points and the figures and areas of large portions of the Moon's surface, or the shape and size of the Moon.

selenoid A satellite of Earth's Moon; a spacecraft in orbit around the Moon, as, for example, NASA's lunar orbiter spacecraft.

See also: LUNAR ORBITER.

selenography The branch of astronomy that deals with Earth's Moon, its surface, composition, motion, and the like. *Selene* is Greek for "Moon."

self-cooled Term applied to a combustion chamber or nozzle in which temperature is controlled or limited by methods that do not involve flow within the wall of coolant supplied from an external source.

self-pressurization Increase of ullage pressure by vaporization or boil-off of contained fluid without the aid of additional pressurant.

semiactive homing guidance A system of homing guidance in which the receiver in the missile uses radiations reflected from a target that has been illuminated by a source outside the missile. For example, a pilot in an aircraft can use a laser designator to mark, or "paint," a particular target. Some of this laser light then is reflected back to the missile, which follows it to the target.

See also: GUIDANCE SYSTEM.

sensible atmosphere That portion of a planet's atmosphere that offers resistance to a body passing through it.

sensible heat The thermal energy (heat) that, when added to or removed from a thermodynamic system, causes a change in temperature. Compare with LATENT HEAT.

sensor In general, a device that detects and/or measures certain types of physically observable phenomena. More specifically, that part of an electronic instrument that detects electromagnetic radiations (or other characteristic emissions, such as nuclear particles) from a target or object at some distance away and then converts these incident radiations (or particles) into a quantity (i.e., an internal electronic signal) that is amplified, measured (quantified), displayed, and/or recorded by another part of the instrument. A passive sensor uses characteristic emissions from the object or target as its input signal. In contrast, an active sensor (like a radar) places a burst of electromagnetic energy on the object or target being observed and then uses the reflected signal as its input.

See also: REMOTE SENSING.

Sentinel An former antiballistic missile (ABM) system that was designed for light-area defense against a low-level ballistic missile attack on the United States. It was developed into the Safeguard system in the late 1960s.

See also: BALLISTIC MISSILE DEFENSE; SAFEGUARD.

separation 1. The action of a fallaway section or companion body as it casts off from the remaining body of a vehicle, or the action of the remaining body as it leaves a fallaway section behind it. 2. The moment at which this action occurs.

separation velocity The velocity at which a rocket, aerospace vehicle, or spacecraft is moving when some part or section is separated from it; specifically, the velocity of a space probe or satellite at the time of separation from the launch vehicle.

Sergeant (MGM-29A) A U.S. Army mobile, inertially guided, solid-propellant, surface-to-surface missile with nuclear capability, designed to attack targets up to a range of about 140 kilometers (85 miles).

service module (SM) The large part of the Apollo spacecraft that contained support equipment; it was attached to the command module (CM) until just before the CM (carrying three astronauts) reentered Earth's atmosphere at the end of a mission.

See also: APOLLO PROJECT.

servo A device that helps control (usually by hydraulic means) a large moment of inertia by the application of a relatively small moment of inertia. Also called a *servomechanism*.

See also: ROBOTICS.

shaft A bar (almost always cylindrical) used to support rotating pieces or to transmit power or motion by rotation.

shake-and-bake test A series of prelaunch tests performed on a spacecraft to simulate the launch vibrations and thermal environment (i.e., temperature extremes) it will experience during the mission. A typical test plan might involve the use of enormous speakers to blast the spacecraft with acoustic vibrations similar to those it will encounter during launch. As part of a typical shake-and-bake test plan, aerospace engineers also will place the spacecraft in a special environmental chamber and subject it to the extreme hot and cold temperatures it will experience during space flight.

shake table Device for subjecting components or assemblies to vibration in order to reveal vibrational mode patterns.

shear strength In materials science, the stress required to produce fracture in the plane of cross section, the conditions of loading being such that the directions of force and of resistance are parallel and opposite, although their paths are offset a specified minimum amount.

shelf life Storage time during which an item, such as a battery or a propellant compound, remains serviceable, that is, will operate satisfactorily when put to use.

shield A quantity of material used to reduce the passage of ionizing radiation. The term "shielding" refers to the arrangement of shields used for a particular nuclear radiation protection circumstance.
See also: SPACE RADIATION ENVIRONMENT.

Shillelagh (MGM-51) A U.S. Army missile system that is mounted on a main battle tank or assault reconnaissance vehicle for use against enemy armor, troops, and field fortifications.

shirt-sleeve environment A space station module or spacecraft cabin in which the atmosphere is similar to that found on the surface of Earth, that is, it does not require a pressure suit.

shock 1. A SHOCK WAVE. 2. A blow, impact, collision, or violent jar. 3. The sudden agitation of a person's mental or emotional state; or the event causing it. 4. The sudden (sometimes fatal) stimulation caused by an electrical discharge on a human being or animal. Also called an *electric shock.*

shock diamonds The diamond-shaped (or wedge-shaped) shock waves that sometimes become distinctly visible in the exhaust of a rocket vehicle during launch ascent.

shock front 1. A SHOCK WAVE regarded as the forward surface of a fluid region having characteristics different from those of the region ahead of it. 2. The boundary between the pressure disturbance created by an explosion (in air, water, or earth) and the ambient atmosphere, water, or earth.

shock isolator A resilient support that tends to isolate a system from applied shock. Also called *shock mount.*

shock layer The layer of fluid between the SHOCK WAVE and the vehicle in which the velocity of the fluid changes from supersonic (or hypersonic) to subsonic.

shock tube A relatively long tube in which brief, high-velocity gas flows are produced by the sudden release of very high-pressure gas into the low-

pressure portion of the tube. This action produces a traveling SHOCK WAVE along the tube with high-speed flow behind the shock.

shock wave 1. A surface of discontinuity (i.e., of abrupt changes in conditions) set up in a supersonic field of flow, through which the fluid undergoes a finite decrease in velocity accompanied by a marked increase in pressure, density, temperature, and ENTROPY. Sometimes called a *shock.* 2. A pressure pulse in air, water, or earth, propagated from an explosion. It has two distinct phases: in the first, or positive, phase, the pressure rises sharply to a peak, then subsides to the normal pressure of the surrounding medium; in the second, or negative, phase, the pressure falls below that of the medium, then returns to normal. A shock wave in air is also called a *blast wave.*

shoot-back In space defense, the technique of defending a space asset by shooting back at an attacker and trying to destroy the attacking objects before they can destroy the targeted space asset.

short-range attack missile (AGM-69) A U.S. Air Force air-to-surface missile that is armed with a nuclear warhead and can be launched from the B-52 and the FB-111 aircraft. The missile's range, speed, and accuracy allow the carrier aircraft to "stand off" from its intended targets and launch this missile while still outside enemy defenses.

short-range ballistic missile A ballistic missile with a range capability up to about 1,100 kilometers (690 miles).

shot A colloquial aerospace term used to describe the act or instance of firing a rocket, especially from Earth's surface; for example, the launch crew prepared for the next *shot* of the space shuttle.

Shrike (AGM-45) An air-launched, antiradiation missile used by the U.S. Navy to home in on and destroy hostile antiaircraft radars. The missile uses a solid-propellant rocket motor, is 3.05 meters (10 feet) long, has a mass of 177 kilograms (390 pounds-mass). It employs a passive radar homing guidance system and contains a conventional warhead.

shroud 1. In general, the protective outer covering for a payload that is being transported into space by a launch vehicle. Once the launch vehicle has left Earth's sensible atmosphere, the shroud is discarded. 2. In the context of BALLISTIC MISSILE DEFENSE (BMD), a shroud would be used with a reentry vehicle (RV) or a postboost vehicle (PBV) to confuse the missile defense system. For example, the RV shroud is a thin envelope that would enclose a reentry vehicle, interfering with the infrared radiation it normally would emit; a PBV shroud is a loose conical device that would be positioned behind a PBV to conceal the deployment of reentry vehicles and decoys.

shutdown 1. In aerospace engineering, the process of decreasing the thrust of a rocket engine to zero. 2. In nuclear engineering, the process of reducing the power level of a nuclear reactor to zero (i.e., the process of stopping the neutron chain reaction).

shutoff valve Valve that terminates the flow of fluid; usually a two-way valve that is either fully open or fully closed.

Shuttle Commonly encountered, shortened name for NASA's space shuttle vehicle or the U.S. Space Transportation System (STS).
See: SPACE TRANSPORTATION SYSTEM.

Shuttle glow A phenomenon first observed on early space shuttle missions in which a visible glow, caused by the optical excitation of the tenuous residual atmosphere of atomic oxygen and molecular nitrogen found between 250 to 300 kilometers (km) (155 to 186 miles [mi]) altitude, is seen around the leading edges of the vehicle. As the space shuttle or other spacecraft flies through these thin gases at orbital velocities (about 8 km (5 mi) per second), the impact of these gases actually gives rise to two phenomena: Some portions of the space vehicle glow while in orbit, while other portions of the space vehicle can erode away slowly due to a chemical interaction with the highly reactive residual atmosphere (i.e., atomic oxygen chemically attacks the surfaces of an orbiting spacecraft).

sideband 1. Either of the two frequency bands on both sides of the carrier frequency within which fall the frequencies of the wave produced by the process of modulation. 2. The wave components lying within such a band.

sidereal Of or pertaining to the stars.

sidereal day The duration of one rotation of Earth on its axis, with respect to the vernal equinox. It is measured by successive transits of the vernal equinox over the upper branch of a meridian. Because of the procession of the equinoxes, the sidereal day so defined is slightly less than the period of rotation with respect to the stars, but the difference is less than 0.01 second. The length of the mean sidereal day is 24 hours of sidereal time or 23 hours 56 minutes 4.091 seconds of mean solar time.

sidereal time Time measured by the rotation of Earth with respect to the stars, which are considered "fixed" in position. Sidereal time may be designated as local or Greenwich, depending on whether the local meridian or the Greenwich meridian is used as the reference.

sidereal year The period of one apparent revolution of Earth around the Sun, with respect to a referenced ("fixed") star. A sidereal year averages 365.25636 days in duration. Because of the precession of the equinoxes, this is about 20 minutes longer than a tropical year. The tropical year is defined as the average period of time between successive passages of the Sun across the vernal equinox.
See also: YEAR.

Sidewinder (AIM-9) A supersonic, heat-seeking, air-to-air missile carried by U.S. Navy, Marine, and Air Force fighter aircraft. The Sidewinder has the following main components: an infrared homing guidance section, an active optical target detector, a high-explosive warhead, and a solid-propellant rocket motor. The heat-seeking infrared guidance system enables the missile to home on a target aircraft's engine exhaust. This infrared seeker also permits the pilot to launch the missile, then leave the area or take evasive action, while the missile guides itself to the target. The AIM-9A, prototype of Sidewinder, was fired successfully first in September 1953. Since then the design of this missile has evolved continuously to where it has become the most widely used air-to-air missile by the United States and its Western allies.

siemens (symbol: S) The SI UNIT of electrical conductance. It is defined as the conductance of an electrical circuit or element that has a resistance of one ohm. In the past this unit sometimes was called the *mho* or *reciprocal ohm*. The unit is named in honor of the German scientist Ernst Werner von Siemens (1816–1892).

sievert (symbol: Sv) The special SI UNIT for dose equivalent (H). In radiation protection, the dose equivalent in sieverts (Sv) is the product of the absorbed dose (D) in grays (Gy) and the quality factor (QF) as well as any other modifying factors considered necessary to characterize and evaluate the biological effects of the ionizing radiation received by human beings or other living creatures. The sievert is related to the traditional dose equivalent unit (rem) as follows: 1 sievert = 100 rem.

See also: DOSE EQUIVALENT; SPACE RADIATION ENVIRONMENT.

signal 1. A visible, audible, or other indication used to convey information. 2. Information to be transmitted over a communications system. 3. Any carrier of information; as opposed to noise. 4. In electronics, any transmitted electrical impulse. The variation of amplitude, frequency, and waveform are used to convey information.

signal-to-noise ratio (SNR) The ratio of the amplitude of the desired signal to the amplitude of noise signals at a given point in time. The higher the signal-to-noise ratio, the less interference with reception of the desired signal.

signature In general, the set of characteristics by which an object or target can be identified; for example, the distinctive type of radiation emitted or reflected by the target that can be used to recognize it. A target's signature might include a characteristic infrared emission, an unusual pattern of motion, or a distinctive radar return.

simulation 1. In general, the art of replicating relevant portions of the "real-world" environment to test equipment, train mission personnel, and prepare for emergencies. Simulations can involve the use of physical mass and energy replicants, high-fidelity (i.e., reasonably close to the original) hardware, and supporting software. With the incredible growth in computer and display technologies, computer-based simulations are assuming an ever-increasing role as aerospace design tools and astronaut training aids. In fact, today's computer-based simulations often are referred to as "reality in a box." Virtual reality systems are extremely versatile simulation tools that can be operated to test equipment and operating procedures and to train personnel safely using a variety of highly interactive mission scenarios. *See also:* VIRTUAL REALITY. 2. In a military context, the art of making a decoy look like a more valuable strategic target.

simulator A heavily computer-dependent training facility that imitates flight-hardware responses and can be used to train flight personnel.

single-event upset (SEU) A bit flip (i.e., a "0" is changed to a "1," or vice versa) in a digital microelectronic circuit. The single-event upset (SEU) is caused by the passage of high-energy ionizing radiation through the silicon material of which the semiconductors are made. These space radiation–induced bit flips (or SEUs) can damage data stored in memory, corrupt operating software, cause the central processing unit (CPU) to write over critical data tables or to halt, and even trigger an unplanned event involving some piece of computer-controlled hardware (e.g., fire a thruster) that then severely impacts the mission. Aerospace engineers deal with the SEU problem in a variety of ways, including: the use of additional shielding around sensitive spacecraft electronics components, the careful selection of electronic components (i.e., using more radiant resistant parts), the use of multiple-redundancy memory units and "polling" electronics, and the regular resetting of the spacecraft's onboard computers.

See also: SPACE RADIATION ENVIRONMENT.

single failure point (SFP) A single element of hardware, the failure of which would lead directly to loss of life, vehicle, or mission. Where safety conditions dictate that abort be initiated when a redundant element fails, that element also is considered a single failure point.

single-stage rocket A rocket vehicle provided with a single rocket propulsion system.

single-stage-to-orbit (SSTO) vehicle Since the early 1960s, aerospace engineers have envisioned building reusable launch vehicles because they offer the potential of relative operational simplicity and reduced costs, when compared with expendable launch vehicles. Until recently, however, the necessary technologies were not available. Now, thanks to aerospace technology improvements, many engineers believe that it is technically feasible to design and produce a single-stage-to-orbit (SSTO) launch vehicle with sufficient payload capacity to meet most government and commercial space transportation requirements.

But despite these recent technology advances, the development of an SSTO space transportation system involves considerable risk. For example, because an SSTO launch vehicle will have no expendable components, it will need to carry more fuel than would be necessary otherwise, if it were shedding mass by dropping (expended) stages during launch. Achieving the propellant mass fraction necessary to reach orbit with a useful payload will require numerous technological advances that improve fuel efficiency and lower structural mass without compromising structural integrity. In addition, completely reusable launch vehicles are technologically much more difficult to achieve because components must be capable of resisting deterioration and surviving multiple launches and reentries.

The difficulties of a horizontal takeoff–horizontal landing vehicle are known from the National Aerospace Plane (NASP) Program. Other candidate SSTO vehicle configurations include vertical takeoff/vertical landing; vertical takeoff/horizontal landing (winged body); and vertical takeoff/horizontal landing (lifting body). NASA's current X-33 program is focusing SSTO vehicle development using a vertical-takeoff/horizontal-landing (lifting body) approach.

See also: X-33.

SI unit(s) *Le Systéme International d'Unités* (the International System of Units, or SI units) is the internationally agreed-upon system of coherent units that is now in use throughout the world for scientific and engineering purposes. The metric (or SI) system was developed originally in France in the late 18th century. Its basic units for length, mass, and time—the meter (m), the kilogram (kg), and the second (s)—were based on natural standards. The modern SI units are still based on natural standards and international agreement, but these standards now are ones that can be measured with greater precision than the previous natural standards. For example, the *meter (m)* [British spelling: *metre*] is the basic SI unit of length. Currently it is defined as being equal to 1,650,763.73 wavelengths in a vacuum of the orange-red line of the spectrum of krypton-86. (Previously the meter had been defined as one ten-millionth the distance from the equator to the North Pole along the meridian nearest Paris.)

Metric measurements play an important part in the global aerospace industry. Unfortunately, a good deal of American aerospace activity still involves the use of another set of units, the English system of measurement (sometimes referred to as the American Engineering system of units). One major advantage of the metric system over the English system is that the metric system uses the number 10 as a base. Therefore, multiples or submultiples of SI units are reached by multiplying or dividing by 10.

The metric system uses the kilogram as the basic unit of mass. In contrast, the English system has a unit called the pound-mass (lbm), which is a *unit of mass*, and another unit, the pound-force (lbf) which is a *unit of force*. Furthermore, these two "pound" units are related by an arbitrary (pre–space age) definition within the English system of measurement that states that a 1 pound-mass object "weighs" 1 pound-force at sea level on Earth. Novices and professionals alike all too often forget that this "pound" equivalency is valid *only* at sea level on the surface of Earth. Therefore, this particular English unit arrangement can cause much confusion in working aerospace engineering problems. For example, in the metric system, a kilogram is a kilogram, whether on Earth or on Mars. However, in the English system, if an object "weighs" one pound* on Earth, it only "weighs" 0.38 pounds* on Mars. Of course, from the basic physical concept of mass, one pound-mass (lbm) on Earth is still one-pound mass (lbm) on Mars. What changes the object's "weight" (as calculated from Newton's second law of motion: force = mass x acceleration) is the difference in the local acceleration due to gravity. On Earth, the sea-level acceleration due to gravity (g) is equal to 9.8 meters per second per second (m/s^2) (or about 32.2 feet per second per second [ft/s^2]); while on the surface of Mars, the local acceleration due to gravity (g$_{Mars}$) is only 3.73 meters per second per second (m/s^2) (or about 12.2 feet per second per second [ft/s^2]). Confusing? That is why the metric system is used extensively throughout this book and why the

---

* To be perfectly correct, we must specify the object's "weight" in pound-force (lbf) units.

companion English units (wherever appropriate) are included in parentheses. A special effort has been made to identify the pound-mass and the pound-force, as separate and distinct units within the English system of measurements. The metric companion unit to the pound-mass is the kilogram (kg), namely 1 kg = 2.205 pounds-mass; while the metric companion unit to the pound-force is the newton (N), namely 1 N = 0.2248 pound-force.

Appendix A provides a summary of contemporary SI units and their conversion factors, the recommended SI unit prefixes, special units used in astronomical investigations, and common metric/English conversion factors.

See also: INTERNATIONAL SYSTEM OF UNITS; APPENDIX A.

skin The outer covering of a rocket, missile, or aerospace vehicle.

skirt The lower outer part of a missile or rocket vehicle.

skirt fog The cloud of steam and water that often surrounds the engines of a rocket being launched from a wet emplacement.

Skylab (SL) The first U.S. space station, which was placed in orbit in 1973 by a two-stage configuration of the Saturn V expendable launch vehicle and then visited by three astronaut crews who worked on scientific experiments in space for a total of approximately 172 days, with the last crew spending 84 days in Earth orbit. (See Figure 115.)

Skylab (SL) was composed of five major parts: the Apollo telescope mount (ATM); the multiple docking adapter (MDA); the airlock module (AM); the instrument unit (IU); and the orbital workshop (OWS), which included the living and working

Figure 115. Major components of NASA's 90-metric-ton Skylab space station. Note in this illustration one of the large solar wings is missing because it was torn off during the launch ascent. The solar parasol erected by the first Skylab crew is also depicted as the "sunshield" instead of the original meteoroid/Sun shield, which was also lost during the uncrewed ride to orbit on May 14, 1973 on top of a two-stage version of the Saturn V rocket. *(Drawing courtesy of NASA)*

SKYLAB MISSION SUMMARY (1973–1974)

Mission	Dates	Crew	Mission Duration	Remarks
Skylab 1	Launched 05/14/73	Unmanned	Re-entered atmosphere 07/11/79	90-metric ton space station visited by three astronaut crews
Skylab 2	05/25/73 to 06/22/73	Charles Conrad, Jr Paul J. Weitz Joseph P. Kerwin (M.D.)	28 days 49 min	Repaired Skylab; 392 hrs experiments; 3 EVAs
Skylab 3	07/28/73 to 09/25/73	Alan L. Bean Jack R. Lousma Owen K. Garriott (Ph.D.)	59 days 11 hrs 3 EVAs	Performed maintenance; 1,081 hrs experiments;
Skylab 4	11/16/73 to 02/08/74	Gerald P. Carr William R. Pogue Edward G. Gibson (Ph.D.)	84 days 1 hr 1,563 hrs experiments	Observed Comet Kohoutek; 4 EVAs;

quarters. The ATM was a solar observatory, and it provided attitude control and experiment pointing for the rest of the cluster. The retrieval and installation of film used in the ATM was accomplished by the astronauts during extravehicular activity (EVA). The MDA served as a dock for the modified Apollo spacecraft that taxied the crews to and from the space station. The airlock module (AM) was located between the docking port (MDA) and the living and working quarters, and contained controls and instrumentation. The instrument unit (IU), which was used only during launch and the initial phases of operation, provided guidance and sequencing functions for the initial deployment of the ATM, its solar arrays, and the like. The orbital workshop (OWS) was a modified Saturn IV-B stage that had been converted into a "two-story" space laboratory with living quarters for a crew of three. This orbital laboratory was capable of unmanned, in-orbit storage, reactivation, and reuse.

There were four launches in the Skylab Program from Complex 39 at the Kennedy Space Center. The first launch was on May 14, 1973. A two-stage Saturn V vehicle placed the unmanned 90-metric ton (100-ton) Skylab space station in an initial 435-kilometer (270-mile) orbit around Earth. As the rocket accelerated past 7,620 meters (25,000 feet), atmospheric drag began clawing at Skylab's meteoroid/Sun shield. This cylindrical metal shield was designed to protect the orbital workshop from tiny particles and the Sun's scorching heat. Sixty-three seconds after launch, the shield ripped away from the spacecraft, trailing an aluminum strap that

caught on one of the unopened solar wings. The shield became tethered to the laboratory while at the same time prying the opposite solar wing partly open. Minutes later, as the booster rocket staged, the partially deployed solar wing and meteoroid/Sun shield were flung into space. With the loss of the meteoroid/Sun shield, temperatures inside Skylab soared, rendering the space station uninhabitable and threatening the food, medicine, and film stored onboard. The Apollo Telescope Mount (ATM), the major piece of scientific equipment, did deploy properly, however, an action that included the successful unfolding of its four solar panels.

The countdown for the launch of the first Skylab crew was halted. NASA engineers worked quickly to devise a solar parasol to cover the workshop and to find a way to free the remaining stuck solar wing. On May 25, 1973, Astronauts Charles "Pete" Conrad. Jr., Dr. Joseph P. Kerwin, and Paul J. Weitz were launched by a Saturn 1B rocket toward Skylab.

After repairing Skylab's broken docking mechanism, which had refused to latch, the astronauts entered the space station and erected a mylar solar parasol through a space access hatch. It shaded part of the area where the protective meteoroid/Sun shield had been ripped away. Temperatures within the spacecraft immediately began dropping, and Skylab soon became habitable without space suits. But the many experiments on board demanded far more electric power than the four ATM solar arrays could generate. Skylab could fulfill its scientific mission only if the first crew freed the remaining crippled solar wing. Using equipment that resembled long-handled pruning shears and a prybar, the astronauts pulled the stuck solar wing free. The space station was now ready to meet its scientific mission objectives.

The duration of the first crewed mission was 28 days. The second astronaut crew—Alan Bean, Jack Lousma, and Dr. Owen Garriott—was launched on July 28, 1973; mission duration on the space station was approximately 59 days and 11 hours. The third Skylab crew—Gerald Carr, William Pogue, and Dr. Edward Gibson—was launched November 16, 1973; mission duration was a little over 84 days. Saturn IB rockets launched all three crews in modified Apollo spacecraft, which also served as their return-to-Earth vehicle. The third and final manned Skylab mission ended with splashdown in the Pacific Ocean on February 8, 1974. (See the table.)

After the last astronaut crew departed the space station in February 1974, it orbited Earth as an abandoned derelict. Unable to maintain its original altitude, the station finally reentered the atmosphere on July 11, 1979, during orbit 34,981. While most of the station was burned up during reentry, some pieces survived and impacted in remote areas of the Indian Ocean and sparsely inhabited portions of Australia.

See also: SPACE STATION.

slenderness ratio A dimensionless number that expresses the ratio of a rocket vehicle's length to its diameter.

slew To change the position of a sensor or an antenna assembly by injecting a signal into the positioning servo-mechanism.

slip flow Flow in the transition regime of gas dynamics, wherein the mean free path of the gas molecules is of the same order of magnitude as the thickness of the boundary layer. The gas in contact with a body surface immersed in the flow is no longer at rest with respect to the surface.

slipstream The flow of fluid around a structure that is moving through the fluid.

sliver The portion of solid-propellant grain remaining at the time of web burnout.

See also: ROCKET.

sloshing The back-and-forth movement of a liquid rocket propellant in its tank(s), creating problems of stability and control in the vehicle. Aerospace engineers often use antislosh baffles in a rocket vehicle's propellant tanks to avoid this problem.

slug A unit of mass in the standard system of measurement (i.e., the foot-pound-second system of units) approximately equal to 32.17 pounds-mass (lbm). It is defined as the amount of mass that, if acted upon by a one-pound force (lbf), would experience an acceleration of one foot per second per second. This unit physically represents an amount of mass (in pound-mass units) that is *numerically* equal to the value of the standard acceleration of gravity at sea level on the surface of Earth (namely, 32.17 feet per second per second).

slurry fuel A rocket fuel consisting of a suspension of fine solid particles in a liquid.

small self-contained payload A research and development payload that is small (i.e., less than 91 kilograms [200 pounds-mass] in mass or 0.14 cubic meter [5 cubic feet] in volume), requires no space shuttle orbiter services, and is flown in the orbiter's cargo bay on a space-available basis. Also called a *Get Away Special* (*GAS*) payload.

See also: GET AWAY SPECIAL.

SNAP An acronym for *Systems for Nuclear Auxiliary Power.* The SNAP program was created by the U.S. Atomic Energy Commission (forerunner of the U.S. Department of Energy) to develop small auxiliary nuclear power sources for specialized outer space, remote land, and sea applications. Two general approaches were pursued. The first approach used the thermal energy from the decay of a radioisotope source to produce electricity directly by thermoelectric or thermionic methods. The second approach used the thermal energy liberated in a small nuclear reactor to produce electricity by either direct conversion methods or dynamic conversion methods.

See also: SPACE NUCLEAR POWER.

Snark A surface-to-surface guided missile developed by the U.S. Air Force in the early 1950s. This now obsolete winged missile had a range of about 8,000 kilometers (5,000 miles) and was capable of carrying a nuclear warhead.

snubber A device used to increase the stiffness of an elastic system (usually by a large factor), whenever the displacement of the system becomes larger than a specified amount.

soft kill In aerospace military operations and ballistic missile defense (BMD), the destruction of an object by, for example, a particle beam or microwave weapon directed against the object's electronic subsystems, such that an outside observer cannot detect any physical change in the object from a distance but the object (target) is, in fact, unable to perform its mission. Also called a *functional kill*.

See also: BALLISTIC MISSILE DEFENSE.

soft landing The act of landing on the surface of a planet without damage to any portion of the space vehicle or payload, except possibly the landing gear. NASA's Surveyor spacecraft and Viking lander spacecraft were designed for soft landings on the Moon and Mars, respectively.

See also: SURVEYOR; VIKING PROJECT.

soft missile base A missile launching base that is not protected against a nuclear explosion.

soft radiation Ionizing radiation that has a low penetrating capability. Frequently, "soft" is applied to X rays of relatively low energy (i.e., long-wavelength, low-frequency X rays). Compare this term with HARD RADIATION.

soft target In strategic nuclear warfare, any target that cannot be hardened (protected) in order to survive a nearby nuclear detonation. Cities, airfields, and large industrial centers are examples of soft targets.

soft X rays Photons with energy from 100 electron volts (eV) to 10 kiloelectron volts (keV).

Sol The Sun.

sol A Martian day (about 24 hours 37 minutes 23 seconds in duration); seven sols equal approximately 7.2 Earth days.

solar 1. Of or pertaining to the Sun or caused by the Sun, as *solar radiation, solar atmospheric tide* 2. Relative to the Sun as a datum or reference, such as *solar time.*

solar activity Any type of variation in the appearance or energy output of the Sun.

Solar and Heliospheric Observatory (SOHO) The primary scientific aims of the European Space Agency's (ESA's) Solar and Heliospheric Observatory (SOHO) are to investigate the physical processes that form and heat the Sun's corona, maintain it, and give rise to the expanding solar wind; and to study the interior structure of the Sun. SOHO is part of the International Solar-Terrestrial Physics Program (ISTP) and involves NASA participation. The 1,350-kilogram (on-orbit dry mass) spacecraft was launched on December 2, 1995 and placed in a halo orbit at the Earth-Sun Lagrangian libration point one (L1) to obtain uninterrupted sunlight. It had a two-year design life, but onboard consumables are sufficient for an extra four years of operation. The spacecraft carries a complement of 12 scientific instruments.

See also: EUROPEAN SPACE AGENCY; LAGRANGIAN LIBRATION POINTS; SUN.

solar cell Solar cells are proven direct energy conversion devices that have been used for over three decades to provide electric power for spacecraft. In a direct energy conversion (DEC) device, electricity is produced directly from the primary energy source without the need for thermodynamic power conversion cycles involving the heat engine principle and the circulation of a working fluid. A solar cell or "photovoltaic system" turns sunlight directly into electricity. The solar cell has no moving parts to wear out and produces no noise, fumes, or other polluting waste products. However, the space environment, especially trapped radiation belts and the energetic particles released in solar flares, can damage solar cells used on spacecraft and reduce their useful lifetime.

See also: PHOTOVOLTAIC MATERIAL; SATELLITE POWER SYSTEM.

solar constant The total amount of the Sun's radiant energy that normally crosses perpendicular to a unit area at the top of Earth's atmosphere (i.e., at one astronomical unit from the Sun). The currently used value of the solar constant is 1,371 ± 5 watts per square meter. The spectral distribution of the Sun's radiant energy resembles that of a BLACKBODY radiator with an effective temperature of 5,800° Kelvin. This means that the most of the Sun's radiant energy lies in the visible portion of the electromagnetic spectrum, with a peak value near 0.45 micrometer (μm).

See also: SUN.

solar cycle The periodic (semiregular) change in the number of sunspots. It is the interval between successive minima and is about 11.1 years (unless the magnetic polarities of the Northern and Southern Hemisphere sunspots are considered; then the 11-year interval is actually part of a 22-year magnetic cycle).

See also: SUN; SUNSPOT.

solar electric propulsion (SEP) A low-thrust propulsion system in which the electricity required to power the ion engines (or other type of electric rocket engines) is generated either by a solar-thermal conversion system or by a solar-photovoltaic conversion system.

See also: ELECTRIC PROPULSION.

solar flare A highly concentrated explosive release of energy within the solar atmosphere. It appears as a sudden, short-lived brightening of a localized area within the Sun's chromosphere. The electromagnetic radiation output from a solar flare ranges from radio to X-ray frequencies. Energetic nuclear particles, primarily electrons, protons, and a few alpha particles, also are ejected during a solar flare.

See also: SUN.

solar mass The mass of the Sun, namely 1.99×10^{30} kilograms; it is commonly used as a unit in comparing stellar masses.

See also: SUN.

Solar Maximum Mission (SMM) A NASA spacecraft designed to provide coordinated observations of solar activity, especially solar flares, during a period of maximum solar activity. The 2,315-kilogram (5,100 pounds-mass) spacecraft was placed in orbit on February 14, 1980. Its scientific payload consisted of seven instruments specifically selected to study the short-wavelength and coronal manifestations of solar flares. Data were obtained on the storage and release of flare energy, particle acceleration, formation of hot plasma, and mass ejection.

In April 1984 space shuttle mission STS 41-C involved on-orbit repair of the SMM spacecraft. During this shuttle mission, the astronauts rendezvoused with the spacecraft while performing an extravehicular activity (EVA) from the orbiter and successfully repaired it. The SMM spacecraft then continued to collect data until November 24, 1989. It reentered Earth's atmosphere on December 2, 1989.

solar nebula The cloud of dust and gas from which the Sun, the planets, and other minor bodies of the solar system are postulated to have formed (condensed).

See also: SUN.

solar panel A winglike set of solar cells used by a spacecraft to convert sunlight directly into electric power; also called a *solar array.*

See also: SOLAR CELL; SOLAR PHOTOVOLTAIC CONVERSION.

solar photovoltaic conversion The direct conversion of sunlight (solar energy) into electrical energy by means of the photovoltaic effect. A single photovoltaic (PV) converter cell is called a *solar cell,* while a combination of cells, designed to increase the electric power output, is called a *solar array* or a *solar panel.*

Since 1958, solar cells have been used to provide electric power for a wide variety of spacecraft. The typical spacecraft solar cell is made of a combination of n-type (*n*egative) and p-type (*p*ositive) semiconductor materials (generally silicon). When this combination of materials is exposed to sunlight, some of the incident electromagnetic radiation removes bound electrons from the semiconductor material atoms, thereby producing free electrons. A hole (positive charge) is left at each location from which a bound electron has been removed. Consequently, an equal number of free electrons and holes are formed. An electrical barrier at the p-n junction causes the newly created free electrons near the barrier to migrate deeper into the n-type material and the matching holes to migrate further into the p-type material.

If electrical contacts are made with the n- and p-type materials and these contacts connected through an external load (conductor), the free electrons will flow from the n-type material to the p-type material. Upon reaching the p-type material, the free electrons will enter existing holes and once again become bound electrons. The flow of free electrons through the external conductor represents an electric current that will continue as long as more free electrons and holes are being created by exposure of the solar cell to sunlight. This is the general principle of solar photovoltaic conversion.

See also: PHOTOVOLTAIC MATERIAL; SOLAR CELL.

Solar Power Satellite (SPS) A proposed concept involving very large orbiting space platforms located in GEOSYNCHRONOUS EARTH ORBIT that would use solar photovoltaic or solar thermal conversion techniques to satisfy terrestrial energy needs. These massive space platforms would intercept sunlight, convert it into electricity, and then beam energy to special receiving stations on Earth either at microwave (RF) or infrared laser wavelengths. More commonly called *Satellite Power System (SPS)*.

See also: SATELLITE POWER SYSTEM.

solar radiation The total electromagnetic radiation emitted by the Sun. The Sun is considered to radiate as a BLACKBODY at a temperature of about 5,770° Kelvin. Approximately 99.9% of this radiated energy lies within the wavelength interval from 0.15 to 4.0 micrometers (μm), with some 50% lying within the visible portion of the electromagnetic spectrum (namely 0.4 to 0.7 μm) and most of the remaining radiated energy in the near-infrared portion of the spectrum.

See also: ELECTROMAGNETIC SPECTRUM; SUN.

solar storm A disturbance in the space environment triggered by an intense solar flare (or flares) that produces bursts of electromagnetic radiation and charged particles. A solar storm can adversely impact human space operations, cause damage to orbiting spacecraft (especially geostationary satellites that are outside of the Earth's magnetosphere), and affect Earth's upper atmosphere and magnetic field. Solar storms are associated with unexpected surges in solar activity.

Periods of intense solar activity present several major problems for orbiting spacecraft. First, a solar storm heats Earth's atmosphere, causing it to expand. This atmospheric expansion increases the drag experienced by low-Earth-orbiting (LEO) satellites, forcing them to use additional altitude control propellant and shortening their operating lifetimes. Second, during a solar storm more energetic charged particles bombard spacecraft, causing electronic upsets and damage to sensors and electronic equipment. Finally, a solar storm involves bursts of electromagnetic radiation that upset Earth's ionosphere and interfere with radio-wave communications.

Also called a *geomagnetic storm.*
See also: SOLAR FLARE; SUN.

solar system When used in the lower case, the term refers to any star and its gravitationally bound collection of planets, asteroids, and comets.

solar system The Sun and the collection of celestial objects that are bound to it gravitationally. These celestial objects include the nine major planets, over 60 known moons, more than 2,000 minor planets or asteroids, and a very large number of comets. Except for the comets, all of these celestial objects orbit around the Sun in the same direction and their orbits lie close to the plane defined by Earth's own orbit and the Sun's equator.

The nine major planets can be divided into two general categories: (1) the terrestrial or Earth-like planets, consisting of Mercury, Venus, Earth and Mars; and (2) the outer or Jovian planets, consisting of the gaseous giants Jupiter, Saturn, Uranus, and Neptune. Tiny Pluto is currently regarded as a "frozen snowball" in a class by itself. Because of the size of its moon, Charon, some astronomers like to consider Pluto and Charon as forming a double-planet system.

As a group, the terrestrial planets are dense, solid bodies with relatively shallow or no atmosphere. In contrast, the Jovian planets are believed to contain modest-size rock cores, surrounded by concentric layers of frozen hydrogen, liquid hydrogen, and gaseous hydrogen, respectively. Their atmospheres also contain such gases as helium, methane and ammonia.

See also: ASTEROID; COMET; EARTH; JUPITER; MARS; MERCURY; NEPTUNE; PLUTO; SATURN; SUN; URANUS; VENUS.

solar thermal conversion The conversion of sunlight (solar energy) into electricity by means of a thermodynamic cycle involving a heat engine. In general, incoming solar energy is concentrated and focused to heat a working fluid. The solar-heated working fluid undergoes a series of changes in its thermodynamic state during which mechanical energy (work) is extracted from the hot fluid. This mechanical work then is used to spin a generator to produce electricity. Thermodynamic cycles that could be used in solar thermal conversion include the Brayton, Rankine, and Stirling cycles.

See also: BRAYTON CYCLE; HEAT ENGINE; RANKINE CYCLE; STIRLING CYCLE.

solar wind The variable stream of electrons, protons, and various atomic nuclei (e.g., alpha particles) that flows continuously outward from the Sun into interplanetary space. The solar wind has typical speeds of a few hundred kilometers per second.
See also: MAGNETOSPHERE; SUN.

solenoid Helical coil of insulated wire that, when conducting electricity, generates a magnetic field that actuates a movable core.

solid angle (symbol: Ω) Three-dimensional angle formed by the vertex of a cone; that portion of the whole of space about a given point, bounded by a conical surface with its vertex at that point and measured by the area cut by the bounding surface from the surface of a sphere of unit radius centered at that point. The steradian (sr) is the SI UNIT of solid angle.

solid lubricant A dry film lubricant.
See also: SPACE TRIBOLOGY.

solid propellant A rocket propellant in solid form, usually containing both fuel and oxidizer combined or mixed, and formed into a monolithic (not powdered or granulated) grain.
See also: PROPELLANT; ROCKET.

solid-propellant rocket A rocket propelled by a chemical mixture or compound of fuel and oxidizer in solid form. Also called a *solid rocket*.
See also: PROPELLANT; ROCKET.

solid rocket booster (SRB) Two solid rocket boosters (SRBs) operate in parallel to augment the thrust of the space shuttle main engines (SSMEs) from the launch pad through the first two minutes of powered flight. These boosters also assist in guiding the entire vehicle during the initial ascent. Following separation, they are recovered (after a parachute-assisted splashdown in the ocean) for refurbishment and reuse. In addition to its basic component, the solid rocket motor (SRM), each booster contains several subsystems: structural, thrust vector control (TVC), separation, recovery, and electrical and instrumentation.

The heart of the solid rocket booster is the solid rocket motor, the first ever developed for use on a crewed launch vehicle. The huge solid rocket motor is composed of a segmented motor case loaded with solid propellants, an ignition system, a movable nozzle, and the necessary instrumentation and integration hardware.

Each SRB develops about 11,790 kilonewtons (2,650,000 pounds-force) at liftoff and contains more than 500,000 kilograms (1.1 million pounds-mass) of propellant. The type of propellant used in the solid rocket motor is known as PBAN, which stands for polybutadiene acrylic acid acrylonitrile terpolymer. In addition to the PBAN (which serves as the binder), the propellant consists of approximately 70% ammonium perchlorate (the oxidizer), 16% powdered aluminum (the fuel), and a trace of iron oxide (a catalyst) to control the burning rate. The cured solid propellant looks and feels like a hard rubber eraser.
See also: PROPELLANT; ROCKET; SPACE TRANSPORTATION SYSTEM.

solid-state device A device that uses the electric, magnetic, and photonic properties of solid materials, mainly semiconductors. It contains no moving parts and depends on the internal movement of charge carriers (i.e., electrons and "positive" holes) for its operation.

solidus temperature The temperature at which melting starts.

sonic 1. In aerodynamics, of or pertaining to the speed of sound; that which moves at acoustic velocity, as in *sonic flow*; designed to operate or perform at the speed of sound, as in a *sonic leading edge*. 2. Of or pertaining to sound, as in *sonic amplifier*. In this sense, "acoustic" is preferred to "sonic."

sonic boom A thunderlike noise caused by a shock wave that emanates from an aircraft, aerospace vehicle, or flying object that is traveling at or above sonic velocity in Earth's atmosphere. As supersonic objects travel through the air, the air molecules are pushed aside with great force, and this action forms a SHOCK WAVE. The bigger and heavier the supersonic object, the more the air is displaced and the stronger the resultant shock waves. Several factors can influence sonic booms—the mass, size, and shape of the supersonic vehicle or object; its altitude, attitude, and flight path; and local weather or atmospheric conditions.

The shock wave forms a cone of pressurized air molecules that moves outward and rearward in all directions and extends to the ground. As the cone spreads across the landscape along the flight path, it creates a continuous sonic boom along the full width of its base.

sophisticated Complex and intricate; making use of advanced technology; requiring special skills to operate.

sorbent A substance or material that takes up gas by absorption, adsorption, chemisorption, or any combination of these processes.
See also: ABSORPTION; ADSORPTION; CHEMISORPTION.

sorption The taking up of gas by absorption, adsorption, chemisorption, or any combination of these processes.
See also: ABSORPTION; ADSORPTION; CHEMISORPTION.

sound In physics, a vibration in an elastic medium that is at a frequency and intensity that can be heard by a human being. The normal human ear can respond to sounds in the frequency range from approximately 20 to 20,000 hertz (Hz). Vibrations lower than this frequency range are called *infrasounds,* while those above this frequency range are called *ultrasounds.*

sounding In geophysics, any penetration of the natural environment for scientific observation. 2. In meteorology, an observation of the upper air; also, a single complete radiosonde observation. A radiosonde is a balloon-borne device for the simultaneous measurement and transmission of meteorological data up to a height of about 30,000 meters (100,000 feet).

sounding rocket A rocket, usually with a solid-propellant motor, used to carry scientific instruments on parabolic trajectories into the upper regions of Earth's sensible atmosphere (i.e., beyond the reach of aircraft and scientific balloons) and into near-Earth space. A sounding rocket basically is divided into two major components: the solid rocket motor and the payload. Payloads typically include: the experiment package, the nose cone, a telemetry system, an attitude control system, a radar tracking beacon, the firing despin module, and the recovery section. Many sounding rocket payloads are recovered for refurbishment and reuse.

Sounding rockets fly vertical trajectories from 48 kilometers (km) (30 miles [mi]) to over 1,285 km

(800 mi) in altitude. The flight normally lasts less than 30 minutes. Sounding rockets come in a wide variety of sizes and types. For example, NASA's sounding rocket fleet ranges from the single-stage Super Arcas (which stands 3 meters [7 feet] high and 11 centimeters [4.5 inches] in diameter) to the single-stage Aries (which stands 11 meters [35 feet] high and 111 centimeters [44 inches] in diameter). The Super Arcas has been used by NASA since 1962 for carrying meteorological measuring devices. It can carry a 4.5-kilogram (10 pound-mass) payload to an altitude of 91 km (57 mi). The four-stage Black Brant XII, the tallest in NASA's fleet, is 20 meters (67 feet) high.

All of NASA's sounding rockets use solid-propellant rocket motors. Furthermore, all of these rocket vehicles are unguided, except the Aries and those that use the S-19 Boost Guidance System. During flight, all sounding rockets except the Aries are imparted with a spinning motion to reduce potential dispersion of the flight trajectory due to vehicle misalignments. NASA conducts between 30 to 35 suborbital sounding rocket flights per year, providing low-cost, quick-response flight opportunities to scientists in the areas of physics and astronomy, microgravity materials processing research, and instrument development. Most of these sounding rocket launches take place at NASA's Wallops Flight Facility, Wallops Island, Virginia.
See also: ROCKET.

South Atlantic Anomaly (SAA) A region of Earth's trapped radiation particle zone that dips close to the planet in the South Atlantic Ocean southeast of the Brazilian coast. This region represents the most significant source of ionizing radiation for space travelers in low-inclination, low-altitude orbits around Earth.
See also: EARTH'S TRAPPED RADIATION BELTS; SPACE RADIATION ENVIRONMENT.

Soyuz launch vehicle The "workhorse" Soviet (and later Russian) launch vehicle that was first used in 1963. With its two cryogenic stages and four cryogenic strap-ons, this vehicle is capable of placing up to 6,900 kilograms into LOW EARTH ORBIT (LEO). At present, it is the most frequently flown launch vehicle in the world. Since 1964 it has been used to launch every Russian human crew space mission.
See also: LAUNCH VEHICLE.

Soyuz spacecraft An evolutionary family of crewed spacecraft that have been used by the Soviet Union and later the Russian Federation on a wide variety of space missions. The word *soyuz* is Russian for "union". The first Soyuz spacecraft, called *Soyuz 1*, was launched in April 1967. Unfortunately, upon reentry a parachute failed to open properly and the spacecraft was destroyed on impact and its occupant, Cosmonaut Vladimir Komarov, killed. The second Russian space tragedy occurred at the end of the *Soyuz 11* mission (June 1971), when a valve malfunctioned as the spacecraft was separating from the *Salyut 1* space station, allowing all the air to escape from the crew compartment. This particular early version of the Soyuz spacecraft did not have sufficient room for the crew to wear their pressure suits during reentry; consequently, the three cosmonauts, Georgi Dobrovolsky, Victor Patseyev, and Vladislav Volkov, suffocated during the reentry operation. They were found dead by the Russian recovery team after touchdown. In July 1975 the *Soyuz 19* spacecraft was used successfully by Cosmonauts Alexei Leonov and Valeri Kubasov in the Apollo-Soyuz Test Project—an international rendezvous and docking mission. The next major variant of this versatile spacecraft, called the Soyuz-T (with the "T" standing for transport), was first flown in December 1979. The Soyuz-TM is a modernized version of the Soyuz-T. It was flown in May 1986 and can be used to ferry crew and supplies to an orbiting station such as the Mir or the International Space Station.

See also: APOLLO-SOYUZ TEST PROJECT; MIR; SALYUT.

space 1. Specifically, the part of the universe lying outside the limits of Earth's atmosphere. 2. More generally, the volume in which all celestial bodies, including Earth, move.

space base A large, permanently inhabited space facility located in orbit around a celestial body or on its surface. The space base would serve as a center of human operations in some particular region of the solar system—supporting exploration, scientific missions, and extraterrestrial resource applications. An orbiting facility also could serve as a space transportation hub, robot repair and maintenance facility, a space construction site, and even a recreation and medical services center for space travelers. With from 10 to perhaps 200 occupants, the space base would have a much larger human population than a space station. Modular construction, the use of extraterrestrial materials for radiation shielding, development of a closed regenerative life support system, and large solar or nuclear power supplies (e.g., 50 to 100 kilowatts-electric or more) are some characteristic design features. For an orbiting facility, artificial gravity would be provided by rotating the crew habitats and certain work areas. For surface bases on the Moon and Mars, the human inhabitants would experience the natural gravity of the particular celestial object.

See also: LUNAR BASE; MARS BASE; SPACE SETTLEMENT; SPACE STATION.

space-based astronomy Astronomical observations conducted by human-crewed or robotic spacecraft above Earth's atmosphere; for example, the excellent cosmic observations performed by the Hubble Space Telescope (a human-tended but remotely operated Earth-orbiting instrument platform) or the solar observations made by the crew of the U.S. Skylab space station (1973–1974).

See also: COMPTON OBSERVATORY; COSMIC BACKGROUND EXPLORER (COBE); HUBBLE SPACE TELESCOPE (HST); SKYLAB.

space-based high-energy laser system A proposed space-based, multimegawatt, high-energy laser (HEL) system that could be used in several modes of operation. In its "weapons mode" with the laser system on high power, it could attack ground, air, and space targets. In its "surveillance mode," it could operate either using the laser at low power levels for active-illumination imaging or with the laser inoperative for passive imaging.

See also: BALLISTIC MISSILE DEFENSE.

space-based interceptor (SBI) A kinetic energy kill rocket vehicle that is based in space.

See also: BALLISTIC MISSILE DEFENSE.

spaceborne imaging radar In general, a synthetic aperture radar (SAR) system that is placed on a spacecraft. The radar is an active remote sensing instrument that transmits pulses of microwave energy toward the planet's surface and measures the amount of energy that is reflected back to the radar antenna. A SAR system therefore provides its own illumination and can produce images of the planet's surface during the day or night, through cloud cover. These types of radar systems have been used to image the cloud-enshrouded surface of Venus and to help scientists study the planet Earth more effectively.

For example, the Spaceborne Imaging Radar-C/X Band Synthetic Aperture Radar (SIR-C/X-SAR) was flown in the space shuttle orbiter's cargo bay during the STS-59 mission (April 1994). This radar system, a joint project of NASA, the German Space Agency (DARA), and the Italian Space Agency (ASI), collected an enormous amount of radar imagery data in support of NASA's MISSION TO PLANET EARTH and other planetary study efforts.

See also: MAGELLAN MISSION; RADAR IMAGING; REMOTE SENSING.

space capsule A container used for conducting an experiment or operation in space, usually involving a human being or other living organisms. The Mercury Project spacecraft were small space capsules designed to carry a single American atronaut into space and return him safely to Earth. As American human-rated spacecraft became a little larger during the Gemini and Apollo projects, the term "space capsule" generally was abandoned in favor of "spacecraft."

See also: MERCURY PROJECT.

space colony An earlier term used to describe a large, permanent space habitat and industrial complex occupied by up to 10,000 persons. Currently the term "space settlement" is preferred.

See also: SPACE SETTLEMENT.

space commerce The commercial sector of space operations and activities. At least six major areas are now associated with the field commonly referred to as space commerce. These areas are: (1) space transportation; (2) satellite communications; (3) satellite-based positioning and navigational services; (4) satellite remote sensing (including geographic information system support); (5) space-based industrial facilities; and (6) materials research and processing in space.

See also: COMMUNICATIONS SATELLITE; GLOBAL POSITIONING SYSTEM; LAUNCH VEHICLE; MATERIALS PROCESSING IN SPACE; REMOTE SENSING; X-33; X-34.

space construction Large structures in space, such as modular space stations, global communication and information services platforms, and satellite power systems (SPSs), will all require on-orbit assembly operations by space construction workers. Space construction requires protection of the

workforce and some materials from the hard vacuum, intense sunlight, and natural radiation environment encountered above Earth's protective atmosphere.

Outer space, however, is also an environment that in many ways is ideal for the construction process. First, because of the absence of significant gravitational force (i.e., the microgravity experienced by the free-fall condition of orbiting objects), the structural loads are quite small, even minute. Structural members may therefore much lighter than terrestrial structures of the same span and stiffness. Second, the absence of gravitational forces greatly facilitates the movement of material and equipment. On Earth, the movement of materials during a construction operation absorbs a large portion of the total work effort expended by construction personnel and their machines. Third, the absence of an atmosphere with its accompanying wind loads, inclement weather, and unpredictable changes permits space work to be planned accurately and executed readily without environmental interruptions (except perhaps due to solar flares, which would increase the radiation hazard).

Automated fabrication is considered to be a key requirement for viable space construction activities. The table identifies some typical space construction hardware and supporting systems. Work in space will require the close interaction of astronaut (i.e., space worker) and very smart machine. For example, the advanced maneuverable spacesuit will be a versatile, self-contained, life-supporting backpack with gaseous-nitrogen-propelled jet thrusters that enable a space worker to travel back and forth to various space construction locations.

TYPICAL SPACE CONSTRUCTION EQUIPMENT AND SUPPORTING SYSTEMS

- Advanced maneuverable spacesuits
- Automated beam builder
- Space structure fabrication system
- Remote astronaut work stations
  "Closed cherry picker"
  "Open cherry picker"
  Free-flyer workstation
- Manned orbital transfer vehicle (MOTV)
- Cargo orbital transfer vehicle (COTV)
- Advanced launch vehicles (for personnel and cargo)

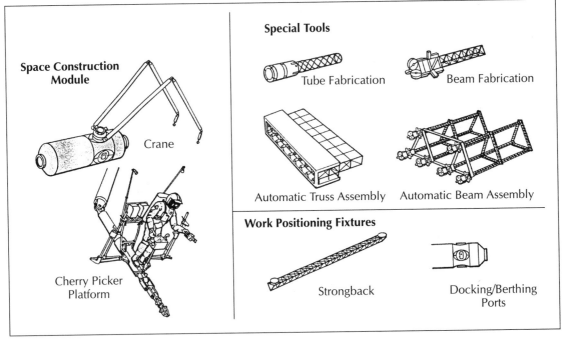

Figure 116. Space construction equipment   *(Drawing courtesy of NASA)*

The automated beam builder is a machine designed for fabricating "building-block" structural beams in space. Combined with a space structure fabrication system, the beam builder will allow space workers to manufacture and assemble structures in LOW EARTH ORBIT (LEO) using the international space station as an early "construction camp." Eventually, as the demand for more sophisticated space construction and assembly efforts grows, permanent space construction bases can be established in LEO and elsewhere in cislunar space. Remote astronaut workstations can be mounted on large manipulator arms attached to the space station or space base. These "open cherry pickers" would have a convenient tool and parts bin, a swing-away control and display panel, and lights for general and point illumination. The closed version of this cherry picker would involve a pressurized human-occupied remote workstation (*space construction module*) that contains life support equipment and controls and displays for operating dexterous manipulators. (See Figure 116.)

See also: LARGE SPACE STRUCTURES, SATELLITE POWER SYSTEM.

space control operations Aerospace operations that provide freedom of action in space for friend-ly forces while, when directed, denying it to an enemy. These operations include the broad aspects of protection of U.S. and allied space systems and negation of enemy space systems. Space control operations also encompass all elements of the space defense mission.

See also: SPACE DEFENSE.

spacecraft In general, a human-occupied or uncrewed platform that is designed to be placed into an orbit about Earth or into a trajectory to another celestial body. The spacecraft is essentially a combination of hardware that forms a space platform. It provides structure, thermal control, wiring, and subsystem functions, such as attitude control, command, data handling, and power. Spacecraft come in all shapes and sizes, each often tailored to meet the needs of a specific mission in space. For example, spacecraft designed and constructed to acquire scientific data are specialized systems intended to function in a specific hostile environment. The complexity of these scientific spacecraft varies greatly. Often they are categorized according to the missions they are intended to fly.

Scientific spacecraft include: flyby spacecraft, orbiter spacecraft, atmospheric probe spacecraft, atmospheric balloon packages, lander spacecraft, surface penetrator spacecraft, and surface rover spacecraft.

Flyby spacecraft follow a continuous trajectory and are not captured into a planetary orbit. These spacecraft have the capability of using their onboard instruments to observe passing celestial targets (e.g., a planet, a moon, an asteroid), even compensating for the target's apparent motion in an optical instrument's field of view. They must be able to transmit data at high rates back to Earth and also must be capable of storing data onboard for those periods when their antennas are not pointing toward Earth. They must be capable of surviving in a powered-down, cruise mode for many years of travel through interplanetary space and then of bringing all their sensing systems to focus rapidly on the target object, during an encounter period that may last only for a few crucial hours or minutes. NASA's *Pioneer 10* and *11* and the *Voyager 1* and *2* are examples of highly successful flyby scientific spacecraft. NASA uses the flyby spacecraft during the initial, or reconnaissance phase, of solar system exploration.

An *orbiter spacecraft* is designed to travel to a distant planet and then orbit around that planet. This type of scientific spacecraft must possess a substantial propulsive capability to decelerate at just the right moment in order to achieve a proper orbit insertion. Aerospace engineers design an orbiter spacecraft recognizing the fact that solar occultations will occur frequently as it orbits the target planet. During these periods of occultation, the spacecraft is shadowed by the planet, cutting off solar array production of electric power and introducing extreme variations of the spacecraft's thermal environment. Generally, a rechargeable battery system augments solar electric power. Active thermal control techniques (e.g., the use of tiny electric-powered heaters) are used to complement traditional passive thermal control design features. The periodic solar occultations also interrupt uplink and downlink communications with Earth, making onboard data storage a necessity. NASA uses orbiter spacecraft as part of the second, in-depth study phase of solar system exploration. The lunar orbiter, Magellan and Galileo spacecraft are examples of successful scientific orbiters.

Some scientific exploration missions involve the use of one or more smaller, instrumented spacecraft, called *atmospheric probe spacecraft.* These probes separate from the main spacecraft prior to closest approach to a planet in order to study the planet's gaseous atmosphere as they descend through it. Usually an atmospheric probe spacecraft is deployed from its "mothership" (i.e., the main spacecraft) by the release of springs or other devices that simply separate it from the mothership without making a significant modification of the probe's trajectory. Following probe release, the mothership usually executes a trajectory correction maneuver to prevent its own atmospheric entry and to help the main spacecraft continue on with its flyby or orbiter mission activities. NASA's Pioneer-Venus (4 probes) and Galileo (1 probe) missions involved the deployment probes into the target planet's atmosphere (i.e., Venus and Jupiter, respectively). Similarly, the Cassini mission to Saturn will involve the deployment of a probe spacecraft into the murky atmosphere of the moon Titan. An aeroshell protects the atmospheric probe spacecraft from the intense heat caused by atmospheric friction during entry. At some point in the descent trajectory, the aeroshell is jettisoned and a parachute then is used to slow the probe's descent sufficiently so it can perform its scientific observations. Data usually are telemetered from the atmospheric probe to the mothership, which then either relays the data back to Earth in real time or else records the data for later transmission to Earth.

An *atmospheric balloon package* is designed for suspension from a buoyant gas–filled bag that can float and travel under the influence of the winds in a planetary atmosphere. Tracking of the balloon package's progress across the face of the target planet will yield data about the general circulation patterns of the planet's atmosphere. A balloon package needs a power supply and a telecommunications system (to relay data and support tracking). It also can be equipped with a variety of scientific instruments to measure the planetary atmosphere's composition, temperature, pressure, and density.

Lander spacecraft are designed to reach the surface of a planet and survive at least long enough to transmit back to Earth useful scientific data, such as: imagery of the landing site, measurement of the local environmental conditions, and an initial examination of soil composition. For example, the Russian Venera lander spacecraft have made brief scientific investigations of the infernolike Venusian surface. In contrast, NASA's Surveyor lander craft extensively explored the lunar surface at several landing sites in preparation for the human Apollo Project landing missions, while NASA's *Viking 1* and 2 lander craft investigated the surface conditions of Mars at two separate sites for many months.

A *surface penetrator spacecraft* is designed to enter the solid body of a planet, an asteroid, or a comet. It must survive a high-velocity impact and then transmit subsurface information back to an orbiting mothership.

Finally, a *surface rover spacecraft* is carried to the surface of a planet, soft-landed, and then deployed. The rover can either be semiautonomous or fully controlled (through teleoperation) by scientists on Earth. Once deployed on the surface, the electrically powered rover can wander a certain distance away from the landing site and take images and perform soil analyses. Data then are telemetered back to Earth by one of several techniques: via the lander spacecraft, via an orbiting mothership, or (depending on size of rover) directly from the rover vehicle. The Soviet Union deployed two highly successful robot surface rovers (called Lunokhod 1 and 2) on the Moon in the 1970s. NASA plans to explore the surface of Mars with a variety of small mobile robots over the next decade.

spacecraft charging In orbit or in deep space, spacecraft and space vehicles can develop an electric potential up to tens of thousands of volts relative to the ambient outer space plasma (the solar wind). Large potential differences (called *differential charging*) also can occur on the space vehicle. One of the consequences is electrical discharge or arcing, a phenomenon that can damage space vehicle surface structures and electronic systems. Many factors contribute to this complex problem, including the spacecraft configuration, the materials from which the spacecraft is made, whether the spacecraft is operating in sunlight or shadow, the altitude at which the spacecraft is performing its mission, and environmental conditions, such as the flux of high-energy solar particles and the level of magnetic storm activity.

Wherever possible, spacecraft designers use conducting surfaces and provide adequate grounding techniques. These design procedures can significantly reduce differential charging, which is generally a more serious problem than the development of a high spacecraft-to-space (plasma) electrical potential.

spacecraft clock Generally, the timing component within the spacecraft's command and data-

handling subsystem; it meters the passing time during the life of the spacecraft and regulates nearly all activity within the spacecraft.

See also: CLOCK.

spacecraft drag A space vehicle or spacecraft operating at an altitude below a few thousand kilometers will encounter a significant number of atmospheric particles (i.e., the residual atmosphere) during each orbit of Earth. These encounters result in drag or friction on the spacecraft, causing it gradually to "slow down" and lose altitude, unless some onboard propellant is expended to overcome this drag and maintain the original orbital altitude. If the density of the residual atmosphere at the space vehicle's altitude increases, so will the drag on the vehicle. Any mechanism that can heat Earth's atmosphere (e.g., a geomagnetic storm) will create density changes in the upper atmosphere that can alter a spacecraft's orbit rapidly and significantly. When the residual upper atmosphere is heated by these solar disturbances, it expands outward and makes its presence felt at even higher (than normal) altitudes.

The significance and severity of spacecraft drag was demonstrated clearly by the rapid and premature demise of the abandoned U.S. Skylab space station. Atmospheric heating during a period of maximum solar activity caused the space station's drag to increase considerably, a situation that then resulted in a much more rapid rate of loss in orbital altitude than had been projected. As a result, the 90 metric ton station (last occupied by an astronaut crew in 1974) experienced a fiery reentry in July 1979, years before its originally projected demise. In fact, NASA had been considering using an early space shuttle mission to "rescue Skylab" by providing a reboost to higher altitude. However, the first shuttle mission (STS-1) was not flown until April 1981, almost two years after Skylab became a "front-page" victim of spacecraft drag.

See also: SKYLAB.

spacecraft navigation In general, navigating a spacecraft involves measuring its radial distance and velocity, the angular distance to the spacecraft, and its velocity in the plane of the sky. From these data, a mathematical model can be developed and maintained that describes the history of the spacecraft's location in three-dimensional space as a function of time. Any necessary corrections to a spacecraft's trajectory or orbit then can be identified based on this mathematical model. A spacecraft's navigational history often is reconstructed and incorporated in its scientific observations during a planetary encounter.

Within NASA, the art of spacecraft navigation draws on tracking data, which include measurements of the DOPPLER SHIFT of the downlink carrier and the pointing angles of antennas in the DEEP SPACE NETWORK (DSN). Such navigational data differ from the telemetry data associated with scientific instruments and spacecraft state-of-health sensors.

The distance to a spacecraft can be measured in the following manner. A uniquely coded ranging pulse can be added to the uplink communications sent to a spacecraft. The transmission time of this specially coded pulse is recorded. When the spacecraft receives the ranging pulse, it then returns the special pulse on its downlink communications transmission. The time it takes the spacecraft to turn the pulse around within its onboard electronics package is known from prelaunch calibration testing. Thus when the specially coded downlink pulse is received at one or several DSN sites, the true travel time elapsed can be determined and the spacecraft's distance from Earth then calculated. When several DSN sites have received this coded downlink transmission, the angular position of the spacecraft also can be determined, using triangulation techniques (since the angles at which the DSN antennas point are recorded with an accuracy of thousandths of a degree). Similarly, a spacecraft's velocity component can be determined by a careful measurement of an induced Doppler shift in the downlink frequency, when a two-way coherent communications mode is being used.

Spacecraft that are equipped with imaging instruments can employ these instruments to perform optical navigation. The imaging instrument observes the spacecraft's target (destination) planet against a known background star field. These images are called *optical navigation (OPNAV) images,* and their interpretation provides as very precise data set that is useful for refining knowledge of a spacecrafts's trajectory.

Once a spacecraft's solar or planetary orbital parameters are known, they are compared to the parameters desired for the flight. A *trajectory correction maneuver (TCM)* then can be planned and executed to correct any discrepancy between a spacecraft's actual and desired/planned trajectory. A TCM typically will involve a spacecraft velocity change (Δ V) on the order of just meters to tens of meters per second because of the limited propellant supply carried by a spacecraft.

Similarly, small changes in a spacecraft's orbit around a planet might be needed to adjust an instrument's field-of-view footprint, to improve sensitivity of a gravity field survey, or to prevent too much orbital decay (i.e., loss of altitude). These orbit changes are called orbit trim maneuvers (OTMs), and generally they are carried out in the same manner as TCMs. For example, to make a change that increases the altitude of perigee, an OTM would be performed that increased the spacecraft's velocity when the craft was at apogee. Finally, slight changes in a spacecraft's orbital plane orientation also can be accomplished using OTMs. However, the magnitude of the orbital plane change often is necessarily small, due to the limited amount of propellant a spacecraft carries for these navigational maneuvers.

space debris Space junk or derelict human-made space objects in orbit around Earth. Space debris represents a hazard to astronauts, spacecraft, and large space facilities such as space stations.

Since the start of the space age in 1957, the natural meteoroid environment has been a design consideration for spacecraft. Meteoroids are part of the interplanetary environment and sweep through Earth orbital space at an average speed of about 20 kilometers (km) per second. Space science data indicate that, at any one moment, a total of approximately 200 kilograms (kg) of meteoroid mass is within some 2,000 km of Earth's surface—the region of space (called LOW EARTH ORBIT, or LEO) most frequently used. The majority of this mass is found in meteoroids about 0.01 centimeter (cm) diameter; however, lesser amounts of this total mass occur in meteoroid sizes both smaller and larger than 0.01 cm. The natural meteoroid flux varies in time as Earth travels around the Sun.

Human-made space debris is also called *orbital debris* and differs from natural meteoroids, because it remains in Earth orbit during its lifetime and is not a transient phenomenon like the meteoroid showers that occur as the Earth travels through interplanetary space around the Sun. The estimated mass of human-made objects orbiting the Earth within about, 2,000 km of its surface is about 3 million kilograms (or about 15,000 times more mass than represented by the natural meteoroid environment). These human-made objects are for the most part in high-inclination orbits and pass one another at an average relative velocity of 10 km per second. Most of this mass is contained in over 3,000 spent rocket stages, inactive satellites, and a comparatively few active satellites. A lesser amount of space debris mass (some 40,000 kg) is distributed in the over 4,000 smaller-size, orbiting objects currently being tracked by space surveillance systems. The majority of these smaller space debris objects are the by-products of over 130 on-orbit fragmentations (satellite breakup events). Recent studies indicate a total mass of at least 1,000 kg for orbital debris sizes of 1 cm or smaller, and about 300 kg for orbital debris smaller than 0.1 cm. The explosion or fragmentation of a large space object also has the potential of producing a large number of smaller objects, objects too small to be detected by contemporary ground-based space surveillance systems. Consequently, this orbital debris environment is now considered more hazardous than the natural meteoroid environment to spacecraft operating in Earth orbit below an altitude of 2,000 km.

Two general types of orbital debris are of concern: (1) large objects (greater than 10 cm in diameter) whose population, while small in absolute terms, is large relative to the population of similar masses in the natural meteoroid environment; and (2) a much greater number of smaller objects (less than 10 cm diameter), whose size distribution approximates the natural meteoroid population and whose numbers add to the "natural debris" environment in those size ranges. The interaction of these two general classes of space debris objects, combined with their long residence time in orbit, creates further concern that new collisions producing additional fragments and causing the total space debris population to grow are inevitable.

An orbiting object loses energy through frictional encounters with the upper limits of Earth's atmosphere and as a result of other orbit-perturbing forces (e.g., gravitational influences). Over time, the object falls into progressively lower orbits and eventually makes a final plunge toward Earth. Once an object enters the sensible atmosphere, atmospheric drag slows it down rapidly and causes it either to burn up completely or to fall through the atmosphere and impact on Earth's surface or in its oceans. A *decayed satellite* (or piece of orbital debris) is one that reenters Earth's atmosphere under the influence of natural forces and phenomena (e.g., atmospheric drag). Space vehi-

cles and satellites that are intentionally removed from orbit are said to have been "deorbited."

One of the most celebrated reentries of a large human-made object occurred on July 11, 1979, when the then-decommissioned and abandoned first American space station, called SKYLAB, came plunging back to Earth over Australia and the Indian Ocean—a somewhat spectacular reentry event that occurred without harm to life or property. In fact, although human-made objects reenter from orbit on the average of more than one per day, only a very small percentage of these reentry events result in debris surviving to reach Earth's surface. The aerodynamic forces and heating associated with reentry processes usually break up and vaporize most incoming space debris.

Solar activity greatly affects the natural decay of Earth-orbiting objects. High levels of solar activity heat Earth's upper atmosphere, causing it to expand further into space and to reduce the orbital lifetimes of space objects found at somewhat higher altitudes in the LEO regime. However, about 600 km altitude, the atmospheric density is sufficiently low and solar activity–induced atmospheric density increases do not noticeably affect the debris population lifetimes. This solar cycle–based natural cleansing process for space debris in LEO is extremely slow and by itself cannot offset the current rate of human-made space debris generation.

The effects of orbital debris impacts on spacecraft and space facilities depend on the velocity and mass of the debris. For debris sizes less than approximately 0.01 cm in diameter, surface pitting and erosion are the primary effects. Over a long period of time, the cumulative effect of individual particles colliding with a satellite could become significant, because the number of such small debris particles is very large in LEO.

For debris larger than about 0.1 cm in diameter, the possibility of structural damage to a satellite or space facility becomes an important consideration. For example, a 0.3-cm-diameter sphere of aluminum traveling at 10 kilometers per second has about the same kinetic energy as a bowling ball traveling at 100 kilometers per hour. Aerospace engineers anticipate significant structural damage to the satellite or space facility if such an impact occurs.

Space system engineers, therefore, find it helpful to distinguish three space debris size ranges in designing spacecraft. These are debris sizes 0.01 cm diameter and below, which produce surface erosion; debris sizes ranging from 0.01 to 1.0 cm diameter, which produce significant impact damage that can be quite serious; and (3) space debris objects greater than 1.0 cm diameter, which can readily produce catastrophic damage in a satellite or space facility.

Today, only about 5% of the cataloged objects in Earth orbit are active, operational spacecraft. The remainder of these human-made space objects represent various types of orbital debris. Space debris often is divided into four general categories: (1) operational debris (about 12%), objects intentionally discarded during satellite delivery or satellite operations (this category includes lens caps, separation and packing devices, spin-up mechanisms, payload shrouds, empty propellant tanks, and a few objects discarded or "lost" during extravehicular activities [EVAs] by astronauts or cosmonauts); (2) spent and intact rocket bodies (14%); (3) inactive (decommissioned or dead) payloads (20%); and (4) fragmentation (on-orbit space object breakup) (49%).

Aerospace engineers consider the growing space debris problem when they design new spacecraft. In an attempt to make these new spacecraft as "litter-free" as possible, new spacecraft are designed with provisions for retrieval or removal at the end of their useful operations. Telerobotic space debris collection systems also have been proposed.

See also: METEOROIDS.

space defense All defensive measures designed to destroy attacking enemy vehicles (including missiles) while they are in space, or to nullify or reduce the effectiveness of such an attack from (or through) space.

Space Detection and Tracking System (SPADATS)

A network of space surveillance sensors operated by the U.S. Air Force. This ground-based network is capable of detecting and tracking space vehicles and objects in orbit around Earth. The orbital characteristics of such objects are reported to a central control facility.

See also: CHEYENNE MOUNTAIN AIR STATION.

space food Eating is a basic survival need that an astronaut or cosmonaut must accomplish in order to make space a suitable place to work and accomplish mission objectives. The *space food* (meals) he or she consumes must be nutritious, safe, lightweight, easily prepared, convenient to use, require

little storage space, need no refrigeration and be psychologically acceptable (especially for crews on long-duration missions).

Since the beginning of human space flight in the early 1960s, eating in space has become more natural and "Earth-like," while better meeting the other criteria. Space flight feeding has progressed from squeezing pastelike foods from "toothpaste" tubes to eating a "sit-down" dinner complete with normal utensils, except for the addition of scissors, which today's astronauts use to cut open packages.

In general, there are five basic approaches to preparing food for use in space: rehydratable food, intermediate-moisture food, thermostabilized food, irradiated food, and natural-form food.

Rehydratable food has been dehydrated by a technique such as freeze drying. In the space shuttle program, for example, foods are dehydrated to meet launch vehicle mass and volume restrictions. They are rehydrated later in orbit when they are ready to be eaten. Water used for rehydration comes from the orbiter vehicle's fuel cells, which produce electricity by combining hydrogen and oxygen; water is the resultant by-product. More than 100 different food items, such as cereals, spaghetti, scrambled eggs, and strawberries, go through this dehydration/rehydration process. For example, when a strawberry is freeze-dried, it remains full size in outline, with its color, texture, and quality intact. The astronaut can then rehydrate the strawberry with either saliva (mouth moisture) as it is chewed or by adding water to the package.

Twenty varieties of drinks, including tea and coffee, also are dehydrated for use in space travel. But pure orange juice and whole milk cannot be included. If water is added to dehydrated orange juice, orange "rocks," form in water; they do not rehydrate. Dehydrated whole milk does not dissolve properly upon rehydration. It floats around in lumps and has a disagreeable taste. So skim milk must be used. Back in the 1960s, General Foods Corporation developed a synthetic orange juice product (called Tang) that could be used in place of orange juice.

Intermediate-moisture food is partially dehydrated food, such as dried apricots, dried pears, or dried peaches. *Thermostabilized food* is cooked at moderate temperatures to destroy bacteria and then sealed in cans or aluminum pouches. This type of space food includes tuna, canned fruit in heavy syrup, and ground beef. *Irradiated food* is preserved by exposure to ionizing radiation. Various types of meat and bread are processed in this manner. Finally, *natural-form food* is low in moisture and taken into space in much the same form as is found on Earth. Peanut butter, nuts, graham crackers, gum, and hard candies are examples. Salt and pepper are packaged in liquid form because crystals would float around the crew cabin and could cause eye irritation or contaminate equipment.

All food in space must be packaged in individual serving portions that allow easy manipulation in the microgravity environment of an orbiting spacecraft. These packages can be off-the-shelf thermostabilized cans, flexible pouches, or semirigid containers.

In the space shuttle program, the variety of food carried into orbit is sufficiently broad that crew members can enjoy a six-day menu cycle. A typical dinner might consist of a shrimp cocktail, steak, broccoli, rice, fruit cocktail, chocolate pudding, and grape drink. Similar types of space foods will be available for crew members on the permanent international space station. Resupply from Earth will provide menu variety and an occasional culinary "surprise" to mark special occasions.

However, long-duration human missions beyond Earth orbit (where resupply is difficult or impossible) will require food supplies capable of extended storage. The menu cycle will have to be greatly expanded to support crew morale and nutritional well-being. A permanent lunar base could have a highly automated greenhouse to provide fresh vegetables and fruits. A rotating "space greenhouse" (to provide an appropriate level of artificial gravity for plant development) might accompany human expeditions to Mars and beyond. A permanent Martian surface base most likely would include an "agricultural facility" as part of its closed environment life support system (CELSS).

space industrialization A new wave in humanity's sociotechnical development in which the special environmental conditions and properties of outer space are used for the economic and social benefit of all people on Earth. Some interesting properties of cislunar space include hard vacuum, microgravity, low vibration levels (in orbiting spacecraft), a wide-view angle of Earth and the heavens, and complete isolation from the terrestrial biosphere. Contemporary studies have suggested long-term space industrialization opportunities

in the following four general categories: (1) information services; (2) "made-in-space" products; (3) energy; and (4) human activities (including space therapeutics and tourism).

See also: SPACE COMMERCE.

Space Infrared Telescope Facility (SIRTF) One of NASA's "great observatory" spacecraft. This Sun-orbiting spacecraft is a planned follow-on to the INFRARED ASTRONOMICAL SATELLITE (IRAS) and the infrared companion to the ADVANCED X-RAY ASTROPHYSICS FACILITY (AXAF), the COMPTON GAMMA RAY OBSERVATORY (GRO), and the HUBBLE SPACE TELESCOPE (HST). The SIRFT will provide astronomers unprecedented spatial and spectral resolution in the infrared portion of the electromagnetic spectrum (from 4 to 180 micrometers wavelength). This long-lived, cryogenically cooled, meter-diameter-class infrared telescope will study the cold regions of space. Specifically, SIRFT will: (1) investigate the location in space where the cosmic gas and dust condense into stars; (2) examine "cool" objects in the solar system, such as new comets and other primitive bodies in the outer solar system; (3) study disks of solid material around nearby stars (i.e., planetary system development); (4) search for brown dwarfs; (5) identify and study powerful infrared-emitting galaxies at the edge of the observable universe; and (6) provide an infrared perspective for the understanding of quasars. As presently planned, the 700-kilogram (1,550 pound-mass) SIRFT will be launched by an expendable Delta 2 vehicle sometime in the year 2001 and placed in an orbit around the Sun, such that it will trail Earth by a distance of about 16 million kilometers (10 million miles). This orbit will place the infrared observatory far away from the infrared radiation emitted by the planet Earth and provide its instruments an uninterrupted view of a large portion of the universe.

See also: INFRARED ASTRONOMY.

space junk A popular aerospace industry expression for space debris or orbital debris.

See also: SPACE DEBRIS.

Spacelab Spacelab was developed by the European Space Agency (ESA) and NASA to be an international gateway to space exploration. Spacelab has met and exceeded the program's initial expectations. Scientists and specialists from universities, industry, and government agencies all

over the world now use this facility to conduct a variety of important "themed" science research programs including: space life sciences, microgravity (µg) research, plasma physics, astronomy, solar physics, atmospheric physics, and high-energy astrophysics.

Spacelab is a unique laboratory facility. Carried in the cargo bay of the space shuttle orbiter, it converts the orbiter into a versatile on-orbit research center. Spacelab features several interchangeable elements that can be put together in various configurations to meet the particular needs of a given flight. The major elements are a habitable module in which scientists can work in a SHIRT-SLEEVE ENVIRONMENT and platforms called pallets that can be placed in the orbiter's cargo bay behind the habitable module. These pallets hold instruments requiring direct exposure to space. (See Figure 117.)

Various configurations of these Spacelab elements can be fitted into the orbiter's cargo bay to meet the needs of any particular mission. The habitable module can be carried alone or with one or more pallets. The pallets also can be carried into space on a mission that uses no habitable module. Even when no habitable module is carried (i.e., in the "pallet-only" configuration), the facility is still called Spacelab.

The habitable module comes in two 4-meter-(m) (13.1-foot [ft]-) diameter segments. The "core segment" houses data processing equipment and utilities for both the pressurized module and pallets when flown together. It also has laboratory fixtures such as air-cooled experiment racks and a workbench. The second section, called the experiment segment, provides more pressurized workspace and additional experiment racks. The core segment can be flown by itself (called the "short-module" configuration), or coupled in tandem with the experiment segment (called the "long-module" configuration). The short module, which consists of the core segment and two cone-shaped end sections, measures 4.26 m (~14 ft) in length. When the two segments are assembled, the maximum outside length, including end cones, is 7 m (23 ft).

The pallets are uniform. Each is a u-shaped aluminum frame and panel platform 4 m (13.1 ft) wide and 3 m (10 ft) long. The experiment equipment is connected to a series of "hard points" on the main structure of the pallet. Up to five pallets may be flown on a single mission. When the pallets are flown without a habitable module aboard, subsystems needed for equipment operation (which normally would be housed in the core segment of the habitable module) are placed in a pressurized cylinder mounted to the front frame of the first pallet. This cylinder is called the *igloo*.

Racks for experiment equipment that goes into the habitable module also are standardized. The 48-centimeter- (19-inch-) wide racks are arranged in single or double assemblies. Generally, the racks and floor are assembled first outside the module, checked out as a unit, then slid into the module where connections are made between the rack-mounted experiment equipment, the subsystems in the core segment, and the primary structure.

Spacelab has other important elements. When a habitable module is flown, an access tunnel connects the module with the middeck level of the orbiter cabin. This access tunnel is about 1 m (3.3 ft) in diameter. The hatch between the orbiter cabin and the access tunnel is left open during a mission, so the orbiter cabin, tunnel, and Spacelab module all share the same pressure and common air. The tunnel has lighting and handrails to allow easy passage between Spacelab and the orbiter middeck, where the Spacelab crew of mission and payload specialists sleep and take their meals. The length of the access tunnel varies with the configuration of the Spacelab in the cargo bay. A tunnel 2.7 m (8.8 ft) in length can be used for missions during which the module is carried in the forward portion of the orbiter's cargo bay. A 5.8 m (~ 19-foot) tunnel is used for missions on which the module is carried in the aft portion of the bay.

A high-quality window-viewport assembly can be carried in the core segment of the habitable

Figure 117. Major elements of Spacelab *(Drawing courtesy of ESA and NASA)*

module. A small viewport is mounted permanently in the aft end cone of the module. A scientific airlock also may be installed in the overhead area of the experiment segment for use in exposing small instruments to the space environment.

Some research performed on Spacelab missions requires that instruments be pointed with very high accuracy and stability at certain stars, the Sun, locations on Earth, or other targets of observation. The instrument pointing system (IPS) provides a versatile pointing system for use on the orbiter to provide precision orientation capability. With its three-axis gimbal system the IPS can orient payloads of up to 2,000 kilograms (4,400 pounds-mass (lbm)) with very high accuracy.

Spacelab mission peculiar equipment support structure (MPESS) carriers provide a variety of resources for unpressurized payloads with the advantage of taking up very little length in the orbiter's cargo bay.

Spacelab also includes the following major subsystems: structure, environment control, electrical power and distribution, command and data management, and common payload support equipment.

See also: EUROPEAN SPACE AGENCY; SPACE TRANSPORTATION SYSTEM.

space launch vehicle(s) The expendable or reusable rocket-propelled vehicle(s) used to lift a payload or spacecraft from the surface of Earth and place it in orbit around the planet or on an interplanetary trajectory.

See also: LAUNCH VEHICLE; SPACE TRANSPORTATION SYSTEM.

spaceman A person, male or female, who travels in outer space. The term "astronaut" is preferred.

See also: ASTRONAUT; COSMONAUT.

space medicine The branch of aerospace medicine concerned specifically with the health of persons who make, or expect to make, flights beyond Earth's sensible (measurable) atmosphere into outer space.

space mine A (hypothetical) military satellite with an explosive charge (either nuclear or nonnuclear) that is designed to position itself within lethal range of a target satellite and then detonate at a preprogrammed condition or time, upon direct command, or when it is attacked.

space nuclear power (SNP) Through the cooperative efforts of the U.S. Department of Energy (DOE), formerly called the Atomic Energy Commission, and NASA, the United States has used nuclear energy in its space program to provide electrical power for many missions, including science stations on the Moon, extensive exploration missions to the outer planets—Jupiter, Saturn, Uranus, Neptune and beyond—and even to search for life on the surface of Mars.

For example, when the *Apollo 12* astronauts departed from the lunar surface on their return trip to Earth (November 1969), they left behind a nuclear-powered science station that sent information back to scientists on Earth for several years. That science station, as well as similar stations left on the Moon by the *Apollo 14* through *17* missions, operated on electrical power supplied by plutonium-238 fueled, radioisotope thermoelectric generators (RTGs). In fact, since 1961 nuclear power systems have helped assure the success of many space missions, including the *Pioneer 10* and *11* missions to Jupiter and Saturn; the *Viking 1* and *2* landers on Mars; the spectacular *Voyager 1* and *2* missions to Jupiter, Saturn, Uranus, Neptune and beyond; the Ulysses mission to the Sun's polar regions; and the Galileo mission to Jupiter. (See Table 1.)

Energy supplies that are reliable, transportable, and abundant represent a very important technology in the development of an extraterrestrial civilization. Space nuclear power systems can play an ever-expanding role in supporting the advanced space exploration and settlement missions of the 21st century, including permanent lunar and Martian surface bases. Even more ambitious space activities, such as asteroid movement and mining, planetary engineering, and human expeditions to the outer regions of the solar system, will require compact energy systems (in advanced space nuclear reactor designs) at the megawatt and gigawatt levels.

Space nuclear power supplies offer several distinct advantages over the more traditional solar and chemical space power systems. These advantages include: compact size; modest mass requirements; very long operating lifetimes; the ability to operate in extremely hostile environments (for e.g., intense trapped radiation belts, the surface of Mars, the moons of the outer planets, and even interstellar space); and the ability to operate independent of distance from the Sun or orientation to the Sun.

Table 1.
SUMMARY OF SPACE NUCLEAR POWER SYSTEMS LAUNCHED BY THE
UNITED STATES (1961–1997)

Power Source	Spacecraft	Mission Type	Launch Date	Status
SNAP-3A	Transit 4A	Navigational	June 29, 1961	Successfully achieved orbit
SNAP-3A	Transit 4B	Navigational	November 15, 1961	Successfully achieved orbit
SNAP-9A	Transit-5BN-1	Navigational	September 28, 1963	Successfully achieved orbit
SNAP-9A	Transit-5BN-2	Navigational	December 5, 1963	Successfully achieved orbit
SNAP-9A	Transit-5BN-3	Navigational	April 21, 1964	Mission aborted: burned up on reentry
SNAP-10A (reactor)	Snapshot	Experimental	April 3, 1965	Successfully achieved orbit
SNAP-19B2	Nimbus-B-1	Meteorological	May 18, 1968	Mission aborted: heat source retrieved
SNAP-19B3	Nimbus III	Meteorological	April 14, 1969	Successfully achieved orbit
SNAP-27	Apollo 12	Lunar	November 14, 1969	Successfully placed on lunar surface
SNAP-27	Apollo 13	Lunar	April 11, 1970	Mission aborted on way to Moon. Heat source returned to South Pacific Ocean
SNAP-27	Apollo 14	Lunar	January 31, 1971	Successfully placed on lunar surface
SNAP-27	Apollo 15	Lunar	July 26, 1971	Successfully placed on Lunar surface
SNAP-19	Pioneer 10	Planetary	March 2, 1972	Successfully operated to Jupiter and beyond; in interstellar space
SNAP-27	Apollo 16	Lunar	April 16, 1972	Successfully placed on lunar surface
Transit-RTG	"Transit" (Triad-01-IX)	Navigational	September 2, 1972	Successfully achieved orbit
SNAP-27	Apollo 17	Lunar	December 7, 1972	Successfully placed on lunar surface
SNAP-19	Pioneer 11	Planetary	April 5, 1973	Successfully operated to Jupiter, Saturn and beyond
SNAP-19	Viking 1	Mars	August 20, 1975	Successfully landed on Mars
SNAP-19	Viking 2	Mars	September 9, 1975	Successfully landed on Mars
MHW	LES 8/9	Communications	March 14, 1976	Successfully achieved orbit
MHW	Voyager 2	Planetary	August 20, 1977	Successfully operated to Jupiter, Saturn, Uranus, Neptune and beyond
MHW	Voyager 1	Planetary	September 5, 1977	Successfully operated to Jupiter, Saturn and beyond
GPHS-RTG	Galileo	Planetary	October 18, 1989	Successfully sent on interplanetary trajectory to Jupiter (1996 arrival)
GPHS-RTG	Ulysses	Solar-Polar	October 6, 1990	Successfully sent on interplanetary trajectory to explore polar regions of Sun (1994–1995)
GPHS-RTG	Cassini	Planetary	October 15, 1997	Successfully sent on interplanetary trajectory to Saturn (July 2004 arrival)

Source: NASA; Department of Energy.

Space nuclear power systems use the thermal energy or heat released by nuclear processes. These processes include the spontaneous (but predictable) decay of radioisotopes, the controlled splitting or fissioning of heavy atomic nuclei (such as fissile uranium-235) in a self-sustained neutron chain reaction, and (eventually) the joining together or fusing of light atomic nuclei (such as deuterium and tritium) in a controlled thermonuclear reaction. This "nuclear" heat then can converted directly or through a variety of thermodynamic (heat-engine) cycles into electric power. Until controlled thermonuclear fusion capabilities are achieved, space nuclear power applications will be based on the use of either radioisotope decay or nuclear fission reactors.

The radioisotope thermoelectric generator consists of two main functional components: the thermoelectric converter and the nuclear heat source. The radioisotope plutonium-238 has been used as the heat source in all U.S. space missions involving radioisotope power supplies. Plutonium-238 has a half-life of about 87.7 years and therefore supports a long operational life. (The half-life is the time required for one-half the number of unstable nuclei present at a given time to undergo radioactive decay.) In the nuclear decay process, plutonium-238 emits primarily alpha radiation that has very

---

Table 2.
SP-100 REFERENCE FLIGHT SYSTEM DESIGN CONCEPT
(SUBSYSTEM CHARACTERISTICS)

Nuclear Subsystems

• Fast spectrum reactor
UN fuel
Lithium cooled
Nb-1Zr vessel

• Radiation Shield
17-degree 1/2-cone angle
LiH neutron attenuation
Tungsten gamma-ray attenuation

• Heat transport
Lithium-pumped loop
Thermoelectric-electromagnetic (TEM) pumps
Thaw-assist heat pipes

• Instrumentation and control
Temperature, position and electrical
    parameter sensing
Multiplex signal transmission

Space Subsystems

• Thermoelectric conversion
Si-Ge/GaP thermoelectrics conductively coupled

• Heat rejection
Lithium pumped loop
TEM pumps
Potassium heat pipe radiator
Self-thaw capability

• Power conditioning and control
200 VDC primary power
Full shunt regulation
Millisecond response to load following
28 volt secondary power

• Structure/mechanical
Titanium/beryllium structures
State-of-the-art mechanics

Source: NASA, Department of Energy, and Department of Defense.

low penetrating power. Consequently, only light-weight shielding is required to protect the space-craft from its nuclear emissions. A thermoelectric converter uses the "thermocouple principle" to directly convert a portion of the nuclear (decay) heat into electricity.

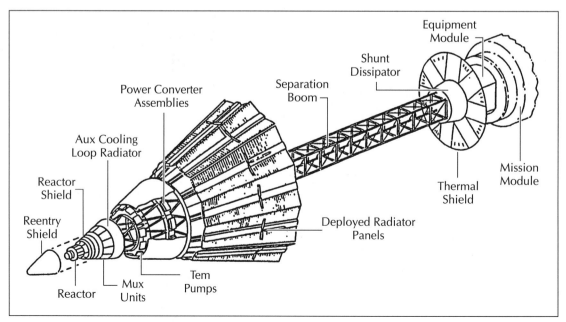

Figure 118. The proposed U.S. 100-kilowatt-electric class SP-100 space reactor in a radiator-deployed, space mission configuration *(Drawing courtesy of DoE, DoD and NASA)*

A nuclear reactor also can be used to provide electric power in space. The Soviet and, later, Russian space program has flown several space nuclear reactors (most recently a system called Topaz). The United States has flown only one space nuclear reactor, an experimental system called the SNAP-10A, which was launched and operated on-orbit in 1965. The objective of the SNAP-10A program was to develop a space nuclear reactor power unit capable of producing a minimum of 500 watts-electric for a period of one year while operating in space. The SNAP-10A reactor was a small zirconium hydride (ZrH) thermal reactor fueled by uranium-235. The SNAP-10A orbital test was successful, although the mission was prematurely (and safely) terminated on-orbit by the failure of an electronic component outside the reactor.

In 1983 a tri-agency (NASA–Department of Defense–DoE) group within the United States Government began development of a 100-kilowatt-electric class space nuclear reactor, called the SP-100. Some of the key features of this advanced space reactor are presented in Table 2. Because of changing space mission needs, however, this program was suspended before a planned flight demonstration test could be performed. (See Figure 118.)

Since the United States first used nuclear power in space, great emphasis has been placed on the safety of people and the protection of the terrestrial environment. A continuing major objective in any new space nuclear power program is to avoid undue risks. In the case of radioisotope power supplies, this means designing the system to contain the radioisotope fuel under all normal and potential accident conditions. For space nuclear reactors, such as the SNAP-10A and more advanced systems, this means launching the reactor in a "cold" (nonoperating) configuration and starting up the reactor only after a safe, stable Earth orbit or interplanetary trajectory has been achieved.

See also: FISSION (NUCLEAR); FUSION (NUCLEAR); NUCLEAR-ELECTRIC PROPULSION (NEP) SYSTEM; RADIOISOTOPE THERMOELECTRIC GENERATOR (RTG); SPACE NUCLEAR PROPULSION.

space nuclear propulsion Nuclear fission reactors can be used in two basic ways to propel a space vehicle: (1) to generate electric power for an electric propulsion unit; and (2) as a thermal energy or heat source to raise a propellant (working material) to extremely high temperature for subsequent

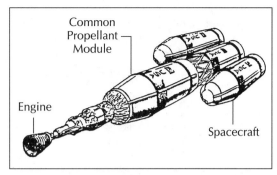

Figure 119. Nuclear Engine Rocket Vehicle Application (NERVA) vehicle *(Drawing courtesy of the U.S. Department of Energy and NASA)*

expulsion out a nozzle. In the second application, the system is often called a *nuclear rocket.* (See Figure 119.)

In a nuclear rocket, chemical combustion is not required. Instead, a single propellant, usually hydrogen, is heated by the energy released in the nuclear fission process, which occurs in a controlled manner in the reactor's core. Conventional rockets, in which chemical fuels are burned, have severe limitations in the specific impulse a given propellant combination can produce. These limitations are imposed by the relatively high molecular weight of the chemical combustion products. At attainable combustion chamber temperatures, the best chemical rockets are limited to specific impulse values of about 4,300 meters per second (440 seconds). Nuclear rocket systems using fission reactions, fusion reactions, and even possibly matter-antimatter annihilation reactions (the "photon rocket") have been proposed because of their much greater propulsion performance capabilities.

Engineering developments will be needed in the 21st century to permit the use of advanced fission reactor systems, such as the gaseous-core reactor rocket or even fusion-powered systems. However, the solid-core nuclear reactor rocket is within a test-flight demonstration of engineering reality. In this nuclear rocket concept, hydrogen propellant is heated to extremely high temperatures while passing through flow channels within the solid-fuel elements of a compact nuclear reactor system that uses uranium-235 as the fuel. The high-temperature gaseous hydrogen then expands through a nozzle to produce propulsive thrust. From the mid-1950s until the early 1970s, the United States conducted a nuclear rocket program called Project Rover. The primary objective of the project was to develop a nuclear rocket for a manned mission to Mars. Unfortunately, despite the technical success of this rocket program, overall space program emphasis changed, and the nuclear rocket and the human-crewed Mars mission planning were discontinued in 1973.

See also: FISSION (NUCLEAR); FUSION (NUCLEAR); ELECTRIC PROPULSION; NERVA; NUCLEAR-ELECTRIC PROPULSION (NEP) SYSTEM; ROVER PROGRAM; SPACE NUCLEAR POWER; SPECIFIC IMPULSE.

space physics The branch of science that investigates the magnetic and electric phenomena that occur in outer space, in the upper atmosphere of planets, and on the Sun. Space physicists use balloons, rockets, satellites, and deep-space probes to study many of these phenomena in situ (i.e., in their place of origin). The scope of space physics ranges from investigating the generation and transport of energy from the Sun, to searching, past the orbit of Pluto, for a magnetic boundary (called the *heliopause*) separating our solar system from the rest of the Milky Way Galaxy. Phenomena such as aurora, trapped radiation belts, the solar wind, solar flares, and sun spots fall within the realm of space physics.

space platform An uncrewed (unmanned), free-flying orbital platform that is dedicated to a specific mission, such as commercial space activities (e.g., materials processing in space) or scientific research (e.g., the Hubble Space Telescope). This platform can be deployed and serviced or retrieved by the space shuttle. In the future, platform servicing can be accomplished by astronauts from the international space station—if the space platform orbits near the station or can be delivered to the vicinity of the space station by a space tug.

See also: HUBBLE SPACE TELESCOPE; SPACE TUG.

spaceport A spaceport is both a doorway to outer space from the surface of a planet and a port of entry from outer space to a planet's surface. At a spaceport we find the sophisticated facilities required for the assembly, testing, launching, and (in the case of reusable aerospace vehicles) landing and postflight refurbishment of space launch vehicles. Typical operations performed at a spaceport include the assembly of space vehicles; preflight preparation of space launch vehicles and their payloads; testing and checkout of space vehicles, spacecraft, and support equipment; coordination

of launch vehicle tracking and data-acquisition requirements; countdown and launch operations; and (in the case of reusable space vehicles) landing operations and refurbishment. A great variety of technical and administrative activities also are needed to support the operation of a spaceport. These include design engineering, safety and security, quality assurance, cryogenic fluids management, toxic and hazardous materials handling, maintenance, logistics, computer operations, communications, and documentation.

Expendable (one-time use) space launch vehicles now can be found at spaceport facilities around the globe. NASA's Kennedy Space Center in Florida is the spaceport for the (partially) reusable aerospace vehicle, the space shuttle. In the next century, highly automated spaceports also will appear on the lunar and Martian surfaces to support permanent human bases on these alien worlds.

See also: CAPE CANAVERAL AIR FORCE STATION; KENNEDY SPACE CENTER.

space radiation environment One of the major concerns associated with the development of a permanent human presence in outer space is the ionizing radiation environment, both natural and human-made. The natural portion of the space radiation environment consists primarily of Earth's trapped radiation belts (also called the Van Allen belts), solar particle events (SPEs), and galactic cosmic rays (GCRs). Ionizing radiation sources associated with human activities can include: space nuclear power systems (fission reactors and radioisotope), the detonation of nuclear explosives in the upper portion of Earth's atmosphere or in outer space (activities currently banned by international treaty), space-based particle accelerators, and radioisotopes used for calibration and scientific activity.

Earth's trapped radiation environment is most intense at altitudes ranging from 1,000 kilometers (km) to 30,000 km. Peak intensities occur at about 4,000 km and 22,000 km. Below approximately 10,000 km altitude, most trapped particles are relatively low-energy electrons (typically, a few million electron volts [MeV]) and protons. In fact, below about 500 km altitude, only the trapped protons and their secondary nuclear interaction products represent a chronic ionizing radiation hazard.

Trapped electrons collide with atoms in the outer skin of a spacecraft creating penetrating X rays and gamma rays (called secondary radiations) that can cause tissue damage. Trapped energetic protons can penetrate several grams of material (typically 1–2 centimeters of aluminum are required to stop them), causing ionization of atoms as they terminate their passage in a series of nuclear collisions. Most human-occupied spacecraft missions in LOW EARTH ORBIT (LEO) are restricted to altitudes below 500 km and inclinations below about 60 degrees to avoid prolonged (chronic) exposure to this type of radiation. For orbits below 500 km altitude and inclinations less than about 60 degrees, the predominant part of an astronaut's overall radiation exposure will be due to trapped protons from the SOUTH ATLANTIC ANOMALY (SAA). The SAA is a region of Earth's inner radiation belts that dips close to the planet over the southern Atlantic Ocean southeast of the Brazilian coast. Passage through the SAA generally represents the most significant source of chronic natural space radiation for space travelers in LEO. Earth's geomagnetic field generally protects astronauts and spacecraft in LEO from cosmic ray and solar flare particles.

However, spacecraft in highly elliptical orbits around Earth will pass through the Van Allen belts each day. Furthermore, those spacecraft with a high-apogee altitude (say greater than 30,000 km) also will experience long exposures to galactic cosmic rays and solar flare environments. Similarly, astronauts traveling through interplanetary space to the Moon or Mars will be exposed to both a continuous galactic cosmic ray environment and a potential solar flare environment (i.e., a solar particle event).

A solar flare is a bright eruption from the Sun's chromosphere that may appear within minutes and then fade within an hour. Solar flares cover a wide range of intensity and size. They eject high-energy protons that represent a serious hazard to astronauts traveling beyond LEO. The SPEs associated with solar flares can last one to two days. Anomalously large solar particle events (ALSPEs), the most intense variety of solar particle event, can deliver potentially lethal doses of energetic particles—even behind modest spacecraft shielding (e.g., 1 to 2 grams per centimeter squared of aluminum). The majority of SPE particles are energetic protons, but heavier nuclei also are present.

Galactic cosmic rays (GCRs) originate outside the solar system. GCR particles are the most energetic of the three general types of natural ionizing radiation in space and contain all elements from atomic number 1 to 92. Specifically, galactic cosmic rays have the following general composition: protons (82–85%), alpha particles (12–14%), and highly ionizing heavy nuclei (1–2%), such as carbon, oxygen, neon, magnesium, silicon, and iron. The ions that are heavier than helium have been given the name HZE particles, meaning high atomic number (Z) and high energy (E). Iron (Fe) ions appear to contribute substantially to the overall HZE population. Galactic cosmic rays range in energy from 10s of MeV to 100s of GeV (a GeV is one billion [10^9] electron volts) and are very difficult to shield against. In particular, HZE particles produce high-dose ionization tracks and kill living cells as they travel through tissue.

An effective space radiation protection program for astronauts on extended missions in interplanetary space or on the lunar or Martian surface should include sufficient permanent shielding (of the spacecraft or surface base habitat modules), adequate active dosimetry, the availability of "solar storm shelters" (zones of increased shielding protection) on crewed spacecraft or on the planetary surface, and an effective solar particle event warning system that monitors the Sun for ALSPEs.

The ionizing radiation environment found in space also can harm sensitive electronic equipment (e.g., a single-event upset) and spacecraft materials. Design precautions, operational planning, localized shielding, device redundancy, and computer-memory "voting" procedures are techniques used by aerospace engineers to overcome or offset space radiation-induced problems that can occur in a spacecraft, especially one operating beyond LEO.

See also: EARTH'S TRAPPED RADIATION BELTS; RADIATION SICKNESS; SINGLE EVENT UPSET.

space resources Generally, when people think about outer space, visions of vast emptiness, devoid of anything useful, come to their minds. However, space is really a new frontier that is rich with resources, including unlimited (solar) energy, a full range of raw materials, and an environment that is both special (e.g., high vacuum, microgravity, physical isolation from the terrestrial biosphere) and reasonably predictable.

Since the start of the space age, preliminary investigations of the MOON, MARS, several asteroids and comets, and meteorites have provided tantalizing hints about the rich mineral potential of the extraterrestrial environment. For example, the U.S. Apollo expeditions to the lunar surface established that the average lunar soil contains more than 90% of the material needed to construct a complicated space industrial facility. The soil in the lunar highlands is rich in anorthosite, a mineral suitable for the extraction of aluminum, silicon, and oxygen. Other lunar soils have been found to contain ore-bearing granules of ferrous metals such as iron, nickel, titanium and chromium. Iron can be concentrated from the lunar soil (called regolith) before the raw material even is refined simply by sweeping magnets over regolith to gather the iron granules scattered within.

Remote sensing data of the lunar surface obtained by the CLEMENTINE spacecraft have encouraged some scientists to suggest that water ice may be trapped in perpetually shaded polar regions. If this holds true, then "ice mines" on the Moon could provide both oxygen and hydrogen—vital resources for permanent lunar settlements and space industrial facilities. The Moon would be able both to export chemical propellants for propulsion systems and to resupply materials for life support systems.

Its vast mineral-resource potential, frozen volatile reservoirs and strategic location will make Mars a critical "supply depot" for human expansion into the mineral-rich ASTEROID belt and to the giant outer planets and their fascinating collection of resource-laden moons. Smart robot explorers will assist the first human settlers on Mars, enabling these "Martians" to assess quickly and efficiently the full resource potential of their new world. As these early settlements mature, they will become economically self-sufficient by exporting propellants, life support system consumables, food, raw materials, and manufactured products to feed the next wave of human expansion to the outer regions of the solar system. Cargo spacecraft also will travel between cislunar space and Mars, carrying specialty items to eager consumer markets in both civilizations.

The asteroids, especially Earth-crossing asteroids, represent another interesting category of space resources. Current remote sensing data and analysis of meteorites (many of which scientists believe originate from broken-up asteroids) indicate that carbonaceous (C-type) asteroids may contain up to 10% water, 6% carbon, significant amount of sulfur, and useful amounts of nitrogen. S-class asteroids, which are common near the inner edge of the main asteroid belt and among the Earth-crossing asteroids, may contain up to 30%

free metals (alloys of iron, nickel, and cobalt, along with high concentrations of precious metals). E-class asteroids may be rich sources of titanium, magnesium, manganese, and other metals. Finally, chondrite asteroids, which are found among the Earth-crossing population, are believed to contain accessible amounts of nickel, perhaps more concentrated than the richest deposits found on Earth.

Using smart machines, possibly including self-replicating systems, space settlers in the 21st century will be able to manipulate large quantities of extraterrestrial matter and move it to wherever it is needed in the solar system. Many of these space resources will be used as the feedstock for the orbiting and planetary surface base industries that will form the basis of interplanetary trade and commerce. For example, atmospheric ("aerostat") mining stations could be set up around JUPITER and SATURN, extracting such materials as hydrogen and helium—especially helium-3, an isotope of great potential value in nuclear fusion research and applications. Similarly, Venus could be "mined" for the carbon dioxide in its atmosphere, Europa for water, and Titan for hydrocarbons. Large fleets of robot spacecraft might even be used to gather chunks of water ice from the Saturnian ring system, while a sister fleet of robot vehicles extracts metals from the main asteroid belt. Even the nuclei of selected COMETs could be intercepted and mined for frozen volatiles, including water ice.

See also: ASTEROID; LUNAR PROSPECTOR.

space settlement A large extraterrestrial habitat where from 1,000 to perhaps 10,000 people would live, work, and play, while supporting space industrialization activity, such as the operation of a large space manufacturing complex or the construction of satellite power systems. One possible design is a spherical space settlement called the *Bernal sphere.* This giant spherical habitat would be approximately 2 kilometers in circumference. Up to 10,000 people would live in residences along the inner surface of the large sphere. Rotation of the settlement at about 1.9 revolutions per minute (RPM) would provide Earth-like gravity levels at the sphere's equator, but there would be essentially microgravity conditions at the poles. Because of the short distances between locations in the equatorial residential zone, passenger vehicles would not be necessary. Instead, the space settlers would travel on foot or perhaps by bicycle. The climb from the residential equatorial area up to the sphere's poles would take about 20 minutes and would lead the hiker past small villages, each at progressively lower levels of artificial gravity. A corridor at the axis would permit residents to float safely in microgravity out to exterior facilities, such as observatories, docking ports, and industrial and agricultural areas. Ringed areas above and below the main sphere in this type of space settlement would be the external agricultural toruses.

See also: BERNAL SPHERE; SATELLITE POWER SYSTEM.

spaceship In general, any crewed vehicle or craft capable of traveling in outer space; specifically, a crewed space vehicle capable of performing an interplanetary (and eventually an interstellar) journey.

space shuttle Space shuttles (i.e., the orbiter vehicles) are the main element of America's Space Transportation System (STS) and are used for space research and applications. The shuttles are the first vehicles capable of being launched into space and returning to Earth on a routine basis.

Space shuttles are used as orbiting laboratories in which scientists and mission specialists conduct a wide variety of scientific experiments. Astronaut crews aboard space shuttles place satellites into orbit. They also rendezvous with satellites to carry out repairs and/or return a malfunctioning spacecraft to Earth for refurbishment. Recently, space shuttles have been used as part of Phase I of the International Space Station program. In this application, orbiter vehicles such as the Atlantis (OV-104) have performed important rendezvous and docking missions with the Russian Mir space station.

Space shuttles are true aerospace vehicles. They leave Earth and its atmosphere under rocket power provided by three liquid-fueled main engines and two solid-propellant boosters attached to an external liquid-propellant tank. After their missions in orbit end, the orbiter vehicles streak back through the atmosphere and are maneuvered to land like an airplane. The shuttles, however, are without power during reentry, and they land on runways much like a glider.

The operational space shuttle fleet consists of the: *Columbia* (OV-102), *Discovery* (OV-103), *Atlantis* (OV-104), and *Endeavour* (OV-105). The *Enterprise* (OV-101) served as a test article but never flew in space. The *Challenger* (OV-99) was lost along with

its crew on January 28, 1986 during the first two minutes of the STS 51-L mission.

See also: SPACE TRANSPORTATION SYSTEM.

space sickness A form of motion sickness experienced by about 50% of astronauts or cosmonauts when they encounter the microgravity ("weightless") environment of an orbiting spacecraft a few minutes or hours after launch. Space sickness symptoms include nausea, vomiting, and general malaise. This condition is generally only temporary (typically lasting no more than a day or so) and can be treated (but not prevented) with medications. When a person enters an extended period of microgravity, the fluids shift from the lower part of the body to the upper part, causing many physical changes to occur. For example, a person's eyes will appear smaller because the face becomes fuller (i.e., puffy or swollen in appearance) and the waistline shrinks a few centimeters. Also referred to as *space adaptation syndrome.*

space simulator A device or facility that stimulates some condition or conditions found in space. It is used for testing equipment or in training programs.

See also: SIMULATOR.

space station A space station is an orbiting space system that is designed to accommodate long-term human habitation in space. The concept of people living and working in artificial habitats in outer space appeared in 19th-century science fiction literature in stories such as Edward Everett Hale's "Brick Moon" (1869) and Jules Verne's "Off on a Comet" (1878).

At the beginning of the 20th century, Konstantin Tsiolkovsky (1857–1935) provided the technical underpinnings for this concept with his truly visionary writings about the use of orbiting stations as a springboard for exploring the cosmos. Tsiolkovsky, the father of Russian astronautics, provided a more technical introduction to the space station concept in his 1895 work *Dreams of Earth and Heaven, Nature and Man.* He greatly expanded on the idea of a space station in his 1903 work entitled "The Rocket into Cosmic Space." In this technical classic, Tsiolkovsky described all the essential ingredients needed for a crewed space station including the use of solar energy, the use of rotation to provide artificial gravity and the use of a closed ecological system complete with "space greenhouse."

Throughout the first half of the 20th century the space station concept continued to technically evolve. For example, the German scientist Hermann Oberth described the potential applications of a space station in his classic treatise: *The Rocket to Interplanetary Space* (German title: *Das Rakete zu den Planetenraumen*) (1923). The suggested applications included the use of a space station as an astronomical observatory, an Earth-monitoring facility, and a scientific research platform. In 1929 an Austrian named Potočnik (pen name Hermann Noordung) introduced the concept of a rotating, wheel-shaped space station. Noordung called his design "Wohnrad" ("Living Wheel.") Another Austrian, Guido von Pirquet, wrote many technical papers on space flight, including the use of a space station as a refueling node for space tugs. In the late 1920s and early 1930s, von Pirquet also suggested the use of multiple space stations at different locations in cislunar space. After World War II Dr. Wernher von Braun (with the help of space artist Chesley Bonestell) popularized the concept

of a wheel-shaped space station in the United States. (See Figure 120.)

The U.S. National Aeronautics and Space Administration (NASA), created in 1958, became the forum for the American space station debate. How long should such an orbiting facility last? What was its primary function? How many crew? What orbital altitude and inclination? Should it be built in space or on the ground and then deployed in space? In 1960 space station advocates from every part of the fledgling space industry gathered in Los Angeles for a Manned Space Station Symposium where they agreed that the space station was a logical goal but disagreed on what it was, where it should be located, or how it should be built.

Then, in 1961, President John F. Kennedy decided that the Moon was a worthy target of the American spirit and heritage. A lunar landing had a definite advantage over a space station: Everyone could agree on the definition of landing on the Moon, but few could agree on the definition of a space station. However, this disagreement was actually beneficial. It forced space station designers

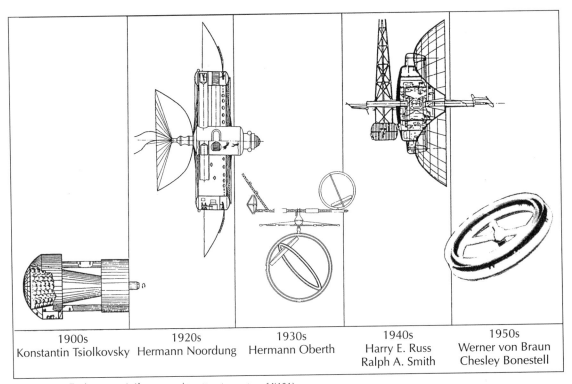

1900s	1920s	1930s	1940s	1950s
Konstantin Tsiolkovsky	Hermann Noordung	Hermann Oberth	Harry E. Russ Ralph A. Smith	Werner von Braun Chesley Bonestell

Figure 120. Early space station concepts   *(Drawing courtesy of NASA)*

and advocates to think about what they could do, the cost of design, and what was necessary to make the project a success. What were the true requirements for a space station? How could they best be met? The space station requirements review process started informally within NASA in 1963 and has continued up to the present day. For over three decades, NASA planners and officials have asked the scientific, engineering, and business communities over and over again. What would you want? What do you need? As answers flowed in, NASA developed a variety of space station concepts to help satisfy these projected requirements. The International Space Station (ISS) is the latest in this evolving series of space station concepts.

Even before the Apollo program had landed men successfully on the Moon, NASA engineers and scientists were considering the next giant step in the U.S. crewed space flight program. That next step became the simultaneous development of two complementary space technology capabilities. One was a safe, reliable transportation system that could provide routine access to space. The other was an orbital space station where human beings could live and work in space. This space station would serve as a base camp from which other, more advanced space technology developments could be initiated. This long-range strategy set the stage for two of the most significant American space activities carried out in the 1970s and 1980s: Skylab and the space shuttle (or Space Transportation System).

On May 14, 1973 the United States launched its first space station, called Skylab. It was launched by a Saturn V booster from the Apollo program. Skylab demonstrated that people could function in space for periods up to 12 weeks and, with proper exercise, could return to Earth with no ill effects.

In particular, the flight of Skylab proved that human beings could operate very effectively in a prolonged microgravity environment and that it was not essential to provide artificial gravity for people to live and work in space (at least for periods up to about six months). (Recent longer-duration flights by Russian cosmonauts and American astronauts on the Mir space station have reinforced and extended these findings.) The Skylab astronauts accomplished a wide range of emergency repairs on station equipment, including freeing a stuck solar panel array (a task that saved the entire mission), replacing rate gyros, and repairing a malfunctioning antenna. On two sepa-

rate occasions the crew installed portable sun shields to replace the original equipment that was lost when Skylab was launched. These on-orbit activities clearly demonstrated the unique and valuable role people have in space.

Unfortunately, Skylab was not designed for a permanent presence in space. For example, the system was not designed to be routinely serviced on orbit—although the Skylab crews were able to perform certain repair functions. Skylab was not equipped to maintain its own orbit—a design deficiency that eventually caused its fiery demise on July 11, 1979 over the Indian Ocean and portions of western Australia. Finally, it was not designed for evolutionary growth and therefore was subject to rapid technological obsolescence. Future space station designs will take these shortcomings into account and effectively use the highly successful Skylab program experience to develop a permanent, evolutionary, and modular space station.

While the United States was concentrating on the Apollo Moon Landing program, the former Soviet Union (now called the Russian Federation) began embarking on an ambitious space station program. As early as 1962 Russian engineers described a space station comprised of modules launched separately and brought together in orbit. The world's first space station, called *Salyut-1*, was launched on April 19, 1971 by a Proton booster. (The Russian word *salyut* means "salute.") The first-generation of Russian space stations had one docking port and could not be resupplied or refueled. The stations were launched uncrewed and later occupied by crews. Two types of early Russian space stations existed: Almaz military stations and Salyut civilian stations. During the cold war, to confuse Western observers the Russians referred to both kinds of station as Salyut. (See Table 1.)

The Almaz military station program was the first approved. When proposed in 1964, it had three parts: the Almaz military surveillance space station, transport logistics spacecraft for delivering military-cosmonauts and cargo, and Proton rockets for launching both. All of these spacecraft were built, but none was actually used as originally planned.

Russian engineers completed several Almaz space station hulls by 1970. The Russian leaders then ordered that the hulls be transferred to a crash program to launch a civilian space station. Work on the transport logistics spacecraft was deferred, and

Table 1.
RUSSIAN SPACE STATION EXPERIENCE

Name	Type	Launched	Remarks
First-Generation Space Stations (1964–1977)			
Salyut-1	Civilian	1971	First space station
Unnamed	Civilian	1972	Failure
Salyut-2	Military	1973	First Almaz station; failure
Cosmos 557	Civilian	1973	Failure
Salyut-3	Military	1974–75	Almaz station
Salyut-4	Civilian	1974–77	
Salyut-5	Military	1976–77	Last Almaz station
Second-Generation Space Stations (1977–1985)			
Salyut-6	Civilian	1977–82	Highly successful
Salyut-7	Civilian	1982–91	Last staffed in 1986
Third-Generation Space Stations (1986–Present)			
Mir	Civilian	1986—Present	First permanent space station

Source: NASA.

the Soyuz spacecraft originally built for the Russian manned Moon program was reapplied to ferry crews to the space stations.

Unfortunately, the early first-generation Russian space stations were plagued by failures. For example, the crew of *Soyuz 10*, the first spacecraft sent to *Salyut-1*, was unable to enter the station because of a docking mechanism problem. The *Soyuz 11* crew lived aboard, *Salyut-1* for three weeks but died during the return to Earth because the air escaped from their spacecraft. Then three first-generation stations failed to reach orbit or broke up in orbit before the cosmonaut crews could reach them. The second failed space station was called *Salyut-2*. It was the first Almaz military space station to fly.

However, the Russians recovered rapidly from these failures. *Salyut-3*, *Salyut-4*, and *Salyut-5* supported a total of five crews. In addition to military surveillance and scientific and industrial experiments, the cosmonauts performed engineering tests to help develop the second-generation stations.

The second-generation Russian space station was introduced with the launch (on September 29, 1977) and successful operation of the *Salyut-6* station. Several important design improvements appeared on this station, including the addition of a second docking port and the use of an automated Progress resupply spacecraft (a space "freighter" derived from the Soyuz spacecraft.)

With the second-generation stations, the Russian space station program evolved from short-duration to long-duration stays. Like the first-generation stations, they were launched uncrewed and their crews arrived later in a Soyuz spacecraft. Second-generation Russian stations had two docking ports. This permitted refueling and resupply by Progress spacecraft, which docked automatically at the aft port. After docking, cosmonauts on the station opened the aft port and unloaded the space freighter. Transfer of fuel to the station was accomplished automatically under supervision from ground controllers.

The availability of a second docking port also meant long-duration resident crews could receive visitors. Visiting crews often included cosmonaut-researchers from the former Soviet bloc countries or countries that were politically sympathetic to the former Soviet Union. For example, the Czech cosmonaut Vladimir Remek visited the *Salyut-6* station in 1978 and became the first space traveler not from either the United States or Russia.

These visiting crews helped relieve the monotony that can accompany a long stay in space. They often traded their Soyuz spacecraft for the one already docked at the station, because the Soyuz spacecraft had only a limited lifetime in orbit. The spacecraft's lifetime was gradually extended from 60 to 90 days for the early *Soyuz Ferry* to more than

180 days for the *Soyuz-TM.* By way of comparison, the Soyuz crew transfer vehicle intended for use with the international space station will have a lifetime of more than a year.

The *Salyut-6* station received 16 cosmonaut crews, including six long-duration crews. The longest stay time for a *Salyut-6* crew was 185 days. The first *Salyut-6* long-duration crew stayed in orbit for 96 days, surpassing the 84-day space endurance record that had been established in 1974 by the last *Skylab* crew. The *Salyut-6* hosted cosmonauts from Hungary, Poland, Romania, Cuba, Mongolia, Vietnam, (East) Germany, as well as Czechoslovakia. Twelve Progress freighter spacecraft delivered more than 20 tons of equipment, supplies, and fuel. An experimental transport logistics spacecraft called *Cosmos 1267* docked with *Salyut-6* in 1982. The transport logistics spacecraft was originally designed for the Almaz program. *Cosmos 1267* demonstrated that a large module could dock automatically with a space station—a major space technology step toward the multimodular Mir station and the international space station. The last cosmonaut crew left the *Salyut-6* station on April 25, 1977. The station reentered the Earth's atmosphere and was destroyed in July 1982.

The *Salyut-7* space station was launched on April 19, 1982 and was a near twin of the *Salyut-6* station. It was home to ten cosmonaut crews, including six long-duration crews. The longest crew stay time was 237 days. Guest cosmonauts from France and India worked aboard the station, as did the first Russian female space traveler (Cosmonaut Svetlana Savitskaya) since 1963; she flew aboard the Soyuz-T-7/Salyut-7 mission. Savitskaya also became the first woman to "walk in space" (i.e., perform an extravehicular activity) during the Soyuz-T-12/Salyut 7 mission in 1984. Unlike the *Salyut-6* station, however, the *Salyut-7* station suffered some major technical problems. In early 1985, for example, Russian ground controllers lost contact with the then unoccupied station. In July 1985 a special crew aboard the *Soyuz-T-13* spacecraft docked with the derelict space station and made emergency repairs that extended its lifetime for another long-duration mission. The *Salyut-7* station finally was abandoned in 1986; it reentered Earth's atmosphere over Argentina in 1991.

During its lifetime on orbit, 13 Progress spacecraft delivered more than 25 tons of equipment, supplies, and fuel to *Salyut-7.* Two experimental transport logistics spacecraft, called *Cosmos 1443* and *Cosmos 1686,* docked with the station. *Cosmos 1686* was a transitional vehicle, a transport logistics spacecraft that had been redesigned to serve as an experimental space station module.

In February 1986 the Russians introduced their third-generation space station, the Mir ("peace") station. More extensive automation, more spacious crew accommodations for resident cosmonauts (i.e., long-duration mission personnel late to include American astronauts), and the addition of a multiport docking adapter at one end of the station highlight some of the major design improvements found on Mir. It is the world's first permanent space station. When docked with the *Progress-M* and *Soyuz-TM* spacecraft, this station measures more than 32.6 meters (107 feet) long and is about 27.4 meters (90 feet) wide across its modules. The orbital complex consists of the Mir core module and a variety of modules including: Kvant ("quantum"), Kvant 2, and Kristall.

The Mir core resembles the *Salyut-7* station but has six ports instead of two. The fore and aft ports are used primarily for docking, while the four radial ports, which are located in a node at the station's front, are used for berthing large modules. When launched in 1986, the core had a mass of about 20 tons. The Kvant module was added to the Mir core's aft port in 1987. This small, 11-ton module contains astrophysics instruments and life support and attitude control equipment. Kvant blocked the core module's aft port but had its own aft port, which then took over duty as the station's aft port.

The 18.5-ton Kvant 2 module was added in 1989. Module design is based on the transport logistics spacecraft originally intended for the Almaz military space station program of the early 1970s. The purpose of Kvant-2 is to provide biological research data, Earth observation data, and extravehicular activity (EVA) capability. It carries an EVA airlock, two solar arrays, and life-support equipment.

The 19.6-ton Krystall module was added in 1990. It carries scientific equipment, retractable solar arrays, and a docking node equipped with a special androgynous docking mechanism designed to receive spacecraft with a mass of up to 100 tons. This docking unit (originally developed for the former Russian space shuttle *Buran*) now is attached to the Docking Module (DM) that is being used by the American space shuttle (*Atlantis*) to link up with the Mir during Phase I of the international space station program.

Three more modules, all carrying American equipment, have been added to the Mir complex as part of the international space station program. These are: the Spektr module, the Priroda module, and the docking module. The Spetkr module carries scientific equipment and solar arrays. (It was severely damaged on June 25, 1997 when a Progress resupply spacecraft collided with it during practice docking operations.)

The Priroda ("Nature") module carries microgravity research and Earth observation equipment. This 19.7-ton module was the last module added to the Mir complex (April 1996). Unlike the other modules, however, Prioroda has none of its own solar power arrays and depends instead on electric power from other portions of the Mir complex.

The docking module was delivered by the space shuttle *Atlantis* during the STS-74 mission (November 1995) and berthed at Kristall's androgynous docking port. The Russian-built DM is now a permanent extension on Mir and provides better clearances for space shuttle orbiter-Mir linkups.

Before describing the International Space Station (ISS), a brief discussion of several NASA space station efforts that originated in the 1980s will prove helpful. In January 1984 President Ronald Reagan called for a space station program as part of his State of the Union address. He said that this space station program was to include participation by U.S. allies. With this presidential mandate, NASA established a Space Station Program Office in April 1984 and requested proposals from the U.S. aerospace industry. By March 1986 the baseline design was the dual-keel configuration, a rectangular framework with a truss across the middle for holding the station's living and working modules and solar arrays.

In the spring of 1985, Japan, Canada, and the European Space Agency (ESA) each signed a bilateral memorandum of understanding with the United States for participation in the space station project. Then, in 1987, the station's dual-keel configuration was revised to take into account a reduced space shuttle flight rate in the wake of the *Challenger* accident. The revised baseline had a single truss with the built-in option to upgrade to the dual-keel design. The need for a space station "lifeboat"—called the assured crew return vehicle—also was identified.

In 1988 President Reagan gave this space station a name, *Freedom*. Space station *Freedom*'s design underwent modifications with each annual budget

Table 2. STATISTICS FOR INTERNATIONAL SPACE STATION (WHEN ASSEMBLY COMPLETED)	
Length	110 meters (361 ft)
Width (end-to-end)	88.4 meters (290 ft)
Mass	419,125 kg (924,200 lb-mass)
Power level	110 kilowatts (electric)
Crew Size (operational)	6
Habitat atmosphere	101.35 kilopascals (14.7 psi)
Orbital altitude	410 kilometers (~250 miles)
Inclination	51.6 degrees (to the equator)

Source: NASA (May 1997).

cycle as the U.S. Congress called for its cost to be reduced. The truss was shortened and the U.S. Habitation and Laboratory modules were reduced in size. The truss was to be launched in sections with subsystems already in place. Despite these redesign efforts, NASA and its contractors produced a substantial amount of hardware. In 1992, in actions that presaged the current increased space cooperation between the United States and the Russian Federation, the United States agreed to purchase Russian Soyuz spacecraft to serve as *Freedom*'s lifeboat. These spacecraft are now called the *Soyuz crew transfer vehicles*. In addition, the shuttle-Mir program (now referred to as Phase I of the international space station) was initiated. This program uses existing assets (primarily U.S. space shuttle orbiters and the Russian Mir space station) to acquire the joint operational experience and to perform the joint research that will lead to the successful construction and operation of an international space station complex.

In 1993 President William Clinton called for Space Station Freedom to be redesigned once again to reduce costs and to include more international involvement. The White House then selected a design option, which was called Space Station Alpha. In its new form, Alpha would use 75% of the hardware designs originally intended for the Freedom program. After the Russians agree to supply major hardware elements (many of which were

Figure 121. The International Space Station (ISS) as currently envisioned (1996–97) *(Artwork courtesy of NASA)*

originally intended for the *Mir 2* space station), Space Station Alpha became known as the International Space Station (ISS). (See Figure 121 and Table 2.)

Table 3.
ASSEMBLY SEQUENCE FOR THE INTERNATIONAL SPACE STATION
(EARLY FLIGHTS)

Flight Designation	Activities/Remarks
1 A/R Functional Cargo Block (FCB)	The Russian-built FCB is a self-supporting active vehicle; it provides: propulsive control capability and power through the early assembly stages; fuel storage capability; rendezvous and docking capability to the Service Module.
1R Service Module	Russian-built Service Module launched passive with PMA-1, PMA-2, and 1 storage rack; PMA-1 provides the interfaces between the U.S. and Russian elements; PMA-2 provides a shuttle docking location.
2R Soyuz (January 1999) Return capability without the orbiter present.	Establishes first station occupancy with 3-person crew; provides assured crew return.
UF-1 MLPM (ISPRs) and PV Module batteries	Provides payload utilization delivering U.S. Lab ISPR racks; 2 storage racks; 2 additional battery sets are delivered and installed on the P6 PV Module, providing a full complement of batteries.
9A ITS SI and CETA Cart A	Delivers the starboard U.S. Central Thermal Control System; radiators remain stowed until the power system is activated on flight 12A; provides second string of S-band capability; the CETA Cart provides EVA crew translation capability along the truss.

Source: NASA

At present, the ISS program is divided into three basic phases. Phase I, an expansion of the shuttle-Mir docking mission program that was initiated in 1992, has provided U.S. and Russian aerospace engineers, flight controllers, and cosmonauts/astronauts with the valuable experience needed to cooperatively assemble and build a structure as complicated as the international space station. Phases II and III involve the actual on-orbit assembly of the station's components. In Phase II, the core of the international space station will be assembled from U.S. and Russian components and early scientific research will begin. Table 3 summarizes some of the highlights of the early portions of the planned ISS Assembly Sequence. Phase III includes utilization flights, during which crews of docked space shuttle orbiters will conduct research inside the station's U.S. Laboratory module. Also during this phase, European, Japanese, Russian, Canadian, and U.S. components will be added to expand the station's capabilities. Phase III will end sometime in 2003 or 2004, when assembly is completed and a planned ten years of operations by international crews begins.

Started at the dawn of a new millennium, the International Space Station is the largest international scientific effort ever undertaken. The United States is now partnered with Russia, Canada, Japan, and the nations of the European Space Agency (including Belgium, Denmark, France, Germany, Italy, the Netherlands, Norway, Spain, and the United Kingdom) in making this long-envisioned space technology dream a constructive pathway for human development and cooperation in the 21st century and beyond.

See also: MIR; SALYUT; SKYLAB; SPACE TRANSPORTATION SYSTEM.

spacesuit Outer space is a very hostile environment. If astronauts/cosmonauts are to survive there, they must take part of Earth's environment with them. Air to breathe, acceptable ambient pressures, and moderate temperatures have to be contained in a shell surrounding the space traveler. This can be accomplished by providing a very large enclosed structure or habitat or, on an individual basis, by encasing the astronaut in a protective flexible capsule called the spacesuit.

Spacesuits used on previous NASA missions from the Mercury Project up through the Apollo Soyuz Test Project have provided effective protection for American astronauts. However, certain design problems have handicapped the suits. These suits were custom-fitted garments. In some suit models, more than 70 different measurements had to be taken of the astronaut in order to manufacture the spacesuit to the proper fit. As a result, a spacesuit could be worn by only one astronaut on only one mission. These early spacesuits were stiff, and even simple motions such as grasping objects quickly drained an astronaut's strength. Even donning the suit was an exhausting process that at times lasted more than an hour and required the help of an assistant.

For example, the Mercury spacesuit was a modified version of a U.S. Navy high-altitude jet aircraft pressure suit. It consisted of an inner layer of Neoprene-coated nylon fabric and a restrain outer layer of aluminized nylon. Joint mobility at the elbows and knees was provided by simple break lines sewn into the suit; but even with these break lines, it was difficult for the wearer to bend arms or legs against the force of a pressurized suit. As an elbow or knee joint was bent, the suit joints folded in on themselves, reducing suit internal volume and increasing pressure. The Mercury spacesuit was worn "soft," or unpressurized, and served only as backup for possible spacecraft cabin pressure loss—an event that never happened.

NASA spacesuit designers then followed the U.S. Air Force approach toward greater suit mobility when they developed the spacesuit for the two-man Gemini Project spacecraft. Instead of fabric-type joints used in the Mercury suit, the Gemini spacesuit had a combination of a pressure bladder and a link-net restraint layer that made the whole suit flexible when pressurized.

The gas-tight, human-shaped pressure bladder was made of Neoprene-coated nylon and covered by load-bearing link-net woven from Dacron and Teflon cords. The net layer, being slightly smaller than the pressure bladder, reduced the stiffness of the suit when pressurized and served as a type of structural shell. Improved arm and shoulder mobility resulted from the multilayer design of the Gemini suit.

Walking on the Moon's surface presented a new set of problems to spacesuit designers. Not only did the spacesuits for the "Moonwalkers" have to offer protection from jagged rocks and the intense heat of the lunar day, but the suits also had to be flexible enough to permit stooping and bending as the Apollo astronauts gathered samples from the Moon and used the lunar rover vehicle for

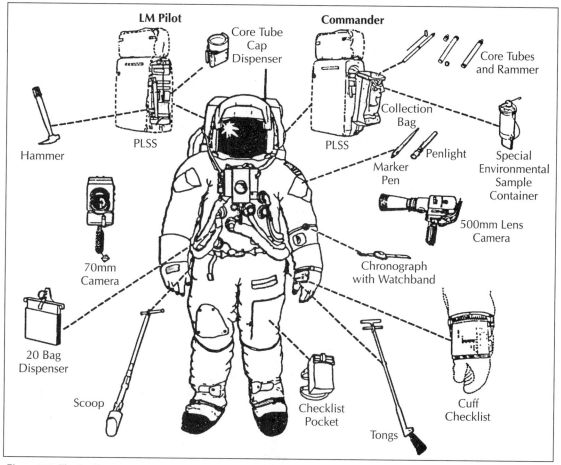

Figure 122. The Apollo astronaut spacesuit and its supporting equipment   *(Drawing courtesy of NASA)*

transportation over the surface of the Moon. (See Figure 122.)

The additional hazard of micrometeoroids that constantly pelt the lunar surface from deep space was met with an outer protective layer on the Apollo spacesuit. A backpack portable life support system provided oxygen for breathing, suit pressurization, and ventilation for moonwalks lasting up to seven hours.

Apollo spacesuit mobility was improved over earlier suits by use of bellowslike molded rubber joints at the shoulders, elbows, hips and knees. Modifications to the suit waist for the *Apollo 15* through *17* missions provided flexibility and made it easier for astronauts to sit on the lunar rover vehicle.

From the skin out, the Apollo A7LB spacesuit began with an astronaut-worn liquid-cooling garment, similar to a pair of longjohns with a network

of spaghettilike tubing sewn onto the fabric. Cool water, circulating through the tubing, transferred metabolic heat from the astronaut's body to the backpack, where it was then radiated away to space. Next came a comfort and donning improvement layer of lightweight nylon, followed by a gastight pressure bladder of Neoprene-coated nylon or bellowslike molded joints components, a nylon restraint layer to prevent the bladder from ballooning, a lightweight thermal superinsulation of alternating layers of thin Kapton and glass-fiber cloth, several layers of Mylar and spacer material, and, finally, protective outer layers of Teflon-coated glass-fiber Beta cloth.

Apollo space helmets were formed from high-strength polycarbonate and were attached to the spacesuit by a pressure-sealing neckring. Unlike Mercury and Gemini helmets, which were closely fitted and moved with the astronaut's head, the Apollo helmet was fixed and the astronaut's head was free to move within it. While walking on the Moon, the Apollo crew wore an outer visor assembly over the polycarbonate helmet to shield against eye-damaging ultraviolet radiation and to maintain head and face thermal comfort.

Lunar gloves and boots completed the Apollo spacesuit. Both were designed for the rigors of exploring; the gloves also could adjust sensitive instruments. The lunar gloves consisted of integral structural restraint and pressure bladders, molded from casts of the crewperson's hands, and covered by multilayered superinsulation for thermal and abrasion protection. Thumb and fingertips were molded of silicone rubber to permit a degree of sensitivity and "feel." Pressure-sealing disconnects, similar to the helmet-to-suit connection, attached the gloves to the spacesuit arms.

The lunar boot was actually an overshoe that the Apollo astronaut slipped on over the integral pressure boot of the spacesuit. The outer layer of the lunar boot was made from metal-woven fabric, except for the ribbed silicone rubber sole; the tongue area was made from Teflon-coated glass-fiber cloth. The boot inner layers were made from Teflon-coated glass-fiber cloth followed by 25 alternating layers of Kapton film and glass-fiber cloth to form an efficient, lightweight thermal insulation.

Modified versions of the Apollo spacesuit were used also during the Skylab Program (1973–1974) and the Apollo-Soyuz Test Project (1975).

A new spacesuit has been developed for shuttle-era astronauts that provides many improvements in comfort, convenience, and mobility over previous models. This suit, which is worn outside the orbiter during extravehicular activity (EVA), is modular and features many interchangeable parts.

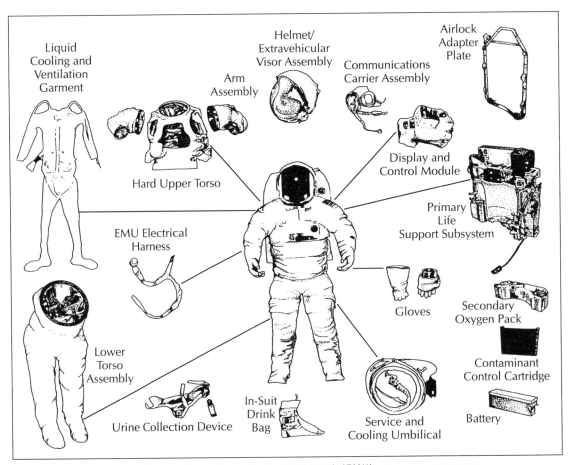

Figure 123. The components of the shuttle-era Extravehicular Mobility Unit (EMU) *(Drawing courtesy of NASA)*

Torso, pants, arms, and gloves come in several different sizes and can be assembled for each mission in the proper combination to suit individual male and female astronauts. The design approach is cost-effective because the suits are reusable and not custom-fitted.

The shuttle spacesuit is called the *Extravehicular Mobility Unit* (*EMU*) and consists of three main parts: liner, pressure vessel, and primary life support system (PLSS). These components are supplemented by a drink bag, communications set, helmet and visor assembly. (See Figure 123.)

Containment of body wastes is a significant problem in spacesuit design. In the shuttle era EMU, the primary life support system (PLSS) handles odors, carbon dioxide, and the containment of gases in the suit's atmosphere. The PLSS is a two-part system consisting of a backpack unit and a control and display unit located on the suit chest. A separate unit is required for urine relief. Two different urine-relief systems have been designed to accommodate both male and female astronauts. Because of the short-time durations for extravehicular activities, fecal containment is considered unnecessary.

The *manned maneuvering unit* (*MMU*) is a one-person, nitrogen-propelled backpack that latches to the EMU spacesuit's PLSS. Using rotational and translational hand controllers, the astronaut can fly with precision in or around the orbiter's cargo bay or to nearby free-flying payloads or structures, and can reach many otherwise inaccessible areas outside the orbiter vehicle. Astronauts wearing MMUs have deployed, serviced, repaired, and retrieved satellite payloads.

The MMU has been called "the world's smallest reusable spacecraft." The MMU propellant (non-contaminating gaseous nitrogen stored under pressure) can be recharged from the orbiter vehicle. The reliability of the unit is guaranteed with a dual parallel system rather than a backup redundant system. In the event of a failure in one parallel system, the system would be shut down and the remaining system would be used to return the MMU to the orbiter's cargo bay. The MMU includes a 35-mm still camera that is operated by the astronaut while working in space.

Shuttle era spacesuits are pressurized at 29.6 kilopascals (4.3 pounds-force per square inch [psi]), while the shuttle cabin pressure is maintained at 101 kilopascals (14.7 psi). Because the gas in the suit is 100% oxygen (instead of 20% oxygen as is found in Earth's atmosphere), the person in the spacesuit actually has more oxygen to breathe than is available at an altitude of 3,000 meters (10,000 feet) or even at sea level without the spacesuit. However, prior to leaving the orbiter to perform tasks in space, an astronaut has to spend several hours breathing pure oxygen. This procedure (called "prebreathing") is necessary to remove nitrogen dissolved in body fluids and thereby prevent its release as gas bubbles when pressure is reduced, a condition commonly referred to as "the bends."

With the advent of an operational International Space Station, work outside the complex will be expanded to provide numerous on-orbit service capabilities not fully achieved in previous space program operations. Therefore, for use on the space station, spacesuits must be: easy to put on and take off (i.e., easy to don and doff); comfortable to wear; capable of fitting different-size astronauts, and easily maintained. They also must permit adequate mobility and range of motion during EVA operations, and provide the necessary protection from radiation, micrometeoroids, space debris, and the overall space environment. A combination of hard- and soft-element suit (called the Mark III suit) and a hard, all-metal suit (called the AX-5) share these common design goals. Both suits have been designed to operate at a pressure of 57.2 kilopascals (8.3 psi). Therefore, the required prebreathing period (which allows the astronaut's body to adapt to the difference in pressure between the spacecraft and the spacesuit) will be shortened considerably or even eliminated. As a result, space station astronauts can prepare for EVA in much less time.

space system Generally, a system consisting of launch vehicle(s), spacecraft, and ground support equipment (GSE).

Spacetrack A global system of radar, optical, and radiometric sensors linked to a computation and analysis center in the North American Aerospace Defense Command (NORAD) combat operations center. The Spacetrack mission is detection, tracking, and cataloging of all human-made objects in orbit around Earth. It is the U.S. Air Force portion of the North American Aerospace Defense Command Space Detection and Tracking system (SPADATS).

See also: NORTH AMERICAN AEROSPACE DEFENSE COMMAND.

Figure 124. The space shuttle *Discovery* lifts off from Pad 39-B at the Kennedy Space Center to start off the STS-26 mission (September 29, 1988). *(NASA)*

Space Transportation System (STS) NASA's name for the overall space shuttle program, including intergovernmental agency requirements and international and joint projects. The major components of the space shuttle system are the winged orbiter vehicle (often referred to as the shuttle or the space shuttle); the three space shuttle main engines (SSMEs); the giant external tank (ET), which feeds liquid hydrogen fuel and liquid oxygen (oxidizer) to the shuttle's three main engines; and the two solid rocket boosters (SRBs).

The orbiter is the only part of the space shuttle system that has a name in addition to a part num-ber. The first orbiter built was the *Enterprise* (OV-101), which was designed for flight tests in the atmosphere rather than operations in space. It is now at the Smithsonian Museum at Dulles Airport outside Washington, D.C. Five operational orbiters were constructed (listed in order of completion): *Columbia* (OV-102), *Challenger* (OV-99),* *Discovery* (OV-103), *Atlantis* (OV-104), and *Endeavour* (OV-105).

Shuttles are launched from either Pad 39A or 39B at the Kennedy Space Center, Florida. Depending

---

* The *Challenger* and its crew were lost in a launch acci-dent on January 28, 1986.

on the requirements of a particular mission, a space shuttle can carry about 22,680 kilograms (kg) (50,000 pounds-mass (lbm)) of payload into LOW EARTH ORBIT (LEO). An assembled shuttle vehicle has a mass of about 2.04 million kg (4.5 million lbm) at liftoff. (See Figure 124).

The two solid rocket boosters (SRBs) are each 45.4 meters (m) (149 feet [ft]) high and 3.7 m (12.1 ft) in diameter. Each has a mass of about 590,000 kg (1.3 million lbm). Their solid propellant consists of a mixture of powdered aluminum (fuel), ammonium perchlorate (oxidizer), and a trace of iron oxide to control the burning rate. The solid mixture is held together with a polymer binder. Each booster produces a thrust of approximately 13.8 million newtons (3.1 million pounds-force [lbf]) for the first few seconds after ignition. The thrust then gradually declines for the remainder of the two-minute burn to avoid overstressing the flight vehicle. Together with the three main liquid-propellant engines on the orbiter, the shuttle vehicle produces a total thrust of 32.5 million newtons (7.3 million lbf) at liftoff.

Typically, the SRBs burn until the shuttle flight vehicle reaches an altitude of about 45 kilometers (km) (28 miles [mi]) and a speed of 4,970 km (3,094 mi) per hour. Then they separate and fall back into the Atlantic Ocean to be retrieved, refurbished, and prepared for another flight. After the solid rocket boosters are jettisoned, the orbiter's three main engines, fed by the huge external tank, continue to burn and provide thrust for another six minutes before they too are shut down at MECO (main engine cut-off). At this point the external tank is jettisoned and falls back to Earth, disintegrating in the atmosphere with any surviving pieces falling into remote ocean waters.

The huge external tank is 47 m (154.2 ft) long and 8.4 m (27.6 ft) in diameter. At launch, it has a total mass of about 760,250 kg (1.676 million lbm). The two inner propellant tanks contain a maximum of 1,458,400 liters (385,300 gallons) of liquid hydrogen (LH_2) and 542,650 liters (143,350 gallons) of liquid oxygen (LO_2). The external tank is the only major shuttle flight vehicle component that is expended on each launch.

The winged orbiter vehicle is both the heart and the brains of America's Space Transportation System. About the same size and mass as a commercial DC-9 aircraft, the orbiter contains the pressurized crew compartment (which can normally carry up to eight crew members), the huge cargo bay (which is 18.3 m long and 4.57 m in diameter [60 x 15 ft]), and the three main engines mounted on its aft end. The orbiter vehicle itself is 37 m (121.4 ft) long, 17 m (56 ft high), and has a wingspan of 24 m (78.7 ft). Since each of the operational vehicles varies slightly in construction, an orbiter generally has an empty mass of between 76,000 to 79,000 kg (~168,000 to 174,000 lbm).

Each of the three main engines on an orbiter vehicle is capable of producing a thrust of 1.668 million newtons (375,000 lbf) at sea level and 2.09 million newtons (470,000 lbf) in the vacuum of space. These engines burn for approximately eight minutes during launch ascent and together consume about 242,250 liters (64,000 gallons) of cryogenic propellants each minute, when all three operate at full power.

An orbiter vehicle also has two smaller orbital maneuvering system (OMS) engines that operate only in space. These engines burn nitrogen tetroxide as the oxidizer and monomethyl hydrazine as the fuel. These propellants are supplied from onboard tanks carried in the two pods at the upper rear portion of the vehicle. The OMS engines are used for major maneuvers in orbit and to slow the orbiter vehicle for reentry at the end of its mission in space. On most missions the orbiter enters an elliptical orbit, then coasts around Earth to the opposite side. The OMS engines then fire just long enough to stabilize and circularize the orbit. On some missions the OMS engines also are fired soon after the external tank separates, to place the orbiter vehicle at a desired altitude for the second OMS burn that then circularizes the orbit. Later OMS engine burns can raise or adjust the orbit to satisfy the needs of a particular mission. A shuttle flight can last from a few days to more than a week or two.

After deploying the payload spacecraft (some of which can have attached upper stages to take them to higher-altitude operational orbits, such as a geostationary orbit), operating the onboard scientific instrument (e.g., Spacelab), making scientific observations of Earth or the heavens, or performing other aerospace activities, the orbiter vehicle reenters Earth's atmosphere and lands. This landing usually occurs at either the Kennedy Space Center in Florida or at Edwards Air Force Base in California (depending on weather conditions at the landing site). Unlike prior manned spacecraft, which followed a ballistic trajectory, the orbiter (now operating like an unpowered glider) has a cross-range capability (i.e., it can move to the right or left off the straight line of its reentry path) of about 2,000 km (1,250 mi). The landing speed is between 340 and 365 km (211 to 226 mi) per hour. After touchdown and rollout, the orbiter vehicle immediately is "safed" by a ground crew with special equipment. This safing operation is also the first step in preparing the orbiter for its next mission in space.

The orbiter's crew cabin has three levels. The uppermost is the flight deck, where the commander and pilot control the mission. The middeck is where the galley, toilet, sleep stations, and storage and experiment lockers are found. Also located in the middeck are the side hatch for passage to and from the orbiter vehicle before launch and after landing, the airlock hatch into the cargo bay and to outer space to support on-orbit extravehicular activities (EVAs). Below the middeck floor is a utility area for air and water tanks. (See Figure 125.)

The orbiter's large cargo bay is adaptable to numerous tasks. It can carry satellites, large space platforms such as the Long-Duration Exposure Facility (LDEF), and even an entire scientific laboratory, such as the European Space Agency's Spacelab to and from LOW EARTH ORBIT. It also serves as a

workstation for astronauts to repair satellites, a foundation from which to erect space structures, and a place to store and hold spacecraft that have been retrieved from orbit for return to Earth.

Mounted on the port (left) side of the orbiter's cargo bay behind the crew quarters is the remote manipulator system (RMS), which was developed and funded by the Canadian government. The RMS is a robot arm and hand with three joints similar to those found in a human being's shoulder, elbow, and wrist. There are two television cameras mounted on the RMS near the "elbow" and "wrist." These cameras provide visual information for the astronauts who are operating the RMS from the aft station on the orbiter's flight deck. The RMS is about 15 m (49 ft) in length and can move anything, from astronauts to satellites, to and from the cargo bay as well as to different points in nearby outer space.

The table provides a brief summary of the space shuttle flights from 1981 to 1998. Despite the tragedy of the 51-L mission, the space shuttle program has been a very important and productive period in the U.S. human space flight program. The on-orbit repair and servicing missions to the HUBBLE SPACE TELESCOPE (1993 and 1997) have improved the value and extended the lifetime of this unique

Figure 125. Layout of the orbiter's crew module *(NASA)*

NASA SPACE SHUTTLE LAUNCHES (1981–1996)

Year	Launches
1981	STS-1, STS-2
1982	STS-3, STS-4, STS-5
1983	STS-6, STS-7, STS-8, STS-9
1984	41-B, 41-C, 41-D, 41-G, 51-A
1985	51-C, 51-D, 51-B, 51-G, 51-F, 51-I, 51-J, 61-A, 61-B
1986	61-C, 51-L (*Challenger* accident)
1987	No launches
1988	STS-26, STS-27
1989	STS-29, STS-30, STS-28, STS-34, STS-33
1990	STS-32, STS-36, STS-31, STS-41, STS-38, STS-35
1991	STS-37, STS-39, STS-40, STS-43, STS-48, STS-44
1992	STS-42, STS-45, STS-49, STS-50, STS-46, STS-47, STS-52, STS-53
1993	STS-54, STS-56, STS-55, STS-57, STS-51, STS-58, STS-61
1994	STS-60, STS-62, STS-59, STS-65, STS-64, STS-68, STS-66
1995	STS-63, STS-67, STS-71, STS-70, STS-69, STS-73, STS-74
1996	STS-72, STS-75, STS-76, STS-77, STS-78, STS-79, STS-80
1997	STS-81, STS-82, STS-83, STS-84, STS-94, STS-85, STS-86, STS-87
1998	STS-89, STS-90, STS-91, STS-88, STS-95, STS-93, STS-96

Source: NASA.

scientific instrument. The rendezvous and docking missions with the Russian Mir space station represent the initial phase of the International Space Station program. The Spacelab missions collectively have returned a wealth of scientific and engineering data over a wide range of technical disciplines. The operational space shuttle fleet will remain the foundation of America's human space flight program well into the next century.

See also: CHALLENGER ACCIDENT; LAUNCH VEHICLE; SPACELAB; SPACE SHUTTLE; SPACE STATION.

space tribology The branch of aerospace engineering that deals with friction, lubrication, and the behavior of lubricants under the harsh environmental conditions encountered during space flight. Space tribology is actually a combination of scientific disciplines: engineering, physics, chemistry, and metallurgy, all focused and concerned with the contact of surfaces in the vacuum of outer space. The space environment often imposes special demands on the moving parts of a spacecraft. Factors such as high vacuum (i.e., very low pressure), radiation, thermal stress, and microgravity all must be considered in developing suitable approaches to reducing friction between moving components of a spacecraft. For example, new liquid lubricants, such as perfluorinated fluids, have been developed with extremely low vapor pres-

sure and a high viscosity index. Physical vapor deposition techniques also have been used to produce thin, highly adherent films of solid lubricant on metal components. Future space missions with extended lifetimes (e.g., five to ten years) and intermittent periods of operation (as might occur in a multiple asteroid encounter mission) will place new demands on the field of space tribology. Lubricants possessing extended lifetimes and increased reliability must be developed to support these new space mission requirements.

See also: LUBRICATION (IN SPACE).

space tug A proposed (but as yet undeveloped) space-based reusable upper-stage vehicle that is capable of delivering, retrieving, and servicing payloads in orbits and trajectories beyond the planned operating altitude of the International Space Station. The space tug would be "hangared" in space, refurbished on orbit, and reused many times.

space vehicle In general, a vehicle or craft capable of traveling through outer space. This vehicle can be occupied by a human crew or uncrewed; capable of returning to Earth or sent on a one-way (expendable) mission. A space vehicle capable of operating both in space and in Earth's atmosphere is called an *aerospace vehicle* (as, for example, the space shuttle orbiter vehicle).

space walk Aerospace jargon used to describe an extravehicular activity (EVA).

See also: EXTRAVEHICULAR ACTIVITY.

space warfare 1. The conduct of offensive and/or defensive operations in outer space, usually resulting in the destruction or negation of an adversary's military space systems; for example, the use of antisatellite (ASAT) systems against capital military space assets. 2. The use of military space systems (e.g., surveillance satellites and secure communications satellites) to support friendly forces during hostile actions in Earth's atmosphere, on land or at sea. 3. The use of military space systems to support ballistic missile defense operations.

See also: ANTISATELLITE (ASAT) OPERATIONS; ANTISATELLITE (ASAT) WEAPON; BALLISTIC MISSILE DEFENSE; SPACE CONTROL OPERATIONS.

space weather Variability of the near-Earth and interplanetary space environment; for example, the development of a solar flare and its potential impact on orbiting space systems.

spalling Flaking off of particles and chunks from the surface of a material as a result of localized stresses.

spare An individual part, subassembly, or assembly supplied for the maintenance or repair of systems or equipment.

Sparrow (AIM-7) The Sparrow is a radar-guided, air-to-air missile with a high-explosive warhead. The versatile missile has all-weather, all-altitude operational capability and can attack high-performance aircraft and missiles from any direction. It is a widely deployed missile used by the forces of the United States and the North Atlantic Treaty Organization (NATO).

The missile has five major sections: radome, radar guidance, warhead, flight control (autopilot plus hydraulic control system), and solid-propellant rocket motor. It has a cylindrical body with four wings at midbody and four tail fins. Although the external dimensions of the Sparrow have remained relatively unchanged from model to model, the internal components of newer missiles represent major improvements with vastly increased capabilities.

The AIM-7F joined air force inventory in 1976 as the primary medium-range, air-to-air missile for the F-15 Eagle. The AIM-7M, the only current operational version, entered service in 1982. It has improved reliability and performance over earlier models at low altitudes and in electronic countermeasures environments. It also has a significantly more lethal warhead. Today the F-4 Phantom, F-15 Eagle, and F-16 Fighting Falcon fighter aircraft carry the AIM-7M Sparrow. U.S. and NATO navies operate a surface-to-air version of this missile called the RIM-7F/M, Sea Sparrow.

See also: SEA SPARROW.

Spartan 1. A nuclear-armed, long-range (midcourse-intercept), surface-to-air guided missile that had been deployed by the United States as part of the former Safeguard ballistic missile defense system in 1975. It was designed to intercept strategic ballistic missile reentry vehicles in space. *See also:* BALLISTIC MISSILE DEFENSE; SAFEGUARD. 2. A free-flying, unmanned space platform developed by NASA to support various scientific studies. A Spartan space platform is launched aboard the space shuttle and deployed from the orbiter vehicle, where it then performs a preprogrammed mission on orbit. Scientific data are collected during each mission, using a tape recorder and (in many cases) film cameras. After the Spartan platform is deployed from the orbiter, there is no command and control capability. At the end of its mission, the platform is retrieved by the orbiter, stowed in the cargo bay, and returned to Earth for data recovery. The platform then is refurbished and made available for a future mission. Power during the deployed phase of the mission is provided by onboard batteries, while platform attitude control is accomplished with pneumatic gas jets.

See also: SPACE TRANSPORTATION SYSTEM.

specific heat capacity (symbol: c) In thermodynamics, a measure of the heat capacity of a substance per unit mass. It is the quantity of thermal energy (heat) required to raise the temperature of a unit mass of a substance by one degree. In the SI UNIT system, specific heat capacity has the units: joules per kilogram-kelvin ($J kg^{-1} K^{-1}$).

For a simple compressible substance, the specific heat at constant volume (c_v) can be defined as: $c_V = (\partial u / \partial T)_V$, where u is internal energy and T is temperature; while the specific heat at constant pressure (c_p) can be defined as: $c_p = (\partial h / \partial T)_p$, where h is enthalpy.

specific impulse (symbol: I_{sp}) An important performance index for rocket propellants. It is defined as the thrust (or thrust force) produced by propellant combustion divided by the propellant mass flow rate. Expressed as an equation, the specific impulse is:

$$I_{sp} = \text{thrust} / \text{mass flow rate} = F_{thrust} / \dot{m}$$

where F_{thrust} is the thrust and m is the mass flow rate of propellant. It is also important to understand the units associated with specific impulse. In the SI UNIT system, thrust is expressed in newtons and mass flow rate in kilograms per second. Since one newton equals one kilogram-meter per second-squared (i.e., $1 \text{ N} = 1 \text{ kg-m/s}^2$), the specific impulse in SI units becomes:

$$I_{sp} = \text{newtons} / (\text{kg/sec}) =$$
$$\text{meter/second (m/s). [SI units]}$$

In the English (or traditional engineering) system of units, thrust is expressed in pounds-force (lbf), while mass flow rate of propellant in pounds-mass per second (lbm/s). Since (by definition), one pound-force is equal to one pound-mass at sea level on the surface of Earth, aerospace engineers often use the following simplification, which is, strictly speaking, valid only at sea level on Earth:

$$I_{sp} = \text{lbf} / (\text{lbm/s}) \approx \text{seconds (s)}$$
$$\text{(traditional engineering units)}$$

See also: PROPELLANT; ROCKET; ROCKET ENGINE.

specific volume (symbol: v) Volume per unit mass of a substance. The reciprocal of density.

spectral line A bright (or dark) line found in the spectrum of some radiant source. Bright lines indicate emission; dark lines indicate absorption.

spectrum 1. In physics, any series of energies arranged according to frequency (or wavelength). 2. The electromagnetic spectrum; the sequence of electromagnetic waves from gamma rays (high frequency) to radio waves (low frequency). 3. The series of images produced when a beam of radiant energy is dispersed.

specular reflection Reflection in which the reflected radiation is not diffused; reflection as if from a mirror. The angle between the normal (perpendicular) to the surface and the incident beam is equal to the angle between the normal to the surface and the reflected beam. Any surface irregularities on a specular reflector must be small compared to the wavelength of the incident radiation.

speed of light (symbol: c) The speed of propagation of electromagnetic radiation (including light) through a perfect vacuum; a universal constant equal to 299,792.458 kilometers per second.

speed of sound The speed at which sound travels in a given medium under specified conditions. The speed of sound at sea level in the International Standard Atmosphere is 1,215 kilometers per hour (1,108 feet per second). Sometimes called the *acoustic velocity.*
See also: ATMOSPHERE.

spherical coordinates A system of coordinates defining a point on a sphere by its angular distances from a primary great circle and from a reference secondary great circle, as latitude and longitude.

spin-off A general term used to describe benefits that have dervived from the (secondary) application of aerospace technologies to terrestrial problems and needs. For example, a special coating material designed to protect a reentry vehicle is also applied to fire-fighting equipment to make it more heat resistant. The manufacturer of the fire-fighting equipment improved the terrestrial product by "spinning-off" aerospace technology.

spin rocket A small rocket that imparts spin to a large rocket vehicle or spacecraft.

spin stabilization Directional stability of a missile or spacecraft obtained by the action of gyroscopic forces that result from spinning the body about its axis of symmetry.

splashdown That portion of a human space mission in which the space capsule (reentry craft) containing the crew lands in the ocean—quite literally, "splashing down." The astronauts then are recovered by a team of helicopters, aircraft, and/or surface ships. This term was used during NASA's Mercury, Gemini, Apollo, Skylab and Apollo-Soyuz projects (1961–1975). In the space shuttle era, the orbiter vehicle returns to Earth by landing much like an aircraft. Consequently, the orbiter vehicle and its crew are said to "touch down."

The term "splashdown" also can be applied to an uncrewed, recoverable space capsule or spacecraft that has been deorbited intentionally and lands in the ocean. Once again, if the space capsule lands on the surface of Earth (under controlled circumstances), the event is described as touching down or making a soft landing. An uncontrolled or destructive landing on Earth's surface is called an impact, hard landing, or crash landing, depending on the circumstances. For example, a piece of space debris is said to "impact"; a space capsule with an undeployed or ripped parachute will either "hard land" or "crash land."

SPOT A family of Earth observation spacecraft developed by French Space Agency (CNES). The acronym "SPOT" stands for *Satellite Pour l'Observation de la Terre*. The *SPOT-1* remote sensing satellite was launched by an Ariane 1 rocket from Kourou, French Guiana on February 22, 1986 into a 825-kilometer altitude, circular polar orbit. The *SPOT-2* satellite was launched by an Ariane 4 rocket from Kourou on January 22, 1990 and placed in an orbit exactly opposite to the *SPOT-1* spacecraft, providing more frequent (every 13 days) repeat visits to scenes on Earth. Imagery from these spacecraft are commercially marketed by a company called SPOT Image.

See also: REMOTE SENSING.

Sprint A high-acceleration, short-range, nuclear-armed, surface-to-air guided missile that was deployed in 1975 as part of the former Safeguard ballistic missile defense system. The Sprint system was designed to intercept strategic ballistic reentry vehicles in the atmosphere during the terminal phase of their flight.

See also: BALLISTIC MISSILE DEFENSE; SAFEGUARD.

Sputnik 1 On October 4, 1957 the former Soviet Union (now called the Russian Federation) launched *Sputnik 1*, the first human-made object to be placed in orbit around Earth. A 29-meter-foot-tall Russian A-1 rocket boosted this artificial satellite into an approximate 230 kilometer by 950 kilometer orbit. The simple, 83.5 kilogram spacecraft was essentially a hollow sphere made of steel that contained batteries and a radio transmitter to which were attached four whip antennas. As it

orbited Earth, *Sputnik 1* provided scientists with information on temperatures and electron densities in Earth's upper atmosphere. It reentered the atmosphere and burned up on January 4, 1958.

The name *Sputnik* means "fellow traveler." Launched during the cold war under the guidance of the Russian aerospace visionary Sergei Korolov (1907–1966), Sputnik represented a technological surprise that sent tremors through the United States and its allies. This launch is often regarded as the birth date of the modern space age. It also marks the beginning of a heated "space race" between the United States and the former Soviet Union—a space technology race that was to culminate in 1969 with an American astronaut becoming the first human to walk on the surface of the Moon.

spy satellite Popular name for a reconnaissance satellite.

See also: RECONNAISSANCE SATELLITE.

squib A small pyrotechnic device that may be used to fire the igniter in a rocket.

stacking Assembling the coolant tubes of a liquid propellant rocket engine's thrust chamber vertically on a mandrel that simulates the chamber/nozzle contour. This procedure facilitates fitting and adjusting the tubes to the required contour prior to brazing.

stage 1. In rocketry, an element of the missile or launch vehicle system that usually separates from the vehicle at burnout or engine cutoff. In multistage rockets, the stages are numbered chronologically in the order of burning (i.e., first stage, second stage, etc.). 2. In mechanical engineering, a set of rotor blades and stator vanes in a turbine or in an axial-flow compressor. 3. In fluid mechanics and thermodynamics, a step or process through which a fluid passes, especially in compression or expansion.

stage-and-a-half A liquid rocket propulsion unit of which only part falls away from the rocket vehicle during flight, as in the case of booster rockets falling away to leave the sustainer engine to consume the remaining fuel.

staged combustion Rocket engine cycle in which propellants are partially burned in a preburner prior to being burned in the main combustion chamber.

staging 1. In rocketry, the process during the flight of a multistage launch vehicle or missile during which a spent stage separates from the remaining vehicle and is free to decelerate or follow its own trajectory 2. In mechanical engineering, the use of two or more stages in a turbine or pump.

stagnation In thermodynamics, a condition in which a flowing fluid is brought to rest isentropically (i.e., with no change in ENTROPY).

stagnation point Point in a flow field about a body immersed in the flowing fluid at which the fluid particles have zero velocity with respect to the body.

stagnation pressure 1. Pressure that a flowing fluid would attain if it is brought to rest isentropically (i.e., with no change in ENTROPY). 2. Pressure of a flowing fluid at a point of zero fluid velocity on a body around which the fluid flows.

stagnation region The region in the vicinity of a stagnation point in a flow field about an immersed body where the fluid velocity is negligible.

stagnation temperature In thermodynamics, the temperature that a flowing fluid would attain if the fluid were brought to rest isentropically (i.e., with no change in ENTROPY).

standard deviation (symbol: σ) A measure of the dispersion of data points around their mean value. It is the positive square root of the arithmetic mean of the squares of the deviation from the arithmetic mean of the population:

$$\sigma = \sqrt{\Sigma\, d^2\, m/n}$$

where d is the deviation from the arithmetic mean, m is the arithmetic mean, and n is the number of data points.

Standard Missile (SM) A U.S. Navy surface-to-air and surface-to-surface missile that is mounted on surface ships. The Standard Missile is produced in two major types: the SM-1 MR/SM-2 (medium range) and the SM-2 (extended range). It is one of the most reliable in the navy's inventory and is used against enemy missiles, aircraft, and ships. The SM joined the fleet more than a decade ago. It replaced the Terrier and Tartar missiles and now is part of the weapons inventory of more than 100

navy ships. The SM-2 (MR) is a medium-range defense weapon for Ticonderoga-class AEGIS cruisers, Arleigh Burke–class AEGIS destroyers, and California- and Virginia-class nuclear cruisers. Oliver Hazard Perry–class frigates use the SM-1 MR.

The SM-1/SM-2 Medium Range (MR) missile has a dual-thrust solid-propellant rocket, a semiactive radar homing guidance system, and a promixity fuse, high-explosive warhead. The SM-2 Extended Range (ER) missile has a two-stage, solid-fuel rocket, an inertial/semiactive radar homing guidance system, and a proximity fuse, high-explosive warhead. The SM-1 MR missile has a range of between 27 and 37 kilometers (km) (17–23 miles [mi]); the SM-2 MR missile, between 74 and 167 km (46–104 miles); and the SM-2 ER missile, between 120 and 185 km (75–115 miles.)

Stanton number A nondimensional number used to express the ratio of heat transferred to a fluid to the heat transported by the fluid.

$$\text{Stanton number} = \frac{\text{heat transferred to fluid}}{\text{heat transported by fluid}} = \frac{h}{\rho\, c_p V}$$

where h is the heat transfer coefficient, ρ is the density, c_p is the specific heat at constant pressure, and V is the flow velocity.

STARDUST mission A planned NASA mission that will fly a spacecraft (called STARDUST) within approximately 100 kilometers (62 miles) of Comet Wild-2 in early 2004 and collect cometary dust and volatile samples. During the cruise phase of its mission, STARDUST also will collect contemporary particles that recently came into the solar system from the interstellar medium. The presence of this interstellar dust in the solar system was first discovered by the *Ulysses* spacecraft in 1993 and later confirmed during the Galileo mission. STARDUST will return to Earth in January 2006 and drop off the samples using a streamlined, low-cost reentry capsule. An air-snatch recovery of this capsule over the White Sands Missile Range by a specially equipped chase aircraft is planned. The launch date for the STARDUST mission currently is set for February 1999.

See also: COMET; INTERSTELLAR MEDIUM.

star grain A hollow, solid-propellant rocket grain with the cross section of the hole having a multipointed star shape.

See also: ROCKET.

star probe A specially designed and instrumented probe spacecraft that is capable of approaching within 1 million kilometers or so of the Sun's surface (photosphere). This close encounter with the Sun, the nearest star, would provide scientists with their first in-situ measurements of the physical conditions in the corona (the Sun's outer atmosphere). The challenging mission requires advanced space technologies (including propulsion, laser communications, thermal protection, etc.) and might be flown in the second or third decade of the 21st century.

See also: SUN.

stars A star is essentially a self-luminous ball of very hot gas that generates energy through thermonuclear fusion reactions that take place in its core.

Stars may be classified as either "normal" or "abnormal." Normal stars, such as the Sun, shine steadily. These stars exhibit a variety of colors: red, orange, yellow, blue, and white. Most stars are smaller than the Sun, and many stars even resemble it. However, a few stars are much larger than the Sun. In addition, astronomers have observed several types of abnormal stars including giants, dwarfs, and a variety of variable stars.

Most stars can be put into one of several general spectral types called O, B, A, F, G, K, and M. (See the table.) This classification is a sequence established in order of decreasing surface temperature.

Our parent star, the Sun, is approximately 1.4 million kilometers (865,000 miles) in diameter and has an effective surface temperature of about 5,800° Kelvin. The Sun, like other stars, is a giant nuclear furnace, in which the temperature, pressure, and density are sufficient to cause light nuclei to join together, or "fuse." For example, deep inside the solar interior, hydrogen, which makes up 90% of the Sun's mass, is fused into helium atoms, releasing large amounts of energy that eventually works its way to the surface and then is radiated throughout the solar system. The Sun is currently in a state of balance, or equilibrium, between two competing forces: gravity (which wants to pull all its mass inward) and the radiation pressure and hot gas pressure resulting from the thermonuclear reactions (which push outward).

Many stars in the galaxy appear to have companions, with which they are gravitationally bound in binary, triple, or even larger systems. Compared to other stars throughout the galaxy, the Sun is slightly unusual. It does not have a known stellar companion. However, the existence of a very distant, massive, dark companion called Nemesis has been postulated by some astrophysicists in an attempt to explain an apparent "cosmic catastrophe cycle" that occurred on Earth about 65 million years ago.

Astrophysicists have discovered what appears to be the life cycle of stars. Stars originate by the condensation of enormous clouds of cosmic dust and hydrogen gas, called nebulae. Gravity is the dominant force behind the birth of a star. According to Newton's Universal Law of Gravitation, all bodies attract each other in proportion to their masses and distance apart. The dust and gas particles found in these huge interstellar clouds attract each other and gradually draw closer together. Eventually enough of these particles join together to form a central clump that is sufficiently massive to bind all the other parts of the cloud by gravitation. At this point, the edges of the cloud start to collapse inward, separating it from the remaining dust and gas in the region.

Initially the cloud contracts rapidly, because the thermal energy release related to contraction is radiated outward easily. However, when the cloud grows smaller and more dense, the heat released at the center cannot escape to the outer surface immediately. This causes a rapid rise in internal temperature, slowing down but not stopping the relentless gravitational contraction.

The actual birth of a star occurs when its interior becomes so dense and its temperature so high that thermonuclear fusion occurs. The heat released in thermonuclear fusion reactions is greater than that released through gravitational contraction, and fusion becomes the star's primary energy-producing mechanism. Gases heated by nuclear fusion at the cloud's center begin to rise, counterbalancing the inward pull of gravity on the outer layers. The star stops collapsing and reaches a state of equilibrium between outward and inward forces. At this point, the star has become what astronomers and astrophysicists call a "main sequence star." Like the Sun, it will remain in this state of equilibrium for billions of years, until all the hydrogen fuel in its core has been converted into helium.

How long a star remains on the main sequence, burning hydrogen for its fuel, depends mostly on its mass. The Sun has an estimated main sequence lifetime of about 10 billion years, of which approximately 5 billion years have now passed. Larger stars burn their fuels faster and at much higher temperatures. These stars, therefore, have short main sequence lifetimes, sometimes as little as 1 million years. In comparison, the "red dwarf stars," which typically have less than one-tenth the mass of the Sun, burn up so slowly that trillions of years must elapse before their hydrogen supply is exhausted. When a star has used up its hydrogen fuel, it leaves the "normal" state or departs the main sequence. This happens when the core of the star has been converted from hydrogen to helium by thermonuclear reactions that have taken place.

When the hydrogen fuel in the core of a main sequence star has been consumed, the core starts to collapse. At the same time, the hydrogen fusion process moves outward from the core into the surrounding outer regions. There the process of converting hydrogen into helium continues, releasing radiant energy. But as this burning process moves into the outer regions, the star's atmosphere expands greatly, and it becomes a "red giant." The term "giant" is quite appropriate. If we put a red giant where the Sun is now, the innermost planet, Mercury, would be engulfed by it; similarly, if we put a larger "red supergiant" there, this supergiant would extend out past the orbit of Mars.

As the star's nuclear evolution continues, it might become a "variable star," pulsating in size and brightness over periods of several months to years. The visual brightness of such an "abnormal" star might now change by a factor of 100, while its total energy output varies by only a factor of 2 or 3.

As an abnormal star grows, its contracting core may become so hot that it ignites and burns nuclear fuels other than hydrogen, beginning with the helium created in millions to perhaps billions of years of main sequence burning. The subsequent behavior of such a star is complex, but in general it can be characterized as a continuing series of gravitational contractions and new nuclear reaction ignitions. Each new series of fusion reactions produces a succession of heavier elements in addition to releasing large quantities of energy. For example, the burning of helium produces carbon, the burning of carbon produces oxygen, and so forth.

Finally, when nuclear burning no longer releases enough radiant energy to support the giant star, it collapses and its dense central core becomes either a compact white dwarf or a tiny neutron star. This collapse also may trigger an explosion of the star's outer layers, which displays itself as a supernova. In exceptional cases with very massive stars, the core (or perhaps even the entire star) might become a black hole.

When a star like the Sun has burned all the nuclear fuels available, it collapses under its own gravity until the collective resistance of the electrons within it finally stops the contraction process. The "dead star" has become a "white dwarf" and may now be about the size of Earth. Its atoms are packed so tightly together that a fragment the size of a sugar cube would have a mass of thousands of kilograms. The white dwarf then cools for perhaps several billion years, going from white, to yellow, to red, and finally becomes a cold, dark sphere sometimes called a "black dwarf." (Note that the white dwarf is not experiencing nuclear burning; rather its light comes from a thin gaseous atmosphere that gradually dissipates its heat to space.) Astrophysicists estimate that there are over 10 billion white dwarf stars in the Milky Way Galaxy alone, many of which have now become black dwarfs. This fate appears to be awaiting our own Sun and most other stars in the galaxy.

However, when a star with a mass of about 1.5 to 3 times the mass of the Sun undergoes collapse, it will contract even further and ends up as a "neutron star," with a diameter of perhaps only 20 kilometers. In neutron stars, intense gravitational forces drive electrons into atomic nuclei, forcing them to combine with protons and transforming this combination into neutrons. Atomic nuclei are, therefore, obliterated in this process, and only the collective resistance of neutrons to compression halts the collapse. At this point, the star's matter is so dense that each cubic centimeter has a mass of several billion tons.

For stars that end their life having more than a few solar masses, even the resistance of neutrons is not enough to stop the unyielding gravitational collapse. In death such massive stars may ultimately become black holes—incredibly dense point masses or singularities that are surrounded by a literal "black region" in which gravitational attraction is so strong that nothing, not even light itself, can escape.

Currently, many scientists relate the astronomical phenomena called supernovae and pulsars with neutron stars and their evolution. The final collapse of a giant star to the neutron stage may give rise to the physical conditions that cause its outer portions to explode, creating a *supernova*. This type of cosmic explosion releases so much energy that its debris products will temporarily outshine all the ordinary stars in the galaxy.

A regular "nova" (the Latin word for "new," the plural of which is *novae*) occurs more frequently and is far less violent and spectacular. One common class, called *recurring novae*, is due to the nuclear ignition of gas being drawn from a companion star to the surface of a white dwarf. Such binary star systems are quite common; sometimes the stars will have orbits that regularly bring them close enough for one to draw off gas from the other.

When a supernova occurs at the end of a massive star's life, the violent explosion fills vast regions of space with matter that may radiate for hundreds or even thousands of years. The debris created by a supernova explosion eventually will cool into dust and gas, become part of a giant interstellar cloud, and perhaps once again be condensed into a star or planet. Most of the heavier elements found on Earth are thought to have originated in supernovae, because the normal thermonuclear fusion processes cannot produce such heavy elements. The violent power of a supernova explosion can, however, combine lighter elements into the heaviest elements found in nature (e.g., lead, thorium, and uranium). Consequently, both the Sun and its planets were most likely enriched by infusions of material hurled into the interstellar void by ancient supernova explosions.

Pulsars, first detected by radio astronomers in 1967, are sources of very accurately spaced bursts, or pulses, of radio signals. These radio signals are so regular, in fact, that the scientists who made the first detections were startled into thinking that they might have intercepted a radio signal from an intelligent alien civilization.

The pulsar, named because its radio-wave signature regularly turns on and off, or pulses, is considered to be a rapidly spinning neutron star. One pulsar is located in the center of the Crab Nebula, where a giant cloud of gas is still glowing from a supernova explosion that occurred in the year A.D. 1054—a spectacular celestial event observed and recorded by ancient Chinese astronomers. The discovery of this pulsar allowed scientists to understand both pulsars and supernovae.

In a supernova explosion, a massive star is literally destroyed in an instant, but the explosive debris lingers and briefly outshines everything in the galaxy. In addition to scattering material all over interstellar space, supernova explosions leave behind a dense collapsed core made of neutrons. This neutron star, with an immense magnetic field, spins many times a second, emitting beams of radio waves, X rays, and other radiations. These radiations may be focused by the pulsar's powerful magnetic field and sweep through space much like a revolving lighthouse beacon. The neutron star, the end product of a violent supernova explosion, becomes a pulsar.

Astrophysicists must develop new theories to explain how pulsars can create intense radio waves, visible light, X rays and gamma rays, all at the same time. Orbiting X-ray observatories have detected X-ray pulsars that are believed to be caused by a neutron star pulling gaseous matter from a normal companion star in a binary star sys-

STELLAR SPECTRAL CLASSES			
Type	Description	Typical Surface Temperatures(K)	Remarks
O	very hot, large blue stars ['hottest]	28,000–40,000	ultraviolet stars; very short lifetimes (3–6 million years)
B	large, hot blue stars	11,000–28,000	example: Rigel
A	blue-white, white stars	7,500–11,000	Vega, Sirius, Altair
F	white stars	6,000–7,500	Canopis, Polaris
G	yellow stars	5,000–6,000	the Sun
K	orange-red stars	3,500–5,000	Arcturus, Aldebaran
M	red stars ['coolest]	<3,500	Antares, Betelgeuse

Source: NASA.

tem. As gas is sucked away from the normal companion to the surface of the neutron star, the gravitational attraction of the neutron star heats up the gas to millions of degrees Kelvin; this causes the gas to emit X rays.

The advent of the space age and the use of powerful orbiting observatories, such as the Hubble Space Telescope (HST), to view the universe as never before possible has greatly increased our knowledge about the many different types of stellar phenomena. Most exciting of all, perhaps, is the fact that this process of astrophysical discovery has really only just begun.

See also: ASTROPHYSICS; BLACK HOLE(S); FUSION; HUBBLE SPACE TELESCOPE; SUN.

starship A space vehicle capable of traveling the great distances between star systems. Even the closest stars in the Milky Way Galaxy are often light-years apart. The term "starship" is generally used to describe an interstellar spaceship capable of carrying intelligent beings to other star systems; robot interstellar spaceships are often referred to as "interstellar probes."

See also: INTERSTELLAR COMMUNICATION AND CONTACT; INTERSTELLAR TRAVEL.

starting pressure In rocketry, the minimum chamber pressure required to establish shock-free flow in the exit plane of a supersonic nozzle.

star tracker An instrument on a missile or spacecraft that locks onto a star (or pattern of "fixed" stars) and provides reference information to the missile or spacecraft's guidance system and/or attitude control system during the flight.

See also: GUIDANCE SYSTEM.

state of the art (SOA) The level to which technology and science have been developed in any given discipline or industry at some designated cutoff time.

static 1. Involving no variation with time. 2. Involving no movement, as in *static test.* 3. Any radio interference heard as unwanted, random noises at the speaker (audio stage) of the radio receiver.

static conversion Energy conversion in which no moving parts or equipment are involved.

See also: DIRECT CONVERSION.

static firing The firing of a rocket engine in a hold-down position. Usually done to measure thrust and to accomplish other performance tests.

static seal Device used to prevent leakage of fluid through a mechanical joint in which there is no relative motion of the mating surfaces other than that induced by changes in the operating environment.

static testing The testing of a rocket or other device in a stationary or hold-down position, either to verify structural design criteria, structural integrity, and the effects of limit loads or to measure the thrust of a rocket engine.

stationary orbit An orbit in which the satellite revolves about the primary at the same angular rate at which the primary rotates on its axis. To an observer on the surface of the primary, the satellite would appear to be stationary over a point on the primary.

See also: GEOSTATIONARY EARTH ORBIT; SYNCHRONOUS SATELLITE.

stationkeeping The sequence of maneuvers that maintains a space vehicle or spacecraft in a predetermined orbit.

stator 1. Part of a turbopump assembly that remains fixed or stationary relative to a rotating or moving part of the assembly. 2. In an alternating current (a.c.) generator, the part that is stationary.

statute mile A distance of 5,280 feet. One statute mile (often called simply "mile") is equal to 1.6093 kilometers. It is also equal to approximately 0.869 nautical mile.

steady flow A flow whose velocity vector components at any point in the fluid do not vary with time.

steady state Condition of a physical system in which parameters of importance (fluid velocity, temperature, pressure, etc.) do not vary significantly with time; in particular, the condition or state of rocket engine operation in which mass, momentum, volume, and pressure of the combustion products in the thrust chamber do not vary significantly with time.

Stefan-Boltzmann law One of the basic laws of radiation heat transfer. This law states that the amount of energy radiated per unit time from a unit surface area of an ideal BLACKBODY radiator is proportional to the fourth power of the absolute temperature of the blackbody. It can be expressed as:

$$E = \varepsilon \, \sigma \, T^4$$

where E is the emittance per unit area (watts per square meter per second [$Wm^{-2}s^{-1}$]) of the blackbody, ε is the emissivity ($\varepsilon = 1$ for a blackbody), σ is the Stefan-Boltzmann constant (5.67×10^{-8} (watts per square meter per degrees Kelvin to the fourth power [$Wm^{-2} K^{-4}$]), and T is the absolute temperature (Kelvin) of the blackbody.

stellar Of or pertaining to the stars.

stellar guidance A system wherein a guided missile may follow a predetermined course with reference primarily to the relative position of the missile and certain preselected celestial bodies.
See also: GUIDANCE SYSTEM.

stellar wind The flux of electromagnetic radiation and energetic particles that stream outward from a star. The stellar wind associated with the Sun is called the *solar wind.*
See also: SOLAR WIND.

step rocket A multistage rocket.

steradian (symbol: sr) The supplementary unit of solid angle in the international (SI) system. One steradian is equal to the solid angle subtended at the center of a sphere by an area of surface equal to the square of the radius. The surface of a sphere subtends a solid angle of 4π steradians about its center.

Stinger A shoulder-fired infrared missile that homes in on the heat (thermal energy) emitted by either jet-or propeller-driven fixed-wing aircraft or helicopters. The Stinger system employs a proportional navigation system that allows it to fly an intercept course to the target. Once the missile has traveled a safe distance from the gunner, its main engine ignites and propels it to the target.

Stirling cycle A thermodynamic cycle for a heat engine in which thermal energy (heat) is added at constant volume, followed by isothermal expansion with heat addition. The heat then is rejected at constant volume, followed by isothermal compression with heat rejection. If a regenerator is used so that the heat rejected during the constant volume process is recovered during heat addition at constant volume, then the thermodynamic efficiency of the Stirling cycle approaches (in the limit) the efficiency of the Carnot cycle. The basic principle of the Stirling engine was first proposed and patented in 1816 by Robert Stirling, a Scottish minister.

Aerospace engineers are investigating the free-piston Stirling engine for space power applications in the 21st century. Invented in 1962, this type of Stirling cycle device is an integrated unit consisting of a free-piston engine to convert thermal energy (e.g., solar or nuclear supplied) into linear motion and an alternator to convert the linear motion into electric power. It has the potential for high reliability and long life—features critical for space use—because it has few moving parts, can use noncontacting gas bearings, and can be hermetically sealed.

The stages in an ideal Stirling cycle are shown in Figure 126. The thermodynamic processes associated with these stages are as follows: (1) Isothermal (constant temperature) compression of the working fluid (gas) from a to b at the lower (sink) temperature T_1. In this stage of the Stirling cycle, work is done on the gas and thermal energy must be removed to maintain a constant temperature.

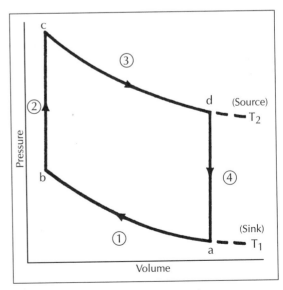

Figure 126. Stages of an ideal Stirling cycle   *(Drawing courtesy of Department of Energy)*

(2) Heat addition to the gas occurs at constant volume from *b* to *c*. During this stage the pressure of the gas rises and its temperature increases to the upper (source) temperature T_2. (3) Isothermal expansion of the working gas takes place from *c* to *d*. During this expansion process heat must be supplied to maintain the gas at a constant temperature (T_2). (4) Thermal energy is removed (rejected) from the gas at constant volume from *d* to *a*. The temperature of the gas falls to the lower (sink) temperature T_1 and the gas returns to its initial thermodynamic state *a*.

See also: CARNOT CYCLE; HEAT ENGINE; THERMODYNAMICS.

stochastic process A statistical process; a process in which there is a random variable.

stoichiometric combustion The burning of fuel and oxidizer in precisely the right proportions required for complete reaction with no excess of either reactant.

Stokes number A nondimensional number used to express the relationship between viscous force and gravity force in a fluid, as follows:

$$\text{Stokes number} = \frac{\text{viscous force}}{\text{gravity force}} = \frac{\mu V}{\rho \, gl^2}$$

where μ is absolute viscosity, V is velocity, ρ is mass density, g is the acceleration of gravity, and l is characteristic length.

storable propellant Rocket propellant (usually liquid) capable of being stored for prolonged periods of time without special temperature or pressure controls.

stowing In aerospace operations, the process of placing a payload in a retained, or attached, position in the space shuttle orbiter's cargo bay for ascent to or return from orbit.

strain In engineering, the change in the shape or volume of an object due to applied forces. There are three basic types of strain: longitudinal, volume, and shear. Longitudinal (or tensile) strain is the change in length per unit length, as occurs, for example, with the stretching of a wire. Volume (or bulk) strain involves a change in volume per unit volume, as occurs, for example, when an object is totally immersed in a liquid and experiences a hydrostatic pressure. Finally, shear strain is the angular deformation of an object without a change in its volume. Shear occurs, for example, when a rectangular block of metal is strained or distorted in such a way that two opposite faces become parallelograms, while the other two opposite do not change their shape.

See also: STRESS.

strategic defense In general, defense against long-range nuclear weapons.

Stratospheric Observatory for Infrared Astronomy (SOFIA) A planned advanced airborne observatory, utilizing a Boeing 747 aircraft, that will provide astronomers routine access to the infrared and submillimeter portions of the electromagnetic spectrum. SOFIA will be an international facility operated by NASA (and based out of the Ames Research Center California) in cooperation with the German Space Agency (DARA). DARA will provide the telescope and NASA will provide the rest of the facilities, including the 747 aircraft. The airborne observatory will begin flight operations by the year 2001.

stress In engineering, a force per unit area on an object that causes it to deform (i.e., experience strain). Stress can be viewed as either the system of external forces applied to deform an object or the system of internal "opposite" forces (a function of the material composition of the object) by which the object resists this deformation. The three basic types of stress are: compressive (or tensile) stress, hydrostatic pressure, and shear stress.

See also: STRAIN.

stretchout An action whereby the time for completing an aerospace activity, especially a contract, is extended beyond the time originally programmed or contracted for. Cost overruns, unanticipated technical delays, and budget cuts are frequent reasons why a stretchout is needed.

stringer A slender, lightweight, lengthwise fill-in structural member in a rocket body. A stringer reinforces and gives shape to the rocket vehicle's skin.

structured attack An attack in which the arrival of (nuclear) warheads on their diverse targets is precisely timed for maximum strategic impact.

See also: BALLISTIC MISSILE DEFENSE.

subassembly A portion of an assembly, consisting of two or more parts, that can be provisioned and replaced as an entity.

subcooled liquid In thermodynamics, a liquid whose temperature is lower than the saturation temperature for the existing pressure.

sublimation In thermodynamics, the direct transition of a material from the solid phase to the vapor phase, and vice versa, without passing through the liquid phase.

subliming ablator An ablative cooling material characterized by sublimation of the thermal protection material at the aerodynamically heated surface.

submarine-launched ballistic missile (SLBM) An intercontinental ballistic missile, usually solid propellant with a nuclear warhead payload, that is launched by a submarine at strategic targets.

See also: POLARIS; TRIDENT MISSILE.

submarine rocket (Subroc) Submerged, submarine-launched, surface-to-surface rocket with nuclear depth charge or homing torpedo payload, primarily used in antisubmarine applications. Also designated by the U.S. Navy as UUM-44A.

subsatellite point Intersection with Earth's (or planet's) surface of the local vertical passing through an orbiting satellite.

subsonic Of or pertaining to speeds less than the speed of sound.

See also: SPEED OF SOUND.

Sun The Sun is our parent star and the massive, luminous celestial object about which all other bodies in the solar system revolve. It provides the light and warmth upon which almost all terrestrial life depends. Its gravitational field determines the movement of the planets and other celestial bodies (e.g., comets). The Sun is a main sequence star of spectral type G-2. Like all main sequence stars, the Sun derives its abundant energy output from thermonuclear fusion reactions involving the conversion of hydrogen to helium and heavier nuclei. Photons associated with these exothermic (energy-releasing) fusion reactions diffuse outward from the Sun's core, until they reach the convective

envelope. Another by-product of the thermonuclear fusion reactions is a flux of neutrinos that freely escape from the Sun.

At the center of the Sun is the core, where energy is released in thermonuclear reactions. Surrounding the core are concentric shells called the radiative zone, the convective envelope (which occurs at approximately 0.8 of the Sun's radius), the photosphere (the layer from which visible radiation emerges), the chromosphere, and, finally, the corona (the Sun's outer atmosphere). Energy is transported outward through the convective envelope by convective (mixing) motions that are organized into cells. The Sun's lower or inner atmosphere, the photosphere, is the region from which energy is radiated directly into space. Solar radiation approximates a Planck distribution (BLACK-BODY source) with an effective temperature of 5,800° Kelvin (K). The table provides a summary of the physical properties of the Sun.

The chromosphere, which extends for a few thousand kilometers above the photosphere, has a maximum temperature of approximately 10,000° K. The corona, which extends several solar radii above the chromosphere, has temperatures of over 1 million° K. These regions emit electromagnetic (EM) radiation in the ultraviolet (UV), extreme ultraviolet (EUV), and X-ray portions of the spectrum. This shorter-wavelength EM radiation, although representing a relatively small portion of the Sun's total energy output, still plays a dominant role in forming planetary ionospheres and in photochemistry reactions occurring in planetary atmospheres.

Since the Sun's outer atmosphere is heated, it expands into the surrounding interplanetary medium. This continuous outflow of plasma is called the *solar wind*. It consists of protons, electrons, and alpha particles as well as small quantities of heavier ions. Typical particle velocities in the solar wind fall between 300 and 400 kilometers per second, but these velocities may get as high as 1,000 kilometers per second.

Although the total energy output of the Sun is remarkably steady, its surface displays many types of irregularities. These include sunspots, faculae, plages (bright areas), filaments, prominences, and flares. (See Figure 127.) All are believed ultimately to be the result of interactions between ionized gases in the solar atmosphere and the Sun's magnetic field. Most solar activity follows the *sunspot cycle*. The number of sunspots varies, with a period

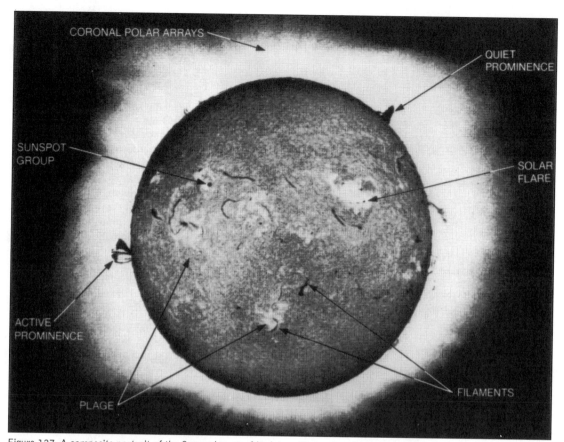

Figure 127. A composite portrait of the Sun and some of its interesting surface features   *(Lockheed-Martin—B&W Photo # 84-22/1)*

of about 11 years. However, this approximately 11-year sunspot cycle is only one aspect of a more general 22-year *solar cycle* that corresponds to a reversal of the polarity patterns of the Sun's magnetic field.

Sunspots were originally observed by Galileo in 1610. They are less bright than the adjacent portions of the Sun's surface, because they are not as hot. A typical sunspot temperature might be 4,500° K compared to the photosphere's temperature of 5,800° K. Sunspots appear to be made up of gases boiling up from the Sun's interior. A small sunspot may be about the size of Earth, while larger ones could hold several hundred or even thousands of Earth-size planets. Extra-bright solar regions, called *plages,* often overlie sunspots. The number and size of sunspots appear to rise and fall through a fundamental 11-year cycle (or in an overall 22-year cycle, if polarity reversals in the Sun's magnetic field are considered). The greatest num-

ber occur in years when the Sun's magnetic field is the most severely twisted (called sunspot maximum). Solar physicists think that sunspot migration causes the Sun's magnetic field to reverse its direction. It then takes another 22 years for the Sun's magnetic field to return to its original configuration.

A *solar flare* is the sudden release of tremendous energy and material from the Sun. A flare may last minutes or hours, and it usually occurs in complex magnetic regions near sunspots. Exactly how or why enormous amounts of energy are liberated in solar flares is still unknown, but scientists think the process is associated with electrical currents generated by changing magnetic fields. The maximum number of solar flares appears to accompany the increased activity of the sunspot cycle. As a flare erupts, it discharges a large quantity of material outward from the Sun. This violent eruption also sends SHOCK WAVES through the SOLAR WIND.

PHYSICAL AND DYNAMIC PROPERTIES OF THE SUN	
Diameter	1.39×10^6 km
Mass	1.99×10^{30} kg
Distance from the Earth (average)	1.496×10^8 km [1 AU] (8.3 light-min)
Luminosity	3.9×10^{26} watts
Density (average)	1.41 g/cm^3
Equivalent blackbody temperature	$5,800°$ Kelvin
Central temperature (approx.)	$15,000,000°$ Kelvin
Rotation period (varies with latitude zones)	27 days (approx.)
Radiant energy output per unit surface area	6.4×10^7 W/m^2
Solar cycle (total cycle of polarity reversals of Sun's magnetic field)	22 years
Sunspot cycle	11 years (approx.)
Solar constant (at 1 AU)	1371 ± 5 W/m^2
Source: NASA.	

Data from space-based solar observatories have indicated that *prominences* (condensed streams of ionized hydrogen atoms) appear to spring from sunspots. Their looping shape suggests that these prominences are controlled by strong magnetic fields. About 100 times as dense as the solar corona, prominences can rise at speeds of hundreds of kilometers per second. Sometimes the upper end of a prominence curves back to the Sun's surface, forming a "bridge" of hot glowing gas hundreds of thousands of kilometers long. On other occasions, the material in the prominence jets out and becomes part of the solar wind.

High-energy particles are released into heliocentric space by solar events, including very large solar flares called anomalously large solar particle events (ALSPEs). Because of their close association with infrequent large flares, these bursts of energetic particles are also relatively infrequent. However, solar flares, especially ALSPEs, represent a potential hazard to astronauts traveling in interplanetary space or working on the surface of the Moon and Mars.

See also: FUSION; SPACE RADIATION ENVIRONMENT; STARS; ULYSSES MISSION.

sunlike stars Yellow, main sequence stars with; surface temperatures of 5,000° to 6,000° Kelvin; spectral type G stars.

See also: STARS; SUN.

sunspot A relatively dark, sharply defined region on the Sun's surface, marked by an umbra (darkest region) that is approximately 2,000° Kelvin (K) cooler than the effective photospheric temperature of the Sun (i.e., 5,800° K). The umbra is surrounded by a less dark, but sharply bounded region, called the penumbra. The average sunspot diameter is about 3,700 kilometers (km), but this diameter can range up to 245,000 km. Most sunspots are found in groups of two or more, but they can occur singly.

See also: SUN.

sun-synchronous orbit A space-based sensor's view of Earth will depend on the characteristics of its orbit and the sensor's field of view (FOV). A sun-synchronous orbit is a special polar orbit that enables a spacecraft's sensor to maintain a fixed relation to the Sun. This feature is particularly important for environmental satellites (i.e., weather satellites) and multispectral imagery remote sensing satellites (such as the Landsat family of spacecraft). Each day a spacecraft in a sun-synchronous orbit around Earth passes over a certain area on the planet's surface at the same local time. One way to characterize sun-synchronous orbits is by the time the spacecraft cross the equator. These equator crossings (called *nodes*) occur at the same local time each day, with the descending (north-to-south) crossings occurring 12 hours (local time) from the ascending (south-to-north) crossings. In aerospace operations, the terms "A.M. polar orbiter" and "P.M. polar orbiter" are used to describe sun-synchronous satellites with morning and afternoon equator crossings, respectively.

An A.M. polar orbiter permits viewing of the land surface with adequate illumination, but before solar heating and the daily cloud buildup occur. Such a "morning platform" also provides an illumination angle that highlights geological features. The P.M. polar orbiter provides an opportunity to study the role of developed clouds in Earth's weather and climate and provides a view of the land surface after it has experienced a good deal of solar heating.

A typical morning meteorological platform might orbit at an altitude of 810 kilometers (km) (500 miles [mi]) at an inclination of 98.86 degrees and would have a period of 101 minutes. This morning platform would have its equatorial crossing time at approximately 0730 (local time). Similarly, an early-afternoon P.M. polar orbiter might orbit the Earth at an altitude of 850 km (530 mi) at an inclination of 98.70 degrees and would have a period of 102 minutes. This early-afternoon platform would cross the equator at approximately 1330 (local time). Each satellite (i.e., the morning and afternoon platform) views the same portion of Earth twice each day, therefore, the pair would provide environmental data collections with approximately six-hour gaps between each collection. In the United States, the afternoon platform is usually considered the primary meteorological mission, while the morning platform is considered to provide supplementary and backup coverage.

See also: ORBITS OF OBJECTS IN SPACE; WEATHER SATELLITE.

superheating In thermodynamics, the heating of a vapor, particularly saturated (wet) steam, to a temperature much higher than the boiling point at the existing pressure. This is done in power plants to improve efficiency and to reduce condensation in the turbines.

See also: HEAT ENGINE; RANKINE CYCLE; THERMODYNAMICS.

superior planets Planets that have orbits around the Sun that lie outside Earth's orbit. These planets include Mars, Jupiter, Saturn, Uranus, Neptune, and Pluto.

superluminal With a speed greater than the speed of light, 3×10^8 meters per second (m/s).

supernova A catastrophic stellar explosion occurring near the end of a star's life in which the star collapses and explodes, manufacturing (by nuclear transmutation) the heavy elements that it spews out into space. During a supernova explosion, the brightness of a star increases by a factor of several million times in a matter of days.

See also: STARS.

supersonic Of or pertaining to speed in excess of the speed of sound.

See also: SPEED OF SOUND.

supersonic compressor A compressor in which a supersonic velocity is imparted to the fluid relative to the rotor blades, the stator blades, or both the rotor and the stator blades, producing oblique shock waves over the blades to obtain a high-pressure rise.

supersonic diffuser A diffuser designed to reduce the velocity and increase the pressure of fluid moving at supersonic velocities.

supersonic flow In aerodynamics, flow of a fluid over a body at speeds greater than the speed of sound (i.e., greater than the acoustic velocity) and in which the shock waves start at the surface of the body.

See also: SPEED OF SOUND.

supersonic nozzle A converging-diverging nozzle designed to accelerate a fluid to supersonic speed.

See also: NOZZLE.

surface penetrator spacecraft A spacecraft probe designed to enter the surface of a celestial body, such as a comet or asteroid. The penetrator is capable of surviving a high-velocity impact and then making in-situ measurements of the penetrated surface. Data are sent back to a mothership for retransmission to scientists on Earth.

See also: PENETRATOR.

surface rover spacecraft An electrically powered robot vehicle designed to explore a planetary surface. Depending on the size of the rover and its level of sophistication, this type of mobile craft is capable of semiautonomous to fully autonomous operation. The rover could perform wide a variety of exploratory functions, including the acquisition of multispectral imagery, soil sampling and analysis, and rock inspection and collection. Data are transmitted back to Earth either directly by the rover vehicle or via a lander spacecraft or orbiting mothership.

See also: LUNAR ROVER(S); MARS PATHFINDER; MARS SURFACE ROVER(S).

surface tension The tendency of a liquid that has a large cohesive force to keep its surface as small as possible, forming spherical drops. Surface tension arises from intermolecular forces and is manifested in such phenomena as the absorption of liquids by porous surfaces, the rise of water (and other fluids) in a capillary tube, and the ability of liquids to "wet" a surface.

See also: HEAT PIPE.

surveillance In general, the systematic observation of places, persons, or things usually accomplished by optical, infrared, radar, or radiometric sensors. These sensors can be placed on a satellite to observe Earth or other regions of space (called *space-based surveillance*); installed on a aircraft platform (called *aerial surveillance*) to observe outer space (i.e., airborne astronomy), the surrounding atmosphere, or Earth's surface; or else situated on fixed or mobile terrestrial platforms to monitor the atmosphere and/or outer space (called *ground-based surveillance*). Surveillance includes tactical observations, strategic warning, and meteorological and environmental assessments.

See also: DEFENSE SUPPORT PROGRAM.

Surveyor Project NASA's highly successful Surveyor Project began in 1960. It consisted of seven unmanned lander spacecraft that were launched between May 1966 and January 1968, as a precursor to the human expeditions to the lunar surface in the Apollo Project. These robot lander craft were used to develop soft-landing techniques, to survey potential Apollo mission landing sites, and to improve scientific understanding of the Moon.

The *Surveyor 1* spacecraft was launched on May 30, 1966 and soft-landed in the Ocean of Storms region of the Moon. It found the bearing strength of the lunar soil was more than adequate to support the Apollo lander spacecraft (called the lunar excursion module, or LEM). This contradicted the then-prevalent hypothesis that the Apollo LEM might sink out of sight in the fine lunar dust. The *Surveyor 1* spacecraft also telecast many pictures from the lunar surface.

The *Surveyor 3* spacecraft was launched on April 17, 1967 and soft-landed on the side of a small crater in another region of the Ocean of Storms. This robot spacecraft used a shovel attached to a mechanical "arm" to dig a trench and discovered that the load-bearing strength of the lunar soil increased with depth. It also transmitted many pictures from the lunar surface.

The *Surveyor 5* spacecraft was launched on September 8, 1967 and soft-landed in the Sea of Tranquility. An alpha-scattering device onboard this craft examined the chemical composition of the lunar soil and revealed a similarity to basalt on Earth.

The *Surveyor 6* was launched on November 7, 1967 and soft-landed in the Sinus Medii (Central Bay) region of the Moon. In addition to performing soil analysis experiments and taking many images of the lunar surface, this spacecraft also performed an extremely critical "hop experiment." NASA engineers back on Earth remotely fired the surveyor's vernier rockets to launch it briefly above the lunar surface. The spacecraft's launch did not create a dust cloud and resulted only in shallow cratering. This important demonstration indicated that the Apollo astronauts could safely lift off from the lunar surface with their rocket-propelled craft (upper portion of the LEM) when their surface exploration mission was completed.

Finally, the *Surveyor 7* spacecraft was launched on January 7, 1968 and landed in a highland area of the Moon, near the Crater Tycho. Its alpha-scattering device showed that the lunar highlands contained less iron than the soil found in the mare regions (lunar plains). Numerous images of the lunar surface also were returned.

Despite the fact that the *Surveyor 2* and *4* spacecraft crashed on the Moon (rather than soft-landed and functioned), the overall Surveyor Project was extremely successful and paved the way for the Apollo surface expeditions that occurred between 1969 and 1972.

See also: APOLLO PROJECT; LANDER (SPACECRAFT); MOON.

survivability The capability of a system to avoid or withstand hostile environments without suffering irreversible impairment of its ability to accomplish its designated mission.

sustainer engine A rocket engine that maintains the velocity of a rocket vehicle once the vehicle has achieved its intended (programmed) velocity by means of a more powerful booster engine or engines (which is/are usually jettisoned). A sustainer engine also is used to provide the small amount of thrust needed to maintain the speed of a spacecraft or orbital glider that dipped into the atmosphere at perigee.

synchronous orbit An orbit over the equator in which the orbital speed of a spacecraft or satellite matches exactly the rotation of Earth on its axis, so that the spacecraft or satellite appears to stay over the same location on Earth's surface.

See also: GEOSYNCHRONOUS ORBIT.

synchronous rotation In astronomy, the rotation of a natural satellite (moon) about its primary in which the orbital period is equal to period of rotation of the satellite about its own axis. As a consequence of this condition, the satellite (moon) always presents the same side (face) to the parent body. The Moon, for example, is in synchronous rotation around Earth. (However, LIBRATION allows slightly more than one hemisphere to be seen from Earth.) Sometimes called *captured rotation.*

synchronous satellite An equatorial west-to-east satellite orbiting Earth at an altitude of approximately 35,900 kilometers (22,300 miles); at this altitude the satellite makes one revolution in 24 hours, synchronous with Earth's rotation.

See also: GEOSYNCHRONOUS ORBIT; GEOSTATIONARY EARTH ORBIT.

synchrotron radiation Electromagnetic radiation (light, ultraviolet, or X ray) produced by very energetic electrons as they spiral around lines of force in a magnetic field.

Syncom A family of NASA spacecraft launched in the 1960s to demonstrate the technologies needed to operate commercial communications satellites in geostationary Earth orbit. *Syncom 1* was launched in February 1963. After a successful launch and injection into a highly elliptical orbit, contact was lost with the spacecraft during the firing of its built-in orbit circularization rocket. *Syncom 2* was launched in July 1963 and provided important operational experience for communications satellites operating at synchronous orbit. *Syncom 3* was launched in August 1964 and successfully provided live coverage of the 1964 Olympic games from Japan.

See also: COMMUNICATIONS SATELLITE.

synoptic Pertaining to or affording an overall view.

synthetic aperture radar (SAR) A radar system that correlates the echoes of signals emitted at different points along a satellite's orbit or an aircraft's flight path. For example, a SAR system on a spacecraft illuminates its target to the side of its direction of movement and travels a known distance in orbit while the reflected, phase shift-coded pulses are returned and collected. With extensive computer processing, this procedure provides the basis for synthesizing an antenna (aperture) on the order of kilometers in size. The highest resolution achievable by such a system is theoretically equivalent to that of a single large antenna as wide as the distance between the most widely spaced points along the orbit that are used for transmitting positions.

See also: MAGELLAN MISSION; RADAR IMAGING; RADARSAT.

system integration The process of uniting the parts (components) of a spacecraft, launch vehicle, or space platform into a complete and functioning system.

tail 1. The tail surfaces of an aircraft, aerospace vehicle, missile, or rocket. 2. The rear portion of a body, as of an aerospace vehicle or rocket. 3. Short for the tail of a comet.

tailoring Modification of a basic solid rocket propellant by adjustment of the propellant properties to meet the requirements of a specific rocket motor.

takeoff 1. The ascent of a rocket vehicle as it departs from the launch pad at any angle. 2. The action of an aircraft as it becomes airborne. Compare this term to LIFTOFF, which refers only to the vertical ascent of a rocket or missile from its launch pad.

tandem launch The launching of two or more spacecraft or satellites using a single launch vehicle.

tank 1. A container incorporated into the structure of a liquid-propellant rocket from which a liquid propellant or propellants are fed into the combustion chamber(s). 2. A container incorporated into the structure of a nuclear rocket from which a monopropellant, such as liquid hydrogen, is fed into the nuclear reactor. 3. A ground-based or space-based container for the storage of liquid hydrogen, liquid oxygen, or other liquid propellants until they are transferred to a rocket's tanks or some other receptacle.

tankage The aggregate of the tanks carried by a liquid-propellant rocket or a nuclear rocket.

tank components 1. Devices for controlling the behavior of propellants, including positioning devices, slosh and vortex suspension devices, baffles, standpipes, and explusion devices. 2 Tank insulation.

tap A unit of impulse intensity, defined as one dyne-second per square centimeter. 1 tap = 0.1 Pascal-second.

taper ratio 1. The ratio of maximum coolant-tube diameter to minimum tube diameter; usually kept below four in modern rocket engine design 2. The ratio of the tip chord length of an airfoil to the root chord length.

target 1. Any object, destination, point, and so on, toward which something is directed. 2. An object that reflects a sufficient amount of radiated signal to produce a return, or echo, signal on detection equipment. 3. The cooperative (usually passive) or noncooperative partner in a space rendezvous operation. 4. In military operations, a geographic area, complex, or installation planned for capture or destruction by military forces. 5. In intelligence usage, a country area, installation, or person against which intelligence operations are directed. 6. In radar, (1) generally, any discrete object that reflects or retransmits energy back to the radar equipment; (2) specifically, an object of radar search or surveillance. 7. In nuclear physics, a material subjected to particle bombardment (as in an accelerator) or neutron irradiation (as in a nuclear reactor) in order to induce a nuclear reaction.

target acquisition The detection, identification, and location of a target in sufficient detail to permit the effective employment of weapons.

target spacecraft The nonmaneuvering spacecraft in rendezvous and proximity operations.

Taurus® A family of new, commercially developed launch vehicles aimed at the small to medium-size payload market. For example, the initial Taurus expendable launch vehicle was designed to place up to 1,360 kilograms (3,000 pounds-mass) into LOW EARTH ORBIT (LEO). The Orbital Sciences Corporation's Taurus® launch vehicle had its maiden flight on March 13, 1994.

telecommunications 1. In general, any transmission, emission, or reception of signs, signals, writings, images, sounds, or information of any nature by wire, radio, visual, or other electromagnetic or electro-optical systems. 2. In aerospace, the flow of data and information (usually by radio signals) between a spacecraft and an Earth-based communications system. A spacecraft has only a limited amount of power available to transmit a signal that sometimes must travel across millions or even billions of kilometers of space before reaching Earth. For example, an interplanetary spacecraft might have a transmitter that has no more than 20 watts of radiating power. One aerospace engineering approach is to concentrate all available power into a narrow radio beam and then to send this narrow beam in just one direction, instead of broadcasting the radio signal in all directions. Often this is accomplished by using a parabolic dish antenna on the order of 1 to 5 meters in diameter. However, even when these concentrated radio signals reach Earth, they are have very small power levels. The other portion of the telecommunications solution is to use special, large-diameter radio receivers on Earth, such as found in NASA's *Deep Space Network.* These sophisticated radio antennas are capable of detecting the very-low-power signals from distant spacecraft.

In telecommunications, the radio signal transmitted to a spacecraft is called the *uplink.* The transmission from the spacecraft to Earth is called the *downlink.* Uplink or downlink communications may consist of a pure radio-frequency (RF) tone (called a carrier), or these carriers may be modified to carry information in each direction. Commands transmitted to a spacecraft sometimes are referred to as an *upload.* Communications with a spacecraft involving only a downlink are called *one-way communications.* When an uplink signal is being received by the spacecraft at the same time that a downlink signal is being received on Earth, the telecommunications mode is often referred to as *two-way.*

Spacecraft carrier signals usually are modulated by shifting each waveform's phase slightly at a given rate. One scheme is to modulate the carrier with a frequency, for example, near 1 megahertz (1 MHz). This 1 MHz modulation is then called a *subcarrier.* The subcarrier is modulated to carry individual phase shifts that are designated to represent binary ones (1s) and zeros (0s)—the spacecraft's telemetry data. The amount of phase shift used in modulating data onto the subcarrier is referred to as the *modulation index* and is measured in degrees. This same type of communications scheme is also on the uplink. Binary digital data modulated onto the uplink are called *command data.* They are received by the spacecraft and either acted upon immediately or stored for future use or execution. Data modulated onto the downlink are called *telemetry* and include science data from the spacecraft's instruments and spacecraft state-of-health data from sensors within the various onboard subsystems (e.g., power, propulsion, thermal control, etc).

Demodulation is the process of detecting the subcarrier and processing it separately from the carrier, detecting the individual binary phase shifts, and registering them as digital data for further processing. The device used for this is called a *modem,* which is short for *mo*dulator/*dem*odulator. These same processes of modulation and demodulation are commonly used with Earth-based computer systems and facsimile (fax) machines to transmit data back and forth over a telephone line. For example, if you have used a personal computer to "chat" over the Internet, your modem used a familiar audio frequency carrier that the telephone system could handle.

The dish-shaped, *high-gain antenna* (HGA) is the type of spacecraft antenna mainly used for communications with Earth. The amount of *gain* achieved by an antenna refers to the amount of incoming radio signal power it can collect and focus into the spacecraft's receiving subsystems. In the frequency ranges used by spacecraft, the high-gain antenna incorporates a large parabolic reflector. Such an antenna may be fixed to the spacecraft bus or steerable. The larger the collecting area of the high-gain antenna, the higher the gain, and the higher the data rate it will support. However, the higher the gain, the more highly directional the antenna becomes. Therefore, when a spacecraft uses a high-gain antenna, the antenna must be pointed within a fraction of a degree of Earth for communications to occur. Once this accurate antenna-pointing is achieved, communications can take place at a high rate over the highly focused radio signal.

The low-gain antenna (LGA) provides wide-angle coverage at the expense of gain. Coverage is nearly omnidirectional, except for areas that may be shadowed by the spacecraft structure. The low-gain antenna is designed for relatively low data rates. It is useful as long as the spacecraft is relatively close to Earth (e.g., within a few astronomical units). Sometimes a spacecraft is given two low-gain antennas to provide full omnidirectional coverage, since the second LGA will avoid the spacecraft structure "blind spots" experienced by the first LGA. The low-gain antenna can be mounted on top of the high-gain antenna's subreflector.

The medium-gain antenna (MGA) represents a compromise in spacecraft engineering. It provides more gain than the low-gain antenna and has wider angle antenna-pointing accuracy requirements (typically 20 to 30 degrees) than the high-gain antenna.

See also: DEEP SPACE NETWORK.

telemetry 1. The process of making measurements at one point and transmitting the data to a distant location for evaluation and use. 2. Data modulated onto a spacecraft's communications downlink, including science data from the spacecraft's instruments and subsystem state-of-health data.

See also: TELECOMMUNICATIONS.

teleoperation The process by which a human worker (usually in a safe and comfortable environment) operates a versatile robot system that is at a distant, often hazardous location. Communications can be accomplished with radio signals, laser beams, or even "cable" (if the distance is not too great and the deployed cable does not interfere with operations or safety). For example, an astronaut onboard the space shuttle (or space station) might "teleoperate" at a safe distance (using radio signals) a free-flying space robot retrieval system. In one space operations scenario, the teleoperated space robot rendezvouses with a damaged, potentially dangerous spacecraft. After initial rendezvous, the human operator uses instruments on the robot system to inspect the target space object. Then, if it appears that repairs can be performed

safely, the human worker uses the space robot to capture it and bring it closer to the shuttle (or space station). Otherwise, again through teleoperations, the human operator uses the retrieval robot system to move the derelict spacecraft to a designated parking (storage) orbit or else put the hunk of "space junk" on a reentry trajectory that will cause it to plunge into Earth's upper atmosphere and burn up harmlessly.

See also: ROBOTICS.

telepresence The use of telecommunications, interactive displays, and a collection of sensor systems on a robot (which is at some distant location) to provide the human operator a sense of being present where the robot system actually is located. Depending on the level of sophistication in the operator's workplace as well as on the robot system, this telepresence experience can vary from a simple "steroscopic" view of the scene to a complete virtual reality activity in which sight, sound, touch, and motion are provided. Telepresence actually combines the technologies of virtual reality with robotics. Some day in the not too distant future, human controllers (on Earth), wearing sensor-laden bodysuits and three-dimensional viewer helmets, will use telepresence actually to "walk" and "work" on the Moon and other planetary bodies through their robot surrogates. Also called *virtual residency*.

See also: ROBOTICS; TELEOPERATION; VIRTUAL REALITY.

telescience A mode of scientific activity in which a distributed set of users (investigators) can interact directly with their instruments, whether in space or ground facilities, with databases, data handling and processing facilities, and with each other.

telescope In general, a device that collects electromagnetic radiation from a distant object so as to form an image of the object or to permit the radiation to be analyzed. Optical (or astronomical) telescopes can be divided into two main classes: *refracting telescopes* and *reflecting telescopes*. The oldest optical telescope is the refracting telescope, first constructed in Holland in 1608 and then developed for astronomical use by Galileo (1564–1642) in 1609. In its simplest form, the refracting telescope (or *refractor*) uses a converging lens (often called the primary lens) to gather and focus incoming light onto an eyepiece, which then magnifies the image. Galileo used a diverging lens in the eyepiece of his *Galilean telescope,* while Johannes Kepler (1571–1630) created an improved telescope in about 1611 by replacing the concave (negative) lens in the eyepiece with a convex (positive) lens. In the reflecting telescope, invented by Sir Isaac Newton (1642–1727) around 1668, a primary concave mirror located at the bottom of the telescope tube is used to collect and focus incoming light back up to a small secondary mirror, usually at a 45-degree angle to the incident light beams. This secondary mirror then reflects the incident light into an eyepiece (mounted on the side of the telescope tube) which magnifies the image. A variety of optical telescopes, consisting of various combinations of mirrors and lenses, have since been developed, including the Cassegrain and Schmidt telescopes. An optical telescope often is described in terms of its resolving power, aperture, and light-gathering power. In addition to optical telescopes, Earth-based observatories use radio telescopes and (in limited locations such as high mountaintops) infrared telescopes. However, space-based observatories (unhampered by the attenuation of Earth's atmosphere) also include infrared telescopes, gamma ray telescopes, X-ray telescopes, and ultraviolet telescopes.

See also: COMPTON OBSERVATORY; HUBBLE SPACE TELESCOPE; INFRARED ASTRONOMICAL SATELLITE (IRAS).

Television and Infrared Observation Satellite (TIROS) The TIROS series of weather satellites carried special television cameras that viewed Earth's cloud cover from a 725-kilometer (450-mile) altitude orbit. The images telemetered back to Earth provided meteorologists with a new tool—a nephanalysis, or cloud chart. On April 1, 1960 *TIROS 1,* the first true weather satellite, was launched into a near-equatorial orbit. By 1965 nine more TIROS satellites were launched. These spacecraft had progressively longer operational times and carried infrared radiometers to study Earth's heat distribution. Several were placed in polar orbits to increase cloud picture coverage. *TIROS 8* had the first Automatic Picture Transmission (APT) equipment. *TIROS 9* and *10* were test satellites of improved spacecraft configurations for the Tiros Operational Satellite (TOS) system. Operational use of the TOS satellites began in 1966. They were placed in Sun-synchronous (polar) orbits, so they could pass over the same location on Earth's surface at exactly the same time each day. This orbit enabled meteorologists to view local cloud changes

on a 24-hour basis. Several Improved TOS Satellites (ITOS) were launched in the 1970s. The ITOS spacecraft served as workhorses for meteorologists of the National Oceanographic and Atmospheric Administration (NOAA), which was responsible for their operation.

See also: WEATHER SATELLITE.

temperature (symbol: T) A thermodynamic property that determines the direction of heat (thermal energy) flow. From the laws of thermodynamics, when two objects or systems are brought together, heat naturally will flow from regions of higher temperature to regions of lower temperature. In statistical mechanics, temperature can be considered as a "macroscopic" measurement of the overall kinetic energy of the individual atoms and molecules of a substance or body.

See also: ABSOLUTE TEMPERATURE; ABSOLUTE TEMPERATURE SCALE.

tera- (symbol: T) A prefix in the INTERNATIONAL SYSTEM OF UNITS meaning multiplied by 10^{12}.

terminal 1. A point at which any element in a circuit may be connected directly to one or more other elements. 2. Pertaining to a final condition or the last division of something, as *terminal guidance* or *terminal ballistics.* 3. In computer operations, an input/output (I/O) device (or station) usually consisting of a video screen or printer for output and a keyboard for input.

terminal guidance 1. The guidance applied to a missile between midcourse guidance and its arrival in the vicinity of the target. 2. With respect to an interplanetary spacecraft, the guidance and navigation performed during its approach to the target planet, which is accomplished by observing the angular position and motion and possibly the apparent size of the target body.

See also: GUIDANCE SYSTEM.

terminal phase The final phase of a ballistic missile trajectory, lasting about a minute or less, during which warheads reenter the atmosphere and detonate at their targets.

See also: BALLISTIC MISSILE DEFENSE.

terminator The boundary line separating the illuminated (i.e., sunlit) and dark portions of a nonluminous celestial body, like the Moon.

Terra A Latin word meaning "Earth."

terrae The highland regions of the Moon. Typically, the terrae are heavily cratered with large, old-appearing craters on a rugged surface with high albedo.
See also: LATIN SPACE DESIGNATIONS; MOON.

terraforming The proposed large-scale modification or manipulation of the environment of a planet, such as Mars or Venus, to make it more suitable for human habitation. Also called *planetary engineering*.

terran Of or relating to the planet Earth; a native of the planet Earth.
See also: TERRESTRIAL.

terrestrial Of or relating to the planet Earth.

terrestrial environment Earth's land area, including its human-made and natural surface and subsurface features, and its interfaces and interactions with the atmosphere and the oceans.
See also: EARTH.

terrestrial planets In addition to Earth itself, the terrestrial (or inner) planets include Mercury, Venus, and Mars. These planets are similar in their general properties and characteristics to the Earth; that is, they are small, relatively high-density bodies, composed of metals and silicates with shallow (or no) atmospheres as compared to the gaseous outer planets.
See also: EARTH; MARS; MERCURY; VENUS.

terrestrial reference guidance The technique of providing information to a missile from certain characteristics of the surface over which the missile is flown, thereby achieving flight along a predetermined path.
See also: GUIDANCE SYSTEM.

Terrier (RIM-2) A U.S. Navy surface-to-air missile with solid-fuel rocket motor. It is equipped with radar beam rider or homing guidance and a nuclear or nonnuclear warhead.

Terrier land weapon system A surface-to-air missile system, using the Terrier RIM-2B and Terrier RIM-2C missile with ground-launching and guidance equipment, developed specifically for operations. This equipment is a lighter and land-mobile version of the U.S. Navy Terrier system.

tesla (symbol: T) The SI UNIT of magnetic flux density. It is defined as one weber of magnetic flux per square meter. The unit is named in honor of Nikola Tesla (1870–1943), a Croatian-American electrical engineer and inventor.

$$1 \text{ tesla} = 1 \text{ weber}/ (\text{meter})^2 = 10^4 \text{ gauss}$$

test 1. A procedure taken to determine under simulated or real conditions the capabilities, limitations, characteristics, effectiveness, reliability, or suitability of a material, device, system, or method. 2. Similarly, the procedure taken to determine the reactions, limitations, abilities, or skills of a person or crew.

test bed 1. A base, mount, or frame within or upon which a piece of equipment, such as an engine or sensor system, is secured for testing. 2. A flying test bed.

test chamber A place or room that has special characteristics where a person or device is subjected to experiment, such as an altitude chamber, wind tunnel, or acoustic chamber.

test firing The firing of a rocket engine, either live or static, with the purpose of making controlled observations of the engine or of an engine component.

test flight A flight to make controlled observations of the operation or performance of an aircraft, aerospace vehicle, rocket, or missile.

Tethered Satellite System (TSS) The Tethered Satellite System (TSS) uses an orbiting space shuttle to deploy a special "satellite" payload at the end of a long cable or tether. In a successful mission, the reusable instrument package would be reeled out from the shuttle's cargo bay on a tether up to a length of about 20 kilometers (12.4 miles). When the mission is completed, the instrumented tethered satellite would be reeled back into the shuttle's cargo bay for refurbishment and use on subsequent missions. The tethered satellite system has been jointly sponsored by NASA and the Italian Space Agency.

During space shuttle *Columbia* mission STS-76 in February 1996, the thin tether for the Tethered Satellite System (called TSS-1R) broke when the tether was almost fully extended to a length of over 19.3 kilometers (12 miles), snapping the satellite off into an orbit increasingly distant from the shuttle. Before the conducting tether snapped, the TSS was, as anticipated, already generating a powerful electrical current as it cut through Earth's magnetic field. This loss of the TSS was the second failed attempt to tow a satellite through space on a tether. An earlier attempt in 1992 (called TSS-1) failed when the tether became caught on a safety bolt in the reel after extending to a length of only about 244 meters (800 feet).

In addition to representing an innovative way of generating electric power on orbit, tethers have been suggested as a way of raising or lowering a spacecraft's altitude without using fuel and also as a way to lower science instruments into regions of Earth's upper atmosphere.

theater defense Defense against nuclear weapons on a regional level (e.g., Europe, Japan, Israel) rather than at the strategic level (i.e., globally or the United States and Russia).

thermal 1. Of or pertaining to heat or temperature. 2. A vertical air current caused by differential heating of the terrain.

thermal conductivity (symbol: k) An intrinsic physical property of a substance, describing its ability to conduct heat (thermal energy) as a consequence molecular motion. Typical units for thermal conductivity are joules/(second-meter-kelvin).

thermal control Regulation of the temperature of a space vehicle is a complex problem because extreme temperatures are encountered during a typical space mission. In the vacuum environment of outer space, radiative heat transfer is the only natural means to transfer thermal energy (heat) into and out of a space vehicle. In some special cir-

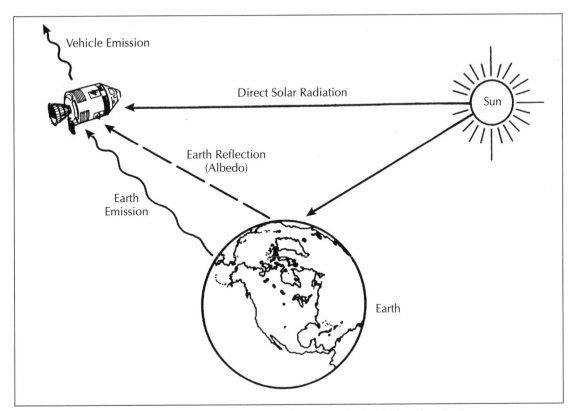

Figure 128. The overall energy balance for a space vehicle traveling near a planetary body, such as Earth   *(Drawing courtesy of NASA)*

cumstances, a gaseous or liquid working fluid could be "dumped" from the space vehicle, to provide a temporary solution to a transient heat load —but this is extreme exception rather than the general design approach. Figure 128 depicts the thermal energy balance for a space vehicle near a planetary body, such as Earth. This overall energy balance is determined by several factors: (1) thermal energy sources within the space vehicle itself; (2) direct solar radiation (the Sun has a characteristic BLACKBODY temperature of about 5770° Kelvin ([K]); (3) direct thermal (infrared) radiation from the planet (e.g., Earth has an average surface temperature of about 288° K); (4) indirect (reflected) solar radiation from the planetary body (e.g., Earth reflection); and (5) vehicle emission, that is, radiation from the surface of space vehicle to the low-temperature sink of outer space. (Deep space has a temperature of about 3° K).

Under these conditions, thermally isolated portions of a space vehicle in orbit around Earth could encounter temperature variations from about 200° K, during Earth-shadowed or darkness periods, to 350° K, while operating in direct sunlight. Spacecraft materials and components can experience thermal fatigue due to repeated temperature cycling during such extremes. Consequently, aerospace engineers need to exercise great care in providing the proper thermal control for a spacecraft. Radiative heat transport is the principal mechanism for heat flow into and out of the spacecraft, while conduction heat transfer generally controls the flow of heat within the spacecraft.

There are two major approaches to spacecraft thermal control: passive and active. Passive thermal control techniques include: the use of special paints and coatings, insulation blankets, radiating fins, Sun shields, heat pipes, as well as the careful selection of the space vehicle's overall geometry (i.e., both the external and internal placement of temperature-sensitive components). Active thermal control techniques include the use of heaters (including small radioisotope sources) and coolers, louvers and shutters, or the closed-loop pumping of cryogenic materials.

An open-loop flow (or "overboard dump") of a rapidly heated working fluid might be used to satisfy a one-time or occasional special mission requirement to remove a large amount of thermal energy in a short period of time. Similarly, a sacrificial ablative surface could be used to handle a singular, large transitory external heat load. But these

transitory (essentially one-shot) thermal control approaches are the exception rather than the aerospace engineering norm.

For interplanetary spacecraft, aerospace engineers often use passive thermal control techniques such as surface coatings, paint, and insulation blankets to provide an acceptable thermal environment throughout the mission. Components painted black will radiate more efficiently. Surfaces covered with white paint or white thermal blankets will reflect sunlight effectively and protect the spacecraft from excessive solar heating. Gold (i.e., gold-foil surfaces) and quartz mirror tiles also are used on the surfaces of special components. Active heating can be used to keep components within tolerable temperature limits. Resistive electric heaters, controlled either autonomously or via command, can be applied to special components to keep them above a certain minimum allowable temperature during the mission. Similarly, radioisotope heat sources (generally containing a small quantity of plutonium-238) can be installed where necessary to provide "at-risk" components with a small, essentially permanent supply of thermal energy.

thermal cycling Exposure of a component to alternating levels of relatively high and low temperatures.

thermal efficiency (symbol: η_{th})
See: THERMODYNAMIC EFFICIENCY.

thermal equilibrium A condition that exists when energy transfer as heat between two thermodynamic systems (e.g., System 1 and System 2) is possible but none occurs. We say that System 1 and System 2 are in thermal equilibrium and that they have the same temperature.
See also: ZEROTH LAW OF THERMODYNAMICS.

thermal inertia (symbol: P) The resistance of a material or substance to temperature change, indicated by the time-dependent variations in temperature during a full heating/cooling cycle (for Earth's surface during a 24-hour day). Thermal inertia is defined as:

$$P = (kc\,\rho)^{0.5}$$

where k is thermal conductivity joules per meter per second per degree Kelvin [J/(m-s-°K)], c is specific heat joules per kilogram per degree Kelvin

[J/(kg-°K)], and ρ is density kilograms per cubic meter (kg/m³).

thermal infrared The infrared region (IR) of the electromagnetic spectrum extending from about 3 to 14 micrometers (μm) wavelength. The thermal IR band most frequently used in remote sensing of Earth (from space) is the 8 to 14 micrometer wavelength band. This band corresponds to windows in the atmospheric absorption bands and, since Earth has an average surface temperature of about 288° Kelvin, its thermal emission peaks near 10 micrometers wavelength.

thermal kill The destruction of a target by heating it, using directed energy (such as a high-energy laser beam), to the degree that structural components fail.

thermal protection system A system designed to protect a space vehicle from undesirable heating. Usually this is accomplished by using a system of special materials that can reject, absorb, or reradiate the unwanted thermal energy.

When a reusable aerospace vehicle, such as the space shuttle orbiter, reenters Earth's atmosphere after a mission in space, aerodynamic heating can produce external temperatures as high as 1650° Celsius (C) (3000° Fahrenheit [F]). Special thermal barriers are required to protect the vehicle and its occupants. NASA selected four basic materials for the original design used on *Columbia*, the first operational orbiter. Each of these thermal protection materials was designed to insulate the orbiter's aluminum and/or graphite epoxy skin against a wide range of extreme temperatures, including a low of -156° C (-250° F). The basic materials were reinforced carbon-carbon (RCC), low-temperature reusable surface insulation (LRSI) tiles, high-temperature reusable surface insulation (HRSI) tiles, and felt reusable surface insulation (FRSI) blankets. Subsequent orbiter vehicle design improvements included use of advanced thermal protection materials in certain areas. These new materials included flexible insulation blankets (FIBs) and fibrous refractory composite insulation (FRCI). The orbiter's nose cone, including the chin panel, and the leading edge of its wings are the hottest areas during reentry. When maximum heating occurs about 20 minutes before touchdown, temperatures on these surfaces reach as high as 1650° C (3000° F).

See also: SPACE TRANSPORTATION SYSTEM.

thermal radiation In general, the electromagnetic radiation emitted by any object as a consequence of its temperature. Thermal radiation ranges in wavelength from the longest infrared wavelengths to the shortest ultraviolet wavelengths and includes the optical (or visible) regions of the spectrum.

See also: PLANCK'S RADIATION LAW.

thermal tagging A target discrimination technique in which a high-powered laser heats up an object; a subsequent measure of its temperature then would help indicate whether the object was light (i.e., displaying a higher temperature after receiving a known heat input) or massive (i.e., exhibiting a lower temperature after receiving a similar heat input). Light objects most likely would be decoys, while the more massive objectives probably would be warhead-carrying reentry vehicles. The targets exhibiting this higher-temperature response to thermal tagging then would either be ignored or else identified for closer inspection by other missile defensive system sensors later in their trajectory, prior to the final commitment of "shoot-down" resources.

See also: BALLISTIC MISSILE DEFENSE.

thermionic conversion The direct conversion of heat (thermal energy) into electricity by evaporating electrons from a hot metal surface and condensing them on a cooler surface. The energy required to remove an electron completely from a

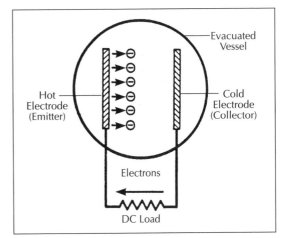

Figure 129. Thermionic conversion principle *(Drawing courtesy of U.S. Department of Energy)*

metal is called the *work function,* which varies with the nature of the metal and its surface condition. The basic thermionic converter consists of two metals (or electrodes) with different work functions sealed in an evacuated chamber. The electrode with the larger work function is maintained at a higher temperature than the one with the smaller work function. (See Figure 129.)

The emitter (or higher-temperature electrode) evaporates electrons, thereby acquiring a positive charge. The collector (or lower-temperature electrode) collects these evaporated or emitted electrons and becomes negatively charged. As a result, a voltage develops between the two electrodes, and a direct electric current will flow in an external circuit (or load) connecting them. The voltage is determined mainly by the difference in the work functions of the electrode materials.

However, the emission of electrons from the higher-temperature electrode can be inhibited as a result of the accumulation of electrons in its vicinity. This phenomenon is called the *space charge effect,* its impact can be reduced by introducing a small quantity of cesium metal into the evacuated thermionic converter chamber that contains the electrodes.

To achieve a substantial electron emission rate per unit area of emitter, the emitter temperature in a thermionic converter containing cesium must be at least 1000° Celsius (1830° Fahrenheit). Thermionic conversion has been suggested for space power generation, especially when used in conjunction with a space nuclear reactor as the heat source.

See also: DIRECT CONVERSION; SPACE NUCLEAR POWER.

thermistor A semiconductor electronic device that uses the temperature-dependent change of resistivity of the substance. The thermistor has a very large negative temperature coefficient of resistance; that is, the electrical resistance decreases as the temperature increases. It can be used for temperature measurements or electronic circuit control.

thermocouple A device consisting essentially of two conductors made of different metals, joined at both ends, producing a loop in which an electric current will flow when there is a difference in temperature between the two junctions. The amount of current that will flow in an attached circuit is dependent on: the temperature difference between

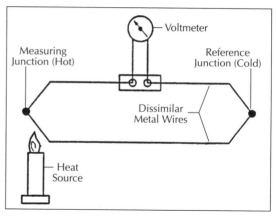

Figure 130. Basic thermocouple circuit   *(Drawing courtesy of U.S. Department of Energy)*

the measurement (hot) and reference (cold) junction; the characteristics of the two different metals used; and the characteristics of the attached circuit. Depending on the different metals chosen, a thermocouple can be used as a thermometer over a certain temperature range. (See Figure 130.)

thermodynamic efficiency (symbol: η_{th}) In thermodynamics, the ratio of work done by a heat engine (W_{out}) to the total heat supplied by the thermal energy source (Q_{in}).

$$\eta_{th} = work_{out}/heat_{in}$$

Also called *thermal efficiency* and *Carnot efficiency.*
See also: HEAT ENGINE; THERMODYNAMICS.

thermodynamics The branch of science that treats the relationships between thermal energy (heat) and mechanical energy. The field of thermodynamics in both physics and engineering involves the study of *systems.* A *thermodynamic system* is simply a collection of matter and space with its boundaries defined in such a way that energy transfer (as work and heat) across the boundaries can be identified and understood easily. The *surroundings* represent everything else that is not included in the thermodynamic system being studied.

Thermodynamic systems usually are placed in one of three groups: closed systems, open systems, and isolated systems. A *closed system* is a system for which only energy (but not matter) can cross the boundaries. An *open system* can experience both matter and energy transfer across its boundaries.

An *isolated system* can experience neither matter nor energy transfer across its boundaries. A *control volume* is a fixed region in space that is defined and studied as a thermodynamic system. Often the control volume is used to help in the analysis of open systems.

Steady state refers to a condition where the properties at any given point within the thermodynamic system are constant over time. Neither mass nor energy accumulate (or deplete) in a steady state system.

A *thermodynamic process* is the succession of physical states that a system passes through. Thermodynamic processes often can described by one of the following terms: cyclic, reversible, irreversible, adiabatic, or isentropic. In a *cyclic process,* the system experiences a series of states and ultimately returns to its original state. The CARNOT CYCLE and the BRAYTON CYCLE are examples. A *reversible process* can proceed in either direction and results in no change in the thermodynamic system or its surroundings. An *irreversible process* can proceed in only one direction; if the process were reversed, there would be a permanent (i.e., irreversible) change made to the system or its surroundings. An *adiabatic process* is one in which there is no flow of heat across the boundaries of the thermodynamic system. An *isentropic process* is one in which the ENTROPY of the thermodynamic system remains constant or unchanged. An isentropic process is actually a reversible adiabatic process.

Thermodynamics is an elegant branch of physics based on two fundamental laws. The FIRST LAW OF THERMODYNAMICS states: *Energy can neither be created nor destroyed, but only altered in form.* This concept often is referred to as the *Conservation of Energy Principle.* In its simplest formulation involving a thermodynamic system, this law can be expressed as:

$$\Sigma \text{ energy}_{in} - \Sigma \text{ energy}_{out} = \Delta \text{ energy}_{storage}$$

This expression often is referred to as an *energy balance* in which the energy flows into a system and out of a system are balanced with respect to any change in energy stored in the system. First-law energy balances are very useful in engineering thermodynamics.

The SECOND LAW OF THERMODYNAMICS involves the concept of entropy and is used to determine the possibility of certain processes and to establish the maximum efficiency of allowed processes. There are many statements of the second law. The statement attributed to the German physicist Rudolph Clausius (1822–1888), which was made in 1850, is considered one of the earliest: *It is impossible to construct a device that operates in a cycle and produces no effect other than the removal of heat from a body at one temperature and the absorption of an equal quantity of heat by a body at a higher temperature.*

The Second Law of Thermodynamics demonstrates that the maximum possible efficiency of a system (e.g., heat engine) is the Carnot efficiency, which is expressed as:

$$\eta_{max} = \eta_{Carnot} = (T_H - T_L)/T_H$$

where T_H is the high (absolute) temperature and T_L is the low (absolute) temperature associated with the system—that is, the temperature at which heat is added to the system (T_H) and the temperature at which heat is rejected from the system (T_L).

Another way of expressing the second law is to look at the possible changes in entropy of an isolated system. From the Second Law of Thermodynamics, we know that the entropy of an isolated system can never decrease; it can only remain constant or increase—that is,

$$\Delta \text{ entropy}_{isolated} \geq 0$$

Thermodynamics plays a very important role in aerospace engineering, especially in defining the limits performance of space power and propulsion systems.

thermoelectric conversion The direct conversion of thermal energy (heat) into electrical energy based on the SEEBECK THERMOELECTRIC EFFECT. In 1821 the Russian-German scientist Thomas Johann Seebeck (1770–1831) was the first person to observe that if two different metals were joined at two locations that were then kept at different temperatures, an electric current will flow in a loop. Such a combination of two materials capable of producing electricity are directly as a result of a temperature difference is called a *thermocouple.*

Figure 131 shows a simple arrangement for achieving thermoelectric conversion. If the thermocouple materials A and B are joined at the hot junction and the other ends are kept cold, an electromotive force is generated between the cold ends. A direct current also will flow in a circuit (or load)

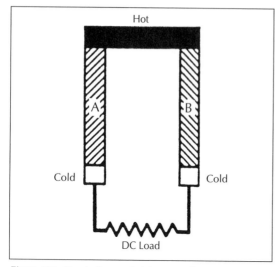

Figure 131. Simple thermoelectric conversion arrangement
(Drawing courtesy of U.S. Department of Energy)

connected between these cold ends. This electric current will continue to flow as long as heat is supplied at the hot junction and removed from the cold ends. For a given thermocouple (using either different metals or semiconductor materials), the voltage and electric power output are increased by increasing the temperature difference between the hot and cold junctions. The practical performance limits of a particular thermoelectric conversion device generally are set by the nature of the thermocouple materials and the (high) temperature of the available heat source. Often, as in space power applications, several thermocouples are connected in series to increase both voltage and power.

See also: SPACE NUCLEAR POWER; THERMOCOUPLE.

thermometer An instrument or device for measuring temperature.

thermonuclear Pertaining to nuclear reactions in which very high temperatures (i.e., millions of degrees Kelvin) are needed to bring about the fusion (joining) of light nuclei, such as deuterium (D) and tritium (T), with the accompanying release of energy.

See also: FUSION (NUCLEAR).

thermonuclear weapon A nuclear weapon in which very high temperatures (from a nuclear fission explosion) are used to bring about the fusion of light nuclei, such as deuterium (D) and tritium

(T), which are isotopes of hydrogen, with the accompanying release of enormous quantities of energy. Sometimes referred to as a *hydrogen bomb.*

Third Law of Thermodynamics Based on the work of Hermann Nernst (1864–1941), Max Planck (1858–1947), Ludwig Boltzmann (1844–1906), Gilbert Lewis (1875–1946), Albert Einstein (1879–1955), and others in the early 1900s, the Third Law of Thermodynamics can be stated as: *The entropy of any pure substance in thermodynamic equilibrium approaches zero as the absolute temperature approaches zero.* The third law is important in that it furnishes a basis for calculating the absolute entropies of substances, either elements or compounds; these data then can be used in analyzing chemical reactions.

See also: THERMODYNAMICS.

Thor An early intermediate-range ballistic missile (IRBM) developed by the U.S. Air Force. This one-stage, liquid-propellant rocket had a range of over 2,700 kilometers (1,700 miles). It was first launched on January 25, 1957 and is now retired from service. Originally developed as a nuclear weapon delivery system, this rocket also served the U.S. Air Force and NASA as a space launch vehicle, especially when combined with a variety of upper-stage vehicles, such as the Agena.

Thousand Astronomical Unit (TAU) mission A proposed future NASA mission involving an advanced-technology robot spacecraft that would be sent on a 50-year journey into very deep space about 1,000 astronomical units (some 160 billion kilometers) away from Earth. The TAU spacecraft would feature an advanced multimegawatt nuclear reactor, ion propulsion, and a laser (optical) communications system. Initially, the TAU spacecraft would be directed for an encounter with Pluto and its moon Charon; followed by passage through the heliopause; perhaps even reaching the inner Oort cloud (the hypothetical region where comets are thought to originate) at the end of its long mission. This advanced robot spacecraft would investigate low-energy cosmic rays, low-frequency radio waves, interstellar gases, and deep-space phenomena. It also would perform high-precision astrometry (the measurement of distances between stars).

threat In general, the anticipated inventory of enemy weapons. In ballistic missile defense

(BMD), the inventory of nuclear weapons and their delivery systems as well as of decoys, penetration aids, and other BMD countermeasures.

See also: BALLISTIC MISSILE DEFENSE.

threat clouds Dense concentrations of both threatening and nonthreatening (i.e., decoy) objects. A defensive system must be capable of distinguishing between objects.

threat tube During the cold war era, a narrow geometrical volume of space, usually over the Arctic, from Soviet missile fields to U.S. targets, within which there would be a high density of reentry vehicles and decoys during a Russian nuclear attack.

three-body problem The problem in classical celestial mechanics that treats the motion of a small body, usually of negligible mass, relative to and under the gravitational influence of two other finite point masses.

three-dimensional grain configuration In rocketry, a solid-propellant grain whose surface is described by three-dimensional analytical geometry (i.e., one that considers end effects).

throat In rocketry, the portion of a convergent/divergent nozzle at which the cross-sectional area is at a minimum. This is the region in which exhaust gases from the combustion chamber transition from subsonic flow to supersonic flow.

See also: NOZZLE.

throttling The varying of the thrust of a rocket engine during powered flight by some technique. Adjusting the propellant flow rate (e.g., tightening of fuel lines), changing of thrust chamber pressure, pulsed thrust, and variation of nozzle expansion are methods to achieve throttling.

throttling process In thermodynamics, an adiabatic process in which the ENTHALPY of a flowing fluid remains constant and no work is done. This process, usually involving a throttling device that restricts fluid flow, leads to a decrease in fluid pressure.

thrust (symbol: T) 1. In general, the forward force provided by a reaction motor. 2. In rocketry, the fundamental thrust equation is:

$$T = \dot{m}\, V_e + (P_e - p_a)\, A_e$$

where T is the thrust (force); $\dot{m}$ is the mass flow rate of propellant; V_e is the exhaust velocity at the nozzle exit; P_e is the exhaust pressure at the nozzle exit; p_e is the ambient pressure; and A_e is exit area of the nozzle. For a well-designed nozzle in which the exhaust gases are properly and completely expanded, $p_e \approx p_a$, so that the thrust becomes approximately represented by the term: $T \approx \dot{m}\, V_e$.

thrust barrel Structure in a rocket vehicle designed to accept the thrust load from two or more engines. Also called the *thrust structure*.

thrust chamber The place in a chemical rocket engine where the propellants are burned (or combusted) to produce the hot, high-pressure gases that are then accelerated and exhausted by the nozzle, thereby creating forward thrust. The combustion chamber and nozzle assembly.

See also: ROCKET.

thrust collector The structure attached to a rocket engine during static (i.e., captive) testing to transmit the engine thrust to thrust-measuring instruments.

thrusted replica A decoy reentry vehicle that has a small rocket which is used upon reentry into the atmosphere. The rocket motor's thrust compensates for atmospheric drag, making it more difficult for the defensive system to discriminate the decoy from the real (warhead-carrying) reentry vehicle.

See also: BALLISTIC MISSILE DEFENSE.

thrust-time profile A plot of thrust level versus time for the duration of firing of a rocket engine or engines.

thrust terminator A device for ending the thrust in a rocket engine, either through propellant cutoff (in the case of a liquid-propellant rocket engine) or through the diversion of the flow of exhaust gases from the nozzle (in the case with a solid-propellant rocket).

thrust vector control (TVC) The intentional change in the direction of the thrust of a rocket engine to guide the vehicle. Thrust vector control can be achieved by using such devices as jet vanes and rings, which deflect the exhaust gas flow as it leaves the rocket's nozzle, or by using gimbaled nozzles and nozzle fluid injection techniques. However, interrupting the nozzle exhaust flow will introduce some degradation in the rocket engine's performance. Therefore, the gimbaled nozzle approach to thrust vector control often is the technique that imposes the minimum engine performance degradation.

time (symbol: t) In general, time is defined as the duration between two instants. The SI UNIT of time is the second, which now is precisely defined using an atomic standard. Time also may be designated as solar time, lunar time, or sidereal time, depending on the astronomical reference used. For example, *solar time* is measured by successive intervals between transits of the Sun across the meridian. *Lunar time* involves phases of Earth's Moon. The *lunar month,* for example, represents the time taken by the Moon to complete one revolution around Earth, as measured from new Moon to new Moon. The lunar month is also called the *synodic month* and is 29.5306 days long. *Sidereal time* is measured by successive transits of the vernal equinox across the local meridian. On Earth, time can be local or *universal time* (UT), which is related to Greenwich meridian.

time line In aerospace operations involving human crews, the planned schedule for astronauts during their space mission.

time tic Markings on telemetry records to indicate time intervals.

time tick A time signal consisting of one or more short audible sounds or beats.

Titan The largest Saturnian moon, approximately 5,150 kilometers in diameter. It has a sidereal period of 15.945 days and orbits at a mean distance of 1,221,850 kilometers from the planet.
See also: SATURN.

Titan (launch vehicle) The family of air force launch vehicles that was started in 1955. The Titan I missile was the first U.S. two-stage intercontinental ballistic missile (ICBM) and the first underground silo-based ICBM. The Titan I vehicle provided many structural and propulsion techniques that were later incorporated in the Titan II vehicle. Years later the Titan IV evolved

from the Titan III family and is similar to the Titan 34D vehicle.

The Titan II was a liquid-propellant, two-stage, intercontinental ballistic missile that was guided to its target by an all-inertial guidance and control system. This missile, designated as LGM-25C, was equipped with a nuclear warhead and designed for deployment in hardened and dispersed underground silos. The air force built more than 140 Titan ICBMs; at one time they served as the foundation of America's nuclear deterrent force during the cold war. The Titan II vehicles also were used as space launch vehicles in NASA's Gemini Project in the mid-1960s. Deactivation of the Titan II ICBM force began in July 1982. The last missile was taken from its silo at Little Rock Air Force Base, Arkansas, on June 23, 1987. The deactivated Titan II missiles then were placed in storage at Norton Air Force Base, California. Some of these retired ICBMs have found new use as space launch vehicles. The Titan II space launch vehicle is a modified Titan II ICBM that is designed to provide low- to medium-mass launch capability into polar LOW EARTH ORBIT (LEO). The modified Titan II is capable of lifting about 1,900 kilograms (kg) (4,200 pounds-mass [lbm]) into polar LEO. With the addition of two strap-on solid rocket motors (i.e., the graphite epoxy motors) to the first stage, the payload capability to polar LEO can be increased to 3,530 kilograms (7,800 lbm).

The versatile Titan III vehicles supported a variety of defense and civilian space launch needs. The Titan IIIA vehicle was developed to test the integrity of the inertially guided three-stage Titan IIIC liquid-propulsion system core vehicle. The Titan IIIB consists of the first two stages of the core Titan III vehicle (without the two strap-on solid rocket motors) with an Agena vehicle used as the third stage. (See Figure 132.) The Titan IIIC consists of the Titan IIIA core vehicle with two solid rocket motors (sometimes called "Stage 0") attached on opposites sides of the liquid-propellant core vehicle. This configuration was developed for space launches from Complex 40 at Cape Canaveral Air Force Station (AFS), Florida. The Titan IIID vehicle, launched from Vandenberg Air Force Base, California, is essentially a Titan IIIC configuration without the Transtage and is radio-guided during launch. The Titan IIIE configuration was developed for NASA and is launched from Complex 41 at Cape Canaveral AFS. The Titan IIIE is basically a standard Titan IIID with a Centaur vehicle used as

Figure 132. A U.S. Air Force Titan-IIIB vehicle with a standard Agena D upper stage lifts off its pad at Vandenberg Air Force Base, California (1967)   *(Photo courtesy of U.S. Air Force)*

the third stage. Finally, the Titan 34D configuration uses a stretched core vehicle in conjunction with larger solid rocket motors to increase booster performance.

The Titan IV is the newest and largest unmanned space booster used by the air force. It was developed to launch the nation's largest, high-

priority, high-value "shuttle-class" defense payloads. This "heavy-lift" vehicle is flexible in that it can be launched with several optional upper stages (such as the Centaur and the Inertia Upper Stage) for greater and more varied spacelift capability. The Titan IV vehicle's first stage consists of an LR87 liquid-propellant rocket that features structurally independent tanks for its fuel (aerozine 50) and oxidizer (nitrogen tetroxide). This design minimizes the hazard of the two propellants mixing if a leak should develop in either tank. Additionally, these liquid propellants can be stored at normal temperature and pressure, eliminating launch pad delays (as often encountered with the boil-off and refilling of cryogenic propellants) and giving the Titan IV vehicle the capability to meet critical defense program and planetary mission launch windows.

The Titan IV vehicle can have a length of up to 61.2 meters (204 feet) and carry up to 17,550 kg (39,000 lbm) into a 144-kilometer (km) (90-mile [mi]) altitude orbit when launched from Cape Canaveral AFS and up to 13,950 kg (31,000 lbm) into a 160-km (100-mi) altitude polar orbit when launched from Vandenberg AFB. Planned solid rocket motor improvements will increase the capability of this versatile heavy-lift space launch vehicle.

See also: LAUNCH VEHICLE.

tolerance The allowable variation in measurements within which the dimensions of an item are judged acceptable.

tolerance stackup Additive effects of all the allowable manufacturing tolerances on the final dimensions of the assembly; also called *tolerance buildup*.

Tomahawk Long-range, subsonic cruise missile used by the U.S. Navy for land attack and for antisurface warfare. Tomahawk is an all-weather submarine or ship-launched antiship or land-attack cruise missile. After launch, a solid-propellant rocket engine propels the missile until a small turbofan engine takes over for the cruise portion of the flight. This cruise missile is a highly survivable weapon. Radar detection is difficult because of its small cross section and low-altitude flight. Similarly, infrared detection is also difficult because the turbofan emits little heat.

Figure 133. The Tomahawk cruise missile system is an All-Up Round (AUR), consisting of the winged-missile that flies the mission, the booster that starts the flight, and the container (canister for ships and capsule for submarines) that protects it during transportation, storage, and stowage. The container also acts as a launch tube for the missile. *(Drawing courtesy of U.S. Department of Defense)*

The antiship variant of Tomahawk uses a combined active radar seeker and passive system to seek out, engage, and destroy a hostile ship at long range. Its modified Harpoon cruise missile guidance system permits the Tomahawk to be launched and fly at low altitudes in the general direction of an enemy warship to avoid radar detection. Then, at a programmed distance, the missile begins an active radar search to seek out, acquire, and hit the target ship.

The land-attack version has inertial and terrain contour matching (TERCOM) guidance. The TERCOM guidance system uses a stored map reference to compare with the actual terrain to help the missile determine its position. If necessary, a course correction is made to place the missile on course to the target.

The basic Tomahawk is 5.56 meters (m) (18.25 feet [ft]) long and has a mass of 1192 kilograms (2,650 pounds-mass [lbm]), not including the booster. It has a diameter of 51.81 centimeters (20.4 inches) and a wing span (when deployed) of 2.67 m (8.75 ft). This missile is subsonic and cruises at about 880 kilometers (km) (550 miles [mi]) per hour. It can carry a conventional or nuclear warhead. In the land-attack (conventional warhead) configuration, it has a range of 1,100 km (about 690 mi); while in the land-attack (nuclear warhead) configuration, it has a range of 2,480 km (1,555 mi). In the antiship role, it has a range of over 460 km (288 mi). This missile was first deployed in 1983. (See Figure 133.)

ton (symbol: T or t) A unit of mass in both the SI and American standard system of units. 1. In the SI UNIT system, one ton (sometimes spelled tonne) is defined as 1,000 kilograms.

$$1 \text{ ton (tonne)} = 1,000 \text{ kilograms} = 2,205 \text{ pounds-mass (lbm)}.$$

Also called the *metric ton.* 2. In the American standard system of units (i.e., the foot-pound-second system), one (short) ton is defined as 2,000 pounds-mass (lbm). In the United Kingdom, an *imperial* (or *long*) *ton* contains approximately 2,240 pounds-mass (lbm).

topside sounder A spacecraft instrument that is designed to measure ion concentration in the ionosphere from above Earth's atmosphere.

torque (symbol: τ) In physics, the moment of a force about an axis; the product of a force and the distance of its line of action from the axis.

torr A unit of pressure named in honor of the Italian physicist Evangelista Torricelli (1608–1647). One standard atmosphere (on Earth) is equal to 760 torr; or 1 torr = 1 millimeter of mercury = 133.32 pascals.

torsion The state of being twisted.

total impulse (symbol: I_T) The integral of the thrust force (T) over an interval of time, t:

$$I_T = \int T \, dt$$

See also: SPECIFIC IMPULSE.

touchdown The (moment of) landing of an aerospace vehicle or spacecraft on the surface of a planet or moon.

toughness In engineering, the ability of a material (especially a metal) to absorb energy and deform plastically before fracturing.

TOW missile The U.S. TOW missile (*Tube-launched Optically Tracked, Wire Command-Link Guided*) is a long-range, heavy antitank system designed to attack and defeat armored vehicles and other targets, such as field fortifications. The TOW 2A missile is 14.91 centimeters (cm) (5.87 inches [in]) in diameter and 128.02 cm (50.40 in) long; the TOW 2B missile is 14.9 cm (5.8 in) in diameter and 121.9 cm (48 in) long. The maximum effective range is about 3.75 kilometers (2.33 miles). The basic TOW weapon system was fielded in 1970. This system is designed to attack and defeat tanks and other armored vehicles. It is used primarily in antitank warfare and is a command to line of sight, wire-guided weapon. The system will operate in all weather conditions and on an obscured battlefield. The TOW 2 launcher is the most recent launcher upgrade. The TOW 2B missile incorporates a new fly-over, shoot-down technology. The TOW missile can be mounted on the Bradley Fighting Vehicle System (BFVS), the Improved TOW Vehicle (ITV), the High Mobility Multipurpose Wheeled Vehicle (HMMWV), and the AH-1S Cobra Helicopter. The TOW missile is also in use by more than 40 nations besides the

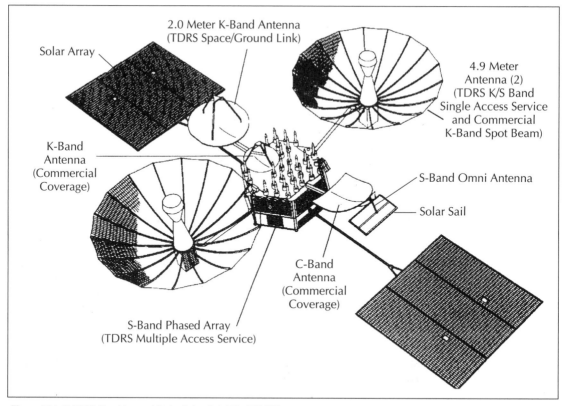

Figure 134. NASA's Tracking and Data Relay Satellite (TDRS) *(Drawing courtesy of NASA)*

United States as their primary heavy antiarmor weapons system.

track 1. (noun) The actual path or line of movement of an aircraft, rocket, aerospace vehicle, and the like over the surface of Earth. It is the projection of the vehicle's flight path on the planet's surface. 2. (verb) To observe or plot the path of something moving, such as an aircraft or rocket, by one means or another, as by telescope or by radar; said of persons or of electronic equipment, as, for example, "the radar *tracked* the satellite while it passed overhead."

tracking 1. The process of following the movement of a satellite, rocket or aerospace vehicle. Tracking usually is accomplished with optical, infrared, radar, or radiosystems. 2. In BALLISTIC MISSILE DEFENSE (BMD), the monitoring of the course of a moving target. Ballistic objects may have their tracks predicted by the defensive system, using several observations and physical laws.

Tracking and Data Relay Satellite (TDRS)
NASA's Tracking and Data Relay Satellite (TDRS) network provides almost full-time coverage not only for the space shuttle but also for up to 24 other orbiting spacecraft simultaneously. Services provided include communications, tracking, telemetry, and data acquisition.

The TDRS satellites orbit geosynchronously at 35,888 kilometers (22,300 miles) above Earth and look down on an orbiting space shuttle or spacecraft. For most of their orbits around Earth, these spacecraft remain in sight of one or more TDRS satellites. In the past, spacecraft could communicate with Earth only when they were in view of a ground tracking station, typically less than 15% of each orbit. The full TDRS constellation enables spacecraft to communicate with Earth for about 85 to 100% of the orbit, depending on their altitude. All space shuttle missions and nearly all other NASA spacecraft in Earth orbit require TDRS support capabilities for mission success.

Each TDRS is a three-axis stabilized satellite measuring 17.4 meters (57 feet) across when its solar panels are fully deployed. The satellite has a mass of 2,268 kilograms (5,000 pounds-mass [lbm]). The spacecraft's design uses three modules. The equipment module, forming the base of the satellite's central hexagon, houses the subsystems that actually control and operate the satellite. Attached solar power arrays generate more than 1,700 watts of electrical power. When TDRS is in the shadow of Earth, nickel-cadmium batteries supply electric power. (See Figure 134.)

The communications payload module is the middle portion of the hexagon and includes the electronic equipment that regulates the flow of transmissions between the satellite's antennas and other communications functions.

Finally, the antenna module is a platform atop the hexagon holding seven antenna systems. TDRS has uplink, or forward, channels that receive transmissions (radio signals) from the ground, amplify them, and retransmit them to user spacecraft. The downlink, or return, channels receive the user spacecraft's transmissions, amplify them, and retransmit them to the ground terminal. The prime transmission link between Earth and TDRS is a 2-meter (6.7-foot) dish antenna attached by a boom to the central hexagon. This parabolic reflector operates in the Ku-band (12–14 gigahertz [GHz]) frequency to relay transmissions to and from the ground terminal. All spacecraft telemetry data downlinked by TDRS is channeled through a highly automated ground station complex at White Sands, New Mexico. This location was chosen for its clear line of sight to the satellites and dry climate. The latter minimizes rain degradation of radio signal transmission.

The TDRS spacecraft with its attached upper stage is launched aboard the space shuttle from the Kennedy Space Center in Florida and deployed from the orbiter's payload bay, nominally about six hours into the mission. To boost the TDRS into a geosynchronous orbit, the Inertial Upper Stage (or IUS) vehicle fires twice. The upper-stage vehicle's first-stage motor fires about an hour after deployment, placing the attached TDRS into an elliptical geotransfer orbit. The first stage then separates. The IUS second-stage motor fires about 12.5 hours into the mission, circularizing the orbit and shifting the flight path so that the satellite is moving above the equator. The IUS second stage and the TDRS then separate at about 13 hours after launch. Once in

geosynchronous orbit its appendages, including the solar panels and parabolic antennas, are deployed. About 24 hours after launch, the satellite is ready for ground controllers to begin checkout procedures. Initially the spacecraft is positioned at an intermediate location (in geosynchronous orbit) for checkout and testing, then it is moved to its final operational location (in geosynchronous orbit).

tracking and pointing In ballistic missile defense (BMD), once a target is detected, it must be followed, or "tracked." When the target is tracked successfully, a high-velocity (kinetic energy weapon) interceptor, high-energy laser (HEL) beam, or neutral particle beam (NPB) is "pointed" at the target. Tracking and pointing frequently are integrated operations.

See also: BALLISTIC MISSILE DEFENSE.

trainer In aerospace, a teaching device or facility that primarily provides a physical representation of flight hardware. The trainer also may have limited computer capabilities. Compare this term with SIMULATOR.

trajectory In general, the path traced by any object or body moving as a result of an externally applied force, considered in three dimensions. *Trajectory* sometimes is used to mean *flight path* or *orbit*, but "orbit" usually means a closed path and "trajectory" means a path that is not closed.

trajectory correction maneuver (TCM) Once a spacecraft's solar or planetary orbital parameters are known, spacecraft controllers on Earth can compare these values to those actually desired for the mission. To correct any discrepancy, a *trajectory correction maneuver* (TCM) can be planned and executed. This process involves computing the direction and magnitude of the vector required to correct to the desired trajectory. An appropriate time then is determined for making the change. The spacecraft is commanded to rotate to the attitude (in three-dimensional space) computed for implementing the change, and its thrusters are fired for the required amount of time. TCMs generally involved a velocity change (or "delta-V") on the order of meters per second or tens of meters per second.

transceiver A combination of *trans*mitter and re*ceiver* in a single housing, with some components being used by both units.

transducer General term for any device that converts one form of energy (usually in some type of signal) to another form of energy. For example, a microphone is an electroacoustic transducer in which sound waves (acoustic signals) are converted into corresponding electrical signals that then can be amplified, recorded, or transmitted to a remote location. The photocell and thermocouple are also transducers, converting light and heat (respectively) into electrical signals.

transfer orbit In interplanetary travel, an elliptical trajectory tangent to the orbits of both the departure planet and target planet (or moon).
See also: HOHMANN TRANSFER ORBIT.

transient The condition of a physical system in which the parameters of importance (e.g., temperature, pressure, fluid velocity, etc.) vary significantly with time; in particular, the condition or state of a rocket engine's operation in which the mass, momentum, volume, and pressure of the combustion products within the thrust chamber vary significantly with time.

transient period The interval from start or ignition to the time when steady-state conditions are reached, as in a rocket engine.

Transit A U.S. Navy navigational satellite system that has provided passive, all-weather, worldwide position information to surface ships (military and commercial) and submarines for over 30 years.

transit time The length of time required by a rocket, missiles, or spacecraft to reach its intended target or destination.

translation Movement in a straight line without rotation.

translunar Of or pertaining to space beyond the Moon's orbit around Earth.

transmission grating A diffraction grating in which incoming signal energy is resolved into spectral components upon transmission through the grating.

transmittance (transmissivity) In radiation heat transfer, the transmittance (commonly used symbol: τ) for a body is defined as the ratio of the incident radiant energy transmitted through the body to the total radiant energy falling upon the body. The body may be *transparent* to the incident radiant energy (i.e., permitting some or all of the radiant energy to travel through the body), or else it may be *opaque* and therefore inhibit or prevent the transmission of incident radiant energy. An ideal BLACKBODY is perfectly opaque; therefore, this blackbody has a transmittance of zero, that is, $\tau_{\text{blackbody}} = 0$. Compare with ABSORPTANCE and REFLECTANCE.

transmitter A device for the generation of signals of any type and form that are to be transmitted. For example, in radio and radar, a transmitter is that portion of the equipment that includes electronic circuits designed to generate, amplify, and shape the radio frequency (RF) energy that is delivered to the antenna where it is radiated out into space. In aerospace applications, the spacecraft's transmitter generates a tone at a single designated frequency, typically in the S-band (about 2 gigahertz) or X-band (about 5 gigahertz) region of the electromagnetic spectrum. This tone is called the *carrier.* The carrier then can be sent from the spacecraft to Earth as it is, or it can be modulated with a data-carrying subcarrier within the transmitter. The signal generated by the spacecraft's transmitter is passed to a power amplifier, where its power typically is boosted several tens of watts. The microwave-band power amplifier can be a solid-state amplifier (SSA) or a traveling wave tube (TWT) amplifier. The output of the power amplifier then is conducted through wave guides to the spacecraft's antenna, often a high-gain antenna (HGA).

transpiration cooling A form of mass transfer cooling that involves controlled injection of a fluid mass through a porous surface. This process basically is limited by the maximum rate at which the coolant material can be pumped through the surface.

transponder A combined receiver and transmitter whose function is to transmit signals automatically when triggered by an appropriate interrogating signal.

trap A part of a solid-propellant rocket engine used to prevent the loss of unburned propellant through the nozzle.

tribology The branch of engineering science that deals with friction, lubrication, and the behavior of lubricants.

Trident missile (D-5) The U.S. Navy's Trident II (D-5) missile is the main armament aboard the Ohio-class fleet ballistic missile submarines (SSBNs), which now have replaced the aging fleet ballistic missile submarines built in the 1960s. The Trident-II (D-5) three-stage, solid-propellant rocket is the latest in a line of fleet ballistic missiles that began with the Polaris (A-1) missile. The Trident-II missile incorporates many state-of-the-art advances in rocketry and electronics, giving this submarine-launched fleet ballistic missile greater range, payload capacity, and accuracy than its predecessors.

triple point In thermodynamics, the temperature of a mixture of a substance that contains the liquid, gaseous, and solid phases of the material in thermal equilibrium at standard pressure. For example, by international agreement, the temperature for the *triple point of water* has been set at 273.16° Kelvin (491.69° Rankine), creating an easily reproducible standard for a one-point absolute temperature scale.

See also: ABSOLUTE TEMPERATURE SCALE.

triplet In rocketry, an injector orifice pattern consisting of one or more sets of three orifices that produce streams converging to a point; usually fuel is injected through the outer orifices and oxidizer is injected through the central orifice.

Trojan group A group of asteroids that lie near the two Lagrangian points in Jupiter's orbit around the Sun. Achilles was the first asteroid in the group to be identified (in 1906); many subsequently discovered members of this group have been named in honor of the heroes, both Greek and Trojan, of the Trojan War.

See also: ASTEROID.

truncation error In computations, the error resulting from the use of only a finite number of terms of an infinite series or from the approximation of operations in the infinitesimal calculus by operations in the calculus of finite differences.

Tsyklon A medium-capacity Russian/Ukranian launch vehicle capable of placing 3,600-kilogram payloads into LOW EARTH ORBIT (LEO). First launched in 1977, this vehicle consists of three hypergolic-propellant stages. It is currently manufactured by NPO Yuzhnoye, Ukraine.

T-time In aerospace operations, any specific time (minus or plus) that is referenced to "launch time," or "zero," at the end of a countdown. T-time is used to refer to times during a countdown sequence that is intended to result in the ignition of a rocket propulsion unit or units to launch a missile or rocket vehicle. For example, one will hear the phrase: "T-minus 20 seconds and counting" during a countdown sequence. This refers to the point in the launch sequence that occurs 20 seconds before the rocket engines are ignited.

tube-wall construction Use of parallel metal tubes that carry coolant to or from the combustion chamber or nozzle wall.

tumble 1. To rotate end over end—said of a rocket, of an ejection capsule, or of a spent propulsion stage that has been jettisoned. 2. Of a gyro, to precess suddenly and to an extreme extent as a result of exceeding its operating limits of pitch.

turbine A machine that converts the energy of a fluid stream into mechanical energy of rotation. The working fluid used to drive a turbine can be gaseous or liquid. For example, a highly compressed gas drives an *expansion turbine,* hot gas drives a *gas turbine,* steam (or other vapor) drives a *steam (or vapor) turbine,* water drives a *hydraulic turbine,* and wind spins a *wind turbine (or windmill).* Generally (except for wind and water turbines), a turbine consists of two sets of curved blades (or vanes) along side each other. One set of vanes is fixed and the other set of vanes can move. The moving vanes are spaced around the circumference of a cylinder or *rotor,* which can rotate about a central shaft. The fixed set of vanes (*the stator*) often is attached to the inside casing that encloses the rotor (or moving portion of the turbine).

In order to make efficient use of the energy of the working fluid, gas and steam turbines often have a series of successive stages. Each stage consists of a set of fixed (stator) and moving (rotor) blades. The pressure of the working fluid decreases as it passes from stage to stage. The overall diameter of each successive stage of the turbine therefore can be increased to maintain a constant torque (or rota-

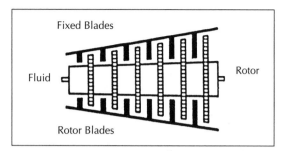

Figure 135. The major components of a typical gas turbine
(Drawing courtesy of U.S. Department of Energy)

tional effect) as the working fluid expands and loses pressure (and energy). (See Figure 135.)

turbopump system In a liquid-propellant rocket, the assembly of components (e.g., propellant pumps, turbine[s], power source, etc.) designed to raise the pressure of the propellants received from the vehicle tanks and deliver them to the main thrust chamber at specified pressures and flow rates.

turbulence A state of fluid flow in which the instantaneous velocities exhibit irregular and apparently random fluctuations so that in practice only statistical properties can be recognized and subjected to analysis. These fluctuations often constitute major deformations of the flow and are capable of transporting momentum, energy, and suspended matter at rates far in excess of the rate of transport by the molecular processes of diffusion and conduction in a nonturbulent or laminar flow.

turbulence ring In a liquid-propellant rocket engine, the circumferential protuberance in the gas-side wall of a combustion chamber intended to generate turbulent flow and thereby enhance the mixing of burning gases.

turbulent flow Fluid flow in which the velocity at a given point fluctuates randomly and irregularly in both magnitude and direction. The opposite of LAMINAR FLOW.

two-body problem The problem in classical celestial mechanics that addresses the relative motion of two point masses under their mutual gravitational attraction.

two-dimensional grain configuration In rocketry, the solid-propellant grain whose burning surface is described by two-dimensional analytical geometry (i.e., the cross section is independent of length).

two-phase flow Simultaneous flow of gases and solid particles (e.g., condensed metal oxides); or the simultaneous flow of liquids and gases (vapors).

ullage The amount that a container, such as a fuel tank, lacks of being full.

ullage pressure Pressure in the ullage space of a container, either supplied or self-generated.

ultra- A prefix meaning "surpassing a specified limit, range, or scope" or "beyond."

ultrahigh frequency (UHF) A radio frequency in the range 0.3 gigahertz to 3.0 gigahertz.

ultrasonic Of or pertaining to frequencies above those that affect the human ear, that is, acoustic waves at frequencies greater than approximately 20,000 hertz; for example, an *ultrasonic vibrator.*

ultraviolet (UV) astronomy Astronomy based on the ultraviolet (UV, 10 to 400 nanometer wavelength) portion of the electromagnetic (EM) spectrum. Because of the strong absorption of UV radiation by Earth's atmosphere, ultraviolet astronomy must be performed using high-altitude balloons, rocket probes, and orbiting observatories. Ultraviolet data gathered from spacecraft are extremely useful in investigating interstellar and intergalactic phenomena. Observations in the ultraviolet wavelengths have shown, for example, that the very-low-density material that can be found in the interstellar medium is quite similar throughout our galaxy but that its distribution is far from homogeneous. In fact, UV data have led some astrophysicists to postulate that low-density cavities, or "bubbles," in interstellar space are caused by supernova explosions and are filled with gases that are much hotter than the surrounding interstellar medium. Ultraviolet data gathered from space-based observatories have revealed that some stars blow off material in irregular bursts and not in a steady flow as originally thought. Ultraviolet data are also of considerable use in studying many of the phenomena that occur in distant galaxies.

See also: ASTROPHYSICS.

ultraviolet (UV) radiation That portion of the electromagnetic spectrum that lies beyond visible (violet) light and is longer in wavelength than X rays. Generally taken as electromagnetic radiation with wavelengths between 400 nanometers (just past violet light in the visible spectrum) and about 10 nanometers (the extreme ultraviolet cutoff and the beginning of X rays).

See also: ELECTROMAGNETIC SPECTRUM.

Ulysses mission An international space project to study the poles of the Sun and the interstellar environment above and below these solar poles. The Ulysses spacecraft was built by Dornier Systems of Germany for the European Space Agency (ESA), which is also responsible for in-space operations of the Ulysses mission. NASA provided launch support using the space shuttle *Discovery* and an upper-stage configuration consisting of a two-stage inertial upper stage (IUS) rocket and a PAM-S (Payload Assist Module) configuration. In addition, the United States, through the Department of Energy, provided the radioisotope thermoelectric generator (RTG) that supplies electric power to this spacecraft. *Ulysses* is tracked and its scientific data collected by NASA's Deep Space Network (DSN). Spacecraft monitoring and control, as well as data reduction and analysis, is performed at NASA's Jet Propulsion Laboratory (JPL) by a joint ESA/JPL team.

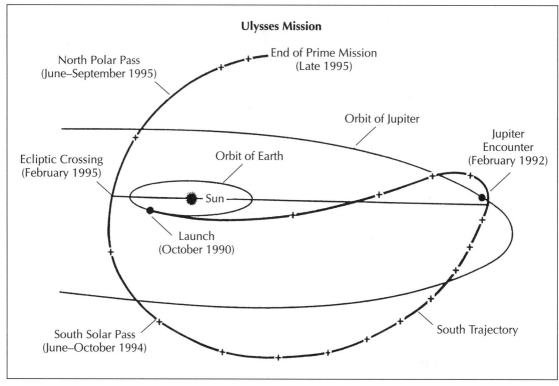

Figure 136. Journey of the Ulysses spacecraft through interplanetary space   *(Drawing courtesy of NASA)*

The Ulysses mission, named for the legendary Greek hero in Homer's epic saga of the Trojan War who wandered into many previously unexplored areas on his return home, is a survey mission designed to examine: the properties of the SOLAR WIND, the structure of the Sun–solar wind interface, the heliospheric magnetic field, solar radio bursts and plasma waves, solar and galactic cosmic rays and the interplanetary/interstellar neutral gas and dust environment—all as a function of solar latitude.

The 370-kilogram (814-pounds-mass [lbm]) spacecraft was carried into LOW EARTH ORBIT (LEO) by *Discovery* on October 6, 1990. Then it was deployed successfully on an interplanetary trajectory that encountered Jupiter (for a gravity-assist maneuver) in February 1992, flew past the southern polar regions of the Sun (80 degrees south solar latitude) in September 1994, and then passed over the northern polar regions of the Sun in the fall 1995, ending the prime mission of this nuclear-powered spacecraft. (See Figure 136.) After completing its first solar orbit on September 29, 1995, the Ulysses spacecraft began its voyage back out to

Jupiter, where it will loop around and return to the vicinity of the Sun in September 2000. At that time the Sun will be in a very active phase of its 11-year solar cycle, and Ulysses will find itself battling through the atmosphere of a star that is no longer docile.

Ulysses is the first spacecraft to explore the third dimension of space over the poles of the Sun. When the spacecraft passed over those polar regions in 1994 and 1995, scientists made some surprising new discoveries. For example, two clearly separate and distinct solar wind regimes exist, with fast wind emerging from the solar poles. Scientists also were surprised to observe how cosmic rays make their way into the solar system from galaxies beyond the MILKY WAY GALAXY (our home galaxy). The magnetic field of the Sun over its poles turned out to be very different from previous expectations, based on observations from Earth. Finally, Ulysses detected a beam of particles from interstellar space that was penetrating the solar system at a velocity of about 80,000 kilometers per hour (50,000 miles per hour). (This beam velocity corresponds to about 22.22 km/s).

This mission was originally called the *International Solar Polar Mission* (*ISPM*). The original mission planned for two spacecraft, one built by NASA and the other by ESA. However, NASA canceled its spacecraft part of the original mission in 1981 and instead provided launch and tracking support for the single spacecraft built by ESA.

See also: SPACE NUCLEAR POWER; SUN.

umbilical An electrical or fluid servicing line between the ground or a tower and an upright rocket vehicle before launch. Also called *umbilical cord.*

UMR injector Injector that produces a uniform mixture ratio (UMR) and thus a combustion region with relatively uniform temperature distribution.

underexpansion A condition in the operation of a rocket nozzle in which the exit area of the nozzle is insufficient to permit proper expansion of the propellant gas. Consequently, the existing gas is at a pressure greater than the ambient pressure, and this leads to the formation of external expansion waves.

unidentified flying object (UFO) A flying object (apparently) seen in Earth's skies by an observer who cannot determine its nature. The vast majority of such "UFO" sightings can, in fact, be explained by known phenomena. However, these phenomena may be beyond the knowledge or experience of the person making the observation. Common phenomena that have given rise to UFO reports include artificial Earth satellites, aircraft, high-altitude weather balloons, certain types of clouds, and the planet Venus.

Modern interest in UFOs appears to have begun with a sighting report made by a private pilot named Kenneth Arnold. In June 1947 he reported seeing a mysterious formation of shining disks in the daytime sky near Mount Rainier in Washington State. When newspaper reporters heard of his account of "shining saucerlike disks," the popular term "flying saucer" was born.

In 1948 the United States Air Force began to investigate these UFO reports. *Project Sign* was the name given by the air force to its initial study of UFO phenomena. In the late 1940s Project Sign was replaced by *Project Grudge,* which in turn became the more familiar *Project Blue Book.* Under Project Blue Book, headquartered at Wright-Patterson Air Force Base in Ohio, the air force investigated many UFO reports from 1952 to 1969. Then on December 17, 1969 the secretary of the air force announced the termination of the project. Of a total of 12,618 sightings reported to Project Blue Book, 701 remained "unidentified."

Since the termination of this project, nothing has occurred that would support a resumption of UFO investigation by the air force. Similarly, while NASA is now the focal point for answering public inquiries to the White House concerning UFOs, it is not engaged in a research program involving these UFO phenomena or sightings.

unit The unit defines a measurement of a physical quantity, such as length, mass, or time. There are two common unit systems in use in aerospace applications today, the International System of Units (SI), which is based on the meter-kilogram-second (mks) set of fundamental units, and the American standard system of units, which is based on the foot-pound-mass-second (fps) set of fundamental units. In the standard system of units, 1 pound-mass (lbm) is defined as equaling 1 pound-force (lbf) on the surface of Earth at sea level. Derived units, such as energy, power, and force, are based on combinations of the fundamental units in accordance with physical laws, such as NEWTON'S LAWS OF MOTION.

See also: INTERNATIONAL SYSTEM OF UNITS.

United States Space Command (USSPACECOM) A unified command of the Department of Defense with headquarters at Peterson Air Force Base, Colorado Springs, Colorado. USSPACECOM was activated on September 23, 1985 to consolidate and operate military assets affecting U.S. activities in space. The command is composed of three components: the Air Force, Naval, and Army Space Commands. The USSPACECOM has three primary missions: space operations, warning, and planning for BALLISTIC MISSILE DEFENSE (BMD). The commander in chief, USSPACECOM, is directly responsible to the president through the secretary of defense and the Joint Chiefs of Staff. USSPACECOM exercises operational command of assigned U.S. military space assets through the air force, navy, and army component space commands.

See also: AIR FORCE SPACE COMMAND.

universal time coordinated (UTC) The worldwide scientific standard of timekeeping, based on carefully maintained atomic clocks. It is kept accurate to within microseconds. The addition (or subtraction) of "leap seconds" as necessary at two opportunities every year keeps UTC in step with Earth's rotation. Its reference point is Greenwich, England. When it is midnight there on Earth's prime meridian, it is midnight (00:00:00.000000) UTC, often referred to as "all balls" in aerospace jargon.

universe Everything that came into being at the moment of the Big Bang, and everything that has evolved from that initial mass of energy; everything that we can (in principle) observe. All energy (radiation), all matter, and the space that contains them.

See also: BIG BANG THEORY.

unmanned Without human crew; *unpersoned* or *uncrewed* are more contemporary terms.

upcomer Nozzle tube in which coolant flows in a direction opposite to that of the exhaust gas flow.

uplink data Information that is passed from a ground station on Earth to a spacecraft, space probe, or space platform.

See also: TELECOMMUNICATIONS.

upper atmosphere The general term applied to outer layers of Earth's atmosphere above the troposphere. It includes the stratosphere, mesosphere, thermosphere, and exosphere. Sounding rockets and Earth-observing satellites often are used to gather scientific data about this region.

See also: ATMOSPHERE; UPPER ATMOSPHERE RESEARCH SATELLITE.

***Upper Atmosphere Research Satellite* (UARS)** The *Upper Atmosphere Research Satellite* (*UARS*) was deployed successfully during Space Shuttle STS-48 mission in September 1991. The UARS was the first major element of NASA's Mission to Planet Earth. The satellite was designed to help scientists learn more about the fragile mixture of gases protecting Earth's biosphere from the harsh environment of space. In particular, UARS provided scientists with their first detailed data set involving the upper atmosphere's chemistry, winds, and energy inputs. Depletion of ozone in the stratosphere was an area of special scientific inquiry. The satellite provided simultaneous, coordinated measurements of

atmospheric internal structure (i.e., trace constituents, physical dynamics, radiative emission, thermal structure, and density) and measurements of the external influences acting upon the upper atmosphere (e.g., solar radiation, tropospheric conditions, and electric fields). The UARS operated in a 585-kilometer (364-mile) nearly circular orbit

Table 1.
SELECTED PHYSICAL AND DYNAMIC PROPERTIES OF THE PLANET URANUS

Diameter (equatorial)	51,120 km
Mass (estimated)	8.7×10^{25} kg
"Surface" gravity	8.69 m/s^2
Mean density (estimated)	1.3 g/cm^3
Albedo (visual)	0.5
Temperature (blackbody)	53° Kelvin
Magnetic field	Yes, intermediate strength (field tilted 60° with respect to axis of rotation)
Atmosphere	Hydrogen (~89%), helium (~11%), methane (ppm)
"Surface" features	Bland and feature less (except for some discrete methane clouds)
Escape velocity	21.3 km/s
Radiation belts	Yes (intensity similar to those at Saturn)
Rotation period	17.24 hours
Eccentricity	0.047
Mean orbital velocity	6.8 km/s
Sidereal year (a Uranian year)	84 years
Inclination of planet's equator to its orbit around the Sun	97.9°
Number of (known) natural satellites	15
Rings	Yes (11)
Average distance from Sun	2.871×10^9 km (19.19 AU) [159.4 light-min]
Solar flux at average distance from Sun	3.7 W/m^2 (approx.)

Source: Based on NASA data.

above Earth, inclined 57 degrees to the equator. This orbit enabled the satellite's sensors to view up to the 80-degree latitude bands, thereby providing essentially global coverage of the stratosphere and mesosphere. From this orbit, upper-atmospheric measurements could be made over the full range of local times at all geographic locations approximately every 36 days.

See also: MISSION TO PLANET EARTH.

upper stage In general, the second, third, or later stage in a multistage rocket. Often getting into LOW EARTH ORBIT (LEO) is only part of the effort against the planet's gravitational forces for geosynchronous satellites and interplanetary spacecraft. Once propelled into LEO by a reusable aerospace vehicle, such as the space shuttle, or an expendable launch vehicle, such as the Delta or Titan, these payloads depend on an upper-stage vehicle to boost them on the next phase of their journey. Upper-stage vehicles carried by the space shuttle are solid-propellant rocket vehicles that provide the extra thrust, or "kick," needed to move spacecraft into higher orbits or interplanetary trajectories. Solid-propellant or liquid-propellant rocket vehicles are used as upper stages with expendable launch vehicles.

The upper-stage vehicle, its payload, and any required supporting hardware (e.g., a special cradle attached to the shuttle's cargo bay or an adapter mounted to the first or second stage of an expendable launch vehicle) are carried into LEO by the launch vehicle. Once in LEO, the upper-stage vehicle and its attached payload separate from the launch vehicle and fire the rocket engine (or

engines) necessary to deliver the payload to its final destination.

See also: AGENA; CENTAUR; INERTIAL UPPER STAGE (IUS); PAYLOAD ASSIST MODULE.

Uranian Of or relating to the planet Uranus.
See also: URANUS.

Uranus Unknown to ancient astronomers, the planet Uranus was discovered by Sir William Herschel in 1781. Initially called *Georgium Sidus* (George's star, after England's King George III) and *Herschel* (after its discoverer), in the 19th century the seventh planet from the Sun was finally named Uranus after the ancient Greek god of the sky and father of the Titan Cronos (Saturn in Roman mythology).

At nearly 3 billion kilometers from the Sun, Uranus is too distant from Earth to permit telescopic imaging of its features by ground-based telescopes. Because of the methane in its upper atmosphere, the planet appears as only a blue-green disk or blob in the most powerful of terrestrial telescopes. On January 24, 1986 a revolution took place in our understanding and knowledge about this planet, as the *Voyager 2* encountered the Uranian system at a relative velocity of over 14 kilometers per second. What we know about Uranus today is largely the result of that spectacular encounter.

Uranus has one particularly interesting property —its axis of rotation lies in the plane of its orbit rather than vertical to the orbital plane, as occurs with the other planets. Because of this curious situation, Uranus moves around the Sun like a barrel

Table 2.
SELECTED PHYSICAL AND DYNAMIC PROPERTY DATA FOR
MAJOR URANIAN MOONS

Name	Diameter (km)	Period (day)	Distance from Center of Uranus (km)	Visual Albedo	Average Density (g/cm³)
Miranda	470	1.414	129,800	0.27	1.3
Ariel	1,160	2.520	191,200	0.34	1.7
Umbriel	1,170	4.144	266,000	0.18	1.5
Titania	1,580	8.706	435,800	0.27	1.7
Oberon	1,520	13,463	582,600	0.24	1.6

Source: Based on NASA data.

Table 3.
SELECTED PHYSICAL AND DYNAMIC PROPERTY DATA FOR
MINOR URANIAN MOONS

Name	Diameter (km)	Period (day)	Distance from Center of Uranus (km)
Cordelia (1986U7)[a]	26	0.335	49,700
Ophelia (1986U8)[a]	32	0.376	53,800
Bianca (1986U9)	44	0.435	59,200
Cressida (1986U4)	66	0.464	61,770
Desdemona (1986U6)	60	0.474	62,700
Juliet (1986U3)	84	0.493	64,360
Portia (1986U1)	110	0.513	66,100
Rosalind (1986U2)	60	0.558	69,930
Belinda (1985U5)	68	0.624	75,300
Puck (1985U1)	154	0.762	86,000

[a] Shepherding moon.

Source: Based on NASA data.

rolling along on its side rather than like a top spinning on its end. In other words, Uranus is tipped over on its side, with its orbiting moons and rings creating the appearance of a giant bull's-eye. The northern and southern polar regions are alternatively exposed to sunlight or to the darkness of space during the planet's 84-year-long orbit around the Sun. At its closest approach, *Voyager 2* came within 81,500 kilometers of the Uranian cloudtops. The spacecraft telemetered back to Earth thousands of spectacular images and large quantities of other scientific data about the planet, its moons, rings, atmosphere, and interior.

The upper atmosphere of Uranus consists mainly of hydrogen (H_2) (about 89%) and helium (He) (about 11%) with small amounts of methane (CH_4), water vapor (H_2O), and ammonia (NH_3). The methane in the upper atmosphere of Uranus and its preferential absorption of red light gives the planet its overall blue-green color.

Table 1 presents selected physical and dynamic property data for Uranus, while Tables 2 and 3 describe some of the physical features of the major and minor Uranian moons, respectively. The large Uranian moons appear to be about 50% water ice, 20% carbon- and nitrogen-based materials, and 30% rock. Their surfaces, almost uniformly dark gray in color, display varying degrees of geologic history. Very ancient, heavily cratered surfaces are apparent on some of the moons, while others show strong evidence of internal geologic activity. Miranda, the innermost of the five large Uranian moons, is considered by scientists to be one of the strangest bodies yet observed in the solar system. *Voyager 2* images revealed an unusual world consisting of huge fault canyons as deep as 20 kilometers terraced layers, and a mixture of old and young surfaces.

See also: VOYAGER.

vacuum The absence of gas or a region in which there is a very low gas pressure. This is a relative term. For example, a *soft vacuum* (or *low vacuum*) has a pressure of about 0.01 pascal (i.e., 10^{-2} pascal); a *hard vacuum* (or *high vacuum*) typically has a pressure between 10^{-2} and 10^{-7} pascal; while pressures below 10^{-7} pascal are referred to as an *ultrahard* (or *ultrahigh*) vacuum.

valve Mechanical device by which the flow of fluid may be started, stopped, or regulated by a movable part that opens, closes, or partially obstructs a passageway in a containing structure, called the *valve housing.*

Van Allen radiation belts A doughnut-shaped zone of high-intensity particulate radiation around Earth from an altitude of about 320 to 32,400 kilometers (200 to 20,000 miles) above the magnetic equator. The radiation of the Van Allen belts is composed of protons and electrons temporarily trapped in Earth's magnetic field. Spacecraft and their occupants or sensitive equipment orbiting within the belts or passing through them must be protected against this ionizing radiation. The existence of the belts was first confirmed by instruments placed on *Explorer I* (the first U.S. Earth satellite) by Dr. James Van Allen (1914–), after whom the region is now named.

See also: EARTH'S TRAPPED RADIATION BELTS; EXPLORER I.

Vandenberg Air Force Base (VAFB) Vandenberg Air Force Base is located 89 kilometers (55 miles) north of Santa Barbara near Lompoc, California. It is the site of all military, NASA, and commercial space launches accomplished on the West Coast of the United States. The base, named in honor of General Hoyt S. Vandenberg (Air Force Chief of Staff from 1948 to 1953), also provides launch facilities for the testing of intercontinental ballistic missiles. The first missile was launched from Vandenberg in 1958 and the world's first polar-orbiting satellite was launched from there aboard a Thor/Agena launch vehicle in 1959.

See also: CAPE CANAVERAL AIR FORCE STATION.

Vanguard Project An early U.S. space project involving a new three-stage rocket (*Vanguard rocket*) and a series of scientific spacecraft (*Vanguard satellites*). The U.S. Navy successfully launched the first satellite in this project, called *Vanguard 1,* on March 17, 1958. This tiny Earth-orbiting satellite provided information leading in 1959 to the identification of the slight, but significant, pear shape of the Earth. An earlier, widely publicized launch attempt had ended in dramatic failure, when the Vanguard rocket exploded just as it lifted off the launch pad. The *Vanguard 2* satellite was launched on February 17, 1959. It transmitted the world's first picture of Earth's cloud cover (as observed from a satellite), but a wobble in the spacecraft due to an inadvertent bump by its launch vehicle resulted in a less than satisfactory picture quality. Finally, the *Vanguard 3* satellite was launched on September 18, 1959. This early spacecraft deepened our understanding of the space environment, including the VAN ALLEN RADIATION BELT and micrometeoroids.

vapor The gaseous phase of a substance; in thermodynamics, this term often is used interchangeably with *gas.*

vaporization In thermodynamics, the transition of a material from the liquid phase to the gaseous (or vapor) phase, generally as a result of heating or pressure change.

vapor pressure 1. The pressure exerted by the atoms or molecules of a given vapor. For a pure substance confined within a container, it is the vapor's pressure on the walls of its containing vessel; for a vapor (or gas) mixed with other vapors (or gases), it is that particular vapor's contribution to the total pressure (i.e., its partial pressure). In meteorology, the term "vapor pressure" generally is used to denote the partial pressure of water vapor in the atmosphere. 2. The sum of the partial pressures of all the vapors in a system.

vapor turbine A turbine in which part of the thermal energy (heat) supplied by a vapor is converted into mechanical work of rotation. The *steam turbine* is a common type of vapor turbine. Sometimes called a *condensing turbine.*
See also: RANKINE CYCLE; TURBINE.

variable-area exhaust nozzle An exhaust nozzle on a jet engine or a rocket engine that has an exhaust opening that can be varied in area by means of some mechanical device.
See also: NOZZLE.

vector Any physical quantity, such as force, velocity, or acceleration, that has both magnitude and direction at each point in space, as opposed to a *scalar,* which has magnitude only.

vector steering A steering method for rockets and spacecraft in which one or more thrust chambers are gimbal-mounted ("gimbaled") so that the direction of the thrust (i.e., the thrust vector) may be tilted in relation to the vehicle's center of gravity to produce a turning movement.

Vega Twin Russian spacecraft that were launched in December 1984 and performed a probe/flyby mission to Venus and then continued on for an encounter with Comet Halley. These spacecraft were modified versions of the Venera spacecraft. In June 1985 the *Vega 1* and *2* spacecraft flew by Venus. Each spacecraft dropped off a probe package (consisting of an instrumented balloon and a lander) and then proceeded, using a gravity assist from Venus, to encounter Comet Halley. *Vega 1*

flew past Comet Halley on March 6, 1986, coming within 9,000 kilometers of its nucleus. During its closest approach, the *Vega 1* spacecraft acquired hundreds of images of the comet, as well as other important scientific data. Similarly, *Vega 2* encountered Comet Halley on March 9, 1986 and also returned many images and important data. The Russians quickly provided these images and data to scientists at the European Space Agency (ESA), so they could make last-minute adjustments in the trajectory of the Giotto spacecraft prior to its encounter with Comet Halley on March 14, 1986. The *Vega* spacecraft are now in orbit around the Sun.
See also: COMET; GIOTTO SPACECRAFT; VENERA; VENUS.

vehicle In general, an aerospace structure, machine, or device (e.g., a rocket) that is designed to carry a payload through the atmosphere and/or space; more specifically a rocket vehicle.
See also: LAUNCH VEHICLE.

vehicle mass ratio In rocketry, the ratio of the final mass of a rocket vehicle (m_f), after all the propellant has been expended, to the initial (fully loaded) mass (m_0):

$$\text{vehicle mass ratio} = m_f/m_0$$

If complete propellant depletion is assumed, then the final vehicle mass (m_f) consists of the payload mass (m_{pl}) and all of the vehicle's total structural mass (m_s)—that is, the mass of the tanks, engine, guidance system, and so on—namely:

$$\text{final vehicle mass } (m_f) = \text{payload mass } (m_{pl}) + \text{total structural mass } (m_s)$$

The *inverse* of the vehicle mass ratio, namely $1/(\text{vehicle mass ratio}) = m_0/m_f$, is also encountered in aerospace engineering. This term is called the *propellant mass ratio* (ζ), or sometimes simply the *mass ratio* (MR), of a rocket vehicle, as is defined as: $\zeta = m_0/m_f$.

vehicle tank Tank that serves both as a primary integral structure of a rocket vehicle (or spacecraft) and as a container of pressurized propellants.

Vela A family of research and development spacecraft launched by the United States in the 1960s and early 1970s to detect nuclear detonations in the atmosphere down to Earth's surface, or in outer space at distances of more than 160 million kilometers (km) (100 million miles [mi]). These spacecraft were jointly developed by the Department of Defense and the Atomic Energy Commission (now Department of Energy) and were placed in pairs, 180 degrees apart in very high altitude (about 115,000 km [71,500 mi]) orbits around Earth. The first pair of Vela spacecraft, called *Vela 1A* and *Vela 1B,* were launched successfully on October 17, 1963. The last pair of these highly successful, 26-sided (polyhedron-shaped) spacecraft, called *Vela 6A* and *Vela 6B,* were launched successfully on April 8, 1970. It is interesting to note that the United States, the former Soviet Union, and the United Kingdom signed the *Limited Nuclear Test Ban Treaty* in October 1963. This treaty prohibits the signatories from testing nuclear weapons in Earth's atmosphere, under water, or in outer space. In addition to supporting important U.S. government nuclear test monitoring objectives, the Vela satellites also supported a modest revolution in astrophysics. Between 1969 and 1972, the Vela satellites detected 16 very short bursts of gamma ray photons with energies of 0.2 to 1.5 million electron volts. These mysterious cosmic gamma ray bursts lasted from less than a tenth of a second to about 30 seconds. Although the Vela instruments were not designed primarily for astrophysical research, simultaneous observations by several spacecraft started astrophysicists on their contemporary hunt for "gamma ray bursters."

See also: GAMMA RAY ASTRONOMY.

velocity A vector quantity that describes the rate of change of position. Velocity has both magnitude (speed) and direction, and it is expressed in terms of units of length per unit of time (e.g., meters per second).

Venera A family of mostly successful robotic space missions flown by Russia (i.e., the former Soviet Union) to the planet Venus between 1961 and 1984. These missions included orbiters, landers, and atmospheric probes. In October 1967, for example, the *Venera 4* spacecraft placed a landing capsule/probe into the Venusian atmosphere, collecting data that indicated the planet's atmosphere was from 90 to 95% carbon dioxide (CO_2). This 380-kilogram (kg) probe descended by parachute for about 94 minutes when data transmissions ceased at an altitude of some 25 kilometers (km). In December 1970 the 495-kg atmospheric probe from the *Venera 7* spacecraft reached the surface of Venus and transmitted data for about 20 minutes. The *Venera 8* spacecraft launched a probe into the Venusian atmosphere in July 1972. This probe, with an improved communications system, successfully landed on the surface and survived for about 50 minutes in the infernolike conditions found on the surface of Venus.

In October 1975 the *Venera 9* and *10* spacecraft sent probes to the surface of Venus that landed successfully and transmitted the first black-and-white images of the planet's rock-strewn surface. *Venera 11* and *12,* launched in 1978, were also lander-probe/flyby missions with improved sensors.

In the 1980s, the Russians launched four more-sophisticated Venera spacecraft to Venus. The *Venera 13* and *14* spacecraft were 5,000-kg flyby/lander configurations sent to the planet at the end of 1981. *Venera 13* landed on Venus on March 1, 1982, and its identical companion, *Venera 14,* touched down on March 5, 1982. These landers returned black-and-white and color images of the Venusian surface. They also performed the first soil analysis of the Venusian surface.

The final pair of Venera spacecraft (called *Venera 15* and *16*), were launched in June 1983. These spacecraft did not carry landers but rather performed mapping missions of the planet's cloud-enshrouded surface, using their synthetic aperture radar (SAR) systems. The spacecraft orbited for about one year and produced detailed radar images of the planet's surface at between one and two kilometers resolution.

See also: VENUS.

vent-and-relief valve Specialized version of a relief valve wherein the valve assembly acts as an outlet for ullage vapor during the filling of a tank (e.g., propellant tank) and then performs as a relief valve during operations.

VentureStar The reusable launch vehicle (RLV) design proposed by the Lockheed-Martin Corporation in response to NASA's X-33 design competition. The VentureStar's design emerged out of Lockheed's "Skunk Works" (known for building such famous aircraft as the U-2, the SR-71, and the F-117 stealth fighter) and contained two features that separated it from the competition: an aerospike engine and a lifting body design. Unlike a conventional rocket engine in which combustion occurs inside the thrust chamber and hot gases

Figure 137. Artist rendering of the Lockheed-Martin reusable launch vehicle (RLV) VentureStar, deploying a payload in low Earth orbit *(Courtesy of NASA and Lockheed Martin)*

then exhaust through a nozzle, in an aerospike engine combustion takes place around the periphery of a central "spike" and the exhaust plume then is shaped by atmospheric pressure and the propellant flow rate. The aerospike engine self-adjusts for changes in atmospheric pressure as the vehicle ascends. In July 1996 Lockheed-Martin won the NASA contract to design and build the X-33 vehicle. Flight tests are now scheduled for 1999. NASA's X-33 is a technology demonstration program that will result in the development of a reusable launch vehicle. (See Figure 137.)

See also: X-33.

venturi tube A short tube having a smaller diameter in the middle than at the ends. This device is used for measuring the quantity of fluid flowing through a pipe. When a fluid flows through such a tube, its pressure decreases and its velocity increases as the diameter becomes smaller. The amount of pressure decrease is proportional to the speed of the flow and the amount of flow restriction.

vent valve Pressure-relieving valve that is operated on external command, as contrasted to a relief valve, which opens automatically when pressure reaches a given level.

Venus Venus is the second planet out from the Sun. Because the planet appears to observers on Earth, as either an evening or a morning star, it is often called the Evening Star or the Morning Star. Venus is named after the Roman goddess of love and beauty. Among the planets in our solar system, it is the only one named after a female mythological deity. It is also called an inferior planet, because it revolves around the Sun within the orbit of Earth. The planet maintains an average distance of about 0.723 astronomical unit (AU) (~108 million kilometers) from the Sun. The table provides physical and dynamic data for Earth's nearest planetary neighbor. At closest approach, Venus is approximately 42 million kilometers from Earth.

Since the 1960s, visits by numerous American and Russian spacecraft have now dispelled the pre–space age romantic fantasies that this cloud-enshrouded planet was a prehistoric world that mirrored a younger Earth. Except for a few physical similarities of size and gravity, Earth and Venus are very different worlds. For example, the surface temperature on Venus approaches 500° Celsius (773° Kelvin), its atmospheric pressure is more than 90 times that of Earth, it has no surface water, and its dense, hostile atmosphere with sulfuric acid clouds and an overabundance of carbon dioxide (about 96%) represents a runaway greenhouse of disastrous proportions.

Cloud-penetrating synthetic aperture radar (SAR) systems carried by the American Pioneer Venus orbiter and Magellan spacecraft and the Russian *Venera 15* and *16* spacecraft have provided a detailed characterization of the previously unobservable Venusian surface. These radar imagery data, especially the high-resolution images collected by the Magellan mission, are now challenging planetary scientists to explain some of the interesting findings.

Scientists generally divide the surface of Venus into three classes of terrain: highlands (or *tesserae*) (10% of surface); rolling uplands (70%); and lowland plains (20%). One very prominent highland region is called Ishtar Terra, after Ishtar, the ancient Babylonian goddess of love. This region is about the size of Australia and stands several kilometers above the average planetary radius. Ishtar Terra contains the highest peaks yet discovered on Venus, including Maxwell Montes, which is often

PHYSICAL AND DYNAMIC PROPERTIES OF VENUS

Diameter (equatorial)	12,100 km
Mass	4.87×10^{24} kg
Density (mean)	5.25 g/cm^3
Surface gravity	8.88 m/sec^2
Escape velocity	10.4 km/sec
Albedo (over visible spectrum)	0.7–0.8
Surface temperature (approx.)	750 K (477° C)
Atmospheric pressure (at surface)	9600 kPa (~1,400 psi)
Atmosphere (main components)	CO_2 (96.4%), N_2 (3.4%)
(minor components)	Sulfur dioxide (150 ppm), argon (70 ppm), water vapor (20 ppm)
Surface wind speeds	0.3–1.0 m/sec
Surface materials	Basaltic rock and altered materials
Magnetic field	Negligible
Radiation belts	None
Number of natural satellites	None
Average distance from Sun	1.082×10^8 km (0.723 AU)
Solar flux (at top of atmosphere)	2,620 W/m^2
Rotation period (a Venusian "day")	243 days (retrograde)
Eccentricity	0.007
Mean orbital velocity	35.0 km/sec
Sidereal year (period of one revolution around Sun)	224.7 days
Earth-to-Venus distances	
Maximum	2.59×10^8 km (1.73 AU)
Minimum	0.42×10^8 km (0.28 AU)

Source: NASA.

regarded as the single most impressive topographical feature on the planet.

The relatively fresh appearance and small number of impact craters suggests to planetary scientists that the surface as a whole is young (by geo-

logic standards). It also appears that Venus experienced a dramatic resurfacing event some 300 to 500 million years ago. But whether this resurfacing phenomenon (which covered most of the planet with lava) was caused by a brief chain of catastrophic events or by the influences of low-level volcanism operating over longer periods of time is currently the subject of scientific investigation and debate. The fractured Venusian highlands, such as Ishtar Terra and Aphroditie Terra, represent the planet's older surface material not covered by younger flows of lava. Maat Mons is the largest volcano on Venus, and it appears to have experienced a recent surge of volcanic activity. A volcanic feature unique to the planet are the *coronae*—large (often hundreds of kilometers across), heavily fractured circular regions that sometimes are surrounded by a trench. The channels, or *canali*, on Venus are long, riverlike surface features where lava once flowed.

Yet despite all the interesting facts that have been revealed about Venus by the American and Russian space missions, equally interesting questions also have been raised by scientists as they examined these new data. Questions such as "What was Venus like before the resurfacing event?" await resolution in the 21st century, when even more rugged probes and landers again visit Earth's nearest planetary neighbor.

See also: MAGELLAN MISSION; PIONEER-VENUS; VENERA.

Venusian Of or pertaining to the planet Venus.

vernier engine A rocket engine of small thrust used primarily to obtain a fine adjustment in the velocity and trajectory or in the attitude of a rocket or aerospace vehicle.

Very Large Array (VLA) The Very Large Array (VLA) is a spatially extended radiotelescope facility at Socorro, New Mexico. It consists of 27 antennas, each 25 meters (82 feet) in diameter, that are configured in a giant "Y" arrangement on railroad tracks over a 20-kilometer (12.5-mile) distance. The VLA is operated by the National Radio Astronomy Observatory and sponsored by the National Science Foundation.

very large scale integration (VLSI) An integrated circuit containing more than 64,000 transistors.

See also: INTEGRATED CIRCUIT.

Viking Project The Viking Project was the culmination of an initial series of American missions to explore Mars in the 1960s and 1970s. This series of interplanetary missions began in 1964 with *Mariner 4*, continued with the *Mariner 6* and *7* flyby missions in 1969, and then the *Mariner 9* orbital mission in 1971 and 1972.

Viking was designed to orbit Mars and to land and operate on the surface of the Red Planet. Two identical spacecraft, each consisting of a lander and an orbiter, were built.

The orbiters carried the following scientific instruments:

1. A pair of cameras with 1,500-millimeter focal length that performed systematic searches for landing sites, then looked at and mapped almost 100% of the Martian surface. Cameras onboard the *Viking 1* and *Viking 2* orbiters took more than 51,000 photographs of Mars.

2. A Mars atmospheric water detector that mapped the Martian atmosphere for water vapor and tracked seasonal changes in the amount of water vapor.

3. An infrared thermal mapper that measured the temperatures of the surface, polar caps, and clouds; it also mapped seasonal changes. In addition, although the Viking orbiter radios were not considered scientific instruments, they were used as such. By measuring the distortion of radio signals as these signals traveled from the Viking orbiter spacecraft to Earth, scientists were able to measure the density of the Martian atmosphere.

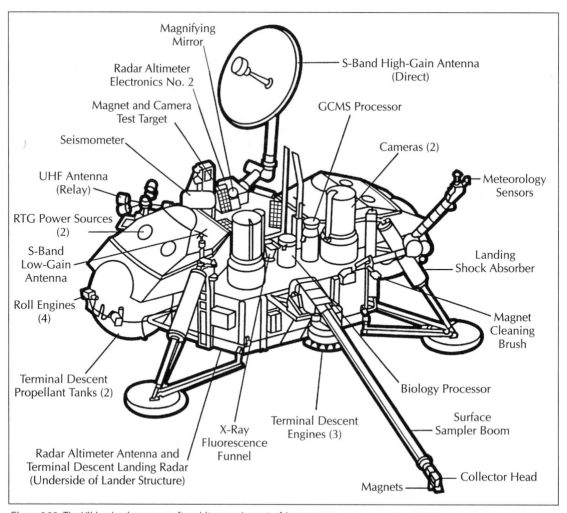

Figure 138. The Viking lander spacecraft and its complement of instruments *(Drawing courtesy of NASA)*

The Viking landers carried the following instruments: (See Figure 138.)

1. The biology instrument, consisting of three separate experiments designed to detect evidence of microbial life in the Martian soil.
2. A gas chromatograph/mass spectrometer (GCMS) that searched the Martian soil for complex organic molecules.
3. An X-ray fluorescence spectrometer that analyzed samples of the Martian soil to determine its elemental composition.
4. A meteorology instrument that measured air temperature and wind speed and direction at the landing sites.
5. A pair of slow-scan cameras that were mounted about 1 meter (3.28 feet) apart on the top of each lander. These cameras provided black-and-white, color, and stereo photographs of the Martian surface.
6. A seismometer had been designed to record any "Marsquakes" that might occur on the Red Planet. Such information would have helped planetary scientists determine the nature of Mars's internal structure. Unfortunately, the seismometer on *Lander 1* did not function after landing and the instrument on Lander 2 observed no clear signs of internal (tectonic) activity.
7. An upper-atmosphere mass spectrometer that conducted its primary measurements as each lander plunged through the Martian atmosphere on its way to the landing site. This instrument made the lander's first important scientific discovery—the presence of nitrogen in the Martian atmosphere.
8. A retarding potential analyzer that measured the Martian ionosphere, again during entry operations.
9. Accelerometers, a stagnation pressure instrument, and a recovery temperature instrument that helped determine the structure of the lower Martian atmosphere as the landers approached the surface.
10. A surface sampler boom that employed its collector head to scoop up small quantities of Martian soil to feed the biology, organic chemistry, and inorganic chemistry instruments. It also provided clues to the soil's physical properties. Magnets attached to the sampler, for example, provided information on the soil's iron content.
11. The lander radios also were used to conduct scientific experiments. Physicists were able to refine their estimates of Mars's orbit by measuring the time for radio signals to travel between Mars and Earth. The great accuracy of these radio-wave measurements also allowed scientists to confirm portions of Einstein's General Theory of Relativity.

Both Viking missions were launched from Cape Canaveral, Florida. *Viking 1* was launched on August 20, 1975, and *Viking 2* on September 9, 1975. The landers were sterilized before launch to prevent contamination of Mars by terrestrial microorganisms. These spacecraft spent nearly a year in transit to the Red Planet. *Viking 1* achieved Mars orbit on June 19, 1976; and *Viking 2* began orbiting Mars on August 7, 1976. The *Viking 1* lander accomplished the first soft landing on Mars on July 20, 1976, on the western slope of Chryse Planitia (the Plains of Gold) at 22.46 degrees north latitude, 48.01 degrees west longitude. The *Viking 2* lander touched down successfully on September 3, 1976, at Utopia Planitia located at 47.96 degrees north latitude, 225.77 degrees west longitude.

The Viking mission was planned to continue for 90 days after landing. Each orbiter and lander, however, operated far beyond its design lifetime. For example, the *Viking 1* orbiter exceeded four years of active flight operations in orbit around Mars.

The Viking Project's primary mission ended on November 15, 1976, just 11 days before Mars passed behind the Sun (an astronomical event called a "superior conjunction"). After conjunction, in mid-December 1976, telemetry and command operations were reestablished and extended mission operations began.

The *Viking 2* orbiter mission ended on July 25, 1978, due to exhaustion of attitude-control system gas. The *Viking 1* orbiter spacecraft also began to run low on attitude-control system gas, but through careful planning it was possible to continue collecting scientific data (at a reduced level) for another two years. Finally, with its control gas supply exhausted, the *Viking 1* orbiter's electrical power was commanded off on August 7, 1980.

The last data from the *Viking 2* lander were received on April 11, 1980. The *Viking 1* lander made its final transmission on November 11, 1982. After over six months of effort to regain contact with the *Viking 1* lander, the Viking mission came to an end on May 23, 1983.

With the single exception of the seismic instruments, the entire complement of scientific instruments of the Viking Project acquired far more data about Mars than ever anticipated. The primary objective of the lander was to determine whether (microbial) life currently exists on Mars. The evidence provided by the landers is still subject to debate, although most scientists feel these results are strongly indicative that life does *not now* exist on Mars. However, recent analyses of Martian meteorites have renewed interest in this very important question, and Mars is once again the target of intense scientific investigation by even more sophisticated scientific spacecraft.

See also: MARINER SPACECRAFT; MARS; MARS GLOBAL SURVEYOR MISSION; MARS PATHFINDER MISSION; MARS SAMPLE RETURN MISSION; MARTIAN METEORITES.

virtual reality (VR) A computer-generated artificial reality that captures and displays in varying degrees of detail the essence or effect of physical reality (i.e., the "real-world" scene, event, or process) being modeled or studied. With the aid of a data glove, headphones, and/or head-mounted stereoscopic display, a person is projected into the three-dimensional world created by the computer.

A virtual reality system generally has several integral parts. There is always a computerized description (i.e., the "database") of the scene or event to be studied or manipulated. It can be a physical place, such as a planet's surface made from digitized images sent back by robot space probes. It can even be more abstract, such as a description of the ozone levels at various heights in Earth's atmosphere or the astrophysical processes occurring inside a pulsar or a black hole.

VR systems also use a special helmet or headset ("goggles") to supply the sights and sounds of the artificial, computer-generated environment. Video displays are coordinated to produce a three-dimensional effect. Headphones make sounds appears to come from any direction. Special sensors track head motions, so that the visual and audio images shift in response.

Most VR systems also include a glove with special electronic sensors. This "data" glove lets a person interact with the virtual world through hand gestures. He or she can move or touch objects in the computer-generated visual display, and these objects then respond as they would in the physical world. Advanced versions of such gloves also provide artificial "tactile" sensations so that an object "feels like the real thing" being touched or manipulated (e.g., smooth or rough, hard or soft, cold or warm, light or heavy, flexible or stiff, etc.).

The field of virtual reality is quite new, and rapid advances should be anticipated over the next decade, as computer techniques, visual displays, and sensory feedback systems (e.g., advanced data gloves) continue to improve in their ability to project and model the real world. VR systems have many potential roles in aerospace. For example, sophisticated virtual reality systems will let scientists "walk on another world" while working safely here on Earth. Future mission planners will identify the best routes (based on safety, resource consumption, and mission objectives) for both robots and humans to explore the surface of the Moon and Mars, before the new missions are even launched. Astronauts will use VR training systems regularly to try out space maintenance and repair tasks and perfect their skills long before they lift off on an actual mission. Aerospace engineers will use VR system as an indispensable design tool to fully examine and test new aerospace hardware, long before any "metal is bent" in building even a prototype model of the item.

viscosity A measure of the internal friction or flow resistance of a fluid when it is subjected to shear stress. The *dynamic viscosity* is defined as the force that must be applied per unit area to permit adjacent layers of fluid to move with unit velocity relative to each other. The dynamic viscosity is sometimes expressed in *poise* (centimeter-gram-second [c.g.s.] system) or in pascal-seconds (SI unit system). One poise is equal to 0.1 newton-second per square meter (i.e., 1 poise = 10^{-1} N s m^{-2}). The *kinematic viscosity* is defined as the dynamic viscosity divided by the fluid's density. The kinematic viscosity can be expressed in *stokes* (centimeter-gram-second [c.g.s.] system) or in square meters per second (SI unit system). One stoke is equal to 10^{-4} m^2 s^{-1}. In general, the viscosity of a liquid usually decreases as the temperature is increased; the viscosity of a gas increases as the temperature increases.

See also: INTERNATIONAL SYSTEM OF UNITS

viscous fluid A fluid whose molecular viscosity is sufficiently large to make the viscous forces a significant part of the total force field in the fluid.

void In rocketry, an air bubble in a cured propellant grain or in a rocket motor insulation.

volt (symbol: V) The SI UNIT of electric potential difference and electromotive force. One volt is equal to the difference of electric potential between two points of a conductor carrying a constant current of 1 ampere when the power dissipated between these points equals 1 watt. This unit is named after the Italian scientist Count Alessandro Volta (1745–1827), who performed pioneering work involving electricity and electric cells.

volume (symbol: V) The space occupied by a solid object or a mass of fluid (liquid or confined gas).

Voskhod An early Russian three-person spacecraft that evolved from the Vostok spacecraft. *Voskhod 1* was launched on October 12, 1964 and carried the first three-person crew into space. The cosmonauts, Vladimir Komarov, Konstantin Feoktistov, and Boris Yegorov, flew on a one-day duration Earth orbital mission. *Voskhod 2* was launched on March 18, 1965 and carried a crew of two cosmonauts, including Alexei Leonov, who performed the world's first "spacewalk" (about 10 minutes in duration) during the orbital mission. *Voskhod* means "sunrise" in Russian.

Vostok The first Russian manned spacecraft. This spacecraft was occupied by a single cosmonaut and consisted of a spherical cabin (about 2.3 meters in diameter) that was attached to a biconical instrument module. *Vostok 1* was launched on April 12, 1961 carrying Cosmonaut Yuri Gagarin, the first human to fly in space. Gagarin's flight made one orbit of Earth and lasted about 108 minutes.

Voyager Once every 176 years the giant outer planets—Jupiter, Saturn, Uranus, and Neptune—align themselves in such a pattern that a spacecraft launched from Earth to Jupiter at just the right time might be able to visit the other three planets on the same mission, using a technique called *gravity assist*. NASA space scientists named this multiple giant planet encounter mission the "Grand Tour" and took advantage of a unique celestial alignment opportunity in 1977 by launching two sophisticated spacecraft, called *Voyager 1* and 2. (See Figure 139.)

Each Voyager spacecraft has a mass of 825 kilograms (1,815 pounds-mass [lbm]) and carries a complement of scientific instruments to investigate

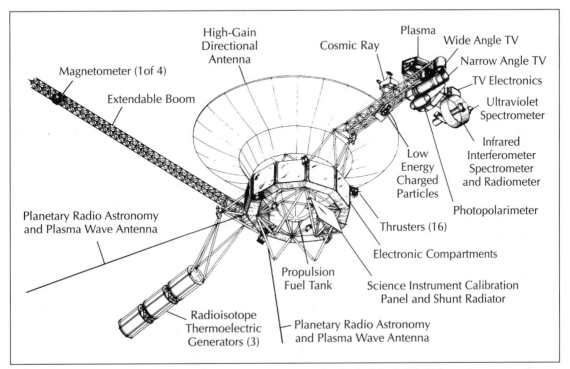

Figure 139. The 825-kilogram Voyager spacecraft and its complement of sophisticated scientific instruments *(Drawing courtesy of NASA)*

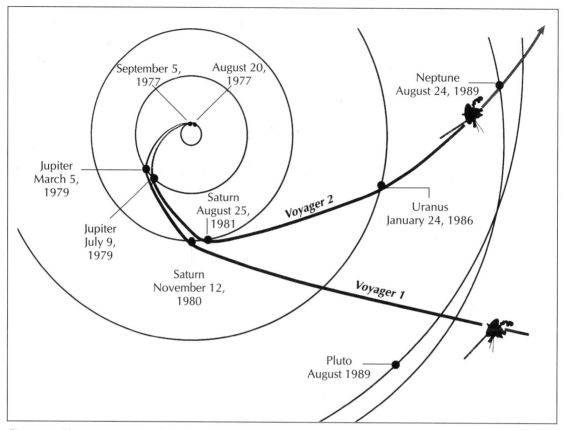

Figure 140. Planetary encounters of the Voyager spacecraft (1977–89)—a Grand Tour exploration epoch of the outer solar system *(Drawing courtesy of NASA)*

the outer planets and their many moons and intriguing ring systems. These instruments, provided electric power by a long-lived nuclear system called a radioisotope thermoelectric generator (RTG), recorded spectacular closeup images of the giant outer planets and their interesting moon systems, explored complex ring systems, and measured properties of the interplanetary medium.

Taking advantage of the 1977 Grand Tour launch window, the *Voyager 2* spacecraft lifted off from Cape Canaveral, Florida on August 20, 1977 onboard a Titan-Centaur rocket. (NASA called the first Voyager spacecraft launched *Voyager 2*, because the second Voyager spacecraft to be launched eventually would overtake it and become *Voyager 1*.) *Voyager 1* was launched on September 5, 1977. This spacecraft followed the same trajectory as its *Voyager 2* twin and overtook its sister ship just after entering the asteroid belt in mid-December 1977.

Voyager 1 made its closest approach to Jupiter on March 5, 1979 and then used Jupiter's gravity to swing itself to Saturn. On November 12, 1980 *Voyager 1* successfully encountered the Saturnian system and then was flung up out of the ecliptic plane on an interstellar trajectory. The *Voyager 2* spacecraft successfully encountered the Jovian system on July 9, 1979 (closest approach) and then used the gravity assist technique to follow *Voyager 1* to Saturn. On August 25, 1981 *Voyager 2* encountered Saturn and then went on to successfully encounter both Uranus (January 24, 1986) and Neptune (August 25, 1989). (See Figure 140.) Space scientists consider the end of *Voyager 2*'s encounter of the Neptunian system as the end of a truly extraordinary epoch in planetary exploration. In the first 12 years since they were launched from Cape Canaveral, these incredible spacecraft contributed more to our understanding of the giant outer planets of our solar system than was accomplished in over three millennia of Earth-based observations. Following its encounter with the Neptunian system, *Voyager 2* also was placed on an interstellar trajectory and (like its *Voyager 1* twin) now continues to travel outward from the Sun.

As the influence of the Sun's magnetic field and SOLAR WIND grow weaker, both Voyager spacecraft eventually will pass out of the heliosphere and into the interstellar medium. Through NASA's Voyager Interstellar Mission (VIM) (which began officially on January 1, 1990), the two Voyager spacecraft will continue to be tracked on their outward journey. The two major objectives of the VIM are: an investigation of the interplanetary and interstellar media, and a characterization of the interaction between the two; and a continuation of the successful Voyager program of ultraviolet astronomy. During the VIM, the spacecraft will search for the heliopause (the outermost extent of the solar wind, beyond which lies interstellar space). It is hoped that one Voyager spacecraft will still be functioning when it penetrates the heliopause and will provide scientists with the first true sampling of the interstellar environment. Barring a catastrophic failure on board either Voyager spacecraft, their nuclear power systems should provide useful levels of electric power until at least 2015.

Since both Voyager spacecraft eventually would journey beyond the solar system, their designers placed a special interstellar message (a record entitled: "The Sounds of Earth") on each in the hope that perhaps millions of years from now, some intelligent alien race will find either spacecraft drifting quietly through the interstellar void. If they are able to decipher the instructions for using this record, they will learn about our contemporary terrestrial civilization and the men and women who sent Voyager on its stellar journey.

See also: JUPITER; NEPTUNE; ORBITS OF OBJECTS IN SPACE; SATURN; URANUS.

V-2 rocket The German V-2 rocket of World War II is the "grandfather" of many of the large missiles flown by the United States. Based on the findings made by the American rocket scientist Dr. Robert H. Goddard (1882–1945) in the 1920s and 1930s, a team of German rocket scientists developed this weapon system at Peenemunde, Germany, and terrorized Allied populations of Europe and Britain until the end of the war. The German program began in early 1940; the first V-2 rocket was launched on July 6, 1942. In the closing days of World War II, the United States captured many German rocket scientists, including Dr. Wernher Von Braun (1912–1977), as part of Operation Paper Clip, and shipped these scientists plus numerous captured V-2 rocket components to the United States. These V-2 rockets were then assembled and tested at the White Sands Missile Range in New Mexico as part of an emerging U.S. missile program.

The V-2 rocket itself had a liquid-propellant engine that burned alcohol and liquid oxygen. It was about 14 meters (46 feet) long and 1.66 meters (5.45 feet) in diameter. After World War II, the United States (using American and captured German rocket personnel) assembled and tested 67 V-2 rockets in New Mexico between 1946 and 1952. This experience provided the technical heritage for many important American rockets, including the Redstone, Jupiter, and Saturn vehicles.

war game A simulation of a military operation involving two or more opposing forces, using rules, data, and procedures designed to depict an actual or assumed real-life situation.

warhead That part of a missile or rocket that contains either the nuclear or thermonuclear system, high-explosive system, chemical or biological agents, or inert materials intended to inflict damage upon the enemy.

warmant passages Passages provided in cryogenic-valve hydraulic actuators to maintain actuator temperatures above specified operating minimums under extended hold conditions.

water vapor feedback An Earth system process in which an increase in the amount of water vapor increases the atmosphere's absorption of infrared radiation, thereby contributing to a warming of the atmosphere. This atmospheric warming, in turn, may result in increased evaporation of water from the planet's surface and, therefore, an increase in the initial water vapor anomaly in the atmosphere. This feedback, along with atmospheric carbon dioxide (CO_2), is considered responsible for the greenhouse effect—an effect that operates virtually continuously in Earth's atmosphere.
See also: GREENHOUSE EFFECT.

watt (symbol: W) The SI UNIT of power (i.e., work per unit time). One watt is defined as 1 joule (J) per second, that is 1 W = 1 J/s. In electrical engineering, 1 watt corresponds to the product of 1 ampere (A) times 1 volt (V), that is, 1 W = 1 A x 1 V. This represents the rate of electric energy dissipation in a circuit in which a current of 1 ampere is flowing through a voltage difference of 1 volt. This unit is named in honor of James Watt (1736–1819), the Scottish engineer who developed the steam engine.

wave A periodic disturbance that is propagated in a medium in such a manner that at any point in the medium, the quantity serving as a measure of the disturbance is a function of time, while at any instant the displacement at a point is a function of the position of the point. At each spatial point there is an oscillation. The number of oscillations that occur per unit time is the *frequency* (symbol: ν). The distance between one wave crest to the next wave crest (or one trough to the next trough) is called the *wavelength* (symbol: λ).
See also: WAVELENGTH.

wavelength (symbol: λ) In general, the mean distance between maxima (or minima) of a periodic pattern. Specifically, the least distance between particles moving in the same phase of oscillation in a wave disturbance. The wavelength is measured along the direction of propagation of the wave, usually from the midpoint of a crest (or trough) to the midpoint of the next crest (or trough). The wavelength (λ) is related to the frequency (ν) and phase speed (c) (i.e., speed of propagation of the wave disturbance) by the simple formula: $\lambda = c/\nu$. The reciprocal of the wavelength is called the *wave number*.

weapon and payload identification 1. The determination of the type of weapon being used in an attack. 2. The discrimination of a reentry vehicle from the penetration aids being used with the reentry vehicle.
See also: ATTACK ASSESSMENT.

weapon debris (nuclear) The residue of a nuclear weapon after it has exploded; that is, the materials used for the casing and other components of the weapon, plus unexpended plutonium or uranium, together with the fission products created in the fission chain reaction and other radioisotopes formed by various phenomena, including neutron capture (activation).

weapon engagement zone In aerospace defense, airspace of defined dimensions within which the responsibility for engagement normally rests with a particular weapon system. Also called: *missile engagement zone* and *short-range air defense engagement zone.*

weapons of mass destruction (WMD) In arms control usage, weapons that are capable of a high order of destruction and/or of being used in such a manner as to destroy large numbers of people. These types of weapons can be nuclear, chemical, biological, or radiological. The term generally excludes the means of transporting or propelling the weapon where such means is a separable and divisible part of the weapon (e.g., a guided missile).

weapon system A delivery vehicle and weapon combination including all related equipment, materials, services, and personnel required so that the system becomes self-sufficient in its intended operational environment.

weather satellite One of the first applications of data and images supplied by Earth-orbiting satellites was to improve the understanding and prediction of weather. The weather satellite (also known as the *meteorological satellite* or the *environmental satellite*) is an uncrewed spacecraft that carries a variety of sensors. Two types of weather satellites generally are encountered: geostationary and polar-orbiting weather satellites, which are named for their types of orbits. (See Figure 141.)

Today weather satellites are used to observe and measure a wide range of atmospheric properties and processes to support increasingly more sophisticated weather warning and forecasting activities. Imaging instruments provide detailed pictures of clouds and cloud motions as well as measurements of sea-surface temperature. Sounders collect data in several infrared or microwave spectral bands that are processed to provide profiles of temperature and moisture as a function of altitude. Radar altimeters, scatterometers, and imagers (i.e., synthetic aperture radar, or SAR) can measure ocean currents, sea-surface winds, and the structure of snow and ice cover.

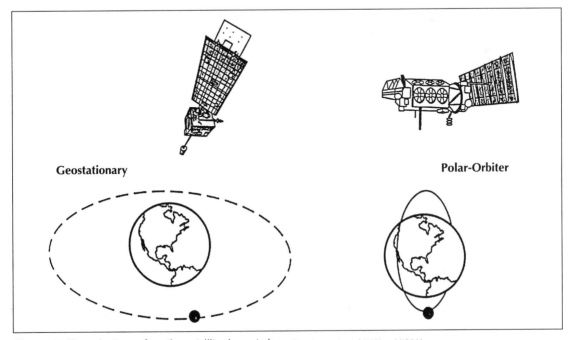

Geostationary   **Polar-Orbiter**

Figure 141. The major types of weather satellites in use today   *(Drawing courtesy of NASA and NOAA)*

In the United States, several federal agencies have distinct but overlapping charters for monitoring and forecasting weather. The National Weather Service (NWS) of the National Oceanic and Atmospheric Administration (NOAA) has the primary responsibility for providing severe storm and flood warnings as well as short and medium-range weather forecasts. The Federal Aviation Administration (FAA) provides specialized forecasts and warnings for aircraft. The Defense Meteorological Satellite Program (DMSP) within the Department of Defense (DoD) supports the specialized needs of the military and intelligence communities, which emphasize global capabilities to monitor clouds and visibility in support of combat and reconnaissance activities and to monitor sea-surface conditions in support of naval operations. NOAA, the air force, and the navy share responsibility for processing the data from NOAA and DMSP satellites: NOAA for soundings, the air force for cloud imagery, and the navy for ocean-surface data.

Global change research strives to monitor and understand the processes of natural and anthropogenic (people-caused) changes in Earth's physical, biological, and human environments. Weather satellites support this research by providing measurements of stratospheric ozone and ozone-depleting chemicals; by providing long-term scientific records of Earth's climate; by monitoring Earth's radiation balance and the concentrations of greenhouse gases and aerosols; by monitoring ocean temperatures, currents, and biological productivity; by monitoring the volume of ice sheets and glaciers; and by monitoring land use and vegetation. These variables provide important information concerning the complex processes and interactions of global environment change, including climate change.

See also: DEFENSE METEOROLOGICAL SATELLITE PROGRAM (DMSP); GEOSTATIONARY OPERATIONAL ENVIRONMENTAL SATELLITE (GOES); GLOBAL CHANGE; POLAR-ORBITING OPERATIONAL ENVIRONMENTAL SATELLITE (POES).

web The minimum thickness of a solid-propellant grain from the initial ignition surface to the insulated case wall or to the intersection of another burning surface at the time when the burning surface undergoes a major change; for an end-burning grain, the length of the grain.

See also: ROCKET; SOLID-PROPELLANT ROCKET.

weber (symbol: Wb) The SI UNIT of magnetic flux. It is defined as the flux that produces an electromotive force of 1 volt when, linking a circuit of one turn, the flux is reduced to zero at a uniform rate in 1 second. Named in honor of Wilhelm Weber, a German physicist (1804–1891) who studied magnetism. 1 weber = 10^8 maxwells.

weight (symbol: w) 1. The force with which a body is attracted toward Earth by gravity. 2. The product of the mass (m) of a body and the gravitational acceleration (g) acting on the body, w = mg. For example, a 1 kilogram (1 kg) mass on the surface of Earth would experience a downward force or "weight" of approximately 9.8 newtons.

In a dynamic situation, the weight can be a multiple of that under resting conditions. Weight also varies on other planets in accordance with their value of gravitational acceleration.

weightlessness The condition of free fall or zero-g, in which objects inside an orbiting, unaccelerated spacecraft are "weightless"—even though the objects and the spacecraft are still under the influence of the celestial object's gravity; the condition in which no acceleration, whether of gravity or other force, can be detected by an observer within the system in question.

See also: G; MICROGRAVITY.

welding The process of joining two or more pieces of metal by applying thermal energy (heat), pressure, or both, with or without filler material to produce a localized union through fusion or recrystallization across the interface.

wet To come in contact with and flow across (a surface, body, or area)—said of a fluid.

wet emplacement A launch pad that provides a deluge of water for cooling the flame bucket and other equipment during the launch of a missile or aerospace vehicle. Compare this term with DRY EMPLACEMENT and FLAME DEFLECTOR.

white room A clean, dust-free room that is used for the assembly, calibration, and (if necessary) repair of delicate spacecraft components and devices, such as gyros and sensor systems.

See also: CLEAN ROOM.

White Sands Missile Range (WSMR) White Sands Missile Range is a multiservice test range whose main function is the support of missile development and test programs for the U.S. Army, Navy, Air Force, NASA, and other government agencies and private firms. WSMR is under operational control of the U.S. Army Test and Evaluation Command (TECOM), Aberdeen Proving Ground, Maryland. The missile range is located in the Tularosa Basin of south-central New Mexico. The range boundaries extend almost 160 kilometers (km) (100 miles [mi]) north to south by about 65 km (40 mi) east to west.

During World War II, the U.S. Army Ordnance Corps recognized the possibilities of rocket warfare and sponsored research and development in methods of missile guidance. The missile range was established on July 9, 1945 as White Sands Proving Ground (the named later changed to White Sands Missile Range) to serve as America's testing range for the development of rocket technology and missile weapons. Following World War II, captured German V-2 rockets were assembled and tested at White Sands. Other rockets such as Nike, Corporal, Lance, and Viking also experienced developmental testing at the range. Launch Complex 33 (LC-33) at WSMR now has been designated as a National Historic Landmark, based on the fact that it was the country's first major rocket launch facility. It is also interesting to note the world's first atomic bomb, the TRINITY shot, was exploded on July 16, 1945 near the northern boundary of the complex.

During the early part of the space shuttle program, Astronauts Jack Lousma and C. Gordon Fullerton landed the orbiter *Columbia* at the Northrup Strip in the Alkali Flats area of the WSMR to successfully end the STS-3 mission (March 30, 1982). Because heavy rains had made the primary shuttle landing site at Edwards Air Force Base, California unacceptably wet, NASA chose the alternate site to support *Columbia*'s return to Earth. After this event, the Northrup Strip was renamed the White Sands Space Harbor. Although STS-3 has been the only shuttle mission (to date) to land at the range, WSMR continues to support ongoing shuttle missions, including support as a contingency or end-of-mission (EOM) landing site.

wick A group or braid of thin fibers that transports (or quite literally "sucks up") a liquid, if the adhesive force between the fiber and the liquid is greater than the liquid's cohesive force.

Wien's displacement law In radiation transport, the statement that the wavelength of maximum radiation intensity (λ_{max}) for a BLACKBODY is inversely proportional to the absolute temperature of the radiating blackbody:

$$\lambda_{max}T = b \text{ (a constant)}$$

If the absolute temperature (T) is in degrees Kelvin and the maximum wavelength (λ_{max}) is in centimeters, then the constant (b) has the value: 0.2898 cm-° K.

"wilco" Aerospace language for "I will comply."

window In general, a gap in a linear continuum. An *atmospheric window,* for example, is a range of wavelengths in the electromagnetic spectrum to which the atmosphere is transparent; a *launch window* is the time interval during which conditions are favorable for launching an aerospace vehicle or spacecraft on a specific mission.

wind tunnel A ground facility that supports aerodynamic testing of aircraft, missiles, propulsion systems, or their components under simulated flight conditions. The concept of a wind tunnel is quite simple: Instead of flying the object (or a precise scale model of the object) through the air at the desired test speed and attitude, it is supported in the test attitude within the wind tunnel, and the air flows past the object at the test speed. Wind tunnels exist in a wide variety of shapes and sizes. One wind tunnel design parameter of particular interest

CLASSIFICATION OF WIND TUNNELS
(ACCORDING TO AIRFLOW SPEED
IN TEST SECTION)

Tunnel class	Free-stream Mach-number[a] range
Low speed	0 to 0.5
High speed	0.5 to 0.9
Transonic	0.7 to 1.4
Supersonic	1.4 to 5.0
Hypersonic	>5.0

[a]Mach number = Local stream velocity / Local velocity of sound

Source: NASA.

is the velocity of airflow, usually given in free-stream Mach number (M) range. (The Mach number is the ratio of the free stream velocity to the local velocity of sound.) The table provides a general classification of wind tunnels according to the speed of the airflow in the test section. The test section in a wind tunnel usually includes windows and appropriate illumination for viewing the test object. Today no aircraft, spacecraft, or space launch or reentry vehicle is built or committed to flight until after its design and components have been thoroughly tested in wind tunnels.

See also: MACH NUMBER.

wing The aerodynamic lifting surface that provides conventional lift and control for an aircraft, winged missile, or aerospace vehicle.

work (symbol: W) In physics and thermodynamics, work (W) is defined as the energy (E) expended by a force (F) acting though a distance (s). Mathematically,

$$\text{Work} = \int F \cdot d\,s$$

In the SI unit system, work is expressed in joules (J). When a force of 1 newton (N) moves through a distance of 1 meter, 1 joule of work is performed; that is, 1 joule = 1 newton-meter.

See also: INTERNATIONAL SYSTEM OF UNITS.

working fluid A fluid (gas or liquid) used as the medium for the transfer of energy from one part of a system to another part.

See also: BRAYTON CYCLE; CARNOT CYCLE; RANKINE CYCLE.

X In aerospace engineering, a prefix used to designate an experimental missile, aerospace vehicle, or rocket. For example, the *X-15 experimental rocket plane.*

X-1 The rocket-powered research aircraft, patterned on the lines of a 50-caliber machine-gun bullet, that was the first human-crewed vehicle to fly faster than the speed of sound. The speed of sound in air varies with altitude. On October 14, 1947 the Bell X-1, named "Glamorous Glennis" and piloted by Captain Charles "Chuck" Yeager, was carried aloft under the bomb bay of a B-29 bomber and then released. The pilot ignited the aircraft's rocket engine, climbed, and accelerated, reaching Mach 1.06, or 1,127 kilometers (km) (700 miles [mi]), per hour as it flew over Edwards Air Force Base in California at an altitude of 13.1 km (8.1 mi). At this altitude, the speed of sound (or Mach 1.00) is 1,078.7 km (670 mi) per hour. The rocket-powered experimental aircraft, having used up all of its propellant, then glided to a landing on its tricycle gear at Muroc Dry Lake in the Mojave Desert.

See also: X-15.

X-15 The North American X-15 was a rocket-powered experimental aircraft 15.24 meters (m) (50 feet [ft]) long with a wingspan of 6.71 m (22 ft). It was a missile-shaped vehicle with an unusual wedge-shaped vertical tail, thin stubby wings, and unique fairings that extended along the side of the fuselage. The X-15 had an empty mass of 6,340 kilograms (kg) (14,000 pounds-mass [lbm]) and a launch mass of 15,420 kg (34,000-lbm). The vehicle's pilot-controlled rocket engine was capable of developing 253,500 newtons (57,000 pounds-force [lbf]) of thrust.

The X-15 research aircraft helped bridge the gap between human flight within the atmosphere and human flight in space. It was developed and flown in the 1960s to provide in-flight information and data on aerodynamics, structures, flight controls, and the physiological aspects of high-speed, high-altitude flight. For flight in the dense air of the lower ("aircraft-usable") portions of the atmosphere, the X-15 employed conventional aerodynamic controls. However, for flight in the thin upper portions of Earth's atmospheric envelope, the X-15 used a ballistic control system. Eight hydrogen peroxide-fueled thruster rockets, located on the nose of the aircraft, provided pitch and yaw control.

Because of its large fuel consumption, the X-15 was air launched from a B-52 aircraft (i.e., a "mothership") at an altitude of about 13,700 m (45,000 ft) and a speed of about 805 kilometers (km) (500 miles [mi]) per hour. Then the pilot ignited the rocket engine, which provided thrust for the first 80 to 120 seconds of flight, depending on the type mission being flown. The remainder of the normal 10- to 11-minute duration flight was powerless and ended with a 322-km (200-mi) per hour glide landing at Edwards Air Force Base in California. Generally, one of two types of X-15 flight profiles was used: a high-altitude flight plan that called for the pilot to maintain a steep rate of climb; or a speed profile that called for the pilot to push over and maintain a level altitude.

First flown in 1959, the three X-15 aircraft made a total of 199 flights. The X-15 flew more than six times the speed of sound and reached a maximum altitude of 107.8 km (67 mi) and a maximum speed of 7,273 km (4,520 mi) per hour. The final flight occurred on October 24, 1968. It is interesting to note that Apollo Astronaut Neil Armstrong (the first human to walk on the Moon) was one of the pilots who flew the X-15 aircraft.

X-20 The name given to an early U.S. Air Force space plane concept whose mission was to explore human flight in the hypersonic and orbital regimes. However, the proposed vehicle did not have a significant payload capacity, and therefore it would not have been suitable in space logistics missions (i.e., in "payload-hauling" missions). The X-20, or DYNA-SOAR, space plane was to be placed into orbit by a Titan booster. When its orbital mission was completed, the military pilot was to control this sleek glider through atmospheric reentry and then land it on a runway, much like a conventional jet fighter. Despite its innovative nature, the project was canceled in December 1963, before the prototype vehicle was ever built.

X-30 The name given in the 1980s to the U.S. National Aerospace Plane (NASP) program, a joint NASA-Department of Defense effort to develop a hypersonic plane capable of flying into orbit and then landing at a conventional airport runway. As formerly conceived, the X-30, with its "scramjet" engines that burned a mixture of hydrogen and air, was to be a horizontal take-off and landing (HOTOL) vehicle. Current U.S. efforts to develop a truly reusable aerospace plane now center around the X-33 and X-34 programs.

See also: X-33; X-34.

X-33 The X-33 technology demonstration is intended to prove the concept of a next-generation reusable launch vehicle (RLV) system that incorporates single-stage-to-orbit (SSTO) characteristics. New maintenance concepts, aircraftlike operations, and advanced fabrication techniques are among the key aspects of this program, which involves a partnership among NASA, the U.S. Air Force, and private industry. Building on ground-based testing as well as X-34 flight test experience, the one-half-scale X-33 demonstrator vehicle is aimed at integrating and testing advanced component technologies necessary to move to a full-scale reusable launch vehicle (now called the VENTURESTAR). The X-33 advanced demonstrator will bring these technologies together for the first time in a proof-of-concept demonstration of the feasibility of an SSTO launch system. Many aerospace experts now think that the SSTO approach offers the greatest potential

savings and performance of any launch vehicle configuration, as measured by such parameters as reusability, operability, reliability, affordability, safety, and mass fraction.

In July 1996 NASA announced that the Lockheed-Martin Corporation had won the competition to design and build the demonstration X-33. The X-33 is a technology demonstration program that will result in the development of a true reusable launch vehicle, called the VentureStar by Lockheed-Martin. The winning design featured a lifting body configuration and an aerospike propulsion system. The vehicle's hydrogen tanks will be made of graphite epoxy composite material and are load bearing. The liquid oxygen (LO_2) tank will be aluminum on the X-33 and graphite epoxy composite material on the reusable launch vehicle.

The X-33's onboard umbilicals are covered by metallic thermal panels for easy access during turnaround on the ground. The reaction control system will use gaseous hydrogen and gaseous oxygen. The use of onboard computers to check the condition of each system on the vehicle will facilitate rapid ground processing. All ground operations will be accomplished in the horizontal position, then the vehicle will be rotated to a vertical position and launched.

The X-33 itself will be light enough to be ferried by the space shuttle carrier aircraft, but the operational RLV (i.e., the VentureStar) will be so heavy that it cannot be ferried; the hangar for any ground work must be at the end of the landing runway. The mass fraction of the vehicle is very critical. The X-33 demonstrator vehicle will be 78% propellant at liftoff, while the true RLV will be 91% propellant at liftoff. The Lockheed-Martin development strategy is to have full traceability from the X-33 to the RLV. The first launch of the X-33 is scheduled for March 1999, and the first launch of the RLV is expected to occur between 2003 and 2004. (See Figure 142.)

See also: REUSABLE LAUNCH VEHICLE; VENTURESTAR; X-34.

X-34 An experimental, flight demonstration vehicle that will provide a basis for realistic assessments of the development and operational costs of a reusable launch vehicle (RLV). The X-34 is being designed as a light payload carrier (i.e., about 450 to 900 kilograms [1,000 to 2,000 pounds-mass [lbm]) to LOW EARTH ORBIT) that will serve as a test-bed for simplifying the operation of a reusable or

System	Space Shuttle	VentureStar	X-33
Length (m)	56.1	38.7	20.4
Width (m)	23.8	39.0	20.7
Gross Takeoff Weight (kg)	2,041,000	991,570	123,800
Fuel	Liquid H_2/Liquid O_2 + solid	Liquid H_2/Liquid O_2	Liquid H_2/Liquid O_2
Fuel Mass (kg)	1,725,000	875,000	95,710
Empty Mass (kg)	269,000	89,360	28,580
Main Propulsion	2 Solid + 3 SSMEs	7Aerospikes	2 Aerospikes
Takeoff Thrust (newtons)	28,467,200	13,388,500	1,823,700
Maximum Speed	Orbital	Orbital	Mach 15 +
Payload Capacity kg (delivered to 160 km/28.5° orb)	23,130	26,760	not applicable
Payload Bay Size (m)	4.57 x 18.29	4.57 x 13.72	1.52 x 3.05

Figure 142. Parametric comparison of Space Transportation System (i.e., space shuttle), X-33, and VentureStar launch systems   *(Line art courtesy of NASA/Lockheed; data developed by author based on data from NASA/Lockheed)*

partly reusable piloted launch vehicle in the early 21st century. In 1995 NASA signed a cooperative agreement with Orbital Sciences Corporation to jointly develop this small, reusable space booster. A launch date in the late 1990s is planned. The X-34 program is part of the current U.S. Reusable Launch Vehicle Technology Program, which is a partnership among NASA, the U.S. Air Force, and private industry to develop world leadership in low-cost space transportation.

See also: X-33.

X ray A penetrating form of electromagnetic radiation of very short wavelength (approximately 0.01 to 10 nanometers or 0.1 to 100 angstroms) and high photon energy (approximately 100 electron volts to some 100 kiloelectron volts). X rays are emitted when either the inner orbital electrons of an excited atom return to their normal energy states (these photons are called *characteristic X rays*) or when a fast-moving charged particle (generally an electron) loses energy in the form of photons upon being accelerated and deflected by the electric field surrounding the nucleus of a high atomic number element (this process is called *bremsstrahlung,* or "braking radiation"). Unlike gamma rays, X rays are nonnuclear in origin.

See also: ADVANCED X-RAY ASTROPHYSICS FACILITY; X-RAY ASTRONOMY.

X-ray astronomy Since Earth's atmosphere absorbs most of the X rays coming from celestial phenomena, astronomers must use orbiting space platforms to study these interesting emissions, which usually are associated with very energetic, violent processes occurring in the universe. In fact, X-ray emissions carry detailed information about the temperature, density, age, and other physical conditions of the celestial objects that have produced them. X-ray astronomy is the most advanced of the three general disciplines associated with high-energy astrophysics: X-ray, gamma ray, and cosmic ray astronomy. The observation of X-ray emissions has been very valuable in the study of high-energy events, such as mass transfer in binary star systems, the interaction of super-

novae remnants with interstellar gas, and the functioning of quasars.

Space-based X-ray observatories provide data allowing scientists to study and understand: stellar structure and evolution, including binary star systems, supernovae remnants, pulsars and BLACK HOLE candidates; large-scale galactic phenomena, including the interstellar medium itself and soft X-ray emissions of local galaxies; the nature of active galaxies, including the spectral characteristics and time variation of X-ray emissions from the central (or nuclear) regions of such galaxies; and rich clusters of galaxies, including their associated X-ray emissions. X-ray emissions also help scientists observe and study solar flares occurring on our parent star, the Sun.

Also see: ADVANCED X-RAY ASTROPHYSICS FACILITY.

X-ray binary The most often encountered type of luminous galactic X-ray source. It is a close binary star system in which material from a large, normal star flows (under gravitational forces) onto a compact stellar companion, such as a neutron star or a black hole (for the most luminous X-ray sources) or perhaps a white dwarf (for less luminous sources).

See also: X-RAY ASTRONOMY.

X-ray Timing Explorer (XTE) A NASA astrophysics mission designed to study the temporal variability in compact X-ray emitting objects. The 3,045-kilogram (6,700 pounds-mass) spacecraft was built at Goddard Space Flight Center, Maryland and carries three special instruments to measure X-ray emissions from deep space: the Proportional Counter Array, the High Energy X-ray Timing Experiment, and the All Sky Monitor. These instruments observe X-ray emissions from the vicinity of BLACK HOLES, from neutron stars, and from white dwarfs, along with telltale radiation from exploding stars and galaxies with active nuclei. The *XTE* was placed in a successful 580-kilometer (360 mile) altitude circular orbit around Earth by an expendable Delta 2 rocket launched from Cape Canaveral Air Force Station, Florida on December 30, 1995.

See also: X-RAY ASTRONOMY.

Y In aerospace engineering, the symbol for prototype. For example, a prototype guided missile would be designated as YGM. Prototype vehicles usually are manufactured in limited quantities and are used to support operational and preproduction tests.

yard (symbol: yd) A fundamental unit of length in the standard (foot-pound-second) system of units. Since 1963, 1 yard has been defined as exactly 0.9144 meter.

$$1 \text{ yard} = 3 \text{ feet} = 0.9144 \text{ meter}$$

yaw The rotation or oscillation of an aircraft, missile, or aerospace vehicle about its vertical axis so as to cause the longitudinal axis of the vehicle to deviate from the flight line or heading in its horizontal plane.

See also: PITCH; ROLL.

year A period of one revolution of Earth around the Sun. The choice of a reference point determines the exact length of a year. The *calendar year* (based on the Gregorian calendar) is made up of an average of 365.2425 mean solar days. For convenience, the calendar year is taken as three successive years of 365 days followed by one "leap" year consisting of 366 days. A *solar day* is defined as the time interval between two successive passages of the Sun across the meridian; while a *mean solar day* of 24 hours is considered as the average value of the solar day for one year. Scientists and astronomers also use other, more specialized definitions. For example, the period of revolution from perihelion to perihelion (point of Earth's closest approach to the Sun) is called the *anomalistic year* and corre-

sponds to approximately 365.259 mean solar days. The *tropical year* is defined as the average period of time between successive passages of the Sun across the vernal equinox (i.e., return of the Sun to the first point in Aries) and corresponds to approximately 365.242 mean solar days. Finally, the *sidereal year* is based on the return passage of certain "fixed" stars and is approximately 365.256 mean solar days.

yield The total energy released in a nuclear explosion. It is usually expressed in equivalent tons of TNT (the quantity of trinitrotohene required to produce a corresponding amount of energy). *Low yield* is generally considered to be less than 20 kilotons; low-intermediate yield, from 20 to 200 kilotons; intermediate yield, from 200 kilotons to 1 megaton. There is no standardized term to describe yields from 1 megaton upward.

YM A prefix often used in aerospace engineering to designate a prototype missile.

Yohkoh A solar X-ray observation satellite launched by the Japanese Institute of Space and Astronautical Sciences (ISAS) on August 30, 1991. The main objective of this satellite is to study the high-energy radiations from solar flares (i.e., hard and soft X rays and energetic neutrons) as well as quiet Sun structures and presolar flare conditions. *Yohkoh*, which means "sunbeam" in Japanese, is a three-axis stabilized observatory-type satellite in a nearly circular Earth orbit, carrying four instruments: two imagers and two spectrometers. The imaging instruments (a hard X-ray telescope [20–80 kiloelectron volts [keV] energy range] and a soft X-ray telescope [0.1–4 keV energy range]) have almost full-Sun fields of view to avoid missing any flares on the visible disk of the Sun. This mission is a cooperative mission of Japan, the United States, and the United Kingdom. For example, *Yohkok*'s soft X-ray telescope (SXT) was developed for NASA by the Lockheed Palo Alto Research Laboratory, in partnership with the National Astronomical Observatory of Japan and the Institute for Astronomy of the University of Tokyo.

See also: SUN.

Z The symbol for *atomic number,* or the number of protons (or electrons) in the atoms of a given element.

Zenit A three-stage Russian launch vehicle capable of placing about 13,700 kilograms in LOW EARTH ORBIT (LEO). It was first launched in 1985.

zenith That point on the celestial sphere vertically overhead. The point 180 degrees from the zenith is called the *nadir.*

zero-g The condition of free fall and weightlessness. When there are no forces on objects in an orbiting spacecraft, they are said to be in zero-g.
See also: G; MICROGRAVITY.

zero-gravity (zero-g) aircraft An aircraft that flies a special parabolic trajectory to create low-gravity conditions (typically 0.01 g) for short periods of time (10–30 seconds), where 1 g here represents the acceleration due to gravity at Earth's surface (9.8 meters per second per second). For example, a modified KC-135 aircraft can simulate up to 40 periods of low-gravity for 25-second intervals during one flight. This aircraft accommodates a variety of experiments and often is used to support crew training and to refine space-flight experiment equipment and techniques. The KC-135, like other "zero-gravity" research aircraft, obtains weightlessness by flying a parabolic trajectory. The plane climbs rapidly at a 45-degree angle (pull-up), slows as it traces a parabola (pushover), and then descends at a 45-degree angle (pull-out). The forces of acceleration and deceleration produce twice the normal gravity during the pull-up and pull-out legs of the flight, while the brief pushover at the top of the parabola produces less than 1% of Earth's sea-level gravity.
See also: MICROGRAVITY.

zero-length launching A technique in which the first motion of the missile or aircraft removes it from the launcher.

Zeroth Law of Thermodynamics Two systems, each in thermal equilibrium with a third system, are in thermal equilibrium with each other. This statement is frequently called the Zeroth Law of Thermodynamics and is actually an implicit part of the concept of temperature. It is important in the field of thermometry and in the establishment of empirical temperature scales.
See also: FIRST LAW OF THERMODYNAMICS; SECOND LAW OF THERMODYNAMICS; THERMODYNAMICS.

zodiacal light A faint cone of light extending upward from the horizon in the direction of the ecliptic. Zodiacal light is seen from the tropical latitudes for a few hours after sunset or before sunrise. It is due to sunlight being reflected by tiny pieces of interplanetary dust in orbit around the Sun.

Zond A family of Russian spacecraft that explored the Moon, Mars, Venus, and interplanetary space in the 1960s. *Zond 1,* a partial success, was launched on April 2, 1964 toward Venus but stopped transmitting about two months before it flew by the planet at a distance of 100,000 kilometers (km). *Zond 3,* launched as a test interplanetary probe on July 18, 1965, flew past the Moon at a distance of 9,200 km and obtained photographs of the lunar farside. The last Zond mission, *Zond 8,* was launched on October 20, 1970. It circled the Moon at a distance of 1,100 km and returned to Earth, splashing down in the Indian Ocean. The Zond lunar circumnavigation missions (i.e., *Zond 5, 6, 7* and *8*) are considered by some space analysts as precursors to Russian manned missions in response to the U.S. Apollo program, during the cold war "race to the Moon" in the late 1960s.

zulu time (symbol: Z) Time based on Greenwich mean time (GMT).

See: GREENWICH MEAN TIME.

APPENDIX A:
Special Reference List

Table A.1
SPECIAL UNITS FOR ASTRONOMICAL INVESTIGATIONS

astronomical unit (AU): The mean distance from Earth to the Sun—
approximately $1.495\ 979 \times 10^{11}$ meters.

light-year (ly): The distance light travels in one year's time—
approximately $9.460\ 55 \times 10^{15}$ meters.

parsec (pc): The parallax shift of one second of arc (3.26 light-years)—
approximately $3.085\ 768 \times 10^{16}$ meters.

speed of light (c): $2.997\ 9 \times 10^{8}$ meters per second.

Source: NASA.

Table A.2
INTERNATIONAL SYSTEM (SI) UNITS AND THEIR CONVERSION FACTORS

Quantity	Name of Unit	Symbol	Conversion Factor
Distance	meter	m	1 km = 0.621 mile
			1 m = 3.28 ft
			1 cm = 0.394 in.
			1 mm = 0.039 in.
			1 μm = 3.9×10^{-5} in. = 10^{4} Å
			1 nm = 10 Å
Mass	kilogram	kg	1 tonne = 1.102 tons
			1 kg = 2.20 lb
			1 gm = 0.0022 lb = 0.035 oz
			1 mg = 2.20×10^{-6} lb = 3.5×10^{-5} oz
Time	second	sec	1 yr = 3.156×10^{7} sec
			1 day = 8.64 10^{4} sec
			1 hr = 3600 sec
Temperature	kelvin	K	273° K = 0° C = 32° F
			373° K = 100° C = 212° F
Area	square meter	m^2	1 m^2 = 10^{4} cm^2 = 10.8 ft^2
Volume	cubic meter	m^3	1 m^3 = 10^{6} cm^3 = 35 ft^3
Frequency	hertz	Hz	1 Hz = 1 cycle/sec
			1 kHz = 1000 cycles/sec
			1 MHz = 10^{6} cycles/sec
Density	kilogram per cubic meter	kg/m^3	1 kg/m^3 = 0.001 gm/cm^3
			1 gm/cm^3 = density of water
Speed, velocity	meter per second	m/sec	1 m/sec = 3.28 ft/sec
			1 km/sec = 2240 mi/hr

Table A.2 (continued)
INTERNATIONAL SYSTEM (SI) UNITS AND THEIR CONVERSION FACTORS

Quantity	Name of Unit	Symbol	Conversion Factor
Force	newton	N	1 N = 10^5 dynes = 0.224 lbf
Pressure	newton per square meter	N/m^2	1 N/m^2 = 1.45 x 10^{-4} lb/in^2
Energy	joule	J	1 J = 0.239 calorie
Photon energy	electron volt	eV	1 eV = 1.60 x 10^{-19} J; 1 J = 10^7 erg
Power	watt	W	1 W = 1 J/sec
Atomic mass	atomic mass unit	amu	1 amu = 1.66 x 10^{-27} kg

Customary Units Used with the SI Units

Quantity	Name of Unit	Symbol	Conversion Factor
Wavelength of light	angstrom	Å	1 Å = 0.1 nm = 10^{-10} m
Acceleration of gravity	g	g	1 g = 9.8 m/sec^2

Source: NASA.

Table A.3
RECOMMENDED SI UNIT PREFIXES

Prefix	Abbreviation	Factor by Which Unit Is Multiplied
tera	T	10^{12}
giga	G	10^9
mega	M	10^6
kilo	k	10^3
hecto	h	10^2
centi	c	10^{-2}
milli	m	10^{-3}
micro	μ	10^{-6}
nano	n	10^{-9}
pico	p	10^{-12}

Table A.4
COMMON METRIC/ENGLISH CONVERSION FACTORS
(FOR SPACE TECHNOLOGY ACTIVITIES)

	Multiply	By	To Obtain
Length:	inches	2.54	centimeters
	centimeters	0.393 7	inches
	feet	0.304 8	meters
	meters	3.281	feet
	statute miles	1.609 3	kilometers
	kilometers	0.621 4	statute miles
	kilometers	0.54	nautical miles

Table A.4 (continued)
COMMON METRIC/ENGLISH CONVERSION FACTORS
(FOR SPACE TECHNOLOGY ACTIVITIES)

	Multiply	By	To Obtain
	nautical miles	1.852	kilometers
	kilometers	3.281.	feet
	feet	0.000 304 8	kilometers
Weight and Mass	ounces	28.350	grams
	grams	0.035 3	ounces
	pounds	0.453 6	kilograms
	kilograms	2.205	pounds
	tons	0.907 2	metric tons
	metric tons	1.102	tons
Liquid Measure	fluid ounces	0.029 6	liters
	gallons	3.785 4	liters
	liters	0.264 2	gallons
	liters	33.814 0	fluid ounces
Temperature	degrees Fahrenheit plus 459.67	0.555 5	kelvins
	degrees Celsius plus 273.16	1.0	kelvins
	kelvins	1.80	degrees Fahrenheit minus 459.67
	kelvins	1.0	degrees Celsius minus 273.16
	degrees Fahrenheit minus 32	0.555 5	degrees Celsius
	degrees Celsius	1.80	degrees Fahrenheit plus 32
Thrust (Force)	pounds force	4.448	newtons
Pressure	newtons	0.225	pounds
	millimeters mercury	133.32	pascals (newtons per square meter)
	pounds per square inch	6.895	kilopascals (1000 pascals)
	pascals	0.007 5	millimeters mercury at 0° C
	kilopascals	0.145 0	pounds per square inch

Source: NASA.

```
┌─────────────────────────────────────────────────────────┐
│  ┌─────────────────────────────────────────────────────┐ │
│  │                                                       │ │
│  │     ╒╤╤PEΠ□ï╳  B:                                      │ │
│  │         Journeys into Cyberspace                      │ │
│  │                                                       │ │
│  └─────────────────────────────────────────────────────┘ │
└─────────────────────────────────────────────────────────┘
```

APPENDIX B:
Journeys into Cyberspace

In recent years, numerous Web sites concerning space exploration and technology have appeared on the Internet. Visits to such sites can provide information about the status of ongoing missions, such as the Cassini mission to Saturn. This book can serve as an important companion, as you explore a new Web site and encounter a word, phrase, or form of space technology that is unfamiliar and not fully discussed within the particular site. To help enrich the content of this book and make your space technology–related travels in cyberspace more enjoyable and productive, the following is a selected list of Web sites that are recommended for your viewing. From these sites you will also be able to link to many other exciting space-related locations on the Web. (Note: This is obviously a partial list of the many space-related Web sites now available. Every effort has been made to ensure the accuracy of the information provided at the time of publication. Any inconvenience you could experience due to the dynamic nature of the Internet is regretted.)

European Space Agency (ESA)	http://www.esrin.esa.it/
National Aeronautics and Space Administration (NASA) (main site)	http://www.nasa.gov/
National Oceanic and Atmospheric Administration (NOAA)	http://www.noaa.gov/

Selected NASA Centers	*Internet Address:*
Ames Research Center, Mountain View, CA	http://www.arc.nasa.gov/
Dryden Flight Research Center, Edwards, CA	http://www.dfrc.nasa.gov/dryden.html
Goddard Space Flight Center, Greenbelt, MD	http://www.gsfc.nasa.gov/
Jet Propulsion Laboratory, Pasadena, CA	http://www.jpl.nasa.gov/
Johnson Space Center, Houston, TX	http://www.jsc.nasa.gov/
Kennedy Space Center, FL	http://www.ksc.nasa.gov/
Langley Research Center, Hampton, VA	http://www.larc.nasa.gov/
Lewis Research Center, Cleveland, OH	http://www.lerc.nasa.gov/
Marshall Space Flight Center, Huntsville, AL	http://www.msfc.nasa.gov/
Stennis Space Center, Mississippi	http://www.ssc.nasa.gov/
Wallops Flight Facility, Wallops Island, VA	http://www.wff.nasa.gov/
White Sands Test Facility, White Sands, NM	http://www.wstf.nasa.gov/

Selected Space Missions

Cassini Mission (Saturn)   http://www.jpl.nasa.gov/cassini/

Galileo Mission (Jupiter)   http://www.jpl.nasa.gov/galileo/

National Space Science Data Center (NSSDC)   http://nssdc.gsfc.nasa.gov/
  (numerous space missions including planetary)

Ulysses Mission (Solar Poles)   http://ulysses.jpl.nasa.gov/

Voyager (Deep Space/Interstellar)   http://vraptor.jpl.nasa.gov/voyager/
                                                                  voyager.html

Military Space

Air Force Space Command (AFSPC)   http://www.spacecom.af.mil/hqafspc/

Ballistic Missile Defense Organization (BMDO)   http://www.acq.osd.mil/bmdo/

45th Space Wing (Cape Canaveral/Patrick AFB)   http://www.pafb.af.mil/

National Reconnaissance Office (NRO)   http://www.nro.odci.gov/

Other Interesting Space Sites

Lunar and Planetary Institute (LPI)   http://cass.jsc.nasa.gov/

National Air and Space Museum   http://ceps.nasm.edu/NASMpage.html
  (Smithsonian Institution)

The Planetary Society   http://planetary.org